Table of Contents

INTRO:

The night air crackled with tension as sirens wailed through the darkness. EMT Sarah Miller gripped the dashboard, her heart pounding in sync with the flashing lights. The dispatcher's voice crackled over the radio: "Multiple vehicle pileup on Highway 101. Entrapment reported. All units respond."

Tires screeched as the ambulance rounded the final bend. The scene unfolded like a nightmare – twisted metal, shattered glass, and the acrid smell of burning rubber. Sarah's training kicked in. She scanned the chaos, triaging patients in her mind.

A man's agonized scream pierced the air. Sarah sprinted toward the sound, her equipment bag bouncing against her back. She found him pinned in the driver's seat, blood oozing from a deep gash in his thigh. The femoral artery – she knew they had minutes, maybe seconds.

With steady hands, Sarah applied a tourniquet, her voice calm as she reassured the terrified driver. She monitored his vitals, administered oxygen, and coordinated with firefighters for extrication. Every action was deliberate, every decision critical.

Hours later, as dawn broke over the horizon, Sarah learned the man would survive. One life saved among many that night – all because she knew exactly what to do when it mattered most.

This is the world of Emergency Medical Services. It's a realm where split-second decisions can mean the difference between life and death. It's challenging, intense, and utterly rewarding. And it all starts with passing the NREMT exam.

This certification is your key to unlocking a career filled with purpose. You'll master crucial skills like airway management, trauma care, and handling medical emergencies. You'll learn to stay cool under pressure and provide comfort in people's darkest hours.

This guide is your roadmap to success. We'll break down complex topics into digestible chunks. You'll find practice questions that mirror the real exam, tips to boost your confidence, and strategies to tackle even the toughest scenarios.

Remember Sarah's story. That could be you, making a real difference when it matters most. The path might seem daunting now, but with dedication and the right tools, you've got this. Your future patients are counting on you. It's time to step up, dive in, and become the hero you're meant to be. Let's get started – your EMT journey begins now.

The National Registry of Emergency Medical Technicians (NREMT) EMT exam serves as the gold standard for EMT certification across the United States. It's designed to ensure that EMTs possess the knowledge and decision-making skills necessary to provide safe and effective emergency care.

The exam uses Computer Adaptive Testing (CAT) technology. This means the difficulty of each question adjusts based on your performance. Answer correctly, and the next question gets tougher. Miss one, and you'll see an easier item. This format allows for a more accurate assessment of your abilities.

You'll face between 70 to 120 questions, with a time limit of 2 hours. The exact number varies because the test ends when it determines your ability level with 95% confidence. This could happen after 70 questions if you're consistently nailing high-difficulty items, or it might take the full 120 if your performance is borderline.

The exam covers five main content areas:

1. Airway, Respiration & Ventilation (18-22% of the exam)

2. Cardiology & Resuscitation (20-24%)
3. Trauma (14-18%)
4. Medical, Obstetrics & Gynecology (27-31%)
5. EMS Operations (10-14%)

Each question is categorized into one of these areas, ensuring a comprehensive evaluation of your skills.

The NREMT uses a scaled scoring system, not a traditional percentage. Your ability is measured against a predetermined standard, not against other test-takers. While the exact passing score isn't published, it typically falls around 70% correct responses at a specific difficulty level.

To be eligible for the exam, you must complete a state-approved EMT course and hold current CPR-BLS certification. Some states have additional requirements, like background checks or age minimums.

Once certified, EMTs must recertify every two years. This involves completing continuing education hours or retaking the cognitive exam. It's a crucial process that ensures EMTs stay current with evolving medical practices.

NREMT certification opens doors. It's recognized nationwide, allowing you to practice in multiple states without retesting. Many employers require it, even in states where it's not mandatory. It's a mark of excellence that sets you apart in the field.

Remember, this exam is your first step into a challenging and rewarding career. It's not just about memorizing facts – it's about proving you can think critically and make sound decisions under pressure. With the right preparation, you'll be well on your way to joining the ranks of certified EMTs across the nation.

To get the most out of this guide, start by understanding its structure. We've aligned each chapter with the NREMT exam content areas, ensuring you're focusing on what matters most. The book kicks off with foundational concepts and builds to more complex topics, mirroring how you'd approach real-life patient care.

Don't just read passively. Engage with the material. When you hit a mnemonic, pause and create a mental image. For case studies, imagine yourself on scene. What would you do first? Why?

We recommend a 6-week study plan, tackling one major content area per week, with the final week for review:

Week 1: Airway, Respiration & Ventilation
Week 2: Cardiology & Resuscitation
Week 3: Trauma
Week 4: Medical, Obstetrics & Gynecology
Week 5: EMS Operations
Week 6: Comprehensive Review

Aim for 2-3 hours of study per day, 5 days a week. Break this into 25-minute focused sessions with 5-minute breaks. This "Pomodoro Technique" helps maintain concentration and prevent burnout.

Incorporate active recall into your routine. After reading a section, close the book and explain the concept out loud, as if teaching someone else. This process, known as the "Feynman Technique," reinforces your understanding and highlights knowledge gaps.

Use spaced repetition to your advantage. Review older material regularly, not just recent chapters. Try creating flashcards for key terms and concepts, shuffling them daily.

The practice questions aren't just for testing – they're learning tools. When you get one wrong, don't just move on. Understand why the correct answer is right and why the others are wrong. This deepens your comprehension and improves critical thinking.

Take full-length mock exams under test-like conditions. Time yourself, find a quiet space, and resist the urge to check answers mid-test. This builds stamina and simulates the pressure you'll face on exam day.

Remember, the NREMT also tests psychomotor skills. While this book focuses on the cognitive exam, supplement your study with hands-on practice. Partner with classmates to run through patient assessment scenarios or practice skills like bag-valve-mask ventilation.

Staying motivated can be tough. Set small, achievable goals and reward yourself when you hit them. Visualize success – picture yourself confidently answering questions and receiving your certification.

If stress creeps in, take a step back. Deep breathing exercises or a quick walk can reset your mind. Remember why you started this journey. Every hour of study brings you closer to saving lives as a certified EMT.

Stay consistent, stay focused, and trust in your abilities. This guide is your roadmap – now it's time to start your engines and drive toward success.

Mastering the NREMT EMT exam requires more than just knowledge – it demands smart test-taking strategies. Let's dive into techniques that'll boost your performance and confidence.

First, understand the computer adaptive format. Each question is a separate challenge – get it right, and the next one's tougher. Miss it, and you'll see an easier item. This means every question counts equally, so don't get hung up on any single item.

Time management is crucial. You've got 2 hours for up to 120 questions. That's about 1 minute per question. If you're stuck, flag it and move on. The test might end after 70 questions if you're consistently correct, so aim for accuracy over speed.

Read each question carefully. Look for keywords like "FIRST," "BEST," or "MOST IMPORTANT." These often point to the correct answer. Don't rush – a misread question can trip up even the most prepared candidate.

When tackling a question:

1. Read the stem and try to answer before looking at choices.
2. Eliminate obviously wrong options.
3. Of the remaining choices, pick the "most right" answer.

If you're unsure, use the "ABCs" (Airway, Breathing, Circulation) as a guide. The correct answer often follows this priority sequence.

For scenario-based questions, imagine yourself on scene. What's your first priority? What additional information do you need?

If you must guess, do it smartly. Eliminate any choices that are clearly wrong. Between two similar answers, the more specific one is often correct.

Test anxiety can be a real challenge. Combat it with these techniques:

- Practice deep breathing: Inhale for 4 counts, hold for 4, exhale for 4.

- Use positive self-talk: Remind yourself, "I've prepared for this. I know this material."
- Progressive muscle relaxation: Tense and relax each muscle group, starting from your toes.

Your pre-exam routine can make or break your performance. In the week before:

- Stick to your study schedule, but don't cram the night before.
- Get plenty of sleep – aim for 7-9 hours nightly.
- Eat balanced meals rich in protein, complex carbs, and omega-3s.
- Stay hydrated and limit caffeine to avoid jitters.

The day before, do a light review and then relax. Visualize yourself succeeding. Prepare your test day kit: ID, snack, water, and any required documents.

On test day:

- Arrive early to settle your nerves.
- Do some light stretching to release tension.
- During the test, take short breaks if needed. Close your eyes and take a few deep breaths.

For different question types:

- Multiple choice: Use process of elimination.
- Ordered response: Think through the sequence of care step-by-step.
- Select all that apply: Treat each option as true/false.

Stay focused by using active reading – underline key parts of each question. If your mind wanders, take a deep breath and refocus.

Remember, you've prepared for this. Trust your knowledge, trust your instincts, and approach each question with confidence. You've got this – now go show that exam what you're made of!

Airway, Respiration & Ventilation

The respiratory system is a marvel of biological engineering, with each structure playing a crucial role in the process of breathing. Let's break it down from top to bottom.

The upper airway starts with the nose and mouth. The nose isn't just for smelling – it's your body's air filter and humidifier. As air rushes in, nasal hairs trap large particles, while the mucous membrane moistens the air and catches smaller debris. This helps protect your lungs from irritants and infection.

Next up is the pharynx, divided into three sections. The nasopharynx sits behind your nose, connecting to your ears via the Eustachian tubes. It's lined with adenoid tissue, which fights off pathogens. The oropharynx is the area behind your mouth, including the soft palate, tonsils, and base of the tongue. It's a crossroads where air and food passages meet. The laryngopharynx is the lowest section, leading to the larynx (voice box) and esophagus.

The larynx houses your vocal cords and the epiglottis – a leaf-shaped flap that covers your airway when you swallow. It's your body's traffic cop, ensuring food goes down the esophagus and air heads to the lungs.

The trachea, or windpipe, is the gateway to the lower airway. It's about 4-5 inches long in adults and lined with tiny hair-like structures called cilia. These cilia wave upward, pushing mucus and trapped particles back towards your throat where you can cough them out.

During normal breathing, these structures work in harmony. You inhale through your nose or mouth, air travels down the pharynx, past the larynx, and into the trachea. The air is warmed, humidified, and filtered along the way.

But in emergencies, this delicate system can be compromised in several ways:

1. Obstruction: Foreign objects, swelling, or trauma can block the airway at any point. A choking victim might have food lodged in their oropharynx. Anaphylaxis can cause rapid swelling of the larynx.
2. Aspiration: When the epiglottis fails to protect the airway, stomach contents or blood can enter the lungs. This is a risk in unconscious patients or those with impaired gag reflexes.
3. Inhalation injuries: Smoke or chemical fumes can damage the delicate tissues of the airway, causing swelling and impaired function.
4. Trauma: Direct injury to the neck can crush the trachea or cause bleeding that obstructs the airway.
5. Infection: Conditions like epiglottitis can cause rapid, life-threatening swelling of airway structures.

As an EMT, you'll need to quickly assess and manage these threats. That might mean performing the Heimlich maneuver on a choking patient, using suction to clear secretions, or assisting ventilations in a patient with compromised breathing.

Remember, in any emergency scenario, maintaining a patent airway is your top priority. Without it, nothing else matters. That's why "A" for Airway comes first in your ABCs of patient care.

Understanding these structures and how they can be compromised will guide your assessment and interventions. It's not just about memorizing anatomy – it's about visualizing how these parts work together and recognizing when that system breaks down. This knowledge forms the foundation of effective airway management, a critical skill for any EMT.

The **Look, Listen, Feel** technique is a fundamental method used in airway assessment to determine if a patient's airway is open and adequate for ventilation. This technique is straightforward and relies on sensory observations to quickly assess and address airway issues.

Look, Listen, Feel Technique
1. **Look**
   - **Visual Inspection**: Observe the chest for rise and fall, which indicates breathing. Look for any foreign objects, blood, vomit, or other obstructions in the mouth or nose.
   - **Cyanosis**: Check for bluish discoloration of the lips, face, or extremities, which can indicate hypoxia.
   - **Effort of Breathing**: Note the use of accessory muscles, nasal flaring, or retractions between the ribs, which suggest difficulty in breathing.
2. **Listen**
   - **Breath Sounds**: Place your ear close to the patient's mouth and nose to hear breath sounds. Normal breath sounds indicate an open airway, while abnormal sounds can signal obstruction.

- **Stridor**: A high-pitched, wheezing sound heard during inspiration, often indicating a partial obstruction of the upper airway (trachea or larynx).
- **Wheezing**: A high-pitched whistling sound, typically heard during expiration, suggesting lower airway obstruction such as bronchoconstriction in asthma.

3. **Feel**
   - **Air Movement**: Place your cheek near the patient's mouth and nose to feel for exhaled air. This confirms that air is moving in and out of the lungs.
   - **Chest Movements**: Feel the chest to ensure it is rising and falling symmetrically.

Indications of Partial vs. Complete Airway Obstruction

- **Partial Airway Obstruction:**
  - **Breathing Sounds**: Stridor or wheezing indicates some air is still moving through the airway.
  - **Coughing**: The patient may be able to cough forcefully, which suggests that some air is passing through.
  - **Voice Changes**: The voice may be hoarse or have a muffled quality due to the obstruction.
  - **Effortful Breathing**: The patient may show signs of increased effort to breathe, such as accessory muscle use.

- **Complete Airway Obstruction:**
  - **No Breath Sounds**: Absence of breath sounds on auscultation.
  - **No Air Movement**: Lack of air movement felt on the cheek.
  - **Silent Cough**: The patient may exhibit an ineffective, silent cough or be unable to speak.
  - **Severe Distress**: Rapid onset of cyanosis and loss of consciousness if not promptly addressed.

Stridor vs. Wheezing

- **Stridor:**
  - **Description**: A high-pitched, harsh sound heard predominantly during inspiration.
  - **Cause**: Indicates a partial obstruction of the upper airway (trachea or larynx).
  - **Conditions**: Common in croup, foreign body aspiration, epiglottitis, or laryngeal edema.

- **Wheezing:**
  - **Description**: A high-pitched whistling sound usually heard during expiration, although it can be present during both inspiration and expiration in severe cases.
  - **Cause**: Indicates a narrowing or obstruction of the lower airways (bronchi).
  - **Conditions**: Common in asthma, chronic obstructive pulmonary disease (COPD), bronchitis, and allergic reactions.

Clinical Implications

Stridor suggests an upper airway obstruction and is often a medical emergency requiring immediate intervention to prevent complete airway closure. Interventions may include positioning, suctioning, administration of nebulized epinephrine, or securing the airway through intubation.

Wheezing, indicative of lower airway obstruction, requires treatments such as bronchodilators (e.g., albuterol), corticosteroids, and in severe cases, advanced airway management if ventilation is compromised.

Understanding the nuances between stridor and wheezing helps EMTs accurately diagnose and treat airway obstructions, ensuring patients receive timely and appropriate care.

Head-Tilt Chin-Lift, Jaw-Thrust, and Modified Jaw-Thrust Maneuvers
Head-Tilt Chin-Lift Maneuver:

Description: The head-tilt chin-lift is the most common method for opening an airway in an unresponsive patient. The rescuer places one hand on the patient's forehead and applies firm backward pressure with the palm to tilt the head back. With the other hand, the rescuer lifts the chin upward by placing fingertips under the bony part of the lower jaw near the chin.

Appropriate Scenarios:
- Use primarily when there is no suspicion of cervical spine injury.
- Ideal for patients who are unconscious due to medical reasons like cardiac arrest, drug overdose, or respiratory arrest.

Risks:

- In patients with suspected cervical spine injuries, this maneuver can cause further spinal damage by hyperextending the neck.

Jaw-Thrust Maneuver:

Description: The jaw-thrust maneuver involves positioning oneself at the head of the patient. The rescuer places their thumbs on the patient's cheeks and uses the index and middle fingers to push the angle of the patient's jaw forward, which lifts the tongue away from the back of the throat without moving the neck.

Appropriate Scenarios:

- Recommended for patients with suspected cervical spine injuries where spinal immobilization is a priority.
- Used in trauma patients with suspected neck injuries.

Risks:

- Can be difficult to perform and maintain, especially if the patient has facial trauma or if the rescuer is not well-practiced.
- May cause discomfort or even exacerbate certain injuries if not performed correctly.

Modified Jaw-Thrust Maneuver:

Description: Similar to the jaw-thrust maneuver, but with the added precaution of minimizing any movement of the cervical spine. The rescuer places their hands behind the angles of the patient's lower jaw and lifts with both hands, one on each side, while avoiding head and neck movement.

Appropriate Scenarios:

- Best suited for patients with suspected cervical spine injuries.
- Used in conjunction with spinal immobilization techniques (e.g., cervical collars, backboards).

Risks:

- Difficult to maintain for extended periods.
- Requires training and practice to perform effectively without causing further injury.

Comparison of Techniques

Indications:

- **Head-Tilt Chin-Lift:** Preferred in non-trauma patients where cervical spine injury is not a concern.
- **Jaw-Thrust and Modified Jaw-Thrust:** Preferred in trauma patients or any situation where cervical spine injury is suspected.

Ease of Use:

- **Head-Tilt Chin-Lift:** Generally easier and quicker to perform for most rescuers.
- **Jaw-Thrust and Modified Jaw-Thrust:** More challenging, especially in maintaining the position without causing discomfort or additional injury.

Safety in Cervical Spine Injury:

- **Head-Tilt Chin-Lift:** Not recommended due to the risk of neck movement and potential spinal damage.
- **Jaw-Thrust and Modified Jaw-Thrust:** Safer options as they minimize cervical spine movement, though they require more skill and practice.

Practical Applications

Medical Emergency Scenario: A patient collapses in a public place with no apparent trauma. The head-tilt chin-lift maneuver is quickly performed to open the airway and begin rescue breathing since there is no risk of spinal injury.

Trauma Scenario: A patient is found unconscious following a car accident. The jaw-thrust or modified jaw-thrust maneuver is used to open the airway while maintaining cervical spine immobilization, reducing the risk of exacerbating a potential spinal injury.

Risks in Cervical Spine Injury

Head-Tilt Chin-Lift:

- Can exacerbate spinal injury by causing hyperextension of the neck.

Jaw-Thrust and Modified Jaw-Thrust:

- While generally safer for cervical spine injuries, these maneuvers require careful execution. Poor technique can still lead to unintended neck movement or discomfort.

Choosing the right airway maneuver depends on the patient's condition and the presence or absence of trauma. The head-tilt chin-lift is effective and easy but should be avoided in suspected cervical spine injuries. The jaw-thrust and modified jaw-thrust maneuvers are safer for trauma patients but require more skill to perform correctly. Proper training and practice in these techniques are essential for EMTs to minimize risks and ensure patient safety.

Inserting an Oropharyngeal Airway (OPA)
Step-by-Step Process
1. **Preparation**:
   - Wash hands and don gloves.
   - Select the appropriate size OPA by measuring from the corner of the patient's mouth to the angle of the mandible.
2. **Open the Airway**:
   - Use the head-tilt, chin-lift maneuver if no cervical spine injury is suspected, or the jaw-thrust maneuver if spinal injury is suspected.
3. **Insertion**:
   - **Adult**: Insert the OPA upside down (with the curve facing up) into the patient's mouth. Once the device reaches the back of the throat, rotate it 180 degrees so that the curve matches the natural curvature of the tongue and pharynx.
   - **Pediatric**: Insert the OPA with the curve oriented correctly from the start to avoid causing trauma to the soft palate.
4. **Placement**:
   - Ensure the flange rests against the patient's lips.
   - Reassess airway patency and ensure the device is not dislodged or causing gagging.
5. **Monitoring**:
   - Continuously monitor the patient's airway and breathing.
   - Be prepared to suction any secretions.

Indications
- Unresponsive patients without a gag reflex.
- Airway maintenance in unconscious patients.

Contraindications
- Conscious or semi-conscious patients with an intact gag reflex.
- Trauma to the oral cavity or recent oral surgery.

Sizing
- Measure from the corner of the mouth to the angle of the mandible.
- Alternatively, measure from the center of the mouth to the earlobe.

Inserting a Nasopharyngeal Airway (NPA)
Step-by-Step Process
1. **Preparation**:
   - Wash hands and don gloves.
   - Select the appropriate size NPA by measuring from the tip of the patient's nose to the earlobe or the angle of the jaw.
   - Lubricate the NPA with a water-based lubricant.
2. **Open the Airway**:
   - Slightly extend the patient's head to align the airway if no cervical spine injury is suspected.
3. **Insertion**:
   - Insert the NPA bevel towards the septum.
   - Gently advance the NPA along the floor of the nasal passage. If resistance is met, slightly rotate or try the other nostril.
   - Ensure the flange rests against the nostril.
4. **Placement**:

- o Confirm the NPA is in place and the patient can breathe through it.
- o Reassess airway patency and ensure the device is not causing discomfort or obstruction.
5. **Monitoring**:
   - o Continuously monitor the patient's airway and breathing.
   - o Be prepared to suction any secretions.

Indications
- Semi-conscious or unconscious patients with a gag reflex.
- Patients with oral trauma or trismus (lockjaw) where OPA cannot be used.

Contraindications
- Severe facial trauma, particularly to the nose or skull base.
- Known or suspected basilar skull fracture (e.g., raccoon eyes, Battle's sign).
- Nasal obstruction or recent nasal surgery.

Sizing
- Measure from the tip of the nose to the earlobe or the angle of the jaw.
- Ensure the diameter of the NPA is appropriate for the patient's nostril size (commonly using sizes 28-34 French).

Summary of Indications and Contraindications
OPA
- **Indications**: Unresponsive patients without a gag reflex.
- **Contraindications**: Conscious patients with a gag reflex, oral trauma.

NPA
- **Indications**: Semi-conscious patients with a gag reflex, oral trauma, trismus.
- **Contraindications**: Severe facial trauma, basilar skull fracture, nasal obstruction.

Proper sizing and insertion techniques for both OPAs and NPAs are crucial to maintaining a patent airway and ensuring patient safety. Monitoring for any complications or signs of obstruction is essential during and after the insertion of these airway adjuncts.

Physiology Behind Suctioning and Its Effects on Patient Oxygenation
Physiology:
Suctioning is a procedure used to remove secretions, blood, vomit, or other substances from a patient's airway to ensure it remains clear. This is crucial for maintaining proper oxygenation and ventilation.

- **Airway Patency:** Secretions or obstructions can block the airway, preventing air from reaching the lungs. Suctioning helps clear these obstructions, allowing for unobstructed airflow.
- **Oxygenation:** By clearing the airway, suctioning improves the ability of the lungs to receive oxygen and expel carbon dioxide, enhancing gas exchange. However, suctioning can temporarily decrease oxygen levels because the procedure can interrupt the supply of air to the lungs. Thus, it should be done efficiently and quickly to minimize hypoxia.
- **Preventing Aspiration:** Suctioning reduces the risk of aspiration, which can lead to serious complications like aspiration pneumonia.

Indications and Contraindications for Suctioning
Indications:
- **Visible Secretions:** When secretions are visible in the airway and are obstructing airflow.
- **Inability to Clear Secretions:** Patients who cannot effectively clear their own secretions due to weakness, unconsciousness, or neurological impairment.
- **Respiratory Distress:** Signs such as gurgling sounds, decreased oxygen saturation (SpO2), and labored breathing that suggest airway obstruction.
- **Artificial Airways:** Routine care for patients with tracheostomies or endotracheal tubes to keep the airway clear.

Contraindications:
- **Head Injury:** In cases of recent head injury or trauma, especially with suspected basal skull fracture, as suctioning can increase intracranial pressure.
- **Bleeding Disorders:** Patients with bleeding disorders or anticoagulation therapy, as suctioning can cause mucosal bleeding.
- **Cardiovascular Instability:** Suctioning can induce vagal responses, potentially causing bradycardia or hypotension, which are risky for unstable cardiovascular patients.

Proper Technique for Suctioning
Preparation:
1. **Assess the Patient:** Check for indications, ensure the patient needs suctioning.
2. **Gather Equipment:** Suction catheter, suction machine, sterile gloves, saline, and oxygen source.
3. **Preoxygenate:** Provide 100% oxygen to the patient for a few minutes before suctioning to reduce the risk of hypoxia.

Procedure:
1. **Positioning:** Place the patient in a semi-Fowler's position if possible to facilitate access and promote drainage.
2. **Sterile Technique:** Use sterile gloves and equipment to reduce the risk of infection.
3. **Catheter Selection:**
   - **Infants:** 6-8 French
   - **Children:** 8-10 French
   - **Adults:** 12-16 French
4. **Suction Pressure:**
   - **Infants:** 60-80 mmHg
   - **Children:** 80-100 mmHg
   - **Adults:** 100-150 mmHg

Steps:
1. **Insert the Catheter:**
   - Do not apply suction while inserting the catheter to avoid mucosal damage and hypoxia.
   - Insert the catheter gently until you meet resistance or the patient coughs.
2. **Apply Suction:**
   - Apply suction by covering the suction control valve (thumb port) intermittently while withdrawing the catheter.
   - Rotate the catheter between your fingers to ensure all areas of the airway are cleared.
3. **Duration:**
   - Suction should be applied for no longer than 10-15 seconds to minimize hypoxia and mucosal trauma.
4. **Post-Suctioning Care:**
   - Reassess the patient's airway, breathing, and oxygen saturation.
   - Reoxygenate the patient after the procedure if necessary.

Repeat if Necessary: If secretions remain or if the patient shows continued signs of airway obstruction, repeat the suctioning process after allowing the patient to rest and recover oxygenation.

Suctioning is a critical procedure in airway management to maintain oxygenation and ventilation. It involves assessing the patient, using appropriate equipment, and performing the procedure efficiently to minimize risks. Understanding the physiology, indications, contraindications, and proper technique ensures effective and safe suctioning, enhancing patient outcomes in emergency and clinical settings.

Anatomy of the Lungs, Pleura, and Respiratory Muscles
Lungs
- **Right Lung:** Composed of three lobes (upper, middle, lower).
- **Left Lung:** Composed of two lobes (upper, lower) and includes the cardiac notch for the heart.
- **Alveoli:** Small air sacs where gas exchange occurs, surrounded by a network of capillaries.

- **Bronchi**: The main passageways into the lungs, branching from the trachea into the bronchioles and finally into alveoli.

Pleura
- **Visceral Pleura**: The inner layer that covers the lungs.
- **Parietal Pleura**: The outer layer that lines the thoracic cavity.
- **Pleural Cavity**: The space between the visceral and parietal pleura, filled with pleural fluid to reduce friction during breathing.

Respiratory Muscles
- **Diaphragm**: The primary muscle for breathing, located below the lungs. Contracts during inhalation, moving downward to increase thoracic cavity volume.
- **Intercostal Muscles**: Muscles between the ribs. The external intercostals contract to lift the ribs upward and outward during inhalation, while internal intercostals assist in forced exhalation.
- **Accessory Muscles**: Include the sternocleidomastoid and scalene muscles, used during deep or labored breathing.

Negative Intrathoracic Pressure and Breathing
Negative intrathoracic pressure is crucial for the mechanics of breathing. Here's how it works:
1. **Inhalation**:
   - The diaphragm contracts and moves downward.
   - External intercostal muscles contract, lifting the ribs.
   - These actions increase the volume of the thoracic cavity.
   - According to Boyle's law, as the volume increases, the pressure decreases.
   - The negative pressure within the thoracic cavity compared to atmospheric pressure causes air to flow into the lungs.
2. **Exhalation**:
   - The diaphragm relaxes and moves upward.
   - External intercostal muscles relax, allowing the ribs to move down and in.
   - This decreases the volume of the thoracic cavity.
   - As the volume decreases, the pressure increases.
   - The higher pressure within the thoracic cavity compared to atmospheric pressure pushes air out of the lungs.

Role of Surfactant in Alveolar Function
Surfactant is a lipoprotein substance produced by type II alveolar cells. It plays a crucial role in maintaining alveolar stability and function:
1. **Reducing Surface Tension**:
   - Surfactant reduces the surface tension within the alveoli, preventing them from collapsing, especially during exhalation.
   - It allows for easier expansion of the alveoli during inhalation, reducing the work of breathing.
2. **Preventing Atelectasis**:
   - By maintaining alveolar stability, surfactant prevents atelectasis (collapse of part or all of a lung).
3. **Enhancing Gas Exchange**:
   - A stable alveolar surface area ensures efficient gas exchange of oxygen and carbon dioxide between the alveoli and the blood.

Relevance of Surfactant in Respiratory Emergencies
1. **Respiratory Distress Syndrome (RDS)**:
   - Common in premature infants whose lungs haven't produced enough surfactant.
   - Results in high surface tension, leading to alveolar collapse and severe difficulty in breathing.
   - Treated with exogenous surfactant therapy and supportive care.
2. **Acute Respiratory Distress Syndrome (ARDS)**:
   - Can occur in adults due to sepsis, trauma, or pneumonia.
   - Damage to alveolar cells reduces surfactant production, leading to stiff lungs and impaired gas exchange.

o   Management includes mechanical ventilation and addressing the underlying cause.

Illustration Description

Imagine an illustration showing:

- The **lungs** with distinct lobes highlighted.
- The **pleura** with labels for the visceral and parietal layers and the pleural cavity.
- The **diaphragm** positioned below the lungs, showing its dome shape at rest and flattened position during contraction.
- The **intercostal muscles** between the ribs, showing their movement during breathing.
- A close-up of an **alveolus** with surfactant lining the inner surface and a network of capillaries surrounding it, illustrating the site of gas exchange.

By understanding the anatomy and physiology of the lungs, pleura, and respiratory muscles, along with the critical role of surfactant, healthcare providers can better assess and manage respiratory conditions, ensuring effective and efficient patient care.

Differentiating Between Normal and Abnormal Breathing Patterns

Normal Breathing Patterns:

- **Eupnea:** This is the term for normal, unlabored breathing. It typically involves a regular rhythm and rate of about 12-20 breaths per minute for adults. Breathing is neither too shallow nor too deep, and there is no apparent effort required.

Abnormal Breathing Patterns

Cheyne-Stokes Respiration:

- **Description:** Characterized by a cyclical pattern of gradual increases and decreases in the depth and rate of breathing, followed by periods of apnea (no breathing).
- **Underlying Conditions:** Often seen in patients with congestive heart failure, stroke, traumatic brain injuries, and conditions that affect the brainstem.
- **EMS Response:**
    o   Monitor and maintain airway patency.
    o   Provide supplemental oxygen if SpO2 levels are low.
    o   Transport promptly to a medical facility for further evaluation and treatment.

Kussmaul Breathing:

- **Description:** Deep, rapid, and labored breathing. This pattern is a response to severe metabolic acidosis, typically diabetic ketoacidosis (DKA).
- **Underlying Conditions:** Diabetic ketoacidosis, renal failure, and other causes of metabolic acidosis.
- **EMS Response:**
    o   Ensure the airway is clear and provide oxygen to maintain adequate oxygenation.
    o   Begin intravenous access and fluid resuscitation if within protocol and trained to do so.
    o   Transport urgently to the hospital for definitive management of the underlying cause.

Agonal Respirations:

- **Description:** Slow, irregular breaths that are often gasping in nature. This pattern usually occurs just before respiratory arrest.
- **Underlying Conditions:** Indicates severe hypoxia and is often seen in the moments preceding cardiac arrest.
- **EMS Response:**
    o   Immediate airway management and assisted ventilation (bag-valve-mask ventilation or advanced airway if trained).
    o   Begin CPR if the patient is in cardiac arrest.
    o   Use an AED or manual defibrillator as indicated.
    o   Rapid transport to an emergency department while continuing resuscitative efforts.

Detailed Examination of Abnormal Breathing Patterns

Cheyne-Stokes Respiration:

- **Cycle Length:** Each cycle typically lasts between 30 seconds to 2 minutes.

- **Significance:** This pattern indicates a significant underlying medical condition, often involving the brain or heart. It may be a sign of worsening heart failure or central nervous system dysfunction.
- **Additional Symptoms:** May include altered mental status, cyanosis, or other signs of cardiac or neurological distress.

Kussmaul Breathing:
- **Characteristics:** The breathing is consistent and does not follow a cyclical pattern like Cheyne-Stokes. Instead, it is continuous and relentless.
- **Significance:** Indicates the body is trying to blow off excess carbon dioxide due to metabolic acidosis. This is a compensatory mechanism and is a medical emergency.
- **Additional Symptoms:** Signs of dehydration, fruity-smelling breath (in DKA), abdominal pain, and altered mental status.

Agonal Respirations:
- **Characteristics:** Often described as "gasping" breaths, these are inadequate for maintaining oxygenation and ventilation.
- **Significance:** Indicates severe brain hypoxia and is often a prelude to cardiac arrest.
- **Additional Symptoms:** Lack of responsiveness, no palpable pulse, and cyanosis.

EMS Provider Response to Abnormal Breathing Patterns
General Approach:
1. **Assessment:**
   - Perform a rapid assessment of airway, breathing, and circulation (ABCs).
   - Determine the patient's level of consciousness using the AVPU scale (Alert, Verbal, Pain, Unresponsive).
2. **Airway Management:**
   - Ensure the airway is clear and secure.
   - Use airway adjuncts (OPA, NPA) if necessary and appropriate for the patient's condition and level of consciousness.
3. **Oxygenation and Ventilation:**
   - Administer high-flow oxygen via non-rebreather mask if SpO2 is low.
   - Assist ventilations with a bag-valve-mask (BVM) if the patient is not breathing adequately.
4. **Monitoring and Transport:**
   - Continuously monitor vital signs and oxygen saturation.
   - Initiate rapid transport to the nearest appropriate medical facility.
   - Provide detailed hand-off to receiving medical personnel, including observed breathing patterns and interventions provided.

Understanding and recognizing these abnormal breathing patterns enable EMS providers to deliver timely and appropriate interventions, potentially improving patient outcomes.

Principles Behind Pulse Oximetry
Pulse oximetry is a non-invasive method used to measure the oxygen saturation (SpO2) of a patient's blood. It relies on spectrophotometry and photoplethysmography to provide real-time data on blood oxygen levels. Here's how it works:
1. **Spectrophotometry:**
   - The pulse oximeter emits two wavelengths of light (red and infrared) through a pulsatile blood flow, typically in a finger, toe, or earlobe.
   - Oxygenated hemoglobin absorbs more infrared light and allows more red light to pass through, whereas deoxygenated hemoglobin absorbs more red light and allows more infrared light to pass.
2. **Photoplethysmography:**
   - A sensor detects the varying absorption levels of these two wavelengths as the light passes through the blood.
   - The device calculates the ratio of oxygenated to deoxygenated hemoglobin, providing the SpO2 reading.

Factors Affecting Accuracy

Several factors can impact the accuracy of pulse oximetry:

1. **Motion Artifacts**:
   - Patient movement can cause fluctuations in the readings.
   - Using a secure attachment site can help minimize this effect.
2. **Poor Perfusion**:
   - Conditions such as hypothermia, shock, or peripheral vascular disease can reduce blood flow to extremities, leading to inaccurate readings.
   - Warming the extremity or choosing an alternative site can improve accuracy.
3. **Ambient Light**:
   - Strong external light sources, such as sunlight or surgical lights, can interfere with the sensor.
   - Shielding the sensor from direct light can mitigate this issue.
4. **Nail Polish or Artificial Nails**:
   - Dark nail polish and artificial nails can absorb light, leading to falsely low readings.
   - Removing nail polish or using an alternative site can help.
5. **Skin Pigmentation and Thickness**:
   - Darker skin pigmentation and thicker skin can affect light absorption and scattering.
   - Newer pulse oximeters are designed to account for these variations, but slight inaccuracies can still occur.
6. **Carbon Monoxide Poisoning**:
   - Carbon monoxide binds to hemoglobin with a higher affinity than oxygen, and pulse oximeters cannot distinguish between the two, potentially giving falsely high readings in cases of CO poisoning.

Interpreting SpO2 Readings

1. **Normal Range**:
   - An SpO2 reading of 95-100% is considered normal for healthy individuals.
   - Values below 90% typically indicate hypoxemia, requiring medical evaluation.
2. **Clinical Context**:
   - SpO2 readings should be interpreted alongside other clinical signs, such as respiratory rate, heart rate, and the presence of cyanosis.
   - In patients with chronic respiratory conditions like COPD, a "normal" SpO2 might be lower (88-92%) and should be evaluated based on their baseline levels.
3. **Supplemental Oxygen**:
   - The effectiveness of oxygen therapy can be monitored with pulse oximetry, ensuring SpO2 remains within the target range set by healthcare providers.

Limitations in Certain Populations

1. **Anemia**:
   - Severe anemia can affect pulse oximetry readings. Although the SpO2 might be normal, the actual oxygen content in the blood may be low due to reduced hemoglobin levels.
2. **Methemoglobinemia**:
   - Abnormal hemoglobin variants, like methemoglobin, can cause inaccurate readings. Methemoglobinemia results in a constant SpO2 reading around 85%, regardless of the actual oxygen saturation.
3. **Neonates**:
   - In newborns, especially premature infants, pulse oximetry may be less accurate due to smaller, more fragile blood vessels and the presence of fetal hemoglobin, which has different light absorption properties.
4. **Critically Ill Patients**:
   - In patients with severe sepsis or multi-organ failure, pulse oximetry can be unreliable due to poor peripheral perfusion and the presence of abnormal hemoglobin.

Understanding the principles, potential inaccuracies, and limitations of pulse oximetry is essential for interpreting SpO2 readings accurately and integrating them into a comprehensive clinical assessment. This approach ensures better patient care and timely identification of respiratory issues.

Comparing and Contrasting Asthma, COPD, Tension Pneumothorax, and Pulmonary Embolism

Asthma

Pathophysiology: Asthma is a chronic inflammatory disorder of the airways characterized by reversible airflow obstruction and bronchospasm. Triggers such as allergens, exercise, or cold air cause inflammation, leading to bronchoconstriction, increased mucus production, and airway edema.

Signs and Symptoms: Patients with asthma typically present with wheezing, shortness of breath, chest tightness, and coughing. Symptoms can vary in severity and often worsen at night or early in the morning.

Emergency Management:

- Administer high-flow oxygen to maintain adequate oxygenation.
- Provide bronchodilators like albuterol via nebulizer or metered-dose inhaler (MDI).
- Administer corticosteroids to reduce inflammation.
- Consider epinephrine for severe cases or if the patient is not responding to initial treatments.
- Monitor for signs of respiratory fatigue and prepare for advanced airway management if necessary.

Impact on Ventilation and Perfusion Ratios: Asthma leads to ventilation-perfusion (V/Q) mismatch primarily due to reduced ventilation in affected airways. The bronchoconstriction and mucus production cause areas of low ventilation, resulting in hypoxemia.

Chronic Obstructive Pulmonary Disease (COPD)

Pathophysiology: COPD is a progressive disease characterized by chronic bronchitis and emphysema. Chronic bronchitis involves inflammation of the bronchial tubes with increased mucus production, while emphysema involves the destruction of alveoli, reducing the surface area for gas exchange.

Signs and Symptoms: Common symptoms include chronic cough, sputum production, dyspnea, and wheezing. Patients may have a barrel chest and use accessory muscles for breathing.

Emergency Management:

- Provide supplemental oxygen cautiously, aiming to maintain SpO2 between 88-92%.
- Administer bronchodilators and corticosteroids as needed.
- Use non-invasive ventilation (NIV) like CPAP or BiPAP for respiratory distress.
- Monitor for signs of CO2 retention and respiratory fatigue.

Impact on Ventilation and Perfusion Ratios: COPD causes both ventilation and perfusion issues. Chronic bronchitis leads to obstructed airways and poor ventilation, while emphysema causes destruction of alveolar-capillary units, leading to areas of poor perfusion. The combined effects result in significant V/Q mismatch and hypoxemia.

Tension Pneumothorax

Pathophysiology: A tension pneumothorax occurs when air enters the pleural space and cannot escape, leading to increased intrapleural pressure. This pressure collapses the affected lung and shifts mediastinal structures, impairing venous return and cardiac output.

Signs and Symptoms: Patients exhibit sudden chest pain and severe dyspnea. Physical findings may include tracheal deviation, distended neck veins, hypotension, decreased or absent breath sounds on the affected side, and subcutaneous emphysema.

Emergency Management:

- Perform needle decompression with a large-bore needle in the second intercostal space at the midclavicular line on the affected side.
- Place a chest tube to re-expand the lung and allow continuous air drainage.
- Provide high-flow oxygen and monitor for signs of shock.

Impact on Ventilation and Perfusion Ratios: Tension pneumothorax creates severe ventilation impairment in the affected lung, leading to significant V/Q mismatch and hypoxemia. The shift of mediastinal structures also impairs perfusion, worsening the overall oxygenation status.

Pulmonary Embolism (PE)

Pathophysiology: A pulmonary embolism occurs when a blood clot, usually from the deep veins of the legs, travels to the pulmonary arteries, causing a blockage. This obstructs blood flow to lung tissue and leads to areas of ventilation without perfusion.

Signs and Symptoms: Patients may present with sudden onset of dyspnea, pleuritic chest pain, tachypnea, tachycardia, and hypoxemia. In severe cases, there may be signs of shock, cyanosis, and right heart strain.

Emergency Management:

- Administer high-flow oxygen to alleviate hypoxemia.
- Anticoagulate with heparin or low molecular weight heparin (LMWH).
- Thrombolytic therapy may be indicated in massive PE with hemodynamic instability.
- Monitor and support cardiovascular function, considering advanced interventions like embolectomy if necessary.

Impact on Ventilation and Perfusion Ratios: Pulmonary embolism causes perfusion defects in the affected areas of the lung, leading to high V/Q ratios (ventilation without perfusion). This results in wasted ventilation and hypoxemia, as well as increased work of breathing.

Summary of Effects on Ventilation and Perfusion Ratios

- **Asthma:** Reduced ventilation due to airway obstruction leads to low V/Q ratios.
- **COPD:** Both ventilation and perfusion are impaired, causing significant V/Q mismatch.
- **Tension Pneumothorax:** Severely impaired ventilation in the affected lung results in low V/Q ratios.
- **Pulmonary Embolism:** Blocked perfusion creates high V/Q ratios and wasted ventilation.

Understanding these conditions' distinct pathophysiologies, signs, symptoms, and management strategies enables effective emergency response, improving patient outcomes.

Indications, Contraindications, and Proper Use of Oxygen Delivery Devices

Nasal Cannula

Indications:

- Mild hypoxemia
- Chronic respiratory conditions like COPD
- Patients who require low to moderate oxygen flow while still being able to eat, drink, and speak

Contraindications:

- Severe hypoxemia or respiratory distress
- Nasal obstruction or injury
- Mouth breathing which may reduce the effectiveness of oxygen delivery

Proper Use:

- Place the prongs into the patient's nostrils and loop the tubing over the ears, securing it under the chin.
- Adjust the flow rate as prescribed, typically between 1-6 liters per minute (L/min).

Oxygen Delivery:

- Delivers a low flow of oxygen
- FiO2 (Fraction of Inspired Oxygen) ranges from 24% to 44%, depending on the flow rate and the patient's breathing pattern.

Non-Rebreather Mask

Indications:

- Moderate to severe hypoxemia
- Acute respiratory distress
- Situations requiring high concentrations of oxygen

Contraindications:

- Chronic CO2 retainers (e.g., some COPD patients) due to the risk of suppressing their respiratory drive
- Patients with facial trauma or burns

Proper Use:

- Place the mask over the patient's nose and mouth, securing it with the elastic strap.

- Ensure the reservoir bag is inflated before placing the mask on the patient.
- Adjust the flow rate to 10-15 L/min to keep the reservoir bag at least one-third inflated during inspiration.

Oxygen Delivery:
- Provides high concentrations of oxygen
- FiO2 ranges from 60% to 100%, depending on the fit of the mask and the flow rate.

Venturi Mask
Indications:
- Patients requiring a precise FiO2
- Chronic respiratory conditions where controlled oxygen therapy is essential (e.g., COPD)
- Situations where accurate oxygen delivery is crucial

Contraindications:
- None specific, but inappropriate for severe hypoxemia requiring higher FiO2 than the mask can deliver

Proper Use:
- Attach the appropriate colored adapter to achieve the desired FiO2 (each color corresponds to a different FiO2 and flow rate).
- Place the mask over the patient's nose and mouth, securing it with the elastic strap.
- Set the oxygen flow rate according to the adapter's specifications.

Oxygen Delivery:
- Delivers a controlled, precise FiO2
- FiO2 ranges from 24% to 60%, depending on the adapter used and the flow rate.

Oxygen Delivery Mechanisms and FiO2 Ranges
- **Nasal Cannula**: Uses low flow rates to deliver supplemental oxygen directly to the nostrils. The FiO2 depends on the flow rate and patient's respiratory rate.
- **Non-Rebreather Mask**: Utilizes a reservoir bag and one-way valves to deliver high concentrations of oxygen. It prevents the inhalation of exhaled gases and ensures a high FiO2.
- **Venturi Mask**: Employs a jet mixing system to mix oxygen with room air, providing a specific FiO2. Different colored adapters allow for precise oxygen delivery.

Hypoxic Drive and Oxygen Administration
Hypoxic Drive:
- In patients with chronic hypercapnia (elevated CO2 levels), such as those with COPD, the body may rely on low oxygen levels (hypoxia) rather than high CO2 levels to regulate breathing. This is known as hypoxic drive.
- High levels of supplemental oxygen can suppress this drive, leading to hypoventilation and further CO2 retention, which can cause respiratory acidosis and respiratory failure.

Relevance in Oxygen Administration:
- For patients with hypoxic drive, oxygen should be administered carefully, starting with low concentrations and titrating to maintain adequate oxygenation without suppressing respiratory drive.
- Monitoring these patients closely with pulse oximetry and, if available, capnography is essential to ensure that oxygen therapy is both effective and safe.

Understanding the specific indications, contraindications, and proper use of each oxygen delivery device ensures appropriate and effective oxygen therapy. Tailoring oxygen delivery to the patient's needs, while being mindful of conditions like hypoxic drive, optimizes respiratory care and enhances patient outcomes.

Bag-Valve-Mask (BVM) Ventilation Techniques
One-Person BVM Ventilation:
Technique:
1. **Preparation:**
   - Select the appropriate mask size.
   - Connect the BVM to an oxygen source and adjust the flow rate to 15 L/min.

- Position the patient supine with their head in the sniffing position (slight extension).
2. **Seal and Ventilation:**
   - Use the "E-C" clamp technique:
     - Place the thumb and index finger in a "C" shape on the top of the mask to create a seal.
     - Use the middle, ring, and little fingers to form an "E" shape, lifting the jaw to open the airway.
   - With the other hand, squeeze the bag gently until the chest rises (approximately 1 second per ventilation).
3. **Ventilation Rate:**
   - Deliver one breath every 5-6 seconds for adults (10-12 breaths per minute).
   - Deliver one breath every 3-5 seconds for children (12-20 breaths per minute).

Two-Person BVM Ventilation:

Technique:
1. **Preparation:**
   - Similar to the one-person technique, ensure all equipment is ready and the patient is in the proper position.
2. **Roles:**
   - **First Rescuer:** Manages the mask and maintains a seal using both hands.
     - Use the "two thumbs down" technique:
       - Place both thumbs on the top of the mask, with fingers encircling the mandible.
       - This creates a more effective seal and better control of the mask.
   - **Second Rescuer:** Squeezes the bag to provide ventilations.
3. **Seal and Ventilation:**
   - The first rescuer focuses on maintaining the mask seal and keeping the airway open.
   - The second rescuer delivers breaths at the appropriate rate and volume.
4. **Ventilation Rate:**
   - Same as in one-person BVM ventilation: one breath every 5-6 seconds for adults and every 3-5 seconds for children.

Common Errors in BVM Use and Avoidance

Errors and Solutions:
1. **Inadequate Mask Seal:**
   - **Error:** Air leaks around the mask due to improper seal.
   - **Solution:** Ensure the mask is the right size and position it correctly. Use the "E-C" or "two thumbs down" techniques effectively.
2. **Improper Head Position:**
   - **Error:** Head not in the sniffing position, causing airway obstruction.
   - **Solution:** Position the patient's head properly with slight extension. Use an airway adjunct like an OPA or NPA if needed.
3. **Excessive Ventilation:**
   - **Error:** Ventilating too quickly or with too much force, leading to gastric insufflation.
   - **Solution:** Squeeze the bag gently and deliver each breath over about 1 second. Watch for chest rise to gauge the appropriate volume.
4. **Inconsistent Ventilation Rate:**
   - **Error:** Inconsistent timing between breaths.
   - **Solution:** Use a timer or count to ensure a regular rate of 10-12 breaths per minute for adults and 12-20 for children.

Assessing the Effectiveness of BVM Ventilation

Key Indicators:
1. **Chest Rise and Fall:**
   - Observe the patient's chest to ensure it rises with each ventilation, indicating air is entering the lungs.

2. **Auscultation:**
   - o Listen to bilateral lung sounds to confirm air entry into both lungs.
3. **Oxygen Saturation:**
   - o Monitor SpO2 levels using a pulse oximeter. Effective ventilation should improve or maintain oxygen saturation.
4. **Capnography:**
   - o Use end-tidal CO2 monitoring if available. A normal range (35-45 mmHg) indicates effective ventilation.
5. **Patient Color and Condition:**
   - o Check for improvements in skin color (e.g., less cyanosis) and overall condition (e.g., reduced respiratory distress).

Troubleshooting Common Issues

No Chest Rise:
- **Cause:** Airway obstruction or poor mask seal.
- **Solution:** Reposition the head, ensure the mask seal is tight, and use airway adjuncts if needed.

Gastric Insufflation:
- **Cause:** Excessive ventilation volume or pressure.
- **Solution:** Reduce the force and speed of bag compressions, ensuring slow and steady breaths.

Low Oxygen Saturation:
- **Cause:** Ineffective ventilations or inadequate oxygen flow.
- **Solution:** Reassess mask seal, check oxygen source and flow rate, and ensure proper head position.

Inadequate Air Entry on One Side:
- **Cause:** Possible pneumothorax or improper head positioning.
- **Solution:** Reassess head position and mask seal. Consider the possibility of a pneumothorax and prepare for appropriate management if suspected.

Using BVM ventilation effectively requires attention to technique, regular reassessment, and prompt troubleshooting to ensure the patient receives adequate ventilation and oxygenation.

Ventilating a Patient with a Tracheostomy or Laryngectomy Stoma

Unique Challenges

1. **Anatomical Differences:**
   - o Patients with tracheostomies or laryngectomy stomas have altered airway anatomy, bypassing the upper airway structures.
   - o Standard airway management techniques (e.g., bag-valve-mask ventilation via the mouth) are ineffective because airflow does not reach the lungs through the upper airway.
2. **Obstruction Risks:**
   - o The stoma or tracheostomy tube can become obstructed with mucus, blood, or foreign material, which requires immediate attention to ensure patency.
3. **Securing the Airway:**
   - o Dislodgement of the tracheostomy tube can lead to loss of the airway, making reintubation challenging.

Techniques for Ventilation

1. **Bag-Valve Ventilation:**
   - o **Directly to the Stoma**: Attach a pediatric or appropriately sized mask directly over the stoma for ventilation.
   - o **Tracheostomy Tube**: If the patient has a tracheostomy tube in place, connect the bag-valve device directly to the tracheostomy tube using an appropriate adapter.
2. **Ensuring Patency:**
   - o **Suctioning**: Use a suction catheter to clear secretions from the tracheostomy tube or stoma regularly. This prevents obstruction and maintains an open airway.

- **Humidification**: Provide humidified oxygen to prevent mucus plugging, which is more common in patients with bypassed upper airways.
  3. **Stoma Care**:
     - Clean the area around the stoma regularly to prevent infection.
     - Ensure the tracheostomy tube is secure and properly positioned.

Specialized Equipment Needed
1. **Tracheostomy Tubes**:
   - Different sizes and types, including cuffed, uncuffed, fenestrated, and non-fenestrated tubes, may be required based on patient needs.
2. **Adapters**:
   - Connectors to attach bag-valve devices or mechanical ventilators directly to the tracheostomy tube.
3. **Suction Equipment**:
   - Suction catheters and a suction machine are essential for clearing secretions from the tracheostomy tube or stoma.
4. **Humidification Systems**:
   - Heated humidifiers or HME (heat and moisture exchanger) filters to provide humidified air and prevent drying of the mucosa.
5. **Oxygen Delivery Devices**:
   - Tracheostomy-specific oxygen masks or tracheostomy collars to deliver supplemental oxygen.

Differences from Standard Airway Management
1. **Ventilation Approach**:
   - Instead of using standard face masks or nasal cannulas, ventilation and oxygen delivery are performed directly through the tracheostomy tube or stoma.
   - In the case of complete upper airway obstruction or altered anatomy, the upper airway routes are bypassed entirely.
2. **Suctioning**:
   - Regular and often more frequent suctioning through the tracheostomy tube is required to keep the airway clear, which is different from the standard oral or nasal suctioning in typical airway management.
3. **Tube Management**:
   - The tracheostomy tube must be managed carefully to avoid dislodgement, which can be more complex compared to standard endotracheal tubes used in intubated patients.
4. **Emergency Situations**:
   - In an emergency where the tracheostomy tube is dislodged, reestablishing the airway might involve re-inserting the tube, using a smaller tube, or ventilating through the stoma with a bag-valve mask directly.
5. **Patient Comfort and Care**:
   - Attention to stoma care, humidification, and comfort measures is critical for these patients, as they are at higher risk for complications like infection and mucus plugging.

Understanding the unique challenges and specialized techniques for ventilating patients with tracheostomies or laryngectomy stomas ensures effective airway management and improves patient outcomes. These patients require tailored approaches that differ significantly from standard airway management practices.

Principles Behind Continuous Positive Airway Pressure (CPAP) Therapy
Continuous Positive Airway Pressure (CPAP) is a non-invasive ventilation therapy that maintains a constant level of positive airway pressure throughout the breathing cycle. It helps keep the airways open and enhances oxygenation and ventilation without the need for intubation. CPAP delivers air (or an air-oxygen mixture) at a constant pressure through a mask, which helps prevent airway collapse, particularly during exhalation.

Physiological Effects of CPAP on the Cardiopulmonary System
1. Improved Oxygenation:

- CPAP increases the functional residual capacity (FRC) by keeping alveoli open, thereby improving gas exchange.
- It reduces the work of breathing by decreasing the resistance against which the patient has to breathe.

2. Enhanced Ventilation:
- By maintaining positive pressure in the airways, CPAP prevents alveolar collapse (atelectasis) and improves ventilation-perfusion (V/Q) matching.
- It helps to clear carbon dioxide more efficiently from the alveoli.

3. Cardiovascular Effects:
- CPAP can reduce preload and afterload in patients with congestive heart failure (CHF), which helps in reducing the workload on the heart.
- By decreasing intrathoracic pressure fluctuations, CPAP can enhance cardiac output in certain heart failure patients.

Indications for CPAP Use

1. Respiratory Distress:
- Acute exacerbations of chronic obstructive pulmonary disease (COPD)
- Acute asthma attacks that do not respond adequately to initial treatment

2. Congestive Heart Failure (CHF):
- Pulmonary edema secondary to left ventricular failure

3. Other Conditions:
- Obstructive sleep apnea
- Pneumonia with significant hypoxemia
- Near-drowning incidents with fluid in the lungs

Contraindications for CPAP Use

1. Respiratory or Cardiac Arrest:
- Patients who are not breathing or are in cardiac arrest require more advanced airway management.

2. Altered Mental Status:
- Patients who cannot protect their airway or are not able to follow commands may not tolerate the CPAP mask and pressure.

3. Severe Facial Trauma:
- Facial fractures or extensive soft tissue injuries may prevent a proper mask seal and increase the risk of air leak.

4. Vomiting:
- Risk of aspiration increases if a patient is actively vomiting.

5. Pneumothorax:
- CPAP can exacerbate a pneumothorax due to increased intrathoracic pressure.

Potential Complications of CPAP Use

1. Barotrauma:
- Excessive airway pressure can cause lung injury, leading to pneumothorax or pneumomediastinum.

2. Gastric Distension:
- Air can be forced into the stomach, causing distension, which can lead to vomiting and aspiration risk.

3. Hypotension:
- CPAP can decrease venous return to the heart, leading to reduced cardiac output and potential hypotension.

4. Skin Breakdown:
- Prolonged use of the CPAP mask can cause pressure sores or skin irritation.

5. Discomfort and Anxiety:
- Some patients may find the mask and pressure uncomfortable or anxiety-inducing, leading to poor compliance.

Implementation in the Prehospital Setting

Procedure:

1. **Assessment:**
   o Evaluate the patient for indications and contraindications.
   o Obtain baseline vital signs, including oxygen saturation.
2. **Preparation:**
   o Explain the procedure to the patient to reduce anxiety.
   o Select the appropriate CPAP device and mask size.
3. **Initiation:**
   o Start with a low pressure setting (e.g., 5 cm H2O) and adjust based on patient response and comfort.
   o Secure the mask to ensure a proper seal and prevent air leaks.
4. **Monitoring:**
   o Continuously monitor the patient's respiratory status, vital signs, and comfort level.
   o Reassess the patient frequently to ensure CPAP is effective and tolerated.
5. **Troubleshooting:**
   o If complications arise, such as hypotension or discomfort, reassess the need for CPAP and adjust or discontinue as necessary.
   o Address any air leaks or discomfort issues promptly.

CPAP therapy can be highly effective in managing various respiratory and cardiac conditions in the prehospital setting. Proper assessment, application, and monitoring are crucial to maximize benefits and minimize potential complications.

Interpreting Capnography Waveforms

Capnography waveforms provide real-time graphical representation of the CO2 levels in the patient's exhaled breath. Understanding these waveforms helps in assessing both ventilation and perfusion status. Here's a breakdown of the waveform phases and their physiological significance:

1. **Phase I (Inspiratory Baseline):**
   o Represents the beginning of exhalation where no CO2 is present, reflecting the air from the anatomical dead space (trachea, bronchi).
   o The waveform starts at a baseline level of 0 mmHg because the initial exhaled breath contains no CO2.
2. **Phase II (Expiratory Upstroke):**
   o As exhalation continues, CO2 from the alveoli begins to mix with the dead space air, leading to a rapid rise in CO2 levels.
   o This phase indicates the transition from the anatomical dead space to alveolar gas, resulting in an upward slope.
3. **Phase III (Alveolar Plateau):**
   o Represents the exhalation of alveolar gas where CO2 levels reach a plateau.
   o This phase is typically flat or slightly sloped upward and represents the alveolar gas exchange, providing an accurate measure of CO2.
4. **Phase 0 (Inspiratory Downstroke):**
   o Indicates the beginning of inhalation as fresh air enters the lungs, causing a rapid drop in CO2 levels back to baseline.
   o This downstroke marks the end of the exhalation phase and the start of inhalation.

End-Tidal CO2 (EtCO2) Monitoring

End-tidal CO2 (EtCO2) is the measurement of CO2 at the end of expiration and is a critical parameter for assessing ventilation and perfusion.

Assessing Ventilation:

- **Hypoventilation:** Elevated EtCO2 (>45 mmHg) indicates inadequate ventilation, potentially due to respiratory depression, obstructive airway diseases, or equipment malfunction.
- **Hyperventilation:** Decreased EtCO2 (<35 mmHg) suggests excessive ventilation, which can occur in conditions like anxiety, pain, or over-ventilation in mechanically ventilated patients.

Assessing Perfusion:

- EtCO2 is also influenced by cardiac output and pulmonary perfusion. For example, low EtCO2 levels can indicate poor perfusion, such as in cases of shock or cardiac arrest.

Confirming Proper Endotracheal Tube Placement

Capnography is a reliable method to confirm endotracheal tube placement:

- **Correct Placement**: Presence of a normal capnographic waveform with consistent EtCO2 readings (typically 35-45 mmHg) confirms that the tube is in the trachea.
- **Esophageal Intubation**: If the tube is placed in the esophagus, the capnography will show a flat line or minimal CO2 levels, indicating no alveolar ventilation.

Monitoring CPR Quality

During cardiopulmonary resuscitation (CPR), capnography provides real-time feedback on the effectiveness of chest compressions:

- **Quality of Compressions**: An EtCO2 reading of 10-20 mmHg during CPR suggests adequate chest compressions. Higher EtCO2 levels (>20 mmHg) are associated with better perfusion and higher chances of return of spontaneous circulation (ROSC).
- **ROSC**: A sudden increase in EtCO2 (>40 mmHg) can indicate ROSC, as effective circulation rapidly restores CO2 delivery to the lungs.

Capnography Waveform Abnormalities

1. **Hypoventilation:**
   - Elevated baseline and plateau (increased EtCO2).
   - Causes: Respiratory depression, airway obstruction, hypoventilation during mechanical ventilation.
2. **Hyperventilation:**
   - Lower baseline and plateau (decreased EtCO2).
   - Causes: Anxiety, pain, metabolic acidosis, over-ventilation.
3. **Obstructive Pattern:**
   - Prolonged expiratory upstroke, "shark fin" appearance.
   - Causes: Asthma, COPD, bronchospasm.
4. **Rebreathing:**
   - Elevated baseline with no return to zero during inhalation.
   - Causes: Inadequate expiratory valve function, insufficient fresh gas flow.

Clinical Application

Capnography is a powerful tool in various clinical scenarios:

- **Assessing Metabolic Status**: Elevated EtCO2 can indicate hypermetabolic states, while decreased EtCO2 can point to metabolic acidosis.
- **Sedation Monitoring**: Ensures patients under sedation are adequately ventilating.
- **Ventilator Management**: Guides adjustments in ventilator settings to ensure appropriate ventilation.
- **Emergency Response**: In prehospital settings, helps paramedics assess respiratory status and confirm tube placement.

Understanding and interpreting capnography waveforms enable healthcare providers to make informed decisions, ensuring effective ventilation, proper airway management, and high-quality patient care.

Concept of Dead Space in Relation to Ventilation

Dead space refers to areas of the respiratory system where air is present but no gas exchange occurs. It can be divided into two main types:

1. **Anatomical Dead Space:** This includes the airways from the nose and mouth down to the terminal bronchioles. In these regions, air is not involved in gas exchange with the blood. This typically accounts for about 150 mL in an adult.
2. **Physiological Dead Space:** This includes anatomical dead space plus any alveolar dead space where alveoli are ventilated but not perfused, meaning no gas exchange occurs. In a healthy person, alveolar dead space is minimal, but it can increase significantly in pathological states.

Effects of Dead Space on Oxygenation and Ventilation

In Normal States:

- **Ventilation:** In normal breathing, air reaching the alveoli participates in gas exchange, while air in the dead space does not. This inefficiency is typically manageable because the body compensates by adjusting tidal volume and respiratory rate to maintain effective alveolar ventilation.
- **Oxygenation:** Oxygenation remains adequate because the majority of inhaled air reaches perfused alveoli. The balance between ventilation and perfusion (V/Q ratio) is well-maintained.

In Pathological States:

- **Increased Dead Space:** Conditions such as pulmonary embolism, emphysema, or severe infections can increase alveolar dead space, leading to V/Q mismatch. This results in more areas where ventilation occurs without perfusion, reducing overall gas exchange efficiency.
- **Reduced Oxygenation:** Increased dead space can lead to hypoxemia (low blood oxygen levels) because less air participates in effective gas exchange.
- **Increased Work of Breathing:** Patients may need to increase their minute ventilation (total volume of air breathed in one minute) to compensate for the increased dead space, which can lead to respiratory fatigue.

Overcoming Increased Physiological Dead Space with Airway Adjuncts and Ventilation Techniques

1. Airway Adjuncts:

- **Oropharyngeal Airway (OPA) and Nasopharyngeal Airway (NPA):**
    - These devices help maintain airway patency, ensuring that air reaches the lower airways effectively, especially in unconscious or semi-conscious patients. This reduces the risk of upper airway obstruction, indirectly optimizing ventilation.
- **Endotracheal Tube (ETT):**
    - In cases where patients cannot maintain their own airway or require mechanical ventilation, an ETT provides a direct route to the lungs, bypassing upper airway obstructions and anatomical dead space.

2. Ventilation Techniques:

- **Positive Pressure Ventilation:**
    - Methods like bag-valve-mask (BVM) ventilation and mechanical ventilation ensure adequate air delivery to the alveoli. Positive pressure helps overcome airway resistance and maintain open alveoli, improving overall ventilation efficiency.
- **Continuous Positive Airway Pressure (CPAP):**
    - CPAP maintains a constant pressure in the airways, keeping alveoli open and reducing alveolar dead space. It is particularly useful in conditions like pulmonary edema or obstructive sleep apnea, where alveolar collapse is a concern.
- **Bi-level Positive Airway Pressure (BiPAP):**
    - BiPAP provides two levels of pressure (inspiratory and expiratory), which can be adjusted to optimize ventilation and oxygenation. It helps in conditions where respiratory muscles are weak or fatigued, ensuring better alveolar ventilation and reducing dead space impact.

3. High-Flow Nasal Cannula (HFNC):

- HFNC delivers a high flow of oxygenated air through nasal prongs, providing a washout effect that reduces anatomical dead space by delivering a higher fraction of inspired oxygen (FiO2) and supporting ventilation in patients with respiratory distress.

Clinical Applications and Considerations

- **Acute Respiratory Distress Syndrome (ARDS):**
    - In ARDS, alveolar dead space increases significantly. Using low tidal volume ventilation strategies and adjuncts like CPAP or BiPAP can help optimize alveolar recruitment and minimize dead space effects.
- **Chronic Obstructive Pulmonary Disease (COPD):**

- Patients with COPD often have increased dead space due to airway obstruction and alveolar destruction. Non-invasive ventilation (NIV) techniques like CPAP and BiPAP are effective in reducing work of breathing and improving alveolar ventilation.
- **Pulmonary Embolism:**
  - PE increases alveolar dead space by blocking pulmonary blood flow. While definitive treatment involves anticoagulation or thrombolysis, supportive ventilation strategies can help maintain adequate oxygenation until the embolism is resolved.

Understanding and managing dead space is crucial in optimizing ventilation and oxygenation, particularly in pathological conditions. Using appropriate airway adjuncts and ventilation techniques can significantly improve patient outcomes by ensuring effective gas exchange and reducing the work of breathing.

Cardiology & Resuscitation

Anatomy and Function of the Heart

Four Chambers

1. **Right Atrium:**
   - **Function:** Receives deoxygenated blood from the body via the superior and inferior vena cava.
   - **Anatomy:** Thin-walled chamber that acts as a reservoir and conduit.
2. **Right Ventricle:**
   - **Function:** Pumps deoxygenated blood to the lungs through the pulmonary artery for oxygenation.
   - **Anatomy:** Thick-walled chamber with muscular walls to generate enough pressure to push blood through the pulmonary circulation.
3. **Left Atrium:**
   - **Function:** Receives oxygenated blood from the lungs via the pulmonary veins.
   - **Anatomy:** Similar to the right atrium but slightly thicker walls due to higher pressure in the pulmonary veins.
4. **Left Ventricle:**
   - **Function:** Pumps oxygenated blood to the entire body through the aorta.
   - **Anatomy:** The thickest-walled chamber, as it needs to generate high pressure to overcome systemic vascular resistance.

Valves

1. **Tricuspid Valve:**
   - **Location:** Between the right atrium and right ventricle.
   - **Function:** Prevents backflow of blood into the right atrium during ventricular contraction.
2. **Pulmonary Valve:**
   - **Location:** Between the right ventricle and pulmonary artery.
   - **Function:** Prevents backflow of blood into the right ventricle after it has been ejected into the pulmonary artery.
3. **Mitral (Bicuspid) Valve:**
   - **Location:** Between the left atrium and left ventricle.
   - **Function:** Prevents backflow of blood into the left atrium during ventricular contraction.
4. **Aortic Valve:**
   - **Location:** Between the left ventricle and aorta.
   - **Function:** Prevents backflow of blood into the left ventricle after it has been ejected into the aorta.

Major Blood Vessels

1. **Superior and Inferior Vena Cava:**
   - **Function:** Bring deoxygenated blood from the body to the right atrium.
2. **Pulmonary Arteries:**
   - **Function:** Carry deoxygenated blood from the right ventricle to the lungs.
3. **Pulmonary Veins:**
   - **Function:** Carry oxygenated blood from the lungs to the left atrium.
4. **Aorta:**
   - **Function:** Distributes oxygenated blood from the left ventricle to the body.

Frank-Starling Mechanism

The Frank-Starling mechanism describes the relationship between stroke volume and end-diastolic volume (EDV). It states that the heart will pump more forcefully when it is filled with more blood during diastole. This intrinsic ability of the heart ensures that the volume of blood ejected (stroke volume) matches the volume of blood entering the heart (venous return).

1. **Increased Preload (EDV):**
   - More blood fills the ventricles, stretching the myocardial fibers.
   - This stretch optimizes actin-myosin overlap, increasing the force of contraction.
   - Results in a higher stroke volume and cardiac output.

2. **Decreased Preload:**
   - o Less blood fills the ventricles, reducing fiber stretch.
   - o Leads to a weaker contraction and lower stroke volume.

Systole and Diastole in Relation to Ventricular Pressure-Volume Loops

The ventricular pressure-volume loop (PV loop) is a graphical representation of the cardiac cycle's phases, illustrating changes in ventricular pressure and volume.

Systole

- **Isovolumetric Contraction:**
  - o Begins with ventricular contraction; pressure rises without a change in volume because all valves are closed.
  - o On the PV loop, this is the vertical line moving upward from the end-diastolic point.

- **Ventricular Ejection:**
  - o When ventricular pressure exceeds aortic pressure, the aortic valve opens, and blood is ejected.
  - o On the PV loop, this phase is represented by the downward-sloping line as volume decreases and pressure slightly decreases or remains constant.

Diastole

- **Isovolumetric Relaxation:**
  - o Following ejection, the ventricles relax, and pressure drops without a change in volume because all valves are closed.
  - o On the PV loop, this is the vertical line moving downward.

- **Ventricular Filling:**
  - o When ventricular pressure falls below atrial pressure, the mitral valve opens, allowing blood to fill the ventricle.
  - o On the PV loop, this phase is represented by the horizontal line moving to the right as volume increases and pressure remains low.

Summary of Phases in the PV Loop

1. **End-Diastolic Volume (EDV):** The volume in the ventricle at the end of filling (diastole), starting point of the loop.
2. **Isovolumetric Contraction:** Vertical rise in pressure with no volume change.
3. **Ventricular Ejection:** Decrease in volume with a slight increase or stable pressure.
4. **End-Systolic Volume (ESV):** The volume remaining in the ventricle after ejection, ending point of ejection.
5. **Isovolumetric Relaxation:** Vertical drop in pressure with no volume change.
6. **Ventricular Filling:** Increase in volume with low pressure.

Understanding the anatomy and function of the heart, the Frank-Starling mechanism, and the phases of the cardiac cycle through PV loops is crucial for comprehending how the heart efficiently pumps blood and adapts to varying physiological demands.

Coronary Circulation

Overview: Coronary circulation refers to the blood supply to the heart muscle (myocardium) itself. The coronary arteries arise from the base of the aorta and encircle the heart, ensuring it receives a constant supply of oxygen-rich blood.

Left Coronary Artery (LCA): The LCA branches into two main arteries:

1. **Left Anterior Descending (LAD) Artery:**
   - o **Supplies:** The anterior wall of the left ventricle, the anterior interventricular septum, and the apex of the heart.
   - o **Branches:** Diagonal branches that supply the left ventricular anterior wall and septal branches that supply the interventricular septum.

2. **Circumflex (LCx) Artery:**
   - o **Supplies:** The lateral wall of the left ventricle and part of the posterior wall.
   - o **Branches:** Obtuse marginal branches that supply the lateral wall of the left ventricle and, in some cases, the posterior descending artery (PDA) if it is a left-dominant heart.

Right Coronary Artery (RCA): The RCA typically supplies the right side of the heart but also has significant contributions to the left ventricle.

- **Supplies:** The right atrium, right ventricle, the sinoatrial (SA) node, and atrioventricular (AV) node. It also supplies parts of the left ventricle and posterior septum.
- **Branches:**
  - **Right Marginal Artery:** Supplies the right ventricle.
  - **Posterior Descending Artery (PDA):** In right-dominant hearts (about 85% of individuals), it supplies the posterior third of the interventricular septum and part of the inferior wall of the left ventricle.

Differences in Coronary Blood Flow

Coronary blood flow has unique characteristics compared to other systemic circulations:

1. **Phasic Flow:** Coronary blood flow is primarily during diastole. During systole, the contraction of the heart muscle compresses the coronary vessels, significantly reducing blood flow.
2. **Autoregulation:** Coronary circulation has a high degree of autoregulation, which allows it to maintain constant blood flow despite changes in perfusion pressure.
3. **Oxygen Extraction:** The myocardium extracts about 70-80% of the oxygen from coronary blood, much higher than other tissues. This means that increased myocardial oxygen demand must be met by increasing blood flow rather than increasing oxygen extraction.

Coronary Steal Syndrome

Concept: Coronary steal syndrome occurs when there is a diversion (or "steal") of blood flow from a diseased coronary artery to a healthier one, typically induced by the administration of vasodilators. This can exacerbate ischemia in areas supplied by the stenotic artery.

Mechanism:

- **Healthy Vessels:** Vasodilators (like adenosine or dipyridamole) cause healthy coronary arteries to dilate, increasing blood flow to well-perfused areas.
- **Stenotic Vessels:** Diseased vessels with significant stenosis are already maximally dilated at baseline to maintain perfusion. When vasodilators are administered, blood is diverted to the healthier vessels, reducing perfusion to the area downstream of the stenosis.

Clinical Significance:

- **Diagnosis:** Coronary steal syndrome can be unmasked during stress tests with vasodilators, indicating the presence of significant coronary artery disease (CAD).
- **Symptoms:** Patients may experience angina or ischemic changes on an ECG due to the decreased perfusion to the myocardial tissue downstream of the stenotic artery.
- **Management:** Recognizing coronary steal is essential for proper treatment planning, including potential revascularization procedures such as percutaneous coronary intervention (PCI) or coronary artery bypass grafting (CABG).

Summary of Coronary Circulation

The coronary arteries and their branches play a vital role in supplying oxygenated blood to the heart muscle. The LCA, with its LAD and LCx branches, primarily supplies the left heart, while the RCA supplies the right heart and parts of the left heart. Unique aspects of coronary circulation, such as its phasic flow and high oxygen extraction rate, distinguish it from other systemic circulations. Coronary steal syndrome highlights the importance of balanced blood flow and can reveal underlying coronary artery disease during diagnostic testing, making it a crucial concept in cardiology.

Cardiac Conduction System

The cardiac conduction system ensures the coordinated contraction of the heart by generating and transmitting electrical impulses. Here's the pathway:

1. **Sinoatrial (SA) Node:**
   - Located in the right atrium near the superior vena cava.
   - Acts as the natural pacemaker, generating impulses at 60-100 beats per minute.
   - Initiates atrial contraction.
2. **Atrioventricular (AV) Node:**

- Located in the interatrial septum near the tricuspid valve.
- Delays the impulse slightly (about 0.1 seconds) to allow complete atrial contraction and ventricular filling.
- Can generate impulses at 40-60 beats per minute if the SA node fails.
3. **Bundle of His**:
   - Located in the interventricular septum.
   - Transmits impulses from the AV node to the ventricles.
   - Divides into right and left bundle branches.
4. **Right and Left Bundle Branches**:
   - Conduct impulses through the interventricular septum to the right and left ventricles.
   - The left bundle branch further divides into anterior and posterior fascicles.
5. **Purkinje Fibers**:
   - Spread throughout the ventricular myocardium.
   - Conduct impulses rapidly (at about 20-40 beats per minute) to ensure coordinated ventricular contraction.

Action Potentials in Nodal vs. Myocardial Cells

Nodal Cells (SA and AV Nodes):

- **Phase 4 (Pacemaker Potential):** Spontaneous depolarization due to slow inward Na+ currents (If), gradually bringing the cell to threshold.
- **Phase 0 (Depolarization):** Rapid depolarization due to Ca2+ influx via voltage-gated L-type calcium channels.
- **Phase 3 (Repolarization):** Outward K+ currents return the membrane potential to its resting state.

Myocardial Cells (Atrial and Ventricular Myocytes):

- **Phase 0 (Depolarization):** Rapid Na+ influx via fast Na+ channels.
- **Phase 1 (Initial Repolarization):** Partial repolarization due to transient outward K+ currents.
- **Phase 2 (Plateau Phase):** Ca2+ influx through L-type calcium channels balanced by K+ efflux, prolonging the action potential.
- **Phase 3 (Repolarization):** Increased K+ efflux via delayed rectifier K+ channels, returning the membrane potential to its resting state.
- **Phase 4 (Resting Potential):** Stable resting potential maintained by inward rectifier K+ currents.

Refractory Periods

Absolute Refractory Period (ARP):

- The period during which a new action potential cannot be initiated, regardless of the stimulus strength.
- Corresponds to the phases 0, 1, 2, and part of 3.
- Ensures that the heart muscle relaxes between contractions, preventing tetany (sustained contraction).

Relative Refractory Period (RRP):

- The period immediately following the ARP, during which a stronger-than-normal stimulus can initiate a new action potential.
- Corresponds to the end of phase 3.
- Action potentials generated during this period may lead to abnormal rhythms.

Importance in Arrhythmia Formation

Refractory periods play a crucial role in maintaining the heart's rhythmic contraction and preventing arrhythmias. Here's how:

1. **Preventing Premature Contractions:**
   - The ARP ensures that cardiac myocytes cannot be re-excited immediately, allowing the heart to fill properly between beats.
2. **Re-entry Circuits:**
   - Abnormalities in refractory periods can lead to re-entry circuits, where an impulse re-excites areas of the myocardium, causing tachyarrhythmias.
   - If the refractory period is shortened or conduction is slowed, re-entry is more likely to occur.
3. **Triggered Activity:**

- Abnormalities during the RRP can cause triggered activity, such as early afterdepolarizations (EADs) or delayed afterdepolarizations (DADs), which can lead to arrhythmias.

Understanding the conduction system, action potential differences, and refractory periods helps in diagnosing and managing arrhythmias effectively, ensuring proper cardiac function.

Proper Technique for Auscultating Korotkoff Sounds During Blood Pressure Measurement

1. Preparation:
- Ensure the patient is seated comfortably with their arm supported at heart level. The patient should be relaxed, and the environment should be quiet.
- Wrap the blood pressure cuff snugly around the upper arm, ensuring it is positioned about 1 inch above the antecubital fossa. The bladder of the cuff should cover at least 80% of the arm circumference.

2. Positioning the Stethoscope:
- Place the diaphragm of the stethoscope over the brachial artery, just below the cuff's edge and medial to the biceps tendon.
- Ensure a proper seal by holding the stethoscope firmly against the skin but not too tightly to avoid muffling the sounds.

3. Inflating the Cuff:
- Inflate the cuff rapidly to about 20-30 mmHg above the point where the radial pulse disappears. This ensures the occlusion of the brachial artery.

4. Deflating the Cuff:
- Slowly release the pressure at a rate of about 2-3 mmHg per second while listening for the Korotkoff sounds.

5. Listening for Korotkoff Sounds:
- **Phase I:** The first appearance of faint, clear tapping sounds. This is the systolic pressure.
- **Phase II:** The sounds become softer and may include a swishing or whooshing sound as the blood flow increases.
- **Phase III:** The sounds become crisper and louder.
- **Phase IV:** The sounds become muffled and softer.
- **Phase V:** The complete disappearance of sounds, marking the diastolic pressure.

Physiological Representation of Korotkoff Sounds
1. **Phase I (Systolic Pressure):**
   - Represents the pressure at which blood begins to flow through the compressed artery. This occurs when the pressure in the cuff is just below the systolic pressure in the artery, allowing a small amount of blood to pass.
2. **Phase II:**
   - Indicates turbulent blood flow through the partially occluded artery. The artery is still compressed, but blood flow is increasing.
3. **Phase III:**
   - Corresponds to the further opening of the artery, where blood flow becomes more streamlined but still exhibits some turbulence.
4. **Phase IV:**
   - Represents the gradual reduction in blood flow turbulence as the artery is almost fully open. The sounds are muffled and softer due to reduced velocity and turbulence of the blood flow.
5. **Phase V (Diastolic Pressure):**
   - Marks the point where the artery is no longer compressed, and blood flow resumes normal laminar flow. The sounds disappear completely, indicating diastolic pressure.

Differentiating Between Auscultatory Gaps and True Diastolic Pressure
Auscultatory Gap:
- **Definition:** A silent interval that may occur between the systolic and diastolic phases during blood pressure measurement. It is a period where Korotkoff sounds disappear and then reappear.

- **Causes:** Can be due to arterial stiffness, atherosclerosis, or other cardiovascular conditions.
- **Identification:** To detect an auscultatory gap, continue to inflate the cuff to a pressure higher than the expected systolic pressure. Note the point where the sounds first appear, then continue to listen for any gaps in the sounds as the cuff pressure is slowly released. Ensure you identify the first reappearance of sounds after any gap to accurately measure diastolic pressure.

True Diastolic Pressure:

- **Definition:** The true diastolic pressure is indicated by the complete disappearance of Korotkoff sounds (Phase V).
- **Measurement:** The true diastolic pressure is noted when the sounds completely disappear. If an auscultatory gap is present, ensure that the disappearance of sounds after the gap is not mistaken for diastolic pressure. True diastolic pressure is the point of last audible sound.

Tips for Accurate Blood Pressure Measurement

- **Proper Cuff Size:** Use the correct cuff size based on the patient's arm circumference. A cuff that is too small or too large can give inaccurate readings.
- **Patient Preparation:** Ensure the patient has rested for at least 5 minutes before measurement. Avoid caffeine, exercise, or smoking 30 minutes prior.
- **Positioning:** The patient's arm should be at heart level, supported, and relaxed. The legs should not be crossed, and the back should be supported.
- **Multiple Readings:** Take multiple readings and average them for more accurate results. Allow at least 1-2 minutes between measurements.

By following these techniques and understanding the physiological significance of Korotkoff sounds, healthcare providers can accurately measure and interpret blood pressure, ensuring proper diagnosis and management of hypertension and other cardiovascular conditions.

Characteristics of Heart Sounds

S1 (First Heart Sound)

- **Characteristics:**
  - Known as "lub."
  - Caused by the closure of the atrioventricular (AV) valves (mitral and tricuspid valves) at the beginning of ventricular systole.
  - Typically a single sound, but can be split in some conditions (physiological or pathological).
- **Best Heard:**
  - At the apex of the heart using the diaphragm of the stethoscope.

S2 (Second Heart Sound)

- **Characteristics:**
  - Known as "dub."
  - Caused by the closure of the semilunar valves (aortic and pulmonary valves) at the beginning of ventricular diastole.
  - Normally split into two components (A2 and P2) due to the slight difference in closure times of the aortic and pulmonary valves.
- **Best Heard:**
  - At the base of the heart (second intercostal space) using the diaphragm of the stethoscope.

S3 (Third Heart Sound)

- **Characteristics:**
  - Known as a "ventricular gallop."
  - Occurs shortly after S2 during the rapid filling phase of early diastole.
  - Low-pitched, often described as a "thud" or "slosh-ing-in."
- **Best Heard:**
  - With the bell of the stethoscope at the apex, especially with the patient in the left lateral decubitus position.

- **Pathological Conditions**:
  - Indicates increased volume in the ventricles or reduced ventricular compliance.
  - Common in heart failure, dilated cardiomyopathy, and conditions causing volume overload (e.g., mitral regurgitation).

S4 (Fourth Heart Sound)
- **Characteristics**:
  - Known as an "atrial gallop."
  - Occurs just before S1, during the atrial contraction phase of late diastole.
  - Low-pitched, often described as a "tenn-es-see."
- **Best Heard**:
  - With the bell of the stethoscope at the apex, especially with the patient in the left lateral decubitus position.
- **Pathological Conditions**:
  - Indicates decreased ventricular compliance.
  - Common in conditions causing left ventricular hypertrophy (e.g., hypertension, aortic stenosis) and ischemic heart disease.

Systolic vs. Diastolic Murmurs
Systolic Murmurs
- **Timing**: Occur between S1 and S2, during ventricular systole.
- **Types**:
  - **Ejection Murmurs**: Caused by turbulent flow through narrowed orifices (e.g., aortic stenosis, pulmonic stenosis).
    - **Example**: Aortic stenosis—heard as a crescendo-decrescendo murmur at the right second intercostal space, radiating to the carotids.
  - **Regurgitant Murmurs**: Caused by backward flow due to incompetent valves (e.g., mitral regurgitation, tricuspid regurgitation).
    - **Example**: Mitral regurgitation—heard as a holosystolic murmur at the apex, radiating to the axilla.

Diastolic Murmurs
- **Timing**: Occur between S2 and S1, during ventricular diastole.
- **Types**:
  - **Early Diastolic Murmurs**: Caused by regurgitation through semilunar valves (e.g., aortic regurgitation, pulmonic regurgitation).
    - **Example**: Aortic regurgitation—heard as a decrescendo murmur at the left sternal border.
  - **Mid-to-Late Diastolic Murmurs**: Caused by turbulent flow through narrowed AV valves (e.g., mitral stenosis, tricuspid stenosis).
    - **Example**: Mitral stenosis—heard as a low-pitched, rumbling murmur at the apex, often with an opening snap.

Summary of Pathological Conditions
- **S3**: Indicates volume overload conditions like heart failure, dilated cardiomyopathy, or mitral regurgitation.
- **S4**: Indicates conditions causing reduced ventricular compliance, such as left ventricular hypertrophy, aortic stenosis, or ischemic heart disease.

Understanding heart sounds and murmurs is crucial for diagnosing various cardiac conditions. Differentiating between systolic and diastolic murmurs, as well as recognizing pathological S3 and S4 sounds, allows for accurate assessment and management of heart diseases.

Proper Placement of ECG Electrodes
3-Lead ECG Electrode Placement
The 3-lead ECG is commonly used for continuous monitoring. The electrodes are placed as follows:

1. **Lead I:**
   - **Negative Electrode (RA):** Right arm, just below the clavicle.
   - **Positive Electrode (LA):** Left arm, just below the clavicle.
2. **Lead II:**
   - **Negative Electrode (RA):** Right arm, just below the clavicle.
   - **Positive Electrode (LL):** Left leg, below the rib cage on the lower chest or upper abdomen.
3. **Lead III:**
   - **Negative Electrode (LA):** Left arm, just below the clavicle.
   - **Positive Electrode (LL):** Left leg, below the rib cage on the lower chest or upper abdomen.

Ground Electrode:
- Typically placed on the right leg (RL) to reduce electrical interference. It is located below the rib cage on the lower chest or upper abdomen.

12-Lead ECG Electrode Placement
The 12-lead ECG provides a comprehensive view of the heart's electrical activity. The placement is as follows:
1. **Limb Leads:**
   - **RA:** Right arm, just below the clavicle.
   - **LA:** Left arm, just below the clavicle.
   - **RL:** Right leg, below the rib cage on the lower chest or upper abdomen (ground electrode).
   - **LL:** Left leg, below the rib cage on the lower chest or upper abdomen.
2. **Precordial (Chest) Leads:**
   - **V1:** Fourth intercostal space, right sternal border.
   - **V2:** Fourth intercostal space, left sternal border.
   - **V3:** Midway between V2 and V4.
   - **V4:** Fifth intercostal space, midclavicular line.
   - **V5:** Fifth intercostal space, anterior axillary line.
   - **V6:** Fifth intercostal space, midaxillary line.

Determining the Electrical Axis of the Heart Using the 12-Lead ECG
1. Overview of Electrical Axis:
- The electrical axis of the heart represents the average direction of the heart's electrical depolarization during ventricular contraction.
- The normal QRS axis ranges from -30° to +90°.

2. Method to Determine Axis:
- **Step 1: Identify the Lead with the Most Isoelectric QRS Complex:**
  - The lead with an isoelectric (or nearly equal positive and negative deflections) QRS complex indicates that the axis is perpendicular to this lead.
- **Step 2: Determine the Perpendicular Lead:**
  - Find the lead perpendicular to the isoelectric lead using the standard hexaxial reference system.
- **Step 3: Assess the QRS Complex in the Perpendicular Lead:**
  - If the QRS complex in this lead is positive, the axis points towards the positive electrode of this lead.
  - If the QRS complex is negative, the axis points towards the negative electrode of this lead.

Example:
- If Lead I is isoelectric, the axis is perpendicular to Lead I, so it lies along a vertical axis (either +90° or -90°).
- To determine the correct direction, look at Lead aVF. If aVF is positive, the axis is +90°. If aVF is negative, the axis is -90°.

Concept of Einthoven's Triangle
1. Definition:
- Einthoven's triangle is a conceptual triangle that illustrates the relationship between the limb leads (Lead I, Lead II, Lead III) in an ECG. It is formed by placing the right arm (RA), left arm (LA), and left leg (LL) electrodes at the corners of the triangle.

2. Relevance to ECG Interpretation:

- **Law of Einthoven:** The law states that the sum of the electrical potentials of Lead I and Lead III equals the potential of Lead II (Lead I + Lead III = Lead II). This relationship helps ensure the accuracy of limb lead placement and the correct recording of ECG tracings.
- **Vector Analysis:** Einthoven's triangle allows for vector analysis of the heart's electrical activity, providing a basis for determining the heart's electrical axis.
- **Clinical Application:** By using Einthoven's triangle, clinicians can quickly assess the direction and magnitude of electrical impulses, aiding in the diagnosis of various cardiac conditions such as axis deviations, myocardial infarctions, and conduction abnormalities.

Understanding the proper placement of ECG electrodes and the principles of Einthoven's triangle is crucial for accurate ECG interpretation and effective diagnosis of cardiac conditions. The 12-lead ECG provides a comprehensive view of the heart's electrical activity, allowing for precise determination of the electrical axis and identification of abnormalities.

ECG Characteristics
Sinus Rhythm
Normal Sinus Rhythm:
- **P Wave:** Present, upright, and precedes each QRS complex. Consistent shape and regular interval.
- **PR Interval:** 0.12-0.20 seconds.
- **QRS Complex:** Narrow, <0.12 seconds.
- **Rate:** 60-100 beats per minute.
- **Rhythm:** Regular, with consistent R-R intervals.

Atrial Fibrillation (AFib)
Atrial Fibrillation:
- **P Wave:** Absent; replaced by erratic, fibrillatory waves.
- **PR Interval:** Not measurable.
- **QRS Complex:** Narrow, <0.12 seconds, unless there is a concurrent conduction abnormality.
- **Rate:** Atrial rate is 350-600 beats per minute; ventricular response can be variable (irregularly irregular).
- **Rhythm:** Irregularly irregular, with no consistent pattern to the R-R intervals.

Ventricular Tachycardia (VTach)
Ventricular Tachycardia:
- **P Wave:** Often absent; if present, no consistent relationship with QRS complexes.
- **PR Interval:** Not measurable.
- **QRS Complex:** Wide, >0.12 seconds, often with a uniform appearance.
- **Rate:** Typically 100-250 beats per minute.
- **Rhythm:** Regular or slightly irregular, with consistent R-R intervals.

Ventricular Fibrillation (VFib)
Ventricular Fibrillation:
- **P Wave:** Absent.
- **PR Interval:** Not measurable.
- **QRS Complex:** Absent; replaced by erratic, chaotic, and irregular electrical activity.
- **Rate:** Not measurable.
- **Rhythm:** Irregular, with no discernible pattern.

Differentiating Supraventricular and Ventricular Rhythms
Supraventricular Rhythms:
- Originate above the ventricles (e.g., sinus node, atria, AV node).
- **QRS Complex:** Typically narrow (<0.12 seconds), unless there is aberrant conduction (e.g., bundle branch block).

- **P Wave**: Present in sinus rhythm and some other supraventricular rhythms; may be absent or abnormal in atrial fibrillation or other atrial arrhythmias.

Ventricular Rhythms:
- Originate within the ventricles.
- **QRS Complex**: Wide (>0.12 seconds) due to abnormal depolarization pathways.
- **P Wave**: Usually absent or dissociated from the QRS complex.

Concept of Aberrancy in ECG Interpretation

Aberrancy:
- Aberrant conduction refers to the abnormal conduction of supraventricular impulses through the ventricles, typically resulting in a wide QRS complex that mimics a ventricular rhythm.
- **Mechanism**: Occurs when a supraventricular impulse is conducted down one bundle branch normally, while the other is refractory (e.g., during a premature atrial contraction), causing delayed conduction and a wide QRS complex.
- **Recognition**: Aberrant conduction can be transient and often resolves with subsequent beats, unlike consistent wide QRS complexes in true ventricular rhythms.

Examples and Differentiation

1. **Atrial Fibrillation with Aberrancy**:
   - Irregularly irregular rhythm with wide QRS complexes.
   - The wide QRS is due to abnormal conduction (e.g., right or left bundle branch block) rather than originating in the ventricles.
2. **Ventricular Tachycardia**:
   - Regular rhythm with wide QRS complexes.
   - No relationship between P waves (if present) and QRS complexes.

Clinical Application

- **Identifying Aberrancy**: Key to distinguishing between supraventricular tachycardia (SVT) with aberrancy and ventricular tachycardia is the presence of pre-existing bundle branch block patterns, fusion beats, or capture beats.
- **Rate Control**: In atrial fibrillation with rapid ventricular response, rate control is crucial, often achieved with medications like beta-blockers or calcium channel blockers.
- **Rhythm Control**: VTach requires prompt treatment, often with antiarrhythmic drugs or electrical cardioversion, depending on the patient's stability.

Summary

- **Sinus Rhythm**: Regular with P wave preceding each QRS.
- **Atrial Fibrillation**: Irregularly irregular with no P waves.
- **Ventricular Tachycardia**: Regular, wide QRS, no relationship between P waves and QRS.
- **Ventricular Fibrillation**: Chaotic, irregular, no discernible waves.

Understanding these ECG characteristics and concepts like aberrancy helps in accurately diagnosing and managing different cardiac arrhythmias, improving patient outcomes through timely and appropriate interventions.

Comparing and Contrasting STEMI and NSTEMI

Pathophysiology:

STEMI (ST-Elevation Myocardial Infarction):
- **Cause:** Complete and persistent occlusion of a coronary artery, leading to full-thickness (transmural) myocardial infarction.
- **Impact:** The blockage causes ischemia and necrosis of the heart muscle supplied by the affected artery.

NSTEMI (Non-ST-Elevation Myocardial Infarction):
- **Cause:** Partial or intermittent occlusion of a coronary artery, resulting in subendocardial infarction (affecting the inner layer of the myocardium).

- **Impact:** The ischemia is less severe compared to STEMI, but it still results in myocardial damage and necrosis.

ECG Findings:

STEMI:
- **ST Elevation:** Significant ST-segment elevation in at least two contiguous leads (≥1 mm in limb leads or ≥2 mm in precordial leads).
- **New Q Waves:** May develop later, indicating necrosis.
- **Reciprocal Changes:** ST-segment depression in opposite leads.

NSTEMI:
- **ST Depression:** ST-segment depression and/or T-wave inversion in multiple leads.
- **No ST Elevation:** No significant ST-segment elevation.
- **Troponin Elevation:** Elevated cardiac biomarkers (troponins) confirm myocardial infarction without ST elevation.

Initial Management:

STEMI:
1. **Reperfusion Therapy:**
   - **Primary PCI (Percutaneous Coronary Intervention):** Preferred method if available within 90 minutes of first medical contact.
   - **Fibrinolytic Therapy:** If PCI is not available within the recommended time frame, and no contraindications exist, administer fibrinolytics within 30 minutes of hospital arrival.
2. **Medications:**
   - **Antiplatelets:** Aspirin and a P2Y12 inhibitor (e.g., clopidogrel, ticagrelor).
   - **Anticoagulants:** Heparin or bivalirudin.
   - **Nitroglycerin:** For chest pain relief.
   - **Beta-Blockers:** If no contraindications.
   - **ACE Inhibitors or ARBs:** For patients with heart failure or reduced ejection fraction.
   - **Statins:** High-intensity statin therapy.

NSTEMI:
1. **Medications:**
   - **Antiplatelets:** Aspirin and a P2Y12 inhibitor.
   - **Anticoagulants:** Heparin or enoxaparin.
   - **Nitroglycerin:** For chest pain relief.
   - **Beta-Blockers:** If no contraindications.
   - **ACE Inhibitors or ARBs:** For patients with heart failure or reduced ejection fraction.
   - **Statins:** High-intensity statin therapy.
2. **Risk Stratification:** Assess risk using scores like TIMI or GRACE to determine the need for early invasive strategies.
3. **Invasive Strategy:** Angiography and possible PCI or CABG (coronary artery bypass grafting) based on risk stratification and patient stability.

Modified Sgarbossa Criteria for Diagnosing STEMI with Left Bundle Branch Block (LBBB)

Background: Diagnosing STEMI in the presence of LBBB can be challenging because LBBB itself causes significant changes in the ECG. The modified Sgarbossa criteria are used to improve the sensitivity and specificity of diagnosing STEMI in these cases.

Original Sgarbossa Criteria:
1. **Concordant ST Elevation:** ≥1 mm of ST elevation in leads with a positive QRS complex.
2. **Concordant ST Depression:** ≥1 mm of ST depression in leads V1-V3.
3. **Discordant ST Elevation:** ≥5 mm of ST elevation in leads with a negative QRS complex.

Modified Sgarbossa Criteria:
1. **Concordant ST Elevation:** ≥1 mm of ST elevation in leads with a positive QRS complex (unchanged).
2. **Concordant ST Depression:** ≥1 mm of ST depression in leads V1-V3 (unchanged).

3. **Excessively Discordant ST Elevation:** ST elevation ≥1 mm in leads with a negative QRS complex where the ST elevation is ≥25% of the depth of the S wave (modification to improve specificity).

Clinical Significance:

- **Enhanced Sensitivity and Specificity:** The modified Sgarbossa criteria help identify true STEMI in patients with LBBB by accounting for the degree of discordance relative to the QRS complex, reducing false positives.
- **Prompt Diagnosis and Treatment:** Accurate diagnosis using these criteria allows for timely reperfusion therapy, which is critical for improving outcomes in STEMI patients with LBBB.

Understanding the differences between STEMI and NSTEMI, along with the application of the modified Sgarbossa criteria, ensures proper diagnosis and management, improving patient care and outcomes in acute coronary syndromes.

Pathophysiology of Acute Decompensated Heart Failure (ADHF)

Acute decompensated heart failure (ADHF) occurs when the heart fails to pump blood effectively, leading to a sudden worsening of heart failure symptoms. The underlying pathophysiology involves the following mechanisms:

1. **Impaired Cardiac Output:**
   - Decreased myocardial contractility due to ischemia, myocardial infarction, or cardiomyopathy.
   - Increased ventricular filling pressures due to volume overload or diastolic dysfunction.
2. **Neurohormonal Activation:**
   - Activation of the sympathetic nervous system and the renin-angiotensin-aldosterone system (RAAS), leading to vasoconstriction, sodium and water retention, and increased heart rate and contractility.
   - These compensatory mechanisms initially maintain perfusion but eventually exacerbate heart failure by increasing afterload and preload, leading to further cardiac stress.
3. **Increased Afterload and Preload:**
   - Elevated systemic vascular resistance (afterload) increases the workload on the heart.
   - Increased venous return (preload) due to fluid retention exacerbates ventricular volume overload and pressure.

Development of Pulmonary Edema

Pulmonary edema is a critical complication of ADHF and develops due to elevated left ventricular filling pressures. Here's how it occurs:

1. **Increased Left Atrial Pressure:**
   - Impaired left ventricular function leads to elevated left ventricular end-diastolic pressure (LVEDP).
   - This pressure is transmitted backward into the left atrium, increasing left atrial pressure.
2. **Elevated Pulmonary Venous Pressure:**
   - The elevated left atrial pressure is further transmitted to the pulmonary veins, increasing pulmonary capillary pressure.
3. **Transudation of Fluid:**
   - When pulmonary capillary pressure exceeds oncotic pressure, fluid leaks from the capillaries into the interstitial and alveolar spaces of the lungs.
   - This results in pulmonary congestion and edema, impairing gas exchange.

Key Assessment Findings in Pulmonary Edema

1. **Respiratory:**
   - Dyspnea (shortness of breath) at rest or on exertion.
   - Orthopnea (difficulty breathing while lying flat).
   - Paroxysmal nocturnal dyspnea (sudden breathlessness at night).
   - Tachypnea (rapid breathing) and use of accessory muscles.
2. **Auscultation:**
   - Crackles (rales) in the lung bases due to fluid in the alveoli.
   - Wheezing (cardiac asthma) from bronchial constriction.
3. **Cardiovascular:**
   - Elevated jugular venous pressure (JVP).
   - S3 gallop (indicative of increased ventricular filling pressures).

4. **Peripheral**:
   - ○ Peripheral edema (swelling of legs and ankles).
   - ○ Cool, clammy skin due to poor perfusion.
5. **Other**:
   - ○ Fatigue, weakness, and confusion due to reduced cardiac output and hypoxia.

Management of Heart Failure: Preload, Afterload, and Contractility

Effective management of heart failure involves optimizing preload, afterload, and contractility to improve cardiac output and relieve symptoms.

1. **Preload Reduction**:
   - ○ **Diuretics**: Reduce fluid volume and venous return to decrease ventricular filling pressures and alleviate pulmonary congestion.
     - ▪ Example: Furosemide (Lasix).
   - ○ **Venodilators**: Reduce venous return by dilating veins, lowering preload.
     - ▪ Example: Nitroglycerin.
2. **Afterload Reduction**:
   - ○ **Arterial Vasodilators**: Decrease systemic vascular resistance, reducing the workload on the heart and improving forward flow.
     - ▪ Example: Hydralazine, ACE inhibitors (e.g., enalapril), and angiotensin II receptor blockers (ARBs, e.g., losartan).
3. **Improving Contractility**:
   - ○ **Positive Inotropes**: Enhance myocardial contractility, improving cardiac output.
     - ▪ Example: Dobutamine, milrinone.
   - ○ **Digoxin**: Increases the force of myocardial contraction and can help control heart rate in atrial fibrillation.

Summary

- **Preload**: Diuretics and venodilators decrease preload by reducing fluid volume and venous return, alleviating congestion.
- **Afterload**: Arterial vasodilators decrease afterload by reducing systemic vascular resistance, easing the heart's workload.
- **Contractility**: Positive inotropes and digoxin improve contractility, enhancing cardiac output.

By managing these three parameters, healthcare providers can stabilize patients with ADHF, relieve symptoms, and prevent further deterioration.

Diagnostic Criteria and Management Principles for Hypertensive Emergencies

Hypertensive Emergency:

- **Diagnostic Criteria**:
  - ○ **Blood Pressure**: Systolic BP ≥180 mmHg and/or diastolic BP ≥120 mmHg.
  - ○ **Target Organ Damage**: Evidence of acute damage to organs such as the brain (encephalopathy, stroke), heart (myocardial infarction, heart failure), kidneys (acute kidney injury), eyes (retinopathy), or blood vessels (aortic dissection).
- **Management Principles**:
  - ○ **Immediate Blood Pressure Reduction**:
    - ▪ **IV Antihypertensives**: Use intravenous medications to lower BP gradually to prevent rapid drops that can lead to ischemia. Common agents include:
      - ▪ Sodium nitroprusside
      - ▪ Labetalol
      - ▪ Nicardipine
      - ▪ Esmolol
    - ▪ **Initial Goal**: Reduce mean arterial pressure (MAP) by no more than 25% within the first hour, then to 160/100-110 mmHg over the next 2-6 hours.

- **Further Reduction:** Gradual reduction to normal BP levels over the following 24-48 hours.
  - ○ **Monitoring and Support:**
    - ▪ **Continuous Monitoring:** Frequent BP checks, continuous cardiac monitoring, and observation in an intensive care setting.
    - ▪ **Identify and Treat Underlying Causes:** Address conditions such as pheochromocytoma, eclampsia, or drug-induced hypertension.
  - ○ **Targeted Treatment:** Specific interventions based on the type of target organ damage.
    - ▪ **Acute Coronary Syndrome:** Use beta-blockers or nitrates.
    - ▪ **Acute Pulmonary Edema:** Use diuretics and vasodilators.
    - ▪ **Acute Renal Failure:** Adjust medications to avoid further renal impairment.

Hypertensive Urgency:
- **Diagnostic Criteria:**
  - ○ **Blood Pressure:** Systolic BP ≥180 mmHg and/or diastolic BP ≥120 mmHg.
  - ○ **No Target Organ Damage:** Unlike hypertensive emergencies, there is no evidence of acute target organ damage.
- **Management Principles:**
  - ○ **Oral Antihypertensives:**
    - ▪ **Medications:** Use oral antihypertensives such as clonidine, captopril, or labetalol to gradually reduce BP over 24-48 hours.
    - ▪ **Monitoring:** Outpatient follow-up within 1-2 days to ensure BP is controlled and to adjust medications if necessary.
  - ○ **No Immediate Hospitalization Required:** Typically managed on an outpatient basis unless there are complicating factors or failed outpatient management.

Difference Between Hypertensive Emergency and Hypertensive Urgency
- **Hypertensive Emergency:**
  - ○ **Severe BP Elevation:** Systolic ≥180 mmHg and/or diastolic ≥120 mmHg.
  - ○ **Target Organ Damage:** Presence of acute organ damage, requiring immediate BP reduction and hospitalization.
  - ○ **Treatment:** IV antihypertensives, close monitoring, and rapid intervention.
- **Hypertensive Urgency:**
  - ○ **Severe BP Elevation:** Systolic ≥180 mmHg and/or diastolic ≥120 mmHg.
  - ○ **No Target Organ Damage:** No evidence of acute organ damage, allowing for gradual BP reduction.
  - ○ **Treatment:** Oral antihypertensives, outpatient management, and follow-up.

Concept of Cerebral Autoregulation and Its Relevance in Managing Hypertensive Emergencies
Cerebral Autoregulation:
- **Definition:** The ability of cerebral blood vessels to maintain consistent blood flow to the brain despite changes in systemic blood pressure. This process ensures stable cerebral perfusion and prevents damage from fluctuations in BP.
- **Mechanism:** Cerebral arteries constrict or dilate in response to changes in BP to keep cerebral blood flow constant.

Relevance in Hypertensive Emergencies:
- **Chronic Hypertension:** Patients with chronic hypertension often have a shifted autoregulation curve, meaning their brains are accustomed to higher BP levels. Rapid reduction in BP can cause cerebral hypoperfusion and ischemia.
- **Gradual BP Reduction:** In hypertensive emergencies, it is crucial to lower BP gradually to avoid surpassing the lower threshold of autoregulation. A rapid drop in BP can overwhelm the autoregulatory mechanisms and lead to cerebral hypoperfusion and potentially ischemic damage.
- **Targeted BP Goals:**

- Initial reduction should not exceed 25% of MAP in the first hour to prevent cerebral hypoperfusion.
- Further reductions should be carefully monitored to avoid crossing the lower autoregulatory limit.

Management Considerations:

- **Individualized Approach:** Tailor BP reduction strategies to each patient's baseline BP and target organ involvement.
- **Close Monitoring:** Frequent neurological assessments and BP monitoring to ensure patient safety and efficacy of the treatment.

Understanding the principles of cerebral autoregulation and the appropriate management strategies for hypertensive emergencies and urgencies ensures effective treatment and prevention of complications. By carefully controlling BP and monitoring patients, clinicians can optimize outcomes and reduce the risk of acute organ damage.

Pathophysiology and Hemodynamic Effects of Cardiogenic Shock

Cardiogenic shock occurs when the heart fails to pump adequately, leading to reduced cardiac output and insufficient perfusion of vital organs. This can be a result of severe myocardial infarction, heart failure, arrhythmias, or structural heart defects.

1. **Impaired Myocardial Contractility:**
   - **Myocardial Infarction:** The most common cause, where a significant portion of the myocardium is damaged, leading to decreased contractile force.
   - **Heart Failure:** Progressive deterioration of myocardial function results in poor cardiac output.
2. **Hemodynamic Effects:**
   - **Decreased Cardiac Output (CO):** The primary issue in cardiogenic shock, leading to reduced blood flow to the body.
   - **Increased Systemic Vascular Resistance (SVR):** As a compensatory mechanism, the body constricts peripheral blood vessels to maintain blood pressure, which further increases the workload on the failing heart.
   - **Elevated Pulmonary Capillary Wedge Pressure (PCWP):** Indicates high left atrial pressure due to left ventricular failure, leading to pulmonary congestion and edema.
   - **Decreased Mixed Venous Oxygen Saturation (SvO2):** Indicates poor tissue perfusion and oxygen extraction by tissues.

Differences from Other Forms of Shock

1. **Hypovolemic Shock:**
   - **Cause:** Loss of blood volume (e.g., hemorrhage, dehydration).
   - **Hemodynamics:** Low preload, low CO, high SVR.
   - **Management:** Fluid resuscitation to restore volume.
2. **Distributive Shock** (e.g., septic shock):
   - **Cause:** Severe vasodilation and increased capillary permeability (e.g., sepsis, anaphylaxis).
   - **Hemodynamics:** Normal or high CO, low SVR, low preload.
   - **Management:** Vasopressors and fluid resuscitation.
3. **Obstructive Shock:**
   - **Cause:** Physical obstruction to blood flow (e.g., pulmonary embolism, cardiac tamponade).
   - **Hemodynamics:** Low CO, high SVR, variable preload.
   - **Management:** Relieving the obstruction.

Management of Cardiogenic Shock

1. **Inotropes:**
   - **Mechanism:** Increase myocardial contractility to enhance cardiac output.
   - **Examples:**
     - **Dobutamine:** β1-adrenergic agonist, increases heart rate and contractility.
     - **Milrinone:** Phosphodiesterase inhibitor, increases contractility and causes vasodilation.
2. **Vasopressors:**
   - **Mechanism:** Constrict blood vessels to increase systemic vascular resistance and blood pressure, ensuring perfusion to vital organs.

- o **Examples:**
  - **Norepinephrine:** α_1 and β_1-adrenergic agonist, increases SVR and has some inotropic effects.
  - **Epinephrine:** α and β-adrenergic agonist, increases heart rate, contractility, and SVR.
  - **Dopamine:** Dose-dependent effects; at higher doses, it acts as a vasopressor.
3. **Mechanical Circulatory Support:**
   - o **Intra-aortic Balloon Pump (IABP):**
     - **Mechanism:** Inflates during diastole to increase coronary perfusion and deflates during systole to reduce afterload and myocardial oxygen demand.
   - o **Ventricular Assist Devices (VADs):**
     - **Mechanism:** Provides mechanical support to the failing ventricle(s), increasing cardiac output and perfusion.
   - o **Extracorporeal Membrane Oxygenation (ECMO):**
     - **Mechanism:** Provides both cardiac and respiratory support, taking over the function of the heart and lungs, allowing them to rest and recover.

Hemodynamic Monitoring and Goals
1. **Hemodynamic Parameters:**
   - o **Cardiac Output (CO)/Cardiac Index (CI):** Aim to increase CO/CI to improve tissue perfusion.
   - o **Systemic Vascular Resistance (SVR):** Manage SVR to optimize afterload and maintain adequate blood pressure.
   - o **Pulmonary Capillary Wedge Pressure (PCWP):** Reduce elevated PCWP to alleviate pulmonary congestion.
   - o **Mixed Venous Oxygen Saturation (SvO2):** Monitor to ensure adequate oxygen delivery and utilization.
2. **Goals of Therapy:**
   - o **Improve Cardiac Output:** Enhance myocardial contractility and reduce afterload.
   - o **Optimize Hemodynamics:** Maintain adequate blood pressure and organ perfusion.
   - o **Relieve Symptoms:** Reduce pulmonary congestion and systemic hypoperfusion.

Clinical Application
Managing cardiogenic shock involves a multifaceted approach that combines pharmacological interventions with mechanical support. Inotropes and vasopressors are used to stabilize hemodynamics, while mechanical devices provide direct support to the failing heart. Continuous hemodynamic monitoring is essential to guide therapy and adjust treatment based on the patient's response. Understanding the pathophysiology and targeted management strategies is critical to improving outcomes in patients with cardiogenic shock.

Signs, Symptoms, and Emergency Management of Cardiac Tamponade
Cardiac Tamponade is a medical emergency where fluid accumulates in the pericardial sac, compressing the heart and impairing its ability to pump blood effectively. This condition can quickly become life-threatening and requires immediate intervention.

Signs and Symptoms:
1. **Beck's Triad:**
   - o **Hypotension:** Due to decreased cardiac output.
   - o **Jugular Venous Distention (JVD):** Elevated central venous pressure because blood cannot return to the heart effectively.
   - o **Muffled Heart Sounds:** Due to the fluid in the pericardial sac dampening the sound.
2. **Additional Symptoms:**
   - o **Pulsus Paradoxus:** A decrease in systolic blood pressure by more than 10 mmHg during inspiration.
   - o **Tachycardia:** Compensatory mechanism to maintain cardiac output.
   - o **Dyspnea and Tachypnea:** Due to decreased cardiac output and pulmonary congestion.
   - o **Chest Pain:** Sharp or stabbing pain that may radiate to the neck, shoulders, or back.
   - o **Anxiety and Restlessness:** Resulting from hypoxia and decreased perfusion.

- Cold, Clammy Skin: Due to peripheral vasoconstriction.

Emergency Management of Cardiac Tamponade
1. **Immediate Stabilization:**
   - **Oxygen Therapy:** Provide supplemental oxygen to improve oxygenation and decrease myocardial oxygen demand.
   - **IV Access:** Establish intravenous access for fluid resuscitation and medication administration.
2. **Hemodynamic Support:**
   - **Volume Expansion:** Administer IV fluids (e.g., normal saline) to increase preload and temporarily improve cardiac output.
3. **Definitive Treatment:**
   - **Pericardiocentesis:** The primary treatment to remove the accumulated fluid from the pericardial sac.

Beck's Triad and Its Relation to Cardiac Tamponade
Beck's Triad is a classic set of clinical signs associated with cardiac tamponade:
- **Hypotension:** Due to decreased ventricular filling and reduced cardiac output.
- **Jugular Venous Distention (JVD):** Elevated venous pressure as blood backs up into the systemic circulation.
- **Muffled Heart Sounds:** Fluid in the pericardium dampens the transmission of heart sounds.

Technique and Indications for Emergency Pericardiocentesis
Indications:
- **Clinical Diagnosis:** Cardiac tamponade diagnosed based on clinical signs (e.g., Beck's triad) and confirmed by imaging (e.g., echocardiography).
- **Hemodynamic Instability:** Patients presenting with signs of hemodynamic compromise, such as severe hypotension, pulsus paradoxus, or shock.

Technique:
1. **Preparation:**
   - **Patient Positioning:** Place the patient in a semi-recumbent position (30-45 degrees) to bring the heart closer to the chest wall.
   - **Sterile Field:** Prepare a sterile field and use sterile gloves and equipment.
2. **Anatomical Landmarks:**
   - Identify the subxiphoid area (below the xiphoid process of the sternum) as the entry site.
3. **Local Anesthesia:**
   - Administer local anesthesia at the puncture site to minimize patient discomfort.
4. **Needle Insertion:**
   - Attach a syringe to a long, large-bore needle (18- or 16-gauge).
   - Insert the needle at a 45-degree angle to the skin, aiming towards the left shoulder.
   - Advance the needle while aspirating continuously until fluid is withdrawn into the syringe.
5. **Fluid Aspiration:**
   - Once pericardial fluid is obtained, continue to aspirate until no more fluid can be withdrawn or hemodynamic stability improves.
6. **Confirmation and Monitoring:**
   - Use echocardiography if available to guide the procedure and confirm the removal of pericardial fluid.
   - Monitor the patient's vital signs and clinical status closely throughout the procedure.

Post-Procedure Care
- **Observation:** Monitor the patient for signs of re-accumulation of fluid or complications such as arrhythmias or pneumothorax.
- **Follow-Up Imaging:** Repeat echocardiography to ensure complete drainage and assess for residual fluid.
- **Definitive Treatment:** Address the underlying cause of the tamponade (e.g., infection, malignancy, trauma) to prevent recurrence.

Cardiac tamponade requires prompt recognition and intervention. Understanding the signs and symptoms, utilizing Beck's triad, and performing emergency pericardiocentesis can be life-saving measures in the management of this critical condition.

Current AHA Guidelines for CPR

The American Heart Association (AHA) guidelines for cardiopulmonary resuscitation (CPR) provide specific instructions tailored to different age groups: adults, children, and infants. Here's a detailed comparison of the current guidelines:

Adult CPR (Ages 8 and Above)
1. **Compression Depth**:
   - At least 2 inches (5 cm) but not more than 2.4 inches (6 cm).
2. **Compression Rate**:
   - 100-120 compressions per minute.
3. **Chest Recoil**:
   - Allow full recoil between compressions to maximize venous return to the heart.
4. **Compression-to-Ventilation Ratio**:
   - 30:2 for single rescuer and two-rescuer CPR.
5. **Hand Placement**:
   - Heel of one hand on the center of the chest (lower half of the sternum), other hand on top, interlocking fingers.

Child CPR (Ages 1 to 8)
1. **Compression Depth**:
   - About 2 inches (5 cm).
2. **Compression Rate**:
   - 100-120 compressions per minute.
3. **Chest Recoil**:
   - Ensure complete chest recoil to allow heart to refill with blood.
4. **Compression-to-Ventilation Ratio**:
   - 30:2 for single rescuer, 15:2 for two-rescuer CPR.
5. **Hand Placement**:
   - One or two hands (depending on the size of the child) on the center of the chest.

Infant CPR (Under 1 Year)
1. **Compression Depth**:
   - About 1.5 inches (4 cm).
2. **Compression Rate**:
   - 100-120 compressions per minute.
3. **Chest Recoil**:
   - Ensure complete chest recoil to facilitate blood flow.
4. **Compression-to-Ventilation Ratio**:
   - 30:2 for single rescuer, 15:2 for two-rescuer CPR.
5. **Hand Placement**:
   - Two fingers in the center of the chest just below the nipple line for single rescuer.
   - Two thumbs encircling hands technique for two-rescuer CPR.

Impact of Compression Depth, Rate, and Chest Recoil on CPR Quality

Compression Depth: Adequate depth ensures sufficient pressure to create blood flow during compressions. Inadequate depth can lead to poor perfusion of vital organs, while excessive depth risks injury.

Compression Rate: Maintaining a rate of 100-120 compressions per minute optimizes blood flow. Too slow or too fast can decrease the effectiveness of compressions.

Chest Recoil: Full chest recoil between compressions is crucial as it allows the heart to refill with blood. Incomplete recoil reduces cardiac output and perfusion to organs.

"Pit Crew" CPR Concept

The "pit crew" CPR approach is a highly organized method of performing resuscitation, modeled after the efficiency of a racing pit crew. Each member of the resuscitation team is assigned specific roles and tasks, enhancing the efficiency and effectiveness of CPR.

Roles and Responsibilities:

- **Compressor**: Performs chest compressions.
- **Airway Manager**: Maintains airway patency and provides ventilations.
- **Team Leader**: Coordinates the resuscitation efforts, ensuring all actions are performed smoothly and according to protocol.
- **Medication Administrator**: Prepares and administers medications.
- **Monitor/Defibrillator Operator**: Manages the defibrillator and monitors patient's rhythm.

Benefits:

- **Efficiency**: Streamlined roles and responsibilities reduce interruptions in chest compressions and improve the overall quality of CPR.
- **Coordination**: Clear communication and predefined roles enhance team coordination and reduce chaos during a resuscitation attempt.
- **Consistency**: Consistent application of resuscitation protocols improves outcomes by ensuring that all necessary steps are followed promptly and accurately.

By understanding and implementing these guidelines and techniques, healthcare providers can significantly improve the chances of survival and recovery for patients experiencing cardiac arrest.

Proper Use of an AED

Automated External Defibrillators (AEDs) are crucial in the early management of cardiac arrest. Here is a detailed guide on their proper use, including pad placement and handling special situations.

Pad Placement:

For Adults:

1. **Upper Right Chest:** Place one pad to the right of the sternum, below the collarbone.
2. **Lower Left Chest:** Place the second pad a few inches below the left armpit, on the side of the chest.

For Children (Under 8 Years or <55 lbs):

1. **Front-Back Placement:** If the child's chest is too small for the standard adult pad placement without them touching, place one pad in the center of the chest and the other on the center of the back. Use pediatric pads if available.

Key Steps in the AED Algorithm

1. **Power On the AED:** Turn on the AED by pressing the power button. Some models power on automatically when the lid is opened.
2. **Attach Pads:** Expose the patient's chest and attach the adhesive pads in the appropriate positions. Ensure the pads have good contact with the skin.
3. **Analyze Rhythm:** The AED will instruct you to stay clear of the patient while it analyzes the heart rhythm. Ensure no one is touching the patient during this time.
4. **Deliver Shock (if advised):** If the AED advises a shock, ensure everyone is clear of the patient and press the shock button. The AED will deliver an electrical shock to the heart.
5. **Resume CPR:** Immediately resume chest compressions and follow the AED's prompts. Continue CPR for 2 minutes before the AED reanalyzes the rhythm.

Managing Special Situations

Implanted Devices:

- **Pacemakers/Defibrillators:** Avoid placing AED pads directly over an implanted device, typically seen as a small bulge under the skin, usually on the upper chest. Adjust the pad placement slightly to the side.
- **Signs:** Look for scars or medical alert bracelets indicating the presence of an implanted device.

Medication Patches:

- **Remove Patches:** Remove any transdermal medication patches from the chest area before placing the AED pads. Use a gloved hand to avoid absorbing the medication.

- **Skin Cleaning:** Wipe the area dry to ensure proper adhesion and function of the AED pads.

Wet or Sweaty Skin:

- **Dry the Chest:** If the patient's chest is wet, dry it off before attaching the pads to ensure they stick properly and deliver the shock effectively.

Hairy Chest:

- **Shave if Necessary:** If the patient has a very hairy chest, quickly shave the area where the pads will be placed to ensure good contact. Some AED kits include a razor for this purpose.

Metal Surfaces:

- **Safety Precautions:** If the patient is on a metal surface, ensure no one is touching the patient or the metal surface when delivering the shock to prevent electrical conduction.

Using an AED promptly and correctly can significantly increase the chances of survival in cardiac arrest cases. Proper pad placement, adherence to the AED algorithm, and managing special situations effectively ensure the best outcomes for patients in these critical moments.

Key Components of Post-Resuscitation Care

Post-resuscitation care is critical to optimizing outcomes for patients who have achieved return of spontaneous circulation (ROSC) after cardiac arrest. The primary goals are to stabilize vital functions, prevent further injury, and improve neurological outcomes. Here are the key components:

1. **Hemodynamic Stabilization:**
   - **Blood Pressure Management:** Maintain adequate blood pressure (e.g., MAP > 65 mmHg) using fluids, vasopressors, or inotropes as needed.
   - **Cardiac Output:** Support cardiac function and address any underlying myocardial dysfunction or ischemia.
2. **Respiratory Support:**
   - **Oxygenation:** Ensure adequate oxygenation (SpO2 > 94%) to prevent hypoxia while avoiding hyperoxia, which can cause oxidative stress.
   - **Ventilation:** Manage ventilation to maintain normal carbon dioxide levels (PaCO2 35-45 mmHg).
3. **Neurological Monitoring and Management:**
   - **Neurological Assessment:** Perform serial neurological exams to monitor for signs of recovery or deterioration.
   - **Targeted Temperature Management (TTM):** Implement TTM to reduce the risk of neurological injury.
4. **Temperature Management:**
   - **Induced Hypothermia (TTM):** Cool the patient to 32-36°C for at least 24 hours.
   - **Rewarming:** Gradually rewarm the patient to normothermia to avoid complications associated with rapid temperature changes.
5. **Glycemic Control:**
   - Maintain blood glucose levels within the normal range (140-180 mg/dL) to avoid both hypoglycemia and hyperglycemia, which can adversely affect outcomes.
6. **Multiorgan Support:**
   - **Renal Support:** Monitor and manage renal function to prevent acute kidney injury.
   - **Liver Function:** Assess and support liver function, as hepatic perfusion can be compromised.
7. **Secondary Prevention:**
   - **Identify and Treat Underlying Causes:** Address reversible causes of cardiac arrest (e.g., myocardial infarction, electrolyte imbalances).
   - **Rehabilitation and Follow-Up:** Plan for long-term follow-up and rehabilitation to support recovery and prevent recurrence.

Neurologically Intact Survival

The concept of "neurologically intact survival" focuses on not only surviving cardiac arrest but also preserving brain function to maintain quality of life. This guides post-resuscitation management by prioritizing interventions that protect and restore neurological function:

- **Early Neurological Assessment**: Conduct thorough and regular assessments to evaluate brain function and identify potential areas of concern.
- **Targeted Temperature Management (TTM)**: Implement TTM to minimize brain injury by reducing metabolic demand and preventing reperfusion injury.
- **Avoiding Secondary Brain Injury**: Manage hemodynamics, oxygenation, and ventilation carefully to prevent further brain damage.

Benefits and Risks of Induced Hypothermia
Benefits:
1. **Neuroprotection**: Reduces metabolic rate and oxygen demand, potentially decreasing the extent of ischemic injury to the brain.
2. **Reduction of Reperfusion Injury**: Minimizes the inflammatory response and oxidative stress associated with reperfusion, which can exacerbate brain damage.
3. **Improved Outcomes**: Clinical trials have shown that TTM can improve survival and neurological outcomes in patients after cardiac arrest.

Risks:
1. **Infection**: Hypothermia can impair immune function, increasing the risk of infections such as pneumonia and sepsis.
2. **Coagulopathy**: Cooling can affect coagulation pathways, leading to increased bleeding risks.
3. **Electrolyte Imbalances**: Hypothermia can cause shifts in electrolytes, necessitating careful monitoring and management.
4. **Cardiac Arrhythmias**: Cooling can increase the risk of arrhythmias, particularly bradycardia.
5. **Shivering**: Can increase metabolic demand and counteract the cooling effects; requires management with sedation and neuromuscular blockade if necessary.

Targeted temperature management and comprehensive post-resuscitation care are vital in optimizing outcomes for cardiac arrest survivors. Balancing the benefits and risks of induced hypothermia is essential for maximizing neurological recovery while minimizing potential complications.

Resuscitation Approaches for Drowning, Severe Hypothermia, and Electrocution
Drowning:
Pathophysiology:
- **Primary Issue:** Drowning leads to hypoxia due to water filling the lungs, impairing gas exchange.
- **Complications:** Can include hypothermia, electrolyte imbalances, and aspiration pneumonia.

Resuscitation Strategy:
1. **Remove from Water:** Ensure the patient is safely removed from the water.
2. **Airway and Breathing:**
   o Check for responsiveness and breathing.
   o Begin rescue breaths immediately if the patient is not breathing. Drowning victims often require ventilation first.
3. **CPR:**
   o Initiate chest compressions if there is no pulse. Use the standard ratio of 30 compressions to 2 breaths.
4. **Defibrillation:**
   o Use an AED if available and follow its prompts. Defibrillation is less commonly required in drowning but should not be delayed if indicated.
5. **Oxygenation and Ventilation:**
   o Provide high-flow oxygen once spontaneous breathing is restored. Use a bag-valve mask or advanced airway management as needed.

Severe Hypothermia:
Pathophysiology:
- **Primary Issue:** Core body temperature drops below 35°C (95°F), leading to slowed metabolism and physiological functions.

- **Complications:** Can include arrhythmias, coagulopathy, and metabolic acidosis.

Resuscitation Strategy:

1. **Gentle Handling:** Avoid rough movements to prevent triggering arrhythmias.
2. **Airway and Breathing:**
   - Ensure airway patency and provide oxygen. Use warmed, humidified oxygen if possible.
3. **CPR:**
   - Initiate chest compressions if there is no pulse. Continue CPR for prolonged periods; hypothermic patients may survive with low blood flow for extended times.
4. **Defibrillation:**
   - Defibrillation is often ineffective below 30°C (86°F). Attempt once, and then focus on rewarming before further attempts.
5. **Rewarming:**
   - Use passive rewarming (blankets, warm environment) for mild hypothermia.
   - Active external rewarming (warm water bottles, heating pads) and active internal rewarming (warm IV fluids, lavage) for severe cases.

Electrocution:

Pathophysiology:

- **Primary Issue:** Electrical injury can cause cardiac arrhythmias, burns, and muscle damage.
- **Complications:** Can include ventricular fibrillation, cardiac arrest, and rhabdomyolysis.

Resuscitation Strategy:

1. **Safety First:** Ensure the electrical source is turned off before approaching the patient.
2. **Airway and Breathing:**
   - Check for responsiveness and breathing. Begin rescue breaths if needed.
3. **CPR:**
   - Initiate chest compressions if there is no pulse. Follow the standard ratio of 30 compressions to 2 breaths.
4. **Defibrillation:**
   - Use an AED as electrical injuries commonly cause arrhythmias. Follow AED prompts for defibrillation.
5. **Ongoing Monitoring:**
   - Monitor for signs of cardiac instability, burn injuries, and muscle damage. Provide advanced cardiac life support (ACLS) as needed.

The Concept of the "Lethal Triad" in Severe Hypothermia

Lethal Triad: The "lethal triad" in severe hypothermia refers to a combination of three critical conditions that significantly complicate resuscitation efforts and can lead to death if not addressed:

1. **Hypothermia:**
   - Low core body temperature impairs normal physiological functions, including enzyme activity, cardiac contractility, and the body's ability to generate heat.
2. **Coagulopathy:**
   - Hypothermia induces a coagulopathic state where the blood's ability to clot is severely impaired. This is due to the direct effects of cold on clotting proteins and platelets, leading to an increased risk of bleeding.
3. **Acidosis:**
   - Cold-induced hypoperfusion and anaerobic metabolism result in metabolic acidosis. The accumulation of lactic acid due to reduced oxygen delivery exacerbates this condition.

Implications for Resuscitation:

1. **Prolonged CPR:** Hypothermic patients may have a better chance of survival despite prolonged cardiac arrest. The low metabolic rate protects organs, so resuscitation efforts should continue until the patient is rewarmed.
2. **Careful Rewarming:** Rapid rewarming can cause rewarming shock and other complications. Controlled rewarming methods are preferred.

3. **Fluid Management:** Warmed IV fluids help in rewarming and managing acidosis. Blood products may be necessary if coagulopathy leads to significant bleeding.
4. **Avoiding Rough Handling:** Minimize movements to reduce the risk of arrhythmias. Hypothermic hearts are highly sensitive to mechanical stimulation.

Resuscitation strategies must be tailored to the specific pathophysiology of drowning, severe hypothermia, and electrocution. Understanding these differences ensures effective treatment and increases the likelihood of patient survival. Managing severe hypothermia requires particular attention to the lethal triad of hypothermia, coagulopathy, and acidosis, which necessitates careful and prolonged resuscitative efforts.

Trauma

Biomechanics of Blunt Trauma in Motor Vehicle Collisions

Motor vehicle collisions (MVCs) are a common cause of blunt trauma, resulting from rapid deceleration and the forces involved. Understanding the biomechanics of these collisions involves applying Newton's laws of motion to the occupant's kinematics.

Newton's Laws of Motion and Occupant Kinematics

1. **First Law (Law of Inertia):**
   - **Principle:** An object at rest stays at rest, and an object in motion stays in motion unless acted upon by an external force.
   - **Application:** In an MVC, occupants continue moving at the vehicle's pre-collision speed until they are stopped by an external force, such as a seatbelt, airbag, or the interior of the vehicle.

2. **Second Law (Law of Acceleration):**
   - **Principle:** The acceleration of an object depends on the mass of the object and the force applied to it ($F = ma$).
   - **Application:** The force exerted on occupants during a collision is a product of the vehicle's deceleration and the occupant's mass. Rapid deceleration results in greater forces exerted on the occupants.

3. **Third Law (Action and Reaction):**
   - **Principle:** For every action, there is an equal and opposite reaction.
   - **Application:** When an occupant's body strikes the interior of the vehicle or a restraint system, the vehicle or restraint system exerts an equal and opposite force on the occupant, causing injuries.

Restrained vs. Unrestrained Occupants

Frontal Impact Collisions

- **Restrained Occupants:**
  - **Seatbelts:** Seatbelts distribute the forces across the stronger parts of the body (pelvis, chest, shoulders), reducing the risk of severe injuries.
  - **Airbags:** Airbags provide a cushion that slows down the occupant's forward motion, decreasing the risk of head and chest injuries.
  - **Kinematics:** The occupant moves forward but is restrained by the seatbelt and cushioned by the airbag, reducing the impact force on critical body parts.

- **Unrestrained Occupants:**
  - **Impact with Interior:** Unrestrained occupants continue moving forward at the vehicle's pre-collision speed until they strike the dashboard, windshield, or steering wheel.
  - **Kinematics:** The abrupt stop can result in severe injuries such as head trauma, facial injuries, rib fractures, and internal organ damage due to high-impact forces.

Side Impact Collisions

- **Restrained Occupants:**
  - **Seatbelts:** Seatbelts help keep the occupant within the protective space of the vehicle, preventing ejection and reducing the risk of contact with intruding structures.
  - **Side Airbags:** Side airbags cushion the impact and reduce the risk of head and thoracic injuries.
  - **Kinematics:** The occupant's body is supported and protected by the side airbags and the seatbelt, minimizing lateral movement and impact forces.

- **Unrestrained Occupants:**
  - **Impact with Interior:** The occupant is thrown sideways toward the point of impact, often colliding with the door, window, or other passengers.
  - **Kinematics:** The lack of restraint leads to a greater risk of lateral impact injuries, including rib fractures, pelvic fractures, and head trauma from hitting the side structures or other occupants.

Rear Impact Collisions

- **Restrained Occupants:**

- - - **Seatbelts**: Seatbelts prevent the occupant from being thrown backward or upward, keeping them in their seat.
    - **Head Restraints**: Properly adjusted head restraints reduce the risk of whiplash injuries by limiting the backward motion of the head and neck.
    - **Kinematics**: The occupant is pushed back into the seat, with the seatbelt and head restraint absorbing much of the force.
  - **Unrestrained Occupants**:
    - **Impact with Interior**: The occupant may be thrown backward into the seat or forward if the vehicle rebounds after the initial impact.
    - **Kinematics**: This can lead to severe injuries, including whiplash, spinal injuries, and head trauma from striking the interior of the vehicle or other passengers.

Summary of Key Differences
- **Frontal Impact**: Restrained occupants are protected by seatbelts and airbags, reducing forward motion and impact forces, whereas unrestrained occupants suffer direct collisions with the interior.
- **Side Impact**: Restrained occupants benefit from seatbelts and side airbags, minimizing lateral injuries, while unrestrained occupants face severe lateral impacts and potential ejection.
- **Rear Impact**: Seatbelts and head restraints protect restrained occupants from whiplash and backward motion, while unrestrained occupants face the risk of severe whiplash and collision with the vehicle's interior.

Understanding these dynamics is crucial for improving vehicle safety features and emergency response strategies, ultimately reducing the severity of injuries sustained in motor vehicle collisions.

Pathophysiology of Penetrating Trauma from Firearms and Stabbing Weapons
Firearms (Projectiles):
Pathophysiology:
- **High-Velocity Projectiles:** Typically include bullets from rifles and some handguns. These projectiles travel at speeds greater than 2,000 feet per second.
  - **Tissue Damage:** High-velocity projectiles cause extensive damage due to their kinetic energy. They create a temporary cavity that is significantly larger than the projectile itself, causing extensive tissue disruption.
  - **Cavitation:** The rapid movement through tissue creates a shock wave, forming a large temporary cavity that collapses, damaging surrounding tissues.
- **Low-Velocity Projectiles:** Include bullets from most handguns and some shotguns, traveling at speeds less than 2,000 feet per second.
  - **Tissue Damage:** Low-velocity projectiles cause damage primarily through the direct path of the bullet. The temporary cavity is smaller, resulting in less extensive tissue disruption compared to high-velocity projectiles.
  - **Cavitation:** Less pronounced, but still present. The damage is more localized to the bullet path.

Stabbing Weapons (Sharp Instruments):
Pathophysiology:
- **Penetration:** Stabbing injuries are caused by sharp objects like knives, which penetrate the skin and underlying tissues.
  - **Tissue Damage:** The damage is primarily along the path of the instrument. The sharp edge cuts through tissues, causing lacerations, and potentially injuring vital organs and blood vessels.
  - **Bleeding:** Significant bleeding can occur if major blood vessels are severed.
  - **Organ Damage:** Vital organs can be punctured, leading to life-threatening conditions such as hemothorax, pneumothorax, or peritonitis.

Cavitation Differences Between Low-Velocity and High-Velocity Projectiles
High-Velocity Projectiles:

- **Temporary Cavity:** The shock wave from a high-velocity projectile creates a large temporary cavity, which can be 30-40 times larger than the diameter of the bullet. This cavity rapidly expands and collapses, causing severe damage to tissues, organs, and blood vessels far from the bullet's path.
- **Permanent Cavity:** The actual path of the bullet, where tissue destruction is complete and irreparable.

Low-Velocity Projectiles:
- **Temporary Cavity:** Smaller and less forceful than that created by high-velocity projectiles. The temporary cavity is only a few times larger than the bullet diameter.
- **Permanent Cavity:** The tissue damage is primarily along the bullet's direct path, with less collateral damage compared to high-velocity projectiles.

Concept of "Yaw" in Ballistics
Yaw:
- **Definition:** Yaw refers to the deviation or wobble of a bullet's longitudinal axis from its line of flight. Instead of traveling point-first, the bullet can tilt and turn sideways, which affects its trajectory and the damage it causes upon impact.

Relevance to Wound Assessment:
- **Increased Damage:** When a bullet yaws, it creates a larger wound channel and can cause more extensive tissue damage. The bullet's sideways orientation increases the surface area impacting the tissues, leading to greater disruption.
- **Unpredictable Trajectory:** Yaw can result in an unpredictable wound path, making it challenging to assess the extent of internal injuries based solely on the entry and exit wounds.
- **Ballistic Stability:** Bullets with high yaw are less ballistically stable, which can cause them to tumble upon entering the body, creating complex wound patterns and more severe trauma.
- **Implications for Treatment:** Understanding yaw is crucial for trauma surgeons and emergency responders, as it affects the approach to wound management, surgical intervention, and the prediction of possible complications.

Clinical Implications
Firearm Injuries:
- **High-Velocity Injuries:** Require prompt assessment for extensive internal damage due to cavitation. Surgical intervention is often necessary to manage hemorrhage and repair damaged organs.
- **Low-Velocity Injuries:** Still serious but may have more localized damage, potentially allowing for less invasive management depending on the injury site and severity.

Stabbing Injuries:
- **Direct Path Damage:** Immediate assessment and intervention are critical to control bleeding and prevent further injury to vital organs. Imaging and exploratory surgery might be necessary to fully evaluate the extent of internal damage.

In both types of trauma, quick and accurate assessment, stabilization, and appropriate surgical intervention are key to improving patient outcomes. Understanding the mechanisms of injury, including the effects of cavitation and yaw, helps in planning effective treatment strategies.

Three Phases of Blast Injuries
Blast injuries can be categorized into three primary phases: primary, secondary, and tertiary, each with distinct mechanisms and clinical presentations.
Primary Blast Injuries
Mechanism:
- Caused by the initial blast wave, a high-pressure shock wave that propagates through the air and impacts the body.
- The **Friedlander waveform** describes the pressure-time profile of a blast wave, characterized by a rapid spike in pressure followed by a rapid exponential decay. This waveform causes sudden and intense pressure changes that affect gas-filled structures and tissues with differential densities in the body.

Injuries:

- **Pulmonary**: Blast lung, characterized by alveolar hemorrhage, pulmonary contusion, and barotrauma.
- **Auditory**: Tympanic membrane rupture and ossicular disruption.
- **Gastrointestinal**: Bowel perforation and hemorrhage.
- **Central Nervous System**: Concussion, traumatic brain injury (TBI), and air embolism.

Secondary Blast Injuries
Mechanism:
- Caused by flying debris and shrapnel propelled by the blast wave.
- Objects can penetrate or lacerate tissues, leading to various traumatic injuries.

Injuries:
- **Penetrating Trauma**: Shrapnel and debris causing cuts, punctures, and impalements.
- **Blunt Trauma**: Debris causing contusions, fractures, and soft tissue injuries.

Tertiary Blast Injuries
Mechanism:
- Caused by the displacement of the body due to the blast wind, the high-energy explosive force that can throw individuals against solid objects.

Injuries:
- **Blunt Trauma**: Impact with ground or other structures leading to fractures, dislocations, and internal injuries.
- **Crush Injuries**: Structural collapse or falling debris trapping or compressing parts of the body.
- **Traumatic Amputations**: Forceful displacement leading to loss of limbs.

Friedlander Waveform and Primary Blast Injuries
The **Friedlander waveform** is crucial in understanding primary blast injuries. The sharp initial pressure spike exerts intense, brief forces on tissues, especially affecting gas-containing structures like lungs and intestines. The rapid decay phase of the waveform can cause rapid expansion and contraction of tissues, leading to barotrauma and shearing injuries. Understanding this waveform helps in anticipating and diagnosing the specific injuries associated with primary blast effects.

Triage and Treatment in Mass Casualty Incidents Involving Explosions
Triage Considerations
1. **Start Triage:**
   o **Simple Triage and Rapid Treatment (START)** system is often used, focusing on quickly categorizing patients based on their breathing, circulation, and mental status.
   o Triage categories include immediate (red), delayed (yellow), minor (green), and expectant (black).
2. **Injury Prioritization:**
   o Immediate life-threatening injuries such as airway obstruction, severe hemorrhage, and tension pneumothorax are prioritized.
   o Secondary blast injuries with significant bleeding or penetrating trauma need prompt attention to prevent deterioration.
   o Tertiary injuries with potential spinal injuries or major fractures require careful handling and stabilization.

Treatment Considerations
1. **Airway Management:**
   o Ensuring a clear airway is crucial, especially in patients with facial or airway trauma. Use of advanced airway techniques may be necessary.
2. **Breathing and Ventilation:**
   o Monitor and treat pulmonary injuries like blast lung. High-flow oxygen, positive pressure ventilation, and chest tube insertion for pneumothorax or hemothorax might be required.
3. **Circulation and Hemorrhage Control:**
   o Rapid identification and control of bleeding are essential. Use of tourniquets, pressure dressings, and fluid resuscitation with blood products as needed.
4. **Neurological Assessment:**

- Monitor for signs of traumatic brain injury and manage intracranial pressure. Frequent neurological assessments are essential.
5. **Wound Care and Infection Prevention**:
   - Secondary blast injuries require thorough wound cleaning, debridement, and antibiotics to prevent infection.
6. **Pain Management**:
   - Effective pain control using appropriate analgesics is necessary to manage patient comfort and reduce stress.
7. **Evacuation and Transport**:
   - Prioritize transport for the most critically injured patients. Ensure continuous monitoring and support during transport to advanced medical facilities.

Unique Considerations for Mass Casualty Incidents

1. **Resource Allocation**:
   - Limited resources must be managed effectively. This involves prioritizing care based on the severity of injuries and the likelihood of survival.
2. **Communication and Coordination**:
   - Effective communication between responders, hospitals, and emergency management teams is critical for a coordinated response.
3. **Decontamination**:
   - In cases involving chemical or radiological blasts, decontamination procedures must be implemented to protect both patients and healthcare providers.
4. **Psychological Support**:
   - Providing psychological first aid and support for survivors and responders is important to address the immediate and long-term mental health impacts.

Understanding the biomechanics of blast injuries and applying appropriate triage and treatment protocols are essential in managing the complex and multifaceted challenges of mass casualty incidents involving explosions.

Assessment and Management of External, Internal, and Concealed Bleeding

External Bleeding:

Assessment:

- **Visible:** Easy to identify by the direct observation of blood loss.
- **Location and Severity:** Determine the source (arterial, venous, or capillary) and amount of blood loss.
- **Signs:** Bright red spurting blood (arterial), dark red flowing blood (venous), or oozing blood (capillary).

Management:

1. **Direct Pressure:** Apply direct pressure to the wound using a sterile dressing or cloth.
2. **Elevation:** Elevate the bleeding extremity above the level of the heart if possible.
3. **Tourniquet:** Apply a tourniquet proximal to the wound if direct pressure fails, especially for limb injuries.
4. **Hemostatic Agents:** Use hemostatic dressings or agents to promote clotting.
5. **Monitor for Shock:** Continuously assess for signs of hypovolemic shock and prepare for rapid transport.

Internal Bleeding:

Assessment:

- **Non-visible:** Bleeding within body cavities (thoracic, abdominal, pelvic) or solid organs.
- **Signs:** Pain, tenderness, swelling, bruising, or rigidity in the affected area. Symptoms like dizziness, fainting, or hypotension may indicate significant blood loss.

Management:

1. **Maintain Airway and Breathing:** Ensure the airway is clear and provide high-flow oxygen.
2. **Fluid Resuscitation:** Establish IV access and administer fluids to maintain perfusion.
3. **Rapid Transport:** Prioritize rapid transport to a facility capable of surgical intervention.
4. **Monitoring:** Continuously monitor vital signs, level of consciousness, and signs of shock.
5. **Imaging:** At the hospital, imaging studies (e.g., ultrasound, CT scan) to identify the source of bleeding.

Concealed Bleeding:

Assessment:

- **Non-visible:** Bleeding within muscle compartments, retroperitoneal space, or after fractures (e.g., pelvic, femur).
- **Signs:** Swelling, pain, and a hard or tense area around the suspected site. Signs of shock without external or obvious internal bleeding sources.

Management:

1. **Maintain Airway and Breathing:** As with internal bleeding, ensure the airway is clear and provide high-flow oxygen.
2. **Fluid Resuscitation:** Establish IV access and administer fluids cautiously.
3. **Immobilization:** Stabilize fractures or injured areas to prevent further bleeding.
4. **Rapid Transport:** Immediate transport to a trauma center for definitive care.
5. **Monitoring:** Continuous monitoring of vital signs and reassessment for signs of compartment syndrome or shock.

Recognizing Early Signs of Significant Blood Loss

Vital Signs:

- **Tachycardia:** Increased heart rate as a compensatory mechanism.
- **Hypotension:** Decreased blood pressure, often a late sign.
- **Tachypnea:** Rapid breathing to compensate for reduced oxygen delivery.

Clinical Signs:

- **Pallor:** Pale or clammy skin indicating poor perfusion.
- **Cool Extremities:** Decreased peripheral perfusion.
- **Delayed Capillary Refill:** More than 2 seconds.
- **Altered Mental Status:** Anxiety, restlessness, or confusion due to reduced cerebral perfusion.
- **Weakness or Fatigue:** Generalized weakness and fatigue as a result of decreased oxygen delivery.

Concept of "Permissive Hypotension"

Definition: Permissive hypotension, or controlled hypotension, is a strategy in trauma care where the patient's blood pressure is allowed to remain lower than normal until surgical control of bleeding is achieved. This approach minimizes further bleeding by avoiding the dislodgement of clots.

Application in Trauma Care:

1. **Target Blood Pressure:**
   - Aim for a systolic BP of approximately 80-90 mmHg, or enough to maintain consciousness and radial pulse in the absence of head injury.
   - For patients with traumatic brain injury, maintain a higher BP (around 110 mmHg) to ensure adequate cerebral perfusion.
2. **Fluid Resuscitation:**
   - Administer fluids judiciously to avoid increasing blood pressure excessively before bleeding is controlled.
   - Use isotonic crystalloids initially, and consider blood products for volume replacement if needed.
3. **Monitoring and Adjustment:**
   - Continuously monitor the patient's vital signs and mental status.
   - Adjust fluid and blood product administration based on ongoing assessment and response to therapy.
4. **Surgical Intervention:**
   - Focus on rapid surgical control of hemorrhage to stabilize the patient definitively.
   - Permissive hypotension is a temporizing measure until definitive surgical care can be provided.

Permissive hypotension is beneficial in reducing the risk of further hemorrhage and improving outcomes in trauma patients. Understanding its application, along with the assessment and management of different types of bleeding, is essential for effective trauma care.

Proper Application of Tourniquets

Tourniquets are essential tools in controlling severe extremity hemorrhage. Here's how to properly apply them:

Indications
1. **Life-Threatening Hemorrhage:**
   - Severe bleeding that cannot be controlled by direct pressure or other means.
   - Situations where immediate hemorrhage control is necessary to prevent shock and death.
2. **Amputation:**
   - Traumatic amputation of an extremity, where rapid blood loss occurs.
3. **Penetrating Trauma:**
   - Deep lacerations or penetrating injuries that damage major blood vessels in the limbs.

Application Procedure
1. **Identify the Bleeding Site:**
   - Assess the location and severity of the bleeding.
   - Ensure the tourniquet is appropriate for the type of injury.
2. **Apply "High and Tight":**
   - Place the tourniquet as high on the limb as possible, proximal to the injury, and close to the torso (e.g., high on the thigh or upper arm).
   - Ensure it is placed over clothing if necessary to avoid delays.
3. **Tighten the Tourniquet:**
   - Tighten the tourniquet until the bleeding stops and there is no distal pulse.
   - Secure the windlass or tightening mechanism to maintain pressure.
4. **Note the Time:**
   - Record the time of application on the tourniquet or the patient's skin to inform subsequent caregivers.
5. **Reassess and Adjust if Necessary:**
   - Ensure the bleeding has stopped and the tourniquet remains tight.
   - Apply a second tourniquet if the first does not fully control the hemorrhage.

Potential Complications
1. **Tissue Damage:**
   - Prolonged application can lead to nerve and muscle damage.
   - Ischemia can occur if left in place for extended periods (typically over 2 hours).
2. **Compartment Syndrome:**
   - Increased pressure within muscle compartments, leading to decreased blood flow and potential tissue necrosis.
3. **Pain:**
   - Tourniquets are often painful, which can be distressing for patients but necessary for life-saving purposes.

Evolution of Tourniquet Use in Civilian EMS
The use of tourniquets has evolved significantly, influenced by military experience in recent conflicts where they proved invaluable in saving lives. Initially controversial in civilian settings due to fears of complications, tourniquets are now widely accepted as a crucial intervention for severe extremity hemorrhage. Changes include:
1. **Increased Acceptance:**
   - Research and military success have demonstrated their efficacy and safety, leading to broader acceptance in civilian EMS protocols.
2. **Education and Training:**
   - EMS providers receive training on the proper use of tourniquets, emphasizing indications, application techniques, and potential complications.
3. **Wider Availability:**
   - Tourniquets are now standard equipment in many civilian EMS kits and are included in public access bleeding control kits.

"HIGH and TIGHT" Principle
The "HIGH and TIGHT" principle is a guideline for the initial placement of tourniquets to control severe bleeding:
1. **High Placement:**

o   Place the tourniquet as proximal as possible on the limb (close to the torso) to ensure it compresses the major blood vessels supplying the entire limb.
o   This reduces the chance of missing more distal arterial branches that could continue to bleed.
2.   **Tight Application**:
o   Tighten the tourniquet until the bleeding stops and there is no detectable distal pulse.
o   Proper tightening is crucial to ensure effective hemostasis and prevent ongoing blood loss.

By applying the tourniquet high on the limb and ensuring it is tight, EMS providers can effectively control severe hemorrhage and stabilize patients for transport to definitive care. This principle, along with proper training and widespread availability of tourniquets, has significantly improved outcomes in trauma care.

Efficacy and Proper Use of Various Hemostatic Agents

Hemostatic agents are designed to rapidly control bleeding, especially in traumatic injuries where traditional methods may be inadequate. Here's an analysis of the efficacy and proper use of some commonly used hemostatic agents:

1. QuikClot:

Mechanism of Action:

- QuikClot contains kaolin, an inert mineral that activates Factor XII in the clotting cascade. This activation leads to the conversion of fibrinogen to fibrin, forming a stable clot.
- The agent also acts as a molecular sieve, concentrating clotting factors and platelets at the bleeding site.

Efficacy:

- QuikClot has been shown to be effective in controlling severe hemorrhage and is widely used by military and civilian first responders.

Proper Use:

- **Application:** Open the package and apply the gauze directly to the wound, ensuring it is in contact with the bleeding source.
- **Pressure:** Apply firm, direct pressure for at least 3-5 minutes to ensure clot formation.
- **Bandaging:** After the bleeding is controlled, secure the gauze in place with a bandage to maintain pressure and prevent displacement.

2. Celox:

Mechanism of Action:

- Celox contains chitosan, a polysaccharide derived from shrimp shells. Chitosan interacts with red blood cells and platelets to form a gel-like clot.
- It works independently of the body's normal clotting mechanisms, making it effective even in patients with coagulopathies.

Efficacy:

- Effective in various bleeding scenarios, including arterial and venous hemorrhage. It has been proven to work in hypothermic and heparinized conditions.

Proper Use:

- **Application:** Pour the granules directly onto the bleeding wound or use Celox gauze. Ensure the agent covers the entire bleeding surface.
- **Pressure:** Apply direct pressure for at least 3-5 minutes to facilitate clotting.
- **Bandaging:** Secure with a bandage to maintain pressure and prevent movement.

3. HemCon:

Mechanism of Action:

- HemCon also uses chitosan, which bonds with red blood cells to form a strong, adhesive clot.
- The chitosan in HemCon provides a mechanical barrier to bleeding and promotes clotting independently of the body's clotting pathways.

Efficacy:

- Demonstrated to be effective in controlling severe bleeding in both military and civilian settings. Suitable for use in various environmental conditions.

Proper Use:

- **Application:** Place the HemCon dressing directly on the wound, ensuring full contact with the bleeding tissue.
- **Pressure:** Apply firm pressure for 3-5 minutes to ensure effective hemostasis.
- **Bandaging:** Secure the dressing with a bandage to maintain continuous pressure.

Considerations for Wound Packing with Hemostatic Gauze

1. Selection of Hemostatic Agent:
- Choose an agent that is appropriate for the type and severity of bleeding.
- Consider patient allergies (e.g., chitosan-based products for patients with shellfish allergies).

2. Technique for Wound Packing:
- **Identify the Source:** Locate the bleeding source within the wound.
- **Pack Tightly:** Use the hemostatic gauze to pack the wound tightly. Ensure that the gauze fills the entire wound cavity and is in direct contact with the bleeding vessel or tissue.
- **Layering:** Pack in layers if necessary, especially in deep or large wounds, ensuring each layer is pressed firmly into the wound.

3. Pressure Application:
- After packing the wound, apply direct pressure for at least 3-5 minutes. This step is crucial for the activation of the hemostatic agent and clot formation.
- Use a pressure dressing or bandage to secure the gauze and maintain continuous pressure.

4. Monitoring and Transport:
- Continuously monitor the patient for signs of bleeding and hemodynamic stability.
- Rapidly transport the patient to a medical facility for further evaluation and definitive care.

5. Reapplication and Reassessment:
- Be prepared to reapply or adjust the packing if bleeding persists.
- Reassess the wound and surrounding area regularly to ensure effective hemostasis and to prevent complications.

Hemostatic agents like QuikClot, Celox, and HemCon are critical tools in controlling severe bleeding. Their mechanisms of action, coupled with proper application techniques, make them highly effective in both military and civilian trauma care. Understanding the specific considerations for wound packing with these agents ensures optimal outcomes in hemorrhage control.

Comparison of Shock Types

Shock is a critical condition characterized by inadequate tissue perfusion and oxygenation. Different types of shock have distinct pathophysiology, signs, symptoms, and management strategies.

Hypovolemic Shock
Pathophysiology:
- Caused by a significant loss of blood or fluids, leading to decreased circulating volume.
- Common causes include hemorrhage, severe dehydration, burns, and traumatic injuries.

Signs and Symptoms:
- Tachycardia
- Hypotension
- Cold, clammy skin
- Decreased urine output
- Altered mental status

Management:
- Rapid fluid resuscitation with crystalloids (e.g., normal saline) or blood products if hemorrhagic.
- Control of bleeding or fluid loss.
- Monitoring and supporting vital functions.

Distributive Shock
Pathophysiology:

- Characterized by vasodilation and increased vascular permeability, leading to relative hypovolemia.
- Common causes include septic shock, anaphylactic shock, and neurogenic shock.

Signs and Symptoms:
- Septic shock: Fever, tachycardia, hypotension, warm flushed skin (early), cool clammy skin (late), altered mental status.
- Anaphylactic shock: Urticaria, angioedema, wheezing, hypotension, tachycardia.
- Neurogenic shock: Bradycardia, hypotension, warm, dry skin.

Management:
- Septic shock: Broad-spectrum antibiotics, fluid resuscitation, vasopressors (e.g., norepinephrine).
- Anaphylactic shock: Epinephrine, antihistamines, corticosteroids, fluid resuscitation.
- Neurogenic shock: Fluid resuscitation, vasopressors, atropine for bradycardia.

Obstructive Shock

Pathophysiology:
- Caused by physical obstruction to blood flow, impeding circulation.
- Common causes include pulmonary embolism, cardiac tamponade, and tension pneumothorax.

Signs and Symptoms:
- Pulmonary embolism: Sudden onset dyspnea, chest pain, tachycardia, hypotension.
- Cardiac tamponade: Muffled heart sounds, jugular venous distention (JVD), pulsus paradoxus, hypotension.
- Tension pneumothorax: Decreased breath sounds on affected side, tracheal deviation, hypotension, tachycardia.

Management:
- Pulmonary embolism: Anticoagulation, thrombolytics, surgical intervention if necessary.
- Cardiac tamponade: Pericardiocentesis to relieve pressure.
- Tension pneumothorax: Needle decompression followed by chest tube insertion.

Cardiogenic Shock

Pathophysiology:
- Caused by the heart's inability to pump effectively, leading to reduced cardiac output.
- Common causes include myocardial infarction, severe heart failure, cardiomyopathy, and arrhythmias.

Signs and Symptoms:
- Tachycardia
- Hypotension
- Cool, clammy skin
- Pulmonary congestion (crackles)
- Jugular venous distention (JVD)
- Altered mental status

Management:
- Inotropes (e.g., dobutamine) to improve contractility.
- Vasopressors (e.g., norepinephrine) to maintain blood pressure.
- Mechanical support devices (e.g., intra-aortic balloon pump, ventricular assist devices).
- Treat underlying cause (e.g., revascularization for myocardial infarction).

Compensatory Mechanisms
- **Hypovolemic Shock:** Increased heart rate, vasoconstriction, activation of the renin-angiotensin-aldosterone system (RAAS) to retain sodium and water.
- **Distributive Shock:** Initial tachycardia, vasodilation in septic and anaphylactic shock (compensation often inadequate due to severe vasodilation).
- **Obstructive Shock:** Increased heart rate, vasoconstriction to maintain perfusion despite mechanical obstruction.

- **Cardiogenic Shock:** Increased heart rate (often ineffective), vasoconstriction, fluid retention to augment preload.

Cryptic Shock
Concept:

- Cryptic shock refers to a state where tissue hypoperfusion and cellular dysfunction are present despite normal vital signs and systemic perfusion parameters.
- Patients may appear stable but have underlying metabolic derangements, such as elevated lactate levels, indicating inadequate cellular oxygen utilization.

Clinical Significance:

- Early recognition and intervention are crucial to prevent progression to overt shock and organ failure.
- Monitoring lactate levels and other markers of tissue perfusion can help identify cryptic shock.
- Interventions may include optimizing oxygen delivery, fluid resuscitation, and addressing underlying causes.

Understanding the different types of shock and their respective pathophysiology, signs, symptoms, and management is essential for effective treatment and improving patient outcomes. Recognizing and addressing compensatory mechanisms and cryptic shock are vital in preventing further deterioration and ensuring comprehensive care.

Wound Assessment Using the "DOTS" Mnemonic

DOTS is a mnemonic that helps healthcare providers systematically assess wounds to determine the severity, appropriate management, and need for further intervention. It stands for Depth, Organs, Tissue type, and Source.
Depth:

- **Superficial Wounds:** Affect only the epidermis and possibly the dermis. These include abrasions and minor lacerations.
- **Partial Thickness:** Involve the epidermis and part of the dermis. Examples include deeper lacerations and puncture wounds.
- **Full Thickness:** Extend through the dermis into subcutaneous tissue, and may involve muscles, bones, and other deeper structures.
- **Assessment:** Determine how deep the wound penetrates by careful inspection and palpation. Consider using sterile probes if necessary, ensuring that probing does not cause further injury.

Organs:

- **Involvement of Vital Structures:** Assess for the involvement of underlying organs and vital structures such as blood vessels, nerves, muscles, bones, and internal organs.
- **Assessment:** Check for signs of organ injury, such as evisceration, or symptoms like severe pain, loss of function, or abnormal movements. For chest and abdominal wounds, be alert to signs of pneumothorax, hemothorax, or peritonitis.

Tissue Type:

- **Type of Tissue Involved:** Identify the type of tissue damaged, which may include skin, subcutaneous fat, muscle, tendon, bone, or internal organs.
- **Assessment:** Examine the wound for different tissue types. For example, exposed fat appears yellow and shiny, while muscle is red and fibrous. Bone exposure indicates a severe injury requiring advanced care.

Source:

- **Cause of the Wound:** Determine the mechanism of injury (e.g., blunt force, sharp object, gunshot wound) to understand the potential extent of damage.
- **Assessment:** Ask the patient or bystanders about the cause of the injury. Analyze the wound edges and characteristics; for instance, jagged edges suggest laceration, while clean cuts suggest incision.

Determining the Need for Wound Exploration in the Field
Indications for Exploration:

- **Uncontrolled Bleeding:** Persistent bleeding despite direct pressure may require exploration to identify and control the bleeding source.

- **Foreign Bodies:** Suspected presence of foreign objects (e.g., glass, wood) necessitates exploration to prevent infection and further damage.
- **Compartment Syndrome:** Signs of increasing pressure and pain, especially in deep or penetrating wounds, may require exploration to relieve pressure.

Contraindications:
- **Involvement of Vital Structures:** Avoid exploration if there is a risk of damaging underlying organs or vital structures, and transport the patient to a higher level of care.
- **Non-urgent Situations:** Stable wounds without signs of severe bleeding, infection, or foreign bodies can be managed with basic first aid and evaluated further in a controlled setting.

Principles of Wound Irrigation and Debridement in the Prehospital Setting
Wound Irrigation:
Purpose:
- Remove debris, bacteria, and contaminants to reduce the risk of infection.

Procedure:
1. **Preparation:**
   - Use sterile or clean equipment and solutions. Normal saline is preferred.
   - Prepare a sufficient volume of irrigating fluid to thoroughly clean the wound.
2. **Irrigation Technique:**
   - Use a syringe with a splash guard or a clean irrigation device.
   - Gently irrigate the wound with moderate pressure, ensuring all areas are flushed.
   - Continue until the wound appears clean, typically using 100-500 mL for smaller wounds and more for larger wounds.
3. **Avoid High Pressure:** High-pressure irrigation can drive contaminants deeper into the tissue and cause additional tissue damage.

Wound Debridement:
Purpose:
- Remove non-viable tissue, which can harbor bacteria and impede healing.

Procedure:
1. **Selective Debridement:**
   - In the field, limit debridement to obvious non-viable tissue that is easily accessible.
   - Use sterile scissors or forceps to gently remove dead tissue.
2. **Avoid Aggressive Debridement:** Only perform minimal debridement to avoid additional trauma and bleeding. Leave extensive debridement to be performed in a controlled medical environment.
3. **Wound Dressing:** After irrigation and debridement, apply a sterile dressing to protect the wound and maintain a clean environment until further medical care is available.

Using the "DOTS" mnemonic helps systematically assess wounds by evaluating their depth, involvement of organs, type of tissue affected, and the source of injury. Deciding whether a wound requires exploration involves considering factors such as uncontrolled bleeding, the presence of foreign bodies, and the risk of compartment syndrome. Wound irrigation and debridement are essential steps to reduce infection risk and promote healing. These procedures should be performed with care to avoid further damage, ensuring the patient is stabilized and prepared for transport to a medical facility for definitive care.

The "Rule of Nines" for Estimating Burn Surface Area
The "Rule of Nines" is a quick method for estimating the total body surface area (TBSA) affected by burns in adults and children. It divides the body into sections, each representing approximately 9% (or multiples thereof) of the body surface area.

Adults
- **Head and Neck**: 9%
- **Each Arm**: 9% (4.5% front, 4.5% back)
- **Each Leg**: 18% (9% front, 9% back)
- **Anterior Trunk**: 18%

- **Posterior Trunk**: 18%
- **Perineum**: 1%

This method is efficient for adults due to the relatively consistent proportions of body parts in adults.

Children

For children, especially those older than infants but not yet fully grown, the proportions differ slightly:

- **Head and Neck**: 18% (due to the larger head size relative to the body)
- **Each Arm**: 9%
- **Each Leg**: 14% (7% front, 7% back)
- **Anterior Trunk**: 18%
- **Posterior Trunk**: 18%
- **Perineum**: 1%

Infants

Infants have different proportions, requiring further adjustments:

- **Head and Neck**: 18%
- **Each Arm**: 9%
- **Each Leg**: 13.5% (6.75% front, 6.75% back)
- **Anterior Trunk**: 18%
- **Posterior Trunk**: 18%
- **Perineum**: 1%

Modifications for the Parkland Formula in Electrical Burns and Inhalation Injuries

Parkland Formula

The Parkland formula is used to calculate fluid resuscitation needs for burn patients within the first 24 hours. The standard formula is:

$$\text{Total fluid (mL)} = 4 \times \text{body weight (kg)} \times \text{TBSA (\%)}$$

Half of this fluid is administered in the first 8 hours, and the remaining half over the next 16 hours.

Modifications for Electrical Burns

Electrical burns often cause deep tissue damage not visible on the surface, leading to underestimated TBSA when using the Rule of Nines. Therefore, the Parkland formula may be modified by:

- Increasing the fluid amount, sometimes doubling the initial estimate to ensure adequate perfusion and renal function.
- Monitoring urine output closely (aiming for 1-2 mL/kg/hr) as a more accurate indicator of tissue perfusion.

Modifications for Inhalation Injuries

Inhalation injuries can complicate fluid management due to airway edema and potential respiratory compromise. Adjustments include:

- Adding extra fluids to the initial resuscitation, though not as much as for electrical burns. An additional 1.5 mL/kg per percentage of TBSA burned may be added.
- Close monitoring of respiratory status, considering the need for intubation and mechanical ventilation due to airway swelling.

Summary of Key Points

- The Rule of Nines simplifies TBSA estimation by assigning body parts percentages that add up to 100%.
- Modifications for infants account for their larger head size relative to body size.
- The Parkland formula is adjusted for electrical burns due to deeper tissue damage and for inhalation injuries due to airway complications.
- Fluid resuscitation aims to prevent shock and ensure adequate organ perfusion, with close monitoring and adjustments based on patient response.

Understanding and applying these methods and modifications appropriately can significantly impact the management and outcomes of burn patients.

Assessment and Management of Open vs. Closed Fractures

Open Fractures:
Assessment:
- **Definition:** An open fracture, also known as a compound fracture, involves a break in the bone that is accompanied by an open wound in the skin.
- **Signs:** Visible bone protrusion, bleeding, and a wound over the fracture site. The wound may be large or small.
- **Risk of Infection:** High due to exposure of bone and tissue to the external environment.
- **Neurovascular Assessment:** Check for distal pulses, capillary refill, sensation, and motor function to identify any neurovascular compromise.

Management:
1. **Control Bleeding:** Apply direct pressure to control bleeding. Use sterile dressings to cover the wound.
2. **Prevent Contamination:** Avoid probing or cleaning the wound excessively in the field. Cover the wound with a sterile dressing.
3. **Immobilization:** Immobilize the fracture with a splint to prevent further injury and reduce pain. Avoid moving the exposed bone.
4. **Pain Management:** Administer analgesics as appropriate and within protocol.
5. **Antibiotics and Tetanus:** Administer broad-spectrum antibiotics and a tetanus booster as soon as possible to reduce infection risk.
6. **Rapid Transport:** Prioritize transport to a medical facility for surgical debridement and definitive care.

Closed Fractures:
Assessment:
- **Definition:** A closed fracture involves a break in the bone without an associated open wound in the skin.
- **Signs:** Swelling, bruising, deformity, pain, and limited function or movement of the affected area.
- **Risk of Compartment Syndrome:** Monitor for signs of increasing pain, swelling, and pressure.
- **Neurovascular Assessment:** Check for distal pulses, capillary refill, sensation, and motor function to identify any neurovascular compromise.

Management:
1. **Immobilization:** Immobilize the fracture with a splint or cast to prevent further injury and reduce pain.
2. **Ice and Elevation:** Apply ice packs to reduce swelling and elevate the affected limb to decrease edema.
3. **Pain Management:** Administer analgesics as appropriate and within protocol.
4. **Monitor for Complications:** Continuously monitor for signs of compartment syndrome or neurovascular compromise.
5. **Follow-Up Care:** Arrange for follow-up care, including imaging and orthopedic evaluation.

Recognizing and Managing Neurovascular Compromise in Extremity Injuries
Recognition:
Signs of Neurovascular Compromise:
- **Pain:** Severe pain that is disproportionate to the injury, especially with passive stretch.
- **Pallor:** Pale or mottled skin indicating poor perfusion.
- **Pulselessness:** Absence of distal pulses.
- **Paresthesia:** Numbness or tingling in the affected limb.
- **Paralysis:** Inability to move the affected limb.
- **Poikilothermia:** The limb feels cooler than the rest of the body.

Assessment:
- **Capillary Refill:** Check capillary refill time, which should be less than 2 seconds.
- **Pulse Check:** Palpate distal pulses (e.g., dorsalis pedis, posterior tibial, radial).
- **Sensation and Movement:** Assess for changes in sensation and ability to move distal to the injury.

Management:
1. **Immediate Intervention:** If neurovascular compromise is suspected, realign the limb to improve perfusion, if possible, before immobilizing.
2. **Immobilization:** Splint the limb in the position of comfort after realignment.

3. **Reassessment:** Continuously monitor the limb for changes in neurovascular status.
4. **Elevation:** Elevate the limb if possible to reduce swelling.
5. **Rapid Transport:** Transport to a medical facility for further evaluation and possible surgical intervention.

Concept of "Reduction to Risk" in Fracture Management

Definition: "Reduction to risk" refers to the decision to reduce (realign) a fracture in the prehospital setting to mitigate the risk of neurovascular compromise or other complications.

Principles:

- **Indications for Reduction:** Perform reduction if there is evidence of neurovascular compromise or if the deformity is severe and causing significant pain.
- **Method:** Gently traction and manipulate the limb to realign the bones, followed by immobilization.
- **Risks vs. Benefits:** Weigh the risks of causing further injury against the potential benefits of improving blood flow and reducing pain.
- **Expertise Required:** Reduction should be performed by trained personnel, with knowledge of the specific techniques for different types of fractures.

Steps in Reduction:

1. **Pain Management:** Administer analgesics to reduce pain and anxiety.
2. **Traction:** Apply gentle, steady traction along the axis of the limb.
3. **Manipulation:** Realign the bone fragments to their anatomical position.
4. **Immobilization:** Splint the limb in the reduced position to maintain alignment and stability.
5. **Monitoring:** Reassess neurovascular status after reduction to ensure perfusion and function are restored.

The assessment and management of open and closed fractures require a systematic approach to identify and treat complications such as neurovascular compromise. Recognizing the signs of significant blood loss and managing the associated risks are crucial in trauma care. The concept of "reduction to risk" guides the decision-making process for prehospital fracture reduction, balancing the need for immediate intervention against the potential risks. Effective management in the field can significantly improve patient outcomes and reduce the risk of long-term complications.

Splinting Techniques for Upper and Lower Extremity Injuries

Splinting is crucial in immobilizing injuries, reducing pain, and preventing further damage. Here are the various techniques:

Upper Extremity Splinting

1. **Forearm/Wrist/Hand Splints:**
   - **Rigid Splints:** Use padded boards, SAM splints, or pre-formed splints.
   - **Application:**
     - Place the splint along the posterior aspect of the forearm.
     - Immobilize the wrist in slight extension and the fingers in a position of function (slightly flexed).
     - Secure with bandages or straps, ensuring not to restrict blood flow.
2. **Elbow Splints:**
   - **Rigid Splints:** Use padded boards or SAM splints.
   - **Application:**
     - Place the splint on the posterior aspect, extending from the upper arm to the forearm.
     - Immobilize the elbow at 90 degrees.
     - Secure with bandages or straps.
3. **Shoulder Splints:**
   - **Sling and Swathe:**
     - Place the arm in a sling with the elbow at 90 degrees.
     - Use a swathe (a broad bandage) to secure the arm against the chest.
     - This immobilizes the shoulder and provides support.

Lower Extremity Splinting

1. **Ankle/Foot Splints:**
   - **Rigid Splints:** Use padded boards or SAM splints.

- o **Application**:
  - Place the splint along the posterior aspect of the leg, extending from the foot to the calf.
  - Secure the ankle in a neutral position (90 degrees).
  - Wrap with bandages or straps, ensuring not to restrict circulation.
2. **Knee Splints**:
   - o **Rigid Splints**: Use padded boards or SAM splints.
   - o **Application**:
     - Place the splint on the posterior aspect, extending from the thigh to the lower leg.
     - Immobilize the knee in a straight position.
     - Secure with bandages or straps.
3. **Femur Fractures**:
   - o **Traction Splints**: Designed to provide constant, gentle traction to align the femur and reduce muscle spasm.
   - o **Types**: Sager, Hare, and Kendrick traction devices.
   - o **Application**:
     - Expose and inspect the leg, ensuring there are no open fractures or contraindications.
     - Measure and adjust the splint to the patient's leg length.
     - Apply the ankle hitch or strap.
     - Attach the splint to the leg, positioning the proximal end against the ischial tuberosity.
     - Apply gentle traction to align the femur.
     - Secure the splint with straps along the leg.
     - Monitor the patient's distal pulses, sensation, and movement.

Key Principles of Effective Splinting
1. **Immobilization**:
   - o Splint the joint above and below the injury.
   - o Ensure the limb is immobilized in a functional position.
2. **Padding**:
   - o Use adequate padding to prevent pressure sores and increase comfort.
3. **Circulation**:
   - o Check distal pulses before and after splinting.
   - o Ensure the splint is not too tight, which could compromise circulation.
4. **Stability**:
   - o Secure the splint firmly to prevent movement.
   - o Avoid excessive tightening that could cause additional injury or discomfort.
5. **Reassessment**:
   - o Frequently reassess circulation, sensation, and motor function distal to the injury.

Pain-Free Passive Range of Motion (PROM)
Concept:
- **Passive Range of Motion (PROM)**: Movement of a joint through its range by an external force (e.g., clinician), without the patient's muscles being used.
- **Pain-Free PROM**: Assessing the range of motion in a joint to the point where the patient experiences no pain.

Importance in Joint Injury Assessment:
- **Diagnosis**: Helps identify the extent and type of injury (e.g., ligamentous vs. muscular).
- **Baseline Measurement**: Establishes a baseline for rehabilitation and recovery.
- **Injury Severity**: Indicates the severity of injury and the need for immobilization or further medical intervention.
- **Rehabilitation**: Guides the safe progression of physical therapy and exercises without causing further harm.

Application in Clinical Practice
- **Joint Stability**: Ensure the joint is stable through PROM without causing pain.

- **Functional Positioning**: Splint or immobilize the joint in a pain-free functional position.
- **Pain Management**: Use pain-free PROM to avoid exacerbating the injury and to facilitate gentle rehabilitation.

By adhering to these principles and techniques, effective splinting can significantly improve patient outcomes, reduce pain, and prevent further injury. Understanding the concept of pain-free PROM aids in accurately assessing joint injuries and planning appropriate treatment strategies.

Pathophysiology, Signs, Symptoms, and Management of Compartment Syndrome
Pathophysiology:
Compartment syndrome occurs when increased pressure within a closed muscle compartment compromises circulation and tissue function within that space. The increase in pressure can be due to internal bleeding, swelling, or external compression, leading to a decrease in blood flow and subsequent ischemia and necrosis of the muscles and nerves.

Causes:
- **Trauma:** Fractures, crush injuries, burns.
- **Reperfusion Injury:** After the restoration of blood flow following ischemia.
- **Tight Bandaging or Casting:** Externally applied pressure can exacerbate the condition.
- **Intensive Exercise:** Can lead to swelling and increased pressure in the muscle compartments.

Signs and Symptoms:
Early Symptoms:
- **Pain:** Severe pain out of proportion to the injury, particularly with passive stretching of the muscles within the compartment.
- **Paresthesia:** Tingling or burning sensation due to nerve compression.

Late Symptoms:
- **Pallor:** Pale appearance of the skin over the affected area.
- **Paralysis:** Weakness or inability to move the muscles within the compartment.
- **Pulselessness:** Weak or absent distal pulses.

The "5 P's" Mnemonic for Compartment Syndrome Assessment
1. **Pain:**
   - **Description:** Disproportionately severe pain that is not relieved by immobilization or analgesia.
   - **Application:** Assess for pain with passive stretching of the muscles in the affected compartment.
2. **Paresthesia:**
   - **Description:** Tingling or burning sensation.
   - **Application:** Check for sensory deficits, particularly in areas served by nerves passing through the compartment.
3. **Pallor:**
   - **Description:** Pale skin indicating compromised circulation.
   - **Application:** Compare the color of the affected limb with the unaffected limb.
4. **Paralysis:**
   - **Description:** Loss of motor function.
   - **Application:** Evaluate motor strength and compare with the unaffected limb. Inability to move muscles within the compartment is a late sign.
5. **Pulselessness:**
   - **Description:** Absence of a pulse distal to the affected compartment.
   - **Application:** Palpate for distal pulses; use a Doppler device if pulses are not palpable.

Diagnostic Tools
Capillary Refill Time (CRT):
- **Normal CRT:** Less than 2 seconds.
- **Application:** Press on a nail bed or the skin of the affected area until it blanches, then release and observe the time it takes for color to return. Prolonged CRT can indicate compromised blood flow.

- **Limitations:** CRT can be affected by factors like cold temperatures and shock, so it should be used in conjunction with other assessments.

Compartment Pressure Measurements:

- **Normal Pressure:** 0-10 mmHg.
- **Critical Pressure:** Pressures above 30 mmHg or a differential pressure (diastolic blood pressure minus compartment pressure) less than 30 mmHg is indicative of compartment syndrome.
- **Application:** Use a compartment pressure monitoring device to measure the pressure within the affected compartment. This is the definitive diagnostic tool for compartment syndrome.
- **Procedure:** Insert a needle connected to a pressure transducer into the compartment and record the pressure.

Management of Compartment Syndrome

1. **Immediate Actions:**
   - **Remove External Constrictions:** Loosen bandages or split open casts to relieve external pressure.
   - **Positioning:** Keep the affected limb at heart level to reduce swelling while ensuring adequate perfusion.
2. **Surgical Intervention:**
   - **Fasciotomy:** The definitive treatment involves surgically opening the fascial compartment to relieve pressure. This procedure should be performed urgently to prevent irreversible damage.
   - **Post-Surgery Care:** Monitor for infection, maintain wound care, and assess for functional recovery.
3. **Supportive Measures:**
   - **Pain Management:** Administer analgesics to manage pain.
   - **Fluids:** Ensure adequate hydration to support circulation and prevent further complications.

Compartment syndrome is a critical condition where increased pressure within a muscle compartment compromises blood flow and tissue viability. The "5 P's" mnemonic helps in the early assessment and identification of this condition, while tools like capillary refill time and compartment pressure measurements aid in diagnosis. Prompt recognition and intervention, primarily through fasciotomy, are essential to prevent permanent damage and improve patient outcomes.

Primary and Secondary Brain Injury Mechanisms in Traumatic Brain Injury (TBI)

Primary Brain Injury

Mechanism:

- **Immediate Impact:** Occurs at the moment of trauma and results from direct mechanical forces to the brain.
- **Types:**
   - **Coup-Contrecoup Injuries:** Brain damage occurring at the site of impact (coup) and directly opposite (contrecoup) due to the brain striking the skull.
   - **Diffuse Axonal Injury (DAI):** Shearing forces cause widespread damage to axons, leading to disruptions in neural communication.
   - **Penetrating Injuries:** Objects such as bullets or shrapnel penetrating the skull and brain tissue.

Effects:

- Structural damage to brain tissues, blood vessels, and the blood-brain barrier.
- Immediate disruption of neural pathways and brain function.

Secondary Brain Injury

Mechanism:

- **Delayed Pathophysiological Changes:** Develops hours to days after the initial trauma due to various biochemical and cellular processes.
- **Types:**
   - **Ischemia and Hypoxia:** Reduced blood flow and oxygen delivery to brain tissues.
   - **Edema:** Swelling of brain tissues leading to increased intracranial pressure (ICP).
   - **Inflammation:** Activation of the inflammatory response causing further damage to brain tissues.

- Excitotoxicity: Excessive release of neurotransmitters (e.g., glutamate) leading to neuronal damage.
- Oxidative Stress: Production of free radicals causing cellular damage.
- Hematomas: Formation of blood clots within the brain (e.g., subdural, epidural, intracerebral).

Effects:
- Progressive worsening of brain injury due to ongoing cellular and molecular damage.
- Increased ICP leading to further neuronal damage and potential herniation.

Monro-Kellie Doctrine and Increased Intracranial Pressure
Monro-Kellie Doctrine:
- **Principle**: The skull is a rigid, fixed-volume container that holds brain tissue, blood, and cerebrospinal fluid (CSF). The sum of these volumes is constant. An increase in one component must be compensated by a decrease in another to maintain stable intracranial pressure (ICP).
- **Components**:
  - **Brain Tissue**: ~80%
  - **Blood**: ~10%
  - **CSF**: ~10%

Relation to Increased ICP:
- **Compensation**: Initial increases in one component (e.g., brain tissue swelling, hematoma formation) are compensated by a reduction in CSF and venous blood volume.
- **Decompensation**: When compensatory mechanisms are exhausted, ICP rises, leading to decreased cerebral perfusion pressure (CPP) and potential brain herniation.
- **Clinical Implications**: Monitoring and managing ICP is crucial in TBI patients to prevent secondary brain injury and improve outcomes.

"Talk and Die" Syndrome and Epidural Hematomas
Concept of "Talk and Die" Syndrome:
- **Definition**: A phenomenon where a patient with an epidural hematoma initially appears lucid and coherent (talks) but rapidly deteriorates and can die if not treated promptly.
- **Mechanism**:
  - **Initial Lucid Interval**: The patient regains consciousness and appears stable after the initial impact due to the temporary absence of significant symptoms.
  - **Delayed Deterioration**: As the hematoma expands, it increases ICP and causes a rapid decline in neurological status, leading to coma and potentially death if not addressed.

Relation to Epidural Hematomas:
- **Epidural Hematoma**:
  - **Location**: Between the dura mater and the skull, often due to arterial bleeding (commonly from the middle meningeal artery).
  - **Symptoms**: Brief loss of consciousness, followed by a lucid interval, and then rapid neurological deterioration (headache, vomiting, drowsiness, seizures).
  - **Diagnosis**: CT scan showing a biconvex, lens-shaped hematoma.
  - **Treatment**: Emergency surgical evacuation to prevent brain herniation and death.

Understanding the mechanisms of primary and secondary brain injury, the implications of the Monro-Kellie doctrine, and the critical nature of conditions like "talk and die" syndrome in epidural hematomas are essential for effective management and improving outcomes in TBI patients. Timely recognition and intervention can significantly influence patient prognosis and recovery.

Full Spinal Motion Restriction (SMR) vs. Selective Spinal Motion Restriction
Full Spinal Motion Restriction:
Indications:
- **High-energy Mechanism of Injury**: Significant trauma mechanisms like falls from height, high-speed motor vehicle accidents, or direct trauma to the spine.

- **Neurological Deficits:** Presence of any new neurological symptoms such as numbness, tingling, or weakness.
- **Altered Mental Status:** Patients with altered consciousness (e.g., intoxication, head injury) where reliable assessment is not possible.
- **Spinal Pain or Tenderness:** Midline spinal pain or tenderness on palpation.
- **Distracting Injuries:** Injuries that could distract from the pain of a spinal injury, making it difficult to assess accurately.

Approach:
- **Equipment:** Use of a cervical collar, rigid spine board, head blocks, and straps to immobilize the entire spine.
- **Patient Positioning:** Maintain the patient in a supine position, ensuring minimal movement during transfer and transport.

Selective Spinal Motion Restriction:
Indications:
- **Low-risk Mechanism of Injury:** Minor falls, low-speed vehicle collisions, or other mechanisms deemed low risk for spinal injury.
- **No Neurological Deficits:** Absence of new neurological symptoms.
- **Alert and Oriented:** Patient is alert, oriented, and able to reliably report symptoms.
- **No Midline Spinal Pain or Tenderness:** No pain or tenderness on palpation of the spine.
- **No Distracting Injuries:** Absence of injuries that could distract from the pain of a potential spinal injury.

Approach:
- **Equipment:** May use a cervical collar alone if there is concern for cervical spine injury but no need for full immobilization.
- **Patient Positioning:** Allowing the patient to self-extricate if able and encouraging movement that minimizes discomfort and pain, which often aligns with natural spinal alignment.

Evolution of Spinal Immobilization Practices

Recent years have seen a shift in the approach to spinal immobilization, moving from routine use of full immobilization for all suspected spinal injuries to more selective use based on clinical criteria. This change is driven by:
- **Evidence of Harm:** Studies have shown that rigid immobilization, especially prolonged use of spine boards, can cause harm, including pressure ulcers, respiratory compromise, and increased pain.
- **Lack of Benefit:** Evidence suggesting that full immobilization does not improve outcomes for all patients, particularly those with low-risk mechanisms of injury.
- **Guideline Updates:** Recommendations from organizations such as the American College of Emergency Physicians (ACEP) and National Association of EMS Physicians (NAEMSP) advocating for selective immobilization based on validated clinical criteria.

NEXUS Criteria and Canadian C-spine Rules
NEXUS Criteria (National Emergency X-Radiography Utilization Study):
Purpose:
- To identify patients at low risk of cervical spine injury who do not need imaging.

Criteria:
1. **No Midline Cervical Tenderness:** Absence of pain on palpation of the midline cervical spine.
2. **No Focal Neurological Deficit:** Absence of new or worsening neurological symptoms.
3. **Normal Alertness:** Patient is fully alert and oriented.
4. **No Intoxication:** Patient is not under the influence of drugs or alcohol.
5. **No Distracting Injuries:** No other injuries that could distract from the pain of a cervical spine injury.

Application:
- If all five criteria are met, the likelihood of significant cervical spine injury is low, and imaging is typically not required.

Canadian C-spine Rules:
Purpose:
- To identify patients at low risk of cervical spine injury who can safely forgo imaging.

Criteria:
1. **High-Risk Factors (any one of the following necessitates imaging):**
   - Age ≥ 65 years.
   - Dangerous mechanism of injury (e.g., fall from height >1 meter, axial load to the head, high-speed motor vehicle collision, motorized recreational vehicle accidents, bicycle collision).
   - Paresthesias in extremities.
2. **Low-Risk Factors (if present, allow safe assessment of range of motion):**
   - Simple rear-end motor vehicle collision.
   - Patient able to sit in the emergency department.
   - Ambulatory at any time post-injury.
   - Delayed onset of neck pain.
   - Absence of midline cervical spine tenderness.
3. **Assessment of Range of Motion:**
   - If the patient can actively rotate their neck 45 degrees to the left and right without pain, imaging is typically not required.

Application:
- Use high-risk and low-risk factors to guide decision-making regarding the need for imaging. If low-risk criteria are met and the patient has full range of motion, imaging can be safely avoided.

The approach to spinal motion restriction has evolved from universal full immobilization to a more selective approach based on clinical criteria. The NEXUS criteria and Canadian C-spine rules provide evidence-based guidelines to help clinicians safely assess and manage patients with potential cervical spine injuries, minimizing unnecessary immobilization and imaging while ensuring patient safety. Understanding and applying these criteria in the prehospital and emergency settings is crucial for optimizing patient outcomes and resource utilization.

Assessment and Management of Open and Closed Chest Injuries
Open Chest Injuries
Assessment:
- **Signs and Symptoms:**
  - Visible wound on the chest wall.
  - Sucking sound on inhalation (sucking chest wound).
  - Dyspnea (difficulty breathing).
  - Decreased or absent breath sounds on the affected side.
  - Hemoptysis (coughing up blood).

Management:
1. **Immediate Care:**
   - **Cover the Wound**: Use an occlusive dressing (e.g., petroleum gauze) to cover the wound. Tape the dressing on three sides to create a one-way valve effect, allowing air to escape but not enter.
   - **Seal and Secure**: Ensure the dressing remains in place, and monitor for signs of tension pneumothorax.
2. **Definitive Care:**
   - **Chest Tube Insertion**: Insert a chest tube to re-expand the lung and drain any accumulated air or blood.
   - **Surgical Repair**: Surgical intervention may be required to repair the chest wall and underlying structures.

Closed Chest Injuries
Assessment:
- **Signs and Symptoms:**
  - Pain at the site of injury.

- Bruising or swelling on the chest wall.
- Dyspnea.
- Decreased or absent breath sounds on the affected side.
- Crepitus (a crackling sensation under the skin).

Management:

1. **Rib Fractures:**
   - **Pain Management:** Provide analgesia to allow effective breathing and coughing.
   - **Supportive Care:** Encourage deep breathing exercises to prevent pneumonia.
2. **Flail Chest:**
   - **Definition:** Occurs when a segment of the rib cage breaks and becomes detached from the chest wall, causing paradoxical movement during breathing.
   - **Management:**
     - **Stabilization:** Stabilize the flail segment with manual pressure or external devices.
     - **Oxygen Therapy:** Provide supplemental oxygen.
     - **Mechanical Ventilation:** In severe cases, intubation and positive pressure ventilation may be necessary.

Tension Pneumothorax
Assessment:

- **Signs and Symptoms:**
  - Severe dyspnea and respiratory distress.
  - Tracheal deviation away from the affected side.
  - Hyperresonance on percussion of the affected side.
  - Decreased or absent breath sounds on the affected side.
  - Jugular venous distension (JVD).
  - Hypotension and signs of shock.

Management:

1. **Needle Decompression:**
   - **Indication:** Perform when tension pneumothorax is suspected and the patient is in severe distress or shock.
   - **Procedure:**
     1. Identify the second intercostal space at the midclavicular line on the affected side.
     2. Prepare the site with antiseptic solution.
     3. Insert a large-bore needle (14-16 gauge) with a catheter over the needle into the second intercostal space just above the third rib to avoid the neurovascular bundle.
     4. Advance the needle until air escapes, then advance the catheter while withdrawing the needle.
     5. Secure the catheter in place and attach it to a one-way valve or a chest drainage system.
   - **Follow-Up:** Insert a chest tube for definitive management after needle decompression.

Flail Chest and Permissive Hypercapnia
Concept of Permissive Hypercapnia:

- **Definition:** Allowing higher levels of carbon dioxide (CO_2) in the blood than normal (hypercapnia) during mechanical ventilation to avoid lung injury.
- **Rationale in Flail Chest:**
  - **Reduced Ventilatory Pressure:** High ventilatory pressures can exacerbate lung injury and increase the risk of barotrauma. Permissive hypercapnia allows for lower ventilatory pressures.
  - **Improved Oxygenation:** By accepting higher CO_2 levels, oxygenation can be maintained with less aggressive ventilation.
  - **Balancing Act:** The goal is to maintain adequate oxygenation while minimizing ventilator-induced lung injury.

Management:

- **Ventilatory Support:**

- o Use gentle ventilation strategies with lower tidal volumes and pressures.
- o Allow for higher levels of CO2 (up to a safe threshold) to reduce ventilatory pressures.
- o Continuous monitoring of blood gases to balance oxygenation and CO2 levels.
- **Pain Control:**
  - o Adequate analgesia to ensure effective breathing and prevent atelectasis and pneumonia.

Effective assessment and management of chest injuries, including techniques like needle decompression for tension pneumothorax and the concept of permissive hypercapnia for flail chest, are essential in preventing complications and improving patient outcomes. These strategies must be tailored to the specific injury and the patient's overall clinical status to ensure optimal care.

Pathophysiology and Management of Crush Injuries and Crush Syndrome
Crush Injuries:
Pathophysiology:

- **Tissue Damage:** Crush injuries occur when a body part is subjected to significant compressive force, leading to damage to muscles, nerves, blood vessels, and bones.
- **Local Effects:** Immediate effects include swelling, bruising, and bleeding within the crushed tissues. Muscle cells (myocytes) are particularly vulnerable, and their damage releases intracellular contents into the bloodstream.

Crush Syndrome:
Pathophysiology:

- **Release of Toxins:** When the compressive force is relieved, damaged muscle cells release their contents, including potassium, myoglobin, creatine kinase (CK), and other intracellular substances, into the bloodstream.
- **Systemic Effects:**
  - o **Hyperkalemia:** Elevated potassium levels can lead to life-threatening cardiac arrhythmias.
  - o **Myoglobinuria:** Myoglobin released from muscle cells can obstruct renal tubules, leading to acute kidney injury (AKI).
  - o **Metabolic Acidosis:** The release of lactic acid and other metabolic byproducts contributes to systemic acidosis.

Reperfusion Injury:

- **Mechanism:** Reperfusion injury occurs when blood flow is restored to previously ischemic tissues. The sudden influx of oxygenated blood leads to the production of reactive oxygen species (ROS) and other inflammatory mediators.
- **Systemic Complications:** ROS and inflammatory mediators can cause further cellular damage, increase vascular permeability, and lead to systemic inflammatory response syndrome (SIRS), multi-organ dysfunction, and shock.

Management of Crush Injuries and Crush Syndrome
Prehospital Care:

1. **Early Recognition and Monitoring:** Identify potential crush injuries and monitor for signs of crush syndrome. Establish IV access and begin continuous cardiac monitoring to detect arrhythmias.
2. **Pain Management:** Administer analgesics as needed.
3. **Fluid Resuscitation:** Initiate aggressive fluid resuscitation before releasing the compressive force to help dilute released toxins and support renal perfusion.

Hospital Management:
Fluid Resuscitation:

- **Purpose:** Prevent renal failure by maintaining adequate urine output and diluting myoglobin and other toxins.
- **Protocol:** Administer isotonic fluids such as normal saline or lactated Ringer's solution. The initial goal is to achieve a urine output of 1-2 mL/kg/hr.
- **Ongoing Monitoring:** Adjust fluid administration based on urine output and hemodynamic status. Monitor for signs of fluid overload, particularly in patients with underlying heart or kidney disease.

Sodium Bicarbonate:
- **Purpose:** Alkalinize the urine to prevent myoglobin precipitation in the renal tubules and to combat metabolic acidosis.
- **Protocol:** Administer sodium bicarbonate (1 ampule = 50 mEq) in 1 liter of D5W at a rate of 100-200 mL/hr. Adjust the infusion rate to maintain urine pH > 6.5 and serum bicarbonate levels within normal range.
- **Monitoring:** Regularly check serum electrolytes, including potassium and bicarbonate levels, to guide ongoing management and avoid complications such as hypernatremia or alkalosis.

Additional Management Strategies:
1. **Electrolyte Management:** Monitor and correct hyperkalemia with medications such as insulin and glucose, calcium gluconate, and sodium polystyrene sulfonate (Kayexalate).
2. **Renal Protection:** Consider the use of mannitol as an osmotic diuretic to maintain urine flow, especially if urine output is inadequate despite aggressive fluid resuscitation.
3. **Dialysis:** Initiate renal replacement therapy if there is evidence of severe acute kidney injury, refractory hyperkalemia, or metabolic acidosis.

Wound Management:
- **Debridement:** Surgically debride necrotic tissue to prevent infection and further systemic complications.
- **Fasciotomy:** Consider fasciotomy to relieve compartment syndrome, which is a common complication of crush injuries.

Crush injuries and crush syndrome involve complex pathophysiological processes, including tissue damage, release of intracellular toxins, and reperfusion injury. Effective management focuses on early recognition, aggressive fluid resuscitation, electrolyte management, and renal protection. Sodium bicarbonate is used to alkalinize urine and prevent myoglobin-induced renal damage. A comprehensive approach, including continuous monitoring and timely interventions, is essential to mitigate systemic complications and improve patient outcomes.

Medical, Obstetrics & Gynecology

Pathophysiology of Ischemic and Hemorrhagic Strokes

Ischemic Stroke

Pathophysiology:

- **Mechanism:** Ischemic stroke occurs due to an obstruction of blood flow to the brain, typically caused by a thrombus (clot) or embolus (traveling clot).
- **Thrombosis:** Formation of a blood clot within a cerebral artery, often due to atherosclerosis.
- **Embolism:** Clot or other debris forms elsewhere in the body (e.g., heart) and travels to the brain, blocking a cerebral artery.
- **Ischemic Cascade:** Lack of blood flow leads to oxygen and glucose deprivation, causing cell death through excitotoxicity, oxidative stress, and inflammation.

Hemorrhagic Stroke

Pathophysiology:

- **Mechanism:** Hemorrhagic stroke occurs when a blood vessel in the brain ruptures, leading to bleeding within or around the brain.
- **Intracerebral Hemorrhage (ICH):** Bleeding within the brain tissue itself, often due to hypertension or arteriovenous malformations.
- **Subarachnoid Hemorrhage (SAH):** Bleeding into the subarachnoid space, often due to a ruptured aneurysm.
- **Effects:** Increased intracranial pressure (ICP), brain tissue compression, and secondary ischemia from disrupted blood flow.

FAST Assessment vs. Cincinnati Prehospital Stroke Scale

FAST (Face, Arms, Speech, Time)

- **Face:** Ask the person to smile. Check for facial droop or uneven smile.
- **Arms:** Ask the person to raise both arms. Look for arm drift or weakness.
- **Speech:** Ask the person to repeat a simple sentence. Listen for slurred speech or difficulty speaking.
- **Time:** Note the time symptoms started and seek emergency help immediately.

Cincinnati Prehospital Stroke Scale (CPSS)

- **Facial Droop:** Ask the person to smile or show teeth. One side does not move as well as the other.
- **Arm Drift:** Ask the person to close eyes and hold both arms out with palms up. One arm drifts down compared to the other.
- **Speech:** Ask the person to repeat a simple sentence. Words are slurred, incorrect, or unable to speak.

Differences:

- **FAST:** Emphasizes the importance of time (last known well) and is more widely recognized for public education.
- **CPSS:** Focuses on specific clinical signs without the explicit time component.

Importance of Last Known Well Time in Stroke Management

Last Known Well (LKW):

- **Definition:** The exact time when the patient was last observed to be at their normal state or symptom-free.
- **Importance:** Critical in determining eligibility for time-sensitive treatments like thrombolytic therapy (e.g., tPA).

Impact on Thrombolytic Therapy Eligibility:

- **Thrombolytic Therapy (tPA):**
  - **Eligibility Window:** Typically, tPA must be administered within 4.5 hours of stroke onset for ischemic strokes.
  - **LKW:** Accurate LKW time ensures that patients within the treatment window receive timely intervention, maximizing the chance of clot dissolution and reperfusion.
  - **Beyond the Window:** If beyond the 4.5-hour window, the risk of complications from tPA, such as hemorrhage, outweighs the potential benefits.

Extended Window:
- **Endovascular Therapy**: Mechanical thrombectomy may be an option for certain patients within 6-24 hours of stroke onset, especially if imaging shows salvageable brain tissue.
- **Imaging Criteria**: Advanced imaging (e.g., CT perfusion, MRI) can identify patients who may benefit from intervention beyond the standard time window.

Understanding the distinct pathophysiology of ischemic and hemorrhagic strokes helps tailor the management approach. The FAST and Cincinnati Prehospital Stroke Scale are tools for early stroke recognition, with the FAST emphasizing the critical nature of time. Accurate determination of the Last Known Well time is pivotal in deciding the eligibility for thrombolytic therapy, influencing treatment decisions and outcomes significantly. Early intervention remains key in minimizing long-term disability and improving survival rates in stroke patients.

Presentations and Management of Seizures
Focal Seizures:
Presentations:
- **Simple Focal Seizures:** These involve a small part of the brain and do not impair consciousness. Symptoms depend on the affected brain area and may include motor symptoms (e.g., twitching), sensory symptoms (e.g., tingling or visual disturbances), or autonomic symptoms (e.g., sweating).
- **Complex Focal Seizures:** These affect a larger part of the brain and impair consciousness. Patients may exhibit automatisms (e.g., lip-smacking, hand-wringing) and may be confused or unaware of their surroundings during the seizure.

Management:
- **Initial Care:** Ensure patient safety, monitor vital signs, and provide reassurance.
- **Medications:** Antiepileptic drugs (AEDs) like carbamazepine, lamotrigine, or levetiracetam are commonly used for long-term control.
- **Emergency Management:** If the seizure persists, administer a benzodiazepine (e.g., lorazepam).

Generalized Seizures:
Presentations:
- **Tonic-Clonic Seizures:** Also known as grand mal seizures, these involve a loss of consciousness and tonic (stiffening) followed by clonic (jerking) phases. Postictal confusion is common.
- **Absence Seizures:** Brief, sudden lapses in consciousness, often described as staring spells. These are more common in children.
- **Myoclonic Seizures:** Sudden, brief muscle jerks, typically without loss of consciousness.
- **Atonic Seizures:** Sudden loss of muscle tone, leading to falls and injuries.

Management:
- **Initial Care:** Ensure the patient is safe and monitor vital signs. Place the patient in the recovery position after the seizure ends.
- **Medications:** AEDs such as valproate, ethosuximide (for absence seizures), or levetiracetam.
- **Emergency Management:** For ongoing seizures, administer benzodiazepines.

Status Epilepticus:
Presentations:
- **Definition:** Seizures lasting more than 5 minutes or two or more seizures without full recovery of consciousness in between.
- **Clinical Picture:** Prolonged convulsive activity or repeated seizures with little to no recovery period.

Management:
- **Immediate Intervention:** Maintain airway, breathing, and circulation (DRABC approach).
- **Medications:** Administer a rapid-acting benzodiazepine (e.g., lorazepam, diazepam) followed by long-acting AEDs (e.g., phenytoin, levetiracetam).
- **Monitoring:** Continuous monitoring in an ICU setting may be required.

DRABC Approach to Seizure Management

DRABC:

1. **Danger:** Ensure the scene is safe for both the patient and the responder.
2. **Response:** Check if the patient is responsive by gently shaking or speaking to them.
3. **Airway:** Ensure the airway is open. Position the patient to prevent aspiration, but do not place anything in their mouth.
4. **Breathing:** Check for breathing. If the patient is not breathing, initiate rescue breathing.
5. **Circulation:** Check for a pulse and signs of circulation. Initiate CPR if needed.

Further Steps:

- **Postictal Care:** Once the seizure ends, place the patient in the recovery position to maintain airway patency and monitor their condition.
- **Documentation:** Record the duration and characteristics of the seizure, including any triggers or injuries.

Differentiating True Seizures from Pseudoseizures

True Seizures:

Characteristics:

- **Electrical Activity:** Abnormal electrical discharges in the brain can be detected with EEG.
- **Clinical Signs:** Rhythmic jerking movements, loss of consciousness, postictal confusion.
- **Autonomic Changes:** Pupillary changes, cyanosis, and tachycardia during the event.

Pseudoseizures (Psychogenic Non-Epileptic Seizures, PNES):

Characteristics:

- **Psychiatric Origin:** Often associated with psychological factors rather than electrical brain activity.
- **Clinical Signs:** May have asynchronous, non-rhythmic movements, and preserved awareness or partial responsiveness.
- **Lack of Postictal State:** Patients may recover immediately without postictal confusion.
- **Triggers:** Often triggered by emotional stress, with more dramatic and prolonged motor activity.

Diagnosis:

- **History and Observation:** Detailed history and observation of seizure events.
- **EEG Monitoring:** Continuous EEG monitoring during suspected events can help differentiate between true seizures and PNES.
- **Psychiatric Evaluation:** Evaluation for underlying psychiatric conditions or stressors.

Management:

- **True Seizures:** Managed with AEDs and addressing underlying neurological conditions.
- **Pseudoseizures:** Managed with psychological therapies, including cognitive-behavioral therapy (CBT) and addressing underlying psychiatric conditions.

Understanding the differences in presentations and management of focal seizures, generalized seizures, and status epilepticus is crucial. The DRABC approach ensures immediate safety and stabilization, while accurate differentiation between true seizures and pseudoseizures guides appropriate treatment and referral.

Differential Diagnosis of Altered Mental Status Using AEIOU-TIPS

The mnemonic AEIOU-TIPS helps healthcare providers systematically consider potential causes of altered mental status (AMS):

1. **A - Alcohol/Acidosis:**
   - **Alcohol:** Intoxication or withdrawal can cause confusion, agitation, or stupor.
   - **Acidosis:** Metabolic disturbances like diabetic ketoacidosis (DKA) or lactic acidosis can alter mental status.
2. **E - Endocrine/Epilepsy/Electrolytes/Encephalopathy:**
   - **Endocrine:** Thyroid disorders (hypo- or hyperthyroidism), adrenal insufficiency.
   - **Epilepsy:** Seizures and postictal states can cause temporary AMS.
   - **Electrolytes:** Imbalances like hyponatremia, hypercalcemia, or hypoglycemia.
   - **Encephalopathy:** Hepatic or uremic encephalopathy can result from liver or kidney failure.
3. **I - Infection:**

- ○ **Infections**: Sepsis, meningitis, encephalitis, urinary tract infections, and pneumonia, especially in the elderly, can cause AMS.
4. **O - Overdose/Oxygen deficiency**:
   - ○ **Overdose**: Intoxication with drugs or medications (e.g., opioids, sedatives).
   - ○ **Oxygen deficiency**: Hypoxia due to respiratory failure, carbon monoxide poisoning.
5. **U - Uremia**:
   - ○ **Uremia**: Accumulation of waste products due to renal failure can cause encephalopathy.
6. **T - Trauma/Tumor/Toxins**:
   - ○ **Trauma**: Head injury leading to concussion, intracranial hemorrhage.
   - ○ **Tumor**: Primary or metastatic brain tumors can affect mental status.
   - ○ **Toxins**: Exposure to environmental toxins or heavy metals.
7. **I - Insulin**:
   - ○ **Insulin**: Hypoglycemia or hyperglycemia can cause confusion, lethargy, or coma.
8. **P - Psychosis/Poisoning**:
   - ○ **Psychosis**: Acute psychiatric conditions like schizophrenia or mania.
   - ○ **Poisoning**: Ingestion of substances like pesticides or antifreeze.
9. **S - Stroke/Seizure/Syncope**:
   - ○ **Stroke**: Ischemic or hemorrhagic stroke leading to focal deficits and AMS.
   - ○ **Seizure**: Status epilepticus or postictal states.
   - ○ **Syncope**: Transient loss of consciousness due to reduced cerebral perfusion.

Glasgow Coma Scale (GCS) and Altered Mental Status
Glasgow Coma Scale (GCS):

- **Purpose**: Assesses a patient's level of consciousness based on eye, verbal, and motor responses.
- **Scoring**: Ranges from 3 (deep coma) to 15 (fully awake).
  - ○ **Eye Opening (E)**:
    - 4: Spontaneous
    - 3: To verbal command
    - 2: To pain
    - 1: No response
  - ○ **Verbal Response (V)**:
    - 5: Oriented
    - 4: Confused conversation
    - 3: Inappropriate words
    - 2: Incomprehensible sounds
    - 1: No response
  - ○ **Motor Response (M)**:
    - 6: Obeys commands
    - 5: Localizes pain
    - 4: Withdraws from pain
    - 3: Abnormal flexion (decorticate)
    - 2: Abnormal extension (decerebrate)
    - 1: No response

Relation to Severity:

- **Mild**: GCS 13-15
- **Moderate**: GCS 9-12
- **Severe**: GCS ≤ 8

A lower GCS score indicates a more severe alteration in consciousness, guiding urgency and type of medical intervention required.

AVPU Scale in Rapid Neurological Assessment
AVPU Scale:

- **A - Alert**: The patient is fully awake and aware.

- **V - Verbal**: The patient responds to verbal stimuli (e.g., spoken commands).
- **P - Pain**: The patient responds to painful stimuli (e.g., pinching).
- **U - Unresponsive**: The patient does not respond to any stimuli.

Use:

- **Rapid Assessment**: Provides a quick and straightforward method to assess the level of consciousness.
- **Baseline Establishment**: Helps to quickly establish a baseline neurological status and detect changes over time.
- **Guide for Intervention**: Helps determine the immediacy and type of intervention needed, especially in emergency settings.

The AVPU scale offers a fast, initial assessment tool, while the GCS provides a more detailed evaluation of consciousness levels and can track changes over time. Both scales are essential in the initial assessment and ongoing monitoring of patients with altered mental status.

Pathophysiology, Signs, Symptoms, and Management of Hypoglycemia, Hyperglycemia, and Diabetic Ketoacidosis
Hypoglycemia:
Pathophysiology:

- **Cause:** Low blood glucose levels, typically below 70 mg/dL.
- **Mechanism:** Excess insulin, inadequate food intake, excessive exercise, or alcohol consumption without adequate carbohydrate intake.

Signs and Symptoms:

- **Adrenergic Symptoms:** Sweating, tremors, palpitations, anxiety, and hunger.
- **Neuroglycopenic Symptoms:** Confusion, headache, dizziness, visual disturbances, difficulty concentrating, and, in severe cases, seizures or loss of consciousness.

Management:

1. **Immediate Treatment:**
    - **Rule of 15:** If the patient is conscious and able to swallow, administer 15 grams of fast-acting carbohydrates (e.g., glucose tablets, juice, regular soda).
    - **Recheck Blood Glucose:** After 15 minutes, recheck blood glucose levels. If still low, repeat the 15 grams of carbohydrates.
    - **Longer-Acting Carbohydrates:** Once blood glucose is normalized, consume a snack with complex carbohydrates and protein (e.g., peanut butter sandwich) to maintain glucose levels.
2. **Severe Hypoglycemia:**
    - **Glucagon:** If the patient is unconscious or unable to swallow, administer glucagon via intramuscular or subcutaneous injection.
    - **Emergency Care:** If there is no response to glucagon or if glucagon is not available, seek emergency medical assistance. In a hospital setting, intravenous dextrose (D50) may be administered.

Hyperglycemia:
Pathophysiology:

- **Cause:** High blood glucose levels, typically above 180 mg/dL.
- **Mechanism:** Insufficient insulin, increased glucose intake, stress, infection, or certain medications.

Signs and Symptoms:

- **Early Symptoms:** Polyuria (frequent urination), polydipsia (excessive thirst), and polyphagia (increased hunger).
- **Later Symptoms:** Fatigue, blurred vision, dry mouth, and unexplained weight loss.

Management:

1. **Monitor Blood Glucose:** Regularly check blood glucose levels to detect and manage hyperglycemia early.
2. **Medication Adjustment:** Adjust insulin or oral hypoglycemic medications as needed based on medical advice.
3. **Hydration:** Increase fluid intake to prevent dehydration.

4. **Dietary Management:** Monitor carbohydrate intake and adjust diet as necessary.
5. **Seek Medical Advice:** If blood glucose levels remain high despite initial management or if ketones are present in the urine, seek medical attention.

Diabetic Ketoacidosis (DKA):
Pathophysiology:
- **Cause:** Severe insulin deficiency, leading to hyperglycemia, ketosis, and metabolic acidosis.
- **Mechanism:** Without insulin, glucose cannot enter cells, leading to fat breakdown for energy. This produces ketones, which accumulate and cause acidosis.

Signs and Symptoms:
- **Early Symptoms:** Polyuria, polydipsia, nausea, vomiting, and abdominal pain.
- **Later Symptoms:** Fruity-scented breath (due to acetone), rapid deep breathing (Kussmaul respirations), confusion, lethargy, and dehydration.
- **Laboratory Findings:** Blood glucose >250 mg/dL, ketonemia, ketonuria, and metabolic acidosis (low bicarbonate, low pH).

Management:
1. **Fluids:** Rapid intravenous rehydration with isotonic saline to correct dehydration.
2. **Insulin:** Continuous IV insulin infusion to reduce blood glucose and stop ketone production.
3. **Electrolytes:** Monitor and correct electrolyte imbalances, especially potassium.
4. **Monitor:** Regular monitoring of blood glucose, ketones, and acid-base status.
5. **Address Underlying Causes:** Identify and treat underlying causes such as infection or missed insulin doses.

Euglycemic DKA
Concept:
- **Definition:** Diabetic ketoacidosis with normal or near-normal blood glucose levels (<250 mg/dL).
- **Causes:** SGLT2 inhibitors (a class of diabetes medications), prolonged fasting, or reduced insulin dosing.

Impact on Assessment and Treatment:
- **Assessment:** Clinicians should consider DKA even if blood glucose levels are not markedly elevated, especially if the patient has symptoms of DKA and a history of diabetes.
- **Treatment:** Management is similar to typical DKA, focusing on fluid resuscitation, insulin administration, and correction of electrolyte imbalances.

The "Rule of 15" in Managing Hypoglycemia
Application:
1. **Administer 15 grams of Fast-Acting Carbohydrates:**
   - Examples include glucose tablets, 4 ounces of juice or regular soda, 1 tablespoon of sugar or honey, or 5-6 hard candies.
2. **Recheck Blood Glucose after 15 Minutes:**
   - If blood glucose remains below 70 mg/dL, repeat the 15 grams of carbohydrates.
3. **Follow with a Snack:**
   - Once blood glucose returns to normal, consume a snack with protein and complex carbohydrates to maintain glucose levels and prevent recurrence.

Benefits:
- **Standardized Approach:** Provides a clear and simple method to rapidly address hypoglycemia.
- **Prevents Over-Treatment:** Helps avoid excessive intake of carbohydrates, which can lead to rebound hyperglycemia.

Hypoglycemia, hyperglycemia, and diabetic ketoacidosis each have distinct pathophysiologies, presentations, and management strategies. Recognizing the signs and symptoms early and understanding appropriate interventions are crucial for effective treatment. Euglycemic DKA presents a diagnostic challenge but follows similar management principles as typical DKA. The "Rule of 15" offers a practical approach to managing hypoglycemia, ensuring quick and effective normalization of blood glucose levels.

Hypothyroidism (Myxedema Coma) vs. Hyperthyroidism (Thyroid Storm)

Presentations

Myxedema Coma (Severe Hypothyroidism):

- **Clinical Features:**
  - **Mental Status**: Severe lethargy, stupor, or coma.
  - **Hypothermia**: Low body temperature.
  - **Bradycardia**: Slow heart rate.
  - **Hypotension**: Low blood pressure.
  - **Hypoventilation**: Respiratory depression, leading to hypercapnia and hypoxia.
  - **Edema**: Generalized swelling, especially non-pitting edema in the face and extremities.
  - **Hyponatremia**: Low sodium levels.
  - **Hypoglycemia**: Low blood sugar levels.
- **Emergency Management:**
  - **Thyroid Hormone Replacement**: Intravenous levothyroxine or liothyronine.
  - **Supportive Care**: Passive rewarming (to avoid rapid temperature shifts), fluid resuscitation, and correction of electrolyte imbalances.
  - **Mechanical Ventilation**: If respiratory failure is present.
  - **Glucocorticoids**: To treat potential adrenal insufficiency and support stress response.

Thyroid Storm (Severe Hyperthyroidism):

- **Clinical Features:**
  - **Mental Status**: Agitation, delirium, or coma.
  - **Hyperthermia**: High fever.
  - **Tachycardia**: Rapid heart rate, often >140 bpm.
  - **Hypertension**: Elevated blood pressure, sometimes followed by hypotension due to heart failure.
  - **Tachypnea**: Rapid breathing.
  - **Diaphoresis**: Excessive sweating.
  - **Gastrointestinal**: Nausea, vomiting, diarrhea.
  - **Neurological**: Tremors, seizures.
- **Emergency Management:**
  - **Beta-Blockers**: Propranolol to control heart rate and reduce adrenergic symptoms.
  - **Antithyroid Medications**: Propylthiouracil (PTU) or methimazole to inhibit thyroid hormone synthesis.
  - **Iodine**: Lugol's solution or potassium iodide to inhibit the release of thyroid hormones.
  - **Glucocorticoids**: Dexamethasone to reduce peripheral conversion of T4 to T3 and treat potential adrenal insufficiency.
  - **Cooling Measures**: External cooling for hyperthermia.
  - **Supportive Care**: Fluid resuscitation, electrolyte correction, and treatment of underlying precipitating factors (e.g., infection).

Apathetic Thyrotoxicosis
Concept:

- **Atypical Presentation**: In elderly patients, hyperthyroidism may present with atypical, muted symptoms, known as apathetic thyrotoxicosis.
- **Symptoms**: Instead of the classic signs of hyperthyroidism, elderly patients may exhibit fatigue, weight loss, depression, or cardiac symptoms like atrial fibrillation or heart failure.
- **Complication in Assessment**: The lack of typical hyperthyroid symptoms (e.g., tremors, heat intolerance, and hyperactivity) can delay diagnosis and treatment, as these symptoms may be mistaken for other age-related conditions or comorbidities.

Comparing and Contrasting Myxedema Coma and Thyroid Storm

- **Mental Status**: Myxedema coma presents with severe lethargy or coma, whereas thyroid storm presents with agitation or delirium.
- **Temperature Regulation**: Myxedema coma is characterized by hypothermia, while thyroid storm is associated with hyperthermia.

- **Heart Rate and Blood Pressure**: Myxedema coma involves bradycardia and hypotension, whereas thyroid storm involves tachycardia and hypertension.
- **Respiratory Function**: Hypoventilation is seen in myxedema coma, leading to respiratory acidosis, whereas tachypnea is common in thyroid storm.
- **Metabolic Features**: Myxedema coma often involves hypoglycemia and hyponatremia, while thyroid storm can present with hyperglycemia and elevated metabolic rates.

The presentation of severe thyroid disorders differs significantly between hypothyroidism and hyperthyroidism, with myxedema coma and thyroid storm being life-threatening emergencies that require prompt recognition and treatment. Apathetic thyrotoxicosis in elderly patients complicates the diagnosis of hyperthyroidism due to atypical presentations, necessitating a high index of suspicion and thorough clinical evaluation.

SAD PERSONS Scale for Suicide Risk Assessment

The SAD PERSONS scale is a clinical tool used to assess the risk of suicide. Each letter in the acronym represents a risk factor, and the presence of these factors can help clinicians determine the level of suicide risk and the need for intervention.

1. **S - Sex**: Male (1 point)
2. **A - Age**: <19 or >45 years (1 point)
3. **D - Depression**: Presence of depression (1 point)
4. **P - Previous attempt**: History of previous suicide attempts (1 point)
5. **E - Ethanol or drug use**: Substance abuse (1 point)
6. **R - Rational thinking loss**: Presence of psychosis or severe mental illness (1 point)
7. **S - Social support lacking**: Lack of social support (1 point)
8. **O - Organized plan**: Having a detailed plan (1 point)
9. **N - No spouse**: Being single, divorced, or widowed (1 point)
10. **S - Sickness**: Chronic illness (1 point)

Scoring and Interpretation:

- **0-4 Points:** Low risk. May require routine follow-up and monitoring.
- **5-6 Points:** Moderate risk. Consider close follow-up and possible mental health referral.
- **7-10 Points:** High risk. Immediate mental health intervention and possible hospitalization.

Differentiating Suicidal Ideation, Intent, and Plan

1. **Suicidal Ideation:**
   - **Definition:** Thoughts about wanting to end one's life or wishing they were dead. These can range from fleeting thoughts to persistent considerations.
   - **Assessment:** Ask the patient about the frequency, duration, and nature of these thoughts.
2. **Suicidal Intent:**
   - **Definition:** The determination to act on suicidal thoughts. It indicates a higher level of risk than mere ideation.
   - **Assessment:** Inquire whether the patient has decided to act on their thoughts and how committed they are to following through.
3. **Suicidal Plan:**
   - **Definition:** A specific, detailed plan about how to commit suicide. This includes the method, time, place, and means to carry out the act.
   - **Assessment:** Ask the patient if they have a specific plan and details about how they intend to execute it. The more detailed and feasible the plan, the higher the risk.

Legal and Ethical Considerations in Managing Patients with Suicidal Behavior
Legal Considerations:

1. **Duty to Protect:**
   - Healthcare providers have a legal obligation to protect patients from self-harm. This may include breaching confidentiality to inform family members or authorities if the patient is at immediate risk.
2. **Involuntary Commitment:**

- If a patient poses a significant risk to themselves, they can be involuntarily committed to a mental health facility for evaluation and treatment. Laws regarding involuntary commitment vary by jurisdiction but generally require evidence of imminent danger.

3. **Documentation:**
   - Thorough documentation of the patient's statements, risk factors, and the clinician's assessment and actions is crucial. This can provide legal protection and ensure continuity of care.

Ethical Considerations:

1. **Confidentiality:**
   - While maintaining patient confidentiality is a core ethical principle, it may be ethically justified to breach confidentiality if it prevents harm. Clear communication with the patient about these boundaries is essential.

2. **Autonomy:**
   - Respecting patient autonomy means considering their wishes and involving them in decision-making as much as possible. However, this must be balanced with the need to prevent harm.

3. **Beneficence and Non-Maleficence:**
   - The principle of beneficence (acting in the patient's best interest) and non-maleficence (doing no harm) guides the management of suicidal patients. Interventions should aim to maximize benefit and minimize harm.

4. **Informed Consent:**
   - Whenever possible, obtain informed consent from the patient for any interventions. This includes discussing the reasons for hospitalization or other treatments and the potential risks and benefits.

5. **Communication and Support:**
   - Provide clear, compassionate communication. Ensure that patients understand they are being supported and that their safety is the primary concern.

The SAD PERSONS scale is a valuable tool for assessing suicide risk, helping to identify individuals who may need immediate intervention. Differentiating between suicidal ideation, intent, and plan is crucial for assessing the level of risk and determining the appropriate response. Managing patients with suicidal behavior involves navigating complex legal and ethical considerations, balancing the need to protect patients with respect for their autonomy and confidentiality. Understanding and applying these principles ensures effective and compassionate care for individuals at risk of suicide.

Excited Delirium Syndrome (ExDS)
Pathophysiology

Excited delirium syndrome (ExDS) is a condition characterized by extreme agitation, aggression, acute distress, and sudden death, often in the context of substance abuse or psychiatric disorders. The exact pathophysiology is not completely understood, but several factors contribute:

1. **Neurotransmitter Imbalance:**
   - Excessive dopamine and norepinephrine activity in the central nervous system.
   - Dysregulation of the autonomic nervous system.

2. **Substance Abuse:**
   - Commonly associated with stimulants such as cocaine, methamphetamine, and synthetic drugs (e.g., bath salts).

3. **Psychiatric Disorders:**
   - Underlying mental health conditions, including schizophrenia and bipolar disorder.

4. **Metabolic Disturbances:**
   - Hyperthermia, metabolic acidosis, and rhabdomyolysis.

Signs and Symptoms

Patients with ExDS often exhibit the following:

- **Severe Agitation:** Extreme restlessness and irritability.
- **Aggression:** Violent behavior, sometimes directed towards others.
- **Paranoia:** Heightened sense of fear or persecution.

- **Hyperthermia**: Elevated body temperature.
- **Tachycardia**: Rapid heart rate.
- **Diaphoresis**: Profuse sweating.
- **Delirium**: Confusion, disorientation, hallucinations.
- **Superhuman Strength**: Perceived or actual increase in strength, often due to adrenaline.
- **Insensitivity to Pain**: Reduced or absent response to painful stimuli.

Management

The management of ExDS focuses on rapidly controlling agitation and addressing underlying pathophysiological issues:

1. **Immediate Control**:
   - **Physical Restraint**: Only if absolutely necessary and with appropriate safety measures to prevent harm.
   - **Chemical Restraint**: Medications to sedate the patient safely.
     - **Benzodiazepines**: Lorazepam or diazepam to reduce agitation and muscle activity.
     - **Antipsychotics**: Haloperidol or droperidol to manage psychotic symptoms.
2. **Supportive Care**:
   - **Cooling Measures**: To address hyperthermia (e.g., ice packs, cool IV fluids).
   - **Fluid Resuscitation**: To correct dehydration and support cardiovascular function.
   - **Monitoring**: Continuous monitoring of vital signs and oxygen saturation.
3. **Treatment of Complications**:
   - **Metabolic Acidosis**: IV bicarbonate if severe acidosis is confirmed.
   - **Rhabdomyolysis**: Aggressive IV hydration and monitoring of renal function.

Metabolic Acidosis and Sudden Death in ExDS

Metabolic Acidosis:

- **Mechanism**: Intense physical activity, hyperthermia, and excessive adrenergic stimulation lead to increased lactate production and decreased pH in the blood.
- **Consequences**: Metabolic acidosis contributes to cardiovascular instability, arrhythmias, and can exacerbate hyperthermia and rhabdomyolysis.

Risk of Sudden Death:

- **Cardiac Arrhythmias**: Acidosis alters myocardial excitability, increasing the risk of fatal arrhythmias.
- **Autonomic Dysfunction**: Dysregulation of the autonomic nervous system can lead to sudden cardiac arrest.
- **Multisystem Failure**: The combined effects of metabolic acidosis, hyperthermia, and rhabdomyolysis can overwhelm the body's compensatory mechanisms, leading to sudden death.

Controversy Surrounding Ketamine Use

Ketamine:

- **Benefits**: Ketamine is a dissociative anesthetic that can provide rapid sedation and control of agitation in ExDS.
  - **Rapid Onset**: Provides quick sedation, which is critical in preventing harm to the patient and others.
  - **Analgesic Properties**: Helps in managing pain and discomfort.
  - **Sympathomimetic Effects**: Maintains airway reflexes and can increase heart rate and blood pressure, which can be beneficial in some scenarios.

Controversies:

- **Safety Concerns**: Potential for adverse effects, such as respiratory depression, laryngospasm, and emergence reactions (e.g., hallucinations).
- **Cardiovascular Effects**: Although ketamine generally supports cardiovascular function, its sympathomimetic properties can exacerbate hypertension and tachycardia in some patients.
- **Lack of Consensus**: Varied guidelines and protocols regarding the appropriate use of ketamine in ExDS, leading to inconsistent practices and potential legal implications.

- **Ethical and Legal Issues**: Concerns about the ethics of using a potent anesthetic in non-hospital settings, potential for misuse, and varying levels of provider training and experience.

While ketamine can be a valuable tool in managing ExDS, its use must be carefully weighed against potential risks, and administered by trained personnel with appropriate monitoring and support available.

Understanding the pathophysiology, signs, symptoms, and management of ExDS is crucial for providing effective and timely care. Addressing metabolic acidosis and using appropriate sedatives like ketamine, while controversial, can be life-saving when used correctly.

Toxidrome Approach to Poisoning and Overdose Assessment

Toxidromes are groups of signs and symptoms associated with specific types of poisoning. Recognizing a toxidrome can help quickly identify the type of poison involved and guide initial management.

1. **Cholinergic Toxidrome (e.g., organophosphates, carbamates):**
   - **Signs and Symptoms:** SLUDGE mnemonic (see below), bradycardia, bronchorrhea, miosis, muscle fasciculations.
   - **Management:** Atropine, pralidoxime, supportive care.
2. **Anticholinergic Toxidrome (e.g., atropine, antihistamines):**
   - **Signs and Symptoms:** Dry mouth, dry skin, hyperthermia, mydriasis, urinary retention, altered mental status, tachycardia.
   - **Management:** Supportive care, benzodiazepines for agitation or seizures, physostigmine (with caution).
3. **Sympathomimetic Toxidrome (e.g., cocaine, amphetamines):**
   - **Signs and Symptoms:** Tachycardia, hypertension, hyperthermia, mydriasis, agitation, seizures.
   - **Management:** Benzodiazepines, cooling measures, supportive care.
4. **Opioid Toxidrome (e.g., heroin, morphine):**
   - **Signs and Symptoms:** Miosis, respiratory depression, altered mental status, bradycardia, hypotension.
   - **Management:** Naloxone, supportive care.
5. **Sedative-Hypnotic Toxidrome (e.g., benzodiazepines, barbiturates):**
   - **Signs and Symptoms:** CNS depression, ataxia, slurred speech, respiratory depression (in severe cases).
   - **Management:** Supportive care, flumazenil (for benzodiazepines, with caution).

Applying the SLUDGE Mnemonic in Cholinergic Toxicity

SLUDGE is a mnemonic used to remember the symptoms of cholinergic toxicity, often caused by organophosphates, carbamates, or certain nerve agents. These substances inhibit acetylcholinesterase, leading to an accumulation of acetylcholine and overstimulation of muscarinic receptors.

1. **S - Salivation:** Excessive drooling or salivation.
2. **L - Lacrimation:** Excessive tearing.
3. **U - Urination:** Frequent urination or incontinence.
4. **D - Defecation/Diarrhea:** Frequent bowel movements or diarrhea.
5. **G - Gastrointestinal upset:** Abdominal cramping, nausea, vomiting.
6. **E - Emesis:** Vomiting.

Management of Cholinergic Toxicity:

- **Atropine:** An anticholinergic agent that competes with acetylcholine at muscarinic receptors, reducing secretions and relieving bronchorrhea and bradycardia.
- **Pralidoxime (2-PAM):** Reverses the inhibition of acetylcholinesterase by organophosphates, restoring normal function.
- **Supportive Care:** Includes airway management, oxygen, and intravenous fluids.

Nomogram in Acetaminophen Overdose Management

Acetaminophen (Paracetamol) Overdose:

- Overdose can lead to hepatotoxicity and potentially fatal liver failure. Early recognition and treatment are crucial.

Rumack-Matthew Nomogram:
- **Purpose:** Assesses the risk of hepatotoxicity after a single acute overdose of acetaminophen.
- **Timeframe:** Useful from 4 to 24 hours post-ingestion.
- **Procedure:**
    1. **Measure Serum Acetaminophen Level:** Obtain a blood sample at least 4 hours after ingestion.
    2. **Plot the Level:** On the nomogram, locate the measured acetaminophen concentration on the y-axis and the time post-ingestion on the x-axis.
    3. **Risk Stratification:**
        - **Above the "Possible Risk" Line:** Indicates a potential for hepatotoxicity; initiate treatment.
        - **Below the Line:** Low risk for hepatotoxicity, but clinical judgment and further monitoring are needed.

Management Based on Nomogram Results:
- **N-Acetylcysteine (NAC):** Administer NAC if the acetaminophen level is above the "possible risk" line. NAC acts as a precursor for glutathione, enhancing detoxification and preventing liver damage.
    - **Oral NAC:** Loading dose of 140 mg/kg followed by 70 mg/kg every 4 hours for 17 doses.
    - **IV NAC:** Loading dose of 150 mg/kg over 1 hour, followed by 50 mg/kg over 4 hours, then 100 mg/kg over 16 hours.
- **Supportive Care:** Includes monitoring liver function tests, coagulation profile, and renal function. Provide symptomatic treatment as needed.

Key Points:
- **Early Treatment:** Administer NAC as soon as possible, ideally within 8 hours of ingestion, for maximum efficacy.
- **Repeat Doses:** If initial treatment was delayed or if severe poisoning is suspected, additional doses or prolonged treatment may be required.

Summary

The toxidrome approach aids in the rapid identification and management of poisonings and overdoses by recognizing characteristic symptom patterns. The SLUDGE mnemonic is specifically useful for cholinergic toxicity, guiding the use of atropine and pralidoxime. In acetaminophen overdose, the Rumack-Matthew nomogram is essential for assessing the risk of hepatotoxicity and guiding the administration of N-acetylcysteine. Understanding these tools and principles ensures effective and timely intervention in poisoning cases.

Pathophysiology of Carbon Monoxide Poisoning

Carbon monoxide (CO) poisoning occurs when CO gas, which is colorless, odorless, and tasteless, is inhaled and binds to hemoglobin in the blood, forming carboxyhemoglobin (COHb). This binding prevents hemoglobin from carrying oxygen, leading to hypoxia and cellular dysfunction.

Mechanisms:
1. **High Affinity for Hemoglobin:** CO binds to hemoglobin with an affinity 200-250 times greater than oxygen, reducing the amount of oxygen transported in the blood.
2. **Leftward Shift of the Oxyhemoglobin Dissociation Curve:** COHb causes hemoglobin to hold onto oxygen more tightly, impeding the release of oxygen to tissues.
3. **Cellular Hypoxia:** Tissues become starved of oxygen, leading to metabolic acidosis and cellular injury.
4. **Binding to Myoglobin and Cytochrome Oxidase:** CO can bind to other heme-containing proteins, impairing muscle function (including the heart) and disrupting cellular respiration in mitochondria.

Clinical Symptoms and Carboxyhemoglobin Levels

Correlation Between COHb Levels and Symptoms:
- **0-10% COHb:** Often asymptomatic or mild symptoms such as headache and dizziness.
- **10-20% COHb:** Mild headache, dizziness, nausea, shortness of breath.
- **20-30% COHb:** Throbbing headache, fatigue, impaired judgment, mild dyspnea.
- **30-40% COHb:** Severe headache, confusion, syncope, tachycardia, dyspnea.

- **40-50% COHb**: Loss of consciousness, tachypnea, increased risk of myocardial ischemia.
- **50-60% COHb**: Seizures, coma, respiratory failure.
- **>60% COHb**: Potentially fatal due to profound hypoxia and cardiac arrest.

Management of Carbon Monoxide Poisoning
1. **Immediate Removal from CO Source**:
   - **Ensure Safety**: Move the patient to fresh air and away from the source of CO exposure.
2. **Oxygen Therapy**:
   - **High-Flow Oxygen**: Administer 100% oxygen via non-rebreather mask to hasten the elimination of CO from the body. This significantly reduces the half-life of COHb from approximately 5 hours on room air to 1-2 hours.
   - **Hyperbaric Oxygen Therapy (HBOT)**: Indicated in severe cases, such as COHb levels >25%, neurological symptoms, cardiovascular dysfunction, or pregnancy. HBOT involves breathing 100% oxygen in a pressurized chamber, reducing the half-life of COHb to 20-30 minutes and improving oxygen delivery to tissues.
3. **Supportive Care**:
   - **Monitoring**: Continuous monitoring of vital signs, cardiac rhythm, and oxygen saturation.
   - **Fluids and Electrolytes**: Administer IV fluids to maintain hydration and electrolyte balance.
   - **Symptomatic Treatment**: Address symptoms like seizures with appropriate medications.

Delayed Neurological Sequelae (DNS)
Concept:
- **Delayed Neurological Sequelae** refer to the development of neurological symptoms days to weeks after the initial recovery from acute CO poisoning. This can occur even after apparent initial recovery and normalization of COHb levels.

Pathophysiology:
1. **Oxidative Stress and Inflammation**: Persistent oxidative damage and inflammation in the brain may contribute to delayed neuronal injury.
2. **Lipid Peroxidation**: CO-induced hypoxia can lead to lipid peroxidation in neuronal cell membranes, disrupting cell function and viability.
3. **White Matter Damage**: Demyelination and axonal injury can occur, affecting brain connectivity and function.

Clinical Manifestations:
- **Cognitive Impairment**: Memory loss, difficulty concentrating, confusion.
- **Psychiatric Symptoms**: Depression, anxiety, personality changes.
- **Motor Dysfunction**: Coordination problems, gait disturbances, tremors.
- **Delayed Symptoms Onset**: Symptoms typically emerge within 2-40 days post-exposure.

Management:
- **Early Identification**: Close monitoring of patients for any new neurological symptoms after the initial exposure.
- **Hyperbaric Oxygen Therapy**: May be considered to mitigate the risk of DNS, though the evidence is mixed.
- **Rehabilitation**: Cognitive and physical rehabilitation programs to address functional deficits.
- **Follow-Up Care**: Regular follow-up with a neurologist or specialist to manage long-term neurological outcomes.

Understanding the pathophysiology and management of CO poisoning, along with the potential for delayed neurological sequelae, is crucial for providing comprehensive care to affected patients. Prompt intervention and continued monitoring can significantly impact patient outcomes and quality of life.

Analysis of the Opioid Crisis and the Role of EMS in Harm Reduction
The Opioid Crisis:
The opioid crisis refers to the rapid increase in the use of both prescription and non-prescription opioid drugs, leading to widespread addiction, overdoses, and deaths. Key factors include:

1. **Prescription Practices:** Over-prescription of opioid pain relievers in the late 1990s.
2. **Illegal Opioids:** Increased availability of illicit opioids such as heroin and synthetic opioids like fentanyl.
3. **Addiction and Dependence:** High potential for addiction with chronic opioid use, leading to dependence and misuse.

Impact:

- **Overdoses:** Significant rise in opioid-related overdoses and deaths.
- **Healthcare System Strain:** Increased burden on emergency services and healthcare facilities.
- **Social and Economic Costs:** Wide-ranging effects on communities, families, and economic productivity.

Role of EMS in Harm Reduction:

1. Emergency Response and Naloxone Administration:

- **Naloxone:** EMS personnel are often the first to administer naloxone, a life-saving medication that reverses opioid overdoses.
- **Training:** EMS providers are trained to recognize opioid overdoses and administer naloxone via intranasal, intramuscular, or intravenous routes.

2. Education and Prevention:

- **Public Education:** EMS can educate the public about the risks of opioid use, safe prescribing practices, and the importance of naloxone availability.
- **Referral to Treatment:** EMS can provide information and referrals to addiction treatment and recovery services.

3. Data Collection and Surveillance:

- **Overdose Tracking:** EMS agencies can contribute to overdose tracking systems, helping public health officials identify trends and target interventions.

4. Community Engagement:

- **Partnerships:** Collaborate with public health organizations, law enforcement, and community groups to address the opioid crisis comprehensively.
- **Harm Reduction Programs:** Support and participate in harm reduction programs such as needle exchange and supervised consumption sites.

Opioid Toxicity Triad

The Opioid Toxicity Triad consists of three key clinical signs that guide the assessment and diagnosis of opioid overdose:

1. **Respiratory Depression:**
   - **Signs:** Slow, shallow, or absent breathing. Hypoxia can lead to cyanosis (bluish discoloration of the skin, particularly around the lips and fingertips).
   - **Assessment:** Monitor respiratory rate, depth, and effort. Use pulse oximetry to measure oxygen saturation.
2. **Central Nervous System Depression:**
   - **Signs:** Altered mental status ranging from drowsiness to coma. Patients may be unresponsive or have minimal response to stimuli.
   - **Assessment:** Evaluate the level of consciousness using the Glasgow Coma Scale (GCS).
3. **Miosis (Constricted Pupils):**
   - **Signs:** Pinpoint pupils, although this may be absent in severe hypoxia or with co-ingestion of other substances.
   - **Assessment:** Examine pupil size and reactivity to light.

Pharmacokinetics and Proper Administration of Intranasal Naloxone

Pharmacokinetics of Naloxone:

1. **Absorption:**
   - **Intranasal Route:** Rapid absorption through the nasal mucosa, providing a quick onset of action.
   - **Bioavailability:** Intranasal naloxone has lower bioavailability compared to intravenous administration but is effective for emergency use.
2. **Distribution:**

- **CNS Penetration:** Naloxone quickly crosses the blood-brain barrier, displacing opioids from their receptors and reversing their effects.
3. **Metabolism:**
   - **Liver:** Naloxone is metabolized in the liver primarily by glucuronidation.
4. **Excretion:**
   - **Kidneys:** The drug and its metabolites are excreted via the kidneys.

Proper Administration of Intranasal Naloxone:
1. **Preparation:**
   - Ensure the intranasal device (e.g., Narcan nasal spray) is readily available and check the expiration date.
   - Assemble the device if necessary (some devices come pre-assembled).
2. **Positioning:**
   - Place the patient in a supine position with their head tilted slightly back to facilitate nasal absorption.
3. **Administration:**
   - **Insert the Device:** Place the nozzle into one nostril, ensuring a proper seal.
   - **Administer the Dose:** Depress the plunger or press the button to deliver the full dose (usually 4 mg).
   - **Alternate Nostrils:** If a second dose is needed, administer it in the other nostril after 2-3 minutes if there is no response.
4. **Post-Administration Monitoring:**
   - **Monitor for Response:** Observe for improved respiratory rate and mental status. Naloxone typically works within 2-3 minutes.
   - **Repeat Doses:** Administer additional doses if there is no response after the initial dose. Follow local protocols for maximum dosage.
   - **Supportive Care:** Provide supplemental oxygen and assist ventilation if needed. Be prepared for withdrawal symptoms and possible agitation once the patient regains consciousness.

Note: Intranasal naloxone is safe and easy to use, making it accessible for use by bystanders, family members, and first responders without advanced medical training.

Conclusion

The opioid crisis necessitates a multifaceted approach involving EMS in emergency response, public education, data collection, and community engagement. Recognizing the opioid toxicity triad is crucial for timely intervention. Intranasal naloxone is an effective tool for reversing opioid overdoses, with proper administration and monitoring being key to successful outcomes. Understanding these concepts and protocols helps EMS providers effectively manage opioid overdoses and contribute to harm reduction efforts.

Pathophysiology, Signs, Symptoms, and Management of Heat Exhaustion and Heat Stroke
Heat Exhaustion
Pathophysiology: Heat exhaustion occurs when the body loses excessive water and salt through sweating, leading to dehydration and an imbalance of electrolytes. This condition typically arises from prolonged exposure to high temperatures, particularly when combined with physical exertion.

Signs and Symptoms:
- **Profuse Sweating**: Excessive sweating as the body attempts to cool down.
- **Weakness and Fatigue**: General feeling of exhaustion.
- **Dizziness and Headache**: Due to dehydration and electrolyte imbalance.
- **Muscle Cramps**: Caused by electrolyte depletion, particularly sodium.
- **Nausea and Vomiting**: Resulting from dehydration and gastrointestinal distress.
- **Tachycardia**: Increased heart rate as the body attempts to maintain adequate blood flow and cooling.
- **Cool, Clammy Skin**: Despite the high external temperature, the skin may feel cool due to evaporation of sweat.

Management:

- **Move to a Cooler Environment**: Immediate removal from the hot environment.
- **Hydration**: Oral rehydration with water or sports drinks to replenish fluids and electrolytes. In severe cases, intravenous fluids may be required.
- **Rest**: Cease physical activity to reduce heat production.
- **Cooling Measures**: Use of fans, cool showers, or wet towels to aid in lowering body temperature.

Heat Stroke

Pathophysiology: Heat stroke is a medical emergency that occurs when the body's thermoregulatory mechanisms fail, leading to a rapid increase in core body temperature (typically above 104°F or 40°C). This condition can cause widespread cellular damage and organ dysfunction.

Signs and Symptoms:
- **Hyperthermia**: Critically elevated core body temperature.
- **Altered Mental Status**: Confusion, agitation, delirium, seizures, or coma due to the effect of high temperature on the brain.
- **Anhidrosis**: Absence of sweating, often seen in classic heat stroke; however, exertional heat stroke may still involve sweating.
- **Hot, Dry Skin**: Especially in classic heat stroke, where sweating mechanisms fail.
- **Tachycardia and Tachypnea**: Rapid heart rate and breathing as the body struggles to cope with the heat stress.
- **Hypotension**: Low blood pressure due to vasodilation and dehydration.
- **Organ Failure**: Potential failure of kidneys, liver, and other organs due to sustained high temperatures and hypoxia.

Management:
- **Immediate Cooling**: Priority is rapid cooling, which can involve immersion in cold water, application of ice packs to major blood vessels (neck, armpits, groin), and evaporative cooling techniques.
- **Hydration**: Intravenous fluids to address dehydration and support cardiovascular function.
- **Monitoring and Support**: Continuous monitoring of vital signs, including core body temperature, and supportive care in an intensive care unit (ICU) setting if necessary.
- **Address Complications**: Management of complications such as seizures, rhabdomyolysis, and electrolyte imbalances.

Critical Thermal Maximum and Core Body Temperature in Heat Stroke

Critical Thermal Maximum: This concept refers to the highest body temperature at which the body's physiological processes can function without failure. Beyond this threshold, enzymatic and cellular functions begin to break down, leading to systemic failure. In heat stroke, surpassing the critical thermal maximum can result in irreversible damage to the brain and other vital organs, emphasizing the urgency of rapid cooling.

Core Body Temperature in Guiding Treatment: Monitoring core body temperature is essential in diagnosing and managing heat-related illnesses. It helps distinguish between heat exhaustion and heat stroke, with the latter typically showing a core temperature above 104°F (40°C). Treatment decisions are guided by core temperature measurements; for instance, aggressive cooling measures are indicated if the core temperature is dangerously high. Continuous monitoring ensures that the cooling interventions are effective and helps prevent overcooling, which can lead to hypothermia. Accurate assessment and timely intervention based on core body temperature are critical in preventing severe complications and improving outcomes in patients with heat stroke.

Assessment and Management of Frostbite Using the Four-Degree Classification System

Frostbite occurs when skin and other tissues freeze due to prolonged exposure to cold temperatures. It is classified into four degrees based on the depth of tissue injury.

First-Degree Frostbite:
- **Assessment**: Involves superficial layers of the skin. Signs include erythema (redness), edema (swelling), and a white or yellowish plaque at the site. The skin may feel firm but remains pliable. Patients often experience a burning sensation or pain followed by numbness.

- **Management:** Rewarm the affected area using warm water (37-39°C or 98.6-102.2°F) for 15-30 minutes. Avoid rubbing or applying direct heat. Administer oral analgesics for pain relief. Protect the area from refreezing and further injury by applying loose, sterile dressings.

Second-Degree Frostbite:
- **Assessment:** Affects deeper skin layers, leading to the formation of clear blisters filled with fluid. The skin may appear red or purple and becomes increasingly painful during rewarming.
- **Management:** Similar to first-degree frostbite, but may require more intensive pain management. Elevate the affected limb to reduce swelling. After rewarming, apply sterile dressings, and consider tetanus prophylaxis. Blisters should be left intact if possible to prevent infection.

Third-Degree Frostbite:
- **Assessment:** Extends into the subcutaneous tissue, characterized by hemorrhagic blisters, indicating deeper tissue damage. The affected area may appear bluish-gray, and there is significant pain during rewarming, followed by potential numbness.
- **Management:** In addition to the measures used for first and second-degree frostbite, consider administering intravenous (IV) analgesics for severe pain. Avoid debridement of blisters in the field. Protect the area with bulky, sterile dressings and elevate to minimize swelling. Seek immediate medical evaluation.

Fourth-Degree Frostbite:
- **Assessment:** Involves full-thickness damage including muscles, tendons, and bone. The affected area may appear black and feel hard or waxy. There is often a complete loss of sensation.
- **Management:** Requires urgent medical attention. Rapid rewarming is critical, along with aggressive pain management using IV analgesics. Protect the area with sterile, non-adherent dressings. Consider IV fluids to support circulation. Immediate evacuation to a specialized medical facility is necessary.

Freeze-Thaw-Freeze Phenomenon

The **freeze-thaw-freeze phenomenon** occurs when frozen tissues are thawed and then refrozen before definitive care. This process significantly exacerbates tissue damage and increases the risk of necrosis.

Impact on Field Treatment Decisions:
- **Avoid Partial Rewarming:** Do not attempt rewarming unless there is absolute certainty that the affected area can be kept warm and will not refreeze.
- **Continuous Protection:** Keep the affected areas protected and insulated to prevent further exposure. If rewarming is not possible, focus on maintaining the current condition until the patient can be evacuated to a proper medical facility.
- **Evacuation Priority:** Prioritize rapid and safe transport to a medical facility capable of providing definitive care and continuous rewarming.

Use of tPA in Severe Frostbite Management

Tissue Plasminogen Activator (tPA) is a thrombolytic agent that has been explored for use in severe frostbite to improve tissue perfusion and reduce the extent of amputation.

Mechanism:
- **Clot Dissolution:** tPA helps dissolve blood clots that may form in the microcirculation of frostbitten tissues, improving blood flow and potentially salvaging tissue that would otherwise become necrotic.

Indications:
- **Severe Frostbite:** Particularly in cases of third and fourth-degree frostbite where there is significant risk of tissue loss.

Administration:
- **Timing:** tPA is most effective when administered within 24 hours of thawing the frostbitten tissue.
- **Protocol:** Administered intravenously, often in conjunction with heparin to prevent new clot formation. Dosing and administration should be managed by a medical professional in a hospital setting.

Considerations:
- **Risk of Bleeding:** tPA carries a risk of serious bleeding and should be used with caution, weighing the potential benefits against the risks.

- **Specialized Care:** Use of tPA for frostbite should be guided by protocols in specialized centers with experience in treating severe frostbite and managing thrombolytic therapy.

Effective assessment and management of frostbite using the four-degree classification system, understanding the freeze-thaw-freeze phenomenon, and the appropriate use of tPA can significantly improve outcomes for patients suffering from severe cold injuries.

Pathophysiology and Management of Drowning and Near-Drowning Incidents

Pathophysiology of Drowning and Near-Drowning

Drowning: Drowning occurs when an individual is submerged in water, leading to respiratory impairment. The pathophysiology of drowning involves several critical stages:

1. **Submersion and Panic:**
   - The individual typically struggles to stay afloat, leading to panic and rapid, ineffective breathing.
2. **Aspiration of Water:**
   - Water enters the airways, leading to laryngospasm (a reflexive closing of the vocal cords), which temporarily prevents further water intake but also restricts airflow.
3. **Hypoxia:**
   - As the individual continues to struggle, hypoxia (lack of oxygen) sets in due to limited air exchange.
4. **Laryngospasm Release:**
   - Prolonged hypoxia eventually relaxes the laryngospasm, leading to further aspiration of water into the lungs.
5. **Pulmonary Damage:**
   - Water in the lungs disrupts the surfactant, leading to alveolar collapse, reduced gas exchange, and pulmonary edema.
6. **Systemic Hypoxia:**
   - Continued hypoxia leads to systemic effects, including cardiac arrhythmias, brain injury, and multi-organ failure.

Near-Drowning: Near-drowning refers to the survival of an individual after a drowning incident, at least temporarily. It involves the same pathophysiological processes but may include varying degrees of hypoxia and organ damage based on the duration and severity of the submersion.

Management of Drowning and Near-Drowning

1. **Immediate Rescue:**
   - Remove the individual from the water as quickly and safely as possible.
2. **Initial Assessment and Stabilization:**
   - Assess airway, breathing, and circulation (ABCs).
   - Provide high-flow oxygen to correct hypoxia.
   - Initiate cardiopulmonary resuscitation (CPR) if the individual is unresponsive and not breathing.
   - Use automated external defibrillators (AEDs) if indicated.
3. **Advanced Care:**
   - Intubation and mechanical ventilation may be necessary for severe respiratory distress or failure.
   - Administer fluids and medications to stabilize hemodynamics.
   - Monitor for and treat complications such as pulmonary edema, aspiration pneumonia, and hypothermia.

Dry Drowning vs. Secondary Drowning

Dry Drowning:

- **Concept:** Dry drowning refers to situations where water does not actually enter the lungs. Instead, the process involves laryngospasm, which leads to asphyxiation due to the closure of the airway.
- **Pathophysiology:** The vocal cords close up due to irritation from water entering the throat, causing a reflex that prevents breathing and results in hypoxia without significant water aspiration.

Secondary Drowning:

- **Concept**: Secondary drowning occurs when water is aspirated into the lungs during a near-drowning incident, leading to pulmonary complications that develop hours to days after the event.
- **Pathophysiology**: The aspirated water disrupts surfactant function, causing inflammation and edema in the lungs, which can progressively worsen and lead to respiratory failure.

Szpilman Drowning Classification System
The Szpilman classification system categorizes drowning incidents based on the severity of the individual's condition at the time of rescue. This system helps prioritize treatment and predict outcomes.

1. **Grade 1**:
   - **Description**: Normal lung auscultation and only mild symptoms such as cough.
   - **Management**: Observation and supportive care, typically no hospital admission needed.
2. **Grade 2**:
   - **Description**: Abnormal lung auscultation with rales in some lung fields and mild to moderate respiratory distress.
   - **Management**: Oxygen therapy, monitoring, and possible hospital admission.
3. **Grade 3**:
   - **Description**: Abnormal lung auscultation with rales in all lung fields and moderate to severe respiratory distress.
   - **Management**: High-flow oxygen, possible intubation, and mechanical ventilation, hospital admission for close monitoring.
4. **Grade 4**:
   - **Description**: Pulmonary edema with pink frothy sputum and severe respiratory distress.
   - **Management**: Immediate intubation and mechanical ventilation, aggressive supportive care, and ICU admission.
5. **Grade 5**:
   - **Description**: Respiratory arrest without cardiac arrest.
   - **Management**: Immediate resuscitation, intubation, mechanical ventilation, and intensive care.
6. **Grade 6**:
   - **Description**: Cardiac arrest.
   - **Management**: Advanced cardiac life support (ACLS) protocols, CPR, defibrillation as needed, and intensive resuscitative efforts.

Impact on Treatment Priorities
The Szpilman classification system provides a structured approach to assessing and managing drowning victims. By categorizing the severity of the patient's condition, it guides clinicians in prioritizing interventions:

- **Grade 1 and 2**: Focus on monitoring and supportive care, with attention to potential delayed complications.
- **Grade 3 and 4**: Immediate respiratory support and hospital admission to manage significant pulmonary injury.
- **Grade 5 and 6**: Aggressive resuscitation efforts, including advanced airway management and cardiovascular support, with ICU care for continued stabilization and monitoring.

Understanding the differences in pathophysiology, signs, and symptoms between dry drowning and secondary drowning, along with the application of the Szpilman classification system, is crucial in providing timely and appropriate care to drowning victims, ultimately improving survival rates and outcomes.

SIRS Criteria and qSOFA Score for Sepsis Recognition
Systemic Inflammatory Response Syndrome (SIRS) Criteria: The SIRS criteria were traditionally used to identify patients at risk of sepsis. A diagnosis of SIRS requires the presence of two or more of the following criteria:

1. **Temperature:** >38°C (100.4°F) or <36°C (96.8°F)
2. **Heart Rate:** >90 beats per minute
3. **Respiratory Rate:** >20 breaths per minute or PaCO2 <32 mm Hg
4. **White Blood Cell Count:** >12,000 cells/mm³, <4,000 cells/mm³, or >10% immature (band) forms

qSOFA (Quick Sequential Organ Failure Assessment) Score: The qSOFA score is a more recent tool used to identify patients with suspected infection who are at greater risk for poor outcomes:

1. **Altered Mental Status:** Glasgow Coma Scale (GCS) score <15
2. **Respiratory Rate:** ≥22 breaths per minute
3. **Systolic Blood Pressure:** ≤100 mm Hg

A qSOFA score of ≥2 suggests a higher risk of adverse outcomes and should prompt further investigation and intervention.

Cryptic Shock and Its Impact on Sepsis Assessment

Cryptic Shock: Cryptic shock refers to a state where a patient with sepsis has normal blood pressure but exhibits signs of inadequate tissue perfusion, such as elevated lactate levels. This condition can complicate the assessment and early recognition of sepsis because the patient does not present with overt hypotension, which is a classic sign of septic shock.

Challenges in Assessment:

- **Normal Blood Pressure:** Patients may appear hemodynamically stable based on blood pressure readings.
- **Inadequate Perfusion:** Despite normal blood pressure, tissues may not be receiving adequate oxygen and nutrients, leading to cellular dysfunction and organ damage.
- **Delayed Recognition:** Without obvious signs of shock, the diagnosis of sepsis may be delayed, impacting the timeliness of treatment and potentially worsening outcomes.

Importance of Lactate Levels in Sepsis Management

Lactate Levels: Lactate is a byproduct of anaerobic metabolism, which increases when tissues are not receiving enough oxygen. Elevated lactate levels in sepsis indicate tissue hypoperfusion and can be used as a marker for severity and prognosis.

Role in Sepsis Management:

- **Risk Stratification:** Elevated lactate levels (>2 mmol/L) suggest a higher risk of mortality and can guide the urgency and intensity of treatment.
- **Monitoring Response:** Serial measurements of lactate levels can help assess the effectiveness of interventions and guide ongoing management.

Sepsis Six Bundle

The Sepsis Six bundle is a set of six key interventions to be initiated within the first hour of recognizing sepsis. These actions are critical in improving outcomes through early management:

1. **Administer High-Flow Oxygen:**
   - Ensure adequate oxygen delivery to tissues. Maintain oxygen saturation >94%.
2. **Take Blood Cultures:**
   - Obtain blood cultures before starting antibiotics to identify the causative organism and guide targeted therapy.
3. **Administer IV Antibiotics:**
   - Start broad-spectrum antibiotics as soon as possible, ideally within the first hour of recognizing sepsis.
4. **Give IV Fluids:**
   - Administer an initial bolus of intravenous crystalloids (e.g., 30 mL/kg) to restore intravascular volume and improve tissue perfusion.
5. **Measure Lactate Levels:**
   - Obtain a baseline lactate level to assess the severity of sepsis and guide resuscitation efforts.
6. **Monitor Urine Output:**
   - Insert a urinary catheter if necessary to accurately measure urine output, which is an important indicator of renal perfusion and overall fluid balance.

Application in Early Management:

- **Timeliness:** The Sepsis Six interventions should be implemented as quickly as possible, ideally within the first hour of sepsis recognition, to maximize their impact on patient outcomes.
- **Continuous Monitoring:** Regular reassessment of vital signs, lactate levels, and clinical status is essential to guide ongoing management and adjust treatment as needed.

By utilizing the SIRS criteria and qSOFA score for early recognition, understanding the implications of cryptic shock, and implementing the Sepsis Six bundle, healthcare providers can improve the identification and management of sepsis, ultimately enhancing patient outcomes.

Presentations and Management of Bacterial, Viral, and Fungal Meningitis
Bacterial Meningitis
Presentations:

- **Symptoms**: Acute onset of fever, severe headache, neck stiffness (nuchal rigidity), photophobia, nausea, vomiting, altered mental status, and possibly seizures.
- **Signs**: Positive Kernig's and Brudzinski signs, petechial rash (particularly with Neisseria meningitidis), and rapid progression to severe illness.

Management:

- **Empiric Antibiotic Therapy**: Immediate administration of broad-spectrum antibiotics (e.g., ceftriaxone, vancomycin, and ampicillin in certain age groups) before confirmation of the pathogen to cover the most likely causative organisms.
- **Corticosteroids**: Dexamethasone may be given before or with the first dose of antibiotics to reduce inflammation and improve outcomes, especially in pneumococcal meningitis.
- **Supportive Care**: Fluids, antipyretics, and management of complications like increased intracranial pressure (ICP) and seizures.

Viral Meningitis
Presentations:

- **Symptoms**: Gradual onset of fever, headache, neck stiffness, photophobia, nausea, vomiting, and general malaise. Less severe than bacterial meningitis and often follows a self-limiting course.
- **Signs**: Kernig's and Brudzinski signs may be positive but are generally less pronounced.

Management:

- **Symptomatic Treatment**: Analgesics, antipyretics, and hydration.
- **Antiviral Therapy**: Specific antivirals (e.g., acyclovir) may be used if herpes simplex virus (HSV) or varicella-zoster virus (VZV) is suspected.
- **Supportive Care**: Close monitoring for complications, although these are less common than in bacterial meningitis.

Fungal Meningitis
Presentations:

- **Symptoms**: Gradual onset with symptoms including headache, fever, neck stiffness, nausea, vomiting, and altered mental status. Often seen in immunocompromised individuals (e.g., HIV/AIDS patients).
- **Signs**: Positive Kernig's and Brudzinski signs may be present.

Management:

- **Antifungal Therapy**: Amphotericin B combined with flucytosine for initial treatment, followed by fluconazole for maintenance therapy.
- **Supportive Care**: Management of symptoms and monitoring for complications.
- **Long-term Therapy**: Extended treatment duration, especially in immunocompromised patients, to prevent relapse.

Kernig's Sign vs. Brudzinski's Sign
Kernig's Sign:

- **Procedure**: With the patient lying supine, the examiner flexes the patient's hip and knee at 90 degrees, then attempts to extend the knee.
- **Positive Sign**: Pain and resistance to knee extension indicate meningeal irritation.

Brudzinski's Sign:

- **Procedure**: With the patient lying supine, the examiner gently lifts the patient's head and neck towards the chest.

- **Positive Sign**: Involuntary flexion of the hips and knees in response to neck flexion indicates meningeal irritation.

Empiric Antibiotic Therapy in Suspected Bacterial Meningitis

Concept: Empiric antibiotic therapy involves the immediate administration of antibiotics based on the most likely causative organisms, rather than waiting for specific culture or laboratory results. This approach is critical in bacterial meningitis due to the rapid progression and high mortality rate associated with the disease.

Key Aspects:
1. **Timing**: Antibiotics should be given as soon as bacterial meningitis is suspected, ideally within the first hour of presentation.
2. **Broad-Spectrum Coverage**: Initial therapy includes antibiotics that cover the most common pathogens (e.g., Streptococcus pneumoniae, Neisseria meningitidis, Haemophilus influenzae, Listeria monocytogenes in certain age groups).
3. **Adjustment Based on Culture Results**: Once the specific pathogen and its antibiotic sensitivities are identified, therapy can be narrowed to target the identified bacteria more effectively.
4. **Combination Therapy**: Often involves the use of multiple antibiotics to ensure broad coverage and address potential resistance.

Example Regimens:
- **Adults:** Ceftriaxone or cefotaxime plus vancomycin, with the addition of ampicillin in older adults or those with immunocompromise to cover Listeria.
- **Neonates:** Ampicillin plus cefotaxime or gentamicin.

Empiric antibiotic therapy in suspected bacterial meningitis is essential to start promptly to reduce morbidity and mortality. This rapid intervention, along with adjunctive therapies like corticosteroids, supportive care, and subsequent tailored antibiotic regimens based on culture results, forms the cornerstone of effective management for bacterial meningitis.

Differential Diagnosis of Acute Abdomen Using the Mnemonic "GET SMACKED"

The mnemonic "GET SMACKED" helps in recalling the common causes of acute abdomen, which is a critical and often life-threatening condition requiring prompt diagnosis and management.

1. **G - Gallbladder:**
   - **Conditions:** Cholecystitis, cholelithiasis, cholangitis
   - **Signs/Symptoms:** Right upper quadrant (RUQ) pain, Murphy's sign, fever, jaundice
2. **E - Ectopic Pregnancy:**
   - **Conditions:** Ectopic pregnancy (usually tubal)
   - **Signs/Symptoms:** Lower abdominal pain, missed period, vaginal bleeding, positive pregnancy test, hemodynamic instability if ruptured
3. **T - Torsion:**
   - **Conditions:** Ovarian torsion, testicular torsion
   - **Signs/Symptoms:** Sudden onset of severe lower abdominal or groin pain, nausea, vomiting, adnexal tenderness (ovarian), scrotal swelling (testicular)
4. **S - Stomach:**
   - **Conditions:** Peptic ulcer disease, gastritis, gastric perforation
   - **Signs/Symptoms:** Epigastric pain, hematemesis, melena, peritonitis if perforated
5. **M - Mesenteric Ischemia:**
   - **Conditions:** Acute mesenteric ischemia, chronic mesenteric ischemia
   - **Signs/Symptoms:** Severe abdominal pain disproportionate to physical findings, vomiting, diarrhea, history of atrial fibrillation or heart disease
6. **A - Appendicitis:**
   - **Conditions:** Acute appendicitis
   - **Signs/Symptoms:** Periumbilical pain migrating to right lower quadrant (RLQ), McBurney's point tenderness, Rovsing's sign, fever, anorexia
7. **C - Crohn's Disease/Colitis:**
   - **Conditions:** Crohn's disease, ulcerative colitis, infectious colitis

- o **Signs/Symptoms:** Abdominal pain, diarrhea, rectal bleeding, weight loss, fever
8. **K - Kidney:**
   - o **Conditions:** Nephrolithiasis, pyelonephritis
   - o **Signs/Symptoms:** Flank pain radiating to groin, hematuria, fever, costovertebral angle tenderness
9. **E - Endometriosis:**
   - o **Conditions:** Endometriosis
   - o **Signs/Symptoms:** Cyclical pelvic pain, dysmenorrhea, dyspareunia, infertility
10. **D - Diverticulitis:**
    - o **Conditions:** Acute diverticulitis
    - o **Signs/Symptoms:** Left lower quadrant (LLQ) pain, fever, altered bowel habits, nausea, vomiting

Referred Pain and Abdominal Assessment

Referred Pain: Referred pain occurs when pain is perceived at a location other than the site of the painful stimulus. This phenomenon complicates abdominal assessment because it can mislead the clinician regarding the true source of pain.

Mechanism:

- **Shared Nerve Pathways:** Pain signals from different organs converge on the same nerve pathways in the spinal cord, leading to the brain misinterpreting the origin of the pain.

Common Examples:

- **Diaphragmatic Irritation:** Pain referred to the shoulder (Kehr's sign).
- **Gallbladder Pain:** Referred to the right shoulder or back.
- **Cardiac Pain:** Referred to the epigastrium or left arm.

Implications:

- **Thorough History and Examination:** Clinicians must consider the possibility of referred pain and correlate it with other clinical findings and history.
- **Differential Diagnosis:** Awareness of referred pain patterns helps in constructing a comprehensive differential diagnosis and avoiding misdiagnosis.

Significance of Murphy's Sign, McBurney's Point, and Rovsing's Sign in Abdominal Examination

Murphy's Sign:

- **Procedure:** Palpate the RUQ and ask the patient to take a deep breath.
- **Positive Sign:** Abrupt cessation of inspiration due to pain indicates cholecystitis.
- **Significance:** Helps differentiate cholecystitis from other causes of RUQ pain.

McBurney's Point:

- **Location:** One-third the distance from the anterior superior iliac spine to the umbilicus on the right side.
- **Tenderness:** Significant tenderness at this point suggests acute appendicitis.
- **Significance:** A key landmark for diagnosing appendicitis, particularly when pain has migrated from the periumbilical region to the RLQ.

Rovsing's Sign:

- **Procedure:** Apply deep palpation to the left lower quadrant (LLQ).
- **Positive Sign:** Pain in the RLQ upon palpation of the LLQ indicates appendicitis.
- **Significance:** Indicates peritoneal irritation and supports the diagnosis of appendicitis.

Understanding the differential diagnosis of acute abdomen using "GET SMACKED," recognizing referred pain, and using specific physical examination signs like Murphy's, McBurney's point, and Rovsing's sign are crucial for accurate diagnosis and effective management of patients presenting with acute abdominal pain.

Differential Diagnosis of Vaginal Bleeding

Non-Pregnant Patients

1. **Menorrhagia:** Excessive menstrual bleeding.
   - o **Causes:** Hormonal imbalances, uterine fibroids, adenomyosis, endometrial polyps, coagulopathies.
2. **Metrorrhagia:** Bleeding between periods.

- - - **Causes**: Endometrial hyperplasia, polyps, infections, malignancies (e.g., endometrial or cervical cancer), hormonal contraceptives.
  3. **Postmenopausal Bleeding**:
     - **Causes**: Atrophic vaginitis, endometrial atrophy, hormone replacement therapy, endometrial cancer.
  4. **Polycystic Ovary Syndrome (PCOS)**:
     - **Causes**: Hormonal imbalances leading to irregular ovulation and bleeding.
  5. **Infections**:
     - **Causes**: Pelvic inflammatory disease (PID), sexually transmitted infections (STIs).
  6. **Iatrogenic Causes**:
     - **Causes**: Intrauterine devices (IUDs), anticoagulant medications.

Pregnant Patients
  1. **First Trimester Bleeding**:
     - **Causes**: Threatened miscarriage, complete or incomplete miscarriage, ectopic pregnancy, molar pregnancy.
  2. **Second and Third Trimester Bleeding**:
     - **Causes**: Placenta previa, placental abruption, vasa previa, preterm labor.
  3. **Ectopic Pregnancy**:
     - **Concept**: A pregnancy that implants outside the uterine cavity, commonly in the fallopian tube.

Ectopic Pregnancy of Unknown Location
Concept:
- **Definition**: An ectopic pregnancy of unknown location (PUL) refers to a clinical situation where a patient has a positive pregnancy test, but the pregnancy is not visible on transvaginal ultrasound (TVUS), and its location cannot be determined.

Impact on Assessment and Treatment:
- **Assessment**:
  - **Serial hCG Measurements**: Serial quantitative beta-hCG levels to assess the pregnancy's viability and location. Normally rising levels suggest intrauterine pregnancy, whereas abnormal rise or plateau suggests ectopic pregnancy.
  - **Transvaginal Ultrasound**: Repeat TVUS to look for intrauterine pregnancy or ectopic pregnancy as hCG levels rise.
  - **Clinical Monitoring**: Assess for symptoms of ectopic pregnancy, such as abdominal pain, shoulder pain, and hemodynamic instability.
- **Treatment**:
  - **Expectant Management**: Close monitoring of hCG levels and symptoms if the patient is stable.
  - **Medical Management**: Methotrexate therapy if ectopic pregnancy is highly suspected and the patient is hemodynamically stable, without significant contraindications.
  - **Surgical Intervention**: Indicated in cases of hemodynamic instability, significant pain, or if the ectopic pregnancy is confirmed and not suitable for medical management.

Use of Bedside Ultrasound in Evaluating Gynecological Emergencies
Role of Bedside Ultrasound:
  1. **Immediate Assessment**:
     - Rapid identification of intrauterine pregnancy or its absence.
     - Detection of ectopic pregnancy, free fluid in the pelvis (suggesting rupture), and other abnormalities.
  2. **Differentiating Causes of Bleeding**:
     - **Intrauterine Gestational Sac**: Confirms intrauterine pregnancy.
     - **No Intrauterine Pregnancy**: Raises suspicion for ectopic pregnancy or very early intrauterine pregnancy.
     - **Endometrial Thickness**: Can provide clues about potential causes like hyperplasia or polyps.
  3. **Assessing for Complications**:

- Free Fluid: Presence of free fluid in the pelvis may indicate hemoperitoneum from a ruptured ectopic pregnancy.
- Ovarian Pathologies: Detection of ovarian cysts, torsion, or masses contributing to pain or bleeding.

Clinical Scenarios:

1. Early Pregnancy Bleeding:
   - Assess for the presence or absence of intrauterine pregnancy.
   - Evaluate for signs of ectopic pregnancy, such as adnexal masses or free fluid.
2. Acute Pelvic Pain:
   - Evaluate for ovarian torsion, hemorrhagic cysts, or ectopic pregnancy.
3. Abnormal Uterine Bleeding in Non-Pregnant Patients:
   - Assess endometrial thickness, uterine fibroids, or polyps.
   - Evaluate for retained products of conception in post-miscarriage patients.

Bedside ultrasound is an invaluable tool in the rapid and accurate assessment of gynecological emergencies, guiding immediate management decisions and improving patient outcomes.

Pyelonephritis and Nephrolithiasis
Pyelonephritis:
Pathophysiology:

- Pyelonephritis is a bacterial infection of the renal pelvis and kidney parenchyma, commonly caused by ascending bacteria from the lower urinary tract, typically E. coli.
- The infection leads to inflammation, which can cause renal edema and, in severe cases, abscess formation or systemic sepsis.

Signs and Symptoms:

- Fever and Chills: Indicative of systemic infection.
- Flank Pain: Often severe, located at the costovertebral angle (CVA).
- Dysuria: Painful urination.
- Frequency and Urgency: Increased need to urinate.
- Nausea and Vomiting: Common systemic response to infection.
- Malaise: General feeling of being unwell.

Management:

1. Antibiotics:
   - Empiric broad-spectrum antibiotics initially, followed by culture-specific antibiotics once sensitivity results are available. Common choices include fluoroquinolones, cephalosporins, or aminoglycosides.
2. Hydration:
   - Encourage fluid intake to ensure adequate urine flow and help flush the urinary system.
3. Pain Management:
   - NSAIDs or acetaminophen for pain and fever control.
4. Hospitalization:
   - Required for severe cases, especially those with high fever, sepsis, or immunocompromised patients.

Nephrolithiasis:
Pathophysiology:

- Nephrolithiasis (kidney stones) involves the formation of crystalline stones within the kidneys due to supersaturation of minerals and salts in the urine, such as calcium oxalate, calcium phosphate, uric acid, or struvite.
- Factors contributing include dehydration, dietary factors, metabolic disorders, and genetic predisposition.

Signs and Symptoms:

- Severe Flank Pain: Sharp, cramping pain that radiates from the flank to the groin, known as renal colic.

- **Hematuria:** Blood in the urine.
- **Nausea and Vomiting:** Common due to severe pain.
- **Frequency and Dysuria:** Increased need to urinate and pain during urination if the stone moves into the ureter.
- **Pain Location:** Often changes as the stone moves through the urinary tract.

Management:

1. **Pain Relief:**
   - NSAIDs (e.g., ibuprofen) or opioids (e.g., morphine) for severe pain.
2. **Hydration:**
   - Encourage oral fluids to help flush the stone.
3. **Medical Expulsive Therapy:**
   - Alpha-blockers (e.g., tamsulosin) or calcium channel blockers to facilitate stone passage.
4. **Imaging:**
   - CT scan without contrast is the gold standard for diagnosis; ultrasound can be used in certain populations.
5. **Surgical Intervention:**
   - Indicated for stones that do not pass with medical management or cause complications (e.g., lithotripsy, ureteroscopy, or percutaneous nephrolithotomy).

Costovertebral Angle Tenderness
Concept:

- **Definition:** Costovertebral angle tenderness (CVAT) is pain elicited by percussion of the area over the kidneys (the angle formed by the vertebral column and the costal margin).
- **Diagnostic Aid:** CVAT is a key physical examination finding that helps distinguish pyelonephritis from other causes of abdominal or flank pain.
- **Procedure:** The examiner places one hand over the CVA and strikes it with the fist of the other hand. A positive sign is the patient's report of pain during this maneuver, indicating inflammation or infection of the kidney.

Use of Pain Assessment Scales in Renal Colic Management
Pain Assessment Scales:

- **Numeric Rating Scale (NRS):**
  - Patients rate their pain on a scale from 0 (no pain) to 10 (worst possible pain). This simple, widely used scale helps quantify pain severity and guide treatment.
- **Visual Analog Scale (VAS):**
  - A 10 cm line with endpoints labeled "no pain" and "worst pain imaginable." Patients mark a point on the line that represents their pain, providing a visual representation of pain intensity.
- **Faces Pain Scale (FPS):**
  - Particularly useful for children or those with communication difficulties, this scale uses facial expressions to indicate pain levels from "no pain" to "worst pain imaginable."

Importance in Renal Colic:

- **Initial Assessment:** Accurately assess pain severity to determine the need for immediate pain relief and the appropriate level of intervention.
- **Monitoring Response:** Track changes in pain levels after treatment to assess the effectiveness of interventions and adjust as necessary.
- **Guiding Treatment:** High pain scores may prompt the use of stronger analgesics or additional diagnostic evaluations, while decreasing scores indicate effective management and potential stone passage.

Recognizing and managing pyelonephritis and nephrolithiasis involve understanding their pathophysiology, signs, symptoms, and treatment options. CVAT is crucial for diagnosing pyelonephritis, while pain assessment scales are essential for managing renal colic effectively. These tools ensure prompt, accurate diagnosis and tailored treatment, improving patient outcomes.

Preeclampsia, Eclampsia, Placenta Previa, and Placental Abruption
Preeclampsia
Pathophysiology:

- **Mechanism**: Abnormal placental development and function lead to systemic endothelial dysfunction and widespread vasospasm.
- **Key Features**: Hypertension and proteinuria after 20 weeks of gestation. Can involve multiple organ systems (e.g., liver, kidneys, brain).

Signs and Symptoms:

- **Hypertension**: Blood pressure ≥ 140/90 mmHg.
- **Proteinuria**: ≥ 300 mg/24-hour urine collection or protein/creatinine ratio ≥ 0.3.
- **Other Symptoms**: Edema, headaches, visual disturbances, epigastric or right upper quadrant pain, elevated liver enzymes, thrombocytopenia.

Management:

- **Monitoring**: Frequent blood pressure checks, urine protein assessment, and fetal monitoring.
- **Medications**: Antihypertensives (e.g., labetalol, nifedipine) and corticosteroids for fetal lung maturity if early delivery is anticipated.
- **Delivery**: The definitive treatment; timing depends on the severity of the disease and gestational age.

Eclampsia
Pathophysiology:

- **Mechanism**: Progression from preeclampsia to seizures or coma.
- **Key Features**: Generalized tonic-clonic seizures in a woman with preeclampsia.

Signs and Symptoms:

- **Seizures**: Without prior neurologic disease.
- **Other Symptoms**: Signs of severe preeclampsia, such as severe hypertension, severe headache, visual changes, epigastric pain.

Management:

- **Seizure Control**: Magnesium sulfate as the first-line treatment.
- **Blood Pressure Control**: Antihypertensives.
- **Delivery**: Expedite delivery once the mother is stabilized.

Placenta Previa
Pathophysiology:

- **Mechanism**: Placenta implants over or near the internal cervical os.
- **Key Features**: Painless vaginal bleeding in the second or third trimester.

Signs and Symptoms:

- **Bleeding**: Sudden onset of painless bright red vaginal bleeding.
- **No Pain**: Typically no abdominal pain or uterine tenderness.

Management:

- **Monitoring**: Ultrasound to confirm placental location.
- **Hospitalization**: For observation and management of bleeding.
- **Delivery Planning**: Cesarean delivery if placenta previa persists near term.

Placental Abruption
Pathophysiology:

- **Mechanism**: Premature separation of a normally implanted placenta from the uterine wall.
- **Key Features**: Painful vaginal bleeding, abdominal pain, uterine tenderness, and contractions.

Signs and Symptoms:

- **Bleeding**: Dark red vaginal bleeding, which may be concealed.
- **Pain**: Severe abdominal pain, uterine tenderness, and contractions.
- **Fetal Distress**: Possible signs of fetal distress or demise.

Management:

- **Stabilization**: Immediate IV access, fluid resuscitation, and blood transfusion if needed.
- **Monitoring**: Continuous fetal and maternal monitoring.
- **Delivery**: Urgent delivery, often via cesarean section, depending on fetal and maternal status.

HELLP Syndrome

Concept:

- **Definition**: A severe form of preeclampsia characterized by Hemolysis, Elevated Liver enzymes, and Low Platelet count.
- **Relation to Preeclampsia**: Indicates a more severe disease with higher risk of complications, necessitating prompt delivery regardless of gestational age.

Signs and Symptoms:

- **Hemolysis**: Anemia, jaundice.
- **Elevated Liver Enzymes**: AST/ALT elevation.
- **Low Platelet Count**: Thrombocytopenia.
- **Other Symptoms**: Epigastric or right upper quadrant pain, nausea, vomiting, headache.

Management:

- **Stabilization**: IV fluids, blood products if necessary.
- **Antihypertensives**: To control severe hypertension.
- **Magnesium Sulfate**: To prevent seizures.
- **Delivery**: Prompt delivery, often via cesarean section.

Magnesium Sulfate in Eclampsia Management

Use:

- **Mechanism**: Acts as a CNS depressant by decreasing acetylcholine release at neuromuscular junctions, thus preventing seizures.
- **Dosage**: Typically administered as a loading dose of 4-6 grams IV over 15-20 minutes, followed by a maintenance infusion of 1-2 grams per hour.

Benefits:

- **Seizure Prophylaxis**: Effective in preventing and treating eclamptic seizures.
- **Neuroprotection**: Reduces the risk of recurrent seizures and maternal morbidity.

Monitoring:

- **Reflexes**: Monitor deep tendon reflexes (DTRs) to assess for magnesium toxicity.
- **Respiratory Function**: Watch for respiratory depression, a sign of toxicity.
- **Urine Output**: Ensure adequate renal function as magnesium is excreted by the kidneys.

Management of Toxicity:

- **Calcium Gluconate**: Administer IV as an antidote for magnesium toxicity.

Understanding these conditions and their management is crucial for the care of pregnant patients presenting with these obstetric emergencies. Early recognition and appropriate intervention can significantly improve maternal and fetal outcomes.

Stages of Normal Labor and Delivery

Labor and delivery are divided into three main stages, each with distinct phases and processes. Understanding these stages and the cardinal movements of labor is crucial for effective management and support during childbirth.

First Stage:

- **Latent Phase:**
  - **Duration:** From the onset of labor until the cervix is dilated to 4 cm.
  - **Characteristics:** Mild, irregular contractions gradually become more regular and stronger. Cervical effacement and slow dilation occur.

- Management: Monitor progress, provide comfort measures, and encourage mobility and hydration.
- **Active Phase:**
    - **Duration:** From 4 cm to full cervical dilation (10 cm).
    - **Characteristics:** Contractions become more intense, frequent (every 2-5 minutes), and last longer (45-60 seconds). Rapid cervical dilation occurs.
    - **Management:** Continuous fetal and maternal monitoring, pain relief options (epidural, IV analgesics), and supportive measures (breathing techniques, position changes).

Second Stage:
- **Pushing Phase:**
    - **Duration:** From full dilation to the delivery of the baby.
    - **Characteristics:** Strong, expulsive contractions. The mother feels the urge to push as the baby moves down the birth canal.
    - **Cardinal Movements:** These are the specific positional changes the fetus undergoes to navigate through the pelvis:
        1. **Engagement:** The fetal head enters the pelvic inlet.
        2. **Descent:** The head moves down through the pelvis.
        3. **Flexion:** The fetal chin moves toward the chest.
        4. **Internal Rotation:** The head rotates to align with the pelvic outlet.
        5. **Extension:** The head extends as it passes under the pubic symphysis.
        6. **External Rotation (Restitution):** The head rotates to align with the shoulders.
        7. **Expulsion:** The rest of the body is delivered.
    - **Management:** Encourage effective pushing, ensure the mother is in a comfortable position, provide support and coaching, and monitor fetal well-being.

Third Stage:
- **Placental Delivery:**
    - **Duration:** From the birth of the baby to the expulsion of the placenta.
    - **Characteristics:** Uterine contractions continue, aiding the separation and expulsion of the placenta.
    - **Signs of Placental Separation:** Gush of blood, lengthening of the umbilical cord, and the uterus becoming firm and globular.
    - **Management:** Gentle traction on the umbilical cord with counterpressure on the uterus, ensuring complete placental expulsion to prevent hemorrhage, and uterine massage to encourage contraction.

Concept of "Bloody Show" and Onset of Labor
"Bloody Show":
- **Definition:** A mixture of blood and mucus discharged from the cervix as it begins to dilate and efface, indicating the early signs of labor.
- **Relation to Labor:** The bloody show is a result of the cervical mucus plug dislodging as the cervix prepares for labor. Its presence signals that labor may begin soon, typically within a few hours to a few days.
- **Characteristics:** It can be pink, red, or brown and is often accompanied by other early signs of labor such as contractions or cramping.

Management of Shoulder Dystocia Using the HELPERR Mnemonic
Shoulder dystocia is a delivery complication where the baby's anterior shoulder gets stuck behind the mother's pubic symphysis after the head has been delivered. The HELPERR mnemonic provides a structured approach to manage this emergency effectively.
HELPERR Mnemonic:
1. **H - Help:**
    - **Call for Additional Help:** Immediately summon additional personnel for assistance. This may include obstetricians, anesthesiologists, and pediatricians.
2. **E - Evaluate for Episiotomy:**

- o **Consider Episiotomy:** Evaluate the need for an episiotomy to provide more space for maneuvering and delivery, although it is not always necessary.
3. **L - Legs (McRoberts Maneuver):**
   - o **Positioning:** Flex and abduct the mother's legs, bringing her knees to her chest (McRoberts position). This position helps straighten the sacrum and widen the pelvis, facilitating the delivery of the shoulders.
4. **P - Pressure (Suprapubic Pressure):**
   - o **Application:** Apply firm, continuous suprapubic pressure just above the pubic bone to dislodge the anterior shoulder. Avoid fundal pressure as it can worsen the impaction.
5. **E - Enter (Internal Maneuvers):**
   - o **Internal Maneuvers:** Use internal rotational maneuvers to reposition the shoulders:
     - **Rubin Maneuver:** Apply pressure on the posterior aspect of the anterior shoulder to push it toward the chest.
     - **Woods Corkscrew Maneuver:** Apply pressure to the anterior aspect of the posterior shoulder to rotate the baby's body, easing the shoulder out.
6. **R - Remove the Posterior Arm:**
   - o **Delivery of Posterior Arm:** Reach into the vagina, grasp the posterior arm, and gently pull it out to reduce the shoulder width, facilitating the delivery of the anterior shoulder.
7. **R - Roll the Patient (Gaskin Maneuver):**
   - o **Position Change:** Roll the patient onto her hands and knees (all-fours position) to change the pelvic dimensions and potentially free the impacted shoulder.

Understanding the stages of labor, the cardinal movements, and specific signs like the "bloody show" is vital for managing childbirth effectively. The HELPERR mnemonic provides a systematic approach to managing shoulder dystocia, a critical obstetric emergency, ensuring prompt and coordinated interventions to reduce the risk of complications for both mother and baby.

Apgar Score Components and Their Significance in Neonatal Resuscitation

The Apgar score is a quick assessment tool used to evaluate the overall health and vital signs of a newborn immediately after birth. It is performed at 1 and 5 minutes after birth and sometimes at 10 minutes if resuscitation is needed. Each of the five components is scored on a scale of 0 to 2, with a maximum score of 10. The components are:

1. **Appearance (Skin Color):**
   - o 0: Blue or pale all over
   - o 1: Pink body with blue extremities (acrocyanosis)
   - o 2: Completely pink
   - o **Significance:** Indicates oxygenation and perfusion. Cyanosis suggests poor oxygenation, while a pink color indicates adequate oxygen delivery.
2. **Pulse (Heart Rate):**
   - o 0: No pulse
   - o 1: Heart rate < 100 beats per minute
   - o 2: Heart rate > 100 beats per minute
   - o **Significance:** Reflects cardiac function. A heart rate below 100 bpm indicates the need for immediate intervention.
3. **Grimace (Reflex Irritability):**
   - o 0: No response to stimulation
   - o 1: Grimace or weak cry when stimulated
   - o 2: Vigorous cry, cough, or sneeze
   - o **Significance:** Measures neurological function and responsiveness. Lack of response suggests poor neurological health.
4. **Activity (Muscle Tone):**
   - o 0: Limp, no movement
   - o 1: Some flexion of extremities
   - o 2: Active motion

- o **Significance**: Assesses neuromuscular activity. Good muscle tone is indicative of a healthy, responsive baby.
5. **Respiration (Breathing Effort)**:
   - o 0: No breathing
   - o 1: Weak, irregular, or gasping breaths
   - o 2: Strong cry
   - o **Significance**: Evaluates respiratory function. Strong crying indicates effective breathing.

Persistent Fetal Circulation

Concept:

- **Definition**: Persistent fetal circulation, also known as persistent pulmonary hypertension of the newborn (PPHN), occurs when a newborn's circulatory system does not adapt to breathing outside the womb, and the blood flow bypasses the lungs, leading to hypoxemia.

- **Impact on Newborn Assessment**:
  - o **Signs**: Cyanosis despite adequate ventilation, respiratory distress, and differential cyanosis (pre- and post-ductal oxygen saturation differences).
  - o **Diagnosis**: Echocardiogram to confirm elevated pulmonary pressures and right-to-left shunting.

- **Impact on Treatment**:
  - o **Oxygen Therapy**: High levels of oxygen to reduce pulmonary vascular resistance.
  - o **Ventilation Support**: Mechanical ventilation or high-frequency oscillatory ventilation.
  - o **Medications**: Inhaled nitric oxide to dilate pulmonary vessels, sildenafil, or extracorporeal membrane oxygenation (ECMO) in severe cases.

Neonatal Resuscitation Program (NRP) Algorithm

The NRP algorithm is a step-by-step guide for the resuscitation of newborns. Key steps include:

1. **Initial Assessment**:
   - o Assess breathing, heart rate, and color immediately after birth.
   - o Provide warmth, position the airway, clear secretions if necessary, dry, and stimulate.
2. **Positive Pressure Ventilation (PPV)**:
   - o Indicated if the baby is apneic, gasping, or if the heart rate is below 100 bpm after initial steps.
   - o Use a bag and mask or T-piece resuscitator to deliver effective breaths.
   - o Monitor for chest rise to ensure effective ventilation.
3. **Chest Compressions**:
   - o Initiate if the heart rate remains below 60 bpm despite adequate ventilation for 30 seconds.
   - o Compression rate is 90 compressions per minute, coordinated with 30 breaths per minute (3:1 ratio).
   - o Continue to reassess every 30 seconds.
4. **Medications**:
   - o Administer epinephrine if the heart rate remains below 60 bpm after 30 seconds of compressions and ventilation.
   - o Consider volume expansion if there is evidence of hypovolemia or shock.

Meconium Aspiration Considerations:

- If meconium-stained amniotic fluid is present, assess the newborn's vigor.
- **Vigorous Newborn**: Proceed with routine care (drying, warming, stimulating).
- **Non-Vigorous Newborn**: Initially clear the airway with a bulb syringe or suction catheter before starting PPV if needed.

The Apgar score provides a rapid assessment of a newborn's health and the need for resuscitative efforts. Persistent fetal circulation (PPHN) presents significant challenges and requires targeted therapies to ensure adequate oxygenation. The NRP algorithm is essential for guiding the resuscitation process, ensuring systematic assessment and intervention, especially in cases of meconium aspiration. Understanding these concepts and protocols is crucial for optimizing outcomes in neonatal care.

EMS Operations

Components of an EMS System

An Emergency Medical Services (EMS) system is a comprehensive network designed to provide emergency medical care to patients. It involves several key components that work together to ensure timely and effective response to emergencies.

1. Dispatch

Role:

- **Call Triage**: Dispatch centers receive emergency calls and triage them based on the severity and type of emergency.
- **Resource Allocation**: Dispatchers determine the appropriate resources to send, including the type and number of EMS units required.
- **Coordination**: Dispatchers coordinate with first responders, guiding them to the incident location and providing real-time updates.

Technology:

- **Computer-Aided Dispatch (CAD)**: Systems that help prioritize calls, track unit status, and optimize dispatching.
- **Geographic Information Systems (GIS)**: Used to provide precise location data and routing information.

2. First Response

Role:

- **Initial Assessment**: First responders (often firefighters or police officers) arrive at the scene quickly to provide an initial assessment of the situation.
- **Basic Life Support (BLS)**: They provide BLS interventions such as CPR, defibrillation, controlling bleeding, and managing airways.
- **Stabilization**: Their primary goal is to stabilize patients until EMS units arrive.

Personnel:

- **Firefighters, Police Officers**: Often trained in BLS and equipped with defibrillators and first aid kits.
- **Emergency Medical Responders (EMRs)**: Specifically trained for medical emergencies and often part of the first response team.

3. Transport

Role:

- **Advanced Life Support (ALS)**: Paramedics and EMTs provide advanced medical care during transport, including IV therapy, medication administration, and advanced airway management.
- **Patient Monitoring**: Continuous monitoring of vital signs and patient condition during transport to the receiving facility.
- **Communication**: Maintain communication with the receiving facility to provide updates and prepare them for the patient's arrival.

Vehicles:

- **Ambulances**: Equipped with medical supplies and equipment for ALS and BLS care.
- **Air Ambulances**: Helicopters or fixed-wing aircraft for rapid transport over long distances or in remote areas.

4. Receiving Facilities

Role:

- **Emergency Departments (EDs)**: The primary receiving facilities equipped to handle a wide range of emergencies.
- **Specialty Centers**: Trauma centers, stroke centers, cardiac care units, and pediatric emergency departments specialized for specific types of emergencies.
- **Patient Handoff**: EMS personnel provide a detailed report to ED staff about the patient's condition, interventions provided, and any changes during transport.

Personnel:
- **Emergency Physicians and Nurses:** Specialize in emergency care and are prepared to take over and continue advanced medical treatment.
- **Specialists:** Available for specific emergencies, such as trauma surgeons, cardiologists, and neurologists.

Medical Direction in EMS Operations

Concept:
- **Medical Direction:** Oversight provided by a physician or group of physicians to ensure the quality and appropriateness of prehospital medical care.

Impact on EMS Operations:
- **Protocols and Guidelines:** Development and implementation of standardized protocols and clinical guidelines for EMS personnel to follow.
- **Training and Education:** Ongoing training and continuing education for EMS providers to ensure they are up-to-date with the latest medical practices.
- **Quality Assurance:** Continuous monitoring and evaluation of the care provided, with feedback mechanisms to improve service quality.
- **Legal and Ethical Oversight:** Ensures that EMS operations comply with legal, ethical, and regulatory standards.

Online vs. Offline Medical Control

Online Medical Control:
- **Definition:** Direct, real-time communication between EMS providers and a medical control physician, usually via radio or telephone.
- **Usage:**
  - **Complex Cases:** When EMS personnel encounter situations beyond the standard protocols or require specific medical orders.
  - **Decision Making:** For decisions such as medication administration, complex medical procedures, or patient transport destinations.
- **Advantages:** Allows for immediate, case-specific medical guidance and decision-making support.

Offline Medical Control:
- **Definition:** Indirect oversight through pre-established protocols, guidelines, training, and quality assurance programs.
- **Usage:**
  - **Standard Protocols:** EMS providers follow predetermined protocols for most situations.
  - **Training:** EMS personnel are trained to handle a wide range of scenarios using these established guidelines.
- **Advantages:** Ensures consistency and standardization in care, reduces the need for real-time communication, and allows for autonomy in routine cases.

In summary, the EMS system is a coordinated effort involving dispatch, first responders, transport units, and receiving facilities, all working under the guidance of medical direction to provide high-quality emergency care. Online and offline medical control both play crucial roles in ensuring that EMS personnel can deliver appropriate and timely care to patients in diverse and dynamic situations.

Legal Concepts of Consent in EMS

1. Expressed Consent:
- **Definition:** Expressed consent is explicit permission granted by a patient to receive medical care or undergo a procedure.
- **Characteristics:** The patient verbally or in writing agrees to the treatment after being informed of the risks, benefits, and alternatives.
- **Application in EMS:**
  - Typically obtained when a patient is conscious, alert, and able to make informed decisions.

- EMS providers explain the necessary treatment, and the patient consents verbally or through a signed document.

2. Implied Consent:

- **Definition:** Implied consent is assumed when a patient is unable to provide expressed consent but needs emergency care to prevent significant harm or death.
- **Characteristics:** Consent is inferred based on the urgent nature of the situation and the presumption that a reasonable person would consent to the treatment if they were able.
- **Application in EMS:**
  - Used in emergencies when patients are unconscious, mentally incapacitated, or otherwise unable to communicate.
  - Allows EMS providers to administer necessary life-saving interventions without formal consent.

3. Involuntary Consent:

- **Definition:** Involuntary consent involves treatment provided against the patient's will or without their ability to consent, often due to legal or medical authority.
- **Characteristics:** Typically applies to patients who are a danger to themselves or others, or who are legally not competent to make their own decisions.
- **Application in EMS:**
  - May involve patients with mental health crises, intoxicated individuals, or minors without a guardian present.
  - Requires appropriate legal or medical authorization, such as a court order or consent from a legal guardian.

Duty to Act
Principle of Duty to Act:

- **Definition:** The legal obligation of healthcare providers, including EMS personnel, to provide care to patients within their scope of practice when on duty.
- **On-Duty EMS Providers:**
  - **Obligation:** EMS providers have a clear duty to act when they are on duty, responding to calls, or within their jurisdiction.
  - **Responsibility:** They must provide care according to established protocols and standards of care, ensuring patient safety and well-being.
- **Off-Duty EMS Providers:**
  - **No Legal Obligation:** Generally, off-duty EMS providers do not have a legal duty to provide care. However, some states or jurisdictions may impose certain obligations under Good Samaritan laws.
  - **Good Samaritan Laws:** These laws protect off-duty EMS providers from liability when they voluntarily provide emergency care in good faith, without gross negligence.

Concept of Abandonment
Abandonment:

- **Definition:** Abandonment occurs when an EMS provider terminates care of a patient without ensuring that care is continued at an appropriate level by another qualified healthcare professional.
- **Legal Implications:**
  - **Breach of Duty:** Abandonment is considered a breach of the duty to act and can result in legal consequences, including malpractice claims.
  - **Harm to Patient:** If abandonment leads to harm or deterioration of the patient's condition, the EMS provider and their employer may be held liable.
- **Prevention:**
  - **Continuity of Care:** EMS providers must ensure that care is transferred to another qualified healthcare professional, such as a nurse, physician, or another EMS provider.
  - **Proper Handoff:** A proper handoff includes providing a thorough report of the patient's condition, treatments administered, and any relevant medical history.

Expressed, implied, and involuntary consent are key concepts in EMS, each applicable in different situations to ensure ethical and legal patient care. The principle of duty to act obligates on-duty EMS providers to offer care within their scope of practice, while off-duty providers may be protected under Good Samaritan laws when providing voluntary assistance. Abandonment is a serious legal issue that can occur if care is inappropriately discontinued, highlighting the importance of ensuring continuity of care through proper handoff procedures. Understanding these concepts helps EMS providers navigate legal and ethical challenges in their practice, ensuring they deliver appropriate and lawful patient care.

Key Components of HIPAA Compliance in EMS Operations

The Health Insurance Portability and Accountability Act (HIPAA) establishes national standards to protect individuals' medical records and other personal health information (PHI). In EMS operations, HIPAA compliance involves several key components:

1. **Privacy Rule**:
   - **Protection of PHI**: Ensures that all patient information is protected and only used or disclosed under permitted circumstances.
   - **Patient Rights**: Patients have the right to access their medical records, request amendments, and receive an accounting of disclosures.
   - **Notice of Privacy Practices**: EMS agencies must provide a notice of privacy practices to patients, explaining how their information will be used and protected.
2. **Security Rule**:
   - **Administrative Safeguards**: Policies and procedures to manage the selection, development, and maintenance of security measures to protect PHI.
   - **Physical Safeguards**: Measures to protect electronic information systems and related buildings and equipment from natural and environmental hazards and unauthorized intrusion.
   - **Technical Safeguards**: Technology and policies to protect electronic PHI (ePHI) and control access to it.
3. **Breach Notification Rule**:
   - **Notification Requirements**: Requires covered entities to notify affected individuals, the Secretary of Health and Human Services (HHS), and, in some cases, the media of breaches of unsecured PHI.
4. **Training and Education**:
   - **Regular Training**: EMS personnel must receive training on HIPAA policies and procedures, with periodic updates to ensure ongoing compliance.
   - **Awareness**: Employees should be aware of their roles and responsibilities in protecting patient information.
5. **Compliance and Enforcement**:
   - **Audits and Monitoring**: Regular audits to ensure compliance with HIPAA regulations.
   - **Sanctions**: Establishment of sanctions for employees who fail to comply with HIPAA policies and procedures.

The Concept of "Minimum Necessary"

Minimum Necessary:

- **Definition**: The "minimum necessary" standard requires that when PHI is used, disclosed, or requested, only the minimum amount of information needed to accomplish the intended purpose should be shared.
- **Application in EMS**:
   - **Patient Care**: Only the information necessary for the treatment of the patient should be accessed or shared among EMS providers.
   - **Billing and Operations**: When disclosing information for billing or operational purposes, only the information relevant to that specific function should be disclosed.
   - **Training and Education**: When using patient information for training, anonymize or de-identify information whenever possible to protect patient privacy.

Covered Entities vs. Business Associates

Covered Entities:

- **Definition**: Covered entities are those who must comply with HIPAA regulations and include healthcare providers, health plans, and healthcare clearinghouses.
- **Examples in EMS**:
  - **Ambulance Services**: EMS agencies that provide medical care and transport are considered covered entities.
  - **Hospitals**: Receiving facilities where EMS patients are transported.

Business Associates:
- **Definition**: Business associates are individuals or entities that perform functions or provide services on behalf of a covered entity that involve access to PHI.
- **Responsibilities**: Must comply with certain HIPAA provisions and enter into Business Associate Agreements (BAAs) with covered entities to ensure proper handling of PHI.
- **Examples in EMS**:
  - **Billing Services**: Companies that handle billing and claims processing for EMS agencies.
  - **IT Service Providers**: Vendors providing electronic health record systems or other IT services that access PHI.

Differences:
- **Scope of Compliance**: Covered entities are directly responsible for complying with all aspects of HIPAA. Business associates must comply with HIPAA provisions relevant to their role and the handling of PHI.
- **Agreements**: Business associates must sign BAAs with covered entities, outlining their responsibilities and ensuring compliance with HIPAA regulations.

In summary, HIPAA compliance in EMS operations involves protecting patient information through strict privacy and security measures, ensuring that only the minimum necessary information is shared, and distinguishing between covered entities and business associates to delineate responsibilities. Regular training, audits, and appropriate handling of PHI are essential to maintaining compliance and safeguarding patient privacy.

Principles of Effective EMS Documentation Using the "CHART" Method
The **CHART** method is a structured approach to EMS documentation, ensuring comprehensive and organized patient care reports. Each letter stands for a specific component of the documentation process:

1. **C - Chief Complaint:**
   - **Definition:** The primary reason the patient called for help, described in their own words.
   - **Importance:** Provides the context for the EMS response and guides the initial assessment and treatment.
2. **H - History:**
   - **History of Present Illness:** Detailed description of the current condition, including onset, duration, location, and characteristics of symptoms.
   - **Past Medical History:** Relevant medical history, including chronic conditions, surgeries, medications, allergies, and recent medical events.
   - **Importance:** Helps in understanding the patient's health background and identifying potential complications or related issues.
3. **A - Assessment:**
   - **Initial Assessment:** Vital signs, primary survey (Airway, Breathing, Circulation), and general impression of the patient.
   - **Detailed Physical Exam:** Findings from a head-to-toe examination, focusing on systems relevant to the chief complaint.
   - **Importance:** Documents the patient's condition upon EMS arrival and provides a baseline for monitoring changes.
4. **R - Rx (Treatment):**
   - **Interventions:** All treatments provided, such as medications administered, procedures performed, and supportive measures taken (e.g., oxygen therapy, IV fluids).
   - **Response to Treatment:** Patient's response to interventions, including improvements, deteriorations, or no changes.

- Importance: Ensures transparency in care provided and allows for evaluation of treatment effectiveness.

5. **T - Transport:**
   - **Mode of Transport:** How the patient was transported (e.g., by ambulance, helicopter) and the level of care provided during transport (e.g., ALS, BLS).
   - **Destination:** Where the patient was taken and any handoff information provided to receiving facility staff.
   - **Importance:** Provides a clear record of the patient's journey and the care continuity.

Contemporaneous Documentation

Contemporaneous Documentation:

- **Definition:** The practice of recording patient care information at or near the time the care is provided.

- **Impact on Patient Care Records:**
  - **Accuracy:** Ensures that the information is accurate and reflective of the actual events and conditions observed.
  - **Detail:** Reduces the risk of omitting critical details due to memory lapses or distractions.
  - **Legal Protection:** Provides a precise and reliable account of care, which is crucial in legal contexts to demonstrate adherence to standards and protocols.

Legal Implications of "If It Wasn't Documented, It Wasn't Done"

Phrase Meaning:

- This phrase underscores the importance of thorough documentation in healthcare. It implies that, legally and clinically, if an action or observation is not documented, it is as if it did not occur.

Legal Implications:

- **Proof of Care:** Documentation serves as the official record of the care provided. In legal disputes, thorough documentation can support the provider's actions and decisions.
- **Accountability:** Poor or incomplete documentation can lead to questions about the quality and completeness of care, potentially resulting in legal and professional repercussions.
- **Regulatory Compliance:** Healthcare providers are required to maintain accurate and complete records to comply with regulatory standards and accreditation requirements.
- **Continuity of Care:** Proper documentation ensures that subsequent healthcare providers have the necessary information to continue appropriate patient care, reducing the risk of errors and omissions.

Summary

The CHART method provides a structured approach to EMS documentation, ensuring all critical aspects of patient care are thoroughly recorded. Contemporaneous documentation enhances the accuracy and reliability of patient care records, which is vital for legal protection, accountability, and continuity of care. The phrase "if it wasn't documented, it wasn't done" highlights the importance of meticulous documentation in establishing a clear and defensible record of the care provided. Effective documentation practices are essential for delivering high-quality patient care and meeting legal and professional standards.

Structure and Function of the Incident Command System (ICS)

The Incident Command System (ICS) is a standardized approach to the command, control, and coordination of emergency response. It allows responders from multiple agencies to work together effectively under a common organizational structure.

Structure of ICS:

1. **Command Staff:**
   - **Incident Commander (IC):** The individual responsible for all incident activities, including the development of strategies and tactics and the ordering and release of resources.
   - **Public Information Officer (PIO):** Provides information to the media and public, ensuring that accurate and timely information is disseminated.
   - **Safety Officer:** Monitors safety conditions and develops measures to ensure the safety of all incident personnel.
   - **Liaison Officer:** Serves as the primary contact for supporting agencies assisting at an incident.

2. **General Staff:**
   o **Operations Section**: Responsible for all tactical operations directly managing the incident.
   o **Planning Section**: Collects, evaluates, and disseminates incident information and develops the Incident Action Plan (IAP).
   o **Logistics Section**: Provides resources and services required to support incident activities.
   o **Finance/Administration Section**: Manages costs related to the incident, including contracts, timekeeping, and compensation for injury or damage.

Span of Control in ICS
Concept of Span of Control:

- **Definition**: Span of control refers to the number of individuals or resources one supervisor can manage effectively. In ICS, the optimal span of control is typically 3 to 7 resources, with 5 being ideal.
- **Influence on ICS Organization:**
  o **Efficiency**: Maintaining an appropriate span of control ensures that supervisors can effectively manage their assigned resources without becoming overwhelmed.
  o **Scalability**: ICS can expand or contract based on the complexity and needs of the incident, adjusting the number of supervisory levels to maintain an effective span of control.
  o **Delegation**: As incidents grow in complexity, the Incident Commander delegates authority to Section Chiefs and Unit Leaders to maintain a manageable span of control.

Roles and Responsibilities of the Command and General Staff in ICS
Command Staff
1. **Incident Commander (IC):**
   o **Role**: Provides overall leadership and management of the incident. Establishes incident objectives and priorities, and is responsible for the overall coordination of incident activities.
   o **Responsibilities:**
     ▪ Develops and implements the Incident Action Plan (IAP).
     ▪ Approves resource orders and demobilization.
     ▪ Coordinates with local, state, and federal authorities as necessary.
2. **Public Information Officer (PIO):**
   o **Role**: Acts as the conduit for information to internal and external stakeholders, including the media.
   o **Responsibilities:**
     ▪ Develops and releases information about the incident to the media, incident personnel, and other agencies.
     ▪ Ensures that information released is accurate and approved by the IC.
3. **Safety Officer:**
   o **Role**: Ensures the safety of incident personnel and oversees the overall safety management of the incident.
   o **Responsibilities:**
     ▪ Identifies and mitigates hazardous situations.
     ▪ Conducts safety briefings and ensures compliance with safety regulations and protocols.
4. **Liaison Officer:**
   o **Role**: Serves as the primary contact for agencies and organizations involved in the incident but not part of the ICS structure.
   o **Responsibilities:**
     ▪ Coordinates with representatives from assisting and cooperating agencies.
     ▪ Maintains a list of assisting and cooperating agencies and their representatives.

General Staff
1. **Operations Section Chief:**
   o **Role**: Manages all tactical operations directly related to the incident.
   o **Responsibilities:**
     ▪ Implements the IAP as developed by the Planning Section.

- Manages operational resources and ensures that operations are conducted safely and effectively.

2. **Planning Section Chief:**
    - **Role:** Oversees the collection, evaluation, and dissemination of incident information.
    - **Responsibilities:**
        - Prepares and documents the IAP.
        - Maintains resource status and situation status boards.
        - Conducts planning meetings and prepares necessary incident documentation.

3. **Logistics Section Chief:**
    - **Role:** Provides all support needs for the incident, including facilities, transportation, supplies, equipment maintenance, and fueling.
    - **Responsibilities:**
        - Orders, receives, stores, and processes incident-related resources.
        - Manages communications and medical support for incident personnel.

4. **Finance/Administration Section Chief:**
    - **Role:** Manages financial, administrative, and cost analysis aspects of the incident.
    - **Responsibilities:**
        - Tracks costs and provides financial and cost analysis information.
        - Manages timekeeping, contract negotiations, and claims related to the incident.

The ICS is designed to be flexible, scalable, and efficient, ensuring that all incident responses are managed effectively and that resources are used optimally. The span of control principle is fundamental in maintaining the system's functionality and effectiveness, allowing for appropriate delegation and management of resources. The roles and responsibilities of the Command and General Staff are clearly defined to ensure that each aspect of the incident is managed by skilled personnel, thereby improving overall incident response and management.

Comparing START and JumpSTART Triage Methods
START Triage (Simple Triage and Rapid Treatment):
- **Purpose:** Designed for use in mass casualty incidents (MCIs) involving adults and children over 8 years old.
- **Process:**
    1. **Assessment of Ambulation:** Direct all patients who can walk to move to a designated area (these patients are tagged green - Minor).
    2. **Respiratory Status:** For non-ambulatory patients, assess breathing. If not breathing, reposition the airway. If still not breathing, tag as black (Deceased). If they begin to breathe, tag as red (Immediate).
    3. **Respiratory Rate:** Count breaths. If >30 breaths per minute, tag as red (Immediate). If <30, move to the next step.
    4. **Perfusion:** Check capillary refill. If >2 seconds, tag as red (Immediate). If <2 seconds, move to the next step.
    5. **Mental Status:** Assess ability to follow simple commands. If unable, tag as red (Immediate). If able, tag as yellow (Delayed).

JumpSTART Triage:
- **Purpose:** Adaptation of START for pediatric patients (ages 1 to 8 years).
- **Process:**
    1. **Assessment of Ambulation:** Similar to START, those who can walk are directed to a designated area (green - Minor).
    2. **Respiratory Status:** If not breathing, open the airway. If still not breathing, check for a pulse:
        - If no pulse, tag as black (Deceased).
        - If pulse present, give five rescue breaths. If they begin to breathe, tag as red (Immediate). If not, tag as black (Deceased).
    3. **Respiratory Rate:** If <15 or >45 breaths per minute, tag as red (Immediate). If within the range, move to the next step.

4. **Perfusion:** Check capillary refill. If >2 seconds, tag as red (Immediate). If <2 seconds, move to the next step.
5. **Mental Status:** Assess using AVPU scale (Alert, responds to Voice, responds to Pain, Unresponsive). If Alert or responds to Voice, tag as yellow (Delayed). If responds to Pain or Unresponsive, tag as red (Immediate).

Secondary Triage
Initial Triage:
- **Purpose:** Quickly classify patients based on severity of injuries and need for immediate care. Conducted at the scene of the incident.
- **Criteria:** Simple criteria (e.g., breathing, circulation, mental status) to rapidly sort large numbers of patients.

Secondary Triage:
- **Purpose:** Reassess patients to refine their triage category and prioritize further based on more detailed assessments.
- **Location:** Typically performed after initial triage, often at treatment areas, casualty collection points, or receiving medical facilities.
- **Criteria:** More comprehensive evaluation, including detailed physical examination, vital signs, and medical history.

Triage Tags and Color Categories
Triage Tags:
- **Function:** Visual tools used to categorize and communicate the triage status of patients.
- **Types:** Can include tear-off tags, stickers, or wristbands with color-coded sections.

Color Categories:
1. **Red (Immediate):**
   - **Criteria:** Life-threatening injuries that require immediate intervention to survive (e.g., severe bleeding, airway obstruction, shock).
   - **Significance:** Highest priority for treatment and transport.
2. **Yellow (Delayed):**
   - **Criteria:** Serious but not immediately life-threatening injuries. These patients can tolerate some delay before receiving definitive care (e.g., fractures, burns without airway compromise).
   - **Significance:** Second priority, treated after red-tagged patients.
3. **Green (Minor):**
   - **Criteria:** Minor injuries that do not require immediate medical attention (e.g., minor cuts, abrasions, sprains).
   - **Significance:** Lowest priority, often referred to as "walking wounded."
4. **Black (Deceased/Expectant):**
   - **Criteria:** Patients who are deceased or have injuries so severe that survival is unlikely given available resources (e.g., massive trauma, prolonged cardiac arrest without resuscitation).
   - **Significance:** No resuscitation efforts are made, focus is on comfort and dignity.

START and JumpSTART triage methods are designed for rapid assessment in mass casualty incidents, with JumpSTART specifically adapted for pediatric patients. Secondary triage provides a more detailed reassessment after initial triage, refining priorities for treatment and transport. Triage tags with color categories are essential tools for visually communicating patient status, guiding efficient and effective care delivery in emergency situations.

Principles of Emergency Vehicle Operation
Emergency vehicle operation requires adherence to specific principles to ensure the safety of both the responders and the public. Key principles include:
1. **Due Regard:**
   - **Definition:** "Due regard" refers to the expectation that emergency vehicle operators will act with reasonable care and caution, prioritizing safety above all.

- o **Application**: Operators must be mindful of other road users, obey traffic laws where possible, and always drive defensively. They should anticipate the actions of other drivers and pedestrians, ensuring they do not pose a hazard while responding to emergencies.
2. **Vehicle Control**:
   - o **Speed Management**: Operators should manage speed to maintain control of the vehicle, particularly in adverse weather conditions, heavy traffic, or when approaching intersections.
   - o **Safe Passing**: When overtaking other vehicles, operators should signal their intentions clearly and ensure the path is clear before proceeding.
   - o **Intersection Approach**: Slow down and ensure the intersection is clear before proceeding, even when using lights and sirens.
3. **Awareness and Communication**:
   - o **Situational Awareness**: Constantly monitor the environment, including road conditions, traffic patterns, and potential hazards.
   - o **Communication**: Use of radio communication to coordinate with dispatch and other responding units, ensuring a coordinated and effective response.

The "Wake Effect" Phenomenon
Concept:
- **Definition**: The "wake effect" refers to the unintentional impact that an emergency vehicle can have on other drivers as it moves through traffic with lights and sirens activated. This effect can cause drivers to react unpredictably, sometimes leading to secondary collisions or incidents in the wake of the emergency vehicle.

Impact on Emergency Driving:
- **Driver Reactions**: Drivers may panic, stop abruptly, or swerve unexpectedly, creating new hazards on the road.
- **Increased Risk**: The wake effect increases the risk of accidents not only for the emergency vehicle but also for other road users who may be affected by sudden changes in traffic flow.
- **Mitigation**: Operators should use their lights and sirens judiciously, maintain a controlled speed, and be prepared for erratic behavior from other drivers.

Legal and Ethical Considerations of Using Lights and Sirens
Legal Considerations:
1. **Jurisdictional Laws**: Operators must be familiar with local and state laws governing the use of lights and sirens, including when and how they can be used.
   - o **Authorized Use**: Typically, lights and sirens are authorized during emergency responses and when transporting patients in critical condition.
   - o **Traffic Laws**: While emergency vehicles are granted certain privileges, they must still comply with laws designed to ensure public safety, such as stopping at red lights and stop signs, and proceeding only when safe.
2. **Due Regard**: Legally, operators must drive with due regard for the safety of all road users. Failure to do so can result in legal liability for any accidents or injuries caused.

Ethical Considerations:
1. **Patient Safety**: The primary responsibility is to the patient. Use of lights and sirens should be based on clinical necessity, balancing the urgency of the patient's condition against the risks posed by high-speed transport.
   - o **Clinical Justification**: Lights and sirens should be used only when the patient's condition justifies rapid transport, such as in cases of severe trauma, cardiac arrest, or other life-threatening emergencies.
2. **Public Safety**: Operators must consider the safety of other road users. Reckless driving or unnecessary use of lights and sirens can endanger the public and erode trust in emergency services.
   - o **Community Perception**: Inappropriate use of lights and sirens can lead to public criticism and a perception of abuse of privileges, impacting the reputation of emergency services.

3. **Resource Allocation**: The use of lights and sirens should be based on the principle of prioritizing limited resources. Non-emergency transport with lights and sirens can divert attention and resources away from true emergencies.

Best Practices:

- **Decision-Making Protocols**: Agencies should establish clear protocols for when to use lights and sirens, including guidelines based on the patient's condition and response priority.
- **Training**: Regular training for emergency vehicle operators on safe driving techniques, the impact of the wake effect, and legal and ethical considerations.
- **Review and Accountability**: Implementing a review process for incidents involving emergency vehicles to ensure compliance with policies and address any issues related to the misuse of lights and sirens.

In summary, effective emergency vehicle operation relies on principles of due regard, awareness of the wake effect, and adherence to legal and ethical standards. Proper use of lights and sirens is critical to balancing the urgency of emergency response with the safety of both the patient and the public.

Hazard Assessment Process Using the SLAM Technique

SLAM is a systematic approach used to ensure safety and manage risks effectively in potentially hazardous environments. It stands for Stop, Look, Assess, and Manage.

1. **Stop:**
   - **Purpose:** Take a moment to pause before entering a potentially hazardous area or starting a task.
   - **Action:** Halt all activities to prevent rushing into a situation that could be dangerous. This pause allows for clear thinking and preparation.
2. **Look:**
   - **Purpose:** Observe the environment for potential hazards.
   - **Action:** Conduct a visual scan of the surroundings. Identify any immediate dangers such as spills, fires, unstable structures, or moving machinery. Pay attention to warning signs and listen for unusual sounds that may indicate a problem.
3. **Assess:**
   - **Purpose:** Evaluate the risks associated with the identified hazards.
   - **Action:** Determine the nature and severity of the hazards. Consider factors such as the type of hazard (chemical, biological, physical), the level of exposure, and the potential impact on people, property, and the environment. Assess whether you have the necessary protective equipment and training to handle the situation safely.
4. **Manage:**
   - **Purpose:** Implement control measures to mitigate the risks.
   - **Action:** Take steps to control or eliminate the hazards. This might involve using personal protective equipment (PPE), following safety protocols, or notifying relevant authorities. Ensure that all team members are aware of the hazards and the measures in place. Continuously monitor the situation and adjust management strategies as needed.

Situational Awareness and Scene Safety

Situational Awareness:

- **Definition:** The ability to perceive, understand, and respond to the environment around you. It involves being aware of what is happening in your surroundings, recognizing potential hazards, and understanding how these hazards could impact you and others.
- **Importance in Scene Safety:**
  - **Proactive Risk Management:** Helps prevent accidents by allowing individuals to anticipate and react to potential dangers before they escalate.
  - **Informed Decision Making:** Enables responders to make informed decisions about how to approach and manage a scene, ensuring the safety of themselves and others.
  - **Dynamic Environment:** Particularly crucial in dynamic environments where conditions can change rapidly, such as in emergency response situations.

Hot, Warm, Cold Zone Model in Hazardous Materials Incidents

The Hot, Warm, and Cold Zone model is used to establish safety perimeters around a hazardous materials (HazMat) incident, helping to manage and control the incident effectively.

1. **Hot Zone:**
   - **Definition:** The area immediately surrounding the hazardous material release, where contamination is present.
   - **Access:** Restricted to trained and properly equipped personnel. Entry and exit points are controlled to prevent the spread of contaminants.
   - **Activities:** Includes identification of the hazard, containment, and initial response actions such as plugging leaks or extinguishing fires. The highest level of PPE is required.

2. **Warm Zone:**
   - **Definition:** Also known as the contamination reduction zone, it surrounds the hot zone and serves as a buffer area where decontamination occurs.
   - **Access:** Limited to personnel involved in decontamination and those transitioning from the hot zone to the cold zone. PPE is still required, but at a reduced level compared to the hot zone.
   - **Activities:** Decontamination of personnel and equipment leaving the hot zone, medical assessment, and minor medical treatment.

3. **Cold Zone:**
   - **Definition:** The safe area outside the warm zone where contamination is not expected.
   - **Access:** Open to all response personnel and support functions. PPE is typically not required.
   - **Activities:** Command and control operations, staging areas for equipment and personnel, medical treatment, and support services. It serves as the coordination hub for the incident response.

Application in Hazardous Materials Incidents
HazMat Incidents:

- **Scene Setup:** Upon arrival at a HazMat incident, responders quickly establish the three zones to ensure a structured and safe response.
- **Perimeter Control:** Ensures that only those with appropriate training and equipment are exposed to the hazards, minimizing the risk of secondary contamination or injury.
- **Efficient Operations:** Facilitates clear communication, resource allocation, and strategic planning by defining specific areas for different response activities.

The SLAM technique, situational awareness, and the hot, warm, cold zone model are fundamental tools in hazard assessment and management. They ensure that risks are systematically identified and controlled, enhancing safety for responders and the public during hazardous materials incidents.

Selection and Use of Personal Protective Equipment (PPE) in EMS Operations
Personal Protective Equipment (PPE) is essential in protecting EMS personnel from exposure to infectious agents and hazardous materials. The selection of appropriate PPE depends on the nature of the call and the potential exposure risks.

Types of PPE in EMS

1. **Gloves:**
   - **Purpose:** Protect hands from contact with blood, body fluids, and other potentially infectious materials.
   - **Use:** Always worn during patient contact, procedures involving body fluids, and handling contaminated items.

2. **Gowns:**
   - **Purpose:** Protect skin and clothing from exposure to blood, body fluids, and other contaminants.
   - **Use:** Worn during procedures that are likely to generate splashes or sprays of blood or body fluids, such as childbirth or trauma care.

3. **Masks:**
   - **Purpose:** Protect the respiratory system from airborne pathogens and reduce the risk of droplet transmission.
   - **Use:** Surgical masks for droplet precautions, and N95 respirators for airborne precautions or when dealing with patients with suspected or confirmed airborne diseases (e.g., tuberculosis).

4. **Eye Protection**:
    - o **Purpose**: Protect mucous membranes of the eyes from splashes, sprays, and respiratory droplets.
    - o **Use**: Goggles or face shields should be worn during procedures that may generate splashes or sprays of blood or body fluids.
5. **Face Shields**:
    - o **Purpose**: Provide comprehensive face protection.
    - o **Use**: Used in conjunction with masks and eye protection in high-risk situations to protect against splashes and sprays.
6. **Respirators (N95 or higher)**:
    - o **Purpose**: Provide a higher level of respiratory protection against airborne pathogens.
    - o **Use**: Required for airborne precautions and high-risk aerosol-generating procedures.
7. **Foot Protection**:
    - o **Purpose**: Prevent contamination of footwear.
    - o **Use**: Shoe covers or dedicated footwear in environments with high contamination risk.

Donning and Doffing

Donning (Putting on PPE):

- **Sequence**: Proper sequence helps ensure full coverage and reduces the risk of contamination.
    1. Hand hygiene
    2. Gown
    3. Mask or respirator
    4. Goggles or face shield
    5. Gloves

Doffing (Removing PPE):

- **Sequence**: Following a proper sequence is critical to avoid self-contamination.
    1. Gloves
    2. Goggles or face shield
    3. Gown
    4. Mask or respirator
    5. Hand hygiene

Impact on Infection Control:

- Proper donning and doffing techniques are essential to prevent self-contamination and the spread of infectious agents. Training and practice in these techniques are crucial for EMS personnel to maintain high standards of infection control.

Standard Precautions vs. Transmission-Based Precautions

Standard Precautions:

- **Definition**: A set of infection control practices used for all patients, regardless of suspected or confirmed infection status.
- **Components**:
    - o Hand hygiene
    - o Use of PPE (gloves, gowns, masks, eye protection) as needed based on anticipated exposure.
    - o Safe injection practices
    - o Safe handling of potentially contaminated equipment or surfaces
    - o Respiratory hygiene and cough etiquette

Transmission-Based Precautions:

- **Definition**: Additional infection control measures used for patients known or suspected to be infected with pathogens that require more than standard precautions to prevent transmission.
- **Types**:
    - o **Contact Precautions**: For infections spread by direct or indirect contact with the patient or the patient's environment (e.g., MRSA, VRE).
        - ▪ PPE: Gloves and gown.

- Practices: Limit patient movement and ensure proper cleaning of equipment and surfaces.
  - o **Droplet Precautions**: For infections spread by large respiratory droplets (e.g., influenza, pertussis).
    - PPE: Surgical mask within 3-6 feet of the patient.
    - Practices: Patient placement in a private room and mask usage for patient transport.
  - o **Airborne Precautions**: For infections spread by small airborne particles (e.g., tuberculosis, measles, COVID-19).
    - PPE: N95 respirator or higher-level protection.
    - Practices: Patient placement in an airborne infection isolation room (AIIR) when possible, or use of a portable HEPA filter if AIIR is not available.

Summary

The selection and use of PPE in EMS operations are guided by the type of exposure anticipated and the infection control needs of each situation. Proper donning and doffing techniques are essential to prevent contamination and the spread of infection. Standard precautions are the foundation of infection control, applied to all patients, while transmission-based precautions provide additional measures to protect against specific pathogens based on their transmission modes. Understanding and adhering to these principles ensures the safety of both EMS personnel and patients.

HAZMAT Recognition and Identification System Using the DOT Emergency Response Guidebook

DOT Emergency Response Guidebook (ERG):

- **Purpose:** The ERG provides first responders with a guide to quickly identify the specific or generic hazards of materials involved in an incident, and to protect themselves and the public during the initial response phase.
- **Structure:** The ERG is divided into color-coded sections to facilitate quick access to vital information.

1. **White Pages:**
   - o **Information:** Contains introductory information, instructions on how to use the guidebook, safety precautions, and an overview of the hazard classification system.
2. **Yellow Pages:**
   - o **UN/NA Number Index:** Lists hazardous materials by their four-digit United Nations (UN) or North American (NA) identification numbers. Each entry provides the corresponding guide number for further information.
3. **Blue Pages:**
   - o **Material Name Index:** Lists hazardous materials alphabetically by name with corresponding UN/NA numbers and guide numbers.
4. **Orange Pages:**
   - o **Guide Pages:** The core of the ERG, providing safety recommendations and emergency response information. Each guide page covers a specific hazard class or material and includes information on potential hazards, public safety measures, and emergency response actions.
5. **Green Pages:**
   - o **Table of Initial Isolation and Protective Action Distances:** Lists materials that are toxic by inhalation and provides guidance on protective actions and isolation distances.

Usage:

- **Recognition:** First responders use the ERG to identify hazards based on placards, labels, container shapes, and UN/NA numbers.
- **Response:** Provides detailed response recommendations, including evacuation distances, firefighting measures, spill control, and first aid.

NFPA 704 Diamond System

NFPA 704 Diamond:

- **Purpose:** The National Fire Protection Association (NFPA) 704 diamond system provides a simple, easily recognizable system for identifying the hazards associated with materials.

- **Design:** The system uses a diamond-shaped symbol with four colored quadrants, each indicating a different type of hazard and its severity.
1. **Blue Quadrant (Health Hazard):**
     - ○ **Indicates:** The potential health risks posed by the material.
     - ○ **Rating Scale:** 0 (no hazard) to 4 (severe hazard).
2. **Red Quadrant (Flammability Hazard):**
     - ○ **Indicates:** The material's susceptibility to burning.
     - ○ **Rating Scale:** 0 (will not burn) to 4 (very flammable).
3. **Yellow Quadrant (Reactivity Hazard):**
     - ○ **Indicates:** The material's potential for chemical reactions or explosions.
     - ○ **Rating Scale:** 0 (stable) to 4 (may detonate).
4. **White Quadrant (Special Hazard):**
     - ○ **Indicates:** Specific hazards such as oxidizers (OX), water-reactive materials (W), or simple asphyxiants.
     - ○ **Symbols:** Specific symbols are used to denote special hazards.

Significance:
- **Quick Assessment:** Provides immediate visual information about the severity and type of hazards present, aiding in rapid decision-making and risk assessment.
- **Safety Measures:** Helps responders implement appropriate safety measures based on the hazards indicated.

UN/NA Numbers in Hazardous Materials Incidents
UN/NA Numbers:
- **Definition:** Four-digit identification numbers assigned by the United Nations Committee of Experts on the Transport of Dangerous Goods or the North American system to identify hazardous materials.
- **Location:** Displayed on placards, labels, and shipping documents.

Significance:
1. **Identification:** Allows for precise identification of hazardous materials involved in an incident, facilitating appropriate response actions.
2. **Reference:** UN/NA numbers are referenced in the ERG, enabling responders to quickly access specific information about the material's hazards, protective measures, and emergency procedures.
3. **International Standardization:** Provides a standardized system recognized internationally, ensuring consistency in hazard communication across borders.
4. **Safety:** Enhances the safety of responders and the public by providing essential information needed to manage hazardous materials incidents effectively.

Example:
- **UN 1203:** Identifies gasoline, a highly flammable liquid. Using the ERG, responders can find detailed information under guide number 128, which provides recommendations for firefighting, spill control, and first aid measures.

Conclusion
The DOT Emergency Response Guidebook, NFPA 704 diamond system, and UN/NA numbers are essential tools for recognizing and identifying hazardous materials. The ERG provides comprehensive response guidance, the NFPA 704 diamond offers quick visual hazard information, and UN/NA numbers ensure precise identification of hazardous substances. Together, these systems enhance the safety and effectiveness of emergency response to hazardous materials incidents.

Principles of Vehicle Extrication
Vehicle extrication is the process of safely removing a trapped or injured person from a vehicle following a collision. Effective extrication requires a combination of specialized tools, techniques, and a focus on patient safety and stabilization.
Tool Selection
1. **Hydraulic Tools:**

- o **Spreaders**: Used to open doors, create space, and lift or move vehicle parts.
- o **Cutters**: Designed to cut through metal parts like roofs, doors, and pillars.
- o **Rams**: Used to push or pull apart vehicle structures to free trapped occupants.
2. **Manual Tools**:
   - o **Pry Bars**: For prying open doors or creating initial access points.
   - o **Glass Management Tools**: Devices like glass hammers or window punches to safely break and remove glass.
3. **Power Tools**:
   - o **Reciprocating Saws**: For cutting through metal and plastic components.
   - o **Rotary Saws**: Used for more precise cutting.
4. **Stabilization Equipment**:
   - o **Struts and Cribbing**: To stabilize the vehicle and prevent movement during extrication.
   - o **Airbags**: Used for lifting and stabilizing heavy vehicle components.

Patient-Centered Extrication
1. **Initial Assessment**:
   - o Conduct a rapid assessment of the patient's condition, including ABCs (Airway, Breathing, Circulation).
   - o Consider spinal immobilization if there is a risk of spinal injury.
2. **Communication**:
   - o Maintain constant communication with the patient to reassure and keep them informed of the extrication process.
   - o Coordinate with medical personnel to provide care during the extrication process.
3. **Minimize Movement**:
   - o Use techniques that minimize movement and prevent further injury.
   - o Use spinal boards, cervical collars, and other immobilization devices as necessary.
4. **Rapid and Safe Removal**:
   - o Balance the need for a quick extrication with the need to avoid causing additional injury.
   - o Prioritize rapid removal in cases where the patient's condition is critical (e.g., airway compromise, major bleeding).

Golden Period and Extrication Priorities
Concept of the Golden Period:
- • **Definition**: The "golden period" (often referred to as the "golden hour") is the critical time period following a traumatic injury during which prompt medical treatment is most likely to improve outcomes.
- • **Influence on Extrication Priorities**:
  - o **Time-Sensitive Care**: Emphasizes the need for quick yet safe extrication to ensure that the patient receives definitive care within the golden period.
  - o **Prioritization**: Extrication teams prioritize techniques that allow for rapid access to and removal of the patient, especially if they have life-threatening injuries.

ABCDE Approach to Vehicle Stabilization
Stabilizing the vehicle before extrication is crucial to ensure the safety of both the patient and the rescuers. The ABCDE approach helps ensure a systematic and thorough stabilization process.
1. **A - Assess the Scene**:
   - o Evaluate the overall safety of the scene, including traffic hazards, potential fire risks, and structural stability of the vehicle.
   - o Ensure that the scene is secure and that responders are protected from oncoming traffic and other dangers.
2. **B - Block the Vehicle**:
   - o Use wheel chocks or other blocking devices to prevent vehicle movement.
   - o Ensure that the parking brake is engaged and the ignition is turned off.
3. **C - Cribbing**:
   - o Place cribbing (wooden or synthetic blocks) under the vehicle at strategic points to stabilize it.

- o Use a combination of wedges, step chocks, and other cribbing materials to prevent any vertical or horizontal movement.

4. **D - Disentangle:**
   - o Plan the extrication process to carefully disentangle the vehicle from around the patient.
   - o Ensure that doors, roofs, and other components are safely removed or repositioned without causing further injury to the patient.

5. **E - Extricate:**
   - o Conduct the final extrication process, ensuring that the patient is carefully removed from the vehicle.
   - o Use appropriate equipment and techniques to minimize movement and maintain spinal alignment if necessary.

The principles of vehicle extrication focus on the safe and rapid removal of trapped patients while minimizing further injury. Tool selection should be appropriate for the specific extrication scenario, and patient-centered care should guide every step of the process. The concept of the "golden period" underscores the importance of timely extrication to improve patient outcomes. Vehicle stabilization, following the ABCDE approach, is essential to create a safe environment for both the rescuers and the patient during the extrication process.

EMS Response to Terrorism and Active Shooter Incidents
EMS Response to Terrorism and Active Shooter Incidents:

- **Initial Actions:** Upon arrival at the scene, EMS personnel must quickly assess the situation, establish a command structure, and communicate with law enforcement and other emergency services.
- **Safety First:** Ensuring the safety of EMS providers is paramount. They must follow instructions from law enforcement, stay in designated safe zones, and wear appropriate personal protective equipment (PPE).
- **Triage:** Rapidly triage victims using mass casualty incident (MCI) protocols such as START or JumpSTART. Focus on identifying and treating those with life-threatening injuries first.
- **Treatment and Transport:** Provide immediate life-saving interventions and prepare for rapid transport to medical facilities. Coordinate with receiving hospitals to ensure they are prepared for the influx of patients.
- **Communication:** Maintain clear and continuous communication with law enforcement, command centers, and hospitals. Ensure that information about the nature of injuries, number of casualties, and required resources is accurately relayed.

Tactical Emergency Casualty Care (TECC) vs. Traditional EMS Care
Tactical Emergency Casualty Care (TECC):

- **Focus:** TECC is designed for high-threat environments, integrating principles from military Tactical Combat Casualty Care (TCCC) adapted for civilian use.
- **Priorities:** Emphasizes immediate life-saving interventions in unsafe or tactical settings, where traditional EMS protocols may not be applicable due to the ongoing threat.
- **Phases of Care:**
  1. **Direct Threat Care (DTC):** Care provided while the threat is ongoing. Focuses on life-saving measures that can be performed quickly, such as tourniquet application and rapid evacuation.
  2. **Indirect Threat Care (ITC):** Care provided once the immediate threat is mitigated but the environment is still potentially dangerous. Allows for more comprehensive medical interventions like airway management and hemorrhage control.
  3. **Evacuation (Evac):** Care provided during the movement of casualties to a safer location or medical facility. Includes continued monitoring and intervention as needed.

Traditional EMS Care:

- **Focus:** Designed for relatively safe environments where providers can work without immediate threat to their safety.
- **Priorities:** Emphasizes thorough assessment, stabilization, and transport of patients following standard protocols.

- **Approach:** Involves detailed assessments, vital sign monitoring, and comprehensive treatments, which may not be feasible in high-threat situations.

Use of the THREAT Acronym in High-Threat Environments

THREAT Acronym: The THREAT acronym provides a structured approach for responders in high-threat situations, particularly in tactical environments like terrorism or active shooter incidents.

1. **T - Threat Suppression:**
   - **Objective:** Neutralize or mitigate the threat to ensure safety for responders and victims.
   - **Action:** Law enforcement focuses on stopping the shooter or terrorist, while EMS personnel remain in secure areas until the scene is safe.

2. **H - Hemorrhage Control:**
   - **Objective:** Address severe bleeding immediately, as uncontrolled hemorrhage is a leading cause of preventable death.
   - **Action:** Apply tourniquets, hemostatic dressings, and direct pressure to control bleeding as quickly as possible.

3. **R - Rapid Extrication to Safety:**
   - **Objective:** Move victims to a safer environment where comprehensive care can be provided.
   - **Action:** Extract casualties from the danger zone to a casualty collection point (CCP) or a safer area for further treatment.

4. **E - Evaluate and Manage Airway:**
   - **Objective:** Ensure open and secure airways for all victims, addressing any breathing difficulties.
   - **Action:** Provide basic airway management techniques such as positioning, suctioning, oropharyngeal/nasopharyngeal airways, and advanced techniques if necessary.

5. **A - Assess for Other Life-Threatening Injuries:**
   - **Objective:** Identify and treat other injuries that could be life-threatening if not addressed promptly.
   - **Action:** Perform rapid assessments and provide interventions for conditions such as tension pneumothorax, flail chest, or penetrating injuries.

6. **T - Transport to Definitive Care:**
   - **Objective:** Ensure rapid transport to medical facilities equipped to provide definitive care.
   - **Action:** Coordinate with transportation resources and receiving hospitals to prioritize the transfer of the most critically injured patients.

EMS response to terrorism and active shooter incidents requires a coordinated, multidisciplinary approach prioritizing safety, rapid assessment, and immediate life-saving interventions. TECC adapts military principles for civilian use in high-threat environments, emphasizing direct threat care, indirect threat care, and evacuation. The THREAT acronym guides responders in managing such situations, focusing on threat suppression, hemorrhage control, rapid extrication, airway management, assessment of other injuries, and transport to definitive care. Understanding and implementing these principles ensures effective and efficient response, minimizing fatalities and improving outcomes in high-threat scenarios.

Components of an EMS Culture of Safety

An effective EMS culture of safety is built on several key components that promote a safe environment for both patients and providers.

Just Culture: Just culture emphasizes accountability and learning over punishment. It distinguishes between human error (unintentional mistakes), at-risk behavior (taking shortcuts), and reckless behavior (disregard for safety protocols). By focusing on understanding why errors occur, just culture encourages reporting mistakes without fear of retribution, which helps identify system issues and fosters continuous improvement.

Error Reporting Systems: Error reporting systems are crucial for tracking incidents and near-misses. These systems enable EMS personnel to report safety events confidentially. The collected data helps identify trends, contributing factors, and opportunities for improvement. A robust reporting system supports transparency, learning, and proactive risk management, ultimately enhancing patient and provider safety.

Human Factors Engineering in EMS

Concept: Human factors engineering (HFE) focuses on designing systems and processes that accommodate human abilities and limitations. By considering factors such as ergonomics, cognitive load, and workflow efficiency, HFE aims to reduce errors and enhance performance.

Impact on Patient Safety: In EMS, HFE can significantly impact patient safety by addressing issues like equipment layout, vehicle design, and the usability of medical devices. For example, intuitive equipment placement in ambulances can reduce the time and effort needed to access critical tools, minimizing delays in patient care. Additionally, HFE principles guide the development of protocols that are easier to follow, reducing the likelihood of errors under stress.

Cognitive Aids and Checklists

Use and Benefits: Cognitive aids and checklists are tools designed to support EMS providers in managing complex tasks and ensuring consistency in patient care. These tools help reduce cognitive load, improve focus, and ensure that critical steps are not overlooked.

Reducing Medical Errors: Checklists standardize procedures and provide a step-by-step guide, which is especially useful during high-pressure situations. For instance, a pre-hospital trauma care checklist ensures that all necessary interventions are performed systematically, reducing the chance of omission.

Cognitive aids, such as flowcharts and algorithms, support decision-making by providing clear guidance on treatment pathways. They are particularly valuable in managing rare or complex conditions, where providers might not have extensive experience.

By integrating just culture principles, robust error reporting systems, human factors engineering, and the use of cognitive aids and checklists, EMS organizations can create a safer environment that minimizes errors and enhances the quality of patient care.

Principles of EMS Resource Management and Deployment

Effective EMS resource management and deployment ensure that emergency medical services are available when and where they are needed most. Key principles include efficient allocation of resources, strategic positioning of units, and ongoing evaluation of system performance. This involves balancing the availability of ambulances and personnel with the demand for services, minimizing response times, and optimizing patient outcomes.

System Status Management:

System Status Management (SSM) is a dynamic approach to deploying EMS resources based on real-time data and predictive analytics. By continuously monitoring and adjusting the status and location of ambulances, SSM aims to improve response times and service efficiency.

Impact on Response Times:

SSM impacts response times by strategically positioning ambulances in high-demand areas during peak periods and reallocating them as demand patterns shift. This proactive approach helps reduce the time it takes for an ambulance to reach a patient, thereby improving the chances of a positive outcome.

Peak-Load Staffing:

Peak-load staffing involves adjusting the number of available EMS units and personnel based on the anticipated demand for services. During periods of high demand, such as weekends, holidays, or specific times of the day, additional staff and units are deployed to ensure adequate coverage.

- **Benefits:** This approach helps manage high call volumes more effectively, reducing strain on resources and improving response times during busy periods.
- **Implementation:** Agencies analyze historical call data to identify peak times and allocate resources accordingly. This may include adding more ambulances, hiring part-time staff, or adjusting shift schedules.

Dynamic Deployment Models:

Dynamic deployment models use real-time data and predictive analytics to position EMS units where they are most likely to be needed. Unlike static deployment, where units are stationed at fixed locations, dynamic deployment continuously adjusts unit positions based on current demand and anticipated call patterns.

- **Real-Time Adjustments:** EMS units are repositioned throughout the day in response to changes in call volume and location. For example, if a high number of calls are expected in a particular area, units may be pre-positioned nearby.

- **Predictive Analytics:** By analyzing trends and patterns in call data, EMS agencies can predict where and when emergencies are likely to occur. This allows for proactive resource allocation, ensuring that units are closer to potential incident sites.

Both peak-load staffing and dynamic deployment models are integral to effective EMS operations, as they enable agencies to respond swiftly and efficiently to emergencies. These strategies not only improve response times but also enhance the overall quality of care provided to patients. By leveraging data and technology, EMS systems can continually optimize their resource management and deployment practices, ensuring they meet the needs of the communities they serve.

Quality Improvement in EMS

Quality improvement (QI) in EMS involves systematic efforts to enhance patient care and operational efficiency. This continuous process uses data-driven strategies to identify areas for improvement and implement changes that lead to better patient outcomes.

Process of Quality Improvement:

1. **Identify Improvement Areas:**
   - Collect data on various aspects of EMS operations, such as response times, clinical interventions, patient outcomes, and provider performance.
   - Use sources like patient care reports, incident debriefs, and feedback from patients and staff.
2. **Set Goals and Objectives:**
   - Define clear, measurable goals based on identified improvement areas.
   - Objectives should align with best practices and regulatory standards.
3. **Develop and Implement Action Plans:**
   - Create action plans that outline specific steps to achieve improvement goals.
   - Involve a multidisciplinary team to ensure comprehensive strategies.
   - Implement changes in protocols, training, equipment, or policies as needed.
4. **Monitor and Measure Performance:**
   - Use clinical performance indicators (CPIs) to assess the impact of implemented changes.
   - CPIs can include response times, adherence to protocols, patient satisfaction, and clinical outcomes like survival rates.
5. **Analyze and Refine:**
   - Regularly review performance data to determine the effectiveness of QI efforts.
   - Make adjustments based on findings and continue monitoring for sustained improvement.

High-Reliability Organizations (HRO) in EMS

Concept: High-reliability organizations (HROs) operate in complex, high-risk environments and consistently maintain a high level of safety and performance. They achieve this through a culture of continuous learning, adaptability, and a commitment to minimizing errors.

Application to EMS Agencies:

- **Preoccupation with Failure:** EMS agencies should always be vigilant for potential errors or failures, encouraging staff to report even minor issues to prevent larger problems.
- **Reluctance to Simplify:** Avoid oversimplifying complex situations. EMS providers should consider all possible factors and nuances in patient care.
- **Sensitivity to Operations:** Maintain an acute awareness of frontline operations. Leadership should stay connected with day-to-day activities to understand challenges and opportunities.
- **Commitment to Resilience:** EMS agencies must be prepared to adapt and respond to unexpected situations effectively, ensuring continuity of high-quality care.
- **Deference to Expertise:** Decision-making should prioritize input from those with the most relevant expertise, regardless of rank or role, to ensure the best outcomes.

Root Cause Analysis in EMS

Role and Importance: Root cause analysis (RCA) is a systematic method used to identify the underlying causes of adverse events or near-misses. By understanding the root causes, EMS agencies can implement targeted interventions to prevent recurrence and improve patient safety.

Process of Root Cause Analysis:
1. **Event Identification and Data Collection**:
   o Collect detailed information about the adverse event, including patient care reports, witness statements, and any relevant environmental factors.
   o Use tools like incident reporting systems and direct interviews.
2. **Event Analysis**:
   o Create a timeline of events leading up to the incident to understand the sequence of actions and decisions.
   o Use techniques such as the "5 Whys" or fishbone diagrams to explore all potential contributing factors.
3. **Identify Root Causes**:
   o Determine the fundamental issues that led to the event, beyond the immediate causes.
   o Consider factors such as system failures, human errors, communication breakdowns, and inadequate training or resources.
4. **Develop Action Plans**:
   o Create strategies to address the root causes, which may include revising protocols, improving training programs, enhancing communication systems, or upgrading equipment.
   o Ensure that action plans are specific, actionable, and measurable.
5. **Implement Changes and Monitor**:
   o Put the action plans into practice and monitor their effectiveness.
   o Regularly review data to ensure that the changes are leading to the desired improvements and adjust as necessary.

By focusing on quality improvement processes, embracing the principles of high-reliability organizations, and conducting thorough root cause analyses, EMS agencies can significantly enhance their performance and patient outcomes.

Ethical Decision-Making in EMS Using the "MORAL" Framework

The **MORAL** framework provides a structured approach for ethical decision-making in EMS, ensuring that decisions are made thoughtfully and systematically. The framework stands for **M**assage the dilemma, **O**utline the options, **R**esolve the dilemma, **A**ct by applying the chosen option, and **L**ook back and evaluate.

1. **M - Massage the Dilemma:**
   o **Identify the Issue:** Clearly define the ethical dilemma, considering all relevant facts and circumstances.
   o **Gather Information:** Collect pertinent information, including patient history, current condition, and input from other healthcare professionals and family members.
2. **O - Outline the Options:**
   o **List Potential Actions:** Identify all possible courses of action. Consider the ethical principles involved, such as autonomy, beneficence, non-maleficence, and justice.
   o **Evaluate the Implications:** Assess the potential outcomes of each option, considering both the benefits and the risks.
3. **R - Resolve the Dilemma:**
   o **Weigh the Options:** Use ethical reasoning to evaluate the options. This may involve consulting with colleagues, ethical committees, or using ethical guidelines.
   o **Make a Decision:** Choose the option that best aligns with ethical principles and the best interests of the patient.
4. **A - Act by Applying the Chosen Option:**
   o **Implement the Decision:** Carry out the chosen course of action with professionalism and compassion.
   o **Communicate Clearly:** Ensure that the patient, family members, and other healthcare providers understand the decision and the reasons behind it.
5. **L - Look Back and Evaluate:**

- Reflect on the Outcome: Evaluate the effectiveness of the decision and its impact on the patient and others involved.
- Learn and Improve: Use the experience to inform future ethical decision-making, identifying any areas for improvement.

Impact of "Futile Care" on End-of-Life Decisions in the Field
Futile Care:
- **Definition:** Medical care that is unlikely to benefit the patient, either because it will not improve their condition or because it only prolongs the dying process without adding quality of life.
- **Impact on Decision-Making:** EMS providers must consider the concept of futile care when making end-of-life decisions. Administering treatments that provide no meaningful benefit to the patient can lead to unnecessary suffering and resource utilization.

Considerations:
- **Patient Autonomy:** Respecting the patient's wishes regarding end-of-life care, including any advance directives or Do Not Resuscitate (DNR) orders.
- **Best Interests:** Balancing the patient's quality of life and the likelihood of a meaningful recovery against the invasiveness and burden of treatments.
- **Professional Judgment:** Using clinical judgment to determine when care may be considered futile and discussing these considerations with the patient and family, if possible.

Ethical Considerations in Termination of Resuscitation Protocols
Termination of Resuscitation (TOR):
- **Definition:** Protocols that guide EMS providers in deciding when to cease resuscitation efforts in cases of cardiac arrest, typically based on specific clinical criteria.

Ethical Considerations:
1. **Clinical Criteria:** TOR protocols are based on evidence-based criteria, such as the absence of return of spontaneous circulation (ROSC) after a specified period of advanced life support, asystole on the ECG, or lack of response to initial interventions.
2. **Patient Wishes:** Respecting advance directives, DNR orders, or other indications of the patient's wishes regarding resuscitation.
3. **Family Involvement:** Communicating clearly and compassionately with family members about the decision to terminate resuscitation, explaining the reasoning and addressing their concerns and emotions.
4. **Provider Support:** Ensuring EMS providers are trained and supported in making TOR decisions, recognizing the emotional and ethical challenges involved.
5. **Documentation:** Thoroughly documenting the decision-making process, the clinical criteria met, and the communication with family and other healthcare providers.

Using the MORAL framework helps EMS providers navigate complex ethical dilemmas by systematically considering all aspects of the situation and making well-informed decisions. The concept of futile care influences end-of-life decisions by guiding providers to avoid unnecessary interventions that do not benefit the patient. Ethical considerations in termination of resuscitation protocols involve respecting patient autonomy, using evidence-based criteria, and communicating effectively with family members, ensuring that decisions are compassionate, justified, and documented.

Principles of Effective Communication in EMS
Effective communication in EMS is critical for ensuring the safety and well-being of patients. It involves clear, concise, and accurate information exchange among EMS providers, between EMS and other healthcare professionals, and with dispatch centers.

Radio Protocols
1. **Clarity and Brevity:**
   - Use clear, concise language and avoid unnecessary details to ensure messages are understood quickly and accurately.
   - Speak slowly and distinctly.
2. **Standardized Codes and Phrases:**

- o Use standardized radio codes and phrases to reduce ambiguity and ensure consistency in communication.
- o Common codes include "10-4" for acknowledgment, "Code 3" for emergency response with lights and sirens, and "ETA" for estimated time of arrival.

3. **Identification**:
   - o Always identify yourself and your unit before transmitting a message to provide context and ensure the message reaches the correct recipient.

4. **Confirmation**:
   - o Confirm receipt of important messages to avoid miscommunication. This can be done by repeating key information back to the sender.

Handoff Reports

1. **Structured Format**:
   - o Use a structured format for handoff reports to ensure all critical information is conveyed. This can include patient demographics, chief complaint, vital signs, interventions provided, and any changes in the patient's condition.

2. **Accuracy**:
   - o Provide accurate and up-to-date information to the receiving healthcare providers to facilitate continuity of care.

3. **Relevance**:
   - o Focus on relevant clinical details that will impact the immediate care and management of the patient.

4. **Interaction**:
   - o Engage in a two-way communication process, allowing the receiving provider to ask questions and clarify details.

Closed-Loop Communication

Concept:

- **Definition**: Closed-loop communication involves sending a message, having the receiver acknowledge and repeat the message back, and then the sender confirming the accuracy of the repeated message.

- **Enhancement of Patient Safety**:
  - o **Error Reduction**: Ensures that information is accurately received and understood, reducing the risk of errors.
  - o **Clarification**: Allows for immediate correction of misunderstandings or miscommunications.
  - o **Verification**: Confirms that all team members are on the same page, which is especially important during high-stress or high-stakes situations.

SBAR Technique in Patient Handoffs

Concept:

- **SBAR (Situation, Background, Assessment, Recommendation)** is a standardized communication framework used to provide clear and concise information during patient handoffs.

Components:

1. **Situation**:
   - o **What is happening now?**: Provide a brief description of the current situation.
   - o Example: "This is EMT John from Unit 52. We are transporting a 68-year-old male with chest pain."

2. **Background**:
   - o **What is the clinical background or context?**: Give relevant medical history and context.
   - o Example: "The patient has a history of hypertension and diabetes. He started experiencing chest pain 30 minutes ago while mowing the lawn."

3. **Assessment**:
   - o **What do you think the problem is?**: Share your clinical findings and assessment.
   - o Example: "The patient is alert but in distress. Blood pressure is 150/90, heart rate is 110, respiratory rate is 22, and oxygen saturation is 94% on room air. He has taken one nitroglycerin tablet with no relief."

4. **Recommendation**:
   - ○ **What do you recommend or need?**: Provide your recommendations or request further actions.
   - ○ Example: "We are en route to your facility with an ETA of 10 minutes. Requesting to have a cardiac monitor and IV access ready."

Benefits:

- **Structured Communication**: Provides a clear and organized method for conveying information.
- **Consistency**: Ensures that all necessary information is covered in every handoff, regardless of the provider.
- **Efficiency**: Saves time by focusing on the most critical information, enabling quick decision-making.

Effective communication in EMS, guided by principles such as radio protocols, structured handoff reports, and techniques like closed-loop communication and SBAR, is essential for delivering safe and efficient patient care. These methods help minimize errors, enhance understanding, and ensure seamless transitions between different phases of patient management.

EMS Response to Special Populations

Bariatric Patients:

Challenges:

- **Transport:** Bariatric patients may require specialized equipment such as bariatric stretchers, wheelchairs, and vehicles.
- **Manual Handling:** Increased risk of injury to both patients and EMS personnel during lifting and moving.
- **Medical Complications:** Higher prevalence of conditions like diabetes, cardiovascular disease, and respiratory issues.

Response Strategies:

- **Specialized Equipment:** Use of bariatric stretchers, lift systems, and additional personnel to safely handle and transport patients.
- **Training:** EMS providers need specific training in lifting techniques and use of bariatric equipment to prevent injuries.
- **Assessment and Monitoring:** Careful monitoring of vital signs, blood sugar levels, and respiratory function, with adjustments in standard protocols to accommodate for the patient's size and potential comorbidities.

Patients with Special Healthcare Needs:

Challenges:

- **Complex Medical Histories:** Patients may have chronic conditions, disabilities, or medical devices such as ventilators or feeding tubes.
- **Communication Barriers:** Cognitive impairments or speech difficulties may complicate the assessment.

Response Strategies:

- **Medical History:** Obtain detailed medical histories from caregivers, medical records, or medical alert devices.
- **Personalized Care:** Tailor interventions to the patient's specific needs, considering their chronic conditions and daily routines.
- **Caregiver Involvement:** Engage with caregivers who can provide valuable information about the patient's normal state and specific care requirements.

Culturally Diverse Communities:

Challenges:

- **Language Barriers:** Communication difficulties due to language differences can impact the accuracy of patient assessment and care.
- **Cultural Sensitivities:** Different beliefs and practices regarding medical care, gender roles, and modesty.

Response Strategies:

- **Cultural Competency Training:** Equip EMS providers with knowledge and skills to respect and effectively interact with diverse cultural backgrounds.

- **Language Services:** Utilize interpretation services to overcome language barriers and ensure clear communication with patients and their families.
- **Community Engagement:** Build relationships with community leaders and organizations to better understand and address the unique needs of diverse populations.

Functional Needs in Emergency Planning and Response

Concept of Functional Needs:
- **Definition:** Functional needs refer to the requirements of individuals who may need additional assistance before, during, and after an emergency due to physical, sensory, mental health, cognitive, or intellectual disabilities, chronic health conditions, or limitations in communication, transportation, supervision, or medical care.

Impact on Emergency Planning and Response:
- **Inclusive Planning:** Emergency plans must consider the specific needs of these individuals, ensuring that they can access evacuation, shelter, and medical services.
- **Resource Allocation:** Allocate resources such as specialized transportation, accessible shelters, and medical equipment to meet the needs of individuals with functional needs.
- **Communication:** Develop clear, accessible communication strategies to inform individuals with functional needs about emergency procedures and available assistance.

Use of Language Interpretation Services in EMS Operations

Importance of Language Interpretation:
- **Effective Communication:** Ensures accurate assessment and treatment by overcoming language barriers between EMS providers and non-English speaking patients.
- **Patient Safety:** Reduces the risk of miscommunication that could lead to incorrect treatment or delayed care.
- **Cultural Sensitivity:** Demonstrates respect for the patient's language and cultural background, fostering trust and cooperation.

Types of Interpretation Services:
- **In-Person Interpreters:** Professional interpreters who can provide face-to-face assistance, especially in critical or sensitive situations.
- **Telephone Interpretation:** Quick and accessible service that allows EMS providers to connect with interpreters via phone, useful in field settings.
- **Video Remote Interpretation (VRI):** Provides visual and auditory interpretation through video calls, enhancing communication when visual cues are important.

Implementation in EMS Operations:
- **Training:** EMS personnel should be trained on how to access and use interpretation services effectively.
- **Protocols:** Develop clear protocols for when and how to use interpretation services, ensuring that all providers are aware of these resources.
- **Equipment:** Ensure that ambulances and response units are equipped with the necessary technology to connect with telephone or video interpreters.
- **Documentation:** Record the use of interpretation services in patient care reports to ensure continuity of care and legal compliance.

EMS response to special populations requires tailored strategies to address the unique challenges presented by bariatric patients, individuals with special healthcare needs, and culturally diverse communities. Incorporating functional needs into emergency planning ensures that all individuals receive appropriate care and assistance. Language interpretation services are essential for effective communication, patient safety, and culturally sensitive care, enhancing the overall quality of EMS operations.

Practice Test Questions

Welcome to the practice exam section of your NREMT Exam Prep Study Guide. This segment is designed to help you solidify your understanding of key concepts, identify areas that may need further review, and ultimately build the confidence needed to excel in your NREMT exam.

Instant Feedback: By providing the answer and explanation immediately after each question, you can quickly assess your understanding of the material. If you answered correctly, the explanation will reinforce your knowledge. If you answered incorrectly, you can instantly learn from your mistake and clarify any misunderstandings.

Efficient Learning: This format eliminates the need to flip back and forth between questions and an answer key, allowing you to focus on the content without breaking your concentration. This streamlined approach helps you maintain momentum as you progress through the practice test.

Enhanced Retention: Research has shown that immediate feedback on your responses can significantly improve learning and retention. By reviewing the answer and explanation right after answering a question, you'll be more likely to remember the information and apply it effectively in the future.

Tips for Success:
- **Hide the Answers:** To simulate a real test environment, consider using a piece of paper or another object to cover the answers as you work through each question. This will help you practice retrieving information from memory before confirming your answer.
- **Repetition of Key Topics:** Some important topics may be covered multiple times in different contexts. This repetition is intentional and helps reinforce crucial concepts and skills.

Remember, the goal of this practice exam is not only to test your knowledge but also to provide a valuable learning experience. Take your time, read each question carefully, and use the explanations to deepen your understanding. Good luck, and let's get started!

1. You are dispatched to a 28-year-old male complaining of sudden onset chest pain. On arrival, you find the patient diaphoretic and clutching his chest. His vital signs are: BP 100/60, HR 110, RR 24, SpO2 94% on room air. The 12-lead ECG shows ST-segment elevation in leads II, III, and aVF. Which of the following is the most appropriate next step in management?
a. Administer aspirin 324 mg and transport to the nearest hospital
b. Perform needle decompression of the left chest
c. Administer nitroglycerin 0.4 mg sublingually
d. Activate a STEMI alert and transport to a PCI-capable center

Answer: d. Activate a STEMI alert and transport to a PCI-capable center. Explanation: The patient's presentation and ECG findings are consistent with an inferior wall ST-elevation myocardial infarction (STEMI). The ST elevations in leads II, III, and aVF indicate involvement of the right coronary artery. While aspirin administration is important, the most crucial next step is to activate the STEMI alert system and transport the patient to a facility capable of performing percutaneous coronary intervention (PCI). This ensures the fastest possible door-to-balloon time, which is critical for myocardial salvage. Needle decompression is not indicated as there are no signs of tension pneumothorax. Nitroglycerin should be avoided in inferior wall MIs due to the risk of profound hypotension, especially if right ventricular involvement is present.

2. You arrive on scene to find an unconscious 45-year-old male with agonal respirations. After opening the airway, you decide to insert an oropharyngeal airway (OPA). Which of the following techniques is most appropriate for OPA insertion in an adult patient?
a. Insert the OPA with the curve facing the tongue, then rotate 180 degrees
b. Measure from the corner of the mouth to the angle of the jaw, then insert with the curve facing the palate
c. Use a tongue depressor to visualize the pharynx, then insert the OPA directly
d. Insert the OPA sideways, then rotate 90 degrees to its final position

Answer: b. Measure from the corner of the mouth to the angle of the jaw, then insert with the curve facing the palate. Explanation: The correct technique for OPA insertion in adults is to measure from the corner of the mouth to the angle of the jaw to ensure proper sizing, then insert the device with the curve facing the palate. This method minimizes the risk of pushing the tongue posteriorly and potentially obstructing the airway. The 180-degree rotation technique is used for pediatric patients. Inserting sideways or using a tongue depressor are not standard practices and may cause trauma or ineffective placement.

3. A 30-year-old female presents with severe respiratory distress due to anaphylaxis. You've administered epinephrine and are preparing to intubate. The physician orders you to perform Sellick's maneuver. What is the primary purpose of this technique?
a. To improve visualization of the vocal cords
b. To prevent aspiration of gastric contents
c. To facilitate easier passage of the endotracheal tube
d. To confirm proper placement of the tube after insertion

Answer: b. To prevent aspiration of gastric contents. Explanation: Sellick's maneuver, also known as cricoid pressure, involves applying backward pressure on the cricoid cartilage during intubation. Its primary purpose is to occlude the esophagus, thereby reducing the risk of passive regurgitation and aspiration of gastric contents. While it was once thought to improve laryngeal view, recent studies have shown it may actually worsen visualization. It's not used to facilitate tube passage or confirm placement. In anaphylaxis cases, where there's an increased risk of vomiting due to histamine release, this technique can be particularly beneficial.

4. You're assessing a 60-year-old male with COPD exacerbation. His SpO2 is 88% on room air, and you're considering oxygen therapy. Which of the following statements is most accurate regarding oxygen administration in this scenario?
a. Withhold oxygen to prevent suppression of hypoxic drive
b. Administer high-flow oxygen via non-rebreather mask to rapidly correct hypoxemia
c. Use a Venturi mask set to 24% FiO2 to provide controlled oxygenation
d. Start with nasal cannula at 6 L/min and titrate based on work of breathing

Answer: c. Use a Venturi mask set to 24% FiO2 to provide controlled oxygenation. Explanation: In COPD patients with chronic hypercapnia, controlled oxygen therapy is crucial to avoid suppressing hypoxic drive while still correcting hypoxemia. A Venturi mask provides precise FiO2 control, making it ideal for these patients. Starting at 24% FiO2 allows for careful titration. Withholding oxygen entirely is dangerous and outdated practice. High-flow oxygen via non-rebreather risks CO2 retention. Nasal cannula at 6 L/min delivers unpredictable FiO2 and may be too high initially for this patient population.

5. During bag-valve-mask ventilation of an unresponsive adult patient, you notice significant gastric distension. Which of the following interventions is most appropriate to address this issue?
a. Increase the rate of ventilations to compensate for poor lung compliance
b. Apply cricoid pressure to prevent further gastric insufflation
c. Insert a nasogastric tube to decompress the stomach
d. Position the patient in Trendelenburg to reduce diaphragmatic pressure

Answer: b. Apply cricoid pressure to prevent further gastric insufflation. Explanation: Cricoid pressure (Sellick's maneuver) can help prevent further gastric insufflation during bag-valve-mask ventilation by compressing the esophagus against the cervical vertebrae. This technique reduces the risk of regurgitation and aspiration. Increasing ventilation rate would likely exacerbate the problem. Nasogastric tube insertion in an unresponsive patient risks aspiration. Trendelenburg position could worsen respiratory mechanics and increase aspiration risk. The key is to address the immediate issue of ongoing gastric insufflation while maintaining effective ventilation.

6. You're preparing to suction the airway of a 70-year-old male with copious secretions. What is the appropriate suction catheter size and maximum suction duration for this patient?
a. 12 French catheter, suction for no more than 10 seconds
b. 14 French catheter, suction for no more than 15 seconds
c. 16 French catheter, suction for no more than 5 seconds
d. 18 French catheter, suction for no more than 20 seconds

Answer: b. 14 French catheter, suction for no more than 15 seconds. Explanation: The appropriate suction catheter size for adults is typically calculated as twice the size of the endotracheal tube's inner diameter. For most adults, this equates to a 14 or 16 French catheter. The maximum duration of suctioning should not exceed 15 seconds to prevent hypoxia. The 14 French catheter provides effective suctioning without being too large, which could cause trauma. The 15-second limit allows for thorough suctioning while minimizing the risk of suction-induced hypoxemia and associated complications.

7. A 25-year-old female is found unresponsive with shallow respirations. After opening the airway, you decide to insert a nasopharyngeal airway (NPA). Which of the following is the most accurate method for sizing an NPA?
a. Measure from the tip of the nose to the tragus of the ear
b. Use a catheter with a French size equal to the patient's age
c. Select a size based on the diameter of the patient's naris
d. Measure from the tip of the nose to the angle of the jaw

Answer: a. Measure from the tip of the nose to the tragus of the ear. Explanation: The correct method for sizing an NPA is to measure from the tip of the nose to the tragus of the ear. This ensures that the airway will be long enough to reach the pharynx without extending into the larynx. The French size-to-age correlation is not a standard practice for NPAs. Selecting based on naris diameter alone doesn't account for proper length. Measuring to the angle of the jaw would result in an NPA that's too long, potentially stimulating the gag reflex or entering the esophagus.

8. During a difficult intubation attempt on a trauma patient, the physician asks you to perform the BURP maneuver. What does this acronym stand for, and what is its primary purpose?
a. Backward, Upward, Rightward Pressure; to improve glottic view
b. Bimanual, Upward, Rotating Pressure; to facilitate tube passage
c. Backward, Upward, Rightward Pressure; to prevent aspiration
d. Bimanual, Unilateral, Rotating Pressure; to align the tracheal axis

Answer: a. Backward, Upward, Rightward Pressure; to improve glottic view. Explanation: BURP stands for Backward, Upward, Rightward Pressure. It's an external laryngeal manipulation technique used to improve visualization of the glottis during difficult intubations. The maneuver involves applying pressure to the thyroid cartilage in a backward, upward, and slightly rightward direction. This can help to bring the larynx into view, especially in cases where the standard view is suboptimal. It's different from cricoid pressure (Sellick's maneuver), which is primarily used to prevent aspiration.

9. You're assessing a 50-year-old male with severe respiratory distress. His SpO2 is 85% on room air, and you note use of accessory muscles. After positioning and supplemental oxygen, you consider CPAP. Which of the following is a contraindication for CPAP use in the prehospital setting?
a. Pulmonary edema
b. COPD exacerbation
c. Pneumothorax
d. Asthma attack

Answer: c. Pneumothorax. Explanation: Pneumothorax is a contraindication for CPAP use because the positive pressure can exacerbate the condition, potentially leading to a tension pneumothorax. CPAP is actually beneficial for pulmonary edema, COPD exacerbations, and asthma attacks as it helps reduce the work of breathing, improves oxygenation, and can help recruit alveoli. However, proper assessment is crucial before initiating CPAP, and patients should be closely monitored for any signs of deterioration or barotrauma.

10. During bag-valve-mask ventilation of a pediatric patient, you notice poor chest rise despite proper head positioning. Which of the following is the most appropriate next step?
a. Increase the tidal volume by squeezing the bag harder
b. Perform a head-tilt, chin-lift maneuver
c. Switch to a larger mask size
d. Use a two-person BVM technique with a jaw-thrust

Answer: d. Use a two-person BVM technique with a jaw-thrust. Explanation: When faced with poor chest rise during BVM ventilation, improving the seal and airway positioning should be the priority. A two-person BVM technique allows one rescuer to focus solely on maintaining an optimal seal and airway position using a jaw-thrust maneuver, while the other manages ventilations. This is particularly effective in pediatric patients. Increasing tidal volume risks barotrauma and gastric insufflation. Head-tilt, chin-lift has already been attempted per the scenario. A larger mask could worsen the seal. The jaw-thrust is preferred in potential cervical spine injuries and often provides better airway patency.

11. A 35-year-old female presents with signs of upper airway obstruction. After unsuccessful attempts at relieving the obstruction, you prepare for a surgical cricothyrotomy. Which of the following landmarks is most crucial to identify for this procedure?
a. Thyroid notch
b. Cricothyroid membrane
c. Sternal notch
d. Hyoid bone

Answer: b. Cricothyroid membrane. Explanation: The cricothyroid membrane is the most crucial landmark to identify for a surgical cricothyrotomy. This membrane is the site where the incision is made to create an emergency surgical airway. It's located between the thyroid cartilage superiorly and the cricoid cartilage inferiorly. Accurate identification of this landmark is essential to avoid damage to surrounding structures such as the vocal cords (above) or the cricoid cartilage (below). The thyroid notch, sternal notch, and hyoid bone are useful reference points but are not the primary landmark for this procedure.

12. A 45-year-old male presents with chest pain and shortness of breath that began suddenly while he was mowing the lawn. He is diaphoretic and appears anxious. His blood pressure is 88/60 mmHg, pulse is 120 bpm, and respiratory rate is 28 breaths per minute. Auscultation reveals clear lung sounds, but his neck veins are distended. What is the most likely diagnosis?
a. Acute myocardial infarction
b. Pulmonary embolism
c. Tension pneumothorax
d. Pericardial tamponade

Answer: d. Pericardial tamponade. Explanation: The combination of hypotension, tachycardia, clear lung sounds, and distended neck veins is indicative of pericardial tamponade, where fluid accumulation in the pericardial sac impairs cardiac filling and output. Pulmonary embolism might present with similar symptoms but typically includes abnormal lung sounds. Tension pneumothorax would usually present with diminished breath sounds on one side. Acute myocardial infarction could also present with hypotension and tachycardia but not with clear lung sounds and distended neck veins unless complicated by right heart failure.

13. A 33-year-old pregnant woman at 30 weeks gestation presents with severe headache, visual disturbances, and swelling of her hands and feet. Her blood pressure is 170/110 mmHg. Urinalysis reveals significant proteinuria. What is the most appropriate initial management?
a. Administer antihypertensive medication and magnesium sulfate
b. Perform an immediate cesarean section
c. Initiate bed rest and oral antihypertensive therapy
d. Administer intravenous fluids and corticosteroids

Answer: a. Administer antihypertensive medication and magnesium sulfate. Explanation: The patient is showing signs of severe preeclampsia, characterized by hypertension, proteinuria, and end-organ dysfunction (headache, visual disturbances). Immediate management includes controlling blood pressure and preventing seizures with magnesium sulfate. Delivery might be necessary but would depend on fetal and maternal stability; immediate cesarean section is not the first step without further evaluation.

14. A 58-year-old male with a history of diabetes and hypertension presents with confusion, slurred speech, and right-sided weakness that started 1 hour ago. His blood glucose level is 65 mg/dL. What is the most appropriate next step in management?
a. Administer intravenous dextrose
b. Perform a CT scan of the head
c. Administer aspirin
d. Start intravenous thrombolytic therapy

Answer: a. Administer intravenous dextrose. Explanation: Although the symptoms are suggestive of a stroke, the low blood glucose level (65 mg/dL) must be corrected first as hypoglycemia can mimic stroke symptoms. Administering dextrose to normalize the blood glucose is the immediate priority. Once hypoglycemia is corrected, further evaluation, including a CT scan, should be performed to rule out stroke or other neurological conditions.

15. A 24-year-old female presents with a high fever, stiff neck, and a petechial rash on her trunk and extremities. She is lethargic and appears acutely ill. What is the most appropriate immediate intervention?
a. Perform a lumbar puncture
b. Administer broad-spectrum intravenous antibiotics
c. Administer antipyretics and observe
d. Isolate the patient and perform blood cultures

Answer: b. Administer broad-spectrum intravenous antibiotics. Explanation: The presentation suggests meningococcal meningitis, a life-threatening condition that requires immediate antibiotic treatment. A lumbar puncture is necessary for definitive diagnosis but should not delay the administration of antibiotics. Isolation and blood cultures are also important but secondary to the immediate need for antibiotic therapy to reduce morbidity and mortality.

16. A 50-year-old male construction worker is brought to the emergency department after falling from a height of 20 feet. He is alert but complains of severe back pain and an inability to move his legs. On examination, there is tenderness over the lower thoracic spine, and his lower extremities are flaccid. What is the most appropriate initial step in his management?
a. Obtain an immediate MRI of the spine
b. Administer high-dose intravenous steroids
c. Immobilize the spine and transport to a trauma center
d. Perform a neurological examination

Answer: c. Immobilize the spine and transport to a trauma center. Explanation: The priority in a patient with a suspected spinal injury is to prevent further damage by immobilizing the spine. Transporting to a trauma center for definitive imaging and management is crucial. While an MRI and neurological examination are important, they come after ensuring the patient's spine is immobilized to prevent further injury. High-dose steroids were historically used for spinal cord injuries, but their use is now controversial and not routinely recommended.

17. A 55-year-old male presents with severe shortness of breath, orthopnea, and bilateral crackles on auscultation. His history includes hypertension and myocardial infarction. Which of the following is the most likely diagnosis?
a. Chronic obstructive pulmonary disease (COPD)
b. Acute pulmonary embolism
c. Congestive heart failure (CHF)
d. Pneumonia

Answer: c. Congestive heart failure (CHF). Explanation: The patient's symptoms of severe shortness of breath, orthopnea (difficulty breathing when lying flat), and bilateral crackles (fluid in the lungs) are classic signs of congestive heart failure, especially given his history of myocardial infarction, which likely led to left ventricular dysfunction.

18. A 42-year-old female with a known history of type 1 diabetes is found unconscious with rapid, deep breathing and a fruity odor on her breath. What is the most appropriate immediate action?
a. Administer insulin
b. Provide high-flow oxygen
c. Administer IV glucose
d. Check blood glucose level

Answer: d. Check blood glucose level. Explanation: Rapid, deep breathing (Kussmaul respirations) and a fruity odor suggest diabetic ketoacidosis (DKA), a complication of type 1 diabetes. The most immediate and crucial step is to check her blood glucose level to confirm DKA and guide further treatment, such as fluid resuscitation and insulin administration.

19. A 70-year-old male experiences sudden onset of chest pain, described as tearing and radiating to his back, along with differential blood pressure in the upper extremities. What is the most likely diagnosis?
a. Acute myocardial infarction
b. Pulmonary embolism
c. Aortic dissection
d. Pericarditis

Answer: c. Aortic dissection. Explanation: Sudden, tearing chest pain radiating to the back and differential blood pressure between the arms are hallmark signs of an aortic dissection, a life-threatening condition requiring immediate medical intervention.

20. A 25-year-old male is involved in a high-speed motor vehicle collision and presents with hypotension, jugular venous distention, and muffled heart sounds. What is the most likely diagnosis?
a. Tension pneumothorax
b. Cardiac tamponade
c. Hemothorax
d. Pulmonary contusion

Answer: b. Cardiac tamponade. Explanation: The triad of hypotension, jugular venous distention, and muffled heart sounds is known as Beck's triad, which is indicative of cardiac tamponade, a condition where fluid accumulates in the pericardium, compressing the heart and impairing its function.

21. A 28-year-old pregnant female at 32 weeks gestation presents with a severe headache, visual disturbances, and epigastric pain. Her blood pressure is 180/110 mmHg. What is the most likely diagnosis?
a. Gestational hypertension
b. Eclampsia
c. Pre-eclampsia
d. HELLP syndrome

Answer: c. Pre-eclampsia. Explanation: The severe headache, visual disturbances, epigastric pain, and significantly elevated blood pressure in a pregnant woman are indicative of pre-eclampsia, a hypertensive disorder of pregnancy that can progress to eclampsia if seizures develop.

22. A 65-year-old female with a history of atrial fibrillation presents with acute onset of left-sided weakness and facial droop. What is the most appropriate initial diagnostic test?
a. MRI of the brain
b. CT scan of the head
c. Carotid Doppler ultrasound
d. Electroencephalogram (EEG)

Answer: b. CT scan of the head. Explanation: In a patient presenting with acute stroke symptoms, the most appropriate initial diagnostic test is a CT scan of the head to quickly rule out hemorrhagic stroke and guide further management, such as thrombolytic therapy for ischemic stroke.

23. A 33-year-old male with a history of asthma presents with severe shortness of breath, wheezing, and a silent chest on auscultation. What is the most appropriate immediate treatment?
a. Administer oral corticosteroids
b. Provide high-flow oxygen
c. Administer nebulized bronchodilators
d. Intubation and mechanical ventilation

Answer: d. Intubation and mechanical ventilation. Explanation: Severe asthma with a silent chest (absence of wheezing due to minimal air movement) indicates life-threatening airway obstruction. Immediate intubation and mechanical ventilation are necessary to secure the airway and provide adequate ventilation.

24. A 45-year-old male presents with chest pain and ST-segment elevation in leads II, III, and aVF on the ECG. What is the most appropriate next step in management?
a. Administer aspirin and heparin
b. Perform immediate percutaneous coronary intervention (PCI)
c. Administer thrombolytics

d. Obtain a chest X-ray

Answer: b. Perform immediate percutaneous coronary intervention (PCI). Explanation: ST-segment elevation in leads II, III, and aVF indicates an inferior myocardial infarction. The most appropriate next step is to perform immediate PCI, the preferred reperfusion strategy for STEMI, to restore coronary blood flow.

25. A 30-year-old female presents with a history of fever, chills, and a painful, swollen right calf. She has a positive Homan's sign. What is the most likely diagnosis?
a. Cellulitis
b. Deep vein thrombosis (DVT)
c. Compartment syndrome
d. Ruptured Baker's cyst

Answer: b. Deep vein thrombosis (DVT). Explanation: Fever, chills, and a painful, swollen calf with a positive Homan's sign (pain in the calf on dorsiflexion of the foot) suggest a deep vein thrombosis, a condition that requires anticoagulation to prevent complications like pulmonary embolism.

26. A 60-year-old female presents with sudden onset of severe epigastric pain radiating to her back, nausea, and vomiting. Her serum lipase is significantly elevated. What is the most likely diagnosis?
a. Acute cholecystitis
b. Acute pancreatitis
c. Peptic ulcer disease
d. Gastritis

Answer: b. Acute pancreatitis. Explanation: Severe epigastric pain radiating to the back, along with nausea, vomiting, and elevated serum lipase levels, are characteristic of acute pancreatitis, an inflammation of the pancreas often associated with alcohol use or gallstones.

27. You arrive on scene to find a 60-year-old male with a history of COPD complaining of increased shortness of breath. On auscultation, you hear low-pitched, rumbling sounds that clear partially with coughing. Which of the following best describes these lung sounds?
a. Wheezes
b. Crackles
c. Rhonchi
d. Stridor

Answer: c. Rhonchi. Explanation: Rhonchi are low-pitched, rumbling lung sounds often described as snoring-like. They are typically caused by secretions or obstruction in larger airways and can often be cleared or changed by coughing. This distinguishes them from wheezes, which are high-pitched, musical sounds typically associated with lower airway narrowing. Crackles are brief, discontinuous popping sounds, while stridor is a high-pitched sound heard mostly during inspiration, typically indicating upper airway obstruction.

28. A 2-month-old infant presents with respiratory distress. You're assessing the work of breathing using the Silverman score. Which of the following is NOT a component of this scoring system?
a. Intercostal retractions
b. Xiphoid retraction
c. Nasal flaring
d. Expiratory grunting

Answer: c. Nasal flaring. Explanation: The Silverman score is a tool used to assess respiratory distress in newborns and young infants. It includes five components: upper chest movement, lower chest retraction, xiphoid retraction, nasal alar flaring, and expiratory grunting. Each component is scored 0-2, with a total possible score of 10 indicating severe distress. Nasal flaring, while an important sign of respiratory distress, is not part of the Silverman score. This question tests the candidate's specific knowledge of this pediatric assessment tool, which is crucial for early recognition of respiratory compromise in infants.

29. You're transporting a 40-year-old female with suspected carbon monoxide poisoning. Her SpO2 reads 99% on room air, but she remains drowsy and confused. What is the most likely explanation for this discrepancy?
a. The pulse oximeter is malfunctioning
b. The patient is hyperventilating
c. Pulse oximetry cannot differentiate between carboxyhemoglobin and oxyhemoglobin
d. The patient has underlying methemoglobinemia

Answer: c. Pulse oximetry cannot differentiate between carboxyhemoglobin and oxyhemoglobin. Explanation: Standard pulse oximetry measures the ratio of light absorption between oxygenated and deoxygenated hemoglobin. However, it cannot distinguish between oxyhemoglobin and carboxyhemoglobin, leading to falsely normal or high SpO2 readings in carbon monoxide poisoning. This limitation is crucial for EMTs to understand, as relying solely on SpO2 can lead to missed diagnosis of CO poisoning. In such cases, clinical presentation (like confusion despite normal SpO2) and history are key. Definitive diagnosis requires measurement with a CO-oximeter or arterial blood gas analysis.

30. During CPR, you're monitoring end-tidal CO2 (EtCO2) via capnography. The waveform suddenly changes from a normal square wave to a low, flattened pattern. What does this most likely indicate?
a. Return of spontaneous circulation
b. Esophageal intubation
c. Hyperventilation
d. Decreased pulmonary blood flow

Answer: d. Decreased pulmonary blood flow. Explanation: A sudden change from a normal square waveform to a low, flattened pattern on capnography during CPR most likely indicates decreased pulmonary blood flow. This could be due to ineffective chest compressions or other factors reducing cardiac output. EtCO2 is a reliable indicator of the effectiveness of CPR, with higher values generally indicating better perfusion. A rise in EtCO2 might indicate ROSC, while a persistently low or absent waveform could suggest esophageal intubation. Hyperventilation typically results in a lower but still present waveform. Understanding capnography interpretation is crucial for assessing CPR quality and detecting physiological changes during resuscitation.

31. A 25-year-old male with diabetic ketoacidosis presents with deep, rapid respirations at a rate of 28 per minute. Which respiratory pattern best describes this presentation?
a. Cheyne-Stokes respiration
b. Biot's respiration
c. Kussmaul respiration
d. Apneustic breathing

Answer: c. Kussmaul respiration. Explanation: Kussmaul respiration is characterized by deep, rapid breathing often seen in metabolic acidosis, particularly diabetic ketoacidosis (DKA). This pattern represents a compensatory mechanism to blow off excess CO_2 and increase blood pH. Cheyne-Stokes respiration is a cyclic pattern of alternating periods of hyperpnea and apnea. Biot's respiration involves irregular deep breaths interspersed with periods of apnea. Apneustic breathing is marked by prolonged inspiratory gasps followed by insufficient expiration, typically seen in severe brainstem injury. Recognizing Kussmaul breathing is crucial for early identification of serious metabolic disturbances like DKA.

32. You're assessing a 70-year-old patient with pneumonia. On auscultation, you hear high-pitched, musical sounds predominantly during expiration. These sounds are best classified as:
a. Fine crackles
b. Wheezes
c. Rhonchi
d. Pleural friction rub

Answer: b. Wheezes. Explanation: Wheezes are high-pitched, musical sounds heard predominantly during expiration. They are caused by air flowing through narrowed airways, creating oscillations in the airway walls. Wheezes are commonly associated with conditions that cause bronchospasm or airway obstruction, such as asthma, COPD, or in this case, pneumonia with associated bronchial inflammation. Fine crackles are short, discontinuous sounds heard on inspiration, often described as "Velcro-like." Rhonchi are low-pitched rumbling sounds that can clear with coughing. A pleural friction rub is a creaking or grating sound heard during both inspiration and expiration, typically associated with pleuritis.

33. A 3-month-old infant presents with respiratory distress. You note intercostal retractions, nasal flaring, and a see-saw breathing pattern. Using the Silverman score, how would you rate the xiphoid retraction if it's visible but not marked?
a. 0
b. 1
c. 2
d. 3

Answer: b. 1. Explanation: In the Silverman score, xiphoid retraction is rated on a scale of 0-2. A score of 0 indicates no retraction, 1 indicates just visible retraction, and 2 indicates marked retraction. Given the scenario describes visible but not marked xiphoid retraction, the correct score is 1. The Silverman score assesses five components of respiratory distress in infants: upper chest movement, lower chest retraction, xiphoid retraction, nasal flaring, and expiratory grunting. Each component is scored 0-2, with a total possible score of 10. Higher scores indicate more severe respiratory distress. This scoring system helps standardize assessment and track the progression of respiratory distress in infants.

34. You're monitoring a patient's capnography waveform during transport. You notice the alpha angle (the angle between the baseline and the upstroke) has become less steep. What does this most likely indicate?
a. Increased airway resistance
b. Decreased cardiac output
c. Hyperventilation
d. Esophageal intubation

Answer: a. Increased airway resistance. Explanation: The alpha angle in capnography represents the rate of CO_2 elimination during exhalation. A less steep alpha angle (more gradual upstroke) typically indicates increased airway resistance, such as in bronchospasm or airway obstruction. This occurs because the increased resistance slows the rate of CO_2 elimination. Decreased cardiac output would more likely result in a lower overall $EtCO_2$ value. Hyperventilation would typically show a steeper alpha angle and lower $EtCO_2$. Esophageal intubation would result in a flat or near-flat capnography waveform. Understanding capnography waveform components is crucial for real-time assessment of ventilation and perfusion status.

35. A 55-year-old male with a history of CHF presents with respiratory distress. You note a breathing pattern characterized by progressively deeper and faster breaths, followed by a period of apnea. This pattern repeats cyclically. Which of the following best describes this respiratory pattern?
a. Kussmaul breathing
b. Biot's respiration
c. Cheyne-Stokes respiration
d. Apneustic breathing

Answer: c. Cheyne-Stokes respiration. Explanation: Cheyne-Stokes respiration is characterized by a cyclic pattern of gradually increasing depth and rate of breathing, followed by a period of apnea. This pattern is often seen in patients with congestive heart failure, as well as in some neurological conditions or at high altitudes. It's caused by delays in the feedback loop between blood CO_2 levels and the respiratory centers in the brain. Kussmaul breathing is deep, rapid breathing associated with metabolic acidosis. Biot's respiration involves irregular deep breaths interspersed with periods of apnea. Apneustic breathing is marked by prolonged inspiratory gasps. Recognizing these patterns is crucial for identifying underlying pathologies and potential deterioration in patient status.

36. During a cardiac arrest, you're using capnography to monitor CPR quality. The patient's initial $EtCO_2$ is 10 mmHg. After 10 minutes of high-quality CPR, the $EtCO_2$ rises to 40 mmHg and remains stable. What does this change most likely indicate?
a. Esophageal intubation
b. Return of spontaneous circulation
c. Hyperventilation
d. Improved CPR quality

Answer: b. Return of spontaneous circulation. Explanation: A sudden and significant rise in EtCO2 during CPR, especially to a normal range (35-45 mmHg), is strongly suggestive of return of spontaneous circulation (ROSC). This occurs because restored cardiac output dramatically increases pulmonary blood flow and thus CO2 delivery to the lungs. An initial low EtCO2 (10 mmHg) is common during cardiac arrest due to minimal pulmonary blood flow. While improved CPR quality can increase EtCO2, it typically doesn't cause such a dramatic rise to normal levels. Esophageal intubation would show very low or absent EtCO2. Hyperventilation tends to lower EtCO2. This scenario highlights the importance of continuous capnography during resuscitation for both monitoring CPR effectiveness and detecting ROSC.

37. A 64-year-old male with a history of COPD presents with shortness of breath. His SpO2 is 85% on room air. Which of the following is the most appropriate initial oxygen therapy?
a. Venturi mask at 60%
b. Non-rebreather mask at 15 L/min
c. Nasal cannula at 2 L/min
d. CPAP at 10 cmH2O

Answer: c. Nasal cannula at 2 L/min. Explanation: For COPD patients, it is crucial to avoid high oxygen concentrations to prevent suppression of the hypoxic drive. Starting with a low flow rate of 2 L/min via nasal cannula is appropriate to improve oxygenation without risking CO2 retention.

38. A patient requires precise FiO2 delivery due to variable respiratory rates. Which oxygen delivery device would be most appropriate?
a. Non-rebreather mask
b. Venturi mask
c. Nasal cannula
d. Simple face mask

Answer: b. Venturi mask. Explanation: The Venturi mask provides a precise FiO2 regardless of the patient's respiratory rate and tidal volume, making it suitable for patients who need specific oxygen concentrations.

39. A 70-year-old female with a history of chronic hypercapnia presents with worsening dyspnea. Her blood gas shows a PaCO2 of 55 mmHg and PaO2 of 50 mmHg. Which oxygen delivery device should be avoided?
a. Non-rebreather mask
b. Venturi mask at 24%
c. Nasal cannula at 1 L/min
d. CPAP at 5 cmH2O

Answer: a. Non-rebreather mask. Explanation: A non-rebreather mask can deliver high concentrations of oxygen (close to 100%), which can suppress the hypoxic drive in patients with chronic CO2 retention, leading to further respiratory depression.

40. A patient is on a Venturi mask set at 40% FiO2 with a flow rate of 8 L/min. What would happen if the flow rate is increased to 12 L/min?
a. FiO2 will increase
b. FiO2 will decrease
c. FiO2 will remain the same
d. The mask will not function properly

Answer: c. FiO2 will remain the same. Explanation: The Venturi mask is designed to deliver a specific FiO2 by mixing oxygen with room air. Increasing the flow rate will not change the FiO2, but will increase the total flow rate to the patient.

41. A 58-year-old male with a history of CHF is experiencing acute pulmonary edema. Which of the following is the most appropriate initial treatment?
a. Nasal cannula at 2 L/min
b. Non-rebreather mask at 10 L/min
c. CPAP at 10 cmH2O
d. Venturi mask at 35%

Answer: c. CPAP at 10 cmH2O. Explanation: CPAP provides continuous positive airway pressure, which helps to open alveoli, improve oxygenation, and reduce the work of breathing in patients with pulmonary edema, making it the preferred initial treatment.

42. In a hypoxic patient with an FiO2 requirement of 50%, which Venturi mask setting is appropriate?
a. Green (35%)
b. Yellow (28%)
c. Blue (24%)
d. Red (50%)

Answer: d. Red (50%). Explanation: Venturi masks are color-coded to deliver specific FiO2 levels. The red adapter typically corresponds to 50% FiO2, which matches the patient's requirement.

43. A patient with COPD is receiving oxygen therapy via nasal cannula at 1 L/min. What is the expected approximate FiO2 delivered?
a. 21%
b. 24%
c. 30%
d. 40%

Answer: b. 24%. Explanation: Each liter per minute of oxygen via nasal cannula increases the FiO2 by approximately 4%. Therefore, 1 L/min provides an FiO2 of about 24%.

44. Which of the following is a contraindication for the use of CPAP?
a. Pulmonary edema
b. Acute asthma exacerbation
c. Severe facial trauma
d. COPD exacerbation

Answer: c. Severe facial trauma. Explanation: CPAP requires a tight-fitting mask to deliver continuous positive airway pressure. Severe facial trauma may prevent an adequate seal and increase the risk of further injury or complications.

45. A patient with severe hypoxia is on a non-rebreather mask, but the reservoir bag collapses completely during inhalation. What should be the immediate action?
a. Increase the oxygen flow rate
b. Switch to a Venturi mask
c. Decrease the oxygen flow rate
d. Remove the mask

Answer: a. Increase the oxygen flow rate. Explanation: If the reservoir bag collapses completely during inhalation, it indicates an inadequate flow rate. Increasing the flow rate ensures the reservoir bag remains inflated, providing a higher concentration of oxygen to the patient.

46. A 65-year-old male with a history of COPD presents with acute respiratory distress. His SpO2 is 88% on a Venturi mask set at 28% FiO2. What is the next best step?
a. Switch to a nasal cannula at 4 L/min
b. Increase the FiO2 on the Venturi mask to 35%
c. Administer a bronchodilator
d. Switch to a non-rebreather mask

Answer: b. Increase the FiO2 on the Venturi mask to 35%. Explanation: Increasing the FiO2 on the Venturi mask allows for better oxygenation while still providing a controlled and precise concentration of oxygen, minimizing the risk of CO2 retention in COPD patients.

47. You're obtaining a 12-lead ECG on a patient with chest pain. Which of the following electrode placements is correct for lead V4?
a. 4th intercostal space, right sternal border
b. 5th intercostal space, left midclavicular line
c. 5th intercostal space, left anterior axillary line
d. 4th intercostal space, left midaxillary line

Answer: b. 5th intercostal space, left midclavicular line. Explanation: V4 is correctly placed in the 5th intercostal space at the left midclavicular line. This placement is crucial for accurate ECG interpretation, especially for anterior wall MI detection. V1 is placed in the 4th intercostal space at the right sternal border, V2 in the 4th intercostal space at the left sternal border, V3 midway between V2 and V4, V5 in the 5th intercostal space at the left anterior axillary line, and V6 in the 5th intercostal space at the left midaxillary line. Proper electrode placement ensures standardized and comparable ECG readings across patients and over time.

48. A 60-year-old male presents with chest pain. His 12-lead ECG shows ST-segment elevation in leads V2-V4 with reciprocal ST depression in leads II, III, and aVF. Which of the following best describes this STEMI location?
a. Inferior wall
b. Anterior wall
c. Lateral wall
d. Posterior wall

Answer: b. Anterior wall. Explanation: The ECG findings describe an anterior wall STEMI. ST-segment elevation in leads V2-V4 is characteristic of anterior wall myocardial infarction, typically due to occlusion of the left anterior descending (LAD) coronary artery. The reciprocal ST depression in the inferior leads (II, III, aVF) further supports this diagnosis. Inferior STEMI would show elevation in II, III, aVF; lateral in I, aVL, V5-V6; and posterior often presents with ST depression in V1-V3 and tall R waves in V1-V2. Recognizing STEMI patterns is crucial for rapid triage and treatment decisions in the prehospital setting.

49. You're assessing a 50-year-old female with palpitations. Her ECG shows a regular, wide-complex tachycardia at 150 bpm. Which of the following features would most strongly suggest ventricular tachycardia (VT) rather than supraventricular tachycardia (SVT) with aberrancy?
a. Presence of fusion beats
b. QRS duration >140 ms
c. Concordance of QRS complexes in precordial leads
d. Presence of capture beats

Answer: c. Concordance of QRS complexes in precordial leads. Explanation: While all options can suggest VT, concordance (all QRS complexes in precordial leads pointing in the same direction, either all positive or all negative) is a strong indicator of VT. This pattern is rarely seen in SVT with aberrancy. Fusion and capture beats are specific for VT but not always present. QRS duration >140 ms favors VT but can occur in SVT with aberrancy. Differentiating VT from SVT with aberrancy is crucial as their management differs significantly. VT often requires immediate cardioversion, while SVT might be managed with vagal maneuvers or adenosine.

50. A patient with known left bundle branch block (LBBB) presents with chest pain. Which of the following Sgarbossa criteria would be most specific for acute MI in the presence of LBBB?
a. ST elevation ≥1 mm concordant with the QRS complex
b. ST depression ≥1 mm in lead V1, V2, or V3
c. ST elevation ≥5 mm discordant with the QRS complex
d. ST elevation ≥1 mm in leads with a positive QRS complex

Answer: a. ST elevation ≥1 mm concordant with the QRS complex. Explanation: The Sgarbossa criteria are used to identify acute MI in the presence of LBBB, where typical STEMI criteria are less reliable. ST elevation ≥1 mm concordant with the QRS complex is the most specific criterion, with a specificity of 98%. ST depression ≥1 mm in V1-V3 is also part of the criteria but less specific. The original criteria included ST elevation ≥5 mm discordant with the QRS, but this has been modified in updated versions to use a proportional approach. ST elevation ≥1 mm in leads with a positive QRS is not part of the Sgarbossa criteria. Understanding these criteria is crucial for accurate STEMI identification in patients with LBBB.

51. You're interpreting an ECG that shows a short PR interval and a slurred upstroke of the QRS complex. What is this slurred upstroke called, and what condition does it suggest?
a. J point elevation, suggesting early repolarization
b. Delta wave, suggesting Wolff-Parkinson-White syndrome
c. Epsilon wave, suggesting arrhythmogenic right ventricular cardiomyopathy
d. U wave, suggesting hypokalemia

Answer: b. Delta wave, suggesting Wolff-Parkinson-White syndrome. Explanation: The described ECG features are characteristic of Wolff-Parkinson-White (WPW) syndrome. The slurred upstroke of the QRS complex is called a delta wave, caused by early ventricular activation via an accessory pathway. This, combined with a short PR interval (<120 ms), is diagnostic of WPW. J point elevation is seen in early repolarization but doesn't cause PR shortening. Epsilon waves are small deflections after the QRS in ARVC. U waves follow the T wave and can be prominent in hypokalemia. Recognizing WPW is crucial as these patients are at risk for rapid conduction of atrial arrhythmias and potential sudden cardiac death.

52. A 55-year-old male presents with chest pain. His ECG shows ST depression in leads V1-V3 with tall R waves in the same leads. What type of myocardial infarction should you suspect?
a. Anterior STEMI
b. Inferior STEMI
c. Lateral STEMI
d. Posterior STEMI

Answer: d. Posterior STEMI. Explanation: The ECG findings described are characteristic of a posterior wall myocardial infarction. ST depression in leads V1-V3, especially when accompanied by tall R waves in these leads, is considered a reciprocal change to posterior wall ST elevation. This occurs because the standard 12-lead ECG doesn't directly view the posterior wall. To confirm, posterior leads (V7-V9) can be used, which would show ST elevation in a true posterior MI. Recognizing these reciprocal changes is crucial for identifying posterior MIs, which might otherwise be missed. Anterior STEMI typically shows ST elevation in V1-V4, inferior in II, III, aVF, and lateral in I, aVL, V5-V6.

53. You're assessing a patient with a wide-complex tachycardia. Which of the following ECG features is most suggestive of ventricular tachycardia (VT) according to the Brugada criteria?
a. QRS duration >140 ms
b. Presence of a northwest axis (-90° to ±180°)
c. RS interval >100 ms in one precordial lead
d. Presence of AV dissociation

Answer: c. RS interval >100 ms in one precordial lead. Explanation: The Brugada criteria are used to differentiate VT from SVT with aberrancy in wide-complex tachycardias. An RS interval >100 ms in one precordial lead is one of the most specific criteria for VT. While QRS duration >140 ms suggests VT, it's less specific. A northwest axis favors VT but isn't part of the Brugada criteria. AV dissociation strongly suggests VT but isn't always visible and isn't part of these specific criteria. The Brugada algorithm states that if there's no RS complex in precordial leads, it's VT. If there is an RS complex and the longest RS interval is >100 ms, it's VT. Understanding these criteria is crucial for accurate rhythm interpretation and appropriate management in emergency situations.

54. A 40-year-old female presents with palpitations. Her ECG shows a regular narrow-complex tachycardia at 150 bpm with no visible P waves. You suspect AVNRT. Which of the following ECG findings would best support this diagnosis?
a. Presence of delta waves
b. Pseudo S waves in inferior leads and pseudo R' in V1
c. Alternating QRS amplitude (electrical alternans)
d. Progressively lengthening PR interval

Answer: b. Pseudo S waves in inferior leads and pseudo R' in V1. Explanation: In Atrioventricular Nodal Reentrant Tachycardia (AVNRT), retrograde P waves often occur simultaneously with the QRS complex, creating a pseudo R' in V1 and pseudo S waves in inferior leads. This is due to the near-simultaneous activation of atria and ventricles. Delta waves suggest Wolff-Parkinson-White syndrome. Electrical alternans is more characteristic of atrial flutter or ventricular tachycardia. A progressively lengthening PR interval is seen in Wenckebach phenomenon (Mobitz Type I AV block), not in AVNRT. Recognizing these subtle ECG findings is crucial for differentiating various supraventricular tachycardias and guiding appropriate management.

55. You're reviewing an ECG from a patient with chest pain and known left bundle branch block (LBBB). Which of the following findings would meet the Modified Sgarbossa criteria for STEMI equivalent?
a. ST elevation ≥1 mm concordant in any lead
b. ST depression ≥1 mm in lead V1, V2, or V3
c. ST/S ratio ≤ -0.25 in leads with QS or rS configuration
d. ST elevation ≥5 mm discordant with the QRS complex

Answer: c. ST/S ratio ≤ -0.25 in leads with QS or rS configuration. Explanation: The Modified Sgarbossa criteria improved upon the original criteria to better identify STEMI in the presence of LBBB. The ST/S ratio ≤ -0.25 in leads with QS or rS configuration replaced the original criterion of ST elevation ≥5 mm discordant with the QRS. This modification improved specificity while maintaining sensitivity. ST elevation ≥1 mm concordant in any lead and ST depression ≥1 mm in V1-V3 are part of both the original and modified criteria. The ≥5 mm discordant ST elevation is no longer used in the modified version. Understanding these criteria is crucial for accurate STEMI identification in patients with LBBB, where traditional STEMI criteria may not apply.

56. A 50-year-old male presents with chest pain. His ECG shows ST elevation in leads V2-V4 with Q waves in the same leads. Based on the OMI (Occlusion Myocardial Infarction) paradigm, which of the following is the most appropriate next step?
a. Administer fibrinolytics immediately
b. Transport to the nearest non-PCI capable hospital
c. Activate the cardiac catheterization lab for emergent PCI

d. Observe for 30 minutes and repeat ECG

Answer: c. Activate the cardiac catheterization lab for emergent PCI. Explanation: The OMI (Occlusion Myocardial Infarction) paradigm emphasizes early recognition of acute coronary occlusion, regardless of whether it meets traditional STEMI criteria. In this case, ST elevation with Q waves in V2-V4 strongly suggests an acute anterior wall MI with possibly some ongoing ischemia. The presence of Q waves doesn't negate the need for emergent reperfusion. The most appropriate action is to activate the cardiac catheterization lab for emergent PCI, as this offers the best chance for myocardial salvage. Fibrinolytics are generally reserved for when PCI isn't available within an appropriate timeframe. Transporting to a non-PCI capable hospital or delaying intervention could result in further myocardial damage. The OMI paradigm aims to reduce delays in reperfusion therapy for acute coronary occlusions.

57. A 60-year-old male presents with chest pain radiating to his left arm, diaphoresis, and nausea. His ECG shows ST-segment elevation in leads V2-V4. What is the most likely diagnosis?
a. Non-ST elevation myocardial infarction (NSTEMI)
b. STEMI
c. Benign early repolarization
d. Pericarditis

Answer: b. STEMI. Explanation: ST-segment elevation in leads V2-V4 indicates an anterior wall myocardial infarction, a type of STEMI. The clinical presentation of chest pain, diaphoresis, and nausea further supports this diagnosis.

58. A patient with a suspected myocardial infarction presents with pulmonary edema, jugular venous distention, and hypotension. According to the Killip classification, in which class does this patient fall?
a. Killip Class I
b. Killip Class II
c. Killip Class III
d. Killip Class IV

Answer: d. Killip Class IV. Explanation: Killip Class IV includes patients with cardiogenic shock, characterized by hypotension and evidence of poor perfusion such as pulmonary edema and jugular venous distention.

59. A 55-year-old female presents with chest pain, hypotension, distended neck veins, and muffled heart sounds. What is the most appropriate initial management step?
a. Administer aspirin
b. Perform pericardiocentesis
c. Administer nitroglycerin
d. Provide high-flow oxygen

Answer: b. Perform pericardiocentesis. Explanation: The triad of hypotension, distended neck veins, and muffled heart sounds (Beck's triad) is indicative of cardiac tamponade. Pericardiocentesis is the immediate treatment to relieve pressure on the heart.

60. A 68-year-old male presents with acute chest pain and an ECG showing diffuse ST-segment elevations and PR-segment depressions. What is the most likely diagnosis?
a. STEMI
b. NSTEMI
c. Pericarditis
d. Benign early repolarization

Answer: c. Pericarditis. Explanation: Diffuse ST-segment elevations with PR-segment depressions on ECG are characteristic findings in pericarditis, differentiating it from localized ST elevations seen in STEMI.

61. Which of the following clinical findings is NOT part of Beck's triad for diagnosing cardiac tamponade?
a. Hypotension
b. Bradycardia
c. Jugular venous distention
d. Muffled heart sounds

Answer: b. Bradycardia. Explanation: Beck's triad for cardiac tamponade includes hypotension, jugular venous distention, and muffled heart sounds. Bradycardia is not part of this triad.

62. A patient with suspected cardiogenic shock has a blood pressure of 80/50 mmHg, a heart rate of 120 bpm, and cool, clammy skin. What is the first-line pharmacologic treatment?
a. Epinephrine
b. Dopamine
c. Nitroglycerin
d. Atropine

Answer: b. Dopamine. Explanation: Dopamine is commonly used to improve cardiac output and increase blood pressure in cardiogenic shock. Epinephrine is more often used in anaphylactic shock, nitroglycerin in ischemic chest pain, and atropine in bradycardia.

63. A 72-year-old male presents with chest pain and his ECG shows ST-segment elevation in leads II, III, and aVF. Which coronary artery is most likely occluded?
a. Left anterior descending artery (LAD)
b. Right coronary artery (RCA)
c. Left circumflex artery (LCX)
d. Posterior descending artery (PDA)

Answer: b. Right coronary artery (RCA). Explanation: ST-segment elevation in leads II, III, and aVF indicates an inferior wall myocardial infarction, typically caused by occlusion of the right coronary artery.

64. Which finding differentiates benign early repolarization from pericarditis on an ECG?
a. ST-segment elevation in V2-V4
b. Absence of reciprocal ST-segment depression
c. PR-segment depression
d. Presence of Q waves

Answer: b. Absence of reciprocal ST-segment depression. Explanation: Benign early repolarization typically does not show reciprocal ST-segment depression, whereas pericarditis does not have reciprocal changes either. However, benign early repolarization usually presents with concave ST elevations and is seen in healthy individuals.

65. A 58-year-old female presents with chest pain and dyspnea. Her ECG shows ST-segment elevation in leads I, aVL, V5, and V6. What is the most likely location of the myocardial infarction?
a. Anterior wall
b. Inferior wall
c. Lateral wall
d. Septal wall

Answer: c. Lateral wall. Explanation: ST-segment elevation in leads I, aVL, V5, and V6 indicates a lateral wall myocardial infarction, typically involving the left circumflex artery.

66. A patient presents with acute myocardial infarction and severe hypotension. Which of the following is NOT a recommended initial treatment?
a. Administering fluids
b. Giving high-dose nitroglycerin
c. Using inotropes like dobutamine
d. Providing supplemental oxygen

Answer: b. Giving high-dose nitroglycerin. Explanation: High-dose nitroglycerin can further lower blood pressure and is not recommended in the setting of severe hypotension. Administering fluids, inotropes, and providing supplemental oxygen are appropriate initial treatments to stabilize the patient.

67. You arrive on scene to find a 25-year-old male victim of a motorcycle crash. He's alert but confused, with cool, pale skin. Vitals: HR 120, BP 100/60, RR 24. Which stage of hypovolemic shock is this patient most likely experiencing?
a. Compensated
b. Uncompensated
c. Irreversible
d. Decompensated

Answer: a. Compensated. Explanation: This patient is exhibiting signs of compensated hypovolemic shock. In this stage, the body's compensatory mechanisms (tachycardia, peripheral vasoconstriction) are maintaining a near-normal blood pressure despite significant blood loss (estimated 15-30% of total blood volume). The tachycardia, slight hypotension, tachypnea, and altered mental status are consistent with this stage. Uncompensated shock would show more severe hypotension, decompensated shock would have profound hypotension and organ failure, while irreversible shock represents end-stage multi-organ failure.

68. A 60-year-old female presents with sudden onset dyspnea and chest pain. She's tachypneic, has JVD, and diminished breath sounds on the right. You suspect tension pneumothorax. Which of the following is NOT a typical finding in tension pneumothorax?
a. Tracheal deviation away from the affected side
b. Hypotension
c. Narrow pulse pressure
d. Bradycardia

Answer: d. Bradycardia. Explanation: Tension pneumothorax typically causes tachycardia, not bradycardia, due to decreased venous return and compensatory sympathetic activation. The other options are consistent with tension pneumothorax: tracheal deviation away from the affected side due to mediastinal shift, hypotension due to decreased venous return, and a narrow pulse pressure due to decreased stroke volume. Tension pneumothorax is a form of obstructive shock, characterized by mechanical obstruction to blood flow. Recognition of these signs is crucial for prompt needle decompression, which can be life-saving in this rapidly progressing condition.

69. You're assessing a 30-year-old male with suspected anaphylaxis. He has diffuse urticaria, wheezing, and lip swelling. Vitals: BP 88/50, HR 120, RR 28, SpO2 92%. What is the most appropriate initial pharmacological intervention?
a. Albuterol 2.5 mg via nebulizer
b. Epinephrine 0.3 mg IM
c. Diphenhydramine 50 mg IV
d. Methylprednisolone 125 mg IV

Answer: b. Epinephrine 0.3 mg IM. Explanation: In anaphylaxis, epinephrine is the first-line treatment and should be administered immediately. The recommended adult dose is 0.3-0.5 mg of 1:1000 concentration, given intramuscularly in the lateral thigh. Epinephrine acts quickly to reverse the pathophysiological effects of anaphylaxis, including vasodilation, increased vascular permeability, and bronchospasm. While albuterol can help with bronchospasm, diphenhydramine with histamine-mediated symptoms, and steroids with preventing biphasic reactions, none of these are as crucial or life-saving as prompt epinephrine administration in anaphylactic shock.

70. A 70-year-old female presents with fever, tachypnea, and altered mental status. You suspect sepsis. Which of the following sets of criteria corresponds to a qSOFA (quick Sequential Organ Failure Assessment) score of 2?
a. RR 24, BP 100/60, GCS 14
b. RR 23, BP 95/55, GCS 13
c. RR 22, BP 90/50, GCS 15
d. RR 25, BP 85/45, GCS 14

Answer: b. RR 23, BP 95/55, GCS 13. Explanation: The qSOFA score is used to rapidly identify patients at risk of poor outcomes due to sepsis. It assigns one point each for: respiratory rate ≥22/min, systolic blood pressure ≤100 mmHg, and altered mental status (GCS <15). A score ≥2 suggests high risk. In this case, the patient meets criteria for respiratory rate (23 > 22) and altered mental status (GCS 13 < 15), but not for hypotension (95 > 100), giving a total score of 2. Understanding and quickly applying qSOFA can help EMTs identify sepsis early and initiate appropriate interventions and transport decisions.

71. You're treating a 45-year-old male in anaphylactic shock who isn't improving after the first dose of IM epinephrine. What is the most appropriate next step in management?
a. Administer a second dose of IM epinephrine after 5 minutes
b. Start an epinephrine IV infusion at 1 mcg/min
c. Administer 2 liters of normal saline bolus
d. Intubate the patient

Answer: a. Administer a second dose of IM epinephrine after 5 minutes. Explanation: In persistent anaphylaxis, a second dose of IM epinephrine can be given 5-15 minutes after the first if there's no improvement. This is the recommended next step before moving to more invasive measures. IV epinephrine infusion is typically reserved for cases refractory to IM epinephrine and is usually initiated in a hospital setting due to the risk of dosing errors. While fluid resuscitation is important in anaphylaxis, it doesn't take precedence over repeat epinephrine. Intubation may eventually be necessary but isn't the next step if oxygenation can be maintained non-invasively. The emphasis is on aggressive early use of IM epinephrine in anaphylaxis management.

72. A 55-year-old male presents with sudden onset dyspnea and chest pain. He's tachycardic, hypotensive, and has clear lung sounds bilaterally. You suspect pulmonary embolism (PE). Which of the following is NOT typically associated with acute PE?
a. Elevated JVD
b. Narrow pulse pressure
c. Unilateral leg swelling
d. Wheezing

Answer: d. Wheezing. Explanation: Wheezing is not typically associated with pulmonary embolism. PE often presents with sudden dyspnea, pleuritic chest pain, tachycardia, and hypotension, but lung sounds are usually clear. Elevated JVD can occur due to right heart strain, narrow pulse pressure from decreased cardiac output, and unilateral leg swelling may be present if the PE originated from a DVT. Understanding the presentation of PE is crucial, as it's a form of obstructive shock that can be easily confused with other conditions like MI or pneumothorax. Recognition of these signs and symptoms helps guide appropriate management and transport decisions.

73. You're assessing a 20-year-old male with a C5 spinal cord injury from a diving accident. His BP is 85/50, HR 50, and he has warm, dry skin. What type of shock is he most likely experiencing?
a. Hypovolemic shock
b. Cardiogenic shock
c. Neurogenic shock
d. Septic shock

Answer: c. Neurogenic shock. Explanation: This patient is exhibiting classic signs of neurogenic shock: hypotension with bradycardia (instead of the tachycardia seen in other forms of shock) and warm, dry skin due to loss of sympathetic tone. Neurogenic shock occurs in high spinal cord injuries (typically above T6) due to the loss of sympathetic nervous system control, leading to vasodilation and loss of cardiac accelerator nerve function. This is different from spinal shock, which refers to the temporary loss of all spinal cord function below the level of injury. Recognition of neurogenic shock is crucial for appropriate management, which often includes careful fluid resuscitation and potentially vasopressors.

74. A 65-year-old female presents with severe shortness of breath 3 days post-op from hip replacement surgery. She's tachypneic, tachycardic, and hypoxic. You suspect pulmonary embolism (PE). Which of the following is the most specific sign of PE in this scenario?
a. Tachycardia >100 bpm
b. Hypoxemia with clear lung sounds
c. Pleuritic chest pain
d. Unilateral leg swelling

Answer: b. Hypoxemia with clear lung sounds. Explanation: While all these signs can be present in PE, hypoxemia with clear lung sounds is the most specific in this context. PE causes ventilation-perfusion mismatch, leading to hypoxemia, but doesn't typically cause audible lung sounds like crackles or wheezes. Tachycardia is common but nonspecific. Pleuritic chest pain occurs in many PE cases but isn't always present. Unilateral leg swelling suggests DVT, a risk factor for PE, but may not be present in all cases. In a post-operative patient with sudden dyspnea, recognizing these signs is crucial for prompt diagnosis and management of this potentially life-threatening condition.

75. You're treating a 40-year-old female in anaphylactic shock. After two doses of IM epinephrine, she remains hypotensive with a BP of 75/40. What is the most appropriate next step in fluid resuscitation?
a. Administer 250 mL normal saline bolus
b. Administer 1 L normal saline bolus
c. Administer 2 L normal saline bolus
d. Start a dopamine drip at 5 mcg/kg/min

Answer: c. Administer 2 L normal saline bolus. Explanation: In anaphylactic shock refractory to IM epinephrine, aggressive fluid resuscitation is crucial. Adults should receive 1-2 L of isotonic crystalloid (like normal saline) rapidly. This large volume is necessary to compensate for the massive fluid shift into the interstitial space caused by increased vascular permeability in anaphylaxis. A 250 mL or 1 L bolus would be insufficient in this scenario. While vasopressors like dopamine may eventually be needed, they're not the next step before adequate fluid resuscitation has been attempted. Recognizing the need for aggressive fluid administration in addition to epinephrine is key in managing severe anaphylaxis.

76. You arrive on scene to find a 50-year-old male with severe burns over 40% of his body surface area. He's alert and oriented with the following vitals: HR 130, BP 95/60, RR 26. Based on the Parkland formula, what is the approximate fluid requirement for the first 8 hours post-burn?
a. 2 liters
b. 4 liters

c. 6 liters
d. 8 liters

Answer: c. 6 liters. Explanation: The Parkland formula estimates fluid requirements in burn patients: 4 mL × patient's weight in kg × % TBSA burned. Half of this calculated amount is given in the first 8 hours post-burn. Assuming an 80 kg patient: 4 × 80 × 40 = 12,800 mL total. Half of this (6,400 mL or about 6 liters) would be given in the first 8 hours. This aggressive fluid resuscitation is crucial in burn shock to replace fluid losses and maintain tissue perfusion. While exact calculations aren't typically done in the field, understanding the massive fluid requirements in severe burns guides initial management and helps in communicating the patient's needs to the receiving facility.

77. A 25-year-old male is found unconscious after a motor vehicle collision. His eyes open to pain, he withdraws from painful stimuli, and he makes incomprehensible sounds. What is his Glasgow Coma Scale (GCS) score?
a. 8
b. 9
c. 10
d. 11

Answer: a. 8. Explanation: The GCS score is calculated as follows: Eye opening to pain = 2, Verbal response with incomprehensible sounds = 2, Motor response with withdrawal from pain = 4. Total GCS score = 2 + 2 + 4 = 8.

78. A 30-year-old female presents with altered mental status after a fall. Using the AVPU scale, she responds to verbal stimuli but not to painful stimuli. How should her level of consciousness be recorded?
a. Alert
b. Verbal
c. Pain
d. Unresponsive

Answer: b. Verbal. Explanation: The AVPU scale assesses level of consciousness as Alert, Verbal (responds to verbal stimuli), Pain (responds to painful stimuli), and Unresponsive. This patient responds to verbal stimuli, so her level of consciousness is recorded as Verbal.

79. Which component of the SAMPLE history focuses on finding out about any medications the patient is currently taking?
a. Signs and symptoms
b. Allergies
c. Medications
d. Past medical history

Answer: c. Medications. Explanation: The "M" in SAMPLE history stands for Medications, which includes any prescriptions, over-the-counter drugs, or supplements the patient is currently taking.

80. During a rapid trauma assessment, what is the primary purpose of the secondary survey?
a. To control external bleeding
b. To assess and manage airway, breathing, and circulation
c. To identify all injuries and conditions after immediate threats to life are addressed
d. To establish patient history and perform a detailed physical examination

Answer: c. To identify all injuries and conditions after immediate threats to life are addressed. Explanation: The secondary survey in trauma assessment aims to identify all injuries and conditions after immediate life-threatening issues have been managed during the primary survey.

81. In a patient with blunt abdominal trauma, which of the following findings on a focused assessment with sonography for trauma (FAST) is most concerning?
a. Presence of free fluid in the Morrison's pouch
b. Absence of free fluid in the perisplenic area
c. Presence of bowel gas shadows
d. Normal cardiac window

Answer: a. Presence of free fluid in the Morrison's pouch. Explanation: Free fluid in the Morrison's pouch (the space between the liver and right kidney) is concerning in the context of blunt abdominal trauma, as it may indicate internal bleeding.

82. A 40-year-old male presents with severe head trauma after a fall. His GCS score is 12. Which of the following GCS components contributes to this score if he opens his eyes to speech and is confused but obeys commands?
a. Eye opening: 3, Verbal response: 4, Motor response: 5
b. Eye opening: 2, Verbal response: 4, Motor response: 6
c. Eye opening: 3, Verbal response: 3, Motor response: 6
d. Eye opening: 4, Verbal response: 2, Motor response: 6

Answer: a. Eye opening: 3, Verbal response: 4, Motor response: 5. Explanation: Eye opening to speech scores 3, confused verbal response scores 4, and obeying commands scores 5. The total GCS score is 3 + 4 + 5 = 12.

83. A 60-year-old female involved in a car accident is unresponsive. What should be the first step in the rapid trauma assessment?
a. Check for external bleeding
b. Perform a detailed head-to-toe examination
c. Assess airway, breathing, and circulation
d. Obtain a SAMPLE history

Answer: c. Assess airway, breathing, and circulation. Explanation: The first step in a rapid trauma assessment is to assess and manage the airway, breathing, and circulation to address any immediate life threats.

84. During a SAMPLE history collection, which of the following would be categorized under "P" for past medical history?
a. The patient's use of antihypertensive medication
b. The patient's allergy to penicillin
c. The patient's history of previous heart attacks
d. The patient's last meal time

Answer: c. The patient's history of previous heart attacks. Explanation: "P" for past medical history includes any significant past illnesses or surgeries, such as a history of heart attacks.

85. In a trauma patient, what is the primary purpose of using the AVPU scale during the initial assessment?
a. To establish the patient's baseline level of consciousness
b. To determine the need for immediate defibrillation
c. To assess pain response for injury severity
d. To check for spinal cord injury

Answer: a. To establish the patient's baseline level of consciousness. Explanation: The AVPU scale helps quickly determine the patient's level of consciousness, which is critical for guiding further assessment and management.

86. A 22-year-old male presents after a motorcycle accident with deformity and severe pain in his left thigh. During the rapid trauma assessment, you find that he has a weak radial pulse and is hypotensive. What is the most appropriate next step?
a. Apply a traction splint to the left leg
b. Perform a needle decompression
c. Administer IV fluids and control external bleeding
d. Obtain a detailed history of the accident

Answer: c. Administer IV fluids and control external bleeding. Explanation: In the context of hypotension and a weak radial pulse, the priority is to manage shock by administering IV fluids and controlling any external bleeding. Splinting the leg should be done after stabilizing the patient's hemodynamic status.

87. You arrive on scene to find a 30-year-old male with a deep laceration to the right thigh from a chainsaw accident. There's pulsatile bleeding, and direct pressure isn't controlling it. What's the most appropriate next step in hemorrhage control?
a. Apply a hemostatic agent
b. Elevate the limb above the heart
c. Apply a tourniquet proximal to the wound
d. Pack the wound with sterile gauze

Answer: c. Apply a tourniquet proximal to the wound. Explanation: In cases of severe, pulsatile extremity bleeding uncontrolled by direct pressure, immediate tourniquet application is the most appropriate next step. Tourniquets are highly effective for controlling life-threatening extremity hemorrhage and should be applied proximal to the wound, as close to the torso as possible. Hemostatic agents are more appropriate for junctional areas where tourniquets can't be applied. Limb elevation is no longer recommended as a primary intervention for severe bleeding. Wound packing alone may be insufficient for this level of arterial bleeding. Early, proper tourniquet use has been shown to significantly improve outcomes in severe extremity hemorrhage.

88. A 25-year-old female presents with a deep groin wound from a stabbing. The wound is actively bleeding despite direct pressure. What's the most appropriate bleeding control technique for this junctional injury?
a. Apply a tourniquet to the proximal thigh
b. Pack the wound with hemostatic gauze
c. Apply a pelvic binder
d. Clamp the bleeding vessel

Answer: b. Pack the wound with hemostatic gauze. Explanation: For junctional hemorrhage in areas like the groin, where tourniquets can't be effectively applied, wound packing with hemostatic gauze is the most appropriate technique. Hemostatic agents enhance clot formation and, when combined with direct pressure, can effectively control severe bleeding in these areas. Tourniquets are not effective for junctional areas. A pelvic binder wouldn't address this specific wound. Clamping vessels in the field is beyond the scope of practice for EMTs and can cause additional damage. Proper wound packing technique involves filling the entire wound cavity with gauze and maintaining firm, direct pressure.

89. You're treating a patient with a suspected pelvic fracture after a motor vehicle collision. The patient is hypotensive and complains of pelvic pain. What's the most appropriate initial management for potential pelvic bleeding?
a. Apply a pelvic binder
b. Position the patient in Trendelenburg
c. Administer tranexamic acid (TXA)
d. Perform external rotation of the hips

Answer: a. Apply a pelvic binder. Explanation: In suspected pelvic fractures with signs of hemodynamic instability, applying a pelvic binder is the most appropriate initial management. Pelvic binders reduce pelvic volume, stabilize the fracture, and can tamponade bleeding from cancellous bone and venous plexuses. This should be done early in the treatment process. Trendelenburg positioning is not recommended for pelvic fractures. While TXA can be beneficial in trauma, it's not the first-line treatment for pelvic fractures. External rotation of the hips could worsen the injury and is contraindicated. Proper application of pelvic binders can significantly reduce mortality in unstable pelvic fractures.

90. A 40-year-old male presents with a penetrating abdominal injury. He's conscious but hypotensive with a BP of 80/50. What's the appropriate blood pressure target for permissive hypotension in this scenario?
a. Systolic BP > 110 mmHg
b. Mean Arterial Pressure > 65 mmHg
c. Systolic BP 80-90 mmHg
d. Maintain baseline BP

Answer: c. Systolic BP 80-90 mmHg. Explanation: In penetrating trauma, permissive hypotension is often employed to balance organ perfusion with the risk of exacerbating bleeding. A target systolic BP of 80-90 mmHg is generally recommended. This approach, also known as "hypotensive resuscitation," aims to maintain critical organ perfusion while avoiding the potential for clot disruption and increased bleeding that can occur with higher pressures. It's important to note that this approach is contraindicated in patients with traumatic brain injury, where higher cerebral perfusion pressures are necessary. The goal is to maintain the minimally acceptable blood pressure until definitive hemorrhage control can be achieved.

91. You've applied a tourniquet to a patient's left arm for severe bleeding. What's the maximum recommended time the tourniquet can remain in place before risking permanent tissue damage?
a. 30 minutes
b. 1 hour
c. 2 hours
d. 4 hours

Answer: c. 2 hours. Explanation: The generally accepted maximum time for continuous tourniquet application is 2 hours. Beyond this time, the risk of permanent neurovascular damage and tissue necrosis increases significantly. However, in a life-threatening situation, saving a life takes precedence over limb preservation. It's crucial to note the time of tourniquet application and communicate this to receiving medical personnel. In prolonged transport situations, reassessing the need for the tourniquet and potentially converting to other hemorrhage control methods under medical direction may be considered. However, this should only be done if bleeding can be controlled by other means and if trained to do so.

92. A 35-year-old female presents with a deep laceration to the scalp that's bleeding profusely. Direct pressure alone isn't controlling the bleeding. What's the most appropriate next step?
a. Apply a tourniquet around the forehead
b. Use hemostatic gauze to pack the wound
c. Apply pressure to bilateral carotid arteries
d. Rapidly infuse 2L of normal saline

Answer: b. Use hemostatic gauze to pack the wound. Explanation: For scalp wounds with profuse bleeding uncontrolled by direct pressure, packing with hemostatic gauze is the most appropriate next step. The scalp is highly vascularized, and hemostatic agents can significantly enhance clot formation. Tourniquets are not applicable to the head. Bilateral carotid artery pressure is dangerous and ineffective for scalp bleeding. Rapid fluid infusion doesn't address the primary problem of blood loss and could exacerbate bleeding by increasing blood pressure. When using hemostatic gauze, it's important to pack the entire wound cavity firmly and maintain direct pressure for at least 3-5 minutes to allow clot formation.

93. You're treating a patient with a gunshot wound to the upper thigh. A tourniquet has been applied, but bleeding persists. What's the most appropriate next step?
a. Apply a second tourniquet proximal to the first
b. Loosen the tourniquet and reapply
c. Replace the tourniquet with a pressure dressing
d. Apply direct digital pressure to the femoral artery

Answer: a. Apply a second tourniquet proximal to the first. Explanation: If bleeding persists after proper application of a tourniquet, the most appropriate next step is to apply a second tourniquet proximal (closer to the torso) to the first. This approach is endorsed by the Committee on Tactical Combat Casualty Care (CoTCCC) for situations where a single tourniquet is ineffective. Loosening and reapplying the original tourniquet could exacerbate bleeding. Replacing with a pressure dressing would be a step backward in hemorrhage control. Direct digital pressure on the femoral artery is not a sustainable or recommended technique. The key is to achieve complete arterial occlusion to stop the bleeding.

94. A 50-year-old male presents with a severe nosebleed following facial trauma. Despite pinching the nose, bleeding continues profusely. What's the most effective next step in managing this hemorrhage?
a. Insert nasal tampons
b. Apply ice to the bridge of the nose
c. Use oxymetazoline nasal spray
d. Perform anterior nasal packing with hemostatic gauze

Answer: d. Perform anterior nasal packing with hemostatic gauze. Explanation: For severe nosebleeds uncontrolled by pinching, anterior nasal packing with hemostatic gauze is the most effective next step. This technique combines the benefits of mechanical pressure with enhanced clot formation provided by hemostatic agents. Nasal tampons without hemostatic properties may be less effective. Ice application can help reduce swelling but isn't a primary hemorrhage control technique. Oxymetazoline can help for minor nosebleeds but is insufficient for severe trauma-related epistaxis. When packing, it's important to use an appropriate amount of gauze to fill the nasal cavity without over-packing, which could damage sensitive structures.

95. You're treating a patient with a pelvic fracture and have applied a pelvic binder. The patient remains hypotensive with a BP of 75/40. What's the most appropriate fluid resuscitation strategy?
a. Rapid infusion of 2L normal saline
b. Administer 250mL normal saline boluses, reassessing after each
c. Start a norepinephrine drip at 0.1 mcg/kg/min
d. Transfuse 2 units of O-negative packed red blood cells

Answer: b. Administer 250mL normal saline boluses, reassessing after each. Explanation: In the setting of suspected ongoing internal bleeding from a pelvic fracture, a cautious fluid resuscitation approach is warranted. Small boluses (250mL) of isotonic crystalloid with reassessment after each is the most appropriate strategy. This allows for some volume replacement while avoiding excessive fluid administration that could exacerbate bleeding by increasing blood pressure and disrupting clot formation. Rapid large-volume infusion could be harmful. Starting vasopressors without adequate volume resuscitation isn't recommended. Blood transfusion might eventually be necessary but isn't typically initiated in the prehospital setting without specific protocols. The goal is to maintain perfusion (often accepting lower-than-normal blood pressures) until definitive hemorrhage control can be achieved.

96. A 28-year-old male presents with a partial amputation of the left hand from a industrial accident. There's severe bleeding from the wound. After applying a tourniquet to the forearm, what's the most appropriate way to manage the amputated part?
a. Place it directly on ice

b. Wrap it in saline-soaked gauze, place in a plastic bag, and put the bag on ice
c. Immerse it in a sterile saline solution
d. Apply a tourniquet to the amputated part to prevent blood loss

Answer: b. Wrap it in saline-soaked gauze, place in a plastic bag, and put the bag on ice. Explanation: Proper management of an amputated part is crucial for potential reattachment. The correct method is to wrap the part in saline-moistened gauze, place it in a clean plastic bag, and then put this bag on ice. This method prevents direct contact with ice (which can cause frostbite damage) while keeping the part cool to reduce metabolic demands. Direct ice contact can cause tissue damage. Simple immersion in saline doesn't provide necessary cooling. Applying a tourniquet to the amputated part is unnecessary and potentially harmful. Proper care of the amputated part, along with effective hemorrhage control and rapid transport, gives the best chance for successful reattachment.

97. A 25-year-old male presents with a painful and swollen ankle after a basketball game. According to the Ottawa ankle rules, which of the following findings would indicate the need for an X-ray?
a. Pain over the medial malleolus
b. Ability to bear weight immediately after injury
c. Pain over the midfoot
d. No pain on palpation of the lateral malleolus

Answer: a. Pain over the medial malleolus. Explanation: The Ottawa ankle rules state that an X-ray is indicated if there is pain at the malleolar zone and tenderness over the posterior edge or tip of either malleolus, or if the patient cannot bear weight both immediately after the injury and in the emergency department.

98. A 68-year-old female presents with a wrist deformity after a fall on an outstretched hand. Her wrist is dorsally displaced and angulated. What type of fracture does she most likely have?
a. Colles' fracture
b. Smith's fracture
c. Barton's fracture
d. Scaphoid fracture

Answer: a. Colles' fracture. Explanation: A Colles' fracture is a distal radius fracture with dorsal displacement and angulation, typically resulting from a fall on an outstretched hand. In contrast, a Smith's fracture involves volar displacement.

99. Which type of pelvic fracture is characterized by anteroposterior compression and involves disruption of the symphysis pubis and widening of the pelvic ring?
a. Lateral compression (LC)
b. Anteroposterior compression (APC)
c. Vertical shear (VS)
d. Open book fracture

Answer: b. Anteroposterior compression (APC). Explanation: Anteroposterior compression (APC) pelvic fractures are characterized by disruption of the symphysis pubis and widening of the pelvic ring, resembling an "open book" appearance on imaging.

100. A 30-year-old male presents with a femur fracture after a motor vehicle collision. Which of the following is a contraindication for applying a traction splint?
a. Closed midshaft femur fracture
b. Open femur fracture with visible bone ends
c. Isolated femur fracture without pelvic injury
d. Femur fracture with neurovascular compromise

Answer: b. Open femur fracture with visible bone ends. Explanation: Traction splints are contraindicated in open femur fractures with visible bone ends, as they can exacerbate the injury and increase the risk of infection.

101. A 45-year-old male presents with an open tibial fracture after falling from a height. What is the first step in the management of this open fracture?
a. Immediate surgical debridement
b. Administration of intravenous antibiotics
c. Application of a plaster cast
d. Perform closed reduction

Answer: b. Administration of intravenous antibiotics. Explanation: The first step in managing an open fracture is to administer intravenous antibiotics as soon as possible to reduce the risk of infection. Surgical debridement and stabilization will follow.

102. A patient presents with knee pain after a fall. According to the Ottawa knee rules, which of the following findings indicates the need for an X-ray?
a. Age 50 years or older
b. Ability to flex the knee to 90 degrees
c. No tenderness at the head of the fibula
d. Ability to bear weight both immediately and in the emergency department

Answer: a. Age 50 years or older. Explanation: The Ottawa knee rules indicate an X-ray is needed if the patient is aged 55 or older, has tenderness at the head of the fibula, isolated tenderness of the patella, cannot flex the knee to 90 degrees, or is unable to bear weight both immediately and in the emergency department.

103. Which of the following traction splinting techniques is most appropriate for a midshaft femur fracture?
a. Hare traction splint
b. Sager traction splint
c. SAM splint
d. Vacuum splint

Answer: a. Hare traction splint. Explanation: The Hare traction splint is specifically designed for midshaft femur fractures, providing continuous traction to align the fracture and reduce pain and further injury.

104. Which of the following antibiotics is commonly used as initial empirical treatment for open fractures?
a. Vancomycin
b. Cefazolin
c. Ciprofloxacin
d. Amoxicillin

Answer: b. Cefazolin. Explanation: Cefazolin is commonly used as initial empirical antibiotic treatment for open fractures due to its broad-spectrum coverage against gram-positive organisms, particularly Staphylococcus aureus.

105. A 22-year-old female presents with a distal radius fracture with volar displacement after falling on her flexed wrist. What type of fracture does she most likely have?
a. Colles' fracture
b. Smith's fracture
c. Barton's fracture
d. Scaphoid fracture

Answer: b. Smith's fracture. Explanation: A Smith's fracture is a distal radius fracture with volar displacement, typically resulting from a fall on a flexed wrist.

106. Which of the following findings differentiates an APC pelvic fracture from an LC pelvic fracture?
a. Disruption of the symphysis pubis
b. Lateral compression forces
c. Vertical displacement of the pelvis
d. Presence of a stable pelvic ring

Answer: a. Disruption of the symphysis pubis. Explanation: Anteroposterior compression (APC) pelvic fractures are characterized by disruption of the symphysis pubis, while lateral compression (LC) fractures are caused by lateral forces compressing the pelvis, and vertical shear (VS) fractures involve vertical displacement.

107. You're assessing a 20-year-old football player who took a hard hit during a game. He's conscious but confused. Which of the following is NOT a component of the SCAT5 (Sport Concussion Assessment Tool 5) immediate assessment?
a. Glasgow Coma Scale
b. Cervical spine assessment
c. Pupillary light reflex
d. Balance examination

Answer: d. Balance examination. Explanation: While balance examination is part of the SCAT5, it's not included in the immediate on-field assessment. The immediate assessment focuses on red flags, observable signs, memory assessment, GCS, and cervical spine assessment. The balance examination is part of the office or off-field assessment. The SCAT5 is designed to provide a standardized approach to concussion assessment, with different components for immediate and later evaluation. Understanding the components and timing of these assessments is crucial for proper concussion management in sports and other settings.

108. A 45-year-old male presents with a severe headache and progressive drowsiness following a fall. CT scan reveals a crescent-shaped hyperdense lesion adjacent to the inner table of the skull. What is the most likely diagnosis?
a. Epidural hematoma
b. Subdural hematoma
c. Subarachnoid hemorrhage
d. Intracerebral hemorrhage

Answer: b. Subdural hematoma. Explanation: The crescent-shaped hyperdense lesion adjacent to the inner table of the skull is characteristic of a subdural hematoma. Subdural hematomas typically result from tearing of bridging veins and can present with a "lucid interval" followed by progressive symptoms. Epidural hematomas are typically lens-shaped and do not cross suture lines. Subarachnoid hemorrhages appear as hyperdense blood in the subarachnoid space. Intracerebral hemorrhages are typically more focal and within the brain parenchyma. Understanding these radiographic appearances is crucial for EMTs in communicating with receiving facilities and anticipating patient needs.

109. You're assessing a 30-year-old female involved in a high-speed MVA. She's alert and oriented with no neurological deficits. Which of the following findings would indicate the need for spinal motion restriction according to the NEXUS criteria?
a. Complaint of neck pain
b. History of osteoporosis
c. Presence of seat belt sign on the neck
d. Ability to rotate neck 45 degrees to each side

Answer: a. Complaint of neck pain. Explanation: According to the NEXUS (National Emergency X-Radiography Utilization Study) criteria, spinal motion restriction is indicated if there is midline cervical spine tenderness. A complaint of neck pain would necessitate further assessment for this tenderness. The NEXUS criteria state that cervical spine imaging (and thus spinal motion restriction) is not necessary if the patient meets all of the following: no midline cervical tenderness, no focal neurologic deficit, normal alertness, no intoxication, and no painful distracting injury. Osteoporosis alone doesn't necessitate restriction. A seat belt sign warrants careful assessment but isn't a NEXUS criterion. Neck rotation is part of the Canadian C-spine Rule, not NEXUS.

110. A 60-year-old male presents with weakness and loss of pain and temperature sensation in the right leg and left arm following a fall. What is the most likely diagnosis?
a. Central cord syndrome
b. Brown-Séquard syndrome
c. Anterior cord syndrome
d. Cauda equina syndrome

Answer: b. Brown-Séquard syndrome. Explanation: The presentation of ipsilateral weakness and contralateral loss of pain and temperature sensation is characteristic of Brown-Séquard syndrome. This syndrome results from a hemisection of the spinal cord, affecting the corticospinal tract (causing ipsilateral weakness) and the spinothalamic tract (causing contralateral loss of pain and temperature sensation). Central cord syndrome typically presents with greater weakness in the upper extremities than lower. Anterior cord syndrome would cause bilateral loss of motor function and pain/temperature sensation below the level of injury. Cauda equina syndrome affects the lumbar nerve roots and typically presents with saddle anesthesia and bowel/bladder dysfunction.

111. A 25-year-old male is brought in unconscious after a motorcycle accident. His left pupil is dilated and nonreactive, and his right arm is extending abnormally. What type of herniation syndrome is this patient most likely experiencing?
a. Central herniation
b. Uncal herniation
c. Tonsillar herniation
d. Upward herniation

Answer: b. Uncal herniation. Explanation: The presentation of a dilated, nonreactive pupil (often called a "blown pupil") combined with abnormal arm extension on the opposite side is highly suggestive of uncal herniation. In this condition, the uncus of the temporal lobe herniates through the tentorial notch, compressing the oculomotor nerve (causing pupillary dilation) and often the cerebral peduncle (causing contralateral motor symptoms). This is a neurosurgical emergency requiring immediate intervention. Central herniation typically presents with bilateral pupillary changes and progressive loss of consciousness. Tonsillar herniation affects the brainstem and can cause respiratory arrest. Upward herniation is rare and typically occurs after decompression of infratentorial lesions.

112. You're assessing a 40-year-old female who fell from a ladder. She complains of neck pain but has no neurological deficits. According to the Canadian C-spine Rule, which of the following would allow you to clear the cervical spine without imaging?
a. Patient age over 65 years
b. Ability to actively rotate neck 45 degrees to each side
c. Presence of paresthesias in the extremities
d. Injury occurred more than 48 hours ago

Answer: b. Ability to actively rotate neck 45 degrees to each side. Explanation: The Canadian C-spine Rule allows clearance of the cervical spine without imaging if the patient can actively rotate their neck 45 degrees to each side, provided they meet other criteria (e.g., no high-risk factors, age < 65). This rule is used in alert and stable trauma patients. Age over 65 is actually a high-risk factor that would necessitate imaging. Paresthesias in the extremities are a concerning symptom requiring further evaluation. The timing of injury (>48 hours) is not a criterion in this rule. Understanding and correctly applying clinical decision rules like the Canadian C-spine Rule can help reduce unnecessary imaging while ensuring patient safety.

113. A 50-year-old male presents with progressive weakness in all four limbs following a fall. The weakness is more pronounced in the upper extremities than the lower. What is the most likely diagnosis?

a. Brown-Séquard syndrome
b. Central cord syndrome
c. Anterior cord syndrome
d. Posterior cord syndrome

Answer: b. Central cord syndrome. Explanation: Central cord syndrome typically presents with greater weakness in the upper extremities compared to the lower extremities, often accompanied by sensory deficits and bladder dysfunction. It's most commonly seen in older individuals with underlying cervical spondylosis who experience hyperextension injuries. Brown-Séquard syndrome would present with ipsilateral weakness and contralateral loss of pain/temperature sensation. Anterior cord syndrome causes bilateral loss of motor function and pain/temperature sensation below the level of injury. Posterior cord syndrome primarily affects proprioception and vibration sense. Recognizing these spinal cord injury patterns is crucial for proper management and early neurosurgical consultation when necessary.

114. You're assessing a 35-year-old male with a head injury. He's confused and becoming progressively drowsy. What's the most appropriate next step in management?
a. Administer mannitol 1 g/kg IV
b. Elevate the head of the bed to 30 degrees
c. Hyperventilate to a target EtCO2 of 30-35 mmHg
d. Ensure SpO2 > 90% and prevent hypotension

Answer: d. Ensure SpO2 > 90% and prevent hypotension. Explanation: In a patient with a head injury showing signs of increased intracranial pressure (confusion, drowsiness), the most crucial initial steps are to ensure adequate oxygenation (SpO2 > 90%) and prevent hypotension (typically maintaining systolic BP > 90 mmHg). These measures help prevent secondary brain injury. Mannitol administration is typically done in hospital settings under specific protocols. While mild head elevation can be beneficial, it's not the most critical first step. Hyperventilation to EtCO2 30-35 mmHg is no longer routinely recommended due to the risk of cerebral vasoconstriction and potential worsening of ischemia. The focus should be on normoventilation (EtCO2 35-45 mmHg) unless there are signs of impending herniation.

115. A 22-year-old female presents with a severe headache and vomiting 12 hours after a minor head injury. She's alert but has a right-sided facial droop. What is the most likely diagnosis?
a. Concussion
b. Epidural hematoma
c. Subdural hematoma
d. Second impact syndrome

Answer: b. Epidural hematoma. Explanation: The presentation of a "lucid interval" followed by rapid neurological deterioration (in this case, facial droop) is classic for an epidural hematoma. Epidural hematomas typically result from tearing of the middle meningeal artery and can present with a brief loss of consciousness, followed by a lucid period, and then rapid decline. This is a neurosurgical emergency requiring immediate intervention. Concussions typically don't cause focal neurological deficits like facial droop. Subdural hematomas usually have a more gradual onset of symptoms. Second impact syndrome occurs when a second concussion is sustained before the first has fully healed and presents differently. Recognition of this classic epidural hematoma presentation is crucial for rapid triage and transport to an appropriate facility.

116. You're assessing a 28-year-old male who fell from a second-story window. He's alert and oriented but complains of severe back pain and can't move his legs. You note a loss of sensation below the umbilicus. What's the most appropriate immediate management?
a. Apply a cervical collar and perform log roll onto a backboard
b. Assist the patient to a seated position to assess lower extremity strength
c. Maintain spinal motion restriction and transport in a supine position
d. Administer high-dose methylprednisolone 30 mg/kg IV bolus

Answer: c. Maintain spinal motion restriction and transport in a supine position. Explanation: In a patient with suspected spinal cord injury (indicated by the motor and sensory deficits), maintaining spinal motion restriction and transporting in a supine position is crucial to prevent further injury. While a cervical collar may be appropriate, log rolling onto a backboard is no longer routinely recommended due to the risk of causing further movement of the spine. Assisting to a seated position could exacerbate the injury. High-dose methylprednisolone is no longer routinely recommended in the prehospital setting for acute spinal cord injury due to limited evidence of benefit and potential risks. The focus should be on maintaining spinal alignment, ensuring adequate oxygenation and perfusion, and rapid transport to a trauma center capable of managing spinal cord injuries.

117. A 45-year-old male presents with severe respiratory distress and unilateral absent breath sounds following a car accident. His blood pressure is 90/60 mmHg, heart rate is 130 bpm, and jugular veins are distended. Where is the most appropriate site for needle decompression in this patient?
a. Second intercostal space, midclavicular line
b. Fourth intercostal space, anterior axillary line
c. Fifth intercostal space, midaxillary line
d. Second intercostal space, midaxillary line

Answer: a. Second intercostal space, midclavicular line. Explanation: The most appropriate site for needle decompression in a tension pneumothorax is the second intercostal space at the midclavicular line, as this site provides rapid decompression to relieve the pressure in the pleural space.

118. A patient presents with paradoxical chest wall movement following a blunt trauma to the chest. What is the most likely diagnosis and initial management?
a. Simple pneumothorax; chest tube insertion
b. Flail chest; positive pressure ventilation
c. Cardiac tamponade; pericardiocentesis
d. Massive hemothorax; immediate thoracotomy

Answer: b. Flail chest; positive pressure ventilation. Explanation: Paradoxical chest wall movement is a hallmark sign of flail chest, which occurs when multiple rib fractures create a segment that moves independently from the rest of the chest wall. Initial management includes positive pressure ventilation to stabilize the chest wall and improve oxygenation.

119. A 60-year-old female presents with chest pain, hypotension, jugular venous distention, and muffled heart sounds. Which condition is most likely present, and what distinguishes it from pericarditis?
a. Cardiac tamponade; presence of Beck's triad
b. Pericarditis; diffuse ST-segment elevation on ECG
c. Cardiac tamponade; PR-segment depression on ECG
d. Pericarditis; pulsus paradoxus

Answer: a. Cardiac tamponade; presence of Beck's triad. Explanation: Cardiac tamponade is characterized by Beck's triad: hypotension, jugular venous distention, and muffled heart sounds. Pericarditis typically presents with diffuse ST-segment elevation and PR-segment depression on ECG, but not Beck's triad.

120. A patient presents with diminished breath sounds on the left side, hypotension, and respiratory distress following a penetrating chest injury. Chest X-ray reveals more than 1,500 mL of blood in the pleural cavity. What is the most appropriate immediate treatment?
a. Chest tube insertion and fluid resuscitation
b. Needle decompression
c. Observation and monitoring
d. Pericardiocentesis

Answer: a. Chest tube insertion and fluid resuscitation. Explanation: A massive hemothorax, defined by the accumulation of more than 1,500 mL of blood in the pleural cavity, requires immediate chest tube insertion to drain the blood and fluid resuscitation to manage shock.

121. A 12-year-old male is struck in the chest by a baseball and collapses. He is found to be pulseless and unresponsive. What is the most likely condition, and what is the first step in management?
a. Cardiac tamponade; pericardiocentesis
b. Tension pneumothorax; needle decompression
c. Commotio cordis; immediate defibrillation
d. Massive hemothorax; chest tube insertion

Answer: c. Commotio cordis; immediate defibrillation. Explanation: Commotio cordis is a sudden cardiac arrest caused by a blunt chest impact, often seen in young athletes. Immediate defibrillation is critical to restore a normal heart rhythm.

122. During the assessment of a patient with blunt chest trauma, you observe paradoxical motion of a segment of the chest wall. Which complication is most commonly associated with this condition?
a. Simple pneumothorax
b. Cardiac tamponade
c. Flail chest
d. Pulmonary contusion

Answer: c. Flail chest. Explanation: Paradoxical motion of a segment of the chest wall indicates flail chest, where multiple rib fractures result in a segment that moves independently from the rest of the chest wall, often leading to underlying pulmonary contusion.

123. A 55-year-old male presents with chest pain and hypotension after a stab wound to the chest. The ECG shows electrical alternans. What condition does this suggest, and what is the definitive treatment?
a. Tension pneumothorax; needle decompression
b. Cardiac tamponade; pericardiocentesis
c. Massive hemothorax; chest tube insertion
d. Myocardial contusion; supportive care

Answer: b. Cardiac tamponade; pericardiocentesis. Explanation: Electrical alternans on ECG, combined with chest pain and hypotension, suggests cardiac tamponade. Pericardiocentesis is the definitive treatment to remove the accumulating fluid around the heart.

124. A 30-year-old female with blunt chest trauma presents with signs of shock and decreased breath sounds on the left side. Her blood pressure is 80/60 mmHg. What is the initial intervention?
a. Needle decompression
b. Chest tube insertion
c. Pericardiocentesis
d. Fluid resuscitation

Answer: b. Chest tube insertion. Explanation: In a patient with blunt chest trauma, signs of shock, and decreased breath sounds, a hemothorax is suspected. The initial intervention is chest tube insertion to drain blood from the pleural space and improve breathing.

125. A patient presents with severe shortness of breath and jugular venous distention following a chest injury. The trachea is deviated to the right. What is the most likely diagnosis?
a. Left-sided tension pneumothorax
b. Cardiac tamponade
c. Right-sided massive hemothorax
d. Flail chest

Answer: a. Left-sided tension pneumothorax. Explanation: Severe shortness of breath, jugular venous distention, and tracheal deviation to the right suggest a left-sided tension pneumothorax, where air trapped in the pleural space increases pressure and shifts mediastinal structures.

126. A 40-year-old male presents with penetrating chest trauma and respiratory distress. Breath sounds are absent on the affected side. Which finding would differentiate a tension pneumothorax from a massive hemothorax?
a. Tracheal deviation towards the affected side

b. Hyperresonance on percussion of the affected side
c. Hypotension and tachycardia
d. Jugular venous distention

Answer: b. Hyperresonance on percussion of the affected side. Explanation: Hyperresonance on percussion indicates the presence of air, which is consistent with a tension pneumothorax. A massive hemothorax would present with dullness to percussion due to the presence of blood in the pleural space.

127. You're assessing a patient involved in a high-speed MVC with complaints of abdominal pain. You note a linear bruise across the abdomen. What is the most concerning potential injury associated with this "seat belt sign"?
a. Liver laceration
b. Splenic rupture
c. Pancreatic injury
d. Small bowel perforation

Answer: d. Small bowel perforation. Explanation: The "seat belt sign," a linear bruise across the abdomen following a MVC, is highly associated with small bowel perforation. This injury occurs due to the sudden deceleration causing the small bowel to tear at fixed points, often where it's compressed against the vertebral column by the seat belt. While liver, splenic, and pancreatic injuries can occur in blunt abdominal trauma, they're less specifically associated with the seat belt sign. The presence of this sign should raise high suspicion for small bowel injury, which may not be immediately apparent on initial assessment or even early imaging studies. Early recognition of this sign is crucial for appropriate triage and management decisions.

128. During a FAST exam on a trauma patient, you observe free fluid in the hepatorenal recess. This space is also known as:
a. Morison's pouch
b. Koller's pouch
c. Rutherford Morison's space
d. Hartmann's pouch

Answer: a. Morison's pouch. Explanation: The hepatorenal recess, commonly known as Morison's pouch, is the potential space between the liver and right kidney. It's a key area examined in the FAST (Focused Assessment with Sonography in Trauma) exam as it's often the first place where free intraperitoneal fluid accumulates in a supine patient. This space is named after James Rutherford Morison, a British surgeon. Koller's pouch is in the female pelvis, Rutherford Morison's space is another name for Morison's pouch (not commonly used), and Hartmann's pouch is part of the gallbladder. Understanding the anatomy and terminology of FAST exam landmarks is crucial for accurate interpretation and communication of findings.

129. A 40-year-old male presents with severe abdominal pain 48 hours after a fall from height. You note bluish discoloration around the umbilicus. What sign is this, and what does it suggest?
a. Grey Turner's sign, suggesting retroperitoneal hemorrhage
b. Cullen's sign, suggesting retroperitoneal hemorrhage
c. Fox's sign, suggesting pancreatic injury

d. Bryant's sign, suggesting splenic rupture

Answer: b. Cullen's sign, suggesting retroperitoneal hemorrhage. Explanation: Bluish discoloration around the umbilicus is known as Cullen's sign. It suggests retroperitoneal hemorrhage, often from a source like a ruptured abdominal aortic aneurysm or pancreatic hemorrhage. The delayed presentation (48 hours post-injury) is typical, as it takes time for blood to track through tissue planes to become visible at the skin surface. Grey Turner's sign presents as bruising on the flanks and also suggests retroperitoneal hemorrhage. Fox's sign (ecchymosis of the inguinal ligament) can indicate retroperitoneal hemorrhage but is less common. Bryant's sign is not a recognized medical term in this context. Recognition of these signs is important for identifying potentially life-threatening internal injuries that may not be immediately apparent.

130. You're performing a FAST exam on a trauma patient. In which quadrant would you be most likely to detect free fluid from a splenic injury?
a. Right upper quadrant
b. Left upper quadrant
c. Right lower quadrant
d. Left lower quadrant

Answer: b. Left upper quadrant. Explanation: In the FAST exam, free fluid from a splenic injury is most likely to be detected in the left upper quadrant, specifically in the splenorenal recess. The FAST exam typically includes four views: right upper quadrant (hepatorenal recess), left upper quadrant (splenorenal recess), pelvic view, and subxiphoid cardiac view. The spleen is located in the left upper quadrant, so fluid from a splenic injury would typically accumulate in this area first. The right upper quadrant view assesses for fluid around the liver, the right lower quadrant is not a standard FAST view, and the left lower quadrant would be part of the pelvic view. Understanding the anatomical correlations in the FAST exam is crucial for accurate interpretation and communication of findings.

131. A patient presents with evisceration following an abdominal stab wound. What is the most appropriate immediate management?
a. Attempt to replace the organs into the abdominal cavity
b. Cover the exposed viscera with dry, sterile dressings
c. Irrigate the exposed organs with sterile saline
d. Cover with moist, sterile dressings and secure with an occlusive dressing

Answer: d. Cover with moist, sterile dressings and secure with an occlusive dressing. Explanation: The most appropriate immediate management for evisceration is to cover the exposed viscera with moist, sterile dressings and secure them with an occlusive dressing. This approach protects the organs from further contamination and prevents desiccation. Attempting to replace the organs risks further injury and contamination. Dry dressings can adhere to the organs and cause damage when removed. While irrigation might seem logical, it's not recommended in the field as it can spread contamination and doesn't provide any significant benefit over moist dressings. The goal is to stabilize the situation for rapid transport to a surgical facility. Remember, do not attempt to remove any impaled objects.

132. During a FAST exam, you observe a hypoechoic stripe between the liver and right kidney. What does this finding most likely indicate?

a. Normal anatomical structure
b. Free intraperitoneal fluid
c. Perinephric hematoma
d. Subcapsular liver hematoma

Answer: b. Free intraperitoneal fluid. Explanation: In a FAST exam, a hypoechoic (dark) stripe between the liver and right kidney in Morison's pouch is indicative of free intraperitoneal fluid. This is a positive FAST exam result and suggests internal bleeding, which could be from various sources including liver, spleen, or mesenteric injuries. Normal anatomical structures typically appear more echogenic (brighter). A perinephric hematoma would appear around the kidney, not between the liver and kidney. A subcapsular liver hematoma would appear within the liver capsule. The ability to recognize and interpret these ultrasound findings is crucial for rapid assessment and triage of trauma patients.

133. A 30-year-old female presents with severe left-sided abdominal pain following a bicycle accident. During your assessment, you note bruising in the left flank area. What is this sign called, and what does it suggest?
a. Cullen's sign, suggesting pancreatic injury
b. Grey Turner's sign, suggesting retroperitoneal hemorrhage
c. Kehr's sign, suggesting splenic rupture
d. Murphy's sign, suggesting gallbladder inflammation

Answer: b. Grey Turner's sign, suggesting retroperitoneal hemorrhage. Explanation: Bruising in the flank area is known as Grey Turner's sign and suggests retroperitoneal hemorrhage. This sign typically appears 24-48 hours after the initial injury as blood tracks through tissue planes. In the context of blunt abdominal trauma, it could indicate injuries to retroperitoneal organs like the kidneys, pancreas, or major blood vessels. Cullen's sign is periumbilical bruising. Kehr's sign is left shoulder pain associated with splenic rupture due to diaphragmatic irritation. Murphy's sign is right upper quadrant pain on deep inspiration, associated with gallbladder inflammation. Recognition of these signs aids in identifying potentially serious internal injuries that may not be immediately apparent on initial examination.

134. You're performing a FAST exam on a trauma patient. Which of the following findings would be considered a positive result?
a. Visible cardiac activity in the subxiphoid view
b. Anechoic area in the hepatorenal space
c. Visible bowel peristalsis in the pelvic view
d. Clear visualization of the splenorenal interface

Answer: b. Anechoic area in the hepatorenal space. Explanation: In a FAST exam, an anechoic (black) area in the hepatorenal space (Morison's pouch) is considered a positive finding, indicating the presence of free intraperitoneal fluid. This fluid could represent blood from solid organ injury or other sources of intraabdominal bleeding. Visible cardiac activity is expected in the subxiphoid view and doesn't indicate injury. Bowel peristalsis is a normal finding. Clear visualization of the splenorenal interface without fluid is a negative finding. A positive FAST exam in an unstable patient typically prompts immediate surgical intervention, while in stable patients it guides further imaging and management decisions.

135. A 45-year-old male presents with severe abdominal pain and distension following a high-speed MVC. During your assessment, you note absent bowel sounds and rigidity of the abdominal wall. What is the most likely underlying injury?
a. Retroperitoneal hematoma
b. Splenic laceration
c. Hollow viscus perforation
d. Mesenteric tear

Answer: c. Hollow viscus perforation. Explanation: The combination of severe abdominal pain, distension, absent bowel sounds, and abdominal rigidity strongly suggests hollow viscus perforation. This could involve the stomach, small intestine, or large intestine. Perforation leads to chemical peritonitis from gastric or intestinal contents spilling into the peritoneal cavity, causing the described symptoms. Retroperitoneal hematoma typically wouldn't cause absent bowel sounds or such marked rigidity. Splenic laceration usually presents with left upper quadrant pain and potentially signs of shock. A mesenteric tear can cause significant bleeding but wouldn't typically result in absent bowel sounds and generalized rigidity. Early recognition of potential hollow viscus injury is crucial as these injuries may not be immediately apparent on initial imaging and can lead to severe sepsis if not promptly addressed.

136. During a FAST exam, you're unable to visualize the spleen clearly. What patient factor might most likely contribute to this difficulty?
a. Recent meal consumption
b. Morbid obesity
c. Pregnancy
d. Subcutaneous emphysema

Answer: b. Morbid obesity. Explanation: Morbid obesity can significantly hinder ultrasound visualization during a FAST exam. Excessive adipose tissue attenuates the ultrasound waves, making it difficult to obtain clear images of deeper structures like the spleen. Recent meal consumption might affect gastric visualization but typically wouldn't impair splenic views. While pregnancy can alter abdominal anatomy, it usually doesn't significantly impact splenic visualization. Subcutaneous emphysema, while problematic for ultrasound, is less common and more likely to affect chest or upper abdominal views. Understanding the limitations of FAST exams in certain patient populations is crucial for accurate interpretation and knowing when additional imaging modalities may be necessary. In obese patients, a negative FAST exam should be interpreted with caution, and other clinical indicators should guide further management decisions.

137. A 30-year-old male sustains burns to his entire left arm, the front of his chest, and his face. Using the Rule of Nines, what is the total body surface area (TBSA) burned?
a. 18%
b. 27%
c. 36%
d. 45%

Answer: b. 27%. Explanation: According to the Rule of Nines, the left arm accounts for 9%, the front of the chest for 9%, and the face for 9%. Adding these together gives a total TBSA of 27%.

138. A 70 kg patient with 40% TBSA burns requires fluid resuscitation using the Parkland formula. How much fluid should be administered in the first 24 hours?
a. 7,000 mL
b. 8,400 mL
c. 10,500 mL
d. 11,200 mL

Answer: c. 11,200 mL. Explanation: The Parkland formula is 4 mL x TBSA (%) x body weight (kg). For this patient: 4 mL x 40 x 70 = 11,200 mL. Half of this amount should be given in the first 8 hours, and the remainder over the next 16 hours.

139. A 45-year-old male with facial burns from a house fire is suspected of having an inhalation injury. Which diagnostic tool is most appropriate for assessing the extent of the injury?
a. Pulse oximetry
b. Chest X-ray
c. Bronchoscopy
d. Arterial blood gas (ABG) analysis

Answer: c. Bronchoscopy. Explanation: Bronchoscopy is the most appropriate diagnostic tool for assessing inhalation injuries as it allows direct visualization of the airway and extent of thermal damage.

140. A patient with circumferential burns to the right lower leg is experiencing compromised distal circulation. What is the most appropriate intervention?
a. Fasciotomy
b. Escharotomy
c. Application of ice packs
d. Elevation of the limb

Answer: b. Escharotomy. Explanation: An escharotomy is indicated to relieve pressure and restore circulation in cases of circumferential burns where the eschar acts like a tourniquet, compromising distal perfusion.

141. A 35-year-old female presents with a chemical burn to her arm caused by a strong acid. What is the first step in managing this type of burn?
a. Apply a neutralizing agent
b. Cover the burn with a sterile dressing
c. Irrigate the burn with copious amounts of water
d. Apply antibiotic ointment

Answer: c. Irrigate the burn with copious amounts of water. Explanation: The first step in managing a chemical burn is to irrigate the area with copious amounts of water to dilute and remove the chemical. Neutralizing agents are not recommended as they may exacerbate the injury.

142. Which of the following signs is most indicative of a severe inhalation injury?
a. Soot around the nostrils
b. Hoarseness
c. Coughing
d. Facial burns

Answer: b. Hoarseness. Explanation: Hoarseness is a sign of airway edema and injury, indicating a severe inhalation injury. Soot around the nostrils, coughing, and facial burns are concerning but not as specific for severe airway injury.

143. A 28-year-old male presents with a partial-thickness burn to the anterior and posterior aspects of his right leg. Using the Rule of Nines, calculate the TBSA affected.
a. 9%
b. 18%
c. 27%
d. 36%

Answer: b. 18%. Explanation: According to the Rule of Nines, each leg accounts for 18% of the TBSA. The anterior and posterior aspects of the right leg each cover 9%, totaling 18%.

144. A patient with significant burn injuries is at risk for hypovolemic shock. Which of the following best explains the pathophysiology behind this risk?
a. Decreased cardiac output
b. Increased vascular permeability
c. Hemolysis of red blood cells
d. Decreased renal perfusion

Answer: b. Increased vascular permeability. Explanation: Burn injuries increase vascular permeability, leading to fluid and protein loss from the intravascular to the interstitial space, which can result in hypovolemic shock.

145. A 50-year-old male sustains a severe electrical burn. Which of the following complications should be most closely monitored?
a. Renal failure
b. Respiratory distress
c. Cardiac arrhythmias
d. Gastrointestinal bleeding

Answer: c. Cardiac arrhythmias. Explanation: Electrical burns can cause significant damage to the cardiac conduction system, resulting in arrhythmias. Close monitoring of the patient's cardiac status is essential.

146. A patient with third-degree burns develops compartment syndrome in the affected limb. Which of the following clinical signs is most indicative of this condition?
a. Decreased sensation in the limb
b. Pain out of proportion to the injury
c. Blisters forming on the skin
d. Redness around the burn

Answer: b. Pain out of proportion to the injury. Explanation: Pain out of proportion to the injury is a hallmark sign of compartment syndrome, indicating increased pressure within the muscle compartments that requires prompt intervention.

147. You respond to a call for a 28-year-old marathon runner who collapsed near the finish line. It's a hot day, and the patient's skin is hot and dry. Their temperature is 105.8°F (41°C). What is the most appropriate initial treatment?
a. Administer oral rehydration solution
b. Apply ice packs to groin and axillae
c. Initiate rapid whole-body cooling with ice water immersion
d. Administer IV normal saline bolus

Answer: c. Initiate rapid whole-body cooling with ice water immersion. Explanation: This patient is exhibiting signs of heat stroke, characterized by an elevated core temperature above 104°F (40°C) and central nervous system dysfunction. Rapid cooling is the primary goal, with ice water immersion being the most effective method, capable of cooling at a rate of 0.2°C per minute. Oral rehydration is inappropriate for an altered patient. While ice packs can help, they're less effective than full immersion. IV fluids are important but secondary to cooling in heat stroke management. The distinction between heat exhaustion (where oral rehydration might be appropriate) and life-threatening heat stroke is crucial for proper emergency management.

148. A 60-year-old hunter is found in the woods with a core temperature of 82°F (27.8°C). He's unconscious but breathing. Which rewarming technique is most appropriate?
a. Passive external rewarming
b. Active external rewarming
c. Active core rewarming
d. Extracorporeal blood rewarming

Answer: b. Active external rewarming. Explanation: This patient is in severe hypothermia (stage III: 82-90°F/28-32°C). For severe hypothermia with preserved circulation, active external rewarming is the most appropriate prehospital technique. This involves applying heat sources to the body surface, such as warm blankets, heating pads, or forced warm air. Passive rewarming is insufficient for this severity. Active core rewarming (e.g., warm IV fluids) can be used in conjunction but isn't the primary method. Extracorporeal rewarming is reserved for the most severe cases (typically <82°F/28°C) and is only available in specialized hospital settings. Understanding hypothermia staging and appropriate rewarming techniques is crucial for effective management and preventing further heat loss or cardiovascular complications.

149. You're treating a patient with suspected frostbite to their feet. The affected area is hard, cold, and white. What grade of frostbite does this represent?
a. Superficial frostbite
b. Partial-thickness frostbite
c. Full-thickness frostbite
d. Deep frostbite

Answer: c. Full-thickness frostbite. Explanation: The description provided aligns with full-thickness (third-degree) frostbite. In this stage, the skin is hard, waxy, and white or yellowish, and the tissue underneath is cold and hard. Superficial frostbite (first-degree) presents with pale, numb skin that blanches. Partial-thickness (second-degree) shows blistering after rewarming. Deep frostbite (fourth-degree) extends into muscle and bone, often appearing blackened, but this isn't apparent until after thawing. Proper classification of frostbite is crucial for determining treatment approach and prognosis. Full-thickness frostbite requires careful rewarming and often results in tissue loss, emphasizing the importance of early recognition and appropriate management to minimize long-term damage.

150. A 5-year-old child is pulled from a swimming pool after being submerged for approximately 3 minutes. The child is unconscious but has a pulse. What is the most critical initial intervention?
a. Begin chest compressions
b. Administer 100% oxygen via non-rebreather mask
c. Perform abdominal thrusts to expel water
d. Initiate rapid rewarming

Answer: b. Administer 100% oxygen via non-rebreather mask. Explanation: In a near-drowning victim with a pulse, the primary concern is hypoxia. Immediate administration of high-flow oxygen is crucial to address potential respiratory failure and prevent secondary drowning. Chest compressions are not indicated if a pulse is present. Abdominal thrusts are not recommended for drowning victims as they delay ventilation and oxygenation, and can increase the risk of aspiration. While hypothermia is a concern in drowning, oxygenation takes precedence over rewarming in the initial management. The "golden hour" following submersion is critical, and early, aggressive oxygenation and ventilation support are key prognostic factors in near-drowning incidents.

151. You're treating a climber at 14,000 feet who complains of severe headache, confusion, and difficulty walking. Which of the following is the most appropriate immediate action?
a. Administer acetazolamide 250 mg orally
b. Begin immediate descent
c. Administer supplemental oxygen at 4 L/min
d. Place in Trendelenburg position

Answer: b. Begin immediate descent. Explanation: The climber is showing signs of High Altitude Cerebral Edema (HACE), a severe form of acute mountain sickness. Immediate descent is the definitive treatment for HACE and can be life-saving. While acetazolamide can help prevent altitude sickness, it's not the primary treatment for established

HACE. Supplemental oxygen can help but doesn't replace the need for descent. The Trendelenburg position is not indicated and could worsen cerebral edema. HACE is a medical emergency that can progress rapidly to coma and death if not treated promptly. Recognizing the symptoms and initiating immediate descent is crucial for preventing severe outcomes in high-altitude environments.

152. A patient presents with painless, white, waxy skin on their fingertips after exposure to cold. Sensation is absent in the affected areas. What is the most appropriate initial management?
a. Rapidly rewarm the affected areas with hot water (104-108°F)
b. Gently massage the affected areas to restore circulation
c. Apply dry heat directly to the affected areas
d. Gradually rewarm at room temperature

Answer: a. Rapidly rewarm the affected areas with hot water (104-108°F). Explanation: The patient is showing signs of frostbite. Rapid rewarming in a water bath at 104-108°F (40-42°C) is the recommended initial treatment. This temperature range is warm enough to reverse tissue freezing quickly without causing thermal injury. Massaging can cause further tissue damage and is contraindicated. Dry heat can lead to uneven rewarming and potential burns. Gradual rewarming at room temperature is too slow and may allow further tissue damage. It's crucial to remember that once rewarming begins, it should not be interrupted, as refreezing can cause severe tissue damage. This question tests understanding of proper frostbite management techniques and the importance of rapid, controlled rewarming.

153. During a summer festival, multiple patients present with similar symptoms: muscle cramps, heavy sweating, and dizziness. Their core temperatures range from 99-101°F (37.2-38.3°C). What is the most likely diagnosis?
a. Heat stroke
b. Heat exhaustion
c. Heat cramps
d. Hyponatremia

Answer: b. Heat exhaustion. Explanation: The presentation is classic for heat exhaustion: muscle cramps, heavy sweating, dizziness, and mildly elevated temperatures (but below 104°F/40°C). Heat stroke would present with significantly higher temperatures (>104°F/40°C) and altered mental status. Heat cramps typically only involve painful muscle spasms without other systemic symptoms. Hyponatremia in an exercise setting (exercise-associated hyponatremia) often presents with nausea, vomiting, headache, and altered mental status, which are not prominent in this scenario. Recognizing heat exhaustion is crucial as it can progress to heat stroke if not properly managed. Treatment focuses on cooling and rehydration, emphasizing the importance of early intervention in heat-related illnesses.

154. A diver surfaces rapidly from a depth of 100 feet, complaining of joint pain and a "pins and needles" sensation. What is the most appropriate initial management?
a. Administer high-flow oxygen via non-rebreather mask
b. Recompress the diver to 60 feet
c. Administer IV fluids for rehydration
d. Perform needle decompression of the chest

Answer: a. Administer high-flow oxygen via non-rebreather mask. Explanation: The diver is showing signs of decompression sickness (DCS), also known as "the bends." The initial management for suspected DCS is administration of 100% oxygen via non-rebreather mask. This helps eliminate inert gas from tissues and can alleviate symptoms. Recompression is the definitive treatment but is performed in a hyperbaric chamber, not in the field. IV fluids can be beneficial but are secondary to oxygen administration. Needle decompression is used for tension pneumothorax, not DCS. Understanding the principles of dive physiology and the management of diving emergencies is crucial for EMS providers, especially in areas where diving is common.

155. You're treating a patient with severe hypothermia (core temperature 82°F/27.8°C) who appears to be in cardiac arrest. How should you modify your CPR approach?
a. Perform CPR at half the normal rate
b. Check for pulse for up to 60 seconds before starting compressions
c. Administer only one shock if ventricular fibrillation is present
d. Withhold epinephrine and other vasopressors

Answer: b. Check for pulse for up to 60 seconds before starting compressions. Explanation: In severe hypothermia, the heart rate and metabolism are extremely slow. Pulse checks should be performed for up to 60 seconds to avoid missing a slow, weak pulse. CPR should be performed at the normal rate if no pulse is detected. Multiple shocks can be administered for VF, as hypothermic hearts may be resistant to defibrillation. While there's debate about medication administration in severe hypothermia, current guidelines do not recommend withholding vasopressors. This question tests understanding of the unique considerations in managing cardiac arrest in severely hypothermic patients, where standard ACLS protocols may need modification.

156. A mountain climber at 16,000 feet altitude presents with a productive cough, shortness of breath, and a low-grade fever. Crackles are heard on lung auscultation. What is the most likely diagnosis?
a. High Altitude Pulmonary Edema (HAPE)
b. High Altitude Cerebral Edema (HACE)
c. Pneumonia
d. Acute mountain sickness

Answer: a. High Altitude Pulmonary Edema (HAPE). Explanation: The symptoms described are classic for High Altitude Pulmonary Edema (HAPE): cough (often productive), dyspnea, and crackles on auscultation. Low-grade fever can also occur. HACE typically presents with severe headache, ataxia, and altered mental status, which are not mentioned here. While pneumonia can present similarly, HAPE is more likely given the high altitude context. Acute mountain sickness usually presents earlier with headache and gastrointestinal symptoms. HAPE is a potentially fatal condition requiring immediate descent and oxygen therapy. Recognizing the difference between various high-altitude illnesses is crucial for proper management and evacuation decisions in remote, high-altitude environments.

157. A 28-year-old male presents with excessive salivation, lacrimation, urination, defecation, gastrointestinal distress, and emesis (SLUDGE syndrome) after exposure to an unknown substance. Which toxidrome is most consistent with his symptoms?
a. Anticholinergic
b. Cholinergic
c. Opioid
d. Sympathomimetic

Answer: b. Cholinergic. Explanation: The SLUDGE syndrome (salivation, lacrimation, urination, defecation, gastrointestinal distress, and emesis) is characteristic of a cholinergic toxidrome, which can occur due to exposure to organophosphates or nerve agents.

158. A 45-year-old female is found unresponsive with pinpoint pupils and respiratory depression. Which of the following is the most appropriate initial intervention?
a. Administer naloxone
b. Administer activated charcoal
c. Perform gastric lavage
d. Administer flumazenil

Answer: a. Administer naloxone. Explanation: The patient's symptoms of pinpoint pupils and respiratory depression suggest an opioid overdose. Naloxone is an opioid antagonist and is the most appropriate initial intervention to reverse opioid toxicity.

159. A patient presents with headache, dizziness, and confusion after being exposed to smoke from a house fire. What diagnostic test is most appropriate to confirm carbon monoxide poisoning?
a. Pulse oximetry
b. Arterial blood gas (ABG)
c. Carboxyhemoglobin (COHb) level
d. Complete blood count (CBC)

Answer: c. Carboxyhemoglobin (COHb) level. Explanation: The most appropriate diagnostic test to confirm carbon monoxide poisoning is measuring the carboxyhemoglobin (COHb) level, as it directly indicates the amount of carbon monoxide bound to hemoglobin.

160. A 35-year-old male presents with altered mental status, wide QRS complexes, and ventricular arrhythmias on ECG after ingesting an unknown quantity of his tricyclic antidepressants. What is the most appropriate treatment for his condition?
a. Sodium bicarbonate
b. Magnesium sulfate
c. Calcium gluconate
d. Potassium chloride

Answer: a. Sodium bicarbonate. Explanation: Sodium bicarbonate is the treatment of choice for tricyclic antidepressant overdose with wide QRS complexes and ventricular arrhythmias, as it helps to stabilize the cardiac membrane and correct acidosis.

161. A 22-year-old female presents to the emergency department 6 hours after ingesting a large quantity of acetaminophen. What is the most appropriate management to prevent liver toxicity?
a. Activated charcoal
b. N-acetylcysteine (NAC)
c. Intravenous fluids
d. Hemodialysis

Answer: b. N-acetylcysteine (NAC). Explanation: N-acetylcysteine (NAC) is the antidote for acetaminophen overdose and is most effective when administered within 8 hours of ingestion to prevent liver toxicity.

162. A 50-year-old male presents with hyperthermia, dry skin, dilated pupils, and delirium after ingesting an unknown substance. Which toxidrome is most consistent with his symptoms?
a. Sympathomimetic
b. Anticholinergic
c. Cholinergic
d. Opioid

Answer: b. Anticholinergic. Explanation: The symptoms of hyperthermia, dry skin, dilated pupils, and delirium are consistent with an anticholinergic toxidrome, which can be caused by substances such as antihistamines, tricyclic antidepressants, and antipsychotics.

163. Which of the following is the primary concern in a patient with a suspected beta-blocker overdose?
a. Tachycardia
b. Hyperthermia
c. Hypotension and bradycardia
d. Seizures

Answer: c. Hypotension and bradycardia. Explanation: Beta-blocker overdose typically presents with hypotension and bradycardia due to the negative inotropic and chronotropic effects of these medications.

164. A 40-year-old male is brought to the emergency department after exposure to an unknown chemical. He presents with miosis, bradycardia, bronchorrhea, and muscle twitching. What is the most appropriate antidote?
a. Atropine and pralidoxime
b. Naloxone
c. Flumazenil
d. Fomepizole

Answer: a. Atropine and pralidoxime. Explanation: The symptoms of miosis, bradycardia, bronchorrhea, and muscle twitching suggest organophosphate poisoning. The appropriate antidotes are atropine and pralidoxime.

165. A 35-year-old female presents with agitation, hypertension, tachycardia, and diaphoresis after ingesting an unknown substance. Which toxidrome is most consistent with her symptoms?
a. Opioid
b. Cholinergic
c. Anticholinergic
d. Sympathomimetic

Answer: d. Sympathomimetic. Explanation: The symptoms of agitation, hypertension, tachycardia, and diaphoresis are consistent with a sympathomimetic toxidrome, which can be caused by substances such as cocaine, amphetamines, and ephedrine.

166. A 25-year-old male presents with altered mental status, ataxia, and nystagmus after ingesting an unknown substance. What is the most appropriate initial diagnostic test?
a. Electrolyte panel
b. Blood glucose level
c. Arterial blood gas (ABG)
d. Serum osmolality

Answer: b. Blood glucose level. Explanation: Altered mental status can be caused by hypoglycemia, which is a life-threatening condition that requires immediate correction. Therefore, checking the blood glucose level is the most appropriate initial diagnostic test.

167. You arrive on scene to find a 65-year-old male with sudden onset right-sided weakness and slurred speech. Which stroke scale is most appropriate for rapid prehospital assessment?
a. NIH Stroke Scale (NIHSS)
b. Cincinnati Prehospital Stroke Scale (CPSS)
c. Los Angeles Prehospital Stroke Screen (LAPSS)
d. Miami Emergency Neurologic Deficit (MEND) exam

Answer: b. Cincinnati Prehospital Stroke Scale (CPSS). Explanation: The Cincinnati Prehospital Stroke Scale (CPSS) is ideal for rapid field assessment of potential stroke patients. It evaluates facial droop, arm drift, and speech abnormalities, making it quick and easy to perform in the prehospital setting. The NIHSS is more comprehensive but time-consuming for field use. LAPSS includes additional criteria like blood glucose and history, which may delay assessment. The MEND exam is more detailed than typically needed for initial prehospital triage. The CPSS's simplicity and effectiveness in identifying stroke symptoms make it a valuable tool for EMTs to expedite stroke recognition and transport decisions.

168. A 30-year-old female presents with a severe headache, neck stiffness, and photophobia. Her temperature is 102.5°F (39.2°C). What is the most likely diagnosis?
a. Migraine headache
b. Subarachnoid hemorrhage
c. Bacterial meningitis
d. Viral encephalitis

Answer: c. Bacterial meningitis. Explanation: The combination of severe headache, neck stiffness (meningismus), photophobia, and high fever strongly suggests bacterial meningitis. This life-threatening infection of the meninges requires immediate recognition and treatment. Migraine can present with similar symptoms but typically without high fever. Subarachnoid hemorrhage usually has a more sudden onset and often lacks fever. Viral encephalitis typically presents with altered mental status as a prominent feature, which isn't mentioned here. In suspected meningitis, rapid transport and early notification to the receiving facility are crucial, as prompt antibiotic administration significantly improves outcomes. EMTs should also consider droplet precautions due to the potentially infectious nature of meningitis.

169. You're treating a patient in status epilepticus who has not responded to initial benzodiazepine administration. What is the most appropriate next step in the prehospital setting?
a. Administer a second dose of benzodiazepines
b. Begin rapid sequence intubation
c. Administer intravenous phenytoin
d. Initiate propofol infusion

Answer: a. Administer a second dose of benzodiazepines. Explanation: In prehospital management of status epilepticus, if the initial dose of benzodiazepines (typically midazolam, lorazepam, or diazepam) is ineffective, the most appropriate next step is to administer a second dose. This approach is supported by current guidelines and has shown efficacy in terminating seizures. Rapid sequence intubation may eventually be necessary but is not the immediate next step. Phenytoin administration is typically reserved for hospital settings due to its potential cardiovascular side effects. Propofol infusion is a hospital-based intervention for refractory status epilepticus. This question tests understanding of the stepwise approach to managing status epilepticus in the prehospital environment.

170. A 55-year-old male presents with right-sided weakness 30 minutes after a witnessed generalized tonic-clonic seizure. His symptoms are gradually improving. What is the most likely diagnosis?
a. Acute ischemic stroke
b. Todd's paralysis
c. Postictal state
d. Conversion disorder

Answer: b. Todd's paralysis. Explanation: The presentation is classic for Todd's paralysis, a transient neurological deficit following a seizure. It typically affects the side of the body contralateral to the seizure focus and gradually improves, usually resolving within 24-48 hours. This condition is important to recognize as it can mimic an acute stroke. The gradual improvement is key in differentiating it from an acute ischemic event. While this is part of the postictal state, the specific term for this phenomenon is Todd's paralysis. Conversion disorder is a diagnosis of exclusion and less likely in this acute, post-seizure setting. Understanding Todd's paralysis is crucial for EMTs to avoid misdiagnosing these patients as having acute strokes, which could lead to unnecessary thrombolytic therapy.

171. You're treating a patient with suspected increased intracranial pressure (ICP). Which of the following interventions is most appropriate to manage ICP in the prehospital setting?

a. Administer mannitol 1g/kg IV
b. Hyperventilate to an EtCO2 of 30-35 mmHg
c. Elevate the head of the bed to 30 degrees
d. Administer 3% hypertonic saline bolus

Answer: c. Elevate the head of the bed to 30 degrees. Explanation: Elevating the head of the bed to 30 degrees is an appropriate and readily implementable measure to help reduce ICP in the prehospital setting. This position promotes venous drainage from the brain without compromising cerebral perfusion pressure. Mannitol and hypertonic saline are typically administered in hospital settings under specific protocols. Hyperventilation to an EtCO2 of 30-35 mmHg is no longer routinely recommended due to the risk of cerebral vasoconstriction and potential worsening of ischemia; current guidelines suggest targeting normal EtCO2 (35-45 mmHg) unless there are signs of impending herniation. This question assesses understanding of practical, non-pharmacological ICP management techniques applicable in the field.

172. Which of the following is a key distinguishing feature between meningitis and encephalitis?
a. Presence of fever
b. Altered mental status
c. Seizure activity
d. Neck stiffness

Answer: b. Altered mental status. Explanation: While both meningitis and encephalitis can present with similar symptoms, altered mental status is more characteristic of encephalitis. Encephalitis primarily affects the brain parenchyma, leading to more prominent cognitive and behavioral changes. Meningitis, an inflammation of the meninges, typically presents with fever, headache, and neck stiffness, but patients often maintain normal mental status, at least initially. Fever and seizures can occur in both conditions. Neck stiffness is more associated with meningitis but can also occur in encephalitis. Understanding these distinctions is crucial for EMTs in recognizing the potential severity of the condition and guiding appropriate management and transport decisions.

173. A 70-year-old female presents with sudden onset left-sided weakness and facial droop. You suspect an acute stroke. What is the most critical piece of information to obtain for potential thrombolytic therapy?
a. Patient's current medications
b. History of recent surgery
c. Last known well time
d. Family history of stroke

Answer: c. Last known well time. Explanation: The last known well time, or the time when the patient was last observed to be normal, is crucial information for potential thrombolytic therapy in acute ischemic stroke. This time determines eligibility for tissue plasminogen activator (tPA), which is typically administered within a 3-4.5 hour window from symptom onset. While other factors like current medications and recent surgical history are important, the time of onset is the most critical for immediate decision-making regarding thrombolytic therapy. Family history, while relevant for risk assessment, doesn't impact acute treatment decisions. EMTs play a vital role in accurately determining and reporting this time to the receiving facility.

174. You're assessing a 45-year-old male with a severe headache that he describes as "the worst headache of my life." Which of the following additional findings would be most concerning for subarachnoid hemorrhage?
a. Gradual onset over 24 hours
b. Associated nausea and vomiting
c. Photophobia and phonophobia
d. Neck stiffness and altered mental status

Answer: d. Neck stiffness and altered mental status. Explanation: In the context of a sudden, severe headache (often described as a "thunderclap headache"), the presence of neck stiffness and altered mental status is highly concerning for subarachnoid hemorrhage (SAH). SAH typically presents with an abrupt onset of severe headache, often accompanied by meningeal irritation (causing neck stiffness) and neurological deficits or altered consciousness. Gradual onset is less consistent with SAH. While nausea, vomiting, photophobia, and phonophobia can occur in SAH, they are also common in other headache disorders and less specific. Recognizing the classic triad of sudden severe headache, neck stiffness, and altered mental status is crucial for EMTs to quickly identify potential SAH cases, which require urgent neurosurgical evaluation.

175. A 60-year-old male with a history of hypertension suddenly develops a severe headache, right-sided weakness, and vomiting. His blood pressure is 220/110 mmHg. What is the most likely diagnosis?
a. Ischemic stroke
b. Hypertensive emergency
c. Intracranial hemorrhage
d. Migraine with aura

Answer: c. Intracranial hemorrhage. Explanation: The presentation of sudden severe headache, focal neurological deficit (right-sided weakness), vomiting, and significantly elevated blood pressure is highly suggestive of an intracranial hemorrhage, particularly a hemorrhagic stroke. While these symptoms can occur in ischemic stroke, the severity of headache and markedly elevated blood pressure are more typical of hemorrhagic events. Hypertensive emergency can cause end-organ damage but typically doesn't present with such acute focal deficits. Migraine with aura rarely causes such severe, persistent weakness. Recognizing the signs of potential intracranial hemorrhage is crucial for EMTs, as these patients require rapid transport to facilities capable of neurosurgical intervention.

176. You're treating a patient in status epilepticus who is not responding to repeated doses of benzodiazepines. What is the most appropriate airway management strategy?
a. Continue bag-valve-mask ventilation
b. Perform nasotracheal intubation
c. Initiate rapid sequence intubation
d. Insert a supraglottic airway device

Answer: c. Initiate rapid sequence intubation. Explanation: In a patient with refractory status epilepticus not responding to benzodiazepines, rapid sequence intubation (RSI) is the most appropriate airway management strategy. RSI allows for definitive airway control, facilitates proper oxygenation and ventilation, and enables the administration of additional anticonvulsant medications if needed. Continued bag-valve-mask ventilation may be inadequate for prolonged management. Nasotracheal intubation is contraindicated in actively seizing patients due to the risk of trauma. While supraglottic devices can be useful in emergency situations, they don't provide the same level of airway protection as endotracheal intubation, which is preferable in this scenario. It's important to note that RSI should only be performed by properly trained personnel under appropriate protocols.

177. A 45-year-old female with a history of type 2 diabetes presents with polyuria, polydipsia, altered mental status, and blood glucose level of 850 mg/dL. Her blood pH is 7.4 and serum osmolality is elevated. What is the most likely diagnosis?
a. Diabetic ketoacidosis (DKA)
b. Hyperosmolar hyperglycemic state (HHS)
c. Hypoglycemia
d. Addisonian crisis

Answer: b. Hyperosmolar hyperglycemic state (HHS). Explanation: HHS is characterized by extreme hyperglycemia, elevated serum osmolality, and a normal blood pH. It typically presents with altered mental status, polyuria, and polydipsia, and lacks the significant acidosis seen in DKA.

178. A 50-year-old male presents with fatigue, weight loss, hypotension, and hyperpigmentation of the skin. Laboratory tests reveal hyponatremia and hyperkalemia. What is the most appropriate initial management?
a. Administer IV insulin
b. Administer IV hydrocortisone
c. Administer oral levothyroxine
d. Administer IV dextrose

Answer: b. Administer IV hydrocortisone. Explanation: The patient's symptoms and laboratory findings are indicative of Addisonian crisis, which is an acute adrenal insufficiency. The initial management includes administering IV hydrocortisone to replace the deficient cortisol.

179. A 35-year-old female with a history of hyperthyroidism presents with fever, tachycardia, delirium, and a palpable goiter. What is the most likely diagnosis?
a. Myxedema coma
b. Addisonian crisis
c. Thyroid storm
d. Pheochromocytoma crisis

Answer: c. Thyroid storm. Explanation: Thyroid storm is a life-threatening exacerbation of hyperthyroidism, characterized by fever, tachycardia, delirium, and goiter. It requires immediate medical intervention.

180. A patient with type 1 diabetes reports feeling shaky, sweaty, and confused. His blood glucose level is 55 mg/dL. What is the first step in management according to the rule of 15?
a. Administer 15 grams of carbohydrates
b. Administer IV insulin
c. Check blood glucose level again in 15 minutes
d. Administer glucagon

Answer: a. Administer 15 grams of carbohydrates. Explanation: According to the rule of 15, the initial management of hypoglycemia involves administering 15 grams of fast-acting carbohydrates, then rechecking the blood glucose level in 15 minutes and repeating if necessary.

181. A 40-year-old female with a history of hypertension presents with severe headache, palpitations, and diaphoresis. Her blood pressure is 220/130 mmHg. What is the most appropriate initial management for suspected pheochromocytoma crisis?
a. Administer beta-blockers
b. Administer alpha-blockers
c. Administer diuretics
d. Administer IV dextrose

Answer: b. Administer alpha-blockers. Explanation: Pheochromocytoma crisis involves the release of excess catecholamines, leading to severe hypertension. The initial management includes administering alpha-blockers to control blood pressure before considering beta-blockers.

182. A 30-year-old male with a history of type 1 diabetes presents with nausea, vomiting, abdominal pain, and Kussmaul respirations. His blood glucose level is 450 mg/dL, and blood pH is 7.2. What is the most likely diagnosis?
a. Diabetic ketoacidosis (DKA)
b. Hyperosmolar hyperglycemic state (HHS)
c. Addisonian crisis
d. Thyroid storm

Answer: a. Diabetic ketoacidosis (DKA). Explanation: DKA is characterized by hyperglycemia, metabolic acidosis (low blood pH), and symptoms such as nausea, vomiting, abdominal pain, and Kussmaul respirations. This patient's presentation is consistent with DKA.

183. A 65-year-old female with hypothyroidism presents with hypothermia, bradycardia, hypotension, and altered mental status. What is the most likely diagnosis?
a. Myxedema coma
b. Addisonian crisis
c. Thyroid storm
d. Pheochromocytoma crisis

Answer: a. Myxedema coma. Explanation: Myxedema coma is a severe form of hypothyroidism presenting with hypothermia, bradycardia, hypotension, and altered mental status. It is a medical emergency requiring immediate treatment.

184. Which of the following laboratory findings is most consistent with Addisonian crisis?

a. Hyperglycemia and hypernatremia
b. Hypoglycemia and hyponatremia
c. Hyperkalemia and hypernatremia
d. Hypokalemia and hyperglycemia

Answer: b. Hypoglycemia and hyponatremia. Explanation: Addisonian crisis is characterized by adrenal insufficiency, leading to low cortisol levels, which can cause hypoglycemia and hyponatremia, along with hyperkalemia.

185. A 55-year-old male with diabetes is found unresponsive with a blood glucose level of 35 mg/dL. After administering IV dextrose, what is the next step in management?
a. Administer long-acting insulin
b. Reassess blood glucose in 15 minutes
c. Start IV fluids
d. Perform a CT scan of the head

Answer: b. Reassess blood glucose in 15 minutes. Explanation: After administering IV dextrose to treat hypoglycemia, the next step is to reassess blood glucose levels in 15 minutes to ensure they have returned to a safe range and to determine if additional intervention is needed.

186. A patient with a known history of pheochromocytoma presents with severe hypertension and a severe headache. Which diagnostic test is most appropriate to confirm a pheochromocytoma crisis?
a. Serum cortisol levels
b. Urinary catecholamines
c. Blood glucose levels
d. Serum thyroid hormone levels

Answer: b. Urinary catecholamines. Explanation: Pheochromocytoma is a tumor that secretes excessive catecholamines. Measuring urinary catecholamines is the most appropriate diagnostic test to confirm a pheochromocytoma crisis.

187. You're assessing a 45-year-old male with sudden onset severe abdominal pain. Which of the following findings is most concerning for a surgical emergency?
a. Pain that improves with eating
b. Diffuse abdominal tenderness
c. Rebound tenderness and guarding
d. Pain that radiates to the back

Answer: c. Rebound tenderness and guarding. Explanation: Rebound tenderness and guarding are signs of peritoneal irritation, often indicating a surgical emergency such as appendicitis, perforated ulcer, or bowel perforation. These findings suggest inflammation of the peritoneum, which can occur with various acute abdominal conditions requiring immediate surgical intervention. Pain improving with eating is more typical of peptic ulcer disease. Diffuse tenderness can occur in various conditions, both surgical and non-surgical. Back radiation can occur in conditions like pancreatitis, which may or may not require surgery. Recognizing signs of peritonitis is crucial for EMTs to appropriately triage and rapidly transport patients needing urgent surgical evaluation.

188. A 60-year-old male presents with hematemesis and melena. His vital signs show tachycardia and hypotension. What is the most appropriate initial management?
a. Administer proton pump inhibitors
b. Initiate rapid crystalloid infusion
c. Perform nasogastric lavage
d. Administer tranexamic acid

Answer: b. Initiate rapid crystalloid infusion. Explanation: In a patient with signs of upper GI bleeding (hematemesis and melena) and evidence of hypovolemic shock (tachycardia and hypotension), the most critical initial step is rapid fluid resuscitation with crystalloids. This helps restore intravascular volume and maintain organ perfusion. While proton pump inhibitors are useful in upper GI bleeds, they don't address the immediate hemodynamic instability. Nasogastric lavage is no longer routinely recommended in the initial management of GI bleeds. Tranexamic acid's role in GI bleeding is still under research and not standard prehospital care. Rapid recognition of shock and immediate fluid resuscitation are key skills for EMTs in managing acute GI bleeds.

189. Which of the following is NOT typically included in the Alvarado score for assessing the likelihood of appendicitis?
a. Migration of pain to the right lower quadrant
b. Anorexia
c. Rebound tenderness
d. Elevated liver enzymes

Answer: d. Elevated liver enzymes. Explanation: The Alvarado score is a clinical scoring system used to estimate the likelihood of appendicitis. It includes migration of pain to the right lower quadrant, anorexia, nausea/vomiting, right lower quadrant tenderness, rebound pain, elevated temperature, leukocytosis, and neutrophil shift to the left. Elevated liver enzymes are not part of this scoring system. While laboratory tests are included (leukocytosis and neutrophil shift), these are typically white blood cell related. Understanding the components of the Alvarado score can help EMTs communicate more effectively with receiving facilities about the likelihood of appendicitis, although the full score calculation is typically done in the hospital setting.

190. A 50-year-old alcoholic male presents with severe epigastric pain radiating to the back, nausea, and vomiting. Which of the following findings would indicate severe acute pancreatitis according to the Ranson criteria?
a. Serum glucose > 200 mg/dL
b. Age > 55 years
c. WBC count > 16,000/mm³
d. Serum calcium < 8 mg/dL

Answer: a. Serum glucose > 200 mg/dL. Explanation: While EMTs don't typically calculate the full Ranson criteria, understanding its components can aid in recognizing potentially severe cases of acute pancreatitis. A serum glucose >

200 mg/dL on admission is one of the Ranson criteria indicating potentially severe pancreatitis. The other options are also part of the criteria, but the question asks for the most severe indicator. Severe hyperglycemia can indicate significant pancreatic dysfunction and systemic stress. Age > 55, WBC > 16,000, and low calcium are also concerning but less specific. Recognizing signs of severe pancreatitis is important for EMTs to appropriately triage and communicate patient status to receiving facilities.

191. You're treating a patient with suspected esophageal varices bleeding. Which of the following positions is most appropriate during transport?
a. Trendelenburg position
b. Left lateral decubitus position
c. Sitting upright at 90 degrees
d. Supine with legs elevated

Answer: b. Left lateral decubitus position. Explanation: For patients with suspected esophageal varices bleeding, the left lateral decubitus position (also known as the recovery position) is most appropriate. This position helps prevent aspiration of blood and stomach contents, which is a significant risk in variceal bleeding. It also may help tamponade the bleeding site if the varices are in the distal esophagus or gastroesophageal junction. The Trendelenburg position can increase the risk of aspiration. Sitting upright might exacerbate bleeding due to increased hydrostatic pressure. Supine with legs elevated doesn't protect the airway. Proper positioning is a crucial aspect of prehospital management for patients with upper GI bleeding, particularly in those with suspected variceal hemorrhage.

192. A 35-year-old female presents with right lower quadrant pain, nausea, and low-grade fever. Her last menstrual period was 6 weeks ago. Which of the following should be highest on your differential diagnosis?
a. Appendicitis
b. Ectopic pregnancy
c. Ovarian torsion
d. Pyelonephritis

Answer: b. Ectopic pregnancy. Explanation: Given the patient's age, location of pain, and notably, the fact that her last menstrual period was 6 weeks ago, ectopic pregnancy should be the highest concern. Ectopic pregnancy is a life-threatening emergency that can present with lower abdominal pain and signs of early pregnancy. While appendicitis is common in this age group, the pregnancy possibility takes precedence. Ovarian torsion typically presents with sudden, severe pain. Pyelonephritis usually causes flank pain rather than lower quadrant pain. EMTs should maintain a high index of suspicion for ectopic pregnancy in any female of childbearing age with abdominal pain, as early recognition and rapid transport can be lifesaving.

193. What is the most appropriate initial management for a patient presenting with massive lower GI bleeding and signs of hypovolemic shock?
a. Administer tranexamic acid
b. Apply abdominal pressure
c. Initiate rapid fluid resuscitation with warm crystalloids
d. Administer vitamin K

Answer: c. Initiate rapid fluid resuscitation with warm crystalloids. Explanation: In a patient with massive lower GI bleeding and signs of hypovolemic shock, the most critical initial step is rapid fluid resuscitation with warm crystalloids. This helps restore intravascular volume, maintain organ perfusion, and prevent complications of shock. Tranexamic acid is not standard treatment for lower GI bleeds in the prehospital setting. Applying abdominal pressure is not effective for internal bleeding and may worsen the condition. Vitamin K is used for reversal of warfarin anticoagulation but doesn't address acute blood loss. Rapid recognition of shock and immediate fluid resuscitation are key skills for EMTs in managing acute GI bleeds, regardless of the source.

194. A 55-year-old male with a history of alcohol abuse presents with severe epigastric pain radiating to the back, nausea, and vomiting. On examination, you note a grey-blue discoloration around the umbilicus. What is this sign called and what does it suggest?
a. Cullen's sign, suggesting pancreatic hemorrhage
b. Grey Turner's sign, suggesting retroperitoneal bleeding
c. Murphy's sign, suggesting cholecystitis
d. McBurney's sign, suggesting appendicitis

Answer: a. Cullen's sign, suggesting pancreatic hemorrhage. Explanation: The grey-blue discoloration around the umbilicus is known as Cullen's sign. In the context of severe epigastric pain radiating to the back in a patient with alcohol abuse history, this sign suggests hemorrhagic pancreatitis. Cullen's sign occurs when blood from the pancreas tracks along the falciform ligament to the umbilicus. Grey Turner's sign is bruising of the flanks, also seen in retroperitoneal bleeding but not specifically around the umbilicus. Murphy's sign (right upper quadrant pain on inspiration) suggests cholecystitis. McBurney's sign (tenderness at McBurney's point) suggests appendicitis. Recognizing these specific signs can help EMTs communicate more effectively with receiving facilities about the potential severity and nature of the abdominal emergency.

195. Which of the following is NOT a typical feature of cholecystitis?
a. Right upper quadrant pain
b. Fever
c. Positive Murphy's sign
d. Jaundice

Answer: d. Jaundice. Explanation: While cholecystitis (inflammation of the gallbladder) typically presents with right upper quadrant pain, fever, and a positive Murphy's sign (pain on palpation of the right upper quadrant during inspiration), jaundice is not a typical feature of uncomplicated cholecystitis. Jaundice is more commonly associated with choledocholithiasis (stones in the common bile duct) or other conditions causing biliary obstruction. Right upper quadrant pain is the hallmark symptom. Fever indicates inflammation. Murphy's sign is a classic physical exam finding in cholecystitis. Understanding the typical presentation of common abdominal emergencies helps EMTs form more accurate differential diagnoses and communicate effectively with receiving facilities.

196. A 40-year-old female presents with severe, colicky abdominal pain that radiates to the right groin. She's nauseous and restless. What is the most likely diagnosis?
a. Appendicitis
b. Renal colic
c. Ovarian torsion
d. Ectopic pregnancy

Answer: b. Renal colic. Explanation: The presentation of severe, colicky abdominal pain radiating to the groin, accompanied by nausea and restlessness, is classic for renal colic, typically caused by kidney stones. The pain often radiates along the path of the ureter as the stone moves. Patients with renal colic are often unable to find a comfortable position, leading to restlessness. Appendicitis typically causes pain localizing to the right lower quadrant without radiation to the groin. Ovarian torsion usually presents with sudden, severe, unilateral pelvic pain. Ectopic pregnancy pain is often accompanied by vaginal bleeding and typically occurs in the lower abdomen or pelvis. Recognizing the characteristic presentation of renal colic is important for EMTs to guide appropriate pain management and fluid administration during transport.

197. A 16-year-old male presents with sudden onset of severe scrotal pain, nausea, and an absent cremasteric reflex on the affected side. What is the most likely diagnosis?
a. Epididymitis
b. Testicular torsion
c. Inguinal hernia
d. Hydrocele

Answer: b. Testicular torsion. Explanation: Testicular torsion is characterized by sudden, severe scrotal pain, nausea, and an absent cremasteric reflex on the affected side. This condition is a surgical emergency requiring immediate intervention to preserve testicular viability.

198. A 45-year-old male with a history of sickle cell disease presents with a painful erection lasting more than 4 hours. What is the first-line treatment for this condition?
a. Oral analgesics
b. Ice packs to the perineum
c. Intracavernosal injection of phenylephrine
d. Urethral catheterization

Answer: c. Intracavernosal injection of phenylephrine. Explanation: Priapism, particularly in patients with sickle cell disease, is treated with intracavernosal injection of phenylephrine to induce detumescence by constricting the penile blood vessels.

199. A 38-year-old male presents with severe, colicky flank pain radiating to the groin, and hematuria. What is the most appropriate initial management for his condition?
a. IV antibiotics
b. IV fluids and pain control with NSAIDs or opioids
c. Surgical intervention
d. Foley catheter insertion

Answer: b. IV fluids and pain control with NSAIDs or opioids. Explanation: The patient's presentation is consistent with nephrolithiasis (kidney stones). Initial management includes IV fluids to facilitate stone passage and pain control with NSAIDs or opioids.

200. A 70-year-old male with benign prostatic hyperplasia (BPH) presents with acute urinary retention. Which technique is most appropriate for catheterization in this patient?
a. Straight catheterization
b. Coude catheterization
c. Suprapubic catheterization
d. Ureteral stent placement

Answer: b. Coude catheterization. Explanation: A Coude catheter, with its curved tip, is often used in patients with BPH to navigate the enlarged prostate and relieve acute urinary retention.

201. A 50-year-old diabetic male presents with severe pain, swelling, and erythema of the perineum and scrotum. There is a foul odor and crepitus on examination. What is the most likely diagnosis and initial treatment?
a. Cellulitis; oral antibiotics
b. Fournier's gangrene; broad-spectrum IV antibiotics and surgical debridement
c. Epididymitis; scrotal elevation and NSAIDs
d. Inguinal hernia; surgical repair

Answer: b. Fournier's gangrene; broad-spectrum IV antibiotics and surgical debridement. Explanation: Fournier's gangrene is a rapidly progressing necrotizing fasciitis of the perineum, often seen in diabetic patients. It requires immediate treatment with broad-spectrum IV antibiotics and urgent surgical debridement.

202. A 22-year-old male presents with scrotal pain that started gradually over the past few days, along with fever and dysuria. On physical examination, the scrotum is swollen and tender with a positive Prehn's sign (pain relief with scrotal elevation). What is the most likely diagnosis?
a. Testicular torsion
b. Epididymitis
c. Inguinal hernia
d. Hydrocele

Answer: b. Epididymitis. Explanation: Epididymitis typically presents with gradual onset of scrotal pain, fever, and dysuria. A positive Prehn's sign (pain relief with scrotal elevation) helps differentiate it from testicular torsion.

203. A 65-year-old male presents with anuria and suprapubic pain. Physical examination reveals a distended bladder. What is the most appropriate initial intervention?
a. Oral diuretics
b. Bladder ultrasound
c. Foley catheter insertion
d. IV fluids

Answer: c. Foley catheter insertion. Explanation: Acute urinary retention with a distended bladder requires immediate relief through Foley catheter insertion to drain the accumulated urine and relieve pain.

204. A patient with a history of nephrolithiasis presents with severe right flank pain, nausea, and vomiting. What is the initial imaging modality of choice to confirm the diagnosis?
a. Abdominal X-ray
b. Ultrasound
c. CT scan without contrast
d. MRI

Answer: c. CT scan without contrast. Explanation: A non-contrast CT scan is the imaging modality of choice for diagnosing nephrolithiasis, as it provides detailed images of the stones and their location without the need for contrast.

205. A 30-year-old male presents with a painless, swollen scrotum. Transillumination reveals a fluid-filled mass. What is the most likely diagnosis?
a. Testicular torsion
b. Epididymitis
c. Hydrocele
d. Varicocele

Answer: c. Hydrocele. Explanation: A hydrocele presents as a painless, swollen scrotum with a fluid-filled mass that transilluminates. It is typically benign and can be managed conservatively or surgically if symptomatic.

206. A 50-year-old male with diabetes presents with fever, chills, and severe pain in the perineal region. On examination, there is swelling and crepitus. What is the most important next step in management?
a. Administer oral antibiotics
b. Schedule elective surgery
c. Immediate surgical consultation
d. Apply local heat therapy

Answer: c. Immediate surgical consultation. Explanation: The presentation of fever, chills, severe pain, swelling, and crepitus in a diabetic patient suggests Fournier's gangrene, a life-threatening emergency that requires immediate surgical consultation for debridement and IV antibiotics.

207. You're assessing a 25-year-old female with lower abdominal pain and vaginal bleeding. Her last menstrual period was 7 weeks ago. What serum β-hCG level, in combination with an empty uterus on transvaginal ultrasound, would be most concerning for ectopic pregnancy?
a. 500 mIU/mL

b. 1,000 mIU/mL
c. 1,500 mIU/mL
d. 2,000 mIU/mL

Answer: c. 1,500 mIU/mL. Explanation: The discriminatory zone for ectopic pregnancy is typically a β-hCG level of 1,500-2,000 mIU/mL with an empty uterus on transvaginal ultrasound. At this level, an intrauterine pregnancy should be visible if present. A level of 1,500 mIU/mL with no visible intrauterine gestational sac is highly suspicious for ectopic pregnancy. Levels below 1,500 mIU/mL may be too early to visualize an intrauterine pregnancy, while 2,000 mIU/mL is at the upper end of the discriminatory zone. While EMTs don't perform or interpret ultrasounds, understanding this concept aids in recognizing high-risk patients and communicating effectively with receiving facilities.

208. Which of the following is NOT one of the CERK criteria for diagnosing Pelvic Inflammatory Disease (PID)?
a. Cervical motion tenderness
b. Elevated ESR or CRP
c. Presence of lower abdominal tenderness
d. Positive pregnancy test

Answer: d. Positive pregnancy test. Explanation: The CERK criteria (Cervical motion tenderness, Elevated ESR or CRP, Right adnexal tenderness, and Knowledge of sexual activity) are used to diagnose PID. A positive pregnancy test is not part of these criteria and, in fact, would suggest an alternative diagnosis such as ectopic pregnancy. Cervical motion tenderness, elevated inflammatory markers, and lower abdominal tenderness are key components of the CERK criteria. While EMTs don't typically perform pelvic exams, understanding these criteria helps in recognizing potential PID cases and communicating relevant information to receiving facilities. Early recognition and treatment of PID are crucial to prevent complications such as infertility and chronic pelvic pain.

209. A 30-year-old female presents with sudden onset of severe, unilateral lower abdominal pain. She reports nausea and vomiting. What is the most concerning diagnosis?
a. Appendicitis
b. Ovarian torsion
c. Ectopic pregnancy
d. Pelvic inflammatory disease

Answer: b. Ovarian torsion. Explanation: The presentation of sudden, severe, unilateral lower abdominal pain accompanied by nausea and vomiting is highly suggestive of ovarian torsion. This condition occurs when an ovary twists on its vascular pedicle, compromising blood flow and potentially leading to necrosis. It's a gynecological emergency requiring rapid diagnosis and surgical intervention. While appendicitis can present similarly, it's typically right-sided and has a more gradual onset. Ectopic pregnancy often presents with vaginal bleeding in addition to pain. PID usually causes bilateral pain and may have a more gradual onset. Recognizing the possibility of ovarian torsion is crucial for EMTs to ensure rapid transport and appropriate hospital notification, as time to surgical intervention significantly impacts outcomes.

210. A 35-year-old female presents with heavy vaginal bleeding, passing large clots, and severe cramping. She's 10 weeks pregnant. What is the most likely diagnosis?
a. Implantation bleeding
b. Threatened miscarriage
c. Ectopic pregnancy
d. Placenta previa

Answer: b. Threatened miscarriage. Explanation: The presentation of heavy vaginal bleeding with large clots and severe cramping at 10 weeks gestation is most consistent with a threatened miscarriage. This occurs in about 20% of pregnancies before 20 weeks. Implantation bleeding is typically light and occurs earlier in pregnancy. Ectopic pregnancy usually presents with lighter bleeding and more unilateral pain. Placenta previa typically causes painless bleeding later in pregnancy. While EMTs can't definitively diagnose these conditions in the field, recognizing the signs of a threatened miscarriage is important for appropriate management, including fluid resuscitation if necessary, and rapid transport. It's crucial to treat all pregnant patients with vaginal bleeding as potentially unstable and requiring urgent evaluation.

211. Which of the following findings would be most concerning for a ruptured ectopic pregnancy?
a. Mild cramping and spotting
b. Shoulder pain when lying flat
c. Bilateral lower abdominal pain
d. Fever and chills

Answer: b. Shoulder pain when lying flat. Explanation: Shoulder pain when lying flat, known as Kehr's sign, is highly concerning for a ruptured ectopic pregnancy. This referred pain occurs due to blood irritating the diaphragm, which shares nerve innervation with the shoulder. It suggests significant intraabdominal bleeding. Mild cramping and spotting can occur in normal early pregnancy or threatened miscarriage. Bilateral lower abdominal pain is more typical of PID. Fever and chills suggest infection rather than ectopic pregnancy. Recognizing signs of ruptured ectopic pregnancy is critical for EMTs, as this condition can rapidly lead to hypovolemic shock and requires immediate surgical intervention. Patients with suspected ruptured ectopic pregnancy should be treated as having potentially severe internal bleeding.

212. A 22-year-old female presents with a painful, swollen mass at the vaginal opening. She reports difficulty walking and sitting. What is the most likely diagnosis?
a. Bartholin's cyst
b. Bartholin's gland abscess
c. Vaginal candidiasis
d. Genital herpes outbreak

Answer: b. Bartholin's gland abscess. Explanation: The presentation of a painful, swollen mass at the vaginal opening causing difficulty with walking and sitting is most consistent with a Bartholin's gland abscess. Bartholin's glands are located at the vaginal opening and can become infected, forming an abscess. This condition is typically more painful and problematic than a simple Bartholin's cyst, which is often asymptomatic. Vaginal candidiasis typically causes itching and discharge rather than a discrete mass. Genital herpes presents with painful vesicles or ulcers, not a large swollen mass. While definitive diagnosis and treatment occur in the hospital setting, EMTs should recognize this condition as potentially requiring incision and drainage, and manage the patient's pain appropriately during transport.

213. A 40-year-old female presents with heavy vaginal bleeding, fatigue, and shortness of breath. She reports her periods have been increasingly heavy over the past year. What is the most likely underlying cause?
a. Cervical cancer
b. Uterine fibroids
c. Endometriosis
d. Ovarian cyst rupture

Answer: b. Uterine fibroids. Explanation: The presentation of progressively heavier menstrual bleeding (menorrhagia) over time, accompanied by fatigue and shortness of breath (suggesting anemia), is most consistent with uterine fibroids. Fibroids are benign tumors of the uterus that commonly cause heavy menstrual bleeding. Cervical cancer typically causes irregular bleeding or postcoital bleeding. Endometriosis more commonly causes painful periods rather than heavy bleeding. Ovarian cyst rupture would cause acute pain and bleeding, not chronic symptoms. While EMTs don't diagnose these conditions, recognizing the possibility of significant blood loss over time is important for appropriate assessment and management, including consideration of the patient's hemodynamic status and potential need for fluid resuscitation.

214. Which of the following is NOT a typical sign or symptom of Pelvic Inflammatory Disease (PID)?
a. Bilateral lower abdominal pain
b. Fever > 101°F (38.3°C)
c. Cervical motion tenderness
d. Painless vaginal bleeding

Answer: d. Painless vaginal bleeding. Explanation: Painless vaginal bleeding is not a typical feature of Pelvic Inflammatory Disease (PID). PID typically presents with bilateral lower abdominal pain, fever, and cervical motion tenderness (although EMTs don't assess this directly). Vaginal discharge may be present, but bleeding is not a primary symptom. Painless vaginal bleeding is more characteristic of conditions like placenta previa or cervical polyps. Understanding the typical presentation of PID is important for EMTs to recognize potentially serious gynecological infections. While definitive diagnosis occurs in the hospital, early recognition can guide appropriate transport decisions and pre-arrival notifications, especially given the risk of long-term complications if PID is not promptly treated.

215. A 28-year-old female presents with severe right lower quadrant pain, nausea, and low-grade fever. Her last menstrual period was 2 weeks ago. Which of the following is the most appropriate initial action?
a. Administer NSAIDs for pain relief
b. Perform a urine pregnancy test
c. Initiate IV antibiotics
d. Apply a heating pad to the affected area

Answer: b. Perform a urine pregnancy test. Explanation: In a female of childbearing age with lower abdominal pain, the most crucial initial step is to rule out pregnancy, particularly ectopic pregnancy, which can be life-threatening. A urine pregnancy test is a quick, non-invasive way to gather this critical information. While pain management is important, NSAIDs should be avoided until pregnancy is ruled out. IV antibiotics aren't indicated without a clear diagnosis. A heating pad could potentially worsen certain conditions if applied indiscriminately. EMTs should always consider the possibility of pregnancy in women of childbearing age presenting with abdominal pain, as this significantly impacts the differential diagnosis and management approach.

216. You're assessing a 35-year-old female with vaginal bleeding at 32 weeks gestation. She reports no pain. What is the most concerning diagnosis?
a. Normal third-trimester spotting
b. Placental abruption
c. Placenta previa
d. Preterm labor

Answer: c. Placenta previa. Explanation: Painless vaginal bleeding in the third trimester is most concerning for placenta previa, a condition where the placenta covers part or all of the cervical os. This is a potentially life-threatening condition for both mother and fetus. Normal third-trimester spotting is not typically heavy. Placental abruption usually presents with painful bleeding. Preterm labor typically involves contractions and may have bloody show, but not usually painless, significant bleeding. EMTs should treat all third-trimester bleeding as potentially serious, positioning the patient on her left side to optimize uterine blood flow, and preparing for possible rapid transport. It's crucial to avoid any digital vaginal examination in suspected placenta previa, as this could provoke severe hemorrhage.

217. A 28-year-old pregnant female at 36 weeks gestation presents with severe headache, visual disturbances, and blood pressure of 170/110 mmHg. Which medication is most appropriate for initial management?
a. Nifedipine
b. Magnesium sulfate
c. Labetalol
d. Hydralazine

Answer: b. Magnesium sulfate. Explanation: Severe preeclampsia is characterized by hypertension, headache, and visual disturbances. Magnesium sulfate is the initial treatment to prevent seizures in preeclampsia, while other antihypertensives like labetalol or hydralazine are used to control blood pressure.

218. A 35-year-old pregnant female at 34 weeks gestation presents with right upper quadrant pain, elevated liver enzymes, low platelet count, and hemolysis on blood tests. What is the most likely diagnosis?
a. Preeclampsia
b. Eclampsia
c. HELLP syndrome
d. Acute fatty liver of pregnancy

Answer: c. HELLP syndrome. Explanation: HELLP syndrome is a severe form of preeclampsia characterized by hemolysis, elevated liver enzymes, and low platelet count. It presents with right upper quadrant pain and requires immediate management.

219. A 30-year-old female at 32 weeks gestation presents with vaginal bleeding and abdominal pain. On examination, the uterus is tender and rigid. What is the most likely diagnosis?
a. Placenta previa
b. Placental abruption
c. Preterm labor
d. Uterine rupture

Answer: b. Placental abruption. Explanation: Placental abruption presents with vaginal bleeding, abdominal pain, and a tender, rigid uterus. It is a separation of the placenta from the uterine wall before delivery, posing risks to both the mother and fetus.

220. A 26-year-old female delivers a baby and experiences significant bleeding post-delivery. Using the 4 T's mnemonic, which of the following is NOT a primary cause of postpartum hemorrhage?
a. Tone (uterine atony)
b. Trauma (lacerations)
c. Thrombosis (clotting disorders)
d. Temperature (hypothermia)

Answer: d. Temperature (hypothermia). Explanation: The 4 T's mnemonic for causes of postpartum hemorrhage includes Tone (uterine atony), Trauma (lacerations), Tissue (retained placenta), and Thrombin (coagulopathies). Temperature is not one of the primary causes.

221. During delivery, the baby's shoulder becomes stuck behind the mother's pubic bone. Using the HELPERR mnemonic, what is the initial maneuver to attempt resolving shoulder dystocia?
a. Episiotomy
b. McRoberts maneuver
c. Suprapubic pressure
d. Delivery of the posterior arm

Answer: b. McRoberts maneuver. Explanation: The McRoberts maneuver, part of the HELPERR mnemonic, involves flexing the mother's hips to her abdomen to widen the pelvic outlet and help release the baby's shoulder in cases of shoulder dystocia.

222. A 32-year-old pregnant female presents with new-onset seizures and a history of hypertension during her pregnancy. What is the most appropriate initial treatment?
a. Diazepam
b. Magnesium sulfate
c. Labetalol
d. Phenytoin

Answer: b. Magnesium sulfate. Explanation: New-onset seizures in a pregnant female with a history of hypertension indicate eclampsia. The first-line treatment for eclampsia is magnesium sulfate to control seizures.

223. A 28-year-old female at 30 weeks gestation presents with painless vaginal bleeding. What is the most likely diagnosis?
a. Placental abruption
b. Placenta previa
c. Preterm labor
d. Cervical insufficiency

Answer: b. Placenta previa. Explanation: Placenta previa presents with painless vaginal bleeding as the placenta covers the cervical os. This contrasts with placental abruption, which typically presents with painful bleeding.

224. A pregnant patient presents with severe preeclampsia and signs of HELLP syndrome. What is the definitive treatment for her condition?
a. Magnesium sulfate administration
b. Immediate delivery of the baby
c. Blood pressure control with antihypertensives
d. Corticosteroids for fetal lung maturity

Answer: b. Immediate delivery of the baby. Explanation: The definitive treatment for severe preeclampsia and HELLP syndrome is the immediate delivery of the baby, regardless of gestational age, to prevent further maternal and fetal complications.

225. During a delivery complicated by shoulder dystocia, which of the following maneuvers involves rotating the baby's shoulder internally to facilitate delivery?
a. McRoberts maneuver
b. Rubin maneuver
c. Suprapubic pressure
d. Delivery of the posterior arm

Answer: b. Rubin maneuver. Explanation: The Rubin maneuver involves rotating the baby's shoulder internally to reduce the shoulder's diameter and facilitate delivery in cases of shoulder dystocia.

226. A 35-year-old female at 38 weeks gestation presents with hypertension, proteinuria, and severe headache. She is diagnosed with severe preeclampsia. Which of the following laboratory findings is most likely to be associated with this condition?
a. Elevated liver enzymes
b. Low serum creatinine
c. Hyperkalemia
d. Elevated white blood cell count

Answer: a. Elevated liver enzymes. Explanation: Severe preeclampsia is often associated with elevated liver enzymes, which indicates liver involvement and potential HELLP syndrome. Other laboratory findings may include thrombocytopenia and elevated serum creatinine.

227. You're assessing a newborn immediately after birth. The infant has a heart rate of 90 bpm, is grimacing in response to stimulation, has some flexion of extremities, is cyanotic, and has irregular, shallow respirations. What would be the 1-minute APGAR score?
a. 4
b. 5
c. 6
d. 7

Answer: b. 5. Explanation: The APGAR score assesses five criteria: Appearance (color), Pulse (heart rate), Grimace (reflex irritability), Activity (muscle tone), and Respiration. Each criterion is scored 0-2. In this case: Appearance (0, cyanotic), Pulse (1, <100 bpm), Grimace (1, grimacing), Activity (1, some flexion), Respiration (1, irregular and shallow). The total score is 5. APGAR scoring is crucial for rapidly assessing newborn status and determining the need for resuscitation. A score of 5 at 1 minute indicates a newborn requiring close monitoring and possible intervention.

228. During a delivery, you notice thick meconium in the amniotic fluid. The newborn is vigorous and crying. What is the most appropriate immediate management?
a. Immediate endotracheal intubation and suctioning
b. Oropharyngeal suctioning before the first breath
c. Routine suctioning of the mouth and nose after delivery
d. No suctioning; proceed with routine newborn care

Answer: d. No suctioning; proceed with routine newborn care. Explanation: Current neonatal resuscitation guidelines recommend against routine suctioning for vigorous newborns born through meconium-stained amniotic fluid. Vigorous newborns are defined as those with good respiratory effort, muscle tone, and heart rate. Immediate intubation and suctioning are no longer recommended as they can cause harm and delay effective ventilation. Oropharyngeal suctioning before the first breath is an outdated practice. Routine suctioning of the mouth and nose is not necessary and can cause vagal stimulation, leading to bradycardia and apnea. This question tests understanding of current evidence-based practices in managing meconium-stained deliveries.

229. A newborn is pale, limp, and not breathing at birth. The heart rate is 40 bpm. What is the most appropriate next step in management?
a. Begin chest compressions
b. Administer epinephrine
c. Provide positive pressure ventilation
d. Apply supplemental oxygen via facemask

Answer: c. Provide positive pressure ventilation. Explanation: According to the Neonatal Resuscitation Program (NRP) algorithm, when a newborn is not breathing and the heart rate is below 100 bpm, the first step is to provide positive pressure ventilation (PPV) for 30 seconds. Chest compressions are only initiated if the heart rate remains below 60 bpm after effective ventilation. Epinephrine is not given until after chest compressions have been initiated and are ineffective. Supplemental oxygen alone is insufficient for a non-breathing newborn. This question assesses knowledge of the critical importance of ventilation as the primary intervention in neonatal resuscitation.

230. You're resuscitating a newborn who remains cyanotic despite 100% oxygen and has a persistent right-to-left shunt. What condition should you suspect?
a. Transient tachypnea of the newborn
b. Respiratory distress syndrome
c. Persistent pulmonary hypertension of the newborn
d. Pneumothorax

Answer: c. Persistent pulmonary hypertension of the newborn. Explanation: Persistent pulmonary hypertension of the newborn (PPHN), also known as persistent fetal circulation, is characterized by continued high pulmonary vascular resistance after birth, leading to right-to-left shunting and severe hypoxemia resistant to oxygen therapy. This condition can be life-threatening and often requires advanced interventions like inhaled nitric oxide or ECMO. Transient tachypnea and respiratory distress syndrome typically improve with oxygen and supportive care. Pneumothorax would cause asymmetric chest movement and breath sounds. Recognizing PPHN is crucial for EMTs to ensure appropriate transport to a facility capable of managing this complex condition.

231. What is the recommended method for maintaining a newborn's temperature during resuscitation?
a. Place under a radiant warmer set to maximum heat
b. Wrap in a pre-warmed blanket
c. Use a chemical warming mattress
d. Place in a polyethylene bag up to the neck

Answer: d. Place in a polyethylene bag up to the neck. Explanation: For premature or very low birth weight infants, placing the newborn in a polyethylene bag or wrap up to the neck, without drying, is the most effective method for preventing heat loss during resuscitation. This technique, known as "plastic bagging," significantly reduces evaporative and convective heat loss. Radiant warmers alone are insufficient for very premature infants. Pre-warmed blankets can help but are less effective than plastic bagging. Chemical warming mattresses are not typically recommended due to the risk of burns. Maintaining normothermia is crucial in neonatal resuscitation, as hypothermia increases mortality and morbidity in newborns.

232. A newborn delivered at term has no respiratory effort and a heart rate of 30 bpm after 30 seconds of positive pressure ventilation. What is the most appropriate next step?
a. Continue positive pressure ventilation for another 30 seconds
b. Begin chest compressions
c. Administer epinephrine
d. Perform endotracheal intubation

Answer: b. Begin chest compressions. Explanation: According to the Neonatal Resuscitation Program (NRP) algorithm, if the heart rate remains below 60 bpm after 30 seconds of effective positive pressure ventilation, chest compressions should be initiated. Compressions are performed at a 3:1 ratio with ventilations, at a rate of 90 compressions and 30 breaths per minute. Continuing ventilation alone is insufficient at this point. Epinephrine is not given until after chest compressions have been initiated and are ineffective. While intubation may be considered, it's not the immediate next step in this scenario. This question tests understanding of the progression of interventions in neonatal resuscitation.

233. What is the correct depth for chest compressions in a newborn?
a. One-third the anterior-posterior diameter of the chest
b. One-half the anterior-posterior diameter of the chest
c. 1 inch (2.5 cm)
d. 1.5 inches (4 cm)

Answer: b. One-half the anterior-posterior diameter of the chest. Explanation: The correct depth for chest compressions in a newborn is approximately one-third to one-half the anterior-posterior diameter of the chest. This typically equates to about 1.5 inches (4 cm) in a term newborn. The one-third depth is considered the minimum, with one-half being the target. Using specific measurements (like 1 inch or 1.5 inches) doesn't account for variations in newborn size. The goal is to depress the sternum sufficiently to generate a palpable pulse. This question assesses understanding of the unique aspects of CPR technique in neonates, which differs from adult or even pediatric CPR.

234. A newborn delivered at 34 weeks gestation has irregular breathing and a heart rate of 110 bpm. What is the most appropriate initial action?
a. Provide supplemental oxygen via facemask
b. Begin positive pressure ventilation
c. Stimulate by drying and rubbing the back
d. Initiate chest compressions

Answer: c. Stimulate by drying and rubbing the back. Explanation: For a newborn with a heart rate above 100 bpm but irregular breathing, the initial step is to provide tactile stimulation by drying and rubbing the back or flicking the soles of the feet. This can often stimulate regular breathing in newborns transitioning to extrauterine life. Supplemental oxygen is not necessary for a newborn with a normal heart rate. Positive pressure ventilation is only initiated if the heart rate drops below 100 bpm or if breathing doesn't improve with stimulation. Chest compressions are not indicated with a heart rate above 60 bpm. This question tests understanding of the initial steps in newborn assessment and the importance of stimulation before more invasive interventions.

235. You're assessing a newborn immediately after birth. Which of the following findings would result in the lowest score (0) for the "Activity" component of the APGAR score?
a. Some flexion of extremities
b. Active motion
c. Flaccid
d. Fully flexed arms and legs

Answer: c. Flaccid. Explanation: In the APGAR scoring system, the "Activity" component assesses muscle tone. A flaccid newborn with no muscle tone receives a score of 0 for this component. Some flexion of extremities would score 1, while active motion or fully flexed arms and legs would score 2. Understanding the nuances of APGAR scoring is crucial for EMTs to accurately assess and communicate a newborn's condition. The Activity component is particularly important as it can indicate neurological status and the need for further intervention.

236. A term newborn is delivered with thick meconium-stained amniotic fluid and is not breathing or moving. What is the most appropriate immediate action?
a. Suction the oropharynx and nasopharynx
b. Begin positive pressure ventilation
c. Perform direct laryngoscopy and suction the trachea
d. Stimulate by drying and rubbing the back

Answer: b. Begin positive pressure ventilation. Explanation: Current neonatal resuscitation guidelines prioritize ventilation for non-vigorous newborns born through meconium-stained amniotic fluid. Immediate positive pressure ventilation should be initiated for a newborn who is not breathing or moving, regardless of the presence of meconium. Routine suctioning of the oropharynx and nasopharynx is no longer recommended. Direct laryngoscopy and tracheal suctioning are no longer routinely performed before initiating ventilation. Stimulation alone is insufficient for a non-breathing newborn. This question tests knowledge of the most up-to-date approach to managing non-vigorous newborns with meconium exposure, emphasizing the critical importance of early ventilation.

237. A 2-year-old child presents with respiratory distress. Using the Pediatric Assessment Triangle (PAT), you note increased work of breathing, decreased level of consciousness, and cyanosis. What is the most appropriate immediate intervention?
a. Administer albuterol
b. Provide blow-by oxygen
c. Initiate bag-valve-mask ventilation
d. Perform chest compressions

Answer: c. Initiate bag-valve-mask ventilation. Explanation: The PAT indicates severe respiratory distress and decreased consciousness, suggesting respiratory failure. Immediate bag-valve-mask ventilation is necessary to provide adequate oxygenation and ventilation.

238. You are using the Broselow tape to determine the correct medication dose for a child who weighs 15 kg. The child falls into the blue zone. What is the correct dose of epinephrine (1:10,000) for cardiac arrest?
a. 0.15 mg
b. 0.3 mg
c. 1.5 mg
d. 0.75 mg

Answer: a. 0.15 mg. Explanation: The Broselow tape indicates that a child in the blue zone weighs approximately 15 kg. The correct dose of epinephrine (1:10,000) for cardiac arrest is 0.01 mg/kg, which equals 0.15 mg for a 15 kg child.

239. A 4-year-old child is being monitored in the emergency department. His PEWS (Pediatric Early Warning Score) is 5. Which of the following actions is most appropriate?
a. Continue routine monitoring
b. Increase the frequency of vital sign checks
c. Prepare for immediate transfer to the pediatric intensive care unit (PICU)
d. Discharge the child home

Answer: c. Prepare for immediate transfer to the pediatric intensive care unit (PICU). Explanation: A PEWS score of 5 indicates significant deterioration and necessitates immediate intervention, which often includes transfer to the PICU for closer monitoring and intensive care.

240. During a routine check-up, you assess a 9-month-old infant. Which of the following developmental milestones should the infant have achieved?
a. Saying single words like "mama" or "dada"
b. Walking independently
c. Sitting without support
d. Using a pincer grasp to pick up small objects

Answer: c. Sitting without support. Explanation: By 9 months, an infant should typically be able to sit without support. Saying single words is expected around 12 months, walking independently around 12-18 months, and using a pincer grasp around 9-12 months.

241. A 3-year-old child presents with multiple bruises in various stages of healing, including on the torso, ears, and neck. What is the most likely cause of these injuries, and which rule helps identify this?
a. Accidental trauma; Denver Developmental Screening Test
b. Non-accidental trauma; TEN-4 rule
c. Hemophilia; rule of nines
d. Nutritional deficiency; PEWS score

Answer: b. Non-accidental trauma; TEN-4 rule. Explanation: The TEN-4 rule helps identify non-accidental trauma, indicating concerning bruising on the Torso, Ears, and Neck in children under 4 years old. These signs are suspicious for abuse and require further investigation.

242. You are using the Pediatric Assessment Triangle (PAT) to assess a 5-year-old with a high fever. You observe a quiet child with a flushed face and rapid, shallow breathing. Which aspect of the PAT does this primarily involve?
a. Appearance
b. Work of breathing
c. Circulation to the skin
d. Neurological status

Answer: b. Work of breathing. Explanation: Rapid, shallow breathing primarily involves the work of breathing aspect of the PAT, indicating respiratory distress possibly due to a high fever or infection.

243. A 6-year-old child with asthma exacerbation is given albuterol based on the Broselow tape's weight estimate. After 15 minutes, there is no improvement, and the child has difficulty speaking. What is the next best step?
a. Administer a second dose of albuterol
b. Start continuous positive airway pressure (CPAP)
c. Administer intravenous magnesium sulfate
d. Prepare for intubation

Answer: a. Administer a second dose of albuterol. Explanation: For an asthma exacerbation not responding to the initial dose, a second dose of albuterol is appropriate. If there is still no improvement, other interventions like CPAP, magnesium sulfate, or intubation may be considered.

244. A 1-year-old child presents with a temperature of 39°C, irritability, and poor feeding. According to the PEWS, which parameter would contribute most to a high score indicating the need for immediate medical attention?
a. Heart rate of 120 bpm
b. Respiratory rate of 30 breaths/min
c. Capillary refill time of 4 seconds
d. Crying but consolable

Answer: c. Capillary refill time of 4 seconds. Explanation: A capillary refill time greater than 3 seconds is a significant indicator of poor perfusion and contributes to a higher PEWS score, indicating the need for immediate medical attention.

245. A 2-year-old is brought to the emergency department after a fall from a height. You note an altered level of consciousness and a bulging fontanelle. Which of the following is the most likely cause?
a. Dehydration
b. Increased intracranial pressure (ICP)
c. Meningitis
d. Simple febrile seizure

Answer: b. Increased intracranial pressure (ICP). Explanation: Altered consciousness and a bulging fontanelle in a young child after trauma suggest increased intracranial pressure, which requires urgent evaluation and management.

246. You are evaluating a 5-month-old infant who has been brought in for excessive crying. Which of the following developmental milestones would be considered delayed if not yet achieved by this age?
a. Rolling over from stomach to back
b. Smiling in response to social interaction
c. Reaching for objects
d. Holding head steady when supported

Answer: b. Smiling in response to social interaction. Explanation: Social smiling typically occurs by 2 months. Delays in social interactions, such as not smiling in response to social interaction by 5 months, would be concerning for developmental delay.

247. You're assessing a 6-month-old with respiratory distress. The infant has a respiratory rate of 60, moderate retractions, and diffuse wheezes. Using the RDAI (Respiratory Distress Assessment Instrument) score, which of the following would be most accurate?
a. Mild distress (score 0-4)
b. Moderate distress (score 5-8)
c. Severe distress (score 9-12)
d. Critical distress (score >12)

Answer: b. Moderate distress (score 5-8). Explanation: The RDAI score assesses wheezing and retractions. With moderate retractions and diffuse wheezes, this infant would likely score in the moderate distress range (5-8). The high respiratory rate supports this assessment. RDAI is particularly useful in assessing bronchiolitis severity. Mild distress typically has minimal retractions and wheezing. Severe distress would show more pronounced retractions and wheezing. The RDAI doesn't have a "critical" category; scores >12 are considered severe. Understanding this scoring system helps EMTs communicate severity effectively and guide treatment decisions, particularly regarding the need for hospital admission.

248. A 3-year-old presents with a barking cough, inspiratory stridor, and mild respiratory distress. The symptoms worsened at night. What is the most likely diagnosis?
a. Epiglottitis
b. Bacterial tracheitis
c. Croup (Laryngotracheobronchitis)
d. Foreign body aspiration

Answer: c. Croup (Laryngotracheobronchitis). Explanation: The presentation of a barking cough, inspiratory stridor, and symptoms worsening at night is classic for croup. Croup is typically viral and affects children aged 6 months to 3 years. Epiglottitis usually presents with more severe distress, drooling, and a preference for sitting forward. Bacterial tracheitis often follows a viral infection and presents with high fever and toxic appearance. Foreign body aspiration typically has a sudden onset and may have unilateral wheezing. Recognizing croup is crucial for EMTs as management differs from other upper airway emergencies, often involving nebulized epinephrine and corticosteroids. The characteristic "barking" cough is often described as "seal-like" and is a key diagnostic feature.

249. You're treating a 4-year-old with sudden onset of choking while eating peanuts. The child is conscious but unable to speak or cough effectively. What is the most appropriate initial action?
a. Perform blind finger sweeps
b. Administer abdominal thrusts
c. Deliver 5 back blows followed by 5 chest thrusts
d. Attempt positive pressure ventilation

Answer: c. Deliver 5 back blows followed by 5 chest thrusts. Explanation: For a choking child over 1 year of age who is conscious but unable to cough effectively, the recommended sequence is 5 back blows followed by 5 chest thrusts. This differs from adult management, which uses abdominal thrusts. Blind finger sweeps are no longer recommended due to the risk of pushing the object further into the airway. Abdominal thrusts are used in adults but not recommended as the initial action in young children. Positive pressure ventilation is not appropriate for a conscious choking victim. This question tests knowledge of age-specific foreign body airway obstruction management, which is crucial for effective emergency care in pediatric patients.

250. A 7-year-old with known asthma presents with moderate respiratory distress. Using the Pediatric Respiratory Assessment Measure (PRAM), which of the following findings would contribute the highest score to the assessment?
a. Oxygen saturation 91-94%
b. Suprasternal retractions
c. Scattered wheezes
d. Decreased air entry

Answer: b. Suprasternal retractions. Explanation: In the PRAM score, suprasternal retractions contribute the highest individual score (3 points). Oxygen saturation of 91-94% scores 1 point, scattered wheezes score 1 point, and decreased air entry scores 1 or 2 points depending on severity. The PRAM score helps quantify asthma severity and guide treatment decisions. A total score of 0-3 indicates mild, 4-7 moderate, and 8-12 severe asthma exacerbation. Understanding this scoring system allows EMTs to more accurately assess and communicate asthma severity, potentially influencing treatment protocols and transport decisions.

251. You're assessing a 2-year-old with fever, cough, and rapid breathing. According to WHO criteria for pneumonia, which respiratory rate would indicate the need for antibiotics in this age group?
a. >40 breaths per minute
b. >50 breaths per minute
c. >60 breaths per minute
d. >70 breaths per minute

Answer: b. >50 breaths per minute. Explanation: The World Health Organization (WHO) criteria for pneumonia in children 1-5 years old define tachypnea as a respiratory rate >40 breaths per minute. However, the threshold for considering antibiotics is set higher at >50 breaths per minute in this age group. For infants 2-12 months, the threshold is >50 breaths per minute, and for children >5 years, it's >30 breaths per minute. These criteria are particularly useful in resource-limited settings but provide a good baseline for assessing pediatric respiratory distress. EMTs should be aware of these age-specific respiratory rate thresholds to accurately assess the severity of respiratory illnesses in children.

252. A 5-month-old presents with rhinorrhea, cough, and increased work of breathing. On auscultation, you hear diffuse crackles and wheezes. What is the most likely diagnosis?
a. Asthma exacerbation
b. Bronchiolitis
c. Pneumonia
d. Croup

Answer: b. Bronchiolitis. Explanation: The presentation of rhinorrhea, cough, increased work of breathing, and diffuse crackles and wheezes in an infant is most consistent with bronchiolitis. This viral lower respiratory tract infection typically affects children under 2 years, with a peak incidence between 3-6 months. Asthma exacerbations are uncommon in infants this young. Pneumonia typically presents with more focal findings on auscultation. Croup primarily affects the upper airway and presents with a characteristic barking cough. Recognizing bronchiolitis is important for EMTs as management focuses on supportive care, including oxygenation and hydration, rather than bronchodilators or steroids which are often ineffective in this condition.

253. You're assessing a 3-year-old with suspected epiglottitis. Which of the following is NOT typically associated with epiglottitis?
a. Preference for sitting upright and leaning forward
b. Barking cough
c. High fever and toxic appearance
d. Drooling and inability to swallow

Answer: b. Barking cough. Explanation: A barking cough is not typically associated with epiglottitis; it's a characteristic feature of croup. Epiglottitis classically presents with rapid onset of high fever, toxic appearance, drooling, and a preference for sitting upright and leaning forward (tripod position) due to airway obstruction. The absence of a barking cough helps differentiate epiglottitis from croup. This distinction is crucial as the management approaches differ significantly. Epiglottitis is a medical emergency requiring careful airway management, often necessitating intubation in a controlled setting. EMTs should be aware that attempts to examine the throat or lay the patient supine can precipitate complete airway obstruction in epiglottitis.

254. An 8-year-old with a history of asthma presents with moderate respiratory distress. Which of the following treatments should be administered first?
a. Inhaled ipratropium bromide
b. Oral prednisone
c. Inhaled albuterol
d. Subcutaneous epinephrine

Answer: c. Inhaled albuterol. Explanation: In a child with known asthma presenting with moderate respiratory distress, inhaled albuterol (a short-acting beta-2 agonist) is the first-line treatment. It provides rapid bronchodilation and symptom relief. Ipratropium bromide can be added to albuterol for severe exacerbations but is not the first choice. Oral prednisone is important for reducing inflammation but takes hours to take effect. Subcutaneous epinephrine is reserved for severe, life-threatening exacerbations unresponsive to other treatments. This question tests knowledge of the stepwise approach to managing pediatric asthma exacerbations, emphasizing the importance of rapid bronchodilation as the initial intervention.

255. A 2-year-old presents with sudden onset of unilateral wheezing and respiratory distress while playing with small toys. What is the most likely diagnosis?
a. Asthma exacerbation
b. Pneumonia
c. Foreign body aspiration

d. Bronchiolitis

Answer: c. Foreign body aspiration. Explanation: The sudden onset of unilateral wheezing and respiratory distress in a toddler playing with small toys is highly suggestive of foreign body aspiration. Unilateral wheezing is a key finding, as it indicates partial obstruction of one main bronchus. Asthma typically causes bilateral wheezing. Pneumonia usually develops more gradually and often has associated fever. Bronchiolitis typically affects younger infants and causes bilateral symptoms. Recognizing the signs of foreign body aspiration is crucial for EMTs, as these cases may require urgent bronchoscopy for removal. The history of playing with small objects provides an important contextual clue in this scenario.

256. You're assessing a 4-month-old with bronchiolitis using the RDAI score. Which of the following would NOT be included in this assessment?
a. Expiratory wheezing
b. Suprasternal retractions
c. Nasal flaring
d. Inspiratory crackles

Answer: d. Inspiratory crackles. Explanation: The Respiratory Distress Assessment Instrument (RDAI) score for bronchiolitis focuses on two main components: wheezing and retractions. It does not include assessment of inspiratory crackles. Expiratory wheezing and suprasternal retractions are key components of the score. While nasal flaring is a sign of respiratory distress, it's not specifically part of the RDAI. Understanding the components of this scoring system is important for EMTs to accurately assess and communicate the severity of bronchiolitis in infants. The RDAI helps in standardizing the assessment of bronchiolitis severity and can guide treatment decisions, including the need for hospital admission.

257. A 2-month-old infant presents with cyanosis and difficulty breathing. On examination, a loud systolic murmur is heard. Which of the following congenital heart defects is most likely responsible for these symptoms?
a. Ventricular septal defect (VSD)
b. Atrial septal defect (ASD)
c. Tetralogy of Fallot
d. Patent ductus arteriosus (PDA)

Answer: c. Tetralogy of Fallot. Explanation: Tetralogy of Fallot is a cyanotic congenital heart defect characterized by four components: ventricular septal defect, pulmonary stenosis, right ventricular hypertrophy, and an overriding aorta. Cyanosis and a loud systolic murmur are common presenting signs.

258. A 6-year-old child presents with prolonged fever, conjunctivitis, and a strawberry tongue. What is the most likely diagnosis, and which complication must be closely monitored?
a. Scarlet fever; rheumatic heart disease
b. Kawasaki disease; coronary artery aneurysms
c. Measles; encephalitis
d. Hand, foot, and mouth disease; dehydration

Answer: b. Kawasaki disease; coronary artery aneurysms. Explanation: Kawasaki disease is characterized by prolonged fever, conjunctivitis, and a strawberry tongue. The most serious complication is the development of coronary artery aneurysms, requiring close monitoring and echocardiography.

259. A 15-year-old male collapses during a basketball game. He is found unresponsive with no pulse. Which of the following is the most likely cause?
a. Ventricular septal defect (VSD)
b. Hypertrophic cardiomyopathy
c. Atrial septal defect (ASD)
d. Patent ductus arteriosus (PDA)

Answer: b. Hypertrophic cardiomyopathy. Explanation: Hypertrophic cardiomyopathy is a common cause of sudden cardiac death in young athletes due to the risk of arrhythmias. It often presents without prior symptoms until a collapse during physical exertion.

260. A 4-year-old presents with lethargy, poor capillary refill, and hypotension. Using the CAP-D assessment for pediatric shock, which type of shock is this child most likely experiencing?
a. Cardiogenic shock
b. Distributive shock
c. Hypovolemic shock
d. Obstructive shock

Answer: c. Hypovolemic shock. Explanation: Hypovolemic shock is characterized by lethargy, poor capillary refill, and hypotension due to significant fluid loss. The CAP-D (Cardiogenic, Anaphylactic/Distributive, Hypovolemic, and Dissociative) mnemonic helps assess and classify pediatric shock.

261. A 5-year-old child with a known history of a congenital heart defect presents with increased work of breathing and cyanosis. Which of the following is the best immediate action?
a. Administer oxygen
b. Perform chest compressions
c. Give intravenous fluids
d. Administer epinephrine

Answer: a. Administer oxygen. Explanation: Increased work of breathing and cyanosis in a child with a congenital heart defect requires immediate administration of oxygen to improve oxygenation and reduce respiratory distress.

262. Which of the following is a hallmark feature of an acyanotic congenital heart defect?
a. Cyanosis
b. Decreased pulmonary blood flow
c. Left-to-right shunt

d. Right-to-left shunt

Answer: c. Left-to-right shunt. Explanation: Acyanotic congenital heart defects typically involve a left-to-right shunt, leading to increased pulmonary blood flow and no cyanosis. Examples include VSD and ASD.

263. In a child with suspected Kawasaki disease, which of the following criteria is NOT part of the diagnostic criteria?
a. Bilateral conjunctival injection
b. Polymorphous rash
c. Arthralgia
d. Cervical lymphadenopathy

Answer: c. Arthralgia. Explanation: The diagnostic criteria for Kawasaki disease include fever for at least 5 days and four of the following: bilateral conjunctival injection, polymorphous rash, cervical lymphadenopathy, changes in the extremities, and oral mucosal changes. Arthralgia is not part of the criteria.

264. A 3-year-old child presents with a fever and a new murmur. An echocardiogram reveals a vegetation on the mitral valve. What is the most likely diagnosis?
a. Rheumatic fever
b. Kawasaki disease
c. Bacterial endocarditis
d. Viral myocarditis

Answer: c. Bacterial endocarditis. Explanation: The presence of fever, a new murmur, and vegetations on the mitral valve seen on echocardiogram are indicative of bacterial endocarditis, a serious infection of the heart valves.

265. Which of the following drugs is the first-line treatment for an infant in cardiogenic shock due to heart failure?
a. Dopamine
b. Epinephrine
c. Norepinephrine
d. Atropine

Answer: a. Dopamine. Explanation: Dopamine is often used as the first-line treatment for infants in cardiogenic shock to increase cardiac output and improve perfusion by its inotropic and vasopressor effects.

266. During a PALS (Pediatric Advanced Life Support) scenario, a 7-year-old is in ventricular fibrillation. After the initial defibrillation, what is the next immediate step?
a. Administer amiodarone
b. Perform chest compressions
c. Give epinephrine
d. Perform endotracheal intubation

Answer: b. Perform chest compressions. Explanation: After the initial defibrillation, the next immediate step in the PALS algorithm for ventricular fibrillation is to perform high-quality chest compressions for 2 minutes before reassessing the rhythm and considering medication administration.

267. You're called to assess a 2-year-old who had a seizure lasting 3 minutes. The child has a temperature of 102.5°F (39.2°C) and no history of seizures. What is the most appropriate initial management?
a. Administer intranasal midazolam
b. Begin cooling measures immediately
c. Perform a finger-stick glucose test
d. Position the child in recovery position and monitor

Answer: d. Position the child in recovery position and monitor. Explanation: This scenario describes a simple febrile seizure, characterized by a seizure lasting less than 15 minutes in a child 6 months to 5 years old with a fever and no underlying neurological issues. Simple febrile seizures typically self-resolve and don't require specific anticonvulsant treatment. The priority is to ensure airway patency and monitor for any complications. Intranasal midazolam is not indicated for simple febrile seizures. Aggressive cooling can trigger rigors and is not recommended. While checking glucose is important in seizures, it's not the most immediate action in a clear febrile seizure scenario. Understanding the management of febrile seizures is crucial for EMTs to avoid unnecessary interventions and provide appropriate reassurance to caregivers.

268. A 6-year-old presents with sudden onset right-sided weakness and speech difficulty. Which of the following findings on the Pediatric NIH Stroke Scale (PedNIHSS) would be most concerning for an acute stroke?
a. Mild pronator drift of the right arm
b. Partial gaze palsy
c. Complete hemiparesis of the right side
d. Mild facial asymmetry

Answer: c. Complete hemiparesis of the right side. Explanation: On the PedNIHSS, complete hemiparesis (a score of 4 on the motor items) is highly concerning for an acute, severe stroke. While all options suggest neurological deficits, complete hemiparesis indicates a large area of brain involvement. Mild pronator drift and partial gaze palsy, while abnormal, are less severe. Mild facial asymmetry could be due to various causes. The PedNIHSS is an adaptation of the adult NIHSS, tailored for pediatric stroke assessment. EMTs should be aware that pediatric stroke, though rare, can occur and requires rapid recognition and transport to a pediatric stroke center. Time is brain, even in children.

269. You're treating a 10-year-old with a severe head injury. The child is unconscious with decorticate posturing. What is the most appropriate immediate intervention to manage potential increased intracranial pressure (ICP)?
a. Administer mannitol 0.5 g/kg IV
b. Hyperventilate to an EtCO2 of 30-35 mmHg
c. Elevate the head of the bed to 30 degrees
d. Administer 3% hypertonic saline bolus

Answer: c. Elevate the head of the bed to 30 degrees. Explanation: In managing potential increased ICP in a pediatric patient, elevating the head of the bed to 30 degrees is the most appropriate immediate intervention. This position helps promote venous drainage from the brain without requiring medication administration or advanced techniques. Mannitol and hypertonic saline are typically administered in hospital settings under specific protocols. Hyperventilation to EtCO2 30-35 mmHg is no longer routinely recommended due to the risk of cerebral vasoconstriction and potential worsening of ischemia. Current guidelines suggest targeting normal EtCO2 (35-45 mmHg) unless there are signs of impending herniation. EMTs should focus on basic measures to control ICP while ensuring rapid transport to a pediatric trauma center.

270. A 3-month-old is brought in by parents concerned about irritability and vomiting. On examination, you note a bulging fontanelle and retinal hemorrhages. What condition should you most strongly suspect?
a. Meningitis
b. Hydrocephalus
c. Shaken Baby Syndrome
d. Intracranial tumor

Answer: c. Shaken Baby Syndrome. Explanation: The combination of irritability, vomiting, bulging fontanelle, and especially retinal hemorrhages in an infant is highly suspicious for Shaken Baby Syndrome, also known as Abusive Head Trauma. Retinal hemorrhages are particularly specific to this condition. While meningitis can cause a bulging fontanelle, it typically doesn't cause retinal hemorrhages. Hydrocephalus would cause a bulging fontanelle but not retinal hemorrhages. Intracranial tumors are rare in this age group and would typically have a more gradual onset. Recognizing signs of potential abuse is crucial for EMTs, as it impacts both immediate medical management and the need for appropriate reporting and child protection measures.

271. You're assessing a 7-year-old with altered mental status following a fall. How would you score eye opening on the Pediatric Glasgow Coma Scale if the child opens eyes only to painful stimuli?
a. 1
b. 2
c. 3
d. 4

Answer: b. 2. Explanation: In the Pediatric Glasgow Coma Scale, eye opening is scored as follows: 4 for spontaneous eye opening, 3 for eye opening to verbal stimuli, 2 for eye opening to pain, and 1 for no eye opening. Therefore, a child who opens eyes only to painful stimuli would score 2 for this component. The Pediatric GCS is similar to the adult version but includes modifications in the verbal response category to account for developmental differences in younger children. Understanding the correct application of the Pediatric GCS is crucial for EMTs to accurately assess and communicate the neurological status of pediatric patients, guiding treatment decisions and triage to appropriate facilities.

272. A 4-year-old presents with headache, vomiting, and ataxia that has worsened over the past week. What is the most likely diagnosis?
a. Migraine
b. Viral meningitis
c. Brain tumor

d. Post-concussion syndrome

Answer: c. Brain tumor. Explanation: The presentation of progressively worsening headache, vomiting, and ataxia over a week is concerning for increased intracranial pressure, with brain tumor being a likely cause in this age group. This triad of symptoms (headache, vomiting, and ataxia) is classic for posterior fossa tumors in children. Migraines typically have a more intermittent pattern. Viral meningitis usually has a more acute onset and often includes fever. Post-concussion syndrome requires a history of recent head trauma. While EMTs don't diagnose brain tumors, recognizing patterns suggestive of serious intracranial pathology is crucial for appropriate triage and transport decisions, ensuring these patients receive timely neurosurgical evaluation.

273. You're assessing a 5-year-old who fell from a height. The child opens eyes spontaneously, is confused, and flexes to pain. What is the Pediatric Glasgow Coma Scale score?
a. 9
b. 10
c. 11
d. 12

Answer: b. 10. Explanation: The Pediatric Glasgow Coma Scale score for this child would be 10. Breaking it down: Eye opening (4 - opens spontaneously), Verbal response (4 - confused, for a child this age), Motor response (3 - flexion to pain). The total score is 4 + 4 + 3 = 11. The Pediatric GCS is crucial for assessing neurological status in children, with some modifications from the adult scale, particularly in the verbal response category to account for developmental differences. A score of 10 indicates moderate brain injury, requiring careful monitoring and likely neuroimaging. EMTs should be proficient in using this scale to accurately communicate a pediatric patient's neurological status to receiving facilities.

274. An 8-year-old presents with sudden onset severe headache, vomiting, and neck stiffness. What is the most appropriate initial management?
a. Administer acetaminophen for pain relief
b. Perform lumbar puncture to rule out meningitis
c. Initiate CT scan to evaluate for subarachnoid hemorrhage
d. Maintain spine immobilization and transport rapidly

Answer: d. Maintain spine immobilization and transport rapidly. Explanation: The presentation of sudden severe headache, vomiting, and neck stiffness in a child is concerning for serious intracranial pathology, including subarachnoid hemorrhage or meningitis. The most appropriate initial management is to maintain spine immobilization (due to neck stiffness) and transport rapidly to a facility capable of advanced neurological assessment and management. Pain relief alone is insufficient. Lumbar puncture and CT scans are hospital-based diagnostic procedures, not field interventions. EMTs should focus on supportive care, maintaining airway and circulation, and rapid transport. The priority is to get the patient to definitive care as quickly as possible while preventing any potential exacerbation of intracranial issues.

275. A 6-month-old presents with irritability, vomiting, and a rapidly enlarging head circumference. What condition should you most strongly suspect?

a. Shaken Baby Syndrome
b. Hydrocephalus
c. Bacterial meningitis
d. Intracranial hemorrhage

Answer: b. Hydrocephalus. Explanation: The combination of irritability, vomiting, and a rapidly enlarging head circumference in an infant is most suggestive of hydrocephalus. This condition involves an accumulation of cerebrospinal fluid in the brain, leading to increased intracranial pressure. The enlarging head circumference is a key finding, as the cranial sutures in infants can separate to accommodate increasing pressure. Shaken Baby Syndrome typically presents with more acute neurological deficits. Bacterial meningitis usually includes fever and more acute onset. Intracranial hemorrhage would likely have a more sudden onset of symptoms. While EMTs don't diagnose hydrocephalus, recognizing these signs is important for appropriate triage and communication with receiving facilities, as hydrocephalus often requires neurosurgical intervention.

276. You're assessing a 3-year-old with altered mental status. The child incomprehensibly mutters and withdraws from pain. What is the Pediatric Glasgow Coma Scale score?
a. 8
b. 9
c. 10
d. 11

Answer: b. 9. Explanation: The Pediatric Glasgow Coma Scale score for this child would be 9. Breaking it down: Eye opening (2 - opens to pain, assumed as not spontaneous or to voice given the altered mental status), Verbal response (3 - inappropriate words/incomprehensible muttering for this age), Motor response (4 - withdraws from pain). The total score is 2 + 3 + 4 = 9. A score of 8 or less indicates severe brain injury, while 9-12 is moderate. This score suggests a significant neurological impairment requiring immediate medical attention. EMTs should be adept at using the Pediatric GCS to accurately assess and communicate a child's neurological status, guiding treatment decisions and the level of urgency in transport and handover to receiving facilities.

277. A 10-year-old child with type 1 diabetes presents with polyuria, polydipsia, and abdominal pain. His blood glucose is 550 mg/dL, pH is 7.1, and serum bicarbonate is 10 mEq/L. What is the most important initial treatment?
a. Administer IV regular insulin
b. Administer IV fluids
c. Administer sodium bicarbonate
d. Administer IV potassium

Answer: b. Administer IV fluids. Explanation: The primary initial treatment for diabetic ketoacidosis (DKA) in children is fluid resuscitation to address dehydration and improve perfusion. Insulin therapy should be started after initial fluid bolus, and electrolyte imbalances corrected based on lab results.

278. A newborn presents with vomiting, dehydration, and hyperpigmentation of the skin. Blood tests show hyponatremia and hyperkalemia. What is the most likely diagnosis?
a. Diabetic ketoacidosis

b. Congenital adrenal hyperplasia
c. Thyroid storm
d. Growth hormone deficiency

Answer: b. Congenital adrenal hyperplasia. Explanation: Congenital adrenal hyperplasia (CAH) often presents in newborns with vomiting, dehydration, hyperpigmentation, hyponatremia, and hyperkalemia due to adrenal insufficiency and deficiency of cortisol and aldosterone.

279. A 12-year-old female with a history of hyperthyroidism presents with fever, tachycardia, and altered mental status. Which of the following is the most appropriate initial treatment?
a. Administer IV levothyroxine
b. Administer IV propranolol
c. Administer IV hydrocortisone
d. Administer IV fluids

Answer: b. Administer IV propranolol. Explanation: In thyroid storm, the immediate treatment involves controlling the adrenergic symptoms with beta-blockers like propranolol. Other treatments, including antithyroid drugs and supportive care, follow after initial stabilization.

280. A 3-year-old male presents with short stature, delayed bone age, and hypoglycemia. Which diagnostic test is most appropriate to confirm growth hormone deficiency?
a. Serum IGF-1 levels
b. Serum cortisol levels
c. Serum TSH levels
d. Random blood glucose

Answer: a. Serum IGF-1 levels. Explanation: Serum IGF-1 levels are used to screen for growth hormone deficiency. Low levels of IGF-1 are indicative of growth hormone deficiency, necessitating further evaluation with growth hormone stimulation tests.

281. An infant presents with jitteriness, irritability, and poor feeding. A bedside glucose check shows a blood sugar level of 30 mg/dL. What is the most appropriate initial treatment?
a. Oral glucose gel
b. Intramuscular glucagon
c. Intravenous dextrose
d. Continuous feeding via nasogastric tube

Answer: c. Intravenous dextrose. Explanation: Hypoglycemia in infants should be treated with intravenous dextrose to rapidly increase blood glucose levels and prevent neurological damage.

282. A child with known congenital adrenal hyperplasia presents with vomiting and severe hypotension. Which of the following is the most important immediate treatment?
a. Oral hydrocortisone
b. Intravenous normal saline
c. Intravenous hydrocortisone
d. Oral glucose

Answer: c. Intravenous hydrocortisone. Explanation: In an adrenal crisis, such as in congenital adrenal hyperplasia, the most important immediate treatment is intravenous hydrocortisone to replace deficient cortisol and stabilize the patient.

283. A 15-year-old female with type 1 diabetes presents with rapid breathing, fruity-smelling breath, and confusion. Blood tests reveal a high blood glucose level and ketones in the urine. What is the first step in managing this condition?
a. Administer subcutaneous insulin
b. Administer IV fluids
c. Administer oral glucose
d. Administer IV sodium bicarbonate

Answer: b. Administer IV fluids. Explanation: The first step in managing diabetic ketoacidosis (DKA) is fluid resuscitation to correct dehydration and improve circulation before starting insulin therapy.

284. A 6-year-old male with a history of hypothyroidism presents with hypothermia, bradycardia, and lethargy. What is the most appropriate initial management?
a. Administer oral levothyroxine
b. Administer IV fluids
c. Administer IV levothyroxine
d. Administer IV dextrose

Answer: c. Administer IV levothyroxine. Explanation: Myxedema coma, a severe form of hypothyroidism, requires immediate treatment with intravenous levothyroxine to replace deficient thyroid hormone and stabilize the patient's condition.

285. A 2-year-old child presents with seizures, hypoglycemia, and elevated insulin levels. Which condition is most likely responsible for these symptoms?
a. Growth hormone deficiency
b. Hyperinsulinism
c. Congenital adrenal hyperplasia
d. Thyroid storm

Answer: b. Hyperinsulinism. Explanation: Hyperinsulinism leads to excessive insulin production, causing severe hypoglycemia and associated symptoms such as seizures. Diagnosis is confirmed by elevated insulin levels during hypoglycemia.

286. A 7-year-old child with type 1 diabetes is found unconscious with a blood glucose level of 25 mg/dL. What is the most appropriate initial treatment?
a. Administer oral glucose
b. Administer subcutaneous insulin
c. Administer intramuscular glucagon
d. Administer IV fluids

Answer: c. Administer intramuscular glucagon. Explanation: In a hypoglycemic emergency with unconsciousness, intramuscular glucagon is administered to rapidly increase blood glucose levels by promoting glycogenolysis in the liver.

287. A 2-year-old presents with sudden onset of drooling and refusal to eat after playing with a remote control. The parents suspect button battery ingestion. What is the most critical immediate action?
a. Administer activated charcoal
b. Induce vomiting with ipecac syrup
c. Obtain an immediate chest X-ray
d. Transport rapidly to the nearest emergency department

Answer: d. Transport rapidly to the nearest emergency department. Explanation: In suspected button battery ingestion, rapid transport to the emergency department is crucial. Button batteries can cause severe tissue damage within 2 hours of ingestion due to electrical current generation and hydroxide production. Activated charcoal is ineffective for battery ingestion. Inducing vomiting is contraindicated as it may cause esophageal injury. While X-ray is important for diagnosis, it shouldn't delay transport. The priority is to get the child to a facility capable of immediate endoscopic removal. EMTs should recognize button battery ingestion as a true emergency requiring rapid intervention to prevent potentially life-threatening complications like esophageal perforation or fistula formation.

288. You're treating a 4-year-old who ingested an unknown amount of acetaminophen 2 hours ago. Which of the following is the most appropriate initial management?
a. Administer N-acetylcysteine (NAC) immediately
b. Perform gastric lavage
c. Obtain a serum acetaminophen level
d. Administer activated charcoal

Answer: c. Obtain a serum acetaminophen level. Explanation: In acetaminophen overdose, the initial management involves obtaining a serum acetaminophen level, ideally 4 hours post-ingestion. This level, plotted on the Rumack-Matthew nomogram, determines the need for N-acetylcysteine (NAC) treatment. While NAC is the antidote, it's not given empirically without knowing the serum level. Gastric lavage is rarely recommended in pediatric poisonings. Activated charcoal can be considered but is not the first step and may interfere with NAC administration if needed. EMTs should focus on supportive care and rapid transport to a facility capable of measuring acetaminophen levels and administering NAC if indicated. Early recognition and proper management of acetaminophen toxicity are crucial to prevent potentially fatal hepatotoxicity.

289. A 3-year-old presents with irritability, developmental regression, and abdominal pain. The family recently moved into an old house. What toxicity should you suspect?
a. Carbon monoxide poisoning
b. Lead poisoning
c. Mercury poisoning
d. Arsenic poisoning

Answer: b. Lead poisoning. Explanation: The combination of irritability, developmental regression, and abdominal pain in a child who recently moved into an old house is highly suggestive of lead poisoning. Lead exposure is common in older homes due to lead-based paint. Symptoms of lead poisoning can be subtle and nonspecific, making it challenging to diagnose. Carbon monoxide poisoning typically has a more acute onset and includes headache and dizziness. Mercury poisoning often presents with neurological symptoms like tremors. Arsenic poisoning usually causes gastrointestinal symptoms and skin changes. While EMTs don't diagnose lead poisoning, recognizing these signs is crucial for appropriate triage and communication with receiving facilities. Lead poisoning requires long-term management and environmental intervention.

290. You're called to assess a 5-year-old who ingested lamp oil. The child is coughing and has shortness of breath. What is the most appropriate initial management?
a. Induce vomiting to remove the hydrocarbon
b. Administer activated charcoal
c. Provide supplemental oxygen and monitor closely
d. Perform gastric lavage

Answer: c. Provide supplemental oxygen and monitor closely. Explanation: In hydrocarbon ingestion, particularly lamp oil which is a low-viscosity hydrocarbon, the primary concern is aspiration pneumonitis. The most appropriate initial management is to provide supplemental oxygen and closely monitor respiratory status. Inducing vomiting is contraindicated as it increases the risk of aspiration. Activated charcoal is not recommended for hydrocarbon ingestions as it doesn't bind well to these substances and may induce vomiting. Gastric lavage is contraindicated due to the high risk of aspiration. EMTs should focus on respiratory support and rapid transport. Even small amounts of ingested hydrocarbons can cause significant respiratory distress, and symptoms may be delayed, necessitating close observation.

291. A family of four, including two children ages 3 and 5, present with headache, nausea, and dizziness. Their home's carbon monoxide detector was beeping. Which of the following findings would be most concerning for severe CO poisoning in the children?
a. SpO2 reading of 99% on room air
b. Cherry-red skin color
c. Confusion and ataxia
d. Tachycardia and hypertension

Answer: c. Confusion and ataxia. Explanation: In carbon monoxide (CO) poisoning, confusion and ataxia are signs of severe toxicity, especially in children. CO poisoning can cause significant neurological effects before other obvious symptoms appear. SpO2 readings are often falsely normal in CO poisoning as pulse oximetry can't differentiate between oxyhemoglobin and carboxyhemoglobin. Cherry-red skin is a late and unreliable sign. Tachycardia and hypertension can occur but are nonspecific. EMTs should have a high index of suspicion for CO poisoning in multiple patients from the same household presenting with similar symptoms. Treatment involves high-flow oxygen and rapid transport to a facility capable of measuring carboxyhemoglobin levels and possibly providing hyperbaric oxygen therapy.

292. A 6-year-old presents with abdominal pain, constipation, and anemia. The child has a history of pica. What toxic exposure should you most strongly suspect?
a. Iron overdose
b. Lead poisoning
c. Copper toxicity
d. Zinc poisoning

Answer: b. Lead poisoning. Explanation: The combination of abdominal pain, constipation, anemia, and a history of pica is highly suggestive of lead poisoning. Pica, the ingestion of non-food items, is a risk factor for lead exposure, especially in children. Lead poisoning can cause a wide range of symptoms, including gastrointestinal issues and anemia. Iron overdose typically presents more acutely with vomiting and gastrointestinal bleeding. Copper toxicity is rare and often associated with Wilson's disease. Zinc poisoning is uncommon and usually causes more prominent gastrointestinal symptoms. While EMTs don't diagnose lead poisoning, recognizing these signs is important for appropriate triage and communication with receiving facilities. Lead poisoning requires long-term management and environmental investigation.

293. You're treating a 2-year-old who ingested an unknown substance found in the garage. The child is lethargic with pinpoint pupils. What is the most appropriate pharmacological intervention?
a. Administer activated charcoal
b. Give naloxone 0.1 mg/kg IV
c. Administer flumazenil 0.01 mg/kg IV
d. Give N-acetylcysteine 140 mg/kg PO

Answer: b. Give naloxone 0.1 mg/kg IV. Explanation: The presentation of lethargy with pinpoint pupils strongly suggests opioid toxicity. Naloxone, an opioid antagonist, is the appropriate antidote. The dose for children is 0.1 mg/kg IV (max 2 mg per dose). Activated charcoal is not effective for opioid overdose and may be dangerous in a lethargic patient. Flumazenil is used for benzodiazepine overdose, which typically causes larger pupils. N-acetylcysteine is the antidote for acetaminophen toxicity. EMTs should be familiar with naloxone administration in pediatric patients, as accidental opioid ingestion can be rapidly fatal in children. It's crucial to maintain respiratory support and be prepared for possible opioid withdrawal symptoms after naloxone administration.

294. An 8-year-old presents with nausea, vomiting, and right upper quadrant pain 24 hours after ingesting "a handful" of acetaminophen tablets. What is the most likely explanation for these symptoms?
a. Acute hepatotoxicity
b. Direct gastrointestinal irritation
c. Renal failure

d. Metabolic acidosis

Answer: a. Acute hepatotoxicity. Explanation: The symptoms of nausea, vomiting, and right upper quadrant pain 24 hours after acetaminophen ingestion are consistent with the onset of acute hepatotoxicity. Acetaminophen overdose can cause liver damage, which typically manifests 24-48 hours post-ingestion. Direct gastrointestinal irritation would occur earlier. Renal failure is a potential complication but usually occurs later. Metabolic acidosis can occur but doesn't typically cause these specific symptoms. This scenario highlights the importance of obtaining an acetaminophen level and initiating N-acetylcysteine therapy within 8 hours of ingestion to prevent hepatotoxicity. EMTs should recognize that the absence of early symptoms doesn't rule out significant acetaminophen toxicity.

295. You're assessing a 5-year-old with suspected button battery ingestion. The child is stable but drooling. What is the most appropriate pre-hospital intervention?
a. Administer honey 10 mL every 10 minutes
b. Give small sips of carbonated beverage
c. Administer oral viscous lidocaine
d. Encourage the child to eat bread or crackers

Answer: a. Administer honey 10 mL every 10 minutes. Explanation: Recent guidelines suggest administering honey in cases of suspected button battery ingestion if it occurred within 12 hours and the child can swallow. Honey may help create a protective barrier and reduce tissue damage until the battery can be removed. The recommended dose is 10 mL every 10 minutes, up to 6 doses. Carbonated beverages don't provide protection. Oral lidocaine isn't recommended and may mask symptoms. Eating solids could worsen the situation. This intervention is specific to button battery ingestion and shouldn't delay transport. EMTs should be aware of this relatively new recommendation while understanding that rapid transport for removal remains the priority.

296. A 3-year-old presents with vomiting and drowsiness after ingesting an unknown amount of her grandmother's "heart pills." What medication should you most strongly suspect?
a. Digoxin
b. Metoprolol
c. Amlodipine
d. Lisinopril

Answer: a. Digoxin. Explanation: In pediatric ingestions of "heart pills," digoxin toxicity should be high on the differential. Digoxin can cause significant toxicity in small doses, particularly in children. Symptoms of digoxin toxicity include vomiting, drowsiness, and can progress to life-threatening arrhythmias. Beta-blockers (like metoprolol) typically cause bradycardia and hypotension. Calcium channel blockers (like amlodipine) often cause hypotension and altered mental status. ACE inhibitors (like lisinopril) are less likely to cause significant toxicity in small ingestions. EMTs should have a high index of suspicion for digoxin toxicity in pediatric patients with access to cardiac medications, as this can be rapidly life-threatening and may require specific antidotal therapy (digoxin-specific antibodies) at the hospital.

297. An 82-year-old female presents with weakness, confusion, and mild epigastric discomfort. She has a history of hypertension and type 2 diabetes. What is the most appropriate next step in her evaluation?

a. Perform a CT scan of the abdomen
b. Check blood glucose levels
c. Perform an ECG
d. Administer antacid and observe

Answer: c. Perform an ECG. Explanation: Elderly patients may present with atypical symptoms of myocardial infarction (MI), such as weakness, confusion, and mild discomfort. An ECG is essential to evaluate for possible MI.

298. A 75-year-old male with a history of multiple medications presents with dizziness and frequent falls. Which tool is most appropriate for assessing his risk of falls?
a. Mini-Mental State Examination (MMSE)
b. STEADI (Stopping Elderly Accidents, Deaths, and Injuries)
c. Glasgow Coma Scale (GCS)
d. APGAR score

Answer: b. STEADI (Stopping Elderly Accidents, Deaths, and Injuries). Explanation: The STEADI tool is specifically designed to assess fall risk in the elderly, considering factors such as balance, medication use, and history of falls.

299. A 78-year-old female is taking multiple medications, including benzodiazepines and antihistamines. According to the Beers Criteria, which of the following is the primary concern with these medications?
a. Increased risk of gastrointestinal bleeding
b. Increased risk of falls and confusion
c. Increased risk of liver toxicity
d. Increased risk of thromboembolism

Answer: b. Increased risk of falls and confusion. Explanation: The Beers Criteria identifies potentially inappropriate medications for older adults. Benzodiazepines and antihistamines are associated with an increased risk of falls and confusion in the elderly.

300. A home health nurse suspects elder abuse in a 79-year-old male who presents with unexplained bruises and a fearful demeanor. What is the most appropriate action?
a. Document the findings and revisit in one month
b. Confront the suspected abuser directly
c. Report the suspected abuse to adult protective services
d. Ignore the signs unless the patient confirms abuse

Answer: c. Report the suspected abuse to adult protective services. Explanation: Healthcare providers are mandated reporters of elder abuse. Suspected abuse should be reported to adult protective services for investigation and intervention.

301. A 77-year-old female presents with acute confusion and agitation that started suddenly. She has a history of mild cognitive impairment. Which of the following is most consistent with delirium?
a. Gradual onset of memory loss
b. Steady decline in cognitive function over months
c. Fluctuating levels of consciousness
d. Consistently poor short-term memory

Answer: c. Fluctuating levels of consciousness. Explanation: Delirium is characterized by an acute onset and fluctuating levels of consciousness, often with agitation and confusion. Dementia, in contrast, presents with a gradual and steady decline in cognitive function.

302. An 80-year-old male presents with increasing forgetfulness and difficulty managing daily activities over the past year. Which of the following findings would most strongly suggest a diagnosis of dementia?
a. Sudden onset of symptoms
b. Stable mental status with periods of confusion
c. Progressive memory loss and impaired executive function
d. Reversible symptoms with treatment

Answer: c. Progressive memory loss and impaired executive function. Explanation: Dementia is characterized by a gradual and progressive decline in memory and executive function. Sudden onset or reversible symptoms are more consistent with delirium.

303. A 76-year-old female with a history of osteoporosis presents after a fall. What is the most appropriate initial imaging study?
a. CT scan of the head
b. MRI of the spine
c. X-ray of the hip and pelvis
d. Ultrasound of the abdomen

Answer: c. X-ray of the hip and pelvis. Explanation: In elderly patients, especially those with osteoporosis, falls often result in hip fractures. An X-ray of the hip and pelvis is the most appropriate initial imaging study to assess for fractures.

304. A 72-year-old male with a history of heart failure presents with confusion, decreased urine output, and swelling in his legs. Which of the following is the most likely cause of his symptoms?
a. Urinary tract infection
b. Heart failure exacerbation
c. Dehydration
d. Hypoglycemia

Answer: b. Heart failure exacerbation. Explanation: The patient's history and symptoms of confusion, decreased urine output, and peripheral edema are indicative of a heart failure exacerbation, a common condition in the elderly.

305. A 70-year-old female is being evaluated for memory loss. Her family reports she has difficulty remembering recent events but can recall details from many years ago. Which test is most appropriate to assess her cognitive function?
a. Electroencephalogram (EEG)
b. Mini-Mental State Examination (MMSE)
c. Serum electrolyte panel
d. MRI of the brain

Answer: b. Mini-Mental State Examination (MMSE). Explanation: The MMSE is a standardized tool used to assess cognitive function, including memory, orientation, and language abilities, and is appropriate for evaluating memory loss in the elderly.

306. A 78-year-old male presents with weight loss, weakness, and easy bruising. He has been taking warfarin for atrial fibrillation. What laboratory test is most important to evaluate his condition?
a. Complete blood count (CBC)
b. Serum creatinine
c. Prothrombin time (PT)/INR
d. Liver function tests

Answer: c. Prothrombin time (PT)/INR. Explanation: PT/INR is essential to evaluate the coagulation status of a patient on warfarin. Easy bruising and weight loss may indicate over-anticoagulation, requiring adjustment of warfarin dosage.

307. You're assessing a 45-year-old male with suicidal ideation. Which of the following factors would contribute the highest score on the SAD PERSONS scale?
a. Male gender
b. Depression diagnosis
c. Previous suicide attempt
d. Rational thinking loss

Answer: c. Previous suicide attempt. Explanation: On the SAD PERSONS scale, a previous suicide attempt contributes the highest individual score (2 points). This scale assesses suicide risk using ten factors, each typically scored 0 or 1, except for previous attempts which scores 2. Male gender, depression, and loss of rational thinking each contribute 1 point. A previous attempt is considered one of the strongest predictors of future suicidal behavior, hence its higher weighting. While EMTs don't typically calculate formal risk scores, understanding these risk factors aids in recognizing high-risk patients and communicating effectively with receiving facilities. This knowledge helps guide decisions about the level of monitoring and interventions needed during transport.

308. A 30-year-old female presents with sudden onset of agitation, hallucinations, and hyperthermia. She's tachycardic and diaphoretic. What is the most likely diagnosis?
a. Schizophrenic episode
b. Excited delirium syndrome
c. Panic attack
d. Acute mania

Answer: b. Excited delirium syndrome. Explanation: The combination of sudden agitation, hallucinations, hyperthermia, tachycardia, and diaphoresis is highly suggestive of excited delirium syndrome. This potentially life-threatening condition is often associated with stimulant use or withdrawal from sedatives. It requires immediate medical intervention due to the risk of sudden cardiopulmonary arrest. Schizophrenic episodes typically don't include such prominent physical symptoms. Panic attacks don't usually involve hallucinations or hyperthermia. Acute mania, while potentially severe, doesn't typically present with this degree of autonomic instability. Recognizing excited delirium is crucial for EMTs as it requires specific management strategies, including rapid sedation and cooling measures, to prevent potentially fatal outcomes.

309. You're assessing an 80-year-old patient with confusion, visual hallucinations, and fluctuating consciousness. These symptoms developed over 24 hours. What is the most likely diagnosis?
a. Acute psychotic episode
b. Delirium
c. Dementia exacerbation
d. Late-onset schizophrenia

Answer: b. Delirium. Explanation: The presentation of acute confusion, visual hallucinations, and fluctuating consciousness developing over 24 hours in an elderly patient is classic for delirium. Delirium is an acute change in mental status characterized by inattention, disorganized thinking, and altered level of consciousness. It often has an underlying medical cause. Acute psychotic episodes typically don't involve fluctuating consciousness. Dementia is a chronic, progressive condition, not an acute change. Late-onset schizophrenia is rare and wouldn't present with such rapid onset. Differentiating delirium from other psychiatric conditions is crucial for EMTs, as delirium often indicates an underlying medical emergency requiring prompt evaluation and treatment.

310. In which of the following scenarios would the Baker Act be most appropriately applied?
a. A patient with alcohol intoxication refusing treatment
b. A patient with suicidal ideation and a specific plan
c. A patient with chronic schizophrenia who is medication non-compliant
d. A patient experiencing opioid withdrawal symptoms

Answer: b. A patient with suicidal ideation and a specific plan. Explanation: The Baker Act (Florida Mental Health Act) allows for involuntary examination of individuals who present a danger to themselves or others due to mental illness. A patient with suicidal ideation and a specific plan meets this criteria, as they present an immediate danger to themselves. Alcohol intoxication alone doesn't qualify; this might fall under the Marchman Act for substance abuse. Chronic schizophrenia without acute danger doesn't necessitate involuntary examination. Opioid withdrawal is a medical condition, not a primary mental health issue. Understanding the appropriate application of involuntary hold laws is crucial for EMTs to ensure patient and public safety while respecting individual rights.

311. A 25-year-old male is exhibiting severe agitation and aggression, posing a risk to himself and others. What is the most appropriate first-line pharmacological intervention for chemical restraint?
a. Haloperidol 5 mg IM
b. Lorazepam 2 mg IV
c. Ketamine 4 mg/kg IM
d. Midazolam 5 mg IM

Answer: d. Midazolam 5 mg IM. Explanation: For acute agitation requiring chemical restraint, midazolam is often considered a first-line agent due to its rapid onset, short duration, and relatively favorable side effect profile. The IM route is preferred in agitated patients where IV access may be challenging. Haloperidol, while effective, has a slower onset and higher risk of extrapyramidal side effects. Lorazepam IV isn't ideal for agitated patients without IV access. Ketamine, while useful in some scenarios, is typically reserved for extreme cases due to its dissociative effects. The choice of agent may vary based on local protocols, but benzodiazepines like midazolam are commonly preferred for their rapid action and safety profile. EMTs should be familiar with their local protocols for chemical restraint and understand the risks and benefits of different agents.

312. You're assessing a 40-year-old female with altered mental status. She's disoriented, having visual hallucinations, and her vital signs show tachycardia and hypertension. What is the most likely underlying cause?
a. Schizophrenia exacerbation
b. Alcohol withdrawal
c. Major depressive disorder
d. Bipolar manic episode

Answer: b. Alcohol withdrawal. Explanation: The combination of disorientation, visual hallucinations, tachycardia, and hypertension is highly suggestive of alcohol withdrawal syndrome. This condition can progress to delirium tremens, a potentially life-threatening state. Schizophrenia exacerbations typically don't include such prominent autonomic symptoms. Major depressive disorder doesn't usually cause hallucinations or significant vital sign changes. While manic episodes can cause agitation, they don't typically cause visual hallucinations or such marked vital sign abnormalities. Recognizing potential alcohol withdrawal is crucial for EMTs, as these patients require close monitoring and may need aggressive treatment to prevent complications like seizures or cardiovascular collapse.

313. A 35-year-old male presents with paranoid delusions and auditory hallucinations. He's agitated but oriented to person, place, and time. What is the most appropriate initial management?
a. Administer haloperidol 5 mg IM immediately
b. Attempt verbal de-escalation in a calm environment
c. Apply physical restraints for safety
d. Administer lorazepam 2 mg IV for sedation

Answer: b. Attempt verbal de-escalation in a calm environment. Explanation: In a patient presenting with psychotic symptoms but who is oriented and not an immediate danger to self or others, verbal de-escalation should be the first approach. Creating a calm, non-threatening environment can often help reduce agitation without the need for pharmacological intervention. Immediate administration of antipsychotics or benzodiazepines should be reserved for cases where verbal de-escalation is ineffective or there's immediate danger. Physical restraints are a last resort due to the potential for escalating agitation and causing physical harm. EMTs should be skilled in verbal de-escalation techniques as they are often the first-line approach in managing patients with acute psychiatric symptoms.

314. You're assessing a 50-year-old female with a history of bipolar disorder who is exhibiting pressured speech, grandiose ideas, and excessive energy. What is the most likely diagnosis?
a. Manic episode
b. Schizophrenic episode
c. Anxiety attack
d. Stimulant intoxication

Answer: a. Manic episode. Explanation: The presentation of pressured speech, grandiose ideas, and excessive energy in a patient with a history of bipolar disorder is classic for a manic episode. Mania is characterized by abnormally elevated mood, increased energy, decreased need for sleep, and often grandiose thinking. Schizophrenic episodes typically involve more prominent thought disorder and hallucinations. Anxiety attacks usually involve fear and physical symptoms of panic. While stimulant intoxication can mimic mania, the history of bipolar disorder makes a manic episode more likely. Recognizing manic episodes is important for EMTs as these patients may require psychiatric evaluation and intervention to prevent potentially dangerous behavior or progression to more severe symptoms.

315. In which of the following scenarios would the Marchman Act be most appropriately applied?
a. A patient with acute psychosis refusing treatment
b. A suicidal patient with a history of depression
c. An intoxicated patient posing a danger to themselves
d. A patient with dementia wandering in public

Answer: c. An intoxicated patient posing a danger to themselves. Explanation: The Marchman Act (Florida's Substance Abuse Impairment Act) allows for involuntary assessment and stabilization of individuals impaired by substance abuse who pose a danger to themselves or others. An intoxicated patient who is a danger to themselves meets this criteria. Acute psychosis and suicidal ideation due to mental illness would fall under the Baker Act. A patient with dementia wandering in public might require intervention, but not necessarily under the Marchman Act. Understanding the distinction between involuntary hold laws for mental health (Baker Act) and substance abuse (Marchman Act) is crucial for EMTs to ensure appropriate care and legal compliance when managing patients with altered mental status or behavioral emergencies.

316. A 28-year-old male presents with sudden onset of severe anxiety, palpitations, and a feeling of impending doom. His vital signs show tachycardia and mild hypertension. What is the most likely diagnosis?
a. Acute coronary syndrome
b. Panic attack
c. Thyroid storm
d. Stimulant overdose

Answer: b. Panic attack. Explanation: The sudden onset of severe anxiety, palpitations, and a feeling of impending doom, accompanied by tachycardia and mild hypertension, is characteristic of a panic attack. Panic attacks can mimic more serious medical conditions, which is why a thorough assessment is crucial. Acute coronary syndrome typically involves chest pain or pressure, which isn't mentioned here. Thyroid storm usually presents with fever and more severe tachycardia and hypertension. Stimulant overdose might cause similar symptoms but usually has additional signs like diaphoresis or agitation. While EMTs should always consider and rule out life-threatening conditions, recognizing panic attacks is important for appropriate management and reassurance of the patient. Treatment typically involves calming techniques and, in some cases, short-acting benzodiazepines under medical direction.

317. A 23-year-old male with a known history of sickle cell disease presents with severe generalized pain, especially in his joints, and reports that it began abruptly a few hours ago. He appears distressed and tachypneic. What is the most appropriate immediate treatment?
a. Administer high-flow oxygen
b. Provide intravenous hydration and analgesia
c. Administer a blood transfusion
d. Start broad-spectrum antibiotics

Answer: b. Provide intravenous hydration and analgesia. Explanation: The patient is experiencing a sickle cell crisis, which is managed by providing intravenous fluids to prevent dehydration and analgesia to control pain. Oxygen and antibiotics may be necessary if there is an associated infection or hypoxia, but they are not the immediate priority. Blood transfusion is reserved for more severe cases or when there is evidence of severe anemia.

318. A 35-year-old female presents with petechiae, bleeding gums, and hematuria. Laboratory results show a platelet count of 15,000/μL. What is the most likely diagnosis?
a. Disseminated intravascular coagulation (DIC)
b. Thrombocytopenia
c. Hemophilia A
d. von Willebrand disease

Answer: b. Thrombocytopenia. Explanation: The presentation of petechiae, bleeding gums, hematuria, and a significantly low platelet count is indicative of thrombocytopenia. DIC would show widespread coagulation and bleeding with abnormal coagulation tests. Hemophilia A and von Willebrand disease typically present with a history of prolonged bleeding but not necessarily with such a low platelet count.

319. A 45-year-old male is brought to the emergency department with severe bleeding following a minor trauma. He has a known history of hemophilia A. What is the most appropriate immediate management?
a. Administer fresh frozen plasma
b. Administer cryoprecipitate
c. Administer factor VIII concentrate
d. Provide vitamin K

Answer: c. Administer factor VIII concentrate. Explanation: Hemophilia A is treated by replacing the deficient clotting factor, which is factor VIII. Fresh frozen plasma and cryoprecipitate can be used in some cases, but factor VIII concentrate is the treatment of choice. Vitamin K is not effective in hemophilia A as it does not address the specific deficiency.

320. A 55-year-old female presents with altered mental status, fever, and renal failure. Laboratory tests show thrombocytopenia and schistocytes on the peripheral smear. What is the most likely diagnosis?
a. Hemolytic uremic syndrome (HUS)
b. Thrombotic thrombocytopenic purpura (TTP)
c. Disseminated intravascular coagulation (DIC)
d. Systemic lupus erythematosus (SLE)

Answer: b. Thrombotic thrombocytopenic purpura (TTP). Explanation: TTP presents with the classic pentad of thrombocytopenia, microangiopathic hemolytic anemia (schistocytes), renal failure, fever, and neurologic symptoms. HUS primarily affects the kidneys and is more common in children. DIC involves widespread coagulation with a consumption of clotting factors. SLE can cause renal failure and thrombocytopenia but typically does not present with the full spectrum seen in TTP.

321. A 4-year-old child is brought to the emergency department with a recent history of bloody diarrhea and is now showing signs of pallor and decreased urine output. Laboratory results reveal thrombocytopenia and hemolytic anemia. What is the most likely diagnosis?
a. Thrombotic thrombocytopenic purpura (TTP)
b. Hemolytic uremic syndrome (HUS)
c. Immune thrombocytopenic purpura (ITP)
d. Acute lymphoblastic leukemia (ALL)

Answer: b. Hemolytic uremic syndrome (HUS). Explanation: HUS typically follows an episode of bloody diarrhea caused by E. coli O157 infection and presents with hemolytic anemia, thrombocytopenia, and acute renal failure. TTP has a similar hematological presentation but typically occurs in adults and presents with neurologic symptoms. ITP usually presents with isolated thrombocytopenia. ALL would show more widespread blood cell abnormalities.

322. A 50-year-old male with a history of recent sepsis presents with bleeding from his IV sites and widespread bruising. Laboratory tests reveal prolonged PT and aPTT, low fibrinogen, and elevated D-dimer. What is the most likely diagnosis?
a. Disseminated intravascular coagulation (DIC)
b. Thrombotic thrombocytopenic purpura (TTP)
c. Hemolytic uremic syndrome (HUS)
d. Immune thrombocytopenic purpura (ITP)

Answer: a. Disseminated intravascular coagulation (DIC). Explanation: DIC is characterized by widespread activation of the coagulation cascade, leading to the consumption of clotting factors and platelets, resulting in prolonged PT and aPTT, low fibrinogen, and elevated D-dimer. TTP and HUS also involve thrombocytopenia and hemolysis but do not show the coagulation abnormalities seen in DIC. ITP primarily presents with isolated thrombocytopenia without the coagulation abnormalities.

323. A 65-year-old female with a history of chronic kidney disease presents with spontaneous bruising and bleeding gums. Laboratory results reveal normal PT and aPTT, but a prolonged bleeding time. What is the most likely diagnosis?
a. Hemophilia A
b. von Willebrand disease
c. Thrombocytopenia
d. Uremic platelet dysfunction

Answer: d. Uremic platelet dysfunction. Explanation: Chronic kidney disease can cause uremic toxins to impair platelet function, leading to prolonged bleeding time with normal PT and aPTT. Hemophilia A and von Willebrand disease would typically show abnormalities in PT, aPTT, or both, and thrombocytopenia would present with low platelet count.

324. A 30-year-old female presents with a history of heavy menstrual bleeding and frequent nosebleeds. Laboratory results show normal PT, aPTT, and platelet count, but a prolonged bleeding time. What is the most likely diagnosis?
a. Hemophilia B
b. von Willebrand disease
c. Immune thrombocytopenic purpura (ITP)
d. Disseminated intravascular coagulation (DIC)

Answer: b. von Willebrand disease. Explanation: von Willebrand disease is the most common inherited bleeding disorder and typically presents with prolonged bleeding time, normal PT, aPTT, and platelet count. Hemophilia B affects factor IX and would present with prolonged aPTT. ITP would show thrombocytopenia, and DIC would present with widespread coagulation abnormalities.

325. A 40-year-old male with a history of recent viral infection presents with petechiae and mucosal bleeding. Laboratory tests show isolated thrombocytopenia with normal PT, aPTT, and fibrinogen levels. What is the most likely diagnosis?
a. Immune thrombocytopenic purpura (ITP)
b. Thrombotic thrombocytopenic purpura (TTP)
c. Hemolytic uremic syndrome (HUS)
d. Disseminated intravascular coagulation (DIC)

Answer: a. Immune thrombocytopenic purpura (ITP). Explanation: ITP is characterized by isolated thrombocytopenia without other coagulation abnormalities, often following a viral infection. TTP and HUS would show additional signs of hemolysis and renal dysfunction. DIC would present with abnormalities in PT, aPTT, and fibrinogen.

326. A 22-year-old male with a history of hemophilia B presents with hemarthrosis after a minor fall. What is the most appropriate treatment?
a. Administer fresh frozen plasma
b. Administer factor IX concentrate
c. Administer desmopressin (DDAVP)

d. Provide vitamin K

Answer: b. Administer factor IX concentrate. Explanation: Hemophilia B, also known as Christmas disease, is treated by replacing the deficient factor IX. Fresh frozen plasma contains multiple clotting factors but is not the treatment of choice. Desmopressin is used for mild hemophilia A and von Willebrand disease but is ineffective for hemophilia B. Vitamin K is not relevant to the treatment of hemophilia.

327. A 25-year-old female presents with difficulty breathing, hives, and swelling of the lips and tongue after eating peanuts. What is the most appropriate initial treatment?
a. Intravenous diphenhydramine
b. Intramuscular epinephrine
c. Oral prednisone
d. Inhaled albuterol

Answer: b. Intramuscular epinephrine. Explanation: Intramuscular epinephrine is the first-line treatment for anaphylaxis as it rapidly reverses airway constriction and cardiovascular collapse. Other treatments can be given as adjuncts after epinephrine.

328. A 40-year-old male presents with swelling of the face, lips, and tongue without hives. Which condition is most likely?
a. Urticaria
b. Anaphylaxis
c. Angioedema
d. Contact dermatitis

Answer: c. Angioedema. Explanation: Angioedema involves deeper swelling, often of the face, lips, and tongue, and is not typically associated with the itchy wheals seen in urticaria.

329. A patient presents with widespread blistering and skin detachment after starting a new medication. Which condition is most likely, and what is the next best step in management?
a. Stevens-Johnson syndrome; discontinue the offending medication
b. Toxic epidermal necrolysis; immediate transfer to a burn unit
c. Erythema multiforme; prescribe oral corticosteroids
d. Bullous pemphigoid; administer IV antibiotics

Answer: b. Toxic epidermal necrolysis; immediate transfer to a burn unit. Explanation: Toxic epidermal necrolysis (TEN) is a severe, life-threatening condition characterized by widespread skin detachment. Immediate transfer to a burn unit is necessary for specialized care.

330. A 55-year-old female who recently underwent a kidney transplant presents with fever, pain over the transplant site, and decreased urine output. What is the most likely diagnosis?
a. Urinary tract infection
b. Acute transplant rejection
c. Pyelonephritis
d. Nephrolithiasis

Answer: b. Acute transplant rejection. Explanation: Fever, pain over the transplant site, and decreased urine output are indicative of acute transplant rejection, requiring immediate medical intervention to prevent graft loss.

331. A patient on immunosuppressive therapy for a liver transplant presents with fever, chills, and a productive cough. What is the most appropriate initial diagnostic test?
a. Chest X-ray
b. Complete blood count (CBC)
c. Sputum culture
d. Blood cultures

Answer: a. Chest X-ray. Explanation: Immunocompromised patients are at high risk for infections. A chest X-ray is the initial diagnostic test to evaluate for pneumonia, a common infection in these patients.

332. A 32-year-old female with a history of asthma presents with sudden onset of wheezing, hives, and hypotension after taking an antibiotic. Which is the correct sequence of treatments for anaphylaxis?
a. IV fluids, epinephrine, diphenhydramine, corticosteroids
b. Epinephrine, IV fluids, albuterol, corticosteroids
c. Albuterol, epinephrine, diphenhydramine, IV fluids
d. Diphenhydramine, epinephrine, corticosteroids, IV fluids

Answer: b. Epinephrine, IV fluids, albuterol, corticosteroids. Explanation: The correct sequence for treating anaphylaxis includes immediate administration of epinephrine, followed by IV fluids for hypotension, albuterol for bronchospasm, and corticosteroids to prevent late-phase reactions.

333. A patient presents with a widespread rash and mucosal involvement, including the eyes and mouth, after starting a new medication. What condition is most likely?
a. Erythema multiforme
b. Stevens-Johnson syndrome
c. Contact dermatitis
d. Psoriasis

Answer: b. Stevens-Johnson syndrome. Explanation: Stevens-Johnson syndrome is a severe hypersensitivity reaction involving widespread rash and mucosal involvement. It is often triggered by medications and requires immediate medical attention.

334. A 70-year-old male with a history of chemotherapy presents with fever and neutropenia. What is the most appropriate initial treatment?
a. Oral antibiotics
b. Intravenous antibiotics
c. Antifungal therapy
d. Antiviral therapy

Answer: b. Intravenous antibiotics. Explanation: Febrile neutropenia is a medical emergency in immunocompromised patients. Immediate treatment with broad-spectrum intravenous antibiotics is crucial to prevent sepsis.

335. A patient presents with a history of HIV and now has a new, progressive cough, fever, and weight loss. What is the most appropriate initial diagnostic test?
a. Chest X-ray
b. Sputum culture
c. Tuberculin skin test
d. Complete blood count (CBC)

Answer: a. Chest X-ray. Explanation: In an immunocompromised patient, symptoms like cough, fever, and weight loss may indicate opportunistic infections like tuberculosis or pneumocystis pneumonia. A chest X-ray is the initial diagnostic test to evaluate the lungs.

336. A 28-year-old female presents with hives, pruritus, and difficulty breathing after a bee sting. What is the first-line treatment?
a. Intramuscular epinephrine
b. Oral diphenhydramine
c. Inhaled albuterol
d. IV corticosteroids

Answer: a. Intramuscular epinephrine. Explanation: Intramuscular epinephrine is the first-line treatment for anaphylaxis following a bee sting. It rapidly reverses the symptoms by causing vasoconstriction, bronchodilation, and reducing edema.

337. A 70-year-old male presents with fever, confusion, respiratory rate of 28 breaths per minute, systolic blood pressure of 90 mmHg, and altered mental status. According to the qSOFA criteria, how many points does he score, and what does this indicate?
a. 1 point, indicating low risk for sepsis
b. 2 points, indicating high risk for sepsis
c. 3 points, indicating high risk for sepsis
d. 4 points, indicating septic shock

Answer: c. 3 points, indicating high risk for sepsis. Explanation: The qSOFA (quick Sequential Organ Failure Assessment) criteria assign 1 point each for systolic blood pressure ≤100 mmHg, respiratory rate ≥22 breaths per minute, and altered mental status. This patient scores 3 points, indicating a high risk for sepsis.

338. A 16-year-old female presents with a high fever, severe headache, neck stiffness, and photophobia. During the physical exam, you notice that when you flex her neck, her hips and knees flex as well. What is this sign called, and what condition does it suggest?
a. Kernig's sign, suggesting meningitis
b. Brudzinski's sign, suggesting meningitis
c. Nuchal rigidity, suggesting encephalitis
d. Babinski's sign, suggesting meningitis

Answer: b. Brudzinski's sign, suggesting meningitis. Explanation: Brudzinski's sign is observed when passive neck flexion leads to involuntary hip and knee flexion. This is a clinical sign suggestive of meningitis. Kernig's sign involves pain in the neck and back when the hip is flexed and the knee is extended.

339. A 25-year-old male steps on a rusty nail and has not received a tetanus booster in the past 10 years. What is the most appropriate prophylactic treatment?
a. Tetanus toxoid alone
b. Tetanus immunoglobulin alone
c. Tetanus toxoid and tetanus immunoglobulin
d. No treatment needed

Answer: c. Tetanus toxoid and tetanus immunoglobulin. Explanation: For patients with a contaminated wound who have not received a tetanus booster in the past 5 years, both tetanus toxoid and tetanus immunoglobulin are recommended to provide immediate and long-term protection against tetanus.

340. A 6-year-old child is bitten by a stray dog. The dog is not captured, and its rabies vaccination status is unknown. What is the most appropriate initial management for rabies post-exposure prophylaxis?
a. Administer rabies vaccine series alone
b. Administer rabies immunoglobulin alone
c. Administer both rabies immunoglobulin and rabies vaccine series
d. Clean the wound thoroughly and observe for symptoms

Answer: c. Administer both rabies immunoglobulin and rabies vaccine series. Explanation: For unprovoked animal bites from a stray dog with unknown rabies status, both rabies immunoglobulin and a full rabies vaccine series should be administered to ensure immediate and long-term immunity.

341. A healthcare worker is donning personal protective equipment (PPE) to care for a patient with Ebola virus disease. Which of the following steps should be performed first?
a. Put on the N95 respirator

b. Put on the gown
c. Perform hand hygiene
d. Put on the gloves

Answer: c. Perform hand hygiene. Explanation: Hand hygiene is the first and most critical step in donning PPE to prevent contamination of the equipment. After hand hygiene, the healthcare worker should proceed with putting on the gown, N95 respirator, and gloves.

342. A 55-year-old female presents with fever, tachycardia, hypotension, and confusion. Blood cultures are pending. Which of the following antibiotics should be initiated empirically to cover a broad spectrum of pathogens, including MRSA and Pseudomonas?
a. Ceftriaxone and vancomycin
b. Piperacillin-tazobactam and vancomycin
c. Meropenem and levofloxacin
d. Clindamycin and ciprofloxacin

Answer: b. Piperacillin-tazobactam and vancomycin. Explanation: Empiric treatment for severe sepsis should cover a broad range of potential pathogens, including MRSA and Pseudomonas. Piperacillin-tazobactam provides broad-spectrum coverage, including Pseudomonas, while vancomycin covers MRSA.

343. A 34-year-old male presents with fever, headache, and a petechial rash. On examination, he has positive Kernig's sign. What is the next best step in the management of this patient?
a. Perform a lumbar puncture immediately
b. Administer broad-spectrum antibiotics
c. Obtain a CT scan of the head
d. Administer corticosteroids

Answer: b. Administer broad-spectrum antibiotics. Explanation: In a patient with signs of meningitis, especially with a petechial rash suggesting meningococcal meningitis, immediate administration of broad-spectrum antibiotics is crucial before performing a lumbar puncture or other diagnostics to reduce mortality.

344. A 28-year-old male healthcare worker is accidentally exposed to a patient with confirmed tuberculosis. He has no symptoms and a negative chest X-ray. What is the most appropriate next step?
a. Start immediate tuberculosis treatment
b. Perform a tuberculin skin test or IGRA
c. Administer BCG vaccine
d. Isolate the healthcare worker

Answer: b. Perform a tuberculin skin test or IGRA. Explanation: In asymptomatic individuals with a known exposure to tuberculosis, performing a tuberculin skin test (TST) or interferon-gamma release assay (IGRA) is the appropriate next step to assess latent TB infection.

345. A 42-year-old male presents with severe muscle spasms and trismus (lockjaw) after sustaining a puncture wound while working in the garden. His immunization history is unknown. What is the most appropriate immediate treatment?
a. Administer tetanus toxoid and tetanus immunoglobulin
b. Administer tetanus toxoid alone
c. Administer tetanus immunoglobulin alone
d. Clean the wound and provide supportive care

Answer: a. Administer tetanus toxoid and tetanus immunoglobulin. Explanation: In patients with suspected tetanus, especially with unknown immunization status, both tetanus toxoid and tetanus immunoglobulin should be administered to provide immediate and long-term protection against the toxin.

346. A 65-year-old female presents with fever, chills, and a productive cough with rusty-colored sputum. Her respiratory rate is 32 breaths per minute, blood pressure is 85/55 mmHg, and she is confused. According to the qSOFA criteria, how many points does she score, and what does this indicate?
a. 1 point, indicating low risk for sepsis
b. 2 points, indicating high risk for sepsis
c. 3 points, indicating high risk for sepsis
d. 4 points, indicating septic shock

Answer: c. 3 points, indicating high risk for sepsis. Explanation: The qSOFA criteria assign 1 point each for systolic blood pressure ≤100 mmHg, respiratory rate ≥22 breaths per minute, and altered mental status. This patient scores 3 points, indicating a high risk for sepsis.

347. A 60-year-old male with a history of non-Hodgkin lymphoma presents with confusion, nausea, and muscle weakness. His lab results show elevated potassium, phosphate, and uric acid levels, and low calcium. What is the most likely diagnosis and initial treatment?
a. Hypercalcemia of malignancy; IV bisphosphonates
b. Tumor lysis syndrome; IV fluids and allopurinol
c. Neutropenic fever; IV antibiotics
d. Spinal cord compression; corticosteroids and MRI

Answer: b. Tumor lysis syndrome; IV fluids and allopurinol. Explanation: Tumor lysis syndrome is characterized by elevated potassium, phosphate, and uric acid levels, and low calcium. Initial treatment includes aggressive IV fluid hydration and allopurinol to prevent uric acid formation.

348. A 55-year-old female undergoing chemotherapy presents with a fever of 101°F, chills, and a white blood cell count of 0.8 x 10^9/L. What is the most appropriate initial management?
a. Oral antibiotics and discharge
b. IV fluids and observation
c. Immediate IV antibiotics and admission

d. Antipyretics and re-evaluation in 24 hours

Answer: c. Immediate IV antibiotics and admission. Explanation: Neutropenic fever is a medical emergency in chemotherapy patients due to their high risk of severe infections. Immediate IV antibiotics and hospital admission are required for prompt treatment.

349. A 65-year-old male with lung cancer presents with facial swelling, shortness of breath, and distended neck veins. Which condition is most likely, and what is the initial treatment?
a. Tension pneumothorax; needle decompression
b. Superior vena cava (SVC) syndrome; elevate the head of the bed and administer steroids
c. Pulmonary embolism; anticoagulation
d. Cardiac tamponade; pericardiocentesis

Answer: b. Superior vena cava (SVC) syndrome; elevate the head of the bed and administer steroids. Explanation: SVC syndrome presents with facial swelling, shortness of breath, and distended neck veins due to obstruction of the SVC. Initial treatment includes elevating the head of the bed to reduce venous pressure and administering steroids to reduce inflammation.

350. A 70-year-old female with metastatic breast cancer presents with new-onset back pain, urinary incontinence, and lower extremity weakness. What is the most likely diagnosis and first step in management?
a. Hypercalcemia of malignancy; IV bisphosphonates
b. Spinal cord compression; corticosteroids and MRI
c. Neutropenic fever; IV antibiotics
d. Tumor lysis syndrome; IV fluids and allopurinol

Answer: b. Spinal cord compression; corticosteroids and MRI. Explanation: Spinal cord compression in cancer patients presents with back pain, urinary incontinence, and lower extremity weakness. Immediate management includes administering corticosteroids to reduce inflammation and obtaining an MRI to confirm the diagnosis and guide further treatment.

351. A 58-year-old male with squamous cell carcinoma of the lung presents with confusion, nausea, and severe constipation. His calcium level is 13.5 mg/dL. What is the most appropriate initial treatment?
a. IV fluids and bisphosphonates
b. Oral calcium supplements
c. IV potassium and phosphate
d. Corticosteroids and antipyretics

Answer: a. IV fluids and bisphosphonates. Explanation: Hypercalcemia of malignancy is treated initially with IV fluids to promote calcium excretion and bisphosphonates to inhibit bone resorption.

352. A 45-year-old female receiving chemotherapy for leukemia develops a fever of 102°F and severe neutropenia. Blood cultures are pending. What is the next best step in her management?
a. Initiate broad-spectrum IV antibiotics immediately
b. Wait for culture results before starting antibiotics
c. Administer antipyretics and observe
d. Discharge with oral antibiotics

Answer: a. Initiate broad-spectrum IV antibiotics immediately. Explanation: In neutropenic fever, prompt initiation of broad-spectrum IV antibiotics is critical to manage potential severe infections, even before culture results are available.

353. A 68-year-old male with renal cell carcinoma presents with nausea, vomiting, polyuria, and confusion. His serum calcium level is 14 mg/dL. What is the most appropriate initial intervention?
a. IV bisphosphonates and hydration
b. Oral bisphosphonates and observation
c. IV calcium gluconate
d. Intramuscular corticosteroids

Answer: a. IV bisphosphonates and hydration. Explanation: The initial management of hypercalcemia of malignancy includes aggressive hydration with IV fluids and administration of IV bisphosphonates to lower serum calcium levels.

354. A 59-year-old female with a history of breast cancer presents with worsening dyspnea, facial swelling, and dilated chest veins. What is the most likely diagnosis and best initial treatment?
a. Pulmonary embolism; thrombolytics
b. Superior vena cava (SVC) syndrome; elevate head and administer diuretics
c. Tension pneumothorax; chest tube insertion
d. Heart failure; IV diuretics and nitrates

Answer: b. Superior vena cava (SVC) syndrome; elevate head and administer diuretics. Explanation: SVC syndrome due to obstruction by a tumor leads to facial swelling, dyspnea, and dilated chest veins. Elevating the head and administering diuretics help reduce symptoms by decreasing venous pressure.

355. A 72-year-old male with prostate cancer presents with new-onset severe lower back pain and difficulty walking. MRI reveals metastatic lesions compressing the spinal cord. What is the most appropriate initial management?
a. IV antibiotics
b. High-dose corticosteroids and urgent neurosurgical consultation
c. Chemotherapy
d. Radiation therapy alone

Answer: b. High-dose corticosteroids and urgent neurosurgical consultation. Explanation: Spinal cord compression requires high-dose corticosteroids to reduce inflammation and urgent neurosurgical consultation for possible decompression surgery or radiation therapy.

356. A 50-year-old male with lymphoma presents with acute renal failure, hyperkalemia, and elevated uric acid following chemotherapy. What is the most likely diagnosis and best initial management?
a. Tumor lysis syndrome; aggressive IV hydration and allopurinol
b. Hypercalcemia of malignancy; IV bisphosphonates and hydration
c. Neutropenic fever; IV antibiotics and fluids
d. Acute kidney injury; dialysis

Answer: a. Tumor lysis syndrome; aggressive IV hydration and allopurinol. Explanation: Tumor lysis syndrome occurs after chemotherapy and is characterized by hyperkalemia, elevated uric acid, and acute renal failure. Management includes aggressive IV hydration and allopurinol to prevent uric acid crystallization.

357. A 45-year-old female with a history of multiple drug allergies, including penicillin, presents with a severe bacterial infection. Which antibiotic would be most appropriate to avoid potential cross-sensitivity reactions?
a. Amoxicillin
b. Ceftriaxone
c. Clindamycin
d. Piperacillin-tazobactam

Answer: c. Clindamycin. Explanation: Clindamycin is a lincosamide antibiotic and does not share cross-sensitivity with penicillins or cephalosporins, making it a safer choice for patients with a history of penicillin allergy.

358. A 60-year-old male presents with chest pain and is found to have a prolonged QT interval on his EKG. Which of the following medications should be avoided due to the risk of exacerbating QT prolongation?
a. Metoprolol
b. Amiodarone
c. Atorvastatin
d. Furosemide

Answer: b. Amiodarone. Explanation: Amiodarone is known to cause QT prolongation and should be avoided in patients who already have a prolonged QT interval to prevent the risk of developing torsades de pointes or other serious arrhythmias.

359. An 80-year-old female with multiple chronic conditions is on several medications. Which of the following is the most important consideration when assessing her medication regimen?
a. Cost of medications
b. Frequency of dosing
c. Potential for drug-drug interactions
d. Route of administration

Answer: c. Potential for drug-drug interactions. Explanation: In elderly patients, polypharmacy increases the risk of drug-drug interactions, which can lead to adverse effects, reduced efficacy, or toxicity. Assessing for interactions is crucial for safe and effective management.

360. A 5-year-old child weighing 20 kg requires an antibiotic for a bacterial infection. The recommended dose is 25 mg/kg/day divided into two doses. How much should be administered per dose?
a. 100 mg
b. 150 mg
c. 250 mg
d. 500 mg

Answer: c. 250 mg. Explanation: The total daily dose is 25 mg/kg x 20 kg = 500 mg/day. Dividing this into two doses gives 250 mg per dose.

361. A 35-year-old male presents with cellulitis. Which antibiotic would be most appropriate for empirical treatment in an EMS setting?
a. Vancomycin
b. Amoxicillin
c. Doxycycline
d. Ciprofloxacin

Answer: c. Doxycycline. Explanation: Doxycycline is effective against common pathogens causing cellulitis, including methicillin-resistant Staphylococcus aureus (MRSA). Vancomycin is typically reserved for more severe cases and inpatient use. Amoxicillin and ciprofloxacin are less effective against MRSA.

362. A 28-year-old female with a history of asthma is experiencing an acute exacerbation. Which of the following medications is contraindicated due to the risk of worsening her condition?
a. Albuterol
b. Ipratropium
c. Propranolol
d. Prednisone

Answer: c. Propranolol. Explanation: Propranolol, a non-selective beta-blocker, can cause bronchoconstriction and worsen asthma symptoms, making it contraindicated in patients with asthma.

363. A 55-year-old male with hypertension and diabetes is prescribed lisinopril. What is a potential adverse effect of this medication that requires monitoring?
a. Hypokalemia
b. Hyperkalemia

c. Bradycardia
d. Hypoglycemia

Answer: b. Hyperkalemia. Explanation: Lisinopril, an ACE inhibitor, can increase potassium levels, potentially leading to hyperkalemia. Regular monitoring of serum potassium is necessary to prevent complications.

364. A 40-year-old male is treated for a severe allergic reaction with an epinephrine auto-injector. What is the correct dose of epinephrine for an adult using an auto-injector?
a. 0.15 mg
b. 0.3 mg
c. 0.5 mg
d. 1 mg

Answer: b. 0.3 mg. Explanation: The standard dose of epinephrine for adults using an auto-injector is 0.3 mg, which is administered intramuscularly, typically into the thigh.

365. A 65-year-old female on digoxin therapy for heart failure presents with nausea, vomiting, and visual disturbances. Which of the following conditions should be suspected?
a. Hypoglycemia
b. Digoxin toxicity
c. Hyperkalemia
d. Hyponatremia

Answer: b. Digoxin toxicity. Explanation: Symptoms such as nausea, vomiting, and visual disturbances are classic signs of digoxin toxicity, which can be life-threatening and requires prompt medical attention.

366. A 50-year-old male with a suspected stroke is in the prehospital setting. Which of the following medications should be administered to manage blood pressure if it exceeds 220/120 mmHg?
a. Labetalol
b. Nifedipine
c. Metoprolol
d. Nitroglycerin

Answer: a. Labetalol. Explanation: Labetalol is often used to manage acute hypertension in the setting of a stroke because it can lower blood pressure effectively without causing significant changes in cerebral blood flow.

367. A 6-year-old child requires intubation. Which size endotracheal tube (ETT) is most appropriate for this patient?
a. 4.0 mm
b. 5.0 mm
c. 6.0 mm

d. 7.0 mm

Answer: b. 5.0 mm. Explanation: The formula for selecting the appropriate ETT size in children is (age/4) + 4. For a 6-year-old, (6/4) + 4 = 5.5. Therefore, a 5.0 or 5.5 mm ETT would be appropriate.

368. A patient presents with a difficult airway, and a decision is made to use a Miller blade for intubation. What is the primary reason for choosing a Miller blade over a Macintosh blade?
a. The Miller blade is better for visualizing the vocal cords.
b. The Miller blade is curved, making it easier to handle.
c. The Miller blade is longer, allowing for deeper insertion.
d. The Miller blade is more flexible than the Macintosh blade.

Answer: a. The Miller blade is better for visualizing the vocal cords. Explanation: The Miller blade is a straight blade that provides better visualization of the vocal cords by directly lifting the epiglottis, making it useful in certain airway scenarios, especially in infants and small children.

369. A 45-year-old male is undergoing emergency airway management, and a supraglottic airway device is being considered. Which of the following is a contraindication for using this device?
a. Patient is unconscious
b. Suspected cervical spine injury
c. Known esophageal disease
d. Cardiac arrest

Answer: c. Known esophageal disease. Explanation: Supraglottic airway devices are contraindicated in patients with known esophageal disease, as they can potentially cause further esophageal injury or be less effective.

370. During a cricothyrotomy, which anatomical structure is incised to establish an airway?
a. Thyroid cartilage
b. Cricoid cartilage
c. Cricothyroid membrane
d. Epiglottis

Answer: c. Cricothyroid membrane. Explanation: A cricothyrotomy involves making an incision through the cricothyroid membrane to establish an airway when other methods are not viable.

371. When using an end-tidal CO2 detector, what color change indicates correct placement of an endotracheal tube in the trachea?
a. Blue to yellow
b. Yellow to blue
c. Purple to red

d. Red to green

Answer: a. Blue to yellow. Explanation: End-tidal CO2 detectors change from blue to yellow when they detect the presence of CO_2, indicating that the endotracheal tube is correctly placed in the trachea and not in the esophagus.

372. A 4-year-old child requires intubation. Which laryngoscope blade is typically preferred in this age group?
a. Miller blade size 2
b. Miller blade size 3
c. Macintosh blade size 2
d. Macintosh blade size 3

Answer: a. Miller blade size 2. Explanation: In pediatric patients, the Miller blade is often preferred due to its straight design, which is more effective in lifting the epiglottis. A size 2 Miller blade is commonly used for a 4-year-old child.

373. Which of the following is a common indication for using a supraglottic airway device?
a. Severe maxillofacial trauma
b. Full stomach with risk of aspiration
c. Routine airway management in cardiac arrest
d. Patients with tracheostomies

Answer: c. Routine airway management in cardiac arrest. Explanation: Supraglottic airway devices are often used in cardiac arrest for quick and effective airway management when endotracheal intubation may be more challenging.

374. A patient with a difficult airway requires a surgical cricothyrotomy. Which of the following items is NOT typically part of a cricothyrotomy kit?
a. Scalpel
b. Tracheal hook
c. Endotracheal tube
d. Laryngoscope

Answer: d. Laryngoscope. Explanation: A cricothyrotomy kit typically includes a scalpel, tracheal hook, and an endotracheal tube or tracheostomy tube. A laryngoscope is not part of the cricothyrotomy kit, as the procedure does not require direct visualization of the vocal cords.

375. A paramedic is using a Broselow tape to determine the appropriate endotracheal tube size for a pediatric patient. The child falls into the "green" zone on the tape. What size ETT should be used?
a. 3.5 mm
b. 4.5 mm
c. 5.5 mm
d. 6.5 mm

Answer: c. 5.5 mm. Explanation: The Broselow tape provides a quick reference for pediatric resuscitation, including appropriate ETT sizes. The "green" zone on the tape typically corresponds to an ETT size of 5.5 mm.

376. In the context of end-tidal CO2 monitoring, which of the following conditions can cause a sudden drop in the detected CO2 level?
a. Hypoventilation
b. Pulmonary embolism
c. Fever
d. Increased cardiac output

Answer: b. Pulmonary embolism. Explanation: A sudden drop in end-tidal CO2 levels can be caused by a pulmonary embolism, which decreases the perfusion of the lungs and, consequently, the amount of CO2 that is exhaled.

377. A 50-year-old male with COPD is experiencing an acute exacerbation. You need to deliver a bronchodilator medication. Which device is most appropriate to ensure effective delivery in this patient?
a. Metered-dose inhaler (MDI) alone
b. MDI with a spacer
c. Dry powder inhaler
d. Oral bronchodilator

Answer: b. MDI with a spacer. Explanation: Using an MDI with a spacer is the most effective way to ensure the medication reaches the lower airways, especially in patients with poor inhalation technique or compromised respiratory function, such as those with COPD.

378. A 70-year-old female with severe pneumonia requires supplemental oxygen. You decide to use a non-rebreather mask. What is the approximate FiO2 delivered by this device?
a. 24-28%
b. 30-40%
c. 60-80%
d. 90-100%

Answer: c. 60-80%. Explanation: A non-rebreather mask can deliver an FiO2 of approximately 60-80%, which is suitable for patients requiring high concentrations of oxygen.

379. A 65-year-old male presents with acute pulmonary edema. You decide to initiate CPAP therapy. Which initial setting is most appropriate?
a. 5 cm H2O
b. 10 cm H2O
c. 15 cm H2O

d. 20 cm H2O

Answer: a. 5 cm H2O. Explanation: The initial CPAP setting is typically around 5 cm H2O, which can be adjusted based on the patient's response and tolerance to therapy. Starting at a lower setting helps prevent discomfort and complications.

380. A 55-year-old female with a history of congestive heart failure is being ventilated using a portable ventilator. Which mode is most appropriate for initial ventilator settings?
a. Assist-Control (AC) mode
b. Synchronized Intermittent Mandatory Ventilation (SIMV) mode
c. Continuous Positive Airway Pressure (CPAP) mode
d. Pressure Support Ventilation (PSV) mode

Answer: a. Assist-Control (AC) mode. Explanation: Assist-Control (AC) mode provides full support for each breath, either initiated by the patient or delivered by the machine, making it suitable for initial management in patients with respiratory failure.

381. A 30-year-old male requires chest tube insertion for a pneumothorax. What is the most important piece of equipment to ensure proper chest tube placement?
a. Sterile gloves
b. Trocar
c. Suction tubing
d. Water seal chamber

Answer: d. Water seal chamber. Explanation: The water seal chamber is crucial for maintaining proper functioning of the chest tube system by preventing air from re-entering the pleural space. Sterile gloves and other equipment are important, but the water seal chamber is essential for the effectiveness of the chest tube.

382. A 45-year-old female with asthma requires nebulized albuterol. What is the key advantage of using a nebulizer over an MDI with a spacer for this patient?
a. Faster delivery of medication
b. Better control over dosing
c. Easier to use during severe exacerbations
d. More portable

Answer: c. Easier to use during severe exacerbations. Explanation: A nebulizer can be easier to use during severe asthma exacerbations when the patient may have difficulty coordinating inhalation with an MDI, even with a spacer.

383. A 70-year-old male with COPD is receiving home oxygen therapy via a nasal cannula. What is the maximum FiO2 that can typically be delivered with a nasal cannula?

a. 24%
b. 36%
c. 44%
d. 60%

Answer: c. 44%. Explanation: A nasal cannula can deliver an FiO2 of up to approximately 44% at flow rates of 6 L/min. Higher concentrations are not typically achievable with this device.

384. A 60-year-old female with acute respiratory distress syndrome (ARDS) is being managed with a portable ventilator. Which mode is generally preferred for this condition?
a. Volume-Controlled Ventilation (VCV)
b. Pressure-Controlled Ventilation (PCV)
c. CPAP
d. SIMV

Answer: b. Pressure-Controlled Ventilation (PCV). Explanation: Pressure-Controlled Ventilation (PCV) is often preferred in ARDS to limit peak airway pressures and reduce the risk of ventilator-induced lung injury.

385. A 30-year-old male with a traumatic chest injury requires emergency chest tube insertion. What is the most appropriate site for the insertion?
a. Second intercostal space, midclavicular line
b. Fourth intercostal space, anterior axillary line
c. Fifth intercostal space, midaxillary line
d. Sixth intercostal space, posterior axillary line

Answer: c. Fifth intercostal space, midaxillary line. Explanation: The fifth intercostal space at the midaxillary line is the most common site for chest tube insertion to treat a pneumothorax or hemothorax, providing optimal access to the pleural space.

386. A 25-year-old female is in severe respiratory distress and requires intubation. You prepare the equipment and choose a size 7.0 endotracheal tube. What is the appropriate depth of insertion for the endotracheal tube in this patient?
a. 15-17 cm
b. 18-20 cm
c. 21-23 cm
d. 24-26 cm

Answer: c. 21-23 cm. Explanation: The appropriate depth of insertion for an endotracheal tube in an adult female is typically around 21-23 cm at the teeth, ensuring proper placement within the trachea while avoiding mainstem bronchus intubation.

387. A patient in cardiac arrest has a large, hairy chest which is interfering with the AED pad adherence. What is the most appropriate initial action?
a. Shave the chest before applying new pads
b. Apply the pads firmly without any modification
c. Place the pads on the back and side of the chest
d. Use alcohol wipes to clean the chest before applying new pads

Answer: a. Shave the chest before applying new pads. Explanation: In cases where chest hair prevents AED pads from adhering properly, shaving the chest is necessary to ensure effective pad placement and electrical conduction.

388. During a 12-lead ECG, you notice that lead V1 shows a flat line. What is the most likely cause and appropriate troubleshooting step?
a. The electrode is not properly attached; ensure V1 electrode contact
b. The machine is malfunctioning; replace the ECG machine
c. The patient has a cardiac condition; perform a repeat ECG
d. The lead cable is disconnected; reattach the cable to the machine

Answer: a. The electrode is not properly attached; ensure V1 electrode contact. Explanation: A flat line in lead V1 likely indicates improper electrode attachment. Checking and ensuring proper contact of the V1 electrode is the appropriate troubleshooting step.

389. A patient with bradycardia is undergoing transcutaneous pacing. The patient experiences discomfort with pacing. Which adjustment should be considered to improve patient comfort while maintaining effective pacing?
a. Decrease the pacing rate
b. Decrease the pacing output
c. Increase the pacing rate
d. Administer analgesia or sedation

Answer: d. Administer analgesia or sedation. Explanation: Transcutaneous pacing can be uncomfortable. Administering analgesia or sedation helps improve patient comfort while maintaining effective pacing.

390. You are called to transport a patient with an intra-aortic balloon pump (IABP). Which principle is crucial to understand about the function of the IABP?
a. It assists in right ventricular function during diastole
b. It inflates during systole to increase cardiac output
c. It inflates during diastole to increase coronary perfusion
d. It assists in reducing afterload during systole

Answer: c. It inflates during diastole to increase coronary perfusion. Explanation: The IABP inflates during diastole to augment coronary perfusion and deflates just before systole to reduce afterload and improve cardiac output.

391. While assessing a patient with a left ventricular assist device (LVAD), you are unable to palpate a pulse. What is the best method to assess the patient's perfusion status?
a. Obtain a manual blood pressure reading
b. Assess capillary refill and mental status
c. Check for carotid artery pulsations
d. Listen for heart sounds using a stethoscope

Answer: b. Assess capillary refill and mental status. Explanation: Patients with an LVAD often do not have a palpable pulse due to continuous flow. Assessing capillary refill and mental status provides a better indication of perfusion status.

392. During cardiac arrest, where should AED pads be placed if a patient has an implanted pacemaker?
a. Directly over the pacemaker
b. At least one inch away from the pacemaker
c. On the back and lower left chest
d. On the upper left chest and lower right chest

Answer: b. At least one inch away from the pacemaker. Explanation: AED pads should be placed at least one inch away from an implanted pacemaker to avoid interference with the device's function and ensure effective defibrillation.

393. While performing a 12-lead ECG, you notice significant interference in all leads. What is the most likely cause and appropriate corrective action?
a. The patient is moving; ask the patient to remain still
b. The ECG machine is malfunctioning; replace the machine
c. The electrodes are incorrectly placed; reattach all electrodes
d. The patient has a pacemaker; reposition the limb leads

Answer: a. The patient is moving; ask the patient to remain still. Explanation: Significant interference in all leads is often caused by patient movement. Asking the patient to remain still can reduce this artifact.

394. You are adjusting the settings on a transcutaneous pacer for a patient with symptomatic bradycardia. What is the correct approach for setting the initial pacing rate and output?
a. Set the rate to 80 bpm and the output to maximum
b. Set the rate to 60 bpm and increase output until capture is achieved
c. Set the rate to 100 bpm and the output to 20 mA
d. Set the rate to 50 bpm and the output to the lowest setting

Answer: b. Set the rate to 60 bpm and increase output until capture is achieved. Explanation: The initial rate should be set to 60 bpm, and the output should be increased until electrical capture is achieved, ensuring effective pacing.

395. During transport, you are monitoring a patient with an LVAD who suddenly becomes unresponsive. What is the immediate next step in management?
a. Check the LVAD device for alarms or malfunctions
b. Begin chest compressions immediately
c. Defibrillate the patient
d. Administer IV fluids

Answer: a. Check the LVAD device for alarms or malfunctions. Explanation: If an LVAD patient becomes unresponsive, the immediate next step is to check the LVAD device for any alarms or malfunctions to determine if the issue is device-related before considering other interventions.

396. When interpreting end-tidal CO_2 (ETCO2) readings during resuscitation, what does a sudden drop in ETCO2 levels indicate?
a. Return of spontaneous circulation (ROSC)
b. Increased cardiac output
c. Airway obstruction or dislodgement
d. Effective chest compressions

Answer: c. Airway obstruction or dislodgement. Explanation: A sudden drop in ETCO2 levels during resuscitation indicates possible airway obstruction or dislodgement, which requires immediate assessment and correction to ensure effective ventilation.

397. A 65-year-old male with hypertension requires frequent blood pressure monitoring. You notice that the readings are consistently higher than expected. Upon examining the equipment, you find that the blood pressure cuff is too small for his arm. What is the likely impact of using an improperly sized cuff?
a. Blood pressure readings will be artificially lower
b. Blood pressure readings will be artificially higher
c. There will be no significant impact on the readings
d. Blood pressure readings will be unpredictable

Answer: b. Blood pressure readings will be artificially higher. Explanation: Using a cuff that is too small for the patient's arm can result in falsely elevated blood pressure readings. The cuff needs to encircle 80% of the arm's circumference to provide accurate measurements.

398. A 45-year-old female undergoing capnography monitoring exhibits a sudden drop in the end-tidal CO_2 (ETCO2) reading. What does this most likely indicate?
a. Hyperventilation
b. Hypoventilation
c. Airway obstruction

d. Cardiac arrest

Answer: d. Cardiac arrest. Explanation: A sudden drop in ETCO2 is often an early indicator of cardiac arrest, reflecting a decrease in cardiac output and subsequent reduction in CO2 delivery to the lungs.

399. A 70-year-old male is being monitored with a pulse oximeter. The reading is consistently low despite the patient showing no signs of respiratory distress. Which alternative placement site might provide a more accurate reading?
a. Earlobe
b. Forehead
c. Wrist
d. Ankle

Answer: a. Earlobe. Explanation: The earlobe is an alternative site for pulse oximetry that can provide accurate readings, particularly when there is poor peripheral perfusion or nail polish/artificial nails interfere with finger readings.

400. A 55-year-old female in the ICU requires continuous invasive blood pressure monitoring. Where should the transducer be leveled to ensure accurate measurements?
a. At the level of the heart (phlebostatic axis)
b. At the level of the diaphragm
c. At the level of the patient's head
d. At the level of the monitoring equipment

Answer: a. At the level of the heart (phlebostatic axis). Explanation: The transducer should be leveled at the phlebostatic axis, which is the fourth intercostal space at the mid-axillary line (level of the heart), to ensure accurate invasive blood pressure measurements.

401. A 50-year-old male undergoing telemetry monitoring complains of chest pain. On examination, you find the leads are incorrectly placed. Where should the V1 lead be placed for accurate ECG readings?
a. Left sternal border, fourth intercostal space
b. Right sternal border, fourth intercostal space
c. Mid-clavicular line, fifth intercostal space
d. Anterior axillary line, fifth intercostal space

Answer: b. Right sternal border, fourth intercostal space. Explanation: The V1 lead should be placed at the right sternal border in the fourth intercostal space to ensure accurate ECG readings and proper detection of cardiac events.

402. A 30-year-old male with a head injury is being monitored for respiratory function using capnography. What characteristic of the capnography waveform indicates effective alveolar ventilation?
a. A rapid, sharp rise in the waveform

b. A prolonged, gradual decline in the waveform
c. A consistent plateau phase
d. A low baseline

Answer: c. A consistent plateau phase. Explanation: A consistent plateau phase in the capnography waveform indicates effective alveolar ventilation, reflecting the proper exchange of CO_2 in the alveoli.

403. A 65-year-old female on continuous pulse oximetry shows fluctuating readings. Which factor is least likely to affect the accuracy of pulse oximetry?
a. Motion artifact
b. Nail polish
c. Skin pigmentation
d. Blood pressure cuff inflation

Answer: c. Skin pigmentation. Explanation: While motion artifact, nail polish, and blood pressure cuff inflation can all affect the accuracy of pulse oximetry readings, skin pigmentation typically does not significantly impact the accuracy of the device.

404. A 75-year-old male requires invasive arterial pressure monitoring. Which of the following best describes the proper maintenance of the pressure transducer setup?
a. Change the tubing every 12 hours
b. Ensure the system is free of air bubbles
c. Place the transducer above the level of the heart
d. Use non-sterile saline for the flush solution

Answer: b. Ensure the system is free of air bubbles. Explanation: To maintain accurate invasive arterial pressure monitoring, the pressure transducer system must be free of air bubbles, which can cause inaccurate readings or even embolism.

405. A 55-year-old female with COPD is monitored using a pulse oximeter. Which condition can cause falsely elevated oxygen saturation readings?
a. Hypovolemia
b. Carbon monoxide poisoning
c. Anemia
d. Hyperthermia

Answer: b. Carbon monoxide poisoning. Explanation: Carbon monoxide poisoning can cause falsely elevated oxygen saturation readings because the pulse oximeter cannot differentiate between oxyhemoglobin and carboxyhemoglobin, leading to misleadingly high readings.

406. A 60-year-old male is being transported with a portable telemetry monitor. He suddenly develops wide QRS complexes on the monitor. What should be your immediate action?
a. Reposition the telemetry leads
b. Administer antiarrhythmic medication
c. Perform synchronized cardioversion
d. Check for pulse and assess the patient

Answer: d. Check for pulse and assess the patient. Explanation: When wide QRS complexes are observed on the telemetry monitor, it is crucial to immediately check for a pulse and assess the patient's clinical condition to determine the appropriate intervention.

407. A 32-year-old male involved in a motor vehicle collision presents with neck pain and potential cervical spine injury. How should you determine the correct size of a cervical collar for this patient?
a. Measure from the clavicle to the chin
b. Measure from the base of the neck to the top of the head
c. Use a one-size-fits-all collar
d. Measure from the sternal notch to the mandible

Answer: d. Measure from the sternal notch to the mandible. Explanation: Correct sizing of a cervical collar is determined by measuring from the sternal notch to the mandible. This ensures appropriate immobilization without causing additional discomfort or injury.

408. A 45-year-old female with a suspected pelvic fracture needs to be immobilized and transported. Which piece of equipment is most appropriate for this situation?
a. Long spine board
b. Scoop stretcher
c. Pelvic binder
d. Traction splint

Answer: b. Scoop stretcher. Explanation: A scoop stretcher is ideal for patients with suspected pelvic fractures because it can be split into two halves and slid under the patient, minimizing movement and further injury.

409. During a football game, a 16-year-old male sustains a midshaft femur fracture. Which immobilization device is most appropriate to use in this case?
a. Pelvic binder
b. Traction splint
c. Long spine board
d. Vacuum splint

Answer: b. Traction splint. Explanation: A traction splint is indicated for midshaft femur fractures to provide alignment and pain relief by applying longitudinal traction. This reduces muscle spasm and prevents further injury.

410. A patient with a suspected unstable pelvic fracture needs stabilization. How should you properly apply a pelvic binder?
a. Position the binder over the iliac crests
b. Place the binder over the lower abdomen
c. Apply the binder below the level of the buttocks
d. Secure the binder around the thighs

Answer: a. Position the binder over the iliac crests. Explanation: The pelvic binder should be positioned over the iliac crests to provide effective stabilization of the pelvic ring and reduce internal bleeding.

411. You are managing a patient with a suspected cervical spine injury. When is it appropriate to use a long spine board?
a. Only for transport to a hospital
b. For immobilization during extrication from a vehicle
c. For long-term immobilization
d. When spinal motion restriction is not a concern

Answer: b. For immobilization during extrication from a vehicle. Explanation: A long spine board is primarily used for immobilization during extrication from a vehicle or other confined spaces. It is not intended for long-term immobilization due to risks such as pressure ulcers and respiratory compromise.

412. When applying a vacuum splint to a patient's fractured limb, what is the correct technique to ensure proper immobilization?
a. Inflate the splint before applying it to the limb
b. Mold the splint to the limb's shape before removing air
c. Apply traction to the limb before placing the splint
d. Use the splint only for upper limb fractures

Answer: b. Mold the splint to the limb's shape before removing air. Explanation: To properly use a vacuum splint, it should be molded to the shape of the injured limb before removing air, ensuring firm and uniform immobilization.

413. A 60-year-old male with a suspected cervical spine injury must be transported over rough terrain. Which immobilization device should be used to ensure maximum stability and comfort?
a. Long spine board
b. Scoop stretcher
c. Vacuum mattress
d. Cervical collar only

Answer: c. Vacuum mattress. Explanation: A vacuum mattress provides better stability and comfort than a rigid spine board, especially during transport over rough terrain. It conforms to the patient's body and reduces the risk of pressure sores.

414. Which of the following is a contraindication for the use of a traction splint?
a. Midshaft femur fracture
b. Open femur fracture with bone protrusion
c. Suspected pelvic fracture
d. Isolated tibia or fibula fracture

Answer: b. Open femur fracture with bone protrusion. Explanation: Traction splints are contraindicated in open femur fractures with bone protrusion due to the risk of worsening the injury and increasing the risk of infection.

415. A 25-year-old female involved in a high-speed collision is found lying supine with an obvious deformity to her pelvis. What is the first step in applying a pelvic binder?
a. Log roll the patient to one side to position the binder
b. Slide the binder under the patient's buttocks
c. Apply the binder directly over the clothing
d. Tighten the binder until the deformity is no longer visible

Answer: b. Slide the binder under the patient's buttocks. Explanation: The first step in applying a pelvic binder is to slide it under the patient's buttocks carefully, ensuring minimal movement and maintaining alignment of the pelvis.

416. A 40-year-old male with a suspected spinal injury is being extricated from a confined space. Which piece of equipment would be most appropriate to use for this patient?
a. Long spine board
b. Scoop stretcher
c. Cervical collar
d. KED (Kendrick Extrication Device)

Answer: d. KED (Kendrick Extrication Device). Explanation: The KED is specifically designed for extricating patients from confined spaces while maintaining spinal immobilization. It provides stability and support during the process of extrication.

417. A 70-year-old male patient with severe COPD needs to be transported from his third-floor apartment to the ambulance. Which piece of equipment is most appropriate for safely transporting him down the stairs?
a. Reeves sleeve
b. Backboard
c. Stair chair
d. Scoop stretcher

Answer: c. Stair chair. Explanation: A stair chair is specifically designed to transport patients down stairs safely and efficiently. It allows for better maneuverability and reduces the risk of injury to both the patient and the rescuers.

418. A 45-year-old female patient weighing 350 lbs requires transport to the hospital for evaluation of abdominal pain. Which special consideration is essential for her safe transport?
a. Use a standard stretcher
b. Ensure the ambulance is equipped with a bariatric stretcher
c. Use a backboard for immobilization
d. Transport her in a stair chair

Answer: b. Ensure the ambulance is equipped with a bariatric stretcher. Explanation: A bariatric stretcher is designed to accommodate larger patients safely, providing adequate support and reducing the risk of injury during transport. Standard stretchers may not be sufficient to handle the weight safely.

419. A 2-day-old neonate requires transport to a specialized facility for further care. What is the most appropriate piece of equipment to use during transport?
a. Pediatric car seat
b. Standard stretcher
c. Neonatal isolette
d. Stair chair

Answer: c. Neonatal isolette. Explanation: A neonatal isolette provides a controlled environment with temperature regulation and protection from environmental factors, making it the most appropriate equipment for transporting a neonate safely.

420. You are preparing to load a critically injured patient into a helicopter for rapid transport to a trauma center. What is the most important consideration during this process?
a. Ensure the patient is secured on a backboard
b. Maintain communication with the flight crew
c. Use a stair chair to load the patient
d. Ensure the patient's vital signs are stable before transport

Answer: b. Maintain communication with the flight crew. Explanation: Effective communication with the flight crew is essential to ensure the patient is loaded safely and efficiently into the helicopter. The flight crew will provide specific instructions and assist with the loading process.

421. During transport, a 60-year-old male patient with a history of spinal injury begins to complain of increased back pain. Which safety feature of the ambulance stretcher should be checked to ensure it is being used correctly?
a. Headrest position
b. Safety straps
c. Stretcher height adjustment

d. Wheel locks

Answer: b. Safety straps. Explanation: Ensuring that the safety straps are properly secured is crucial to prevent the patient from shifting during transport, which can exacerbate spinal pain and increase the risk of further injury.

422. A 75-year-old female with limited mobility needs to be transported from her bed to the ambulance. The distance from her bed to the front door involves navigating narrow hallways. Which piece of equipment is most appropriate for this scenario?
a. Backboard
b. Stair chair
c. Reeves sleeve
d. Scoop stretcher

Answer: c. Reeves sleeve. Explanation: A Reeves sleeve is flexible and can navigate narrow spaces easily, making it ideal for situations where space is limited. It provides adequate support and safety for patients with limited mobility.

423. A 50-year-old bariatric patient needs to be moved from the ambulance to the hospital bed. Which of the following actions is most important to ensure safety during this transfer?
a. Use a standard stretcher and additional personnel
b. Use a bariatric stretcher with hydraulic lift capabilities
c. Utilize a stair chair for the transfer
d. Manually lift the patient with additional personnel

Answer: b. Use a bariatric stretcher with hydraulic lift capabilities. Explanation: A bariatric stretcher with hydraulic lift capabilities ensures safe and efficient transfer of bariatric patients, reducing the risk of injury to both the patient and the healthcare providers.

424. A neonate in an isolette requires transport during cold weather. What additional precaution should be taken to ensure the neonate's safety?
a. Use extra blankets inside the isolette
b. Pre-warm the isolette before placing the neonate inside
c. Place the neonate on a standard stretcher with blankets
d. Adjust the isolette to a higher temperature after transport begins

Answer: b. Pre-warm the isolette before placing the neonate inside. Explanation: Pre-warming the isolette ensures that the neonate is placed in an environment that is already at the appropriate temperature, preventing hypothermia during transport.

425. While transporting a patient with a suspected pelvic fracture, what is the most appropriate piece of equipment to use?

a. Scoop stretcher
b. Backboard
c. Stair chair
d. Reeves sleeve

Answer: a. Scoop stretcher. Explanation: A scoop stretcher is designed to split into two halves, allowing it to be positioned under the patient without causing further movement, which is ideal for patients with suspected pelvic fractures to minimize pain and prevent further injury.

426. A 65-year-old male patient requires helicopter transport from a remote location. What is the primary reason for using a helicopter in this scenario?
a. To provide a more comfortable ride
b. To ensure direct transport to a specialized facility
c. To reduce the time to definitive care
d. To allow for more advanced medical equipment during transport

Answer: c. To reduce the time to definitive care. Explanation: Helicopter transport is often used in remote locations to significantly reduce the time to definitive care, which is critical for improving outcomes in patients with severe or time-sensitive medical conditions.

427. A 58-year-old male with a history of diabetes presents with altered mental status. You decide to check his blood glucose level using a glucometer. What is the most important step to ensure an accurate reading?
a. Squeeze the finger to get a larger blood sample
b. Use the first drop of blood obtained
c. Ensure the glucometer is properly calibrated
d. Apply the blood sample to the glucometer strip immediately

Answer: c. Ensure the glucometer is properly calibrated. Explanation: Proper calibration of the glucometer is crucial to ensure accurate readings. Using the first drop of blood or squeezing the finger can lead to inaccurate results, and applying the blood sample immediately is important, but calibration is key for accuracy.

428. During a trauma assessment, you perform a FAST (Focused Assessment with Sonography for Trauma) exam. Where should you place the ultrasound probe to assess for free fluid in the right upper quadrant?
a. Midline just below the xiphoid process
b. Right midaxillary line at the level of the 9th intercostal space
c. Left lower quadrant just above the iliac crest
d. Right lower quadrant at McBurney's point

Answer: b. Right midaxillary line at the level of the 9th intercostal space. Explanation: The right upper quadrant view of the FAST exam is performed by placing the probe in the right midaxillary line at the level of the 9th intercostal space to visualize the liver and the area around the kidney for free fluid.

429. You are using a CO-oximeter to measure a patient's carboxyhemoglobin level. Which situation would most likely cause an elevated reading?
a. Chronic obstructive pulmonary disease (COPD)
b. Acute asthma exacerbation
c. Carbon monoxide poisoning
d. Diabetic ketoacidosis (DKA)

Answer: c. Carbon monoxide poisoning. Explanation: A CO-oximeter is used to measure carboxyhemoglobin levels, which are elevated in cases of carbon monoxide poisoning. COPD, asthma exacerbation, and DKA do not typically cause elevated carboxyhemoglobin levels.

430. During a 12-lead ECG, where should the V3 electrode be placed?
a. Directly between V1 and V2
b. Directly between V2 and V4
c. Directly below the left clavicle
d. On the left midaxillary line

Answer: b. Directly between V2 and V4. Explanation: The V3 electrode is placed directly between the positions of V2 and V4 to capture the electrical activity of the heart from that specific viewpoint.

431. A patient in septic shock requires monitoring of lactate levels using a point-of-care lactate meter. What is the significance of elevated lactate levels in this patient?
a. Indicates adequate tissue perfusion
b. Suggests hypoperfusion and anaerobic metabolism
c. Confirms metabolic alkalosis
d. Reflects improved oxygenation status

Answer: b. Suggests hypoperfusion and anaerobic metabolism. Explanation: Elevated lactate levels in a patient in septic shock indicate hypoperfusion and anaerobic metabolism, suggesting that tissues are not receiving adequate oxygen.

432. While using a glucometer, you notice that the quality control solution is expired. What is the best course of action?
a. Use the solution anyway, but document the expiration date
b. Perform a test without using the quality control solution
c. Obtain a new quality control solution before testing
d. Use a different glucometer

Answer: c. Obtain a new quality control solution before testing. Explanation: Using an expired quality control solution can lead to inaccurate glucometer readings. It is important to obtain a new quality control solution to ensure the accuracy of the test results.

433. During a FAST exam, you need to assess the pelvic region for free fluid. Where should you place the ultrasound probe?
a. Suprapubic area in the midline
b. Right upper quadrant at the midaxillary line
c. Left upper quadrant below the costal margin
d. Right lower quadrant near McBurney's point

Answer: a. Suprapubic area in the midline. Explanation: The pelvic view in a FAST exam involves placing the ultrasound probe in the suprapubic area in the midline to assess for free fluid in the pelvic cavity.

434. You are interpreting a CO-oximeter reading and notice elevated methemoglobin levels. Which condition is most likely associated with this finding?
a. Carbon monoxide poisoning
b. Cyanide poisoning
c. Methemoglobinemia
d. Iron deficiency anemia

Answer: c. Methemoglobinemia. Explanation: Elevated methemoglobin levels are indicative of methemoglobinemia, a condition where hemoglobin is unable to release oxygen effectively to body tissues.

435. When performing a 12-lead ECG, the patient's right arm electrode is misplaced on the left arm. How will this affect the ECG reading?
a. It will have no significant impact
b. It will result in inaccurate limb lead readings
c. It will cause artifact in precordial leads
d. It will affect only the aVR lead

Answer: b. It will result in inaccurate limb lead readings. Explanation: Misplacing the right arm electrode on the left arm will result in inaccurate readings for the limb leads (I, II, III, aVR, aVL, and aVF) due to improper electrode placement.

436. A trauma patient requires a point-of-care lactate measurement. Which of the following conditions could falsely elevate lactate levels?
a. Hypothermia
b. Hyperventilation
c. Severe anemia
d. Liver dysfunction

Answer: d. Liver dysfunction. Explanation: Liver dysfunction can cause elevated lactate levels due to impaired lactate clearance. Conditions like hypothermia, hyperventilation, and severe anemia do not typically cause false elevation of lactate levels.

437. A 60-year-old male in shock requires rapid IV fluid resuscitation. Which IV catheter size is most appropriate for this purpose?
a. 22 gauge
b. 20 gauge
c. 18 gauge
d. 24 gauge

Answer: c. 18 gauge. Explanation: An 18-gauge catheter is appropriate for rapid IV fluid resuscitation due to its larger bore, allowing for higher flow rates of fluids compared to smaller gauge catheters like 20 or 22 gauge. A 24-gauge catheter is too small for effective fluid resuscitation in shock.

438. A 7-year-old child requires intraosseous (IO) access due to failed IV attempts. What is the most appropriate site for IO insertion in this age group?
a. Proximal tibia
b. Distal femur
c. Proximal humerus
d. Distal radius

Answer: a. Proximal tibia. Explanation: The proximal tibia is the preferred site for intraosseous access in children due to its ease of access and the presence of a large, flat bone surface. The distal femur and proximal humerus are alternative sites but are more commonly used in infants and adults, respectively. The distal radius is not a recommended IO site.

439. A 35-year-old female with asthma requires albuterol nebulization. How should the medication be prepared and administered?
a. Mix albuterol with normal saline and administer over 5-10 minutes
b. Administer albuterol directly without dilution
c. Mix albuterol with sterile water and administer over 15-20 minutes
d. Administer albuterol via metered-dose inhaler (MDI) with spacer

Answer: a. Mix albuterol with normal saline and administer over 5-10 minutes. Explanation: Albuterol should be mixed with normal saline to a total volume of 3-5 mL and administered via a nebulizer over 5-10 minutes for effective bronchodilation. Sterile water is not recommended for nebulization, and an MDI with a spacer is an alternative delivery method, not a preparation technique for nebulization.

440. A 50-year-old male is experiencing severe pain and requires intranasal fentanyl. What is the correct administration technique?
a. Administer the medication slowly over 1 minute
b. Divide the dose between both nostrils
c. Administer the entire dose in one nostril
d. Dilute the medication before administration

Answer: b. Divide the dose between both nostrils. Explanation: Intranasal medications should be divided between both nostrils to maximize absorption and minimize irritation. Administering the medication in one nostril can reduce absorption efficiency, and intranasal medications should not be diluted.

441. A 22-year-old male with a known severe peanut allergy is experiencing anaphylaxis. Which auto-injector is appropriate for immediate use?
a. Glucagon auto-injector
b. Naloxone auto-injector
c. Epinephrine auto-injector
d. Diazepam auto-injector

Answer: c. Epinephrine auto-injector. Explanation: An epinephrine auto-injector is the first-line treatment for anaphylaxis, providing rapid administration of epinephrine to counteract severe allergic reactions. Glucagon, naloxone, and diazepam auto-injectors are used for different emergencies.

442. A 45-year-old female requires IV access for medication administration, but she has small, fragile veins. Which IV catheter size is most appropriate for minimizing vein trauma?
a. 16 gauge
b. 18 gauge
c. 20 gauge
d. 24 gauge

Answer: d. 24 gauge. Explanation: A 24-gauge catheter is the smallest size and is appropriate for patients with small, fragile veins to minimize trauma during insertion and reduce the risk of vein rupture or infiltration.

443. A 6-month-old infant requires intraosseous access in an emergency. What is the most appropriate site for IO insertion in this age group?
a. Distal tibia
b. Proximal humerus
c. Proximal femur
d. Proximal tibia

Answer: d. Proximal tibia. Explanation: In infants, the proximal tibia is the preferred site for intraosseous access due to its easy accessibility and large, flat bone surface suitable for IO needle placement.

444. A 30-year-old female requires administration of naloxone for suspected opioid overdose. What is the appropriate intranasal dose of naloxone?
a. 0.1 mg in one nostril
b. 0.4 mg in one nostril
c. 2 mg divided between both nostrils
d. 4 mg divided between both nostrils

Answer: c. 2 mg divided between both nostrils. Explanation: The standard intranasal dose of naloxone is 2 mg, which should be divided between both nostrils to ensure optimal absorption and rapid reversal of opioid effects.

445. A 40-year-old male with a history of severe allergic reactions is prescribed an epinephrine auto-injector. What is the recommended dose for an adult using an epinephrine auto-injector?
a. 0.1 mg
b. 0.3 mg
c. 0.5 mg
d. 1 mg

Answer: b. 0.3 mg. Explanation: The recommended dose of epinephrine for adults using an auto-injector is 0.3 mg, which is administered intramuscularly, typically into the thigh, to provide rapid onset of action during anaphylaxis.

446. A 55-year-old male requires administration of a bronchodilator via nebulizer for acute asthma exacerbation. What should you do if the patient cannot sit upright?
a. Administer the medication with the patient lying flat
b. Administer the medication using an MDI with a spacer
c. Elevate the head of the bed and administer the nebulizer treatment
d. Hold the nebulizer treatment until the patient can sit upright

Answer: c. Elevate the head of the bed and administer the nebulizer treatment. Explanation: If the patient cannot sit upright, elevating the head of the bed allows for effective administration of the nebulized medication while maintaining patient comfort and optimizing lung expansion for better medication delivery.

447. A 25-year-old male presents with a deep laceration on his forearm. What is the recommended pressure range for effective wound irrigation to minimize infection risk?
a. 1-5 psi
b. 6-10 psi
c. 11-15 psi
d. 16-20 psi

Answer: b. 6-10 psi. Explanation: Effective wound irrigation to minimize infection risk should be performed at a pressure range of 6-10 psi. This pressure is sufficient to remove debris and bacteria without causing further tissue damage.

448. A 35-year-old male is brought to the emergency department with a sucking chest wound. Which type of dressing is most appropriate to apply initially?
a. Gauze dressing
b. Occlusive dressing
c. Transparent film dressing
d. Absorbent pad

Answer: b. Occlusive dressing. Explanation: An occlusive dressing is most appropriate for a sucking chest wound as it prevents air from entering the chest cavity, reducing the risk of tension pneumothorax. It should be sealed on three sides to allow air to escape during exhalation.

449. A 40-year-old female sustains partial-thickness burns on her right arm. Which type of dressing is most suitable for this type of burn?
a. Dry gauze
b. Non-adherent dressing with a hydrogel
c. Occlusive dressing
d. Adhesive bandage

Answer: b. Non-adherent dressing with a hydrogel. Explanation: Partial-thickness burns benefit from a non-adherent dressing with a hydrogel, which maintains a moist environment, reduces pain, and promotes healing.

450. A 30-year-old male suffers a severe laceration with significant arterial bleeding. Where should the tourniquet be placed in relation to the wound, and how should the timing of application be documented?
a. Directly over the wound; document the time every 30 minutes
b. 2-3 inches distal to the wound; document the time of application once
c. 2-3 inches proximal to the wound; document the time of application once
d. Directly over the wound; document the time every 60 minutes

Answer: c. 2-3 inches proximal to the wound; document the time of application once. Explanation: The tourniquet should be placed 2-3 inches proximal to the wound to effectively control arterial bleeding. The time of application should be documented once to ensure timely reassessment and prevent complications from prolonged tourniquet use.

451. A 50-year-old male with a deep, actively bleeding wound requires hemostatic agent application. What is the proper technique for applying a hemostatic agent?
a. Sprinkle the agent over the wound and cover with a dry gauze
b. Apply the agent directly into the wound and apply firm pressure
c. Place the agent on top of the wound and secure with a bandage

d. Mix the agent with saline and pour into the wound

Answer: b. Apply the agent directly into the wound and apply firm pressure. Explanation: Hemostatic agents should be applied directly into the wound with firm pressure to promote clotting and effectively control bleeding.

452. A 45-year-old female with a history of diabetes presents with a chronic foot ulcer. Which irrigation solution is most appropriate for cleaning the wound?
a. Hydrogen peroxide
b. Betadine solution
c. Sterile normal saline
d. Alcohol

Answer: c. Sterile normal saline. Explanation: Sterile normal saline is the preferred irrigation solution for cleaning wounds, including chronic ulcers, as it is isotonic and does not harm tissue or delay healing.

453. A 22-year-old male sustains a puncture wound to the abdomen with bowel evisceration. What is the most appropriate dressing to apply?
a. Dry sterile dressing
b. Occlusive dressing
c. Moist sterile dressing
d. Transparent film dressing

Answer: c. Moist sterile dressing. Explanation: A moist sterile dressing is appropriate for a puncture wound with bowel evisceration to keep the exposed organs moist and prevent further damage until surgical intervention.

454. A patient with a gunshot wound to the leg has severe bleeding that is not controlled by direct pressure. What is the next step in managing the bleeding?
a. Apply an adhesive bandage
b. Use a tourniquet above the wound
c. Elevate the leg
d. Apply a cold pack to the wound

Answer: b. Use a tourniquet above the wound. Explanation: If severe bleeding is not controlled by direct pressure, a tourniquet should be applied above the wound to control arterial bleeding and prevent hemorrhagic shock.

455. A 60-year-old male with a scalp laceration requires a dressing. Which type of dressing is most appropriate for a scalp wound?
a. Non-adherent dressing
b. Occlusive dressing
c. Pressure dressing

d. Transparent film dressing

Answer: c. Pressure dressing. Explanation: A pressure dressing is most appropriate for a scalp wound to control bleeding and secure the wound. The scalp is highly vascular, and a pressure dressing helps to manage hemostasis.

456. A patient requires wound closure after a minor laceration. What is the best method to clean the wound before closure?
a. Soak the wound in betadine
b. Irrigate the wound with high-pressure sterile water
c. Clean the wound with sterile saline and gauze
d. Apply hydrogen peroxide and cover with a sterile dressing

Answer: c. Clean the wound with sterile saline and gauze. Explanation: Cleaning the wound with sterile saline and gauze is the best method to ensure the wound is free of debris and contaminants before closure, promoting optimal healing conditions.

457. Upon arriving at the scene of a chemical spill, you observe a placard with a blue background and the number "3" in the lower quadrant. What does this indicate regarding the type of hazard present?
a. Flammability hazard
b. Health hazard
c. Reactivity hazard
d. Radioactivity hazard

Answer: b. Health hazard. Explanation: The blue quadrant on a hazardous materials placard indicates a health hazard. The number "3" represents a high level of health hazard, meaning that the substance could cause serious or permanent injury with short exposure.

458. You are responding to an active shooter incident at a large shopping mall. What is the most appropriate initial action upon arrival?
a. Immediately enter the mall to locate the shooter
b. Set up a command post and establish communication with law enforcement
c. Begin triaging and treating victims at the entrance
d. Evacuate all civilians from the mall

Answer: b. Set up a command post and establish communication with law enforcement. Explanation: Establishing a command post and communication with law enforcement is critical to coordinate a safe and effective response. Entering the mall without a tactical plan can be dangerous, and triaging or evacuating should be done only after ensuring the scene is secure.

459. While responding to a multi-vehicle collision on a busy highway, you need to manage traffic to ensure the safety of the scene. Which technique is most appropriate to achieve this?
a. Use your vehicle to block all lanes of traffic
b. Set up flares and cones to divert traffic away from the scene
c. Park your vehicle facing oncoming traffic with emergency lights activated
d. Stand in the middle of the road to direct traffic manually

Answer: b. Set up flares and cones to divert traffic away from the scene. Explanation: Setting up flares and cones is an effective way to divert traffic and protect the scene. Blocking all lanes or standing in the middle of the road is unsafe. Parking your vehicle facing oncoming traffic can provide some protection but is not as effective as diverting traffic.

460. You arrive at the scene of a house fire and see multiple bystanders attempting to re-enter the building to rescue pets. What is your primary concern?
a. Assisting the bystanders in rescuing the pets
b. Assessing the stability of the building structure
c. Ensuring the safety of the bystanders and preventing re-entry
d. Identifying the source of the fire

Answer: c. Ensuring the safety of the bystanders and preventing re-entry. Explanation: The primary concern is the safety of the bystanders. Preventing re-entry into a burning building is crucial to avoid further injuries or fatalities. Firefighters should be the ones to assess the structure and handle the rescue efforts.

461. During a PENMAN scene size-up, what does the "E" represent, and what action should you take related to it?
a. Environment; assess weather conditions
b. Equipment; gather necessary medical supplies
c. Exposure; identify potential hazardous materials
d. Extrication; determine need for additional resources

Answer: c. Exposure; identify potential hazardous materials. Explanation: The "E" in PENMAN stands for Exposure, which involves identifying potential hazardous materials or environmental dangers that could pose a risk to responders and patients.

462. You arrive at the scene of an industrial accident where a worker is trapped under heavy machinery. What personal protective equipment (PPE) is essential for ensuring your safety?
a. N95 mask, gown, and gloves
b. Hard hat, safety glasses, and steel-toed boots
c. SCBA (self-contained breathing apparatus), turnout gear, and helmet
d. Surgical mask, face shield, and boot covers

Answer: b. Hard hat, safety glasses, and steel-toed boots. Explanation: For an industrial accident, appropriate PPE includes a hard hat, safety glasses, and steel-toed boots to protect against falling debris, eye injuries, and foot injuries from heavy machinery.

463. You are the first responder to a scene involving a potential hazardous material spill on the roadway. What is the initial step you should take upon arrival?
a. Begin immediate decontamination of affected individuals
b. Identify the hazardous material using the Emergency Response Guidebook (ERG)
c. Evacuate all personnel within a 1-mile radius
d. Contact the National Response Center for guidance

Answer: b. Identify the hazardous material using the Emergency Response Guidebook (ERG). Explanation: The initial step is to identify the hazardous material using the ERG to determine the appropriate actions for ensuring safety, such as evacuation distances and protective measures.

464. At the scene of an active shooter, what specific strategy should EMS personnel use to enhance safety and efficiency during the response?
a. Operate independently from law enforcement
b. Use a rescue task force (RTF) model
c. Focus solely on patient care within the hot zone
d. Transport all victims immediately to the nearest hospital

Answer: b. Use a rescue task force (RTF) model. Explanation: The rescue task force (RTF) model involves integrated operations between EMS and law enforcement to ensure safe and efficient care and evacuation of victims from the warm zone. This model enhances safety by providing protection to medical personnel while delivering care.

465. While responding to a scene where hazardous materials are involved, you notice a placard with the numbers "4" on the red quadrant and "2" on the yellow quadrant. What do these numbers indicate?
a. High health hazard and moderate reactivity hazard
b. High flammability hazard and moderate health hazard
c. High flammability hazard and moderate reactivity hazard
d. High reactivity hazard and moderate health hazard

Answer: c. High flammability hazard and moderate reactivity hazard. Explanation: The red quadrant indicates flammability, and a "4" represents a high flammability hazard. The yellow quadrant indicates reactivity, and a "2" represents a moderate reactivity hazard.

466. You are the first to arrive at the scene of a traffic collision involving multiple vehicles. What should be your initial action to ensure scene safety?
a. Begin triage and treatment of victims
b. Position your vehicle to protect the scene and establish a safety zone
c. Move all vehicles to the side of the road

d. Interview bystanders to gather information about the incident

Answer: b. Position your vehicle to protect the scene and establish a safety zone. Explanation: The initial action is to position your vehicle to protect the scene and establish a safety zone. This helps prevent further accidents and ensures the safety of both the responders and the victims.

467. A 40-year-old male involved in a motor vehicle collision is unresponsive. During the primary survey using the ABCDE approach, what is the first priority?
a. Check for severe bleeding
b. Assess for a patent airway
c. Evaluate circulation and pulses
d. Perform a neurological assessment

Answer: b. Assess for a patent airway. Explanation: The primary survey using the ABCDE approach prioritizes airway assessment and management first, as a patent airway is crucial for oxygenation and ventilation. Following airway assessment, breathing, circulation, disability (neurological status), and exposure are evaluated.

468. During a secondary survey, you discover a large, deep laceration on the patient's thigh. Which step should you take next?
a. Document the finding and continue the assessment
b. Apply direct pressure to control bleeding
c. Reassess the patient's airway and breathing
d. Administer intravenous fluids immediately

Answer: b. Apply direct pressure to control bleeding. Explanation: In the secondary survey, any life-threatening injuries found should be addressed immediately. Applying direct pressure to control bleeding from a deep laceration is essential to prevent further blood loss and stabilize the patient.

469. A 30-year-old female has fallen from a height of 20 feet. What type of assessment should be performed first?
a. Focused assessment
b. Rapid trauma assessment
c. Detailed physical exam
d. Neurological assessment

Answer: b. Rapid trauma assessment. Explanation: For a patient who has experienced a significant mechanism of injury, such as a fall from a height, a rapid trauma assessment should be performed first to quickly identify and manage life-threatening injuries.

470. A 5-year-old child presents with respiratory distress. Using the Pediatric Assessment Triangle (PAT), you note increased work of breathing, pallor, and lethargy. What is the next step?

a. Perform a focused respiratory exam
b. Administer supplemental oxygen
c. Begin chest compressions
d. Obtain a detailed medical history

Answer: b. Administer supplemental oxygen. Explanation: The PAT helps quickly assess the severity of a pediatric patient's condition. Increased work of breathing, pallor, and lethargy indicate a need for immediate intervention, such as administering supplemental oxygen to improve oxygenation and perfusion.

471. An 80-year-old male presents with confusion, dehydration, and poor skin turgor. What is an important consideration in the geriatric assessment of this patient?
a. Assume the confusion is due to age
b. Perform a rapid trauma assessment
c. Consider underlying infection or metabolic disturbances
d. Focus solely on rehydration

Answer: c. Consider underlying infection or metabolic disturbances. Explanation: In geriatric patients, symptoms like confusion and dehydration can be signs of underlying issues such as infection or metabolic disturbances. It is important to consider these possibilities and conduct a thorough assessment to identify the root cause.

472. A 25-year-old male presents with a gunshot wound to the abdomen. What is the first step in your assessment?
a. Perform a focused abdominal exam
b. Establish intravenous access
c. Assess airway, breathing, and circulation
d. Obtain a detailed medical history

Answer: c. Assess airway, breathing, and circulation. Explanation: In trauma patients, the primary survey begins with assessing airway, breathing, and circulation to identify and manage any immediate life-threatening conditions.

473. A 70-year-old female presents with generalized weakness and a history of hypertension and diabetes. During your assessment, she becomes unresponsive. What should you do first?
a. Administer glucose
b. Check for a pulse
c. Begin chest compressions
d. Administer oxygen

Answer: b. Check for a pulse. Explanation: When a patient becomes unresponsive, the first step is to check for a pulse to determine if there is cardiac activity. If no pulse is present, initiate chest compressions.

474. During a focused assessment, you note that a 60-year-old male with chest pain has diminished breath sounds on one side and jugular venous distension. What is the most likely diagnosis?
a. Myocardial infarction
b. Pulmonary embolism
c. Tension pneumothorax
d. Congestive heart failure

Answer: c. Tension pneumothorax. Explanation: Diminished breath sounds on one side and jugular venous distension are indicative of a tension pneumothorax, which is a life-threatening condition that requires immediate intervention.

475. A pediatric patient presents with a high fever, lethargy, and a bulging fontanelle. What is the most likely diagnosis, and what should be your next step?
a. Meningitis; perform a lumbar puncture
b. Dehydration; administer intravenous fluids
c. Sepsis; administer broad-spectrum antibiotics
d. Febrile seizure; administer antipyretics

Answer: c. Sepsis; administer broad-spectrum antibiotics. Explanation: High fever, lethargy, and a bulging fontanelle in a pediatric patient are suggestive of sepsis or meningitis. Immediate administration of broad-spectrum antibiotics is crucial to treat the underlying infection and prevent further complications.

476. A 45-year-old male with a history of COPD presents with shortness of breath and wheezing. During the assessment, his respiratory rate increases to 30 breaths per minute, and he becomes cyanotic. What is the most appropriate initial intervention?
a. Administer a beta-blocker
b. Provide high-flow oxygen
c. Perform endotracheal intubation
d. Administer an albuterol nebulizer treatment

Answer: d. Administer an albuterol nebulizer treatment. Explanation: In a patient with COPD experiencing an acute exacerbation, administering a bronchodilator like albuterol can help relieve bronchospasm and improve breathing. Providing supplemental oxygen is also important but should be carefully titrated to avoid suppressing respiratory drive.

477. You are providing a radio report to the receiving hospital using the SBAR technique. Which of the following correctly represents the "B" in SBAR?
a. The patient is a 45-year-old male with a history of hypertension and diabetes
b. The patient has a blood pressure of 140/90 mmHg, heart rate of 110 bpm, and respiratory rate of 22 breaths per minute
c. Requesting an IV line and cardiac monitoring upon arrival
d. The patient requires immediate transport due to chest pain and shortness of breath

Answer: a. The patient is a 45-year-old male with a history of hypertension and diabetes. Explanation: The "B" in SBAR stands for Background, which includes relevant patient history and context that provide the receiving team with necessary information about the patient's medical history.

478. During a hand-off report, you use the IPASS mnemonic. What does the "P" in IPASS represent, and which information should be included under this component?
a. Patient details; includes the patient's age, gender, and medical history
b. Plan; includes the intended next steps in the patient's care
c. Problems; includes the patient's current problems and diagnosis
d. Procedures; includes the procedures performed during transport

Answer: b. Plan; includes the intended next steps in the patient's care. Explanation: The "P" in IPASS stands for Plan, which includes the next steps or intended actions in the patient's care, ensuring continuity and clarity during the hand-off process.

479. You encounter a patient who is becoming increasingly agitated. What is the most effective initial de-escalation technique to employ?
a. Raise your voice to assert control
b. Use open-ended questions to understand their concerns
c. Stand close to the patient to establish presence
d. Avoid eye contact to prevent confrontation

Answer: b. Use open-ended questions to understand their concerns. Explanation: Using open-ended questions helps to understand the patient's concerns and shows that you are listening, which can effectively de-escalate the situation by making the patient feel heard and respected.

480. While treating a patient who does not speak English, what strategy can best ensure effective communication?
a. Speak slowly and loudly in English
b. Use a family member to translate
c. Utilize a professional medical interpreter
d. Use gestures and body language to convey messages

Answer: c. Utilize a professional medical interpreter. Explanation: Using a professional medical interpreter ensures accurate and effective communication, reducing the risk of miscommunication and ensuring that the patient receives appropriate care.

481. When documenting a patient encounter, which element is most crucial to ensure completeness and accuracy?
a. The time of arrival at the scene
b. A detailed narrative of the patient's chief complaint
c. The name and contact information of witnesses
d. The weather conditions at the time of the incident

Answer: b. A detailed narrative of the patient's chief complaint. Explanation: A detailed narrative of the patient's chief complaint is crucial for medical documentation as it provides essential information about the patient's condition and the care provided, aiding in continuity of care and legal documentation.

482. You are preparing to give a radio report using the SBAR technique. What should be included in the "S" component?
a. The patient's vital signs
b. The patient's current situation, including symptoms and chief complaint
c. The patient's medical history
d. The requested interventions

Answer: b. The patient's current situation, including symptoms and chief complaint. Explanation: The "S" in SBAR stands for Situation, which includes the patient's current condition, symptoms, and chief complaint, providing the receiving team with an immediate understanding of the situation.

483. During the hand-off report using the IPASS mnemonic, what does the "I" stand for and what should it include?
a. Introduction; includes introducing yourself and your role
b. Injuries; includes details about any injuries the patient has sustained
c. Impression; includes your clinical impression and assessment findings
d. Interventions; includes treatments and actions taken so far

Answer: a. Introduction; includes introducing yourself and your role. Explanation: The "I" in IPASS stands for Introduction, which includes introducing yourself and your role to ensure that the receiving team knows who is providing the report and their authority.

484. You are managing a patient with a significant language barrier. Which method should be avoided to ensure accurate communication?
a. Using a bilingual family member to translate
b. Writing down instructions in English
c. Using a professional medical interpreter
d. Utilizing visual aids to assist in communication

Answer: a. Using a bilingual family member to translate. Explanation: Using a family member to translate can lead to inaccuracies and confidentiality issues. It is best to use a professional medical interpreter to ensure accurate and private communication.

485. What is the primary purpose of documenting the time of all significant events during a patient encounter?
a. To provide a detailed timeline for legal records
b. To ensure the accuracy of the narrative

c. To assist in billing and reimbursement processes
d. To enhance communication with the patient's family

Answer: a. To provide a detailed timeline for legal records. Explanation: Documenting the time of all significant events provides a detailed timeline that is crucial for legal records, ensuring that there is an accurate and accountable record of the care provided.

486. When communicating with an agitated patient, which approach should be taken to ensure effective de-escalation?
a. Maintain a calm and empathetic tone
b. Use authoritative language to establish control
c. Stand over the patient to show dominance
d. Avoid addressing their concerns directly

Answer: a. Maintain a calm and empathetic tone. Explanation: Maintaining a calm and empathetic tone helps to de-escalate the situation by demonstrating that you are approachable and understanding, which can help to calm the patient and reduce their agitation.

487. A mass casualty incident (MCI) occurs at a large outdoor concert. Using the START triage method, you encounter an adult patient who is unconscious, has a respiratory rate of 8 breaths per minute, and a weak radial pulse. What is the appropriate triage category for this patient?
a. Minor (Green)
b. Delayed (Yellow)
c. Immediate (Red)
d. Deceased/Expectant (Black)

Answer: c. Immediate (Red). Explanation: According to the START triage method, an adult patient with a respiratory rate below 10 breaths per minute and a weak radial pulse is categorized as Immediate (Red) due to compromised airway, breathing, and circulation, requiring urgent medical intervention.

488. At a school bus accident, you are using the JumpSTART pediatric triage system. You find a 7-year-old child who is not breathing after opening the airway. What is your next step?
a. Tag the child as Deceased/Expectant (Black)
b. Deliver five rescue breaths and reassess
c. Move on to the next patient
d. Begin chest compressions

Answer: b. Deliver five rescue breaths and reassess. Explanation: The JumpSTART pediatric triage system recommends delivering five rescue breaths to apneic children. If they begin breathing after rescue breaths, they are categorized appropriately; if not, they are tagged as Deceased/Expectant (Black).

489. During an evacuation scenario following a building collapse, you are instructed to perform reverse triage. Which patients should you prioritize for evacuation first?
a. Those with the most severe injuries
b. Those with minor injuries
c. Those who are ambulatory
d. Those who are unresponsive

Answer: c. Those who are ambulatory. Explanation: Reverse triage prioritizes the evacuation of ambulatory patients first, as they can move independently and do not require immediate assistance, allowing rescuers to focus on those needing urgent care later.

490. In a chemical plant explosion, you apply the SALT triage method. You encounter a patient who can walk but has severe burns. How should this patient be categorized?
a. Minimal (Green)
b. Delayed (Yellow)
c. Immediate (Red)
d. Expectant (Gray)

Answer: b. Delayed (Yellow). Explanation: In the SALT triage method, patients who can walk are initially considered Minimal (Green) but need further evaluation. Severe burns without immediate life-threatening conditions would reclassify them as Delayed (Yellow).

491. During a prolonged incident with limited resources, what is the primary purpose of secondary triage?
a. To reevaluate patients and adjust their triage categories as needed
b. To document patient information for legal purposes
c. To identify deceased patients for the morgue
d. To provide psychological support to victims

Answer: a. To reevaluate patients and adjust their triage categories as needed. Explanation: Secondary triage involves continuous reassessment of patients' conditions to ensure they receive appropriate care as their medical status changes and resources become available.

492. A multiple vehicle collision results in numerous casualties. Using the START triage method, you find an adult patient who is able to follow commands, has a respiratory rate of 22 breaths per minute, and a strong radial pulse. What is the appropriate triage category for this patient?
a. Minor (Green)
b. Delayed (Yellow)
c. Immediate (Red)
d. Deceased/Expectant (Black)

Answer: b. Delayed (Yellow). Explanation: An adult patient who can follow commands, has a respiratory rate within the normal range, and a strong radial pulse is categorized as Delayed (Yellow) in the START triage method, indicating that they can wait for treatment.

493. During a JumpSTART pediatric triage, you assess an 8-year-old child who is not breathing and has no pulse. What is the correct triage category for this child?
a. Minor (Green)
b. Delayed (Yellow)
c. Immediate (Red)
d. Deceased/Expectant (Black)

Answer: d. Deceased/Expectant (Black). Explanation: In the JumpSTART pediatric triage system, a child who is not breathing and has no pulse is categorized as Deceased/Expectant (Black), indicating no signs of life.

494. At a train derailment with multiple injuries, you are applying the SALT triage method. You come across a patient with severe bleeding, unable to follow commands, but has a pulse. What is their triage category?
a. Minimal (Green)
b. Delayed (Yellow)
c. Immediate (Red)
d. Expectant (Gray)

Answer: c. Immediate (Red). Explanation: In the SALT triage method, a patient with severe bleeding and inability to follow commands but still has a pulse is categorized as Immediate (Red) due to the severity of their condition requiring urgent treatment.

495. After an earthquake, you perform reverse triage in a partially collapsed building. You find a conscious patient trapped under debris with minor injuries. What should be your initial action?
a. Attempt to extricate the patient immediately
b. Provide reassurance and move to the next patient
c. Mark the patient for delayed extrication
d. Administer pain relief and continue extrication

Answer: b. Provide reassurance and move to the next patient. Explanation: In reverse triage, ambulatory patients with minor injuries are reassured and moved to the next patient, prioritizing those who can be quickly moved or require urgent care.

496. You are managing a prolonged incident at a mass gathering with limited medical resources. What key factor should be considered when performing secondary triage?
a. The patient's insurance status
b. The availability of family members
c. The patient's initial triage category
d. The potential for deterioration or improvement

Answer: d. The potential for deterioration or improvement. Explanation: Secondary triage focuses on continuous reassessment to identify any changes in patients' conditions that may necessitate re-triage based on the potential for deterioration or improvement.

497. You are assigned as the Operations Section Chief in an Incident Command System (ICS) structure. Which of the following best describes your primary responsibility?
a. Developing the incident objectives and strategies
b. Providing support and resources to operational personnel
c. Directing all tactical operations to achieve the incident objectives
d. Ensuring effective communication within the command staff

Answer: c. Directing all tactical operations to achieve the incident objectives. Explanation: The Operations Section Chief is responsible for directing all tactical operations to achieve the incident objectives set by the Incident Commander. This role involves managing resources and ensuring that field activities are aligned with the overall strategy.

498. During a large-scale disaster response, multiple agencies are involved. Which aspect of the ICS structure ensures that all agencies work together effectively?
a. Incident Action Plan (IAP)
b. Span of control
c. Unified Command
d. Resource typing

Answer: c. Unified Command. Explanation: Unified Command is a structure within ICS that allows multiple agencies with different legal, geographic, and functional authorities to work together effectively without losing their individual authority, responsibility, or accountability.

499. In the context of ICS, what is the optimal span of control for any supervisor?
a. 3 to 7 individuals
b. 5 to 10 individuals
c. 1 to 3 individuals
d. 10 to 15 individuals

Answer: a. 3 to 7 individuals. Explanation: The optimal span of control within ICS is between 3 to 7 individuals, with 5 being ideal. This range ensures that supervisors can effectively manage their resources without becoming overwhelmed.

500. A specific type of resource has been requested for a wildfire incident. Which ICS concept ensures that the resource meets the necessary qualifications and capabilities?

a. Incident Action Plan (IAP)
b. Resource typing
c. Span of control
d. Staging area management

Answer: b. Resource typing. Explanation: Resource typing is the categorization and description of resources by capability to ensure that the resources requested and deployed are appropriate for the specific needs of the incident.

501. As part of the planning process in ICS, an Incident Action Plan (IAP) is developed. Which of the following elements is NOT typically included in an IAP?
a. Incident objectives
b. Communication plan
c. Personnel compensation details
d. Safety message

Answer: c. Personnel compensation details. Explanation: An IAP typically includes incident objectives, a communication plan, and a safety message, among other elements. Personnel compensation details are not part of the IAP but are handled through administrative channels.

502. You are the Incident Commander at a mass casualty incident. To maintain an effective span of control, you decide to delegate tasks. Which ICS position should be created to manage resources and logistics?
a. Operations Section Chief
b. Planning Section Chief
c. Logistics Section Chief
d. Safety Officer

Answer: c. Logistics Section Chief. Explanation: The Logistics Section Chief is responsible for managing all logistics and resource support for the incident, ensuring that operations have the necessary supplies and support to function effectively.

503. Which principle ensures that all resources are accounted for and efficiently deployed during an incident?
a. Unity of command
b. Resource typing
c. Span of control
d. Check-in/check-out procedures

Answer: d. Check-in/check-out procedures. Explanation: Check-in/check-out procedures ensure that all resources are accounted for and their deployment is tracked, which helps maintain an organized and efficient response effort.

504. In an ICS structure, who is responsible for developing and updating the Incident Action Plan (IAP)?

a. Planning Section Chief
b. Operations Section Chief
c. Logistics Section Chief
d. Incident Commander

Answer: a. Planning Section Chief. Explanation: The Planning Section Chief is responsible for developing and updating the Incident Action Plan (IAP), which outlines the strategies, tactics, and resources needed to achieve the incident objectives.

505. During a multi-agency response, how does the Unified Command structure help to improve coordination?
a. By allowing each agency to have an independent command structure
b. By integrating all agencies under a single Incident Commander
c. By ensuring that each agency maintains its own objectives
d. By enabling agencies to work together with shared objectives and strategies

Answer: d. By enabling agencies to work together with shared objectives and strategies. Explanation: Unified Command allows agencies to work together with shared objectives and strategies, improving coordination and reducing conflicts between different agencies' goals.

506. Which ICS position is responsible for monitoring and assessing safety hazards and developing measures for ensuring personnel safety?
a. Public Information Officer
b. Safety Officer
c. Logistics Section Chief
d. Operations Section Chief

Answer: b. Safety Officer. Explanation: The Safety Officer is responsible for monitoring and assessing safety hazards and developing measures to ensure the safety of all personnel involved in the incident response.

507. A 35-year-old male is trapped in a vehicle following a high-speed collision. Which tool is most appropriate for cutting through the vehicle's metal to extricate the patient?
a. Hydraulic spreaders
b. Hydraulic cutters
c. Reciprocating saw
d. Glass master tool

Answer: b. Hydraulic cutters. Explanation: Hydraulic cutters are specifically designed to cut through the metal of vehicles during extrication, making them ideal for freeing a trapped patient quickly and efficiently.

508. You are part of a team performing a confined space rescue in an industrial setting. What is the primary precaution that must be taken before entering the confined space?
a. Ensure all rescuers are wearing hard hats
b. Test the atmosphere for hazardous gases and ensure proper ventilation
c. Remove any obstructions from the entry point
d. Establish a communication plan with the team

Answer: b. Test the atmosphere for hazardous gases and ensure proper ventilation. Explanation: Confined spaces can contain hazardous gases or lack sufficient oxygen. Testing the atmosphere and ensuring proper ventilation is crucial to the safety of rescuers and the trapped individual.

509. During a water rescue, you are tasked with reaching a drowning victim in a fast-moving river. Which piece of equipment is most appropriate to use?
a. Throw bag
b. Life ring
c. Rescue board
d. Inflatable raft

Answer: a. Throw bag. Explanation: A throw bag, which contains a length of rope, is suitable for reaching a drowning victim in a fast-moving river, allowing the rescuer to stay on shore while providing a lifeline to the victim.

510. You are responding to an incident requiring a high-angle rescue. Which principle is essential to ensure the safety of both the rescuer and the victim?
a. Always use a single rope for speed
b. Rely solely on the rescuer's strength to lower the victim
c. Use a system of pulleys and redundant safety lines
d. Prioritize rapid descent over safety

Answer: c. Use a system of pulleys and redundant safety lines. Explanation: High-angle rescues require the use of pulleys and redundant safety lines to distribute weight and provide backup support, ensuring the safety of both the rescuer and the victim.

511. During a trench rescue, what is the primary purpose of shoring techniques?
a. To provide a pathway for rescuers
b. To prevent further collapse of the trench walls
c. To create a space for medical treatment
d. To improve ventilation within the trench

Answer: b. To prevent further collapse of the trench walls. Explanation: Shoring techniques are used to stabilize trench walls and prevent further collapse, protecting both the victim and rescuers during the rescue operation.

512. A car has overturned in a ditch, trapping a passenger inside. Which extrication technique should be prioritized to safely remove the passenger?
a. Use of a hydraulic jack to lift the car
b. Stabilization of the vehicle followed by door removal
c. Breaking the windshield to access the passenger
d. Cutting through the roof immediately

Answer: b. Stabilization of the vehicle followed by door removal. Explanation: Stabilizing the vehicle to prevent further movement is the first priority, followed by door removal to create a safe and effective access point for extrication.

513. You are involved in a confined space rescue where the atmosphere is tested and found to be low in oxygen. What equipment is essential for rescuers entering this environment?
a. Self-contained breathing apparatus (SCBA)
b. Dust masks
c. Full-face shields
d. Ear protection

Answer: a. Self-contained breathing apparatus (SCBA). Explanation: An SCBA provides a clean air supply to rescuers in environments with low oxygen levels, ensuring their safety while performing the rescue.

514. During a water rescue operation, what is the most important safety measure for rescuers entering the water?
a. Wearing a bright-colored uniform
b. Using a buddy system
c. Carrying a knife
d. Wearing a personal flotation device (PFD)

Answer: d. Wearing a personal flotation device (PFD). Explanation: Wearing a PFD is crucial for rescuers entering the water, providing buoyancy and reducing the risk of drowning during the rescue operation.

515. In a high-angle rescue, what type of knot is commonly used to secure the rope to the anchor point?
a. Square knot
b. Clove hitch
c. Bowline
d. Sheet bend

Answer: c. Bowline. Explanation: The bowline knot is commonly used in high-angle rescues to secure the rope to an anchor point because it is easy to tie and untie, even under load.

516. During a trench rescue, you notice that the soil is starting to shift. What is the immediate action that should be taken?
a. Continue the rescue operation as quickly as possible
b. Halt the operation and evacuate all personnel from the trench
c. Apply additional shoring to stabilize the trench walls
d. Remove the victim immediately without regard for safety

Answer: b. Halt the operation and evacuate all personnel from the trench. Explanation: If the soil begins to shift, it indicates an imminent risk of collapse. The immediate action should be to halt the operation and evacuate all personnel to ensure safety before reassessing and reinforcing the shoring.

517. You are the first responder to a chemical spill on the highway. Using the DOT Emergency Response Guidebook (ERG), you identify the material as UN 1090, acetone. What is the initial isolation distance for a small spill?
a. 50 meters (150 feet)
b. 100 meters (330 feet)
c. 150 meters (500 feet)
d. 200 meters (660 feet)

Answer: b. 100 meters (330 feet). Explanation: According to the DOT ERG, the initial isolation distance for a small spill of acetone (UN 1090) is 100 meters (330 feet) in all directions to ensure the safety of responders and the public.

518. Upon arrival at a hazardous materials incident, you must establish hot, warm, and cold zones. Which zone is designated for contamination reduction and decontamination?
a. Hot zone
b. Warm zone
c. Cold zone
d. Evacuation zone

Answer: b. Warm zone. Explanation: The warm zone, also known as the contamination reduction zone, is where decontamination procedures occur. It is located between the hot zone (where the hazardous material is present) and the cold zone (the safe area).

519. At a chemical spill site, you are tasked with setting up a decontamination corridor. Which of the following is the most critical first step in this process?
a. Establishing the cold zone
b. Identifying the contaminants
c. Setting up decontamination pools
d. Donning appropriate PPE

Answer: d. Donning appropriate PPE. Explanation: Before setting up a decontamination corridor, it is essential to don appropriate personal protective equipment (PPE) to protect responders from exposure to hazardous materials.

520. You encounter a storage tank with an NFPA 704 diamond that has a "4" in the blue quadrant, a "3" in the red quadrant, and a "2" in the yellow quadrant. What does this indicate about the material?
a. Extreme health hazard, high flammability, moderate reactivity
b. High health hazard, extreme flammability, low reactivity
c. Moderate health hazard, low flammability, extreme reactivity
d. Extreme health hazard, moderate flammability, high reactivity

Answer: a. Extreme health hazard, high flammability, moderate reactivity. Explanation: The NFPA 704 diamond's blue quadrant indicates health hazard, red indicates flammability, and yellow indicates reactivity. A "4" in the blue quadrant means extreme health hazard, a "3" in the red quadrant means high flammability, and a "2" in the yellow quadrant means moderate reactivity.

521. You are selecting chemical protective clothing for a response to a known hazardous material spill. Which level of protection is required when the highest level of respiratory protection is needed but a lower level of skin protection is sufficient?
a. Level A
b. Level B
c. Level C
d. Level D

Answer: b. Level B. Explanation: Level B protection is required when the highest level of respiratory protection is needed, but a lower level of skin protection is sufficient. It includes SCBA and chemical-resistant clothing, but it does not require a fully encapsulating suit.

522. You are the incident commander at a hazardous materials incident involving an unknown chemical release. What is the first action you should take to protect your crew and the public?
a. Begin immediate decontamination procedures
b. Evacuate the surrounding area
c. Identify the chemical using the ERG
d. Establish initial isolation and protective action distances

Answer: d. Establish initial isolation and protective action distances. Explanation: The first action should be to establish initial isolation and protective action distances to ensure the safety of responders and the public. This helps prevent exposure while further information about the chemical is obtained.

523. At a hazardous materials incident, you need to set up zones for response. Which zone is where the command post and support functions are located?
a. Hot zone
b. Warm zone
c. Cold zone
d. Exclusion zone

Answer: c. Cold zone. Explanation: The cold zone is where the command post and support functions are located. It is the safe area outside the warm and hot zones, where decontamination and hazardous materials are handled.

524. You respond to a scene with a leaking container displaying a placard with the number "1203." Using the DOT ERG, what material is involved, and what are the primary hazards?
a. Diesel fuel, fire and explosion
b. Gasoline, fire and explosion
c. Kerosene, health hazard
d. Acetone, health hazard

Answer: b. Gasoline, fire and explosion. Explanation: The placard number "1203" identifies the material as gasoline. The primary hazards associated with gasoline are fire and explosion, as indicated in the DOT ERG.

525. You are assessing the scene of a hazardous materials spill at a manufacturing plant. What is the purpose of resource typing in this context?
a. To classify hazardous materials by their chemical properties
b. To determine the necessary isolation distance
c. To categorize and order resources based on their capabilities
d. To identify the level of PPE required

Answer: c. To categorize and order resources based on their capabilities. Explanation: Resource typing categorizes and orders resources based on their capabilities to ensure that the appropriate resources are requested and deployed effectively during a hazardous materials response.

526. A hazardous material has spilled in a lab, and the NFPA 704 diamond indicates a "3" in the red quadrant. What is the primary concern for responders?
a. High health hazard
b. High flammability hazard
c. High reactivity hazard
d. High radioactivity hazard

Answer: b. High flammability hazard. Explanation: A "3" in the red quadrant of the NFPA 704 diamond indicates a high flammability hazard, meaning the material can easily ignite and pose a significant fire risk.

527. A 35-year-old male is trapped in a vehicle following a high-speed collision. Which tool is most appropriate for cutting through the vehicle's metal to extricate the patient?
a. Hydraulic spreaders
b. Hydraulic cutters
c. Reciprocating saw

d. Glass master tool

Answer: b. Hydraulic cutters. Explanation: Hydraulic cutters are specifically designed to cut through the metal of vehicles during extrication, making them ideal for freeing a trapped patient quickly and efficiently.

528. You are part of a team performing a confined space rescue in an industrial setting. What is the primary precaution that must be taken before entering the confined space?
a. Ensure all rescuers are wearing hard hats
b. Test the atmosphere for hazardous gases and ensure proper ventilation
c. Remove any obstructions from the entry point
d. Establish a communication plan with the team

Answer: b. Test the atmosphere for hazardous gases and ensure proper ventilation. Explanation: Confined spaces can contain hazardous gases or lack sufficient oxygen. Testing the atmosphere and ensuring proper ventilation is crucial to the safety of rescuers and the trapped individual.

529. During a water rescue, you are tasked with reaching a drowning victim in a fast-moving river. Which piece of equipment is most appropriate to use?
a. Throw bag
b. Life ring
c. Rescue board
d. Inflatable raft

Answer: a. Throw bag. Explanation: A throw bag, which contains a length of rope, is suitable for reaching a drowning victim in a fast-moving river, allowing the rescuer to stay on shore while providing a lifeline to the victim.

530. You are responding to an incident requiring a high-angle rescue. Which principle is essential to ensure the safety of both the rescuer and the victim?
a. Always use a single rope for speed
b. Rely solely on the rescuer's strength to lower the victim
c. Use a system of pulleys and redundant safety lines
d. Prioritize rapid descent over safety

Answer: c. Use a system of pulleys and redundant safety lines. Explanation: High-angle rescues require the use of pulleys and redundant safety lines to distribute weight and provide backup support, ensuring the safety of both the rescuer and the victim.

531. During a trench rescue, what is the primary purpose of shoring techniques?
a. To provide a pathway for rescuers
b. To prevent further collapse of the trench walls

c. To create a space for medical treatment
d. To improve ventilation within the trench

Answer: b. To prevent further collapse of the trench walls. Explanation: Shoring techniques are used to stabilize trench walls and prevent further collapse, protecting both the victim and rescuers during the rescue operation.

532. A car has overturned in a ditch, trapping a passenger inside. Which extrication technique should be prioritized to safely remove the passenger?
a. Use of a hydraulic jack to lift the car
b. Stabilization of the vehicle followed by door removal
c. Breaking the windshield to access the passenger
d. Cutting through the roof immediately

Answer: b. Stabilization of the vehicle followed by door removal. Explanation: Stabilizing the vehicle to prevent further movement is the first priority, followed by door removal to create a safe and effective access point for extrication.

533. You are involved in a confined space rescue where the atmosphere is tested and found to be low in oxygen. What equipment is essential for rescuers entering this environment?
a. Self-contained breathing apparatus (SCBA)
b. Dust masks
c. Full-face shields
d. Ear protection

Answer: a. Self-contained breathing apparatus (SCBA). Explanation: An SCBA provides a clean air supply to rescuers in environments with low oxygen levels, ensuring their safety while performing the rescue.

534. During a water rescue operation, what is the most important safety measure for rescuers entering the water?
a. Wearing a bright-colored uniform
b. Using a buddy system
c. Carrying a knife
d. Wearing a personal flotation device (PFD)

Answer: d. Wearing a personal flotation device (PFD). Explanation: Wearing a PFD is crucial for rescuers entering the water, providing buoyancy and reducing the risk of drowning during the rescue operation.

535. In a high-angle rescue, what type of knot is commonly used to secure the rope to the anchor point?
a. Square knot
b. Clove hitch
c. Bowline

d. Sheet bend

Answer: c. Bowline. Explanation: The bowline knot is commonly used in high-angle rescues to secure the rope to an anchor point because it is easy to tie and untie, even under load.

536. During a trench rescue, you notice that the soil is starting to shift. What is the immediate action that should be taken?
a. Continue the rescue operation as quickly as possible
b. Halt the operation and evacuate all personnel from the trench
c. Apply additional shoring to stabilize the trench walls
d. Remove the victim immediately without regard for safety

Answer: b. Halt the operation and evacuate all personnel from the trench. Explanation: If the soil begins to shift, it indicates an imminent risk of collapse. The immediate action should be to halt the operation and evacuate all personnel to ensure safety before reassessing and reinforcing the shoring.

537. An explosion occurs at a large public event, and you are the first responder on scene. What criterion must be met to declare a mass casualty incident (MCI)?
a. Presence of hazardous materials
b. Number of casualties exceeds available resources
c. Presence of law enforcement
d. Activation of the National Guard

Answer: b. Number of casualties exceeds available resources. Explanation: An MCI is declared when the number of casualties exceeds the available resources, requiring a coordinated response and allocation of additional resources to manage the incident effectively.

538. During an MCI, what is the most effective method for tracking patients?
a. Verbal communication with each patient
b. Written notes on individual patient conditions
c. Use of a standardized triage tag system
d. Recording information on a handheld device

Answer: c. Use of a standardized triage tag system. Explanation: A standardized triage tag system is the most effective method for tracking patients during an MCI, providing a consistent way to document and communicate patient conditions and priorities for care.

539. A natural disaster has caused widespread injuries in a community. What is a key strategy for managing resources during this MCI?
a. Prioritize care based on the first-come, first-served basis

b. Utilize local resources only and avoid requesting external aid

c. Establish a centralized command to coordinate resources and response efforts

d. Focus all efforts on the most critically injured patients

Answer: c. Establish a centralized command to coordinate resources and response efforts. Explanation: Establishing a centralized command allows for efficient coordination of resources, communication, and response efforts, ensuring that resources are used effectively to manage the incident.

540. You arrive at a mass casualty incident (MCI) and begin triaging patients using the START triage system. A 30-year-old male is conscious, has a respiratory rate of 24 breaths per minute, a radial pulse present, and is able to follow commands. Which triage tag color should be assigned to this patient?

a. Red

b. Yellow

c. Green

d. Black

Answer: b. Yellow. Explanation: In the START triage system, a patient with a respiratory rate under 30 breaths per minute, a radial pulse present, and the ability to follow commands is tagged as "yellow," indicating delayed treatment is needed.

541. You are part of a team setting up a field hospital after a natural disaster. What is the most critical consideration when selecting the location for the field hospital?

a. Proximity to the disaster site

b. Availability of running water

c. Accessibility for supply deliveries

d. Communication infrastructure

Answer: a. Proximity to the disaster site. Explanation: While all these factors are important, the proximity to the disaster site is the most critical consideration to ensure that the field hospital can quickly and efficiently serve the affected population.

542. A push-pack is being deployed to a disaster area. What type of resources can you expect to find in a push-pack?

a. Food and water supplies

b. Communication equipment

c. Medical supplies and pharmaceuticals

d. Heavy machinery for debris removal

Answer: c. Medical supplies and pharmaceuticals. Explanation: Push-packs are pre-packaged sets of medical supplies and pharmaceuticals designed for rapid deployment to support medical response in disaster situations.

543. You are coordinating with a Disaster Medical Assistance Team (DMAT). Which of the following best describes the composition and capabilities of a DMAT?
a. A team of logistics experts providing supply chain management
b. A team of medical professionals providing rapid-response medical care
c. A team of engineers focused on infrastructure repair
d. A team of military personnel providing security and crowd control

Answer: b. A team of medical professionals providing rapid-response medical care. Explanation: DMATs are composed of medical professionals who provide rapid-response medical care during disasters, including triage, stabilization, and evacuation of patients.

544. The National Disaster Medical System (NDMS) has been activated. What is the primary purpose of NDMS activation in a disaster response?
a. To provide financial aid to affected individuals
b. To coordinate the deployment of military forces
c. To manage the transportation and care of patients
d. To restore public infrastructure

Answer: c. To manage the transportation and care of patients. Explanation: The primary purpose of NDMS activation is to coordinate the transportation and care of patients, ensuring that they receive necessary medical treatment and are transported to appropriate facilities.

545. During a disaster response, you are assigned to manage the triage area. Which documentation practice is most important for maintaining accurate records of patient triage and treatment?
a. Using electronic health records (EHR) exclusively
b. Ensuring each patient receives a unique identifier and triage tag
c. Taking detailed notes on patient symptoms verbally
d. Recording patient information on a whiteboard in the command center

Answer: b. Ensuring each patient receives a unique identifier and triage tag. Explanation: Using unique identifiers and triage tags for each patient is crucial for maintaining accurate records of patient triage and treatment during a disaster response.

546. You are setting up a decontamination area at a field hospital. Which of the following is a key consideration for the setup?
a. The area should be located upwind and uphill from the treatment area
b. The area should be located near the main entrance of the hospital
c. The area should be adjacent to the pharmacy
d. The area should have limited access to ensure privacy

Answer: a. The area should be located upwind and uphill from the treatment area. Explanation: The decontamination area should be located upwind and uphill from the treatment area to prevent contamination of the treatment area and ensure the safety of both patients and responders.

547. In a mass casualty incident, what is the purpose of using color-coded triage tags?
a. To identify the patient's name and contact information
b. To prioritize treatment based on the severity of injuries
c. To track the patient's financial status
d. To determine the patient's insurance coverage

Answer: b. To prioritize treatment based on the severity of injuries. Explanation: Color-coded triage tags are used to prioritize treatment based on the severity of injuries, helping to ensure that patients who need immediate care are treated first.

548. You are part of a team deploying a field hospital in response to a hurricane. What is an essential component to consider for maintaining communication with other response teams?
a. Satellite phones
b. Walkie-talkies
c. Cellular phones
d. Landline telephones

Answer: a. Satellite phones. Explanation: Satellite phones are essential for maintaining communication with other response teams in disaster areas where traditional communication infrastructure may be damaged or unavailable.

549. During an NDMS activation, you are assigned to coordinate patient transport. What is a key factor in ensuring the efficient and safe transport of patients to receiving facilities?
a. Prioritizing transport for patients with minor injuries
b. Coordinating with local law enforcement for security
c. Ensuring the receiving facilities have adequate resources
d. Using personal vehicles for patient transport

Answer: c. Ensuring the receiving facilities have adequate resources. Explanation: Coordinating with receiving facilities to ensure they have adequate resources to care for incoming patients is crucial for the efficient and safe transport of patients during an NDMS activation.

550. A 45-year-old bariatric patient weighing 450 lbs requires transport to the hospital. What is the most appropriate handling technique to ensure safety for both the patient and rescuers?
a. Use a standard stretcher with additional personnel
b. Utilize a bariatric stretcher and lifting device
c. Ask the patient to walk to the ambulance
d. Use a scoop stretcher with a stair chair

Answer: b. Utilize a bariatric stretcher and lifting device. Explanation: Bariatric stretchers and lifting devices are specifically designed to safely transport patients with significant weight, minimizing the risk of injury to both the patient and rescuers.

551. You are called to assist a child with autism spectrum disorder (ASD) who is having a medical emergency. Which approach is most appropriate?
a. Speak loudly and quickly to ensure the child understands
b. Use simple, direct language and allow extra time for responses
c. Avoid any physical contact to prevent distress
d. Assume the child will understand complex medical terms

Answer: b. Use simple, direct language and allow extra time for responses. Explanation: Children with ASD may have difficulty processing complex information and responding quickly. Using simple, direct language and allowing extra time for responses can help in effectively communicating with the child.

552. During an assessment of a hearing-impaired patient, which communication strategy is most effective?
a. Shout to ensure the patient can hear you
b. Write down questions and instructions
c. Use medical jargon and abbreviations
d. Turn away from the patient to avoid visual distractions

Answer: b. Write down questions and instructions. Explanation: Writing down questions and instructions helps ensure clear communication with hearing-impaired patients, allowing them to read and understand the information being conveyed.

553. You are assessing a homeless patient who presents with multiple chronic conditions. What is a key consideration during your assessment?
a. Assume the patient has regular access to medications
b. Focus solely on the patient's immediate medical needs
c. Consider the patient's social and environmental factors
d. Avoid discussing the patient's living situation

Answer: c. Consider the patient's social and environmental factors. Explanation: Homeless patients often face unique social and environmental challenges that can impact their health. Considering these factors is essential for providing comprehensive care and addressing underlying issues.

554. A 17-year-old female presents with signs of physical abuse and is accompanied by an older male who answers all questions for her. What is the most appropriate action?
a. Ignore the signs and continue the assessment
b. Ask the male to leave the room to speak privately with the patient

c. Document the interaction and take no further action
d. Assume the patient is not in immediate danger

Answer: b. Ask the male to leave the room to speak privately with the patient. Explanation: To accurately assess for human trafficking and ensure the patient's safety, it is crucial to speak with the patient privately without the presence of the potential abuser or trafficker.

555. A bariatric patient in cardiac arrest requires chest compressions. Which adjustment should be made to ensure effective CPR?
a. Use the standard compression depth of 2 inches
b. Place the patient in a lateral position
c. Increase the compression depth to 2.5 inches
d. Utilize an automated compression device if available

Answer: d. Utilize an automated compression device if available. Explanation: Automated compression devices can deliver consistent and effective compressions, especially in bariatric patients where manual compressions may be more challenging.

556. When assessing a patient with autism spectrum disorder, which environmental modification can help reduce anxiety and improve cooperation?
a. Increase lighting and noise levels
b. Use bright, flashing lights to gain attention
c. Minimize sensory stimuli and create a calm environment
d. Play loud music to distract the patient

Answer: c. Minimize sensory stimuli and create a calm environment. Explanation: Reducing sensory stimuli and creating a calm environment can help reduce anxiety and improve cooperation in patients with autism spectrum disorder.

557. A hearing-impaired patient requires transport to the hospital. Which action will best facilitate effective communication during transport?
a. Speak loudly and use exaggerated mouth movements
b. Use a sign language interpreter if available
c. Rely on the patient's ability to read lips exclusively
d. Avoid using visual aids to prevent confusion

Answer: b. Use a sign language interpreter if available. Explanation: Using a sign language interpreter ensures clear and accurate communication with a hearing-impaired patient, facilitating effective interaction during transport.

558. When assessing a homeless patient, what is an important factor to consider in addition to their immediate medical condition?
a. Their ability to pay for services
b. Their nutritional status and access to food
c. The cleanliness of their clothing
d. The duration of their homelessness

Answer: b. Their nutritional status and access to food. Explanation: Homeless patients often have limited access to food and proper nutrition, which can significantly impact their overall health and recovery.

559. You suspect a patient is a victim of human trafficking based on physical signs and their interaction with a controlling companion. What is the most important immediate step to take?
a. Confront the companion about your suspicions
b. Contact law enforcement or social services discreetly
c. Administer necessary medical care and discharge
d. Inform the patient that they are likely a trafficking victim

Answer: b. Contact law enforcement or social services discreetly. Explanation: If you suspect a patient is a victim of human trafficking, it is crucial to contact law enforcement or social services discreetly to ensure the patient's safety and initiate appropriate intervention measures.

560. A 45-year-old Muslim woman is brought to the emergency room after a car accident. She is conscious and oriented but refuses to let the male paramedic touch her for the examination. What is the most appropriate action for the paramedic to take?
a. Ignore her request and proceed with the examination to ensure her safety
b. Ask a female colleague to perform the examination
c. Explain that it is necessary for him to perform the examination immediately
d. Wait for a family member to arrive and ask for their permission

Answer: b. Ask a female colleague to perform the examination. Explanation: Respecting the patient's cultural and religious beliefs is crucial in providing patient-centered care. Many Muslim women prefer to be examined by female healthcare providers, and accommodating this request when possible is important for maintaining trust and cooperation.

561. A 60-year-old Orthodox Jewish man is admitted to the hospital with chest pain on a Friday afternoon. He mentions that he observes the Sabbath, which begins at sundown on Friday. Which of the following actions should you consider regarding his care?
a. Schedule all necessary tests and treatments immediately, regardless of the time
b. Explain that his medical needs take precedence over religious practices
c. Discuss his condition with him and coordinate care to respect his Sabbath observance where possible
d. Delay all medical interventions until after the Sabbath

Answer: c. Discuss his condition with him and coordinate care to respect his Sabbath observance where possible. Explanation: Understanding and respecting religious practices while ensuring necessary medical care is a key aspect of culturally competent care. Discussing with the patient helps balance his religious observance and medical needs.

562. A 32-year-old Hispanic woman with limited English proficiency presents with abdominal pain. Her daughter, who is bilingual, offers to translate. What should you do?
a. Accept the daughter's offer to translate
b. Use a professional medical interpreter
c. Communicate directly with the patient using simple English
d. Ask another staff member who speaks Spanish to assist

Answer: b. Use a professional medical interpreter. Explanation: Using a professional medical interpreter ensures accurate communication and maintains patient confidentiality and comfort. Family members may not be familiar with medical terminology or may inadvertently alter the information.

563. A 55-year-old Asian man with type 2 diabetes mentions that he uses traditional herbs as part of his treatment regimen. What should you do?
a. Advise him to stop using the herbs immediately
b. Explain that traditional remedies are not effective and only use prescribed medication
c. Ask for details about the herbs and consider any potential interactions with his current medication
d. Ignore his use of traditional herbs as it is not relevant to his care

Answer: c. Ask for details about the herbs and consider any potential interactions with his current medication. Explanation: Understanding and considering a patient's use of traditional remedies can help identify potential interactions with prescribed medications and respect their cultural practices.

564. A 28-year-old transgender woman presents with a complaint of severe headaches. During the examination, she mentions she has been on hormone replacement therapy for the past three years. How should you proceed?
a. Focus solely on the headache and ignore her mention of hormone therapy
b. Document her hormone therapy and consider it in your differential diagnosis
c. Refer her to a specialist without further assessment
d. Discontinue her hormone therapy immediately

Answer: b. Document her hormone therapy and consider it in your differential diagnosis. Explanation: Understanding the patient's hormone therapy is crucial for providing comprehensive care. Hormone therapy can have various effects on the body, which should be considered when diagnosing and treating her symptoms.

565. You are called to the home of a 70-year-old Hindu woman who has collapsed. Upon arrival, her family requests that she not be taken to the hospital because they believe in Ayurvedic treatments. What should you do?
a. Respect the family's wishes and leave the patient at home
b. Explain the importance of hospital care in a medical emergency and transport her

c. Ask the family to sign a waiver before leaving her at home

d. Offer to call an Ayurvedic practitioner to the scene

Answer: b. Explain the importance of hospital care in a medical emergency and transport her. Explanation: In a medical emergency, it is crucial to explain the need for hospital care while respecting cultural beliefs. Ensuring the patient receives necessary emergency care takes precedence, but clear communication with the family is essential.

566. A 40-year-old vegan patient is admitted with a fractured leg. What dietary consideration should be made during his hospital stay?

a. Provide a standard hospital diet

b. Ensure all meals are free of animal products

c. Offer a low-carbohydrate diet

d. Include dairy products for calcium intake

Answer: b. Ensure all meals are free of animal products. Explanation: Respecting the patient's dietary preferences by providing vegan meals is crucial for their comfort and compliance with hospital nutrition protocols.

567. A 65-year-old Native American patient with diabetes insists on using traditional healing practices in addition to prescribed medication. How should the healthcare provider respond?

a. Dismiss the traditional practices as ineffective

b. Encourage the patient to use only prescribed medication

c. Incorporate the traditional practices into the patient's care plan, ensuring they do not interfere with the medication

d. Report the patient's use of traditional practices to the medical board

Answer: c. Incorporate the traditional practices into the patient's care plan, ensuring they do not interfere with the medication. Explanation: Integrating the patient's traditional healing practices with modern medicine can improve adherence and respect cultural beliefs while ensuring effective treatment.

568. During a patient assessment, you discover that the 50-year-old male patient practices Islam and is currently observing Ramadan, which involves fasting from sunrise to sunset. He has been feeling dizzy and weak. What is the most appropriate action?

a. Advise him to continue fasting as it is part of his religious practice

b. Suggest he breaks his fast to maintain his health

c. Refer him to a religious leader for guidance

d. Provide care without addressing the fasting

Answer: b. Suggest he breaks his fast to maintain his health. Explanation: Patient safety and well-being are paramount. In cases where fasting poses a significant health risk, it is appropriate to advise the patient to break their fast and ensure they understand the medical reasons.

569. A 34-year-old patient from a rural area presents with symptoms of depression. She mentions that mental health issues are stigmatized in her community and prefers to seek help from a traditional healer. What is the best approach to her care?
a. Dismiss the traditional healer's role and focus solely on medical treatment
b. Educate the patient about the benefits of modern mental health treatment while respecting her preference for traditional healing
c. Ignore her mental health concerns due to cultural differences
d. Refer her immediately to a psychiatrist without discussing her preferences

Answer: b. Educate the patient about the benefits of modern mental health treatment while respecting her preference for traditional healing. Explanation: Balancing respect for cultural practices with education about the benefits of modern treatment can help the patient feel understood and may increase her willingness to engage in mental health care.

570. A patient refuses medical care after a minor motor vehicle accident. As an EMT, what is the most important documentation to include in your patient care report?
a. The patient's full medical history
b. A detailed description of the accident scene
c. The patient's mental status and their explicit refusal of care
d. The names and contact information of bystanders

Answer: c. The patient's mental status and their explicit refusal of care. Explanation: Documenting the patient's mental status and their explicit refusal of care is crucial for legal protection and to demonstrate that the patient was competent to make that decision. It is also important to include that the patient was informed of the potential risks of refusing care.

571. During a call, you are asked to transport a patient with a serious medical condition. As you prepare the patient for transport, a bystander requests information about the patient's condition. How should you respond to comply with HIPAA regulations?
a. Provide the bystander with the requested information
b. Direct the bystander to the patient's family
c. Inform the bystander that you cannot share any patient information
d. Ask the patient if it is okay to share their condition with the bystander

Answer: c. Inform the bystander that you cannot share any patient information. Explanation: HIPAA regulations strictly prohibit sharing patient information without consent. Informing the bystander that you cannot share any information protects patient confidentiality and ensures compliance with HIPAA.

572. You arrive at the scene of a cardiac arrest. After resuscitation efforts, the patient is revived and begins to regain consciousness. The patient is confused and combative, refusing further treatment. What type of consent allows you to continue treatment?
a. Informed consent
b. Implied consent

c. Expressed consent

d. None of the above

Answer: b. Implied consent. Explanation: In emergency situations where the patient is unable to provide informed consent due to their medical condition, implied consent allows healthcare providers to continue necessary treatment to prevent further harm.

573. An EMT witnesses a car accident while off-duty and provides initial care until on-duty personnel arrive. What legal principle obligates the EMT to act in this scenario?

a. Good Samaritan laws

b. Duty to act

c. Standard of care

d. Abandonment

Answer: b. Duty to act. Explanation: The duty to act obligates an EMT to provide care when they come upon a scene where someone is in need, especially if they are off-duty but have initiated care. This principle ensures that EMTs respond to emergencies ethically and responsibly.

574. A 16-year-old patient with a minor injury refuses treatment. Under what circumstance can the EMT provide care despite the refusal?

a. The patient's parent or legal guardian consents to treatment

b. The patient has a history of refusing medical care

c. The patient is not in immediate danger

d. The patient is known to the EMT personally

Answer: a. The patient's parent or legal guardian consents to treatment. Explanation: Minors cannot legally refuse treatment on their own; consent must be obtained from a parent or legal guardian. If the guardian consents, EMTs can provide care despite the minor's refusal.

575. While documenting a case where a patient refused care, what must be included to ensure legal and ethical compliance?

a. A summary of the patient's health insurance details

b. A note about the patient's cooperation level

c. Detailed information on the patient's condition, the risks explained, and the refusal

d. The time of day the patient refused care

Answer: c. Detailed information on the patient's condition, the risks explained, and the refusal. Explanation: To protect both the patient and the EMT legally, the report must include details of the patient's condition, the risks of refusing care as explained to the patient, and their explicit refusal.

576. An EMT suspects that a child is being abused during a routine call. What action should the EMT take in accordance with mandatory reporting requirements?
a. Confront the guardians about the suspected abuse
b. Document the suspicion in the patient care report and take no further action
c. Report the suspicion to the appropriate authorities immediately
d. Wait until confirming the suspicion before reporting

Answer: c. Report the suspicion to the appropriate authorities immediately. Explanation: EMTs are required by law to report any suspicions of child abuse to the appropriate authorities. This action helps protect the child and ensures that the proper investigation can take place.

577. A patient with a known mental illness is refusing care after an accident. What must the EMT assess to determine if the patient's refusal is legally valid?
a. The patient's willingness to sign a refusal form
b. The patient's understanding of their condition and the consequences of refusal
c. The patient's medical history and previous refusals
d. The patient's physical ability to leave the scene

Answer: b. The patient's understanding of their condition and the consequences of refusal. Explanation: To determine if a refusal is legally valid, the EMT must assess whether the patient is mentally competent to understand their condition and the potential risks of refusing care.

578. An EMT is treating an unconscious patient without any identification and no family members are present. Under what consent is the EMT legally allowed to provide care?
a. Informed consent
b. Implied consent
c. Verbal consent
d. Proxy consent

Answer: b. Implied consent. Explanation: In situations where a patient is unconscious and unable to give consent, implied consent allows EMTs to provide necessary emergency care to save the patient's life or prevent further harm.

579. During a transport, an EMT discusses a patient's condition with another crew member in a public area where others can overhear. What HIPAA violation has occurred?
a. Failing to document patient care accurately
b. Improper disposal of patient information
c. Unauthorized disclosure of protected health information
d. Unprofessional behavior

Answer: c. Unauthorized disclosure of protected health information. Explanation: Discussing a patient's condition in a public area where it can be overheard by unauthorized individuals is a violation of HIPAA, as it breaches the confidentiality of the patient's health information.

580. A recent EMS study examines the efficacy of a new prehospital treatment for acute asthma exacerbations. The study uses a randomized controlled trial (RCT) design. Why is an RCT considered the gold standard in clinical research?
a. It is the easiest and cheapest study design to conduct
b. It minimizes bias and allows for a clear comparison between interventions and controls
c. It involves the most participants, making the results more reliable
d. It guarantees positive outcomes for the intervention being tested

Answer: b. It minimizes bias and allows for a clear comparison between interventions and controls. Explanation: RCTs randomly assign participants to either the intervention or control group, reducing selection bias and allowing for a more accurate assessment of the treatment's efficacy.

581. An EMS agency is implementing a new evidence-based protocol for the management of sepsis. What is the most important first step in this process?
a. Training all EMS personnel on the new protocol
b. Collecting baseline data on current sepsis management outcomes
c. Distributing copies of the protocol to all EMS stations
d. Conducting a cost analysis of the new protocol

Answer: b. Collecting baseline data on current sepsis management outcomes. Explanation: Baseline data collection is essential for measuring the impact of the new protocol and assessing its effectiveness compared to previous practices.

582. A paramedic is conducting a quality improvement project on response times. Which data collection method is most appropriate for this type of project?
a. Patient satisfaction surveys
b. Chart reviews of patient care reports
c. Direct observation of EMS crews
d. Interviews with hospital staff

Answer: b. Chart reviews of patient care reports. Explanation: Chart reviews allow for the systematic collection of quantitative data on response times, which can be analyzed to identify areas for improvement.

583. When developing clinical practice guidelines for prehospital stroke care, what source of evidence should be considered most reliable?
a. Expert opinions from seasoned EMS professionals
b. Case studies of individual stroke patients
c. Systematic reviews and meta-analyses of relevant research

d. Anecdotal experiences from other EMS agencies

Answer: c. Systematic reviews and meta-analyses of relevant research. Explanation: Systematic reviews and meta-analyses synthesize data from multiple studies, providing a higher level of evidence for developing clinical practice guidelines.

584. To meet continuing education requirements, an EMT attends a workshop on the latest research in cardiac arrest management. How can the EMT ensure the information is evidence-based?
a. Verify that the presenter is a well-known expert in the field
b. Check if the workshop content is published in a peer-reviewed journal
c. Confirm that the workshop is sponsored by a reputable EMS agency
d. Ensure that the information is consistent with current EMS protocols

Answer: b. Check if the workshop content is published in a peer-reviewed journal. Explanation: Peer-reviewed publications are vetted by experts in the field, ensuring that the information is based on rigorous scientific research.

585. A new EMS research study aims to evaluate the impact of advanced airway management on patient outcomes during cardiac arrest. What is the primary outcome measure that should be used in this study?
a. Patient satisfaction with care provided
b. Cost of advanced airway equipment
c. Return of spontaneous circulation (ROSC)
d. Number of advanced airway attempts

Answer: c. Return of spontaneous circulation (ROSC). Explanation: ROSC is a key indicator of the immediate effectiveness of cardiac arrest interventions and is a primary outcome measure in cardiac arrest studies.

586. An EMS quality improvement project finds that the implementation of a new pain management protocol has led to improved patient outcomes. What is the next step to ensure continuous improvement?
a. Stop the quality improvement project as goals have been met
b. Share the findings with other EMS agencies
c. Regularly monitor and review patient outcomes related to pain management
d. Implement a completely new protocol to address other issues

Answer: c. Regularly monitor and review patient outcomes related to pain management. Explanation: Continuous monitoring and review are essential to ensure sustained improvement and to identify any areas needing further adjustment.

587. A paramedic is reviewing an article about a new medication for controlling severe asthma attacks in the prehospital setting. What should the paramedic look for to determine if the study's findings are applicable to their practice?

a. The author's credentials and affiliations
b. The sample size and population characteristics
c. The publication date of the article
d. The length of the study

Answer: b. The sample size and population characteristics. Explanation: The sample size and population characteristics determine the generalizability of the study findings to similar patient populations in the paramedic's practice.

588. During an EMS research project, it is found that prehospital administration of IV fluids in trauma patients is associated with increased mortality. What should EMS providers do in light of this evidence?
a. Immediately stop administering IV fluids to trauma patients
b. Consult with medical directors to review and potentially revise protocols
c. Continue current practices until the research is widely accepted
d. Only administer IV fluids to trauma patients in critical condition

Answer: b. Consult with medical directors to review and potentially revise protocols. Explanation: Changes to clinical practice should be made in consultation with medical directors and based on a comprehensive review of the evidence.

589. An EMS agency is collecting data for a study on the impact of bystander CPR training programs. What type of study design would best assess the effectiveness of these programs?
a. Case-control study
b. Cohort study
c. Cross-sectional survey
d. Randomized controlled trial

Answer: b. Cohort study. Explanation: A cohort study can follow participants over time to assess the impact of bystander CPR training on outcomes such as survival rates and neurological function after cardiac arrest.

590. During a busy shift, you notice increasing tension between two EMTs over their assigned tasks. What is the most effective conflict resolution strategy to address this situation?
a. Ignore the issue and let the EMTs work it out themselves
b. Reassign one of the EMTs to a different task immediately
c. Hold a private meeting with both EMTs to discuss their concerns and mediate a solution
d. Document the conflict and report it to higher management without intervention

Answer: c. Hold a private meeting with both EMTs to discuss their concerns and mediate a solution. Explanation: Effective conflict resolution involves addressing the issue directly and mediating a solution. Holding a private meeting allows both EMTs to express their concerns in a controlled environment and work towards a resolution with the help of a mediator.

591. You are tasked with conducting a performance evaluation for an EMT who has been underperforming. What is the most important element to include in your evaluation to promote improvement?
a. A comparison of their performance to their peers
b. Specific, actionable feedback on areas needing improvement
c. A summary of the EMT's overall attitude and demeanor
d. General comments on their work ethic and dedication

Answer: b. Specific, actionable feedback on areas needing improvement. Explanation: Providing specific, actionable feedback helps the EMT understand exactly what needs improvement and how to achieve it. This approach is more constructive and beneficial for professional development compared to general comments or comparisons.

592. During a critical call, a paramedic fails to follow a protocol, leading to a delay in patient care. Which crew resource management principle should be emphasized to prevent this in the future?
a. Task delegation
b. Communication and assertiveness
c. Stress management
d. Equipment familiarity

Answer: b. Communication and assertiveness. Explanation: Emphasizing the importance of clear communication and assertiveness can prevent protocol deviations. Crew members should feel empowered to speak up if they notice an issue, ensuring adherence to protocols and timely patient care.

593. An EMT team has been consistently over-budget on medical supplies for the past three months. What is the first step in managing this budget issue?
a. Reduce the quality of supplies being ordered
b. Conduct a detailed inventory and usage review
c. Cut the budget for other operational areas
d. Implement stricter control on supply usage without review

Answer: b. Conduct a detailed inventory and usage review. Explanation: Conducting a detailed inventory and usage review helps identify where supplies are being overused or wasted. Understanding the root cause of the budget issue is crucial before implementing any cost-saving measures.

594. During an evaluation, you notice that your team frequently runs out of critical supplies. What inventory control method would help prevent this issue?
a. Periodic manual inventory checks
b. Just-in-time inventory management
c. Automatic restocking based on usage patterns
d. Increasing order quantities for all supplies

Answer: c. Automatic restocking based on usage patterns. Explanation: Implementing an automatic restocking system based on usage patterns ensures that supplies are replenished before they run out. This method is efficient and helps maintain a consistent inventory of critical supplies.

595. A new piece of equipment has been introduced to your EMS station, but usage has been inconsistent among the staff. How can you ensure that all EMTs are proficient in using the new equipment?
a. Mandate that all EMTs read the equipment manual
b. Assign one EMT to train others as needed
c. Schedule mandatory hands-on training sessions for all staff
d. Include the equipment in daily briefings without further action

Answer: c. Schedule mandatory hands-on training sessions for all staff. Explanation: Hands-on training sessions ensure that all EMTs have practical experience with the new equipment, promoting proficiency and consistency in its usage. This approach is more effective than simply reading manuals or relying on informal training.

596. An EMT supervisor notices that the team's response times have increased over the past quarter. What performance evaluation technique should be used to address this issue?
a. Comparing the team's response times to industry benchmarks
b. Holding individual meetings to discuss performance with each team member
c. Implementing a new dispatch system without evaluation
d. Providing general feedback to the team about response times

Answer: a. Comparing the team's response times to industry benchmarks. Explanation: Using industry benchmarks to evaluate response times provides a standard for comparison, helping to identify areas for improvement and setting realistic goals for the team.

597. A senior EMT frequently dismisses input from newer team members, leading to decreased morale. Which leadership principle can help address this issue?
a. Encouraging open dialogue and inclusive decision-making
b. Reinforcing the senior EMT's authority
c. Separating new members from experienced members during shifts
d. Implementing a strict hierarchy for decision-making

Answer: a. Encouraging open dialogue and inclusive decision-making. Explanation: Promoting open dialogue and inclusive decision-making fosters a collaborative environment where all team members feel valued and heard, improving morale and team cohesion.

598. You are responsible for preparing the budget for the next fiscal year. Which factor is most critical to consider for accurate budget management?
a. The previous year's budget totals
b. Anticipated changes in call volume and service demand

c. Preferences of the EMT staff for new equipment

d. Historical data on equipment failures

Answer: b. Anticipated changes in call volume and service demand. Explanation: Accurately predicting changes in call volume and service demand is crucial for effective budget management, as it directly impacts resource allocation and operational needs. This foresight allows for more precise planning and budgeting.

599. An EMT team is struggling with effective communication during high-stress calls. What crew resource management strategy can improve their performance?

a. Assigning permanent roles to each team member

b. Conducting regular stress management workshops

c. Implementing structured communication protocols

d. Reducing the number of high-stress calls they respond to

Answer: c. Implementing structured communication protocols. Explanation: Structured communication protocols, such as SBAR (Situation, Background, Assessment, Recommendation), can enhance clarity and efficiency during high-stress calls, ensuring that critical information is accurately conveyed and understood by all team members.

600. An EMS educator is designing a continuing education program that incorporates adult learning principles. Which of the following strategies aligns with these principles?

a. Utilizing lectures as the primary method of instruction

b. Incorporating hands-on, scenario-based learning activities

c. Requiring rote memorization of protocols

d. Providing extensive reading materials without interactive components

Answer: b. Incorporating hands-on, scenario-based learning activities. Explanation: Adult learning principles emphasize the importance of experiential learning and practical application. Scenario-based activities allow adult learners to apply knowledge in a realistic context, enhancing retention and understanding.

601. A paramedic preceptor notices that a trainee consistently struggles with patient assessments. What is the most effective remediation strategy?

a. Allow the trainee to continue without intervention to learn from experience

b. Provide immediate corrective feedback and additional practice opportunities

c. Reassign the trainee to a different preceptor

d. Suggest the trainee review the assessment procedures independently

Answer: b. Provide immediate corrective feedback and additional practice opportunities. Explanation: Effective remediation involves timely feedback and practice to correct deficiencies. This approach ensures that the trainee can develop the necessary skills with guided support.

602. During a simulation-based training session, a trainee hesitates and makes several errors while performing an advanced airway procedure. What should the instructor do to address this issue?
a. Stop the simulation and publicly correct the trainee
b. Allow the trainee to finish and then privately review their performance
c. Take over the procedure and complete it correctly
d. Ignore the errors and focus on other aspects of the training

Answer: b. Allow the trainee to finish and then privately review their performance. Explanation: Providing feedback in a supportive and private manner helps maintain the trainee's confidence while addressing errors constructively. This approach fosters a positive learning environment.

603. An EMS agency is developing a continuing education program to improve cardiac arrest management. What element is essential for ensuring the program's effectiveness?
a. Ensuring all training materials are text-based
b. Including real-time feedback during practical exercises
c. Scheduling sessions infrequently to prevent burnout
d. Focusing solely on theoretical knowledge

Answer: b. Including real-time feedback during practical exercises. Explanation: Real-time feedback during practical exercises allows learners to immediately understand and correct their mistakes, enhancing the effectiveness of the training.

604. A new EMT is struggling to apply their classroom knowledge in the field. As a preceptor, how should you help them bridge this gap?
a. Give them additional reading materials
b. Pair them with an experienced EMT to observe and learn
c. Assign them to less critical tasks until they gain confidence
d. Allow them to make mistakes without intervention

Answer: b. Pair them with an experienced EMT to observe and learn. Explanation: Observing an experienced EMT in action helps the new EMT see how theoretical knowledge is applied in real-life situations, facilitating a smoother transition from classroom to field.

605. In developing a simulation-based training scenario for multi-casualty incidents, what factor should be prioritized to ensure realism and educational value?
a. Simplicity and predictability of scenarios
b. Complexity and unpredictability of scenarios
c. Minimal participant involvement to reduce stress
d. Focus solely on individual skills without team dynamics

Answer: b. Complexity and unpredictability of scenarios. Explanation: Realistic training scenarios should mimic the unpredictability and complexity of actual multi-casualty incidents, challenging participants to think critically and work effectively as a team.

606. When designing a continuing education program for EMS providers, which of the following elements is most important to include to ensure the program meets educational standards?
a. A variety of learning activities, including lectures, hands-on practice, and discussions
b. A focus solely on advanced theoretical concepts
c. Limited opportunities for participant interaction
d. A single, standardized instructional method

Answer: a. A variety of learning activities, including lectures, hands-on practice, and discussions. Explanation: A well-rounded continuing education program incorporates multiple instructional methods to cater to different learning styles and reinforce knowledge through various approaches.

607. An EMS preceptor is responsible for evaluating a trainee's performance. What is the best practice for providing effective evaluations?
a. Giving feedback only at the end of the training period
b. Offering continuous feedback throughout the training
c. Avoiding feedback to prevent discouraging the trainee
d. Focusing solely on positive aspects of the trainee's performance

Answer: b. Offering continuous feedback throughout the training. Explanation: Continuous feedback helps trainees understand their progress and areas for improvement in real-time, facilitating more effective learning and skill development.

608. An experienced paramedic is tasked with creating a new training module on pediatric emergencies. What should be the primary focus to ensure the module's success?
a. Incorporating extensive technical jargon
b. Using detailed case studies and interactive scenarios
c. Relying exclusively on written materials
d. Limiting the module to theoretical knowledge

Answer: b. Using detailed case studies and interactive scenarios. Explanation: Detailed case studies and interactive scenarios provide realistic and engaging learning experiences, helping paramedics better understand and manage pediatric emergencies.

609. An EMT who is also a preceptor wants to encourage a trainee's critical thinking skills during patient assessments. Which technique is most effective for this purpose?
a. Providing direct answers to all trainee questions
b. Asking open-ended questions that prompt the trainee to think and analyze
c. Limiting the trainee's involvement in patient care decisions

d. Focusing only on rote memorization of assessment protocols

Answer: b. Asking open-ended questions that prompt the trainee to think and analyze. Explanation: Open-ended questions encourage trainees to consider various aspects of patient care, promoting critical thinking and deeper understanding of assessment processes.

610. A 70-year-old patient with a history of congestive heart failure and diabetes is being managed by community paramedics. During a home visit, you notice that the patient's legs are swollen, and they are short of breath. What is the most appropriate next step?
a. Advise the patient to take an extra dose of their diuretic medication
b. Call the patient's primary care provider to report the findings
c. Instruct the patient to elevate their legs and rest
d. Suggest the patient monitor their symptoms for the next 24 hours

Answer: b. Call the patient's primary care provider to report the findings. Explanation: The patient's symptoms indicate potential worsening of congestive heart failure. It is critical to inform the primary care provider for further evaluation and management. Advising medication changes or waiting could be harmful without proper medical guidance.

611. During a home safety assessment for an elderly patient, which of the following is the most critical hazard to address first?
a. Loose rugs in the living room
b. Expired food in the refrigerator
c. Low lighting in the hallway
d. Lack of grab bars in the bathroom

Answer: a. Loose rugs in the living room. Explanation: Loose rugs are a significant fall hazard, particularly for elderly patients. Falls are a leading cause of injury in this population, so addressing loose rugs first is a priority to prevent immediate harm.

612. A community paramedic is assisting a patient with chronic obstructive pulmonary disease (COPD) in managing their condition. Which strategy is most effective in preventing exacerbations?
a. Regular use of prescribed inhalers
b. Weekly pulmonary function tests
c. Daily use of over-the-counter cough suppressants
d. Avoiding all physical activity

Answer: a. Regular use of prescribed inhalers. Explanation: Regular use of prescribed inhalers helps to manage symptoms and prevent exacerbations in patients with COPD. Monitoring lung function and activity level are important, but the primary prevention method is adherence to prescribed medication regimens.

613. While conducting a social determinants of health evaluation, you learn that a patient frequently misses medical appointments due to lack of transportation. What is the best course of action?
a. Suggest the patient reschedule their appointments to a more convenient time
b. Provide the patient with a list of local transportation services and resources
c. Encourage the patient to find a friend or family member to drive them
d. Recommend the patient only schedule necessary appointments

Answer: b. Provide the patient with a list of local transportation services and resources. Explanation: Providing information on local transportation services addresses the root cause of the missed appointments and helps ensure the patient can access needed medical care, improving overall health outcomes.

614. A patient with multiple chronic conditions is taking several medications prescribed by different doctors. What is the first step in the medication reconciliation process?
a. Contact each prescribing doctor to verify the medications
b. Review the patient's medication list with them during a home visit
c. Dispose of any duplicate or unnecessary medications
d. Educate the patient on the importance of taking their medications as prescribed

Answer: b. Review the patient's medication list with them during a home visit. Explanation: The first step in medication reconciliation is to review the patient's current medication list to identify any discrepancies, duplications, or potential interactions. This process ensures that all medications are appropriate and safe for the patient.

615. When coordinating care with a primary care provider for a patient with diabetes, which of the following actions is most important?
a. Scheduling regular follow-up visits with the community paramedic
b. Ensuring the patient has access to healthy food options
c. Monitoring the patient's blood glucose levels daily
d. Communicating any changes in the patient's condition to the primary care provider

Answer: d. Communicating any changes in the patient's condition to the primary care provider. Explanation: Effective care coordination involves clear communication with the primary care provider about any changes in the patient's condition. This ensures that the primary care provider can adjust treatment plans as necessary.

616. A community paramedic is conducting a home visit for a patient with hypertension. What is the most important factor to assess during the visit?
a. The patient's daily exercise routine
b. The patient's dietary habits and sodium intake
c. The patient's sleeping patterns
d. The patient's social support network

Answer: b. The patient's dietary habits and sodium intake. Explanation: Dietary habits, particularly sodium intake, have a significant impact on blood pressure control. Assessing and addressing dietary factors is crucial in managing hypertension.

617. During a follow-up visit, a patient with a history of non-compliance with medication admits to not taking their prescribed antihypertensives. What is the most appropriate response?
a. Scold the patient for not following medical advice
b. Educate the patient on the importance of medication adherence and explore barriers to compliance
c. Inform the patient that their condition will worsen without the medication
d. Schedule another visit to check on compliance

Answer: b. Educate the patient on the importance of medication adherence and explore barriers to compliance. Explanation: Education and understanding the reasons behind non-compliance are key to improving medication adherence. This approach addresses any barriers and helps the patient understand the importance of their medication.

618. A patient with congestive heart failure has been hospitalized twice in the past month due to fluid overload. What preventive measure should the community paramedic prioritize?
a. Increasing the patient's diuretic dosage without consulting a doctor
b. Educating the patient on daily weight monitoring and when to seek medical help
c. Advising the patient to restrict all physical activity
d. Scheduling weekly home visits to check on the patient's condition

Answer: b. Educating the patient on daily weight monitoring and when to seek medical help. Explanation: Daily weight monitoring helps detect early signs of fluid overload, allowing for timely intervention. Educating the patient on this preventive measure can reduce the risk of hospitalization.

619. A community paramedic is working with a patient who has recently been diagnosed with diabetes. What is the most effective strategy for managing this patient's condition?
a. Providing the patient with detailed written instructions on diabetes care
b. Conducting a one-time comprehensive education session
c. Establishing regular follow-up visits to monitor the patient's progress and provide ongoing education
d. Recommending that the patient attend a support group

Answer: c. Establishing regular follow-up visits to monitor the patient's progress and provide ongoing education. Explanation: Regular follow-up visits allow for continuous monitoring and education, which are essential for effective diabetes management. This approach ensures the patient receives the support needed to manage their condition effectively.

620. A tactical EMS team is responding to an active shooter situation. Which principle of Tactical Combat Casualty Care (TCCC) should be prioritized first when treating casualties in the hot zone?
a. Airway management

b. Circulation assessment
c. Hemorrhage control
d. Hypothermia prevention

Answer: c. Hemorrhage control. Explanation: In a tactical environment, hemorrhage control is the first priority because severe bleeding is the leading cause of preventable death on the battlefield. Effective control of life-threatening hemorrhage can be achieved using tourniquets, hemostatic agents, and pressure dressings.

621. When selecting ballistic protection for a tactical EMS operation, which factor is most critical to consider?
a. Weight of the protective gear
b. Level of protection required against specific threats
c. Cost of the equipment
d. Comfort and fit of the gear

Answer: b. Level of protection required against specific threats. Explanation: The level of ballistic protection needed depends on the specific threats likely to be encountered, such as handgun or rifle rounds. Ensuring that the gear meets the required protection level is paramount for the safety of EMS personnel in tactical operations.

622. A tactical EMS team is tasked with extracting a casualty from a hot zone. What is the most appropriate technique to use?
a. One-person drag
b. Fireman's carry
c. Two-person carry
d. Use of a tactical evacuation litter

Answer: d. Use of a tactical evacuation litter. Explanation: A tactical evacuation litter allows for a more stable and efficient extraction of casualties from dangerous areas, minimizing movement and potential further injury while providing better protection to the rescuers.

623. In a tactical environment, which method is most appropriate for controlling severe extremity hemorrhage when a tourniquet is not available?
a. Applying a pressure dressing
b. Elevating the limb
c. Using direct pressure with hands
d. Applying a cold compress

Answer: a. Applying a pressure dressing. Explanation: When a tourniquet is not available, a pressure dressing can effectively control severe extremity hemorrhage by applying continuous pressure directly to the wound, thereby reducing blood flow and promoting clotting.

624. What is a key difference between Tactical Combat Casualty Care (TCCC) and Tactical Emergency Casualty Care (TECC) protocols?
a. TCCC is designed for military use, while TECC is adapted for civilian settings
b. TCCC emphasizes airway management first, while TECC focuses on hemorrhage control
c. TCCC protocols are less flexible than TECC protocols
d. TECC requires more advanced medical training than TCCC

Answer: a. TCCC is designed for military use, while TECC is adapted for civilian settings. Explanation: TCCC protocols were initially developed for military combat scenarios, while TECC has been adapted for civilian tactical environments, such as law enforcement or mass casualty incidents, considering the differences in operational context and available resources.

625. During a tactical operation, an EMS provider needs to apply a tourniquet to a casualty's upper arm. What is the correct placement for the tourniquet?
a. Directly over the wound
b. Just above the elbow joint
c. As high as possible on the limb, above the wound
d. Just below the shoulder joint

Answer: c. As high as possible on the limb, above the wound. Explanation: When applying a tourniquet in a tactical environment, it should be placed as high as possible on the limb to ensure that it effectively occludes the major arteries and stops arterial blood flow, especially when the exact location of the injury may be obscured.

626. A tactical EMS provider is treating a casualty with a suspected tension pneumothorax in a combat zone. What is the recommended intervention for this condition in the field?
a. Applying a chest seal
b. Performing needle decompression
c. Administering high-flow oxygen
d. Elevating the casualty's head

Answer: b. Performing needle decompression. Explanation: Needle decompression is the recommended field intervention for suspected tension pneumothorax in a tactical environment. It involves inserting a needle into the pleural space to relieve pressure and prevent cardiovascular collapse.

627. In a tactical EMS scenario, which type of airway management device is preferred for a casualty with severe facial trauma?
a. Nasopharyngeal airway (NPA)
b. Oropharyngeal airway (OPA)
c. Supraglottic airway device
d. Endotracheal tube (ETT)

Answer: c. Supraglottic airway device. Explanation: A supraglottic airway device is often preferred in cases of severe facial trauma because it can be inserted without requiring visualization of the airway and can bypass obstructed or damaged upper airway structures more effectively than NPAs or OPAs.

628. What is the primary goal of tactical casualty care during the Care Under Fire phase?
a. Initiating IV fluid resuscitation
b. Providing comprehensive medical treatment
c. Achieving tactical superiority and extracting the casualty
d. Preventing further casualties and ensuring scene safety

Answer: d. Preventing further casualties and ensuring scene safety. Explanation: During the Care Under Fire phase, the priority is to minimize additional casualties by maintaining cover, returning fire if necessary, and ensuring scene safety before providing medical care.

629. A tactical EMS team needs to prevent hypothermia in a casualty during prolonged field care. Which method is most effective?
a. Using a space blanket
b. Administering warm IV fluids
c. Moving the casualty to a warmer environment
d. Applying chemical heat packs to the casualty's body

Answer: b. Administering warm IV fluids. Explanation: Administering warm IV fluids helps to prevent hypothermia by warming the casualty from the inside out, which is more effective than external methods alone, especially during prolonged field care when environmental factors can rapidly lead to hypothermia.

630. A hiker has sustained a lower leg fracture in a remote wilderness area with limited medical supplies. What is the most appropriate improvised splinting technique?
a. Use a SAM splint if available and secure it with triangular bandages
b. Immobilize the leg using two sturdy branches and cloth strips
c. Use a sleeping pad rolled around the leg and secured with duct tape
d. Utilize the patient's backpack frame to immobilize the leg

Answer: b. Immobilize the leg using two sturdy branches and cloth strips. Explanation: In a wilderness setting with limited supplies, using sturdy branches as splints and securing them with cloth strips is an effective way to immobilize a fracture. This method uses readily available materials and provides adequate stabilization until further medical care is accessible.

631. During a multi-day trek at high altitude, a team member begins to show signs of acute mountain sickness (AMS). What is the initial treatment priority?
a. Administer supplemental oxygen and continue the trek
b. Increase fluid intake and reduce physical activity
c. Descend to a lower altitude immediately

d. Provide acetazolamide and continue monitoring

Answer: c. Descend to a lower altitude immediately. Explanation: The primary treatment for acute mountain sickness is to descend to a lower altitude. This reduces the body's exposure to hypoxia and alleviates symptoms. Supplemental oxygen and medications like acetazolamide can be supportive, but descent is the most effective intervention.

632. A wilderness EMT is treating a patient with deep lacerations from a bear attack. What is the first priority in managing these wounds?
a. Irrigate the wounds with clean water
b. Apply a tourniquet to control bleeding
c. Immobilize the affected limb
d. Administer prophylactic antibiotics

Answer: a. Irrigate the wounds with clean water. Explanation: The first priority in managing bear attack wounds is thorough irrigation to reduce the risk of infection. Controlling bleeding and immobilization are also important but secondary to cleaning the wounds. Prophylactic antibiotics can be administered later if necessary.

633. A climber has been struck by lightning and is unresponsive. What is the initial step in patient assessment and management?
a. Begin CPR immediately if the patient is pulseless
b. Move the patient to a sheltered location
c. Check for entrance and exit wounds from the lightning strike
d. Apply an AED and follow its prompts

Answer: a. Begin CPR immediately if the patient is pulseless. Explanation: The initial step in managing a lightning strike victim who is unresponsive and pulseless is to begin CPR immediately. Quick initiation of resuscitative efforts can be life-saving in these cases. Moving the patient and other assessments are important but secondary.

634. You are leading a group in a remote area when one member suffers a severe asthma attack. What evacuation criteria should you consider to determine if immediate evacuation is necessary?
a. The patient's response to initial albuterol treatment
b. The distance to the nearest medical facility
c. The availability of additional asthma medications
d. The patient's ability to walk without assistance

Answer: a. The patient's response to initial albuterol treatment. Explanation: Evaluating the patient's response to initial albuterol treatment helps determine the severity of the asthma attack. If the patient does not respond adequately, immediate evacuation is necessary to access advanced medical care. Other factors are secondary considerations.

635. A patient at high altitude experiences confusion, ataxia, and severe headache. What is the most likely diagnosis, and what should be the immediate treatment?
a. Acute mountain sickness; administer acetazolamide and monitor
b. High altitude pulmonary edema; provide supplemental oxygen
c. High altitude cerebral edema; initiate descent immediately
d. Dehydration; increase fluid intake and rest

Answer: c. High altitude cerebral edema; initiate descent immediately. Explanation: Confusion, ataxia, and severe headache at high altitude are indicative of high altitude cerebral edema (HACE), a life-threatening condition. The immediate treatment is rapid descent to a lower altitude to reduce intracranial pressure and prevent further deterioration.

636. While camping, a member of your group is struck by a falling tree branch, resulting in a suspected spinal injury. How should you safely evacuate this patient?
a. Use a makeshift stretcher to carry the patient to the nearest road
b. Walk the patient out with assistance
c. Secure the patient to a rigid board and coordinate a helicopter evacuation
d. Allow the patient to rest and reassess in a few hours

Answer: c. Secure the patient to a rigid board and coordinate a helicopter evacuation. Explanation: For suspected spinal injuries, the patient should be secured to a rigid board to prevent further spinal movement and injury. Helicopter evacuation is preferred to minimize jostling and provide rapid transport to advanced medical care.

637. During a backpacking trip, a participant develops symptoms of high altitude pulmonary edema (HAPE). What is the recommended treatment in the wilderness setting?
a. Administer high-flow oxygen and continue monitoring
b. Immediate descent to a lower altitude
c. Provide diuretics and continue the hike slowly
d. Encourage deep breathing exercises to improve oxygenation

Answer: b. Immediate descent to a lower altitude. Explanation: The most effective treatment for high altitude pulmonary edema (HAPE) is immediate descent to a lower altitude. This helps alleviate the hypoxia causing pulmonary edema. High-flow oxygen can be supportive if available, but descent is the priority.

638. A patient in a remote area is showing signs of severe dehydration. What is the most appropriate initial intervention?
a. Administer oral rehydration solution (ORS)
b. Start an IV with normal saline
c. Encourage the patient to drink plain water
d. Provide small, frequent sips of juice

Answer: a. Administer oral rehydration solution (ORS). Explanation: Oral rehydration solution (ORS) is the most effective initial treatment for severe dehydration in a wilderness setting. It helps replenish electrolytes and fluids more efficiently than plain water or juice. Starting an IV may not be feasible in remote areas.

639. A wilderness EMT is assessing a hiker who was found disoriented and stumbling. The hiker reports a history of type 1 diabetes. What should be the first step in managing this patient?
a. Check the patient's blood glucose level
b. Provide high-carbohydrate snacks
c. Administer insulin if available
d. Encourage the patient to rest and hydrate

Answer: a. Check the patient's blood glucose level. Explanation: The first step in managing a diabetic patient presenting with disorientation and stumbling is to check their blood glucose level. This will determine if the patient is hypoglycemic or hyperglycemic and guide appropriate treatment.

640. A flight paramedic is responding to a scene and must set up a landing zone for the helicopter. What is the minimum size required for a safe landing zone?
a. 50 feet by 50 feet
b. 75 feet by 75 feet
c. 100 feet by 100 feet
d. 150 feet by 150 feet

Answer: c. 100 feet by 100 feet. Explanation: A landing zone of at least 100 feet by 100 feet is recommended to provide adequate space for safe helicopter landing and takeoff, ensuring there is enough clearance from obstacles.

641. During an aeromedical transport, a patient begins to experience shortness of breath and chest pain. Which condition is the flight paramedic most concerned about, considering the altitude and pressure changes?
a. Acute myocardial infarction
b. Tension pneumothorax
c. Pulmonary embolism
d. Asthma exacerbation

Answer: b. Tension pneumothorax. Explanation: Changes in altitude and pressure can exacerbate a pneumothorax, potentially leading to a tension pneumothorax. This condition can be life-threatening and requires immediate intervention.

642. A flight paramedic is preparing to load a patient onto a helicopter. Which of the following safety considerations is most important?
a. Ensuring the patient is comfortable before boarding
b. Securing all loose items on the patient and stretcher
c. Allowing family members to board with the patient
d. Checking the patient's vital signs one last time before loading

Answer: b. Securing all loose items on the patient and stretcher. Explanation: In the rotor wash and confined space of a helicopter, unsecured items can become projectiles, posing a danger to the patient and crew. Securing all loose items is essential for safety.

643. A patient being transported by air is receiving IV fluids. Due to changes in altitude, the IV flow rate increases unexpectedly. What physiological principle explains this occurrence?
a. Decreased air pressure increases IV flow rate
b. Increased air pressure decreases IV flow rate
c. Increased temperature increases IV flow rate
d. Decreased temperature decreases IV flow rate

Answer: a. Decreased air pressure increases IV flow rate. Explanation: At higher altitudes, the decrease in air pressure can cause IV fluids to flow more quickly due to the pressure difference between the IV bag and the patient's veins.

644. What is the minimum visibility requirement for a helicopter to safely take off and land during daylight operations?
a. 1/2 mile
b. 1 mile
c. 2 miles
d. 3 miles

Answer: b. 1 mile. Explanation: The minimum visibility requirement for helicopter operations during daylight is generally 1 mile. This ensures that pilots have adequate visibility to navigate and land safely.

645. A flight paramedic must be aware of the physiological changes that occur during flight. Which condition is most likely to be exacerbated by the decreased partial pressure of oxygen at higher altitudes?
a. Hypoglycemia
b. Hypothermia
c. Hypoxia
d. Hypertension

Answer: c. Hypoxia. Explanation: The decreased partial pressure of oxygen at higher altitudes can exacerbate hypoxia, making it critical for flight paramedics to monitor and manage oxygen levels in patients during transport.

646. While preparing for a night flight, a flight paramedic checks the helicopter's external lighting. Which of the following lights is essential for identifying the helicopter's orientation to other aircraft?
a. Landing light
b. Anti-collision light
c. Navigation lights

d. Searchlight

Answer: c. Navigation lights. Explanation: Navigation lights, typically red on the left, green on the right, and white at the rear, help other aircraft identify the helicopter's orientation and position, crucial for preventing mid-air collisions.

647. During a high-altitude flight, a patient with a known cardiac condition begins to show signs of acute distress. What is the first action the flight paramedic should take?
a. Increase the IV fluid rate
b. Administer high-flow oxygen
c. Perform chest compressions
d. Defibrillate the patient

Answer: b. Administer high-flow oxygen. Explanation: At high altitudes, the reduced oxygen levels can worsen cardiac conditions. Administering high-flow oxygen helps to counteract hypoxia and stabilize the patient.

648. A flight paramedic is conducting a pre-flight inspection and notices that the weather forecast predicts turbulence. What is the most appropriate action to ensure patient safety during transport?
a. Cancel the flight and arrange for ground transport
b. Secure the patient more firmly to the stretcher
c. Administer anti-anxiety medication to the patient
d. Ensure all medical equipment is securely fastened

Answer: a. Cancel the flight and arrange for ground transport. Explanation: If turbulence is predicted, the safest course of action is to cancel the flight and arrange for ground transport to avoid risking patient and crew safety.

649. During an in-flight emergency, the pilot becomes incapacitated. What is the flight paramedic's immediate priority?
a. Attempt to land the helicopter
b. Provide medical assistance to the pilot
c. Contact air traffic control for assistance
d. Ensure the safety of the patient and crew

Answer: d. Ensure the safety of the patient and crew. Explanation: The immediate priority is to ensure the safety of the patient and crew, which includes stabilizing the situation and coordinating with other team members or air traffic control for further assistance.

650. A patient on a mechanical ventilator is being transported to a tertiary care facility. During transport, the high-pressure alarm on the ventilator starts to sound. What is the most appropriate initial action?
a. Increase the tidal volume
b. Check for kinks or obstructions in the ventilator tubing

c. Decrease the respiratory rate
d. Increase the PEEP setting

Answer: b. Check for kinks or obstructions in the ventilator tubing. Explanation: High-pressure alarms typically indicate a blockage or resistance in the ventilator circuit. The initial action should be to check for kinks or obstructions in the tubing to ensure adequate airflow to the patient. Adjusting ventilator settings without addressing potential obstructions could worsen the problem.

651. You are transporting a patient on a norepinephrine drip at 8 mcg/min for hypotension. Suddenly, the patient's blood pressure drops to 70/40 mmHg. What should be your first action?
a. Increase the norepinephrine dose
b. Administer a fluid bolus
c. Reassess the intravenous (IV) site for patency
d. Switch to a different vasopressor

Answer: c. Reassess the intravenous (IV) site for patency. Explanation: Before increasing the dose or administering additional medications, it is crucial to ensure that the IV site is patent and the medication is being delivered properly. An infiltration or occlusion could cause a sudden drop in blood pressure due to the lack of medication delivery.

652. During transport, a patient with an intra-aortic balloon pump (IABP) experiences a sudden drop in augmented diastolic pressure. What should be your first step in troubleshooting the IABP?
a. Increase the augmentation setting
b. Check the helium supply
c. Reposition the patient
d. Assess for signs of aortic dissection

Answer: b. Check the helium supply. Explanation: A sudden drop in augmented diastolic pressure could indicate an issue with the helium supply, which is essential for the balloon's inflation and deflation. Ensuring the helium supply is intact and functioning properly is the first step in troubleshooting.

653. A patient on a transport ventilator with an FiO2 of 100% shows signs of hypoxemia with a SpO2 of 85%. What adjustment should be made to improve oxygenation?
a. Increase the FiO2 to 120%
b. Increase the PEEP setting
c. Decrease the tidal volume
d. Decrease the inspiratory time

Answer: b. Increase the PEEP setting. Explanation: Increasing the positive end-expiratory pressure (PEEP) can improve oxygenation by preventing alveolar collapse and improving gas exchange. Since the FiO2 is already at 100%, increasing it further is not an option, and decreasing tidal volume or inspiratory time could worsen hypoxemia.

654. While transporting a patient with a pulmonary artery catheter, you notice the waveform suddenly becomes dampened. What is the most appropriate action?
a. Flush the catheter with heparinized saline
b. Reposition the catheter
c. Zero the transducer
d. Increase the infusion rate of fluids

Answer: a. Flush the catheter with heparinized saline. Explanation: A dampened waveform can indicate a clot or occlusion in the catheter. Flushing the catheter with heparinized saline can help clear any blockage and restore accurate pressure readings.

655. You are calculating a dopamine drip for a patient weighing 70 kg to maintain a blood pressure of 90/60 mmHg. The order is for 5 mcg/kg/min. What is the correct infusion rate if the concentration is 400 mg in 250 mL of D5W?
a. 10 mL/hr
b. 13.1 mL/hr
c. 21.9 mL/hr
d. 26.3 mL/hr

Answer: b.

656. A patient with septic shock is on a vasopressin infusion at 0.04 units/min. During transport, the patient's blood pressure remains low despite maximum vasopressin dosage. What is the next appropriate step?
a. Increase the vasopressin dose
b. Add an additional vasopressor
c. Administer a steroid bolus
d. Decrease the fluid infusion rate

Answer: b. Add an additional vasopressor. Explanation: When the maximum dose of vasopressin is reached and the patient remains hypotensive, adding another vasopressor (such as norepinephrine) can help achieve better hemodynamic stability. Increasing the vasopressin dose beyond the maximum recommended level can lead to adverse effects.

657. During transport, a patient's end-tidal CO2 (EtCO2) suddenly drops from 35 mmHg to 20 mmHg. What is the most likely cause?
a. Increased metabolic rate
b. Pulmonary embolism
c. Hypoventilation
d. Malfunction of the capnography monitor

Answer: b. Pulmonary embolism. Explanation: A sudden drop in end-tidal CO2 is often indicative of a pulmonary embolism, as it obstructs blood flow to the lungs, reducing CO2 exchange. While equipment malfunction is possible, a clinical correlation should first be considered.

658. You are transporting a patient with a history of heart failure who suddenly develops acute respiratory distress and frothy sputum. What intervention is most appropriate?
a. Increase the FiO2 on the ventilator
b. Administer a diuretic
c. Perform an emergency thoracotomy
d. Decrease the tidal volume on the ventilator

Answer: b. Administer a diuretic. Explanation: Acute respiratory distress with frothy sputum in a heart failure patient suggests pulmonary edema. Administering a diuretic can help reduce fluid overload in the lungs. Adjusting ventilator settings or performing a thoracotomy is not appropriate for managing pulmonary edema.

659. A patient on a nitroglycerin drip for chest pain has their infusion set at 20 mcg/min. If the concentration of nitroglycerin is 50 mg in 250 mL of D5W, what is the infusion rate in mL/hr?
a. 6 mL/hr
b. 10 mL/hr
c. 15 mL/hr
d. 20 mL/hr

Answer: b.

660. During a neonatal transport, the paramedic needs to ensure proper thermoregulation for a premature infant. What is the most effective method to prevent hypothermia during transport?
a. Wrapping the infant in multiple blankets
b. Using a neonatal isolette with a controlled temperature environment
c. Placing the infant under a heat lamp
d. Keeping the transport vehicle at a higher ambient temperature

Answer: b. Using a neonatal isolette with a controlled temperature environment. Explanation: A neonatal isolette provides a controlled temperature environment that is essential for maintaining thermoregulation in premature infants, preventing hypothermia more effectively than blankets or ambient temperature adjustments.

661. A paramedic is preparing to transport a neonate with respiratory distress syndrome (RDS). Which respiratory support method is most appropriate for this condition?
a. Nasal cannula at 2 L/min
b. Continuous Positive Airway Pressure (CPAP)
c. Non-rebreather mask at 15 L/min
d. Simple face mask at 6 L/min

Answer: b. Continuous Positive Airway Pressure (CPAP). Explanation: CPAP is the preferred method for managing respiratory distress syndrome in neonates as it helps keep the alveoli open and improves oxygenation without the need for invasive ventilation.

662. When managing an umbilical line during neonatal transport, which precaution is most important to prevent complications?
a. Flushing the line every 15 minutes with saline
b. Keeping the line clamped and secured to prevent dislodgement
c. Administering medications through the line at a rapid rate
d. Repositioning the line frequently to prevent clot formation

Answer: b. Keeping the line clamped and secured to prevent dislodgement. Explanation: Properly securing the umbilical line and keeping it clamped when not in use helps prevent dislodgement and associated complications, such as bleeding or infection.

663. A neonate weighing 2 kg requires a dose of epinephrine during transport. The recommended dose is 0.01 mg/kg. How much epinephrine should the paramedic administer?
a. 0.01 mg
b. 0.02 mg
c. 0.05 mg
d. 0.1 mg

Answer: b. 0.02 mg. Explanation: The correct dose calculation is 0.01 mg/kg x 2 kg = 0.02 mg. Accurate medication dosing is crucial in neonatal care to avoid underdosing or overdosing.

664. During transport, a neonate exhibits signs of hypoglycemia. What is the most appropriate initial intervention?
a. Administering a bolus of 10% dextrose solution intravenously
b. Giving oral glucose gel
c. Starting an infusion of 0.9% normal saline
d. Providing a feeding of formula or breast milk

Answer: a. Administering a bolus of 10% dextrose solution intravenously. Explanation: Intravenous administration of a 10% dextrose solution is the most effective and immediate intervention for neonatal hypoglycemia, providing rapid correction of blood glucose levels.

665. A paramedic is preparing to intubate a neonate during transport. What size endotracheal tube (ETT) is most appropriate for a full-term neonate?
a. 2.0 mm
b. 2.5 mm
c. 3.0 mm

d. 3.5 mm

Answer: d. 3.5 mm. Explanation: For a full-term neonate, an endotracheal tube size of 3.5 mm is typically appropriate, ensuring adequate ventilation without causing excessive trauma to the airway.

666. During neonatal transport, which method is recommended for monitoring oxygen saturation levels?
a. Arterial blood gas analysis
b. Transcutaneous oxygen monitoring
c. Pulse oximetry
d. End-tidal CO2 monitoring

Answer: c. Pulse oximetry. Explanation: Pulse oximetry is the standard method for continuous, non-invasive monitoring of oxygen saturation levels in neonates during transport, providing real-time data on their respiratory status.

667. A neonate with suspected sepsis is being transported. What initial antibiotic therapy is commonly recommended?
a. Amoxicillin and clavulanic acid
b. Ceftriaxone and vancomycin
c. Ampicillin and gentamicin
d. Ciprofloxacin and metronidazole

Answer: c. Ampicillin and gentamicin. Explanation: Ampicillin and gentamicin are commonly used as initial empirical antibiotic therapy for suspected neonatal sepsis, covering a broad range of potential pathogens.

668. What is the most important consideration when calculating medication dosages for neonates during transport?
a. Using the same dosages as for older children
b. Rounding doses to the nearest milligram
c. Basing dosages on the neonate's weight in kilograms
d. Adjusting dosages based on transport time

Answer: c. Basing dosages on the neonate's weight in kilograms. Explanation: Medication dosages for neonates must be carefully calculated based on their weight in kilograms to ensure accurate and safe administration, considering their small size and developing organ systems.

669. A neonate with a heart rate of 80 beats per minute is being transported. What intervention should be performed first?
a. Start chest compressions
b. Administer epinephrine
c. Provide positive pressure ventilation

d. Establish an intravenous line

Answer: c. Provide positive pressure ventilation. Explanation: In neonates, a heart rate below 100 beats per minute often indicates the need for positive pressure ventilation, which can help improve oxygenation and circulation before other interventions like chest compressions or medication are considered.

670. A patient is being transferred from a community hospital to a trauma center under EMTALA guidelines. Which of the following must be ensured before transport?
a. The patient has received a full diagnostic workup
b. The receiving facility has agreed to accept the patient and has the capability to provide appropriate care
c. The patient's insurance information is confirmed and documented
d. The patient has been stabilized to the point where no further treatment is needed

Answer: b. The receiving facility has agreed to accept the patient and has the capability to provide appropriate care. Explanation: Under EMTALA, it is crucial that the receiving facility agrees to accept the patient and can provide the necessary level of care. This ensures continuity of appropriate medical treatment during the transfer process.

671. During an interfacility transport, you are responsible for a patient with a suspected acute myocardial infarction. What is the most appropriate level of transport team composition for this patient?
a. Basic Life Support (BLS) team with additional cardiac monitoring equipment
b. Advanced Life Support (ALS) team with a paramedic
c. Critical Care Transport (CCT) team with a critical care nurse and paramedic
d. Air transport with a flight nurse and physician

Answer: c. Critical Care Transport (CCT) team with a critical care nurse and paramedic. Explanation: A patient with a suspected acute myocardial infarction requires advanced monitoring and the ability to perform complex interventions, making a Critical Care Transport team the most appropriate choice. This ensures that any complications during transport can be promptly managed.

672. When preparing to transport a patient to a tertiary care center, you are informed that the receiving facility has a bed available but the specific unit requested is currently full. What should you do next?
a. Proceed with the transport since a bed is available
b. Delay transport until the specific unit has an available bed
c. Confirm with the receiving facility that the patient can be accommodated in an alternate unit
d. Transfer the patient to a different facility with the requested unit availability

Answer: c. Confirm with the receiving facility that the patient can be accommodated in an alternate unit. Explanation: It is essential to ensure that the patient can be appropriately accommodated even if the specific unit is full. Confirming with the receiving facility allows for adjustments to be made to ensure the patient's needs are met upon arrival.

673. A patient with severe sepsis is being transferred to an ICU at another hospital. What is the most important factor in determining the patient's acuity level for transport?
a. The patient's vital signs and need for continuous monitoring
b. The distance to the receiving facility
c. The patient's insurance coverage and transfer authorization
d. The time of day and traffic conditions

Answer: a. The patient's vital signs and need for continuous monitoring. Explanation: The patient's acuity level is primarily determined by their current clinical status, including vital signs and the need for continuous monitoring or interventions. This ensures that the appropriate level of care is provided during transport.

674. When arranging an interfacility transfer, what is the first step in confirming bed availability at the receiving facility?
a. Calling the receiving facility's admissions office
b. Contacting the receiving facility's bed control or capacity management team
c. Checking the receiving facility's online bed availability system
d. Confirming with the receiving facility's charge nurse on the receiving unit

Answer: b. Contacting the receiving facility's bed control or capacity management team. Explanation: The bed control or capacity management team at the receiving facility is responsible for managing and allocating beds. They provide the most accurate and up-to-date information regarding bed availability.

675. You are tasked with ensuring compliance with EMTALA during an interfacility transfer. What documentation is essential to meet EMTALA requirements?
a. Detailed financial consent forms
b. A completed patient satisfaction survey
c. A physician's certification of the medical necessity for transfer and patient's consent to transfer
d. A copy of the receiving facility's capabilities and resources

Answer: c. A physician's certification of the medical necessity for transfer and patient's consent to transfer. Explanation: EMTALA requires a physician's certification stating the medical necessity of the transfer and the patient's informed consent. This ensures that the transfer is appropriate and that the patient has been informed about the risks and benefits.

676. A neonatal patient requires transfer to a specialized pediatric unit. What team composition is most appropriate for this transport?
a. BLS team with additional pediatric training
b. ALS team with a paramedic and pediatric experience
c. Neonatal transport team with a neonatologist and neonatal nurse
d. Air transport with a flight nurse and EMT

Answer: c. Neonatal transport team with a neonatologist and neonatal nurse. Explanation: A neonatal patient requires specialized care that can be provided by a neonatal transport team. This team has the expertise and equipment necessary to manage the unique needs of neonatal patients during transport.

677. During transport, a patient's condition deteriorates, requiring advanced airway management. What is the most appropriate action?
a. Perform endotracheal intubation if within the scope of practice and transport protocols
b. Administer sedatives and increase oxygen flow
c. Divert to the nearest hospital for airway management
d. Continue monitoring and provide supplemental oxygen

Answer: a. Perform endotracheal intubation if within the scope of practice and transport protocols. Explanation: Advanced airway management, such as endotracheal intubation, should be performed if it is within the provider's scope of practice and follows transport protocols. This ensures the patient receives the necessary intervention promptly.

678. You are coordinating the transfer of a critically ill patient who requires continuous infusion of multiple medications. What is a key consideration when planning this transport?
a. The availability of family members to accompany the patient
b. The compatibility of infusion pumps between facilities
c. The estimated cost of the transfer
d. The availability of a wheelchair at the receiving facility

Answer: b. The compatibility of infusion pumps between facilities. Explanation: Ensuring that infusion pumps are compatible between facilities is crucial to avoid interruption of medication administration during transfer. This maintains the continuity of care and the patient's stability.

679. A patient with a suspected spinal cord injury needs to be transferred to a trauma center. What is the most critical aspect of their transport?
a. Ensuring the patient is comfortable during the ride
b. Using a vehicle with advanced GPS navigation
c. Maintaining spinal immobilization throughout the transfer
d. Confirming the availability of parking at the receiving facility

Answer: c. Maintaining spinal immobilization throughout the transfer. Explanation: For a patient with a suspected spinal cord injury, maintaining spinal immobilization is critical to prevent further injury. This ensures that the patient's condition does not worsen during transport.

680. A large music festival expects an attendance of 50,000 people. As part of the medical planning team, what is the estimated patient presentation rate you should plan for?
a. 0.5% of attendees

b. 1.5% of attendees
c. 5% of attendees
d. 10% of attendees

Answer: b. 1.5% of attendees. Explanation: For large events, an estimated patient presentation rate of 1.5% is commonly used to plan medical resources, accounting for the typical range of minor to moderate medical issues that might arise in such a crowd.

681. When setting up an on-site treatment area for a mass gathering, what is the most important consideration for its location?
a. Proximity to food vendors
b. Central location with easy access for emergency vehicles
c. Close to the main stage or event area
d. Near the entrance gate

Answer: b. Central location with easy access for emergency vehicles. Explanation: The treatment area should be centrally located to ensure rapid access for emergency vehicles and to allow medical personnel to reach patients quickly from any part of the event.

682. A sporting event organizer requests a medical team to cover a VIP section. What special considerations should be included in the planning for VIP medical coverage?
a. Extra security measures and discreet access to medical care
b. Additional medical supplies for potential substance abuse
c. Smaller, less equipped medical kits
d. High visibility of medical staff

Answer: a. Extra security measures and discreet access to medical care. Explanation: VIP areas often require enhanced security and discreet medical access to ensure privacy and safety while providing adequate medical coverage without drawing attention.

683. In the context of a mass gathering, what is the primary purpose of establishing a robust communication system?
a. To manage ticket sales and crowd control
b. To ensure efficient coordination between medical teams and event organizers
c. To provide entertainment updates to attendees
d. To facilitate lost and found services

Answer: b. To ensure efficient coordination between medical teams and event organizers. Explanation: A robust communication system is essential for efficient coordination between medical teams, event organizers, and other emergency services to ensure timely and effective response to medical incidents.

684. During a mass gathering, which type of injury or condition is most commonly expected, and thus should be a primary focus of preparedness?
a. Cardiac emergencies
b. Traumatic injuries
c. Heat-related illnesses
d. Infectious disease outbreaks

Answer: c. Heat-related illnesses. Explanation: Heat-related illnesses are common in mass gatherings, especially outdoor events in warm climates, and should be a primary focus of medical preparedness, including ensuring hydration and cooling measures are in place.

685. When estimating the number of medical staff needed for a mass gathering, which factor is most important to consider?
a. Duration of the event
b. Number of event performers
c. Ticket price
d. Number of food and drink vendors

Answer: a. Duration of the event. Explanation: The duration of the event is a critical factor in estimating the number of medical staff needed, as longer events increase the likelihood of medical incidents and require shifts to ensure continuous coverage.

686. For a mass gathering event, what is the recommended minimum ratio of medical personnel to attendees?
a. 1:1000
b. 1:500
c. 1:250
d. 1:100

Answer: a. 1:1000. Explanation: A commonly recommended minimum ratio is 1 medical staff member per 1000 attendees, though this can vary based on the nature of the event and anticipated risks.

687. In planning for a large outdoor concert, what is a critical aspect of the on-site treatment area setup to handle potential weather-related issues?
a. Setting up tents or shelters for shade and protection from rain
b. Providing sunscreen and hats to attendees
c. Offering free water bottles
d. Placing the treatment area next to the stage

Answer: a. Setting up tents or shelters for shade and protection from rain. Explanation: Tents or shelters are essential to protect patients and medical staff from extreme weather conditions, such as heat or rain, ensuring a safe and functional treatment area.

688. A mass gathering event includes high-profile VIP attendees. What is a key component of the medical coverage plan for this group?
a. Special access to general event medical services
b. Dedicated medical team assigned specifically to the VIPs
c. Reduced medical presence to maintain privacy
d. Prioritizing VIP medical needs over general attendees

Answer: b. Dedicated medical team assigned specifically to the VIPs. Explanation: A dedicated medical team ensures that VIPs receive immediate and tailored medical attention, balancing their need for privacy and prompt care without affecting the general attendees.

689. To ensure the safety of attendees at a large festival, what is the best practice for determining the number and location of on-site medical treatment areas?
a. One large central treatment area
b. Multiple smaller treatment areas strategically located around the event
c. Treatment areas placed near food and beverage stands
d. Treatment areas located at the event entrances

Answer: b. Multiple smaller treatment areas strategically located around the event. Explanation: Multiple smaller treatment areas allow for faster medical response times by reducing the distance staff must travel to reach patients, ensuring comprehensive coverage throughout the event.

690. During a telemedicine consultation, the video feed from the patient's end is blurry and intermittently freezing. What is the most appropriate initial troubleshooting step?
a. Reboot the telehealth equipment
b. Check the internet connection and signal strength
c. Adjust the lighting in the patient's environment
d. Switch to an audio-only consultation

Answer: b. Check the internet connection and signal strength. Explanation: Blurry and freezing video is often due to poor internet connectivity. Checking and improving the internet connection is the first step to resolving these issues and ensuring a clear and stable video feed.

691. A paramedic is performing a remote assessment of a patient with chest pain via telemedicine. Which of the following techniques is essential for an accurate assessment?
a. Directing the patient to perform a self-exam and describe findings
b. Using a remote stethoscope to auscultate heart and lung sounds
c. Asking the patient to email recent medical records
d. Requesting the patient to measure their blood pressure manually

Answer: b. Using a remote stethoscope to auscultate heart and lung sounds. Explanation: A remote stethoscope allows the paramedic to directly assess heart and lung sounds, which is crucial for evaluating a patient with chest pain. This technique provides objective data that can significantly aid in diagnosis and management.

692. During a telemedicine session, a patient begins to experience severe shortness of breath. What is the paramedic's primary legal consideration in this situation?
a. Ensuring that the telemedicine session is properly documented
b. Informing the patient about the limitations of telemedicine
c. Advising the patient to immediately call 911 or an ambulance for in-person care
d. Verifying the patient's insurance coverage for emergency services

Answer: c. Advising the patient to immediately call 911 or an ambulance for in-person care. Explanation: In cases of severe medical emergencies, it is critical to advise the patient to seek immediate in-person care. This action ensures patient safety and complies with legal and ethical responsibilities to provide appropriate care.

693. When documenting a telemedicine consultation, which of the following information is essential to include in the ePCR?
a. The time and date of the teleconsultation
b. The patient's demographic information
c. The weather conditions during the consultation
d. The patient's next scheduled medical appointment

Answer: a. The time and date of the teleconsultation. Explanation: Documenting the time and date of the teleconsultation is essential for medical records and legal purposes. It provides a clear timeline of when the patient was assessed and what recommendations or treatments were given.

694. How should telemedicine data be integrated into an ePCR system to ensure continuity of care?
a. Manually enter the telemedicine notes into the ePCR
b. Attach the telemedicine session recording to the ePCR
c. Utilize compatible software that allows direct transfer of telemedicine data into the ePCR
d. Print and scan the telemedicine consultation summary into the ePCR

Answer: c. Utilize compatible software that allows direct transfer of telemedicine data into the ePCR. Explanation: Using compatible software that directly transfers telemedicine data into the ePCR ensures accurate and seamless integration. This method maintains data integrity and facilitates comprehensive documentation.

695. A paramedic is setting up telehealth equipment for a remote consultation. What is the first step to ensure proper equipment functionality?
a. Test the audio and video components
b. Ensure the patient's medical history is loaded in the system
c. Connect the equipment to a power source

d. Calibrate the telehealth peripheral devices

Answer: c. Connect the equipment to a power source. Explanation: Ensuring the telehealth equipment is connected to a power source is the first step. Without power, none of the other components can function. Once powered, the paramedic can proceed with testing and calibration.

696. In a telemedicine consultation, what is a critical step to maintain patient confidentiality?
a. Conducting the consultation in a private, secure environment
b. Using a speakerphone for better audio clarity
c. Recording the consultation for future reference
d. Sharing the consultation link with family members

Answer: a. Conducting the consultation in a private, secure environment. Explanation: To maintain patient confidentiality, it is crucial to conduct the telemedicine consultation in a private and secure environment. This ensures that patient information is not inadvertently disclosed to unauthorized individuals.

697. A paramedic receives a teleconsultation request from a patient experiencing mild abdominal pain. What remote patient assessment technique should be prioritized?
a. Instructing the patient to apply pressure to different areas of the abdomen and describe the pain
b. Asking the patient to perform a series of physical exercises
c. Requesting the patient to measure their temperature and pulse
d. Directing the patient to take an over-the-counter pain reliever

Answer: a. Instructing the patient to apply pressure to different areas of the abdomen and describe the pain. Explanation: Instructing the patient to apply pressure to different areas of the abdomen and describe the pain helps identify the location and severity of the issue. This technique provides valuable information that can guide further recommendations.

698. During a telemedicine session, a paramedic needs to assess a patient's respiratory status. Which piece of telehealth equipment is most useful for this assessment?
a. A remote thermometer
b. A pulse oximeter
c. An electronic blood pressure monitor
d. A digital scale

Answer: b. A pulse oximeter. Explanation: A pulse oximeter is crucial for assessing a patient's respiratory status as it provides real-time data on oxygen saturation and pulse rate, which are key indicators of respiratory function.

699. What documentation requirement is specific to teleconsultations compared to traditional in-person consultations?

a. Detailed description of the patient's symptoms
b. Documentation of the patient's consent for the telemedicine format
c. Recording the patient's vital signs
d. Noting the medications prescribed during the consultation

Answer: b. Documentation of the patient's consent for the telemedicine format. Explanation: It is important to document the patient's consent for using telemedicine, as this ensures that the patient agrees to and understands the nature of the remote consultation. This step is specific to teleconsultations and is a key legal requirement.

700. During transport, which ambulance safety feature is designed to protect both the patient and EMS personnel in the event of a collision?
a. Enhanced emergency lights and sirens
b. Patient compartment roll cage
c. Anti-lock braking system (ABS)
d. Securement systems for equipment and patients

Answer: d. Securement systems for equipment and patients. Explanation: Securement systems ensure that both patients and equipment remain safely in place during transport, reducing the risk of injury to patients and EMS personnel in the event of a collision.

701. Upon arriving at the scene of a motor vehicle accident, what is the first step in assessing scene safety?
a. Checking for downed power lines
b. Determining the number of patients
c. Ensuring personal protective equipment (PPE) is worn
d. Conducting a 360-degree assessment of the scene

Answer: d. Conducting a 360-degree assessment of the scene. Explanation: A 360-degree assessment allows EMS personnel to identify potential hazards from all angles, ensuring a comprehensive evaluation of scene safety before proceeding with patient care.

702. Which of the following techniques is recommended to minimize the risk of injury while lifting a patient?
a. Using a straight back and lifting with the legs
b. Bending at the waist and lifting with the arms
c. Lifting with a twisting motion to gain leverage
d. Holding the patient away from the body for better control

Answer: a. Using a straight back and lifting with the legs. Explanation: Maintaining a straight back and using the legs to lift helps distribute the weight evenly and reduces the risk of musculoskeletal injuries.

703. What is a key strategy for managing stress and preventing burnout among EMS professionals?

a. Working longer shifts to gain more experience
b. Limiting breaks to maintain a high level of productivity
c. Engaging in regular physical exercise and mindfulness practices
d. Avoiding discussions about stressful experiences with colleagues

Answer: c. Engaging in regular physical exercise and mindfulness practices. Explanation: Regular physical exercise and mindfulness practices are effective strategies for managing stress and preventing burnout, promoting overall well-being and resilience among EMS professionals.

704. In the context of infection control, which type of personal protective equipment (PPE) is most important when treating a patient with a suspected airborne infection?
a. Surgical mask
b. N95 respirator
c. Face shield
d. Gown

Answer: b. N95 respirator. Explanation: An N95 respirator provides a higher level of protection against airborne pathogens compared to a surgical mask, making it essential when treating patients with suspected airborne infections.

705. During a call, an EMS crew encounters a patient with a large open wound. What is the appropriate infection control procedure to follow?
a. Use sterile gloves only
b. Apply a face mask and sterile gloves
c. Wear gloves, gown, face shield, and mask
d. Disinfect the wound immediately

Answer: c. Wear gloves, gown, face shield, and mask. Explanation: Comprehensive PPE, including gloves, gown, face shield, and mask, provides maximal protection against exposure to bloodborne pathogens and other infectious agents.

706. An EMS professional is experiencing symptoms of burnout, including irritability and decreased job satisfaction. What is the most appropriate course of action?
a. Take a leave of absence and seek professional help
b. Increase work hours to stay busy
c. Avoid discussing feelings with colleagues or supervisors
d. Ignore the symptoms and continue working

Answer: a. Take a leave of absence and seek professional help. Explanation: Taking a leave of absence and seeking professional help allows the EMS professional to address burnout symptoms effectively and regain their mental and physical health.

707. When approaching a scene with hazardous materials, what is the initial action EMS personnel should take?
a. Begin patient assessment immediately
b. Don appropriate PPE and approach the scene
c. Wait for the hazardous materials (HAZMAT) team to secure the area
d. Attempt to contain the hazardous material

Answer: c. Wait for the hazardous materials (HAZMAT) team to secure the area. Explanation: The HAZMAT team is specially trained to handle hazardous materials, and EMS personnel should wait for them to secure the area before providing patient care to ensure their own safety.

708. What is the best method for cleaning and disinfecting ambulance surfaces after transporting a patient with a communicable disease?
a. Using soap and water
b. Applying an alcohol-based sanitizer
c. Using a hospital-grade disinfectant
d. Wiping surfaces with a dry cloth

Answer: c. Using a hospital-grade disinfectant. Explanation: Hospital-grade disinfectants are specifically formulated to eliminate a wide range of pathogens, making them the most effective choice for cleaning and disinfecting ambulance surfaces after transporting a patient with a communicable disease.

709. While on scene, an EMS crew needs to move a patient from a confined space. What technique should be employed to safely extricate the patient?
a. Dragging the patient by the arms
b. Using a long spine board with multiple rescuers
c. Lifting the patient with a single rescuer
d. Rolling the patient onto a stretcher

Answer: b. Using a long spine board with multiple rescuers. Explanation: A long spine board provides stability and support, while multiple rescuers ensure the patient is moved safely and securely, minimizing the risk of further injury to both the patient and rescuers.

710. An EMS agency is developing clinical performance indicators to improve patient outcomes. Which of the following is the most effective method for selecting these indicators?
a. Choosing indicators based on the most frequently treated conditions
b. Selecting indicators that are easily measurable
c. Using national benchmarks and evidence-based guidelines
d. Asking for input from all EMS personnel on preferred indicators

Answer: c. Using national benchmarks and evidence-based guidelines. Explanation: Clinical performance indicators should be based on national benchmarks and evidence-based guidelines to ensure they reflect best practices and allow for meaningful comparisons. This approach ensures the indicators are relevant and aligned with industry standards.

711. During the implementation of a peer review process, what is the primary goal?
a. To identify and punish poor performance
b. To provide constructive feedback and promote professional growth
c. To compare individual performance to agency averages
d. To ensure all personnel follow protocols exactly as written

Answer: b. To provide constructive feedback and promote professional growth. Explanation: The primary goal of the peer review process is to provide constructive feedback that fosters professional growth and improves clinical practice. It is a supportive mechanism aimed at enhancing skills and patient care quality.

712. In conducting a root cause analysis (RCA) for a medication error, what is the most important first step?
a. Identifying the individuals involved in the error
b. Mapping out the process to understand where the error occurred
c. Implementing immediate corrective actions
d. Reviewing similar past incidents

Answer: b. Mapping out the process to understand where the error occurred. Explanation: The first step in an RCA is to map out the process to identify where the error occurred. This helps in understanding the sequence of events and the contributing factors, allowing for a thorough analysis and development of effective solutions.

713. An EMS agency is applying the continuous quality improvement (CQI) cycle. What is the initial phase of this cycle?
a. Implementing changes based on data
b. Collecting data on current performance
c. Analyzing data to identify areas for improvement
d. Planning and setting improvement goals

Answer: d. Planning and setting improvement goals. Explanation: The initial phase of the CQI cycle is planning, which involves setting improvement goals and developing a strategy to achieve them. This phase lays the foundation for subsequent data collection, analysis, and implementation of changes.

714. What is the primary purpose of designing patient satisfaction surveys in EMS?
a. To compare the performance of different EMS crews
b. To identify areas where patient care can be improved
c. To gather data for marketing purposes
d. To meet accreditation requirements

Answer: b. To identify areas where patient care can be improved. Explanation: Patient satisfaction surveys are designed to gather feedback on patient experiences and identify areas for improvement in patient care. This information is crucial for enhancing service quality and patient outcomes.

715. In analyzing patient satisfaction survey results, which statistical method is most appropriate for identifying significant trends?
a. Descriptive statistics
b. Inferential statistics
c. Qualitative analysis
d. Content analysis

Answer: b. Inferential statistics. Explanation: Inferential statistics are used to identify significant trends and draw conclusions from the survey data. This method allows for the assessment of relationships and differences within the data, providing insights into areas needing improvement.

716. When developing clinical performance indicators, what is an essential characteristic to ensure their effectiveness?
a. Simplicity in measurement
b. Relevance to patient outcomes
c. Consistency with staff preferences
d. Ease of implementation

Answer: b. Relevance to patient outcomes. Explanation: Clinical performance indicators must be relevant to patient outcomes to effectively measure and improve the quality of care provided. Indicators that directly impact patient health and safety are the most valuable for performance improvement.

717. What is a key element in the successful implementation of a peer review process?
a. Transparency and confidentiality in reviews
b. Rigid adherence to protocol without flexibility
c. Frequent punitive measures for mistakes
d. Sole focus on negative feedback

Answer: a. Transparency and confidentiality in reviews. Explanation: Successful peer review processes rely on transparency and confidentiality to build trust and encourage honest feedback. This approach ensures that the process is constructive and supports professional development.

718. During a root cause analysis, you identify that a lack of training contributed to a patient care error. What should be your next step?
a. Implement immediate mandatory training for all staff
b. Document the finding and move on to the next issue

c. Develop a comprehensive training program addressing the identified gap

d. Conduct a survey to determine training needs

Answer: c. Develop a comprehensive training program addressing the identified gap. Explanation: Once a lack of training is identified as a root cause, developing a comprehensive training program to address the gap ensures that staff are equipped with the necessary knowledge and skills to prevent similar errors in the future.

719. In the continuous quality improvement cycle, how often should performance data be reviewed to ensure ongoing improvement?

a. Annually

b. Quarterly

c. Monthly

d. Weekly

Answer: b. Quarterly. Explanation: Reviewing performance data quarterly provides a balanced approach to monitoring progress and making timely adjustments. This frequency allows for the identification of trends and issues while providing enough time to implement and assess the impact of changes.

720. During a review of EMS response times, it is determined that the average response time in an urban area is 10 minutes. What is the most effective strategy to reduce this response time?

a. Increase the number of ambulances on duty during peak hours

b. Reduce the speed limits for ambulances

c. Limit the response area for each ambulance

d. Decrease the number of stops ambulances make

Answer: a. Increase the number of ambulances on duty during peak hours. Explanation: Increasing the number of ambulances on duty during peak hours can reduce response times by ensuring that more resources are available to respond to calls promptly.

721. When managing system status, what principle helps ensure optimal coverage and resource utilization?

a. Static deployment

b. Dynamic deployment

c. First-in, first-out response

d. Last-in, first-out response

Answer: b. Dynamic deployment. Explanation: Dynamic deployment involves strategically positioning ambulances based on real-time data and anticipated demand, ensuring optimal coverage and efficient use of resources.

722. A mutual aid agreement is being developed between two neighboring EMS agencies. What is a critical component that must be included in this agreement?

a. Agreement to share all resources equally
b. A detailed protocol for requesting and providing aid
c. Provision for rotating shifts between the two agencies
d. A schedule for regular joint training exercises

Answer: b. A detailed protocol for requesting and providing aid. Explanation: A mutual aid agreement should include a clear protocol for how and when to request and provide assistance to ensure a coordinated and effective response during emergencies.

723. To implement a public access defibrillation program, what is the first step EMS leadership should take?
a. Train the general public on CPR and AED use
b. Purchase AEDs and distribute them throughout the community
c. Identify high-traffic areas and locations with high risk of cardiac arrest
d. Develop a maintenance plan for the AEDs

Answer: c. Identify high-traffic areas and locations with high risk of cardiac arrest. Explanation: Identifying strategic locations for AED placement ensures that the devices are readily accessible where they are most likely to be needed, maximizing their potential to save lives.

724. In designing a community paramedic program, which factor is most important to consider for its success?
a. Ensuring all paramedics receive basic EMT training
b. Focusing solely on emergency response capabilities
c. Establishing strong partnerships with local healthcare providers
d. Limiting the scope of practice to transportation services only

Answer: c. Establishing strong partnerships with local healthcare providers. Explanation: Strong partnerships with local healthcare providers are crucial for a community paramedic program, enabling integrated care and effective coordination of services to address community health needs.

725. A new EMS system is being designed to improve response times. Which data analysis method is most appropriate for determining optimal ambulance deployment locations?
a. Random sampling of past response locations
b. Geospatial analysis of call data
c. Surveying public opinion on ambulance placement
d. Reviewing the average driving speed in different areas

Answer: b. Geospatial analysis of call data. Explanation: Geospatial analysis of call data helps identify patterns and high-demand areas, allowing for strategic placement of ambulances to optimize response times.

726. To ensure effective system status management, what is a key performance indicator (KPI) that should be monitored regularly?
a. Number of calls received per day
b. Average response time to emergency calls
c. Number of paramedics on duty
d. Total mileage driven by ambulances

Answer: b. Average response time to emergency calls. Explanation: Monitoring the average response time to emergency calls is a critical KPI for evaluating the efficiency and effectiveness of the EMS system in meeting community needs.

727. A mutual aid agreement between two EMS agencies includes a clause for cost reimbursement. What is the main purpose of this clause?
a. To ensure that the agencies have identical budgets
b. To provide financial compensation for the agency providing aid
c. To require agencies to share all resources equally
d. To establish a competitive relationship between the agencies

Answer: b. To provide financial compensation for the agency providing aid. Explanation: A cost reimbursement clause ensures that the agency providing mutual aid is compensated for its expenses, promoting fair and sustainable cooperation between the agencies.

728. In the context of a public access defibrillation program, what is the role of EMS in community education?
a. Exclusively training medical professionals on AED use
b. Conducting widespread public training sessions on CPR and AED use
c. Replacing all community AEDs annually
d. Limiting AED use to trained personnel only

Answer: b. Conducting widespread public training sessions on CPR and AED use. Explanation: EMS plays a vital role in educating the public on CPR and AED use, increasing community readiness and confidence to respond effectively to cardiac emergencies.

729. When planning a community paramedic program, what is a primary goal for the program?
a. Reducing the number of emergency calls
b. Enhancing the overall health and wellness of the community
c. Increasing hospital admissions
d. Limiting the scope of EMS services

Answer: b. Enhancing the overall health and wellness of the community. Explanation: The primary goal of a community paramedic program is to improve the health and wellness of the community by providing preventive care, education, and integrated healthcare services outside of emergency situations.

730. A rural EMS agency is preparing to apply for a grant to fund new equipment. Which of the following elements is most important to include in the grant proposal to increase the chances of receiving funding?
a. A detailed history of the EMS agency
b. Testimonials from satisfied patients
c. A clear description of the community's needs and how the new equipment will address them
d. A list of all past grants received by the agency

Answer: c. A clear description of the community's needs and how the new equipment will address them. Explanation: Grant proposals are more likely to be funded if they clearly describe the specific needs of the community and how the requested equipment will address those needs. This demonstrates the direct impact and relevance of the funding request.

731. An EMS agency wants to calculate its cost-per-transport to evaluate financial performance. Which of the following costs should be included in this calculation?
a. Only the direct costs, such as fuel and medical supplies
b. Only the indirect costs, such as administrative salaries
c. Both direct and indirect costs, including fuel, medical supplies, and administrative expenses
d. Only the variable costs, such as overtime wages

Answer: c. Both direct and indirect costs, including fuel, medical supplies, and administrative expenses. Explanation: To accurately calculate the cost-per-transport, the agency must include both direct costs (e.g., fuel, medical supplies) and indirect costs (e.g., administrative salaries, overhead expenses). This comprehensive approach provides a true picture of the cost structure.

732. An EMS agency is implementing a charity care policy. What is the primary purpose of this policy?
a. To reduce the amount of paperwork for patients
b. To provide free or discounted services to patients who cannot afford to pay
c. To increase the agency's revenue through charitable donations
d. To streamline the billing process for insured patients

Answer: b. To provide free or discounted services to patients who cannot afford to pay. Explanation: The primary purpose of a charity care policy is to ensure that patients who are unable to afford medical services still receive necessary care. This policy supports the community by providing access to healthcare regardless of financial status.

733. Under the Medicare ambulance fee schedule, what determines the payment rate for a specific transport?
a. The distance traveled during the transport
b. The patient's insurance status
c. The level of service provided and the geographical location of the transport
d. The time of day the transport occurs

Answer: c. The level of service provided and the geographical location of the transport. Explanation: The Medicare ambulance fee schedule bases payment rates on the level of service provided (e.g., basic life support, advanced life support) and the geographical location (urban, rural, super-rural) of the transport. These factors account for differences in costs and resource utilization.

734. To optimize revenue cycle management, which process should an EMS agency prioritize?
a. Expanding the range of services offered
b. Reducing the number of staff members to cut costs
c. Streamlining the billing and collections process
d. Increasing the prices of all services

Answer: c. Streamlining the billing and collections process. Explanation: Optimizing revenue cycle management involves making the billing and collections process more efficient. This ensures timely and accurate reimbursement, reduces administrative burdens, and improves cash flow.

735. When developing a grant proposal budget, which of the following is most important to justify the funding request?
a. A detailed breakdown of projected costs and how each expense supports the project goals
b. A general estimate of the total project cost without specifics
c. A comparison of the proposed budget with past budgets
d. A list of other funding sources that have been approached

Answer: a. A detailed breakdown of projected costs and how each expense supports the project goals. Explanation: A detailed breakdown of projected costs with justification for each expense shows funders exactly how the money will be used to achieve project goals. This transparency increases the likelihood of funding approval.

736. An EMS agency is calculating the cost-per-transport and finds that the total annual costs are $1,200,000 with 6,000 transports per year. What is the cost-per-transport?
a. $150
b. $200
c. $250
d. $300

Answer: b. $200. Explanation: To calculate the cost-per-transport, divide the total annual costs by the number of transports per year:

737. 1
738. ,
739. 200
740. ,
741. 000
742. 6

743. ,
744. 000
745. =
746. 200
747. 6,000
748. 1,200,000
749.
750. =200. Therefore, the cost-per-transport is $200.

751. Which of the following strategies can help an EMS agency improve its Medicare reimbursement rates?
a. Increasing the number of transports without changing the level of service
b. Ensuring accurate documentation and coding for each transport
c. Reducing the amount of charity care provided
d. Raising the prices for non-Medicare patients

Answer: b. Ensuring accurate documentation and coding for each transport. Explanation: Accurate documentation and coding are critical for maximizing Medicare reimbursement rates. Proper coding ensures that the agency is reimbursed at the appropriate level for the services provided.

752. An EMS agency is applying for a grant to improve its emergency response capabilities. What type of data should be included to support the need for this funding?
a. Historical weather patterns in the area
b. Community demographics and emergency response statistics
c. The agency's financial statements
d. Testimonials from the agency's board members

Answer: b. Community demographics and emergency response statistics. Explanation: Including community demographics and emergency response statistics provides a data-driven rationale for the grant request. This information demonstrates the specific needs of the community and how the funding will enhance the agency's ability to meet those needs.

753. In developing a charity care policy, what key element should be included to ensure it is effective?
a. A limit on the number of patients eligible for charity care
b. A clear definition of eligibility criteria based on financial need
c. A requirement for patients to reapply for charity care every month
d. A provision for reducing services to charity care patients

Answer: b. A clear definition of eligibility criteria based on financial need. Explanation: A clear definition of eligibility criteria based on financial need ensures that the charity care policy is applied consistently and fairly. This clarity helps both the agency and patients understand who qualifies for assistance.

754. An EMS agency is selecting an electronic patient care reporting (ePCR) system. What is the most important factor to consider when choosing this system?

a. Cost of the system
b. User interface simplicity
c. Integration with other healthcare systems
d. Availability of customer support

Answer: c. Integration with other healthcare systems. Explanation: The ability of an ePCR system to integrate with other healthcare systems ensures seamless data sharing and continuity of care, which is crucial for patient outcomes and operational efficiency.

755. A GPS-based dispatch system is being implemented in an EMS agency. How does this technology improve emergency response times?
a. By providing real-time tracking and optimal routing for ambulances
b. By reducing the need for trained dispatch personnel
c. By automatically prioritizing lower acuity calls
d. By increasing the range of communication with field units

Answer: a. By providing real-time tracking and optimal routing for ambulances. Explanation: GPS-based dispatch systems improve response times by allowing dispatchers to track ambulances in real-time and provide the quickest route to the scene, reducing travel time and improving efficiency.

756. In integrating telemedicine equipment into EMS operations, what is a key benefit of using this technology during patient transport?
a. Reducing the need for on-board medical supplies
b. Allowing real-time consultation with specialists
c. Eliminating the need for paramedic intervention
d. Increasing patient privacy and confidentiality

Answer: b. Allowing real-time consultation with specialists. Explanation: Telemedicine enables paramedics to consult with medical specialists in real-time during transport, providing advanced care and making informed decisions that can improve patient outcomes.

757. An EMS agency is developing a policy for the use of body-worn cameras by paramedics. What is a critical component to include in this policy?
a. Guidelines for the maintenance and repair of cameras
b. Procedures for reviewing and storing footage
c. Training requirements for paramedics on video editing
d. Restrictions on camera use during patient care

Answer: b. Procedures for reviewing and storing footage. Explanation: Clear procedures for reviewing and storing footage are essential for ensuring compliance with legal, privacy, and operational standards, while also providing a framework for accountability and quality improvement.

758. An EMS agency is considering the implementation of an RFID asset tracking system. What is the primary advantage of using RFID technology for tracking EMS equipment?
a. Reducing the cost of equipment
b. Increasing the lifespan of equipment
c. Providing real-time location and inventory management
d. Enhancing the visual appeal of equipment storage areas

Answer: c. Providing real-time location and inventory management. Explanation: RFID technology enables real-time tracking and management of EMS equipment, ensuring that all necessary assets are accounted for and readily available when needed, thereby improving operational efficiency.

759. When implementing a new ePCR system, what is an essential step to ensure successful adoption by EMS personnel?
a. Limiting access to the system to only a few users
b. Conducting comprehensive training sessions for all users
c. Using the system only for high-acuity patients initially
d. Reducing the number of required data fields

Answer: b. Conducting comprehensive training sessions for all users. Explanation: Comprehensive training ensures that all EMS personnel are proficient in using the new ePCR system, leading to smoother adoption, fewer errors, and more accurate documentation.

760. During an EMS operation, the GPS-based dispatch system indicates a faster route through an area known for heavy traffic. What should the paramedic consider before following the suggested route?
a. The type of call and patient condition
b. The fuel efficiency of the ambulance
c. The proximity to the nearest hospital
d. The availability of parking at the scene

Answer: a. The type of call and patient condition. Explanation: The paramedic should consider the urgency of the call and the patient's condition when deciding whether to follow the suggested route, ensuring that the decision prioritizes patient care and safety.

761. A telemedicine system is being used to monitor a patient with suspected cardiac issues en route to the hospital. Which parameter is most critical to transmit in real-time to the receiving physician?
a. Patient's oxygen saturation
b. Patient's blood glucose levels
c. 12-lead ECG readings
d. Patient's temperature

Answer: c. 12-lead ECG readings. Explanation: Transmitting 12-lead ECG readings in real-time allows the receiving physician to assess the patient's cardiac status promptly, facilitating immediate intervention if necessary and improving patient outcomes.

762. What is a significant concern when developing a body-worn camera policy for EMS personnel?
a. The cost of implementing the camera system
b. The potential impact on patient privacy
c. The technical specifications of the cameras
d. The color and design of the cameras

Answer: b. The potential impact on patient privacy. Explanation: Ensuring patient privacy is a significant concern with body-worn cameras. Policies must address how to handle and protect patient information captured during EMS operations to comply with legal and ethical standards.

763. In an RFID asset tracking system, what is the primary function of the RFID tags?
a. Enhancing the aesthetic appeal of equipment
b. Providing a power source for the equipment
c. Transmitting location data to a central system
d. Increasing the durability of equipment

Answer: c. Transmitting location data to a central system. Explanation: RFID tags transmit location data to a central system, enabling real-time tracking and management of assets, ensuring that equipment is easily located and efficiently utilized.

764. A new EMS education program is developing its curriculum. What is the first step in the curriculum development process?
a. Selecting textbooks and instructional materials
b. Identifying the learning objectives and outcomes
c. Assigning instructors to each course
d. Scheduling the classes and clinical rotations

Answer: b. Identifying the learning objectives and outcomes. Explanation: The first step in curriculum development is identifying the learning objectives and outcomes. These guide the structure of the curriculum, ensuring that all instructional materials, teaching methods, and assessments align with the desired competencies.

765. When revising an EMS education program's curriculum, which stakeholder feedback is most critical to consider?
a. Feedback from former students
b. Input from current instructors
c. Recommendations from accreditation bodies
d. Suggestions from employers of program graduates

Answer: d. Suggestions from employers of program graduates. Explanation: Feedback from employers of program graduates is critical as it reflects the real-world effectiveness and relevance of the curriculum. Employers can provide insights into the strengths and weaknesses of graduates, guiding curriculum improvements.

766. In establishing student selection criteria for an EMS education program, what factor is most important to ensure a fair and effective process?
a. Prioritizing applicants with the highest GPAs
b. Ensuring criteria are transparent and consistently applied
c. Favoring candidates with prior healthcare experience
d. Giving preference to applicants from underrepresented communities

Answer: b. Ensuring criteria are transparent and consistently applied. Explanation: Ensuring that selection criteria are transparent and consistently applied promotes fairness and equity in the admissions process. This approach helps maintain program integrity and supports a diverse student body.

767. Coordinating clinical and field internship sites involves ensuring that students gain exposure to a variety of patient populations. What is the primary benefit of this strategy?
a. Increasing student enrollment numbers
b. Enhancing the program's reputation in the community
c. Providing students with comprehensive clinical experience
d. Reducing the workload on specific clinical sites

Answer: c. Providing students with comprehensive clinical experience. Explanation: Exposing students to a variety of patient populations ensures they gain comprehensive clinical experience, preparing them to handle diverse situations and conditions they will encounter in their professional practice.

768. What is the most important consideration when maintaining program accreditation?
a. Ensuring compliance with accreditation standards and documentation requirements
b. Regularly updating the program's website with accreditation information
c. Attending accreditation workshops and conferences
d. Increasing the program's marketing efforts

Answer: a. Ensuring compliance with accreditation standards and documentation requirements. Explanation: Maintaining program accreditation requires strict adherence to the standards set by accrediting bodies and proper documentation of compliance. This ensures the program meets quality benchmarks and remains accredited.

769. During instructor recruitment for an EMS education program, what quality is most crucial to look for in potential candidates?
a. Extensive experience in EMS education
b. Advanced degrees in related fields

c. Strong communication and teaching skills
d. Membership in professional EMS organizations

Answer: c. Strong communication and teaching skills. Explanation: While experience and advanced degrees are valuable, strong communication and teaching skills are crucial for effective instruction. Instructors must be able to convey complex information clearly and engage students in the learning process.

770. A student in an EMS education program is struggling to meet clinical competencies. What is the most appropriate initial intervention?
a. Recommending the student for dismissal from the program
b. Providing additional resources and targeted support
c. Allowing the student to progress with their cohort without intervention
d. Reducing the number of required clinical hours for the student

Answer: b. Providing additional resources and targeted support. Explanation: Offering additional resources and targeted support helps the student address specific areas of difficulty, promoting their success in meeting clinical competencies and ensuring they are well-prepared for professional practice.

771. In coordinating clinical internship sites, how should an EMS education program ensure quality and consistency across different sites?
a. Standardizing evaluation tools and criteria for all sites
b. Assigning the same preceptor to all students
c. Limiting the number of clinical sites to a few select locations
d. Frequently rotating students between sites

Answer: a. Standardizing evaluation tools and criteria for all sites. Explanation: Standardizing evaluation tools and criteria ensures that all students are assessed consistently regardless of their clinical site. This maintains the quality and fairness of the clinical education experience.

772. To maintain accreditation, an EMS education program must conduct regular self-assessments. What is the primary purpose of these self-assessments?
a. To identify areas for improvement and ensure continuous compliance with standards
b. To prepare for upcoming accreditation site visits
c. To compare the program's performance with other institutions
d. To generate data for marketing and recruitment purposes

Answer: a. To identify areas for improvement and ensure continuous compliance with standards. Explanation: Regular self-assessments help programs identify areas needing improvement and ensure ongoing compliance with accreditation standards. This process supports continuous quality enhancement and readiness for accreditation reviews.

773. When developing a patient satisfaction survey for field internship experiences, what type of question is most effective for gathering actionable feedback?
a. Open-ended questions about the overall experience
b. Multiple-choice questions rating specific aspects of care
c. Demographic questions about the patient
d. Yes/no questions about satisfaction with the experience

Answer: b. Multiple-choice questions rating specific aspects of care. Explanation: Multiple-choice questions that rate specific aspects of care provide structured, quantifiable data that can be analyzed for trends and areas needing improvement. This type of question facilitates actionable feedback for program enhancement.

774. A paramedic is planning to conduct a study on the effectiveness of a new CPR technique. What is the first step in navigating the Institutional Review Board (IRB) approval process?
a. Collect preliminary data
b. Submit a detailed research proposal
c. Conduct a literature review
d. Recruit study participants

Answer: b. Submit a detailed research proposal. Explanation: The first step in the IRB approval process is to submit a detailed research proposal outlining the study's objectives, methodology, and ethical considerations. This ensures the study is reviewed for compliance with ethical standards before data collection begins.

775. When formulating a research question, which characteristic is most important to ensure the question is scientifically valuable?
a. Broad and open-ended
b. Focused and specific
c. Based on anecdotal evidence
d. Easily answered with yes or no

Answer: b. Focused and specific. Explanation: A focused and specific research question allows for a clear and concise study design, making it easier to collect and analyze data effectively, thereby yielding scientifically valuable results.

776. A researcher is designing a data collection tool for an EMS study. What is a key consideration to ensure the tool's reliability?
a. Including a wide variety of questions
b. Ensuring questions are relevant and consistently measure the same concepts
c. Making the tool as brief as possible
d. Allowing open-ended responses

Answer: b. Ensuring questions are relevant and consistently measure the same concepts. Explanation: Reliability refers to the consistency of a measurement tool. Ensuring that questions are relevant and consistently measure the same concepts helps maintain the reliability of the data collected.

777. In selecting a statistical analysis method for comparing the effectiveness of two EMS interventions, which method is most appropriate for analyzing continuous data?
a. Chi-square test
b. T-test
c. Logistic regression
d. Fisher's exact test

Answer: b. T-test. Explanation: A t-test is used to compare the means of two groups with continuous data, making it appropriate for determining the effectiveness of two different EMS interventions.

778. When writing a research grant proposal, what section is critical for justifying the need for the study and demonstrating its potential impact?
a. Budget justification
b. Methodology
c. Literature review
d. Abstract

Answer: c. Literature review. Explanation: The literature review section justifies the need for the study by summarizing existing research, identifying gaps in knowledge, and demonstrating how the proposed study will address these gaps and potentially impact the field.

779. A paramedic wants to investigate the correlation between response times and patient outcomes. Which type of study design is most appropriate for this research question?
a. Randomized controlled trial
b. Cross-sectional study
c. Cohort study
d. Case study

Answer: c. Cohort study. Explanation: A cohort study is appropriate for investigating correlations as it follows a group of individuals over time to observe the relationship between different variables, such as response times and patient outcomes.

780. During the IRB approval process, what is a primary ethical consideration that must be addressed in the research proposal?
a. Cost of the study
b. Researcher's credentials
c. Informed consent process
d. Data collection tools

Answer: c. Informed consent process. Explanation: Ensuring that participants provide informed consent is a primary ethical consideration in research. The proposal must detail how participants will be informed about the study and their rights, ensuring voluntary participation.

781. What is a major advantage of using validated data collection tools in EMS research?
a. Reducing the time needed for data collection
b. Ensuring comparability of results across different studies
c. Allowing for subjective interpretation of responses
d. Limiting the scope of the study to narrow research questions

Answer: b. Ensuring comparability of results across different studies. Explanation: Using validated data collection tools enhances the reliability and validity of the data, allowing results to be compared across different studies and contributing to a broader understanding of the research topic.

782. In preparing a statistical analysis for an EMS study, why is it important to check for normal distribution of data?
a. To determine the appropriate sample size
b. To select the correct statistical tests
c. To simplify data interpretation
d. To identify outliers in the data set

Answer: b. To select the correct statistical tests. Explanation: Many statistical tests assume that the data are normally distributed. Checking for normal distribution helps researchers choose appropriate tests, ensuring the validity of the analysis.

783. When writing a research grant proposal, which element is essential to demonstrate the feasibility of the study?
a. Hypothesis
b. Detailed budget
c. Theoretical framework
d. Research question

Answer: b. Detailed budget. Explanation: A detailed budget outlines the financial requirements of the study and demonstrates that the research team has carefully considered the resources needed, thereby supporting the feasibility and practicality of the proposed research.

784. A paramedic is called to testify as an expert witness in a malpractice case involving an alleged breach of the EMS scope of practice. What is the primary role of the paramedic in this context?
a. To provide opinions on the legal aspects of the case
b. To explain the standards of care and scope of practice relevant to the case
c. To advocate for the defendant

d. To determine the guilt or innocence of the defendant

Answer: b. To explain the standards of care and scope of practice relevant to the case. Explanation: As an expert witness, the paramedic's role is to provide specialized knowledge about the standards of care and scope of practice. This helps the court understand whether the care provided was appropriate and within legal boundaries.

785. An EMS agency is developing a policy for the use of new medical technologies in the field. Which legislative consideration is most important?
a. The cost of implementing the new technologies
b. Compliance with state and federal regulations governing EMS practices
c. The popularity of the technologies among EMS personnel
d. The potential for reducing response times

Answer: b. Compliance with state and federal regulations governing EMS practices. Explanation: When developing policies for new medical technologies, ensuring compliance with relevant state and federal regulations is crucial. This ensures that the use of new technologies is legally sanctioned and adheres to established EMS standards.

786. A new EMS practice act has been introduced in a state legislature that will impact paramedic scope of practice. What is the best strategy for EMS professionals to advocate for their interests?
a. Lobbying legislators directly and providing testimony during hearings
b. Organizing a public demonstration to raise awareness
c. Writing opinion pieces in local newspapers
d. Petitioning the governor to veto the act

Answer: a. Lobbying legislators directly and providing testimony during hearings. Explanation: Direct lobbying and providing testimony during legislative hearings are effective advocacy strategies. These actions allow EMS professionals to present their expertise and perspectives directly to decision-makers, influencing the legislative process.

787. During a review of state EMS regulations, you find discrepancies between the EMS practice act and current EMS agency protocols. What should be your immediate course of action?
a. Update the agency protocols to align with the EMS practice act
b. Ignore the discrepancies if they have not caused any issues
c. Seek clarification from the state EMS office
d. Continue following current protocols until the next scheduled review

Answer: a. Update the agency protocols to align with the EMS practice act. Explanation: Ensuring that agency protocols align with the EMS practice act is essential for legal compliance and the safety of both patients and providers. Updating protocols to match regulatory requirements prevents legal issues and maintains professional standards.

788. An EMS provider is unsure whether a specific medical procedure is within their scope of practice. What is the best resource to consult for clarification?
a. The medical director of the EMS agency
b. The state EMS office or regulatory body
c. Online EMS forums and discussion groups
d. Peers and colleagues with more experience

Answer: b. The state EMS office or regulatory body. Explanation: The state EMS office or regulatory body is the authoritative source for determining scope of practice. These entities provide official guidelines and can offer definitive clarification on whether a specific procedure is permitted.

789. A policy development committee is tasked with addressing emerging issues in EMS, such as opioid overdoses. What is the first step the committee should take?
a. Drafting new protocols for handling opioid overdoses
b. Reviewing current data and trends related to opioid overdoses
c. Consulting with EMS providers for their input
d. Implementing training programs on opioid overdose management

Answer: b. Reviewing current data and trends related to opioid overdoses. Explanation: The first step in policy development is to review current data and trends. This provides a factual basis for understanding the issue and informs the development of effective, evidence-based policies.

790. During a legislative session, a bill is introduced that would significantly reduce EMS funding. What is the most effective way for EMS leaders to respond?
a. Conducting a cost-benefit analysis of EMS services
b. Mobilizing community support through awareness campaigns
c. Meeting with legislators to discuss the impact of funding cuts
d. Increasing service fees to compensate for potential budget shortfalls

Answer: c. Meeting with legislators to discuss the impact of funding cuts. Explanation: Engaging directly with legislators to discuss the potential impact of funding cuts is the most effective way to influence legislative decisions. This approach allows EMS leaders to present evidence and arguments for maintaining or increasing funding.

791. A paramedic is reviewing the EMS practice act to ensure their actions are within legal bounds. Which component of the act is most crucial for understanding their limitations?
a. Definitions of terms used in the act
b. Scope of practice section
c. Penalties for non-compliance
d. History of amendments to the act

Answer: b. Scope of practice section. Explanation: The scope of practice section outlines the specific procedures and actions that EMS providers are legally permitted to perform. Understanding this section is crucial for ensuring that all actions taken are within legal and professional boundaries.

792. An EMS agency is preparing for an accreditation review. Which legal document is essential for demonstrating compliance with state regulations?
a. The agency's strategic plan
b. The state EMS practice act
c. Individual provider certifications
d. Records of patient care reports

Answer: b. The state EMS practice act. Explanation: The state EMS practice act provides the legal framework and regulations governing EMS operations. Demonstrating compliance with this document is essential for accreditation, as it shows that the agency operates within legal requirements.

793. An EMS provider is subpoenaed to provide expert witness testimony in a case involving an EMS-related injury. What preparation is most important for the provider?
a. Reviewing personal experiences related to the case
b. Consulting legal counsel to understand the scope of testimony
c. Practicing answers to potential questions
d. Reading the patient care reports involved in the case

Answer: b. Consulting legal counsel to understand the scope of testimony. Explanation: Consulting with legal counsel helps the EMS provider understand the scope and limitations of their testimony, ensuring that their statements are relevant, accurate, and within legal parameters. This preparation is crucial for effective and appropriate expert witness testimony.

794. An EMS agency is planning to implement a community vaccination program. What is the first step to ensure its success?
a. Purchase a large supply of vaccines
b. Develop educational materials about the benefits of vaccination
c. Identify target populations for the program
d. Train EMS personnel on vaccine administration

Answer: c. Identify target populations for the program. Explanation: Identifying target populations ensures that the vaccination program addresses the specific needs of the community and prioritizes those who are most at risk, enhancing the program's overall effectiveness.

795. To reduce the incidence of opioid overdoses in the community, which strategy should be prioritized by the EMS agency?
a. Increasing the number of paramedics on duty
b. Distributing educational pamphlets on opioid risks

c. Implementing a naloxone distribution program

d. Limiting access to pain medications

Answer: c. Implementing a naloxone distribution program. Explanation: Naloxone is an effective antidote for opioid overdoses. Distributing naloxone and training community members on its use can significantly reduce opioid-related fatalities.

796. A paramedic is designing a community CPR training program. Which factor is most important to consider to ensure the program's success?

a. Providing free training materials

b. Ensuring sessions are available at convenient times and locations

c. Requiring advanced registration for all participants

d. Limiting class sizes to a maximum of five people

Answer: b. Ensuring sessions are available at convenient times and locations. Explanation: Making training sessions accessible in terms of time and location encourages higher participation rates, ensuring more community members are trained in CPR.

797. In developing a falls prevention program for the elderly, what is the most effective approach to reduce fall risk?

a. Installing handrails in all community buildings

b. Conducting home safety assessments and modifications

c. Providing information on proper footwear

d. Encouraging regular physical activity

Answer: b. Conducting home safety assessments and modifications. Explanation: Home safety assessments identify hazards that can lead to falls. Modifying the home environment based on these assessments is a targeted approach to reducing fall risks in the elderly.

798. What is a critical component of managing a public access naloxone program to ensure its effectiveness?

a. Distributing naloxone without any training

b. Partnering with pharmacies and community organizations for distribution

c. Keeping the program limited to healthcare facilities

d. Only allowing EMS personnel to carry and administer naloxone

Answer: b. Partnering with pharmacies and community organizations for distribution. Explanation: Collaborating with pharmacies and community organizations expands access to naloxone, ensuring it is widely available and that individuals are properly trained on its use.

799. When implementing a vaccination program, how can EMS agencies increase public trust and participation?

a. Mandating vaccinations for all residents

b. Providing transparent information about vaccine safety and efficacy

c. Offering incentives for getting vaccinated

d. Limiting vaccinations to healthcare workers only

Answer: b. Providing transparent information about vaccine safety and efficacy. Explanation: Transparency about vaccine safety and efficacy helps build public trust, addressing concerns and misinformation, and encouraging higher participation rates in the vaccination program.

800. To effectively prevent opioid overdoses, what is an essential component of an EMS-led public health initiative?

a. Increasing penalties for opioid possession

b. Providing overdose education and naloxone to at-risk populations

c. Reducing the availability of naloxone

d. Limiting EMS response to confirmed overdoses only

Answer: b. Providing overdose education and naloxone to at-risk populations. Explanation: Educating at-risk populations about overdose prevention and ensuring they have access to naloxone empowers them to respond effectively in an emergency, reducing opioid overdose deaths.

801. A community CPR training program aims to improve bystander response during cardiac emergencies. What key metric should be tracked to evaluate the program's effectiveness?

a. Number of CPR instructors trained

b. Percentage increase in community CPR certifications

c. Average duration of CPR training sessions

d. Number of CPR manikins available

Answer: b. Percentage increase in community CPR certifications. Explanation: Tracking the percentage increase in CPR certifications helps measure the program's reach and impact, indicating how many community members are now trained and prepared to respond to cardiac emergencies.

802. For a falls prevention program targeting the elderly, what is an effective strategy to ensure long-term success?

a. Hosting one-time safety seminars

b. Establishing ongoing exercise classes focused on balance and strength

c. Distributing pamphlets on fall prevention

d. Recommending annual home safety inspections

Answer: b. Establishing ongoing exercise classes focused on balance and strength. Explanation: Regular exercise classes that focus on improving balance and strength help elderly individuals maintain their physical abilities, reducing the risk of falls over the long term.

803. When managing a public access naloxone program, what is a critical factor to monitor to assess the program's impact?
a. Number of naloxone kits distributed
b. Cost of naloxone kits
c. Number of training sessions held
d. Rate of opioid overdose reversals reported

Answer: d. Rate of opioid overdose reversals reported. Explanation: Monitoring the rate of opioid overdose reversals provides direct evidence of the program's effectiveness, indicating how often naloxone is successfully used to save lives.

804. You are responding to a call for a 5-year-old child experiencing respiratory distress. Upon arrival, you find the child in the tripod position, using accessory muscles to breathe, and with audible wheezing. What is the most appropriate initial action?
a. Administer high-flow oxygen via non-rebreather mask
b. Provide a nebulized albuterol treatment
c. Perform a rapid sequence intubation
d. Start CPR immediately

Answer: a. Administer high-flow oxygen via non-rebreather mask. Explanation: The initial action for a child in severe respiratory distress is to administer high-flow oxygen to ensure adequate oxygenation. This stabilizes the child's condition while preparing for further treatments such as nebulized albuterol.

805. You need to administer a dose of 0.1 mg/kg of epinephrine to a 22-pound (10 kg) child experiencing anaphylaxis. What is the correct dose of epinephrine to administer?
a. 0.01 mg
b. 0.1 mg
c. 1 mg
d. 10 mg

Answer: b. 0.1 mg. Explanation: The correct dose is calculated by multiplying the child's weight (10 kg) by 0.1 mg/kg, resulting in a dose of 0.1 mg of epinephrine.

806. A 3-year-old presents with multiple bruises in various stages of healing and a spiral fracture of the humerus. What is the most important next step?
a. Splint the arm and discharge the child home
b. Contact child protective services (CPS) to report suspected abuse
c. Obtain a detailed history from the parents about the injury
d. Refer the child for an orthopedic evaluation

Answer: b. Contact child protective services (CPS) to report suspected abuse. Explanation: Multiple bruises in various stages of healing and a spiral fracture are highly suspicious for child abuse. It is critical to report the suspected abuse to CPS immediately to ensure the child's safety.

807. When preparing to transport a pediatric patient in an ambulance, what is the key consideration regarding pediatric-specific equipment?
a. Ensuring all equipment is color-coded
b. Having adult-sized equipment available just in case
c. Using appropriately sized pediatric equipment and restraints
d. Securing the child on an adult stretcher

Answer: c. Using appropriately sized pediatric equipment and restraints. Explanation: It is crucial to use pediatric-specific equipment and restraints that are appropriately sized to ensure the child's safety and provide effective care during transport.

808. A 7-year-old child with a known seizure disorder is having a generalized tonic-clonic seizure lasting more than 5 minutes. What medication and dose should you prepare to administer?
a. 2 mg lorazepam IV
b. 0.5 mg/kg diazepam rectally
c. 10 mg midazolam IM
d. 1 mg/kg phenobarbital IV

Answer: b. 0.5 mg/kg diazepam rectally. Explanation: For prolonged seizures in children, rectal diazepam is often used, and the dose is 0.5 mg/kg. This route is effective and can be administered quickly.

809. What is the most important principle of family-centered care in pediatric emergencies?
a. Allowing family members to observe procedures to ensure transparency
b. Involving family members in the decision-making process and respecting their input
c. Ensuring the family remains in the waiting room to reduce stress
d. Prioritizing medical interventions over family involvement

Answer: b. Involving family members in the decision-making process and respecting their input. Explanation: Family-centered care emphasizes involving family members in care decisions and respecting their input, which helps reduce anxiety and improves the overall experience for both the child and the family.

810. During a mass casualty incident (MCI) involving children, what is the primary consideration in pediatric disaster preparedness planning?
a. Treating children the same as adults to streamline the process
b. Prioritizing evacuation of children over adults
c. Having pediatric-specific triage protocols and equipment
d. Ensuring that children are kept together regardless of medical needs

Answer: c. Having pediatric-specific triage protocols and equipment. Explanation: Pediatric disaster preparedness planning must include pediatric-specific triage protocols and equipment to ensure that children's unique medical and emotional needs are met during an MCI.

811. A paramedic is educating new EMS recruits on the recognition of child abuse. Which sign should be highlighted as highly indicative of possible child abuse?
a. A single bruise on the shin from a fall
b. A consistent explanation of injuries from the caregiver
c. Multiple fractures in different stages of healing
d. An injury that occurred while the child was playing sports

Answer: c. Multiple fractures in different stages of healing. Explanation: Multiple fractures in different stages of healing are a red flag for child abuse and should be investigated further to protect the child.

812. When using a Broselow tape to estimate medication doses for a pediatric patient, what is the primary advantage of this tool?
a. It reduces the need for calculating doses manually
b. It provides accurate weight-based doses for all medications
c. It eliminates the need for medical oversight
d. It ensures that all children receive the same dose

Answer: a. It reduces the need for calculating doses manually. Explanation: The Broselow tape helps quickly estimate weight-based medication doses, reducing the risk of calculation errors and speeding up the administration process in emergency situations.

813. You are managing the care of a 6-month-old infant with bronchiolitis. What is the most appropriate initial management step?
a. Administering antibiotics to treat the infection
b. Providing supportive care, including suctioning and oxygen therapy
c. Starting corticosteroids to reduce inflammation
d. Initiating immediate intubation and mechanical ventilation

Answer: b. Providing supportive care, including suctioning and oxygen therapy. Explanation: The initial management of bronchiolitis involves supportive care, such as suctioning to clear the airways and providing oxygen therapy to maintain adequate oxygenation. Antibiotics and corticosteroids are not typically indicated unless there is a secondary bacterial infection or severe respiratory distress.

814. An EMS provider contacts online medical control for guidance during a cardiac arrest call. What is the most effective communication technique to ensure clarity and accuracy?
a. Using technical medical jargon extensively

b. Speaking quickly to convey urgency

c. Providing a clear, concise summary of the patient's condition and interventions performed

d. Asking for guidance after each intervention

Answer: c. Providing a clear, concise summary of the patient's condition and interventions performed. Explanation: Clear and concise communication ensures that medical control understands the patient's current status and the interventions already performed, allowing them to give accurate and relevant instructions.

815. During the revision of offline protocols, what is a critical factor to consider to ensure the protocols remain current and effective?

a. Limiting input to senior EMS administrators

b. Reviewing recent evidence-based research and clinical guidelines

c. Using protocols from neighboring EMS systems without modification

d. Keeping protocols unchanged to maintain consistency

Answer: b. Reviewing recent evidence-based research and clinical guidelines. Explanation: Incorporating recent evidence-based research and clinical guidelines ensures that the protocols reflect the latest standards of care and best practices, improving patient outcomes.

816. When conducting a quality assurance case review, what is the primary objective?

a. Identifying and disciplining providers who made errors

b. Highlighting positive outcomes to boost morale

c. Analyzing cases to identify trends and areas for improvement

d. Comparing provider performance to national averages

Answer: c. Analyzing cases to identify trends and areas for improvement. Explanation: The primary objective of quality assurance case reviews is to identify patterns, trends, and areas for improvement to enhance the overall quality of care provided by the EMS system.

817. A remediation program for an EMS provider who has demonstrated a pattern of clinical errors should include which key component?

a. Immediate suspension from all duties

b. Development of a personalized education and training plan

c. Mandatory participation in a peer review committee

d. Reduction of responsibilities until improvement is shown

Answer: b. Development of a personalized education and training plan. Explanation: A personalized education and training plan addresses the specific areas where the provider needs improvement, ensuring targeted and effective remediation.

818. What is the first step in the approval process for introducing a new technology or treatment in an EMS system?
a. Training all EMS providers on the new technology or treatment
b. Conducting a cost-benefit analysis
c. Submitting a proposal to the medical director for review
d. Implementing a pilot program without prior approval

Answer: c. Submitting a proposal to the medical director for review. Explanation: Submitting a detailed proposal to the medical director is the first step in gaining approval for a new technology or treatment, ensuring it is thoroughly evaluated for safety, efficacy, and cost-effectiveness.

819. When an EMS provider needs to consult online medical control during a mass casualty incident (MCI), what information is most critical to communicate first?
a. The total number of patients
b. The estimated time of arrival at the hospital
c. The current triage status and immediate needs of the most critical patients
d. The types of injuries observed

Answer: c. The current triage status and immediate needs of the most critical patients. Explanation: Communicating the triage status and immediate needs of the most critical patients allows medical control to prioritize and coordinate appropriate resources and interventions quickly.

820. In developing offline protocols, how can EMS agencies ensure that the protocols are practical and applicable in the field?
a. Consulting only with medical directors
b. Involving frontline EMS providers in the protocol development process
c. Adopting protocols from leading national organizations without modification
d. Limiting the protocols to basic life support (BLS) interventions

Answer: b. Involving frontline EMS providers in the protocol development process. Explanation: Involving frontline EMS providers ensures that the protocols are realistic, practical, and applicable, as these providers bring firsthand experience and insights into the challenges faced in the field.

821. During a quality assurance review, an EMS provider consistently demonstrates excellent clinical skills but struggles with documentation. What is an appropriate recommendation for this provider?
a. Requiring additional clinical training
b. Implementing a documentation improvement plan and offering additional training on proper documentation techniques
c. Placing the provider on probation
d. Reducing the provider's clinical responsibilities

Answer: b. Implementing a documentation improvement plan and offering additional training on proper documentation techniques. Explanation: Focusing on documentation improvement and providing targeted training helps the provider enhance their documentation skills while continuing to excel clinically.

822. When designing an EMS provider remediation program, what is an important element to include to ensure its effectiveness?
a. A one-size-fits-all training module
b. Regular progress evaluations and feedback sessions
c. Immediate return to full duties upon program completion
d. Publicly documenting the provider's errors

Answer: b. Regular progress evaluations and feedback sessions. Explanation: Regular evaluations and feedback ensure that the provider is progressing and allows for adjustments to the remediation plan as needed, promoting effective learning and improvement.

823. In the context of introducing a new treatment protocol, what role does the medical director play in the approval process?
a. Providing the initial concept for the new protocol
b. Conducting all training sessions for EMS providers
c. Reviewing and approving the proposed protocol based on clinical evidence
d. Implementing the protocol without additional input

Answer: c. Reviewing and approving the proposed protocol based on clinical evidence. Explanation: The medical director reviews and approves new treatment protocols to ensure they are based on sound clinical evidence and align with the overall standards of care, safeguarding patient safety and treatment efficacy.

824. An EMS agency is facing high turnover rates. Which recruitment and retention strategy is most likely to improve employee satisfaction and reduce turnover?
a. Offering higher salaries than competing agencies
b. Providing ongoing professional development and career advancement opportunities
c. Implementing strict discipline policies to ensure compliance
d. Reducing the number of shifts to decrease workload

Answer: b. Providing ongoing professional development and career advancement opportunities. Explanation: Offering professional development and career advancement opportunities enhances job satisfaction and loyalty, leading to lower turnover rates. While salary increases can help, they are often not enough to ensure long-term retention.

825. In developing a performance evaluation system, which method provides the most comprehensive assessment of an EMS employee's capabilities?
a. A single annual review based on supervisor observations
b. Peer reviews and self-assessments combined with supervisor evaluations
c. Customer satisfaction surveys

d. Quarterly reviews focusing only on call response times

Answer: b. Peer reviews and self-assessments combined with supervisor evaluations. Explanation: Combining peer reviews, self-assessments, and supervisor evaluations provides a well-rounded view of an employee's performance. This method incorporates multiple perspectives and offers a more comprehensive assessment.

826. An EMS agency is implementing a progressive discipline policy. What is the primary goal of this policy?
a. To ensure consistent punishment for all infractions
b. To provide a structured framework for corrective action and improvement
c. To quickly terminate underperforming employees
d. To create a record of employee infractions for legal protection

Answer: b. To provide a structured framework for corrective action and improvement. Explanation: The primary goal of a progressive discipline policy is to offer a structured approach to address performance issues and encourage improvement. This policy ensures fairness and provides employees with opportunities to correct their behavior.

827. Following a critical incident, what is the most appropriate first step in critical incident stress management (CISM) for EMS personnel?
a. Conducting a formal debriefing session within 24-72 hours
b. Offering mandatory counseling sessions for all involved
c. Implementing immediate disciplinary action for any errors made
d. Encouraging employees to take personal time off

Answer: a. Conducting a formal debriefing session within 24-72 hours. Explanation: Conducting a formal debriefing session within 24-72 hours allows EMS personnel to process the incident in a structured environment. This step is crucial in CISM to help mitigate stress and support mental health.

828. When designing an employee wellness program for EMS personnel, what should be the primary focus?
a. Offering financial incentives for participation
b. Providing comprehensive mental health support and physical fitness resources
c. Ensuring that participation is mandatory for all employees
d. Creating a competitive environment to motivate employees

Answer: b. Providing comprehensive mental health support and physical fitness resources. Explanation: A successful wellness program should focus on mental health support and physical fitness, addressing the unique stressors and physical demands of EMS work. This holistic approach promotes overall well-being and job satisfaction.

829. An EMS agency is struggling with recruiting new employees. Which strategy is likely to attract high-quality candidates?
a. Reducing the requirements for application to increase the applicant pool

b. Enhancing the agency's presence at job fairs and through social media
c. Offering signing bonuses without additional long-term incentives
d. Limiting recruitment efforts to within the local community

Answer: b. Enhancing the agency's presence at job fairs and through social media. Explanation: Expanding recruitment efforts through job fairs and social media broadens the reach and visibility of the agency, attracting a larger pool of high-quality candidates from diverse backgrounds.

830. In evaluating the effectiveness of an employee wellness program, which metric is most indicative of success?
a. The number of employees participating in the program
b. The overall reduction in employee sick leave and absenteeism
c. The amount of money spent on wellness program activities
d. The number of wellness workshops offered annually

Answer: b. The overall reduction in employee sick leave and absenteeism. Explanation: A reduction in sick leave and absenteeism indicates improved employee health and well-being, making it a key metric for evaluating the success of a wellness program.

831. What is a key component of a performance evaluation system that promotes continuous improvement?
a. Annual performance reviews with no follow-up
b. Real-time feedback and regular check-ins throughout the year
c. Focus solely on areas needing improvement
d. Relying on a single performance metric for evaluation

Answer: b. Real-time feedback and regular check-ins throughout the year. Explanation: Real-time feedback and regular check-ins promote continuous improvement by addressing issues promptly and providing ongoing support and guidance, which helps employees develop and perform better.

832. An EMS provider shows signs of burnout and decreased job performance. What is the most effective initial intervention?
a. Disciplining the employee for poor performance
b. Referring the employee to the employee assistance program (EAP) for support
c. Increasing the employee's workload to encourage productivity
d. Ignoring the signs and hoping they improve on their own

Answer: b. Referring the employee to the employee assistance program (EAP) for support. Explanation: Referring the employee to the EAP provides access to resources and support to address burnout and improve job performance. This proactive approach helps the employee manage stress and regain effectiveness.

833. To ensure fair and consistent application of the progressive discipline policy, what is an essential practice for supervisors?
a. Documenting all infractions and disciplinary actions thoroughly
b. Applying disciplinary actions based on personal judgment
c. Allowing flexibility in how policies are enforced
d. Avoiding documentation to maintain a positive work environment

Answer: a. Documenting all infractions and disciplinary actions thoroughly. Explanation: Thorough documentation ensures transparency and consistency in applying the progressive discipline policy. This practice protects the agency legally and ensures fair treatment of all employees.

834. An EMS agency is developing a fleet maintenance schedule. What is the most important factor to consider to ensure vehicles remain operational and safe?
a. Cost of maintenance
b. Frequency of vehicle usage
c. Availability of replacement parts
d. Color of the vehicles

Answer: b. Frequency of vehicle usage. Explanation: Vehicles that are used more frequently require more regular maintenance to ensure they remain operational and safe, minimizing the risk of breakdowns and ensuring reliability during emergencies.

835. When planning an equipment replacement cycle, what is the primary criterion to determine when equipment should be replaced?
a. The age of the equipment
b. The cost of the equipment
c. The frequency of equipment usage
d. The manufacturer's recommended lifespan

Answer: d. The manufacturer's recommended lifespan. Explanation: Following the manufacturer's recommended lifespan ensures that equipment is replaced before it becomes unreliable or unsafe, maintaining the highest standards of care and safety.

836. An EMS agency is implementing an inventory management system. Which feature is most critical to ensure efficient tracking and restocking of supplies?
a. Barcode scanning capability
b. Manual entry of inventory data
c. Automated email reminders for low stock
d. Monthly physical inventory checks

Answer: a. Barcode scanning capability. Explanation: Barcode scanning streamlines the process of tracking and managing inventory, reducing errors, and ensuring accurate and efficient restocking of supplies.

837. In developing vehicle specifications for a new fleet of ambulances, what is a key consideration to ensure the vehicles meet operational needs?
a. Exterior design and branding
b. Fuel efficiency and environmental impact
c. Interior layout and storage capacity
d. Initial purchase cost

Answer: c. Interior layout and storage capacity. Explanation: Ensuring the interior layout and storage capacity meet operational needs is crucial for the efficient and effective use of space, allowing EMS providers to access equipment quickly and provide optimal patient care.

838. An EMS agency is analyzing a recent equipment failure during a call. What is the first step in conducting a failure analysis?
a. Interviewing the personnel involved in the incident
b. Reviewing the maintenance records of the equipment
c. Identifying the cost of the equipment
d. Contacting the equipment manufacturer

Answer: b. Reviewing the maintenance records of the equipment. Explanation: Reviewing maintenance records helps identify any patterns or lapses in maintenance that may have contributed to the equipment failure, providing insight into potential preventative measures.

839. When developing a fleet maintenance schedule, what should be included to address both preventive and corrective maintenance needs?
a. Only routine oil changes and tire rotations
b. A combination of regular inspections, servicing, and as-needed repairs
c. Monthly cleaning of vehicle interiors
d. Annual repainting of vehicles

Answer: b. A combination of regular inspections, servicing, and as-needed repairs. Explanation: A comprehensive maintenance schedule that includes regular inspections, servicing, and as-needed repairs ensures both preventive and corrective maintenance needs are addressed, promoting vehicle reliability and safety.

840. For an inventory management system, why is real-time tracking of supplies critical?
a. To reduce the workload on administrative staff
b. To ensure immediate availability of necessary equipment and supplies
c. To minimize the cost of supplies
d. To allow flexibility in restocking schedules

Answer: b. To ensure immediate availability of necessary equipment and supplies. Explanation: Real-time tracking ensures that supplies are always available when needed, preventing delays in patient care due to shortages or out-of-stock items.

841. An EMS vehicle specification includes the requirement for advanced life support (ALS) equipment. What is an essential consideration for this specification?
a. The weight of the ALS equipment
b. The compatibility of the ALS equipment with existing protocols
c. The aesthetic design of the equipment
d. The color of the ALS equipment

Answer: b. The compatibility of the ALS equipment with existing protocols. Explanation: Ensuring that the ALS equipment is compatible with existing protocols is essential for seamless integration into EMS operations, allowing providers to deliver advanced care effectively.

842. In analyzing an equipment failure, what is a critical component to identify the root cause?
a. The age of the equipment
b. The training level of the personnel using the equipment
c. The environmental conditions at the time of failure
d. The original purchase cost of the equipment

Answer: c. The environmental conditions at the time of failure. Explanation: Understanding the environmental conditions can provide insight into whether external factors, such as temperature or humidity, contributed to the equipment failure, aiding in identifying the root cause and preventing future incidents.

843. When planning the replacement cycle for EMS equipment, why is it important to consider both the manufacturer's recommended lifespan and the actual usage patterns?
a. To reduce overall spending on equipment
b. To ensure compliance with state regulations
c. To optimize the timing of replacements based on wear and tear
d. To limit the variety of equipment in use

Answer: c. To optimize the timing of replacements based on wear and tear. Explanation: Considering both the manufacturer's recommended lifespan and actual usage patterns ensures that equipment is replaced at the optimal time, balancing safety, reliability, and cost-effectiveness.

844. An EMS agency is planning to improve radio system interoperability with neighboring jurisdictions. What is the primary consideration in this planning process?
a. Ensuring all agencies use the same brand of radios
b. Establishing shared frequencies and protocols for communication

c. Reducing the overall number of radio channels

d. Standardizing the encryption methods used by each agency

Answer: b. Establishing shared frequencies and protocols for communication. Explanation: Interoperability relies on having shared frequencies and protocols that enable different agencies to communicate seamlessly. This ensures effective coordination during multi-agency responses.

845. When designing a new dispatch center, what is the most important factor to consider for optimal performance?
a. The color scheme of the dispatch center
b. The proximity of the dispatch center to major hospitals
c. The ergonomic layout and adequate staffing levels to handle peak call volumes
d. The number of windows in the dispatch center

Answer: c. The ergonomic layout and adequate staffing levels to handle peak call volumes. Explanation: An ergonomic layout and sufficient staffing ensure that dispatchers can work efficiently and comfortably, particularly during high-stress periods with peak call volumes, enhancing overall performance and response times.

846. In implementing Next-generation 911 (NG911), what technological advancement is most significant?
a. Transitioning from analog to digital radio systems
b. Incorporating text, video, and data capabilities in addition to voice communication
c. Reducing the size of the dispatch center
d. Limiting 911 access to only emergency personnel

Answer: b. Incorporating text, video, and data capabilities in addition to voice communication. Explanation: NG911 enhances emergency response by enabling the transmission of text, video, and data, providing more detailed information to responders and improving situational awareness.

847. An EMS agency wants to optimize the use of Mobile Data Terminals (MDTs) in its vehicles. Which feature is most beneficial for improving field operations?
a. The ability to play music for crew members
b. Integration with electronic patient care reporting (ePCR) systems
c. The option to browse the internet
d. Real-time weather updates

Answer: b. Integration with electronic patient care reporting (ePCR) systems. Explanation: Integration with ePCR systems allows for seamless data entry and access to patient records, improving documentation accuracy and efficiency in the field.

848. What is the primary advantage of having a satellite communication backup system for EMS communications?
a. Reducing costs associated with traditional communication systems

b. Ensuring communication capability in remote areas or during disasters when other systems fail

c. Providing high-speed internet access to EMS personnel

d. Eliminating the need for regular radio maintenance

Answer: b. Ensuring communication capability in remote areas or during disasters when other systems fail. Explanation: Satellite communication backup systems provide reliable communication options in areas with poor coverage or during situations where traditional communication infrastructure is compromised, ensuring continuous connectivity.

849. A new dispatch center is being staffed. What is the key criterion for selecting dispatch personnel?

a. Previous experience in healthcare administration

b. Strong communication skills and the ability to remain calm under pressure

c. Advanced knowledge of local geography

d. Proficiency in multiple languages

Answer: b. Strong communication skills and the ability to remain calm under pressure. Explanation: Dispatch personnel must have excellent communication skills and the ability to stay calm and make decisions under pressure, ensuring effective handling of emergency calls and coordination of response efforts.

850. When planning for radio system interoperability, which challenge is most critical to address?

a. The cost of new radio equipment

b. Compatibility issues between different radio systems and manufacturers

c. Training personnel on proper radio usage

d. Securing radio frequencies from interference

Answer: b. Compatibility issues between different radio systems and manufacturers. Explanation: Ensuring compatibility between different radio systems and manufacturers is crucial for effective interoperability. Addressing this challenge involves selecting compatible technologies and establishing standardized protocols.

851. In an NG911 system, what is a major benefit of integrating geographic information systems (GIS)?

a. Reducing the overall cost of the 911 system

b. Improving the accuracy of caller location information

c. Allowing dispatchers to work remotely

d. Providing a backup communication method

Answer: b. Improving the accuracy of caller location information. Explanation: Integrating GIS into NG911 systems enhances the accuracy of caller location data, enabling more precise dispatching of emergency services and reducing response times.

852. What is the most important consideration when using Mobile Data Terminals (MDTs) for dispatch communications?
a. Ensuring that MDTs are equipped with entertainment options
b. Maintaining secure and reliable data transmission
c. Allowing for the customization of user interfaces
d. Reducing the size of the MDT screens

Answer: b. Maintaining secure and reliable data transmission. Explanation: Secure and reliable data transmission is essential for ensuring that sensitive information is accurately and safely communicated between dispatch and field units, maintaining the integrity and confidentiality of operations.

853. When developing a critical incident stress management (CISM) program for dispatch personnel, what is the primary objective?
a. Increasing the workload to build resilience
b. Providing support and resources to help manage stress and prevent burnout
c. Encouraging dispatch personnel to work longer hours
d. Implementing a strict disciplinary policy for handling mistakes

Answer: b. Providing support and resources to help manage stress and prevent burnout. Explanation: The primary objective of a CISM program is to offer support and resources to dispatch personnel, helping them manage stress and reduce the risk of burnout, which enhances their overall well-being and job performance.

854. An EMS agency is working to ensure compliance with the NEMSIS data standard. What is the primary purpose of NEMSIS?
a. To create a universal protocol for EMS patient care
b. To provide a standardized framework for collecting, storing, and sharing EMS data
c. To establish national guidelines for EMS vehicle maintenance
d. To develop a uniform certification process for EMS providers

Answer: b. To provide a standardized framework for collecting, storing, and sharing EMS data. Explanation: The National EMS Information System (NEMSIS) establishes a standardized framework that enables consistent data collection, storage, and sharing across EMS agencies, improving data quality and interoperability.

855. How can data analytics be used to improve EMS operational performance?
a. By manually reviewing individual case reports for errors
b. By identifying trends and patterns in response times and patient outcomes
c. By increasing the number of available ambulances
d. By reducing the number of data points collected

Answer: b. By identifying trends and patterns in response times and patient outcomes. Explanation: Data analytics allows EMS agencies to identify trends and patterns, such as peak call times and common patient outcomes, enabling targeted operational improvements and better resource allocation.

856. An EMS agency participates in a syndromic surveillance system. What is the primary benefit of this participation?
a. Increasing revenue through data sharing
b. Early detection of and response to public health threats
c. Reducing the workload of EMS personnel
d. Simplifying the billing process

Answer: b. Early detection of and response to public health threats. Explanation: Syndromic surveillance systems help detect and monitor public health threats, such as disease outbreaks, in real-time, allowing for timely interventions and improved public health responses.

857. What is a critical component of developing a data security and privacy policy for an EMS agency?
a. Setting strict access controls and encryption measures for all data
b. Sharing data with as many stakeholders as possible
c. Limiting the collection of data to only patient demographics
d. Storing all data on local servers without backups

Answer: a. Setting strict access controls and encryption measures for all data. Explanation: Implementing strict access controls and encryption ensures that sensitive EMS data is protected from unauthorized access and breaches, maintaining patient confidentiality and data integrity.

858. An EMS agency is creating an interagency data sharing agreement. What should be included to ensure effective collaboration?
a. A list of equipment to be shared between agencies
b. Protocols for how and when data will be shared, including security measures
c. Procedures for regular interagency meetings
d. A detailed financial agreement outlining cost-sharing

Answer: b. Protocols for how and when data will be shared, including security measures. Explanation: Clear protocols for data sharing, including security measures, ensure that data is exchanged efficiently, securely, and in compliance with privacy regulations, fostering effective collaboration.

859. In analyzing EMS data for quality improvement, which metric is most important to assess the effectiveness of patient care?
a. Number of calls received
b. Average response time
c. Total miles driven by ambulances
d. Patient survival rates

Answer: d. Patient survival rates. Explanation: Patient survival rates are a direct measure of the effectiveness of EMS care, providing insight into the quality of medical interventions and overall patient outcomes.

860. An EMS agency is developing a policy to comply with the Health Insurance Portability and Accountability Act (HIPAA). What is a key aspect of this policy?
a. Providing unrestricted access to patient data for all EMS staff
b. Ensuring data is only accessed and shared on a need-to-know basis
c. Collecting minimal patient information to reduce data management tasks
d. Allowing patients to edit their own medical records

Answer: b. Ensuring data is only accessed and shared on a need-to-know basis. Explanation: Limiting access to patient data to only those who need it for their role ensures compliance with HIPAA, protecting patient privacy and maintaining data security.

861. When implementing an electronic patient care reporting (ePCR) system, what is a significant benefit for data management?
a. Increased time spent on documentation
b. Improved accuracy and accessibility of patient records
c. Reduced need for EMS provider training
d. Higher costs for system maintenance

Answer: b. Improved accuracy and accessibility of patient records. Explanation: An ePCR system enhances data accuracy and accessibility, facilitating better patient care and streamlined data management processes.

862. What is a primary goal of using real-time data analytics in EMS operations?
a. To delay decision-making processes
b. To provide immediate feedback and support to EMS personnel in the field
c. To increase the complexity of data collection
d. To eliminate the need for traditional documentation

Answer: b. To provide immediate feedback and support to EMS personnel in the field. Explanation: Real-time data analytics enables EMS personnel to receive immediate feedback and support, enhancing decision-making and patient care during emergencies.

863. During an EMS quality assurance review, what data source is most valuable for identifying areas for clinical improvement?
a. Financial records of the EMS agency
b. Detailed patient care reports (PCRs)
c. Maintenance logs of EMS vehicles
d. Schedules of EMS personnel

Answer: b. Detailed patient care reports (PCRs). Explanation: Patient care reports provide comprehensive data on clinical interventions and patient outcomes, allowing for thorough analysis and identification of areas needing improvement in clinical practices.

864. An EMS agency is developing an all-hazards response plan. What is the most important element to include to ensure comprehensive preparedness?
a. Detailed response procedures for each specific type of hazard
b. A generic response outline applicable to all hazards
c. A list of contacts for local emergency services
d. A plan for community education on emergency preparedness

Answer: a. Detailed response procedures for each specific type of hazard. Explanation: While an all-hazards approach provides a framework, detailed response procedures for each specific type of hazard ensure that responders have clear, actionable steps to follow in various scenarios, enhancing preparedness and response effectiveness.

865. When creating a continuity of operations plan (COOP) for an EMS agency, what is a critical component to ensure operational resilience during a disruption?
a. Identifying essential functions and personnel required to maintain them
b. Reducing the number of non-essential staff
c. Increasing the budget for operational expenses
d. Limiting the use of technology to prevent reliance

Answer: a. Identifying essential functions and personnel required to maintain them. Explanation: A COOP must identify essential functions and the personnel required to maintain these functions during a disruption. This ensures that the most critical operations continue, even under adverse conditions.

866. In protecting critical infrastructure, which strategy is most effective for an EMS agency?
a. Enhancing physical security measures at all facilities
b. Reducing the use of critical infrastructure to prevent over-reliance
c. Conducting regular drills without modifying current security protocols
d. Implementing redundant systems and diversifying resources

Answer: d. Implementing redundant systems and diversifying resources. Explanation: Redundancy and resource diversification ensure that critical infrastructure remains functional even if one component fails. This strategy enhances resilience and minimizes the impact of disruptions on EMS operations.

867. A cyberattack compromises the electronic patient care reporting (ePCR) system of an EMS agency. What is the immediate priority to mitigate this cybersecurity threat?
a. Shutting down all electronic systems to prevent further damage

b. Switching to paper documentation until the system is secure
c. Contacting law enforcement to report the attack
d. Notifying patients that their data may have been compromised

Answer: b. Switching to paper documentation until the system is secure. Explanation: Switching to paper documentation ensures continuity of patient care and data recording while the ePCR system is being secured and restored. This mitigates the immediate impact of the cyberattack on operations.

868. To prepare for potential supply chain disruptions, what proactive measure should an EMS agency take?
a. Stockpiling large quantities of all supplies
b. Establishing relationships with multiple suppliers and maintaining a diverse inventory
c. Reducing the overall use of consumable supplies
d. Increasing the frequency of supply orders

Answer: b. Establishing relationships with multiple suppliers and maintaining a diverse inventory. Explanation: Developing relationships with multiple suppliers and maintaining a diverse inventory ensures that the agency can obtain necessary supplies from different sources if one supply chain is disrupted, enhancing preparedness and operational continuity.

869. During an all-hazards response exercise, what is the primary objective of conducting a tabletop drill?
a. To physically deploy all EMS resources
b. To simulate real-time response to an incident in a controlled environment
c. To assess the physical fitness of EMS personnel
d. To evaluate the financial impact of emergency responses

Answer: b. To simulate real-time response to an incident in a controlled environment. Explanation: A tabletop drill allows participants to discuss and simulate the response to an incident in a controlled environment, testing the effectiveness of plans and identifying areas for improvement without deploying physical resources.

870. What is a key consideration in the development of a continuity of operations plan (COOP) specific to EMS communication systems?
a. Minimizing the use of communication technology to avoid dependency
b. Ensuring backup communication systems are in place and regularly tested
c. Limiting the number of personnel trained on communication equipment
d. Reducing communication between field units and dispatch

Answer: b. Ensuring backup communication systems are in place and regularly tested. Explanation: Backup communication systems are essential for maintaining operations if primary systems fail. Regular testing ensures these systems are functional and reliable during an emergency.

871. When addressing cybersecurity threats, what is a fundamental component of an EMS agency's cybersecurity policy?
a. Limiting internet access for all employees
b. Implementing strong password policies and regular system updates
c. Reducing the use of digital systems to minimize risks
d. Disabling all wireless networks

Answer: b. Implementing strong password policies and regular system updates. Explanation: Strong password policies and regular system updates are critical components of cybersecurity. These measures protect against unauthorized access and vulnerabilities, enhancing the overall security of digital systems.

872. In the event of a large-scale disaster, what strategy should an EMS agency employ to ensure critical infrastructure remains operational?
a. Centralizing all operations to a single location
b. Decentralizing operations and utilizing multiple locations
c. Reducing staff to essential personnel only
d. Limiting communication to prevent information overload

Answer: b. Decentralizing operations and utilizing multiple locations. Explanation: Decentralizing operations and using multiple locations prevents the complete loss of functionality if one site is compromised, ensuring continuity of critical services during a large-scale disaster.

873. An EMS agency is reviewing its supply chain management practices. What is an essential practice to improve resilience against disruptions?
a. Increasing the volume of each order to reduce ordering frequency
b. Implementing just-in-time (JIT) inventory management to minimize costs
c. Conducting regular risk assessments and inventory audits
d. Limiting the number of suppliers to streamline procurement

Answer: c. Conducting regular risk assessments and inventory audits. Explanation: Regular risk assessments and inventory audits help identify vulnerabilities in the supply chain and ensure that inventory levels are adequate to meet demand during disruptions, enhancing overall preparedness and resilience.

874. During an active shooter incident, what is the primary role of EMS when integrating with law enforcement on scene?
a. Securing the perimeter
b. Providing immediate medical care in the warm zone
c. Engaging the shooter to neutralize the threat
d. Collecting evidence

Answer: b. Providing immediate medical care in the warm zone. Explanation: EMS personnel are trained to provide immediate medical care in the warm zone, which is secured by law enforcement but may still pose some risk. This ensures that critical care is delivered quickly to those in need while maintaining safety.

875. In developing joint training exercises for EMS and law enforcement, what is a key element to include to ensure effective collaboration?
a. Conducting separate training sessions for each agency
b. Using standardized scenarios that mimic real-life situations
c. Limiting participation to senior staff only
d. Focusing solely on medical response protocols

Answer: b. Using standardized scenarios that mimic real-life situations. Explanation: Joint training exercises should use realistic scenarios to practice and improve coordination and communication between EMS and law enforcement, ensuring a cohesive and efficient response during actual incidents.

876. An EMS agency and a law enforcement agency are establishing an information-sharing protocol. What is a crucial aspect to include in this protocol?
a. Limiting the information shared to administrative details
b. Ensuring compliance with privacy and confidentiality regulations
c. Using informal communication channels for rapid information exchange
d. Sharing all data regardless of relevance

Answer: b. Ensuring compliance with privacy and confidentiality regulations. Explanation: The information-sharing protocol must comply with privacy and confidentiality regulations, such as HIPAA, to protect patient information while facilitating effective communication between agencies.

877. When forming a tactical EMS team, what is an essential qualification for team members?
a. Previous military experience
b. Advanced training in tactical emergency medical support (TEMS)
c. Experience in administrative roles
d. Basic life support (BLS) certification

Answer: b. Advanced training in tactical emergency medical support (TEMS). Explanation: Team members must have advanced training in tactical emergency medical support to effectively integrate with law enforcement and provide care in high-risk environments.

878. During an active shooter response, what is the most critical consideration for EMS providers when entering a scene to render aid?
a. Speed of response
b. Availability of medical supplies
c. Scene safety and security
d. Number of casualties

Answer: c. Scene safety and security. Explanation: Ensuring scene safety and security is paramount for EMS providers to avoid becoming victims themselves and to effectively render aid to those injured.

879. What is the primary purpose of evidence preservation training for EMS providers?
a. To assist law enforcement in criminal investigations
b. To reduce the EMS response time
c. To improve patient care techniques
d. To streamline EMS documentation procedures

Answer: a. To assist law enforcement in criminal investigations. Explanation: Evidence preservation training helps EMS providers understand how to avoid contaminating or destroying potential evidence while delivering patient care, thereby aiding law enforcement in their investigations.

880. When integrating tactical EMS teams into law enforcement operations, what is a critical factor to ensure team effectiveness?
a. Assigning the team to administrative duties
b. Conducting regular joint tactical training sessions
c. Limiting the team's deployment to low-risk situations
d. Providing the team with basic medical supplies only

Answer: b. Conducting regular joint tactical training sessions. Explanation: Regular joint tactical training sessions ensure that EMS and law enforcement teams are well-coordinated, understand each other's roles, and can operate effectively together during high-risk situations.

881. What should be included in a joint training exercise to enhance coordination between EMS and law enforcement during an active shooter scenario?
a. Separate debriefing sessions for EMS and law enforcement
b. Role-playing exercises that simulate communication challenges
c. Focus solely on law enforcement tactics
d. Exclusive use of EMS protocols

Answer: b. Role-playing exercises that simulate communication challenges. Explanation: Role-playing exercises that simulate communication challenges help both EMS and law enforcement personnel practice overcoming barriers, improving coordination and effectiveness during real incidents.

882. In establishing a tactical EMS team, what type of equipment is essential for team members to carry?
a. Basic first aid kits
b. Tactical medical gear, including tourniquets, hemostatic agents, and chest seals
c. Administrative paperwork

d. Heavy weaponry

Answer: b. Tactical medical gear, including tourniquets, hemostatic agents, and chest seals. Explanation: Tactical medical gear is essential for providing immediate life-saving interventions in high-risk environments, addressing severe injuries that are common in tactical situations.

883. During joint operations, how can EMS and law enforcement ensure effective communication and information sharing?
a. Using separate communication channels
b. Establishing a unified command and communication system
c. Limiting communication to critical incidents only
d. Using personal mobile phones for updates

Answer: b. Establishing a unified command and communication system. Explanation: A unified command and communication system ensures that all parties are on the same page, facilitating efficient and effective coordination and information sharing during joint operations.

884. An EMS and fire service are developing a combined response protocol for cardiac arrest calls. What is the most important consideration for this protocol?
a. Ensuring that the fire service arrives first to the scene
b. Defining clear roles and responsibilities for each responding team
c. Minimizing the number of personnel on scene to reduce confusion
d. Using the same communication devices for both services

Answer: b. Defining clear roles and responsibilities for each responding team. Explanation: Clear roles and responsibilities prevent confusion and ensure that all necessary tasks are performed efficiently during a cardiac arrest response, maximizing the chances of patient survival.

885. To implement a cross-training program between EMS and fire service personnel, what is the key benefit of such a program?
a. Reducing the need for specialized training courses
b. Improving overall operational flexibility and efficiency
c. Minimizing the number of personnel required on each call
d. Standardizing uniforms and equipment for both services

Answer: b. Improving overall operational flexibility and efficiency. Explanation: Cross-training allows EMS and fire service personnel to understand each other's roles and responsibilities, improving coordination, flexibility, and efficiency during joint responses.

886. When creating a resource sharing agreement between EMS and fire services, what is the most critical element to include?
a. The process for billing and financial reimbursement
b. The contact information of all participating personnel
c. A detailed inventory list of shared resources
d. The protocol for regular joint training exercises

Answer: c. A detailed inventory list of shared resources. Explanation: A detailed inventory list ensures that both EMS and fire services know exactly what resources are available, preventing duplication and ensuring that necessary equipment is accessible when needed.

887. In designing an integrated dispatch system for EMS and fire services, what feature is most important to ensure effective communication?
a. A user-friendly interface for dispatchers
b. The ability to automatically route calls to the nearest available unit
c. Real-time communication and data sharing between services
d. Integration with social media platforms for public updates

Answer: c. Real-time communication and data sharing between services. Explanation: Real-time communication and data sharing ensure that both EMS and fire services are fully informed and can coordinate their responses effectively, improving overall response efficiency and effectiveness.

888. What is a key component of planning a joint quality improvement initiative between EMS and fire services?
a. Increasing the number of calls handled by each service
b. Establishing shared performance metrics and goals
c. Reducing the training requirements for new recruits
d. Limiting quality improvement activities to EMS personnel only

Answer: b. Establishing shared performance metrics and goals. Explanation: Shared performance metrics and goals ensure that both EMS and fire services are aligned in their improvement efforts, fostering collaboration and achieving better outcomes for the communities they serve.

889. An EMS and fire service are developing a combined response protocol for hazardous materials (HAZMAT) incidents. What is the primary consideration for this protocol?
a. Ensuring that EMS personnel take the lead in all HAZMAT situations
b. Providing specialized HAZMAT training to both EMS and fire personnel
c. Reducing the number of personnel on scene to minimize exposure risk
d. Using the same type of personal protective equipment (PPE) for both services

Answer: b. Providing specialized HAZMAT training to both EMS and fire personnel. Explanation: Specialized HAZMAT training ensures that both EMS and fire personnel can safely and effectively manage hazardous materials incidents, protecting themselves and the public from potential harm.

890. To enhance collaboration between EMS and fire services, what is the most effective strategy for joint training exercises?
a. Conducting separate training sessions for each service
b. Simulating real-life scenarios that require coordinated responses
c. Focusing solely on theoretical knowledge and classroom instruction
d. Limiting joint training to once a year to reduce costs

Answer: b. Simulating real-life scenarios that require coordinated responses. Explanation: Real-life scenario simulations help both EMS and fire personnel practice working together in realistic situations, improving their ability to coordinate effectively during actual emergencies.

891. When establishing an integrated dispatch system, what is a critical factor to consider for ensuring dispatcher proficiency?
a. Hiring dispatchers with experience in either EMS or fire service
b. Providing comprehensive training on both EMS and fire service protocols
c. Rotating dispatchers between different roles frequently
d. Implementing a single protocol for all types of emergency calls

Answer: b. Providing comprehensive training on both EMS and fire service protocols. Explanation: Comprehensive training ensures that dispatchers understand the unique protocols and needs of both EMS and fire services, enabling them to make informed decisions and dispatch the appropriate resources effectively.

892. What is a primary goal of a resource sharing agreement between EMS and fire services?
a. Increasing the operational budget for both services
b. Enhancing the efficiency and effectiveness of emergency responses
c. Reducing the workload for EMS personnel
d. Standardizing the equipment used by both services

Answer: b. Enhancing the efficiency and effectiveness of emergency responses. Explanation: Resource sharing agreements aim to maximize the use of available resources, improving the overall efficiency and effectiveness of emergency responses and ensuring better service to the community.

893. In planning a joint quality improvement initiative, what method is most effective for identifying areas that need improvement?
a. Reviewing past incident reports and response outcomes
b. Conducting anonymous surveys among community members
c. Increasing the number of mandatory training hours
d. Implementing a new software system for data collection

Answer: a. Reviewing past incident reports and response outcomes. Explanation: Analyzing past incident reports and response outcomes helps identify specific areas where improvements are needed, providing a data-driven basis for quality improvement initiatives and ensuring targeted, effective changes.

894. A 70-year-old patient with terminal cancer presents an advance directive stating that they do not wish to receive resuscitative efforts. The patient goes into cardiac arrest during transport. What should the EMS provider do?
a. Initiate full resuscitative efforts
b. Ignore the advance directive and consult medical control
c. Follow the advance directive and withhold resuscitation
d. Ask the family members for their opinion

Answer: c. Follow the advance directive and withhold resuscitation. Explanation: Advance directives are legal documents that specify a patient's wishes regarding medical treatment. The EMS provider should honor the patient's advance directive to withhold resuscitation in accordance with ethical guidelines and legal obligations.

895. In developing a futile care policy, what is a key consideration to ensure ethical decision-making?
a. Prioritizing the opinions of healthcare providers over patients and families
b. Establishing clear criteria for determining when care is considered futile
c. Ensuring that all patients receive maximum medical intervention regardless of prognosis
d. Limiting communication with the patient's family to avoid conflicts

Answer: b. Establishing clear criteria for determining when care is considered futile. Explanation: Clear criteria help define when medical interventions are unlikely to benefit the patient, ensuring that decisions about futile care are made consistently and ethically, respecting both patient autonomy and medical judgment.

896. During a cardiac arrest call, the patient is identified as a registered organ donor. What is the EMS provider's role in facilitating the organ donation process?
a. Discussing organ donation with the family at the scene
b. Ensuring the patient's wishes are communicated to the receiving hospital
c. Performing on-site organ retrieval procedures
d. Ignoring the organ donor status to focus on resuscitation efforts

Answer: b. Ensuring the patient's wishes are communicated to the receiving hospital. Explanation: The EMS provider should communicate the patient's organ donor status to the receiving hospital to ensure the patient's wishes are honored and appropriate steps are taken to facilitate organ donation.

897. What is an important consideration when delivering a death notification to a family member?
a. Using medical jargon to convey the situation accurately
b. Providing the notification over the phone to save time

c. Being compassionate, direct, and using simple language
d. Avoiding eye contact to maintain professionalism

Answer: c. Being compassionate, direct, and using simple language. Explanation: Delivering a death notification requires sensitivity and empathy. Being compassionate, direct, and using simple language helps the family understand the situation while providing emotional support.

898. An EMS provider is faced with an ethical dilemma regarding the care of a terminally ill patient. What framework can be used to guide ethical decision-making?
a. Utilitarianism alone
b. The provider's personal beliefs
c. The Four Principles of Biomedical Ethics: autonomy, beneficence, non-maleficence, and justice
d. Following the instructions of the most senior medical personnel present

Answer: c. The Four Principles of Biomedical Ethics: autonomy, beneficence, non-maleficence, and justice. Explanation: These principles provide a comprehensive framework for making ethical decisions in healthcare by balancing respect for patient autonomy, the duty to do good and avoid harm, and ensuring fairness.

899. A patient with a Do Not Resuscitate (DNR) order experiences respiratory distress but is not in cardiac arrest. What should the EMS provider do?
a. Withhold all medical interventions
b. Provide supportive care, including oxygen and comfort measures
c. Initiate full resuscitative efforts
d. Contact medical control for instructions

Answer: b. Provide supportive care, including oxygen and comfort measures. Explanation: A DNR order typically applies to resuscitative efforts in the event of cardiac arrest. For respiratory distress, providing supportive care and comfort measures is appropriate and aligns with the patient's overall care plan.

900. What should an EMS provider consider when interpreting an advance directive during an emergency?
a. The convenience of following the directive
b. The patient's current condition and the specifics of the directive
c. The presence of family members
d. The potential for legal repercussions

Answer: b. The patient's current condition and the specifics of the directive. Explanation: The EMS provider must carefully interpret the advance directive in the context of the patient's current condition, ensuring that the patient's wishes are respected and appropriately applied to the situation.

901. An EMS provider is involved in the development of a futile care policy. Which stakeholder is most important to include in the policy development process?
a. Hospital administrators
b. Legal counsel
c. Patients and their families
d. Equipment suppliers

Answer: c. Patients and their families. Explanation: Including patients and their families in the policy development process ensures that their perspectives and values are considered, making the policy more patient-centered and ethically sound.

902. During a critical care transport, the patient's family requests that all possible measures be taken to prolong life, despite the patient's advance directive stating otherwise. What should the EMS provider do?
a. Follow the family's wishes to avoid conflict
b. Follow the advance directive and explain the legal and ethical obligations to the family
c. Delay care until the issue is resolved
d. Consult with the receiving hospital for guidance

Answer: b. Follow the advance directive and explain the legal and ethical obligations to the family. Explanation: The EMS provider must follow the advance directive, which is a legal document expressing the patient's wishes, and explain to the family the importance of respecting those wishes.

903. In the context of ethical decision-making, what is the significance of the principle of non-maleficence for EMS providers?
a. Ensuring equal treatment for all patients
b. Acting in the best interest of the patient
c. Avoiding harm to the patient
d. Respecting the patient's autonomy

Answer: c. Avoiding harm to the patient. Explanation: Non-maleficence is the principle of "do no harm," which is fundamental in healthcare. EMS providers must strive to avoid causing harm to patients through their actions or interventions.

904. A paramedic has been exhibiting signs of severe stress, including insomnia and irritability, following a traumatic call. Which PTSD screening and intervention strategy is most appropriate for the EMS agency to implement first?
a. Conducting mandatory weekly mental health check-ins for all staff
b. Encouraging the paramedic to take a leave of absence
c. Offering an anonymous PTSD screening tool and access to counseling services
d. Assigning the paramedic to administrative duties to reduce stress

Answer: c. Offering an anonymous PTSD screening tool and access to counseling services. Explanation: Providing an anonymous screening tool allows the paramedic to assess their symptoms privately and access counseling services for professional help. This approach supports early intervention while respecting the paramedic's privacy.

905. An EMS agency is developing a suicide prevention program. What is the most important component to include for it to be effective?
a. Strict confidentiality policies
b. Regularly scheduled team-building activities
c. Mandatory training on recognizing and responding to suicide risk
d. Increased physical fitness requirements

Answer: c. Mandatory training on recognizing and responding to suicide risk. Explanation: Training EMS personnel to recognize the signs of suicide risk and how to respond appropriately is crucial. This ensures that colleagues can identify and assist those in need, potentially saving lives.

906. During a routine evaluation, an EMT confides in a peer about increasing alcohol use to cope with job stress. What is the most appropriate action for the peer to take?
a. Ignore the situation to respect the EMT's privacy
b. Report the EMT to their supervisor for disciplinary action
c. Refer the EMT to the agency's substance abuse support program
d. Offer personal advice on how to manage stress

Answer: c. Refer the EMT to the agency's substance abuse support program. Explanation: Referring the EMT to a support program provides professional help to address substance abuse issues. This approach ensures that the EMT receives the necessary resources to manage stress healthily and safely.

907. A newly developed peer support team is being trained. What is the key focus area to ensure the team's effectiveness?
a. Developing strong leadership within the team
b. Training team members in active listening and empathy
c. Ensuring team members have advanced medical training
d. Scheduling regular social events for the team

Answer: b. Training team members in active listening and empathy. Explanation: Active listening and empathy are essential skills for peer support team members. These skills enable them to provide emotional support and understanding, helping colleagues cope with mental health challenges.

908. An EMS agency wants to promote work-life balance among its staff. What strategy is most effective for achieving this goal?
a. Increasing the number of required overtime shifts
b. Implementing flexible scheduling options
c. Offering bonuses for extended work hours

d. Mandating participation in wellness programs

Answer: b. Implementing flexible scheduling options. Explanation: Flexible scheduling allows staff to balance work demands with personal life, reducing stress and burnout. This approach supports overall well-being and job satisfaction.

909. A paramedic is showing signs of burnout, including chronic fatigue and decreased job performance. What is the most appropriate intervention?
a. Reassigning the paramedic to a less demanding role
b. Providing the paramedic with additional training opportunities
c. Encouraging the paramedic to take a short-term leave of absence
d. Increasing the paramedic's workload to enhance resilience

Answer: c. Encouraging the paramedic to take a short-term leave of absence. Explanation: A short-term leave of absence allows the paramedic to rest and recover from burnout. This intervention supports mental health and helps prevent long-term negative effects on job performance and personal well-being.

910. An EMS agency is implementing a PTSD intervention strategy. What is a key component to ensure its success?
a. Limiting the intervention to high-ranking personnel only
b. Providing ongoing education about PTSD and its effects
c. Mandating participation in intervention programs
d. Reducing the overall workload for all staff

Answer: b. Providing ongoing education about PTSD and its effects. Explanation: Ongoing education helps staff understand PTSD, recognize its symptoms, and know how to seek help. This approach fosters a supportive environment and encourages early intervention.

911. A paramedic frequently arrives late to shifts and has been found sleeping on the job. What is the most appropriate first step in addressing this behavior?
a. Issuing a formal written warning
b. Conducting a private discussion to explore underlying issues
c. Reducing the paramedic's working hours
d. Terminating the paramedic's employment

Answer: b. Conducting a private discussion to explore underlying issues. Explanation: A private discussion allows supervisors to understand any underlying issues contributing to the paramedic's behavior. This approach provides an opportunity for support and intervention before taking disciplinary action.

912. An EMS agency is creating a wellness program aimed at improving mental health. What should be the primary focus of this program?

a. Increasing physical fitness requirements for all staff
b. Providing access to mental health resources and support services
c. Offering financial incentives for participation
d. Mandating attendance at weekly wellness seminars

Answer: b. Providing access to mental health resources and support services. Explanation: Ensuring that staff have access to mental health resources and support services is crucial for a wellness program. This focus addresses the specific mental health needs of EMS personnel and promotes overall well-being.

913. What is the most effective way for an EMS agency to ensure the success of a peer support team?
a. Providing regular professional training and development for team members
b. Limiting the team to senior staff only
c. Requiring mandatory participation from all employees
d. Reducing the workload for peer support team members

Answer: a. Providing regular professional training and development for team members. Explanation: Ongoing professional training and development ensure that peer support team members are equipped with the necessary skills and knowledge to provide effective support, enhancing the team's overall success.

914. An EMS agency is designing a mobile integrated healthcare (MIH) program. What is the primary goal of this program?
a. To increase the number of emergency room visits
b. To provide preventative and follow-up care in the community
c. To reduce the number of EMS personnel required
d. To focus solely on transportation services

Answer: b. To provide preventative and follow-up care in the community. Explanation: The primary goal of an MIH program is to extend healthcare services into the community, focusing on preventative care, chronic disease management, and follow-up care to reduce hospital readmissions and improve patient outcomes.

915. When planning the use of drones in EMS operations, what is a critical factor to consider for successful implementation?
a. The aesthetic design of the drones
b. Compliance with FAA regulations and airspace restrictions
c. The weight of the drone batteries
d. The brand of the drones

Answer: b. Compliance with FAA regulations and airspace restrictions. Explanation: Compliance with FAA regulations and airspace restrictions is essential to ensure the safe and legal operation of drones in EMS, preventing potential conflicts with other aircraft and ensuring public safety.

916. How can artificial intelligence (AI) be effectively applied in EMS dispatch?
a. By reducing the need for human dispatchers
b. By enhancing decision-making through predictive analytics and real-time data processing
c. By creating automated responses for non-emergency calls
d. By scheduling EMS personnel shifts

Answer: b. By enhancing decision-making through predictive analytics and real-time data processing. Explanation: AI can improve EMS dispatch by analyzing real-time data and using predictive analytics to optimize resource allocation, improve response times, and enhance overall decision-making.

917. What is a potential benefit of using robotic exoskeletons in EMS operations?
a. Increasing the speed of patient transport
b. Reducing physical strain on EMS providers during patient lifting and moving
c. Allowing patients to walk independently
d. Eliminating the need for traditional stretchers

Answer: b. Reducing physical strain on EMS providers during patient lifting and moving. Explanation: Robotic exoskeletons can assist EMS providers by reducing the physical strain associated with lifting and moving patients, decreasing the risk of injury and improving provider safety.

918. In developing a virtual reality (VR) training program for EMS personnel, what is a key advantage of using VR technology?
a. Lowering the cost of training programs
b. Providing immersive, realistic simulations for skill development and decision-making practice
c. Reducing the need for physical training facilities
d. Simplifying the certification process

Answer: b. Providing immersive, realistic simulations for skill development and decision-making practice. Explanation: VR technology offers immersive, realistic training scenarios that can enhance skill development and decision-making, allowing EMS personnel to practice in a safe and controlled environment.

919. A mobile integrated healthcare (MIH) program aims to reduce hospital readmissions. Which strategy is most effective in achieving this goal?
a. Increasing the frequency of emergency department visits
b. Providing home visits and telehealth services for chronic disease management
c. Focusing solely on emergency response calls
d. Limiting patient education on disease management

Answer: b. Providing home visits and telehealth services for chronic disease management. Explanation: Home visits and telehealth services enable continuous monitoring and management of chronic diseases, reducing the likelihood of hospital readmissions by addressing issues before they escalate.

920. In the context of using drones for EMS, what is a significant advantage of deploying drones for medical supply delivery in remote areas?
a. Reducing the cost of medical supplies
b. Enhancing the speed and accessibility of critical medical supplies in hard-to-reach locations
c. Increasing the visibility of the EMS agency
d. Limiting the need for skilled EMS personnel

Answer: b. Enhancing the speed and accessibility of critical medical supplies in hard-to-reach locations. Explanation: Drones can quickly deliver medical supplies to remote or inaccessible areas, improving response times and ensuring that critical resources reach patients in need.

921. When integrating artificial intelligence (AI) into EMS dispatch systems, what is a primary ethical consideration?
a. Ensuring that AI replaces human decision-making entirely
b. Maintaining patient confidentiality and data security
c. Reducing the number of dispatch calls handled
d. Using AI to make all medical decisions autonomously

Answer: b. Maintaining patient confidentiality and data security. Explanation: Ensuring patient confidentiality and data security is a primary ethical consideration when integrating AI into EMS dispatch, as it involves handling sensitive patient information.

922. How can robotic exoskeletons improve the quality of care provided by EMS personnel?
a. By increasing the speed of patient assessments
b. By allowing EMS personnel to perform tasks without assistance
c. By enhancing the physical capabilities of EMS personnel, reducing the risk of injury during patient handling
d. By reducing the need for medical equipment

Answer: c. By enhancing the physical capabilities of EMS personnel, reducing the risk of injury during patient handling. Explanation: Robotic exoskeletons enhance the physical capabilities of EMS personnel, reducing the risk of musculoskeletal injuries during patient lifting and handling, thereby improving the quality of care.

923. What is a key benefit of using virtual reality (VR) in EMS training for high-stress scenarios?
a. Lowering training costs significantly
b. Creating a controlled environment to practice high-stress scenarios safely
c. Reducing the need for written exams
d. Simplifying the accreditation process for EMS providers

Answer: b. Creating a controlled environment to practice high-stress scenarios safely. Explanation: VR allows EMS personnel to practice responding to high-stress scenarios in a controlled, safe environment, enhancing their ability to perform effectively under real-life stress and improving overall preparedness.

924. You are preparing for an international EMS deployment to a country affected by a natural disaster. What is the most important aspect of your pre-deployment preparation?
a. Learning the local language fluently
b. Receiving comprehensive vaccinations and health screenings
c. Familiarizing yourself with the country's entertainment and recreation options
d. Packing enough personal supplies for an extended stay

Answer: b. Receiving comprehensive vaccinations and health screenings. Explanation: Ensuring that you have received the necessary vaccinations and health screenings is critical for your safety and the safety of those you will be assisting. This preparation minimizes the risk of illness and allows you to work effectively in the disaster-affected area.

925. During a humanitarian mission, you encounter a patient with a condition that requires a medical procedure not commonly practiced in your home country. What is the best course of action?
a. Perform the procedure based on your knowledge from training
b. Consult with local medical professionals who are familiar with the procedure
c. Refuse to perform the procedure due to lack of experience
d. Search for instructional videos online to guide you

Answer: b. Consult with local medical professionals who are familiar with the procedure. Explanation: Consulting with local medical professionals ensures that the patient receives appropriate care based on local practices and expertise. This collaboration enhances patient outcomes and respects local medical protocols.

926. In an austere environment, you are tasked with providing care to multiple patients with limited resources. What is the most critical principle to follow?
a. Using all available resources on the most critically injured patient
b. Prioritizing care based on the principles of triage
c. Saving resources for potential future patients
d. Referring all patients to a higher-level facility

Answer: b. Prioritizing care based on the principles of triage. Explanation: In austere environments, it is essential to prioritize care using triage principles to ensure that resources are allocated effectively to maximize the number of lives saved. This approach helps manage limited resources efficiently.

927. You are part of an EMS team partnering with an NGO for a global health initiative. What strategy is most effective for developing a successful partnership?
a. Ensuring the NGO follows all of your agency's protocols
b. Establishing clear communication channels and shared goals

c. Requiring the NGO to provide all necessary funding
d. Maintaining independence from the NGO's activities

Answer: b. Establishing clear communication channels and shared goals. Explanation: Clear communication and shared goals are essential for a successful partnership. This strategy ensures that both parties are aligned in their objectives and can work collaboratively to achieve them.

928. After a major disaster, you are involved in rebuilding the local EMS system. What is the most important first step?
a. Rebuilding physical infrastructure such as ambulance stations
b. Training local EMS personnel in advanced medical techniques
c. Assessing the needs and capabilities of the current EMS system
d. Establishing new EMS protocols based on your home country's standards

Answer: c. Assessing the needs and capabilities of the current EMS system. Explanation: Assessing the needs and capabilities of the current EMS system provides a clear understanding of what is required to rebuild and improve the system effectively. This assessment ensures that efforts are targeted and appropriate.

929. When providing medical care in a culturally diverse environment, what is the key component of cultural competency training?
a. Learning common phrases in the local language
b. Understanding and respecting local customs and beliefs related to healthcare
c. Wearing traditional local clothing
d. Avoiding all physical contact with patients

Answer: b. Understanding and respecting local customs and beliefs related to healthcare. Explanation: Cultural competency involves understanding and respecting local customs and beliefs, which is essential for providing respectful and effective care. This understanding helps build trust and improve patient outcomes.

930. In preparing for an international EMS deployment, what is the primary purpose of a security briefing?
a. To learn about local tourist attractions
b. To understand potential risks and safety protocols
c. To obtain local currency exchange rates
d. To review the mission's success metrics

Answer: b. To understand potential risks and safety protocols. Explanation: A security briefing provides crucial information on potential risks and safety protocols, ensuring that personnel are aware of how to protect themselves and others in the deployment area.

931. During a humanitarian mission, you encounter a language barrier with a patient. What is the most effective approach to overcome this challenge?
a. Using hand signals and gestures to communicate
b. Finding a translator or using translation technology
c. Speaking slowly and loudly in your own language
d. Writing down instructions for the patient to read

Answer: b. Finding a translator or using translation technology. Explanation: Using a translator or translation technology ensures accurate communication, which is vital for understanding the patient's condition and providing appropriate care. This approach minimizes misunderstandings and errors.

932. In a post-disaster scenario, you are tasked with managing the EMS supply chain. What is the most important factor to consider?
a. Ensuring all supplies come from a single, trusted source
b. Prioritizing the distribution of supplies based on immediate needs
c. Keeping detailed records of all supplies used
d. Limiting the use of supplies to prevent shortages

Answer: b. Prioritizing the distribution of supplies based on immediate needs. Explanation: Prioritizing the distribution of supplies based on immediate needs ensures that critical resources are allocated where they are most needed, improving patient care and overall response effectiveness.

933. While working with an NGO in a remote area, you notice that the local population has specific health beliefs that conflict with your medical training. What is the best way to handle this situation?
a. Insist on providing care based solely on your medical training
b. Collaborate with local healthcare providers to find acceptable treatment options
c. Avoid providing care to avoid conflict
d. Teach the local population about your medical practices and insist they follow them

Answer: b. Collaborate with local healthcare providers to find acceptable treatment options. Explanation: Collaborating with local healthcare providers respects the local population's health beliefs and ensures that care is provided in a culturally sensitive manner. This approach improves patient acceptance and outcomes.

As we come to the end of this NREMT Exam Prep Study Guide, let's take a moment to reflect on the journey we've taken together. You've delved into the depths of emergency medical care, mastering the principles and protocols essential to becoming a proficient EMT. From understanding complex medical concepts to learning how to handle high-pressure situations with grace and confidence, you've equipped yourself with the knowledge and skills needed to save lives.

Remember the fundamental lessons we've covered:

1. **Core Medical Knowledge:** You've reviewed critical areas such as cardiovascular emergencies, respiratory issues, trauma management, and more. This foundational knowledge is crucial for providing effective care in any situation.
2. **Practical Skills:** From performing CPR and using an AED to handling airway obstructions and administering medications, you've practiced the hands-on skills that are vital in the field.
3. **Critical Thinking:** You've honed your ability to assess situations quickly and make sound decisions under pressure. This skill will serve you well in every emergency you encounter.
4. **Patient Interaction:** You've learned the importance of communication and empathy when dealing with patients and their families. Remember, your presence can provide comfort and reassurance in times of crisis.
5. **Ethics and Legal Considerations:** You've explored the ethical principles and legal responsibilities that guide your practice. Upholding these standards is key to maintaining trust and integrity in your profession.

As you prepare to take the NREMT exam, keep these lessons close to heart. The road ahead may seem daunting, but remember that you are well-prepared. Trust in the knowledge and skills you've gained. Embrace the challenge with the same dedication and passion that brought you here.

In the words of those who believe in you, you have the power to make a difference. You have the strength to overcome any obstacle and the compassion to touch lives in meaningful ways. Your journey as an EMT is just beginning, and it's a journey filled with opportunities to learn, grow, and make a profound impact on the world.

Good luck on your NREMT exam. Believe in yourself, stay focused, and remember why you chose this path. Your dedication and hard work will not only help you succeed but will also pave the way for countless lives saved and changed for the better.

You've got this. Go out there and show the world what you're capable of.

Made in United States
Orlando, FL
18 September 2024